child psychology

behavior and development

third edition

child psychology

behavior and development

RONALD C. JOHNSON
University of Hawaii
GENE R. MEDINNUS
San Jose State University

JOHN WILEY & SONS | new york · london · sydney · toronto

Library of Congress Cataloging in Publication Data:

Johnson, Ronald Charles.
Child psychology; behavior and development.

1. Child study. I. Medinnus, Gene Roland, joint author. II. Title. [DNLM: 1. Child psychology. WS105 J68c 1974]

BF721.J53 1974 155.4 73-22298
ISBN 0-471-44624-6

Printed in the United States of America

10 9 8 7 6 5 4 3 2

---

to John E. Anderson
whose ideas influenced this book and

to Carol and Colleen
whose patience and goodness
smoothed our way,

and to
Roni, Mark, Steven, Lisa, Laura, David, and Christopher,
young people whose behavior
is a spur to research,
since it is only minimally predictable
in the light of our present knowledge.

preface to the third edition

We again thank our students and colleagues for providing us with opportunities to learn; we thank the various researchers cited herein for providing the data needed to arrive at conclusions concerning the nature of the developmental process. And we thank each other for a long friendship and an easy working relationship.

Honolulu, Hawaii — *Ronald C. Johnson*

San Jose, California — *Gene R. Medinnus*

preface to the second edition

The basic format of the second edition is like that of the first. New data, published since the first edition, have caused us to change our minds on some issues, as may be noted herein. Our position regarding other issues has been supported by new data, and this, too, is reflected in the present edition. We have tried to write a book that is data oriented and that is directed toward presenting a solid body of information rather than defending a specific theoretical position.

We thank our students and our colleagues for continuing to educate us. We thank those critics of our first edition who pointed out areas in which we did not clearly explicate our point of view. We thank our wives for their tolerance, since writing is a lonely craft. Finally, we thank each other for suggestions, support, and forebearance.

Ronald C. Johnson

October 1968 *Gene R. Medinnus*

preface to the first edition

Child psychology is inextricably linked with other psychological fields, such as experimental psychology, the psychology of individual differences, social psychology, learning, and personality. It is also multidisciplinary, since it draws on data gathered in such diverse fields as sociology, anthropology, behavioral genetics, pediatrics, and some areas of home economics. From these different areas of specialization we have gathered data dealing with two major aspects: first, those ways in which all humans are similar to one another in their potentialities, patterns of development, and behavior; and, second, the differences among human beings in capabilities and in behavior as these differences are manifested within the basic core of similarity.

We see two forces operating to produce similarity. The first is our biological nature, which makes humans the moderately large, omnivorous, tough, stimulation-seeking, problem-solving, symbol-using organisms that we are. The second is that necessary core of culture based on such aspects of the human condition as a long period of dependency that in turn demands a stable family structure, considerable instruction, and considerable psychological support if the immature organism is to survive. Within the limits imposed by these two forces, individual differences in behavior occur as a result of hereditary and environmental variability.

We have attempted to present a sound body of facts within the context of those ideas and theories that influence our view of development. We can discuss and raise questions, but the reader must interact with real children to understand the reasons for our interest, our discussion, and our questions.

The basic motivation of any science is to understand fully and accurately those natural phenomena that are the object of study within that science. We have tried to present data that will help the individual in the task of understanding the processes involved in human development. We have tried as best we could to weight the evidence in our interpretations and explanations of psychological phenomena. There are points where our position is not the only one available, and future research may demonstrate that we are clearly wrong, but, at this time, we believe our view to be supported by the preponderance of the evidence. Perhaps some reader will provide the crucial experimental data that will resolve some of the still unanswered questions concerning the psychology of human development.

We wish to express our gratitude to our teachers, John E. Anderson, Gene Gollin, Bryng Bryngelson, Dale B. Harris, Arnold Rose, George Strother, and Donald M. Johnson; to our colleagues, especially Harold Keely, James L. McGaugh, and Karl Mueller, who provided aid; and to our students. We wish to thank the authors whose research makes up this volume, and the publishers who granted us permission to quote some of these research findings. And finally, our thanks go to Henry Angelino, University of Oklahoma, and Aubrey Roden, University of Alberta, Calgary, for their invaluable criticisms. The task of writing has been evenly divided (there is no "first" or "second" author except in an alphabetical sense), and we are grateful to each other for the comments and encouragement that shaped the structure of this book and brought it to completion.

Ronald C. Johnson

October 1964 *Gene R. Medinnus*

contents

section I

introduction

Children, their development and their behavior, have been observed for countless centuries. A great many explanations have been offered to account for the behavior of children. Consequently, a large body of information and misinformation has accumulated. Some of this knowledge has been based on fairly accurate observation, with conclusions carefully drawn. Other data, stemming in part from the "spirit of the times" prevailing in a society at any given moment, provide a distorted and inaccurate view of the process of development. Phrased differently, the values and goals held by a society determine, to some extent, the ways in which that society views children, childhood, and the causes or roots of behavior, quite apart from the accuracy of the information available.

A scientific approach to the study and understanding of child behavior does not ensure that society will deal with children in a wise and reasonable manner. It does mean, however, that the views of individuals and the policies they advocate regarding children can be based on accurate facts and information. The current social issue of law-and-order, with its effect on our perceptions of, and attitudes toward, the causes and treatment of criminal behavior, is a clear example of the way in which prevailing attitudes play a more important role than scientific information in dictating policy.

Scientifically obtained information can form a sound basis for examining a whole host of commonly held assumptions about child behavior. Examples: *Children misbehave because they are mean; babying fosters dependency in children; sexual deviation is caused by too-early exposure to sex information. Too much parental permissiveness has led to the current rejection of adult values by a sizable proportion of young people. Viewing of violence on television causes violent and criminal behavior later.*

This opening section of the book, consisting of a single chapter, considers the scientific method and how child psychologists have developed techniques for observation and experimentation that have yielded a clearer, less biased, and more systematic understanding of human behavior and have enhanced predictive powers. A review of these processes also discloses the historical development of child psychology as a scientific discipline. It is to that review that the next several pages pay close attention.

chapter 1

learning about child psychology

chapter 1

learning about child psychology

chapter 1

learning about child psychology

One of the many reasons a person seeks knowledge is to understand the world around him. By learning the *why* of what he sees, he acquires some proficiency at discerning orderly sequences of events and predicting the future from the present. Through understanding the causes of events, an individual may at times change the sequence and produce a different end result. Understanding leads to prediction and often, ultimately, to control of the environment. But there is a great difference between common, ordinary, everyday understanding and scientific understanding. The latter is achieved by application of what is widely known as the scientific method. Let us therefore explore this method to learn how scientific understanding, prediction, and control develop, in distinction to the more personal, day-to-day understanding of the universe that is shared by all manner of men. And then let us see how scientific techniques develop valuable findings in child development.

SCIENTIFIC METHOD

Observation

The raw data of scientific knowledge are facts, and scientific undertakings usually begin with observation. Astronomy, the first of the sciences, grew out of the keen observations of Egyptian and Babylonian priests. To them, the orderly sequences of day and night and of the seasons might have suggested an orderliness, that is, a predictability, in the physical world. Careful observation led to knowledge of planetary movement and of fixed stars; this knowledge enabled these priestly astronomers to make practical predictions, such as the time at which the Nile would flood. Because they also believed in astrology, they made less valid predictions too—such as "Beware of a dark-haired man next Tuesday." In all probability, the science of astronomy resulted from false notions about the influence of celestial bodies on human behavior as much as from a belief in an orderly universe. Yet the information collected by these early observers was substantially correct, even when their interpretations fell short of the mark.

Since these initial probings of the unknown, knowledge of the world has progressed a long way to its present state. In this advance, observation has played a major role: *knowledge, in fact, has depended on observation.* Although the ability to observe is widespread, scientific observation differs from ordinary observation in several respects. Scientific observation is systematic; it dwells on a particular phenomenon. This phenomenon may be the movement of the planets as observed by the ancients, or it may be the social relations of two-year-olds as observed by child psychologists. In either instance, as in any scientific undertaking, the observation is restricted to one or, at the most, a few kinds of object or event; it does not extend to all things. Moreover, this kind of observation concentrates on *all* aspects of the particular kinds of event, whereas everyday observation may take in only part of many events.

Take the bias found in the casual observation of the relation between physical characteristics and behavior. Redheads have hot tempers, we hear; people with big ears are generous; long fingers denote the artist. If these views were valid, we could easily predict appropriate behavior toward redheads, whom to approach for a loan, and which child would perform in Carnegie Hall. This is hazardous terrain. It leads from fallacies concerning the most observable characteristics of people with big ears to the quicksand of characteristics believed to be evident among members of racial or religious groups. These questionable beliefs result from the human tendency *not* to observe negative manifestations. People prefer to notice only those things that confirm their beliefs; if an event runs counter to a belief, they are more likely to forget or distort the event than to change the belief. This tendency may be seen in a vast number of studies cited by Rapaport (1942), and more recently in the work of Festinger (1957), centered in his theory of cognitive dissonance. Scientific method, in contrast, is aimed at ensuring complete, accurate observation and inclusion of even negative findings. The observation of these instances—the cases that do not fit the expectation—is the very essence of science.

Observation leads to the formation of hypotheses, which may be considered educated guesses or suppositions. If these hypotheses are so linked that a test of any one of them yields information not only about itself but also about the other hypotheses dependent in whole or in part upon it, a theory exists. Sometimes the information bears no essential relation to any specific hypothesis and hence no essential relation to the theory. For example, the difference in average sentence length in the speech of two-year-olds and three-year-olds may have some value for other purposes, but it suggests no new ideas and leads no further to basic understanding of the child. Other data, however, may help to find out whether a hypothesis conforms to reality; such data permit new predictions, which in turn provide new insights about the world. Scientific procedure benefits greatly from findings of this kind and the experimental processes uncovering them, but all scientific investigations must start with the accumulation of facts from observation and then test hypotheses against these facts.

If a theory or a hypothesis does not fit the observed facts, it must be discarded, whether it concerns a folk belief like the temper of redheads or a cosmological issue such as the question of whether the universe is expanding or standing still. The rejection of a theory generally results from systematic, close observation of *all* cases. Sometimes the facts fit the theory fairly well, but not well enough. Here the negating instances indicate where a theory is weak and where it must be revised promptly to improve its accuracy. The next result is a fuller, clearer understanding of the world, which sharpens the skill of predicting the future more precisely.

Prediction

All scientific endeavor is concerned with making observations that lead to accurate predictions—predictions ranging from what may result from a change in the structure of a molecule to what new attitudes may develop among race-prejudiced persons exposed to close contact with another race, as in an integrated teen-aged boys' camp.

Prediction, however, is never certain. It is merely a statement of probability. The form in which it is used in all sciences is often called *actuarial prediction*. This term is borrowed from the insurance field, whose actuaries can tell—barring great, unexpected catastrophes such as wars—the number of individuals in a given age group who will die in a particular year. An actuarial statement sets forth the odds, the chances that a specific thing will happen. In child psychology, for example, an actuarial statement might hold that "a child of IQ 70 at age 12 has less than one chance in 100 of completing a conventional high-school course curriculum by age 20." The chance is there (Baller, 1936), but it is a long shot.

This form of prediction is also known as *nomothetic prediction*—that is, arising from or based on law—a distinction noted by Allport (1937). A nomothetic statement, like an actuarial statement, asserts the odds; it is a statement of probability.

A statement like "Republicans worry more about a balanced budget than do Democrats" is a nomothetic statement. It may very well be true, based on a theory of budgeting that has influenced many Democrats, but it is only a matter of probability for any individual member of either party. Even though the odds in its favor are excellent, the statement is still not a certainty.

A second type of prediction, limited almost entirely to the social sciences, applies to the individual case. This is *idiographic prediction*, roughly a "drawing or graphing of an individual," and it is aimed at understanding a particular individual. Idiographic prediction makes use of nomothetic knowledge, but is concerned only with one individual. To the applied psychologist, it is the predictive technique *par excellence:* "Mr. X will not commit suicide"; "Miss A will do better in group therapy than in analysis"; "Mr. K is not a good parole risk." Such predictions are often wrong. They are based on knowledge acquired by nomothetic means which only imply the odds. Nevertheless, the social scientist must make these predictions, for, although they often provide inaccurate, they are frequently more precise than the predictions made by others. Indeed, considering the present state of knowledge and the complexity of subject matter, the proportion of accuracy in prediction is remarkable.

Whether nomothetic or idiographic, the accuracy of a prediction supplies cues to the truth of a belief. The most wonderful thing about science, believed M. R. Cohen (1949), is that built into it is the notion that unless ideas accurately portray reality, they must be changed. If, for example, one of two theories makes more accurate predictions about the phenomena with which both deal, the more accurate theory is accepted and the other is rejected. If the two predict equally well, the more *parsimonious* theory, the one making fewer assumptions, takes precedence. Should a new theory be developed that outshines either of the other two, both prior theories are discarded. No truth is sacred, universal, or immutable to science or the scientist. This attitude of disrespect for any authority other than nature, observed systematically and without bias, is what has enabled science to change rapidly and relinquish old ideas for better—that is, more accurate or more truthful—new ones. Certainly this applies to many of the ideas discussed in this book; they are likely to be superseded in time by more reliable interpretations.

If the goal of psychology is highly accurate prediction, how closely has this been approached? Not very closely, but progress is being made. There are several reasons why success in psychological prediction has only been moderate. First, the subject matter of psychology is more complex than the subject matter of many other sciences; at least psychologists claim this to be so. Second, psychology is a comparatively young science. One of the early American students of Wilhelm Wundt, a founder of modern psychology, died only recently. This makes one realize, as does nothing else, how young this science is. Psychology may not mature for hundreds of years, and it must suffer the problems of growing up; but there are aspects of the young science that can be changed, aspects that at present contribute to a deficiency in skill.

One change desired by most psychologists and toward which they are working is an increase in the reliability and validity of measuring devices. In its simplest form, reliability means that a device used to measure a stable characteristic, such as the height of an adult, will give the same information on every occasion. If a yardstick expanded or contracted capriciously, what would measure 5 feet, 10 inches today might measure 3 feet, 6 inches or 9 feet, 8 inches at some future date. Obviously this yardstick would be unreliable as a measuring device, and because of its unreliability growth trends could not be predicted with any accuracy over intervals of time. The reliability of many measuring instruments is indeed low, especially the tests for measuring personality. Perhaps personality characteristics are basically unstable and individual personality varies greatly at different points in time. If, however, this lack of reliability is largely the fault of inadequate tests rather than of actual personality change, continued efforts to increase the reliability of psychological tests should make their results more dependable and therefore better instruments for predicting behavior.

A test is valid if it measures what it set out to measure. It is invalid if it measures other things and not what it was designed to test. Suppose we measured the height of members of a psychology class and graded them on the basis of height. The measurements would be highly reliable on the subject of height, but they would not be valid for achievement, since tallness is hardly a good measure of ability. Whereas a reliable measure may not be valid, as in the foregoing example, a measure cannot be highly valid unless it is highly reliable. As better testing methods are used and reliability grows, the validity of measurements increases. But more important, the validity of the measuring device can be checked by comparing its findings with reality. Does the person who does well in a test of creativity, for example, actually behave creatively? Only when behavior in the real world is predictable from test results does a test become a valid predictive device. Development of tests at once reliable and valid increases the power to predict.

Phenotype and Genotype. Psychology also stands to gain in both understanding and predictability from an increasing awareness of *genotypic* variation as opposed to *phenotypic* variation between individuals. (It should be noted that the words genotype and phenotype are used here, as among psychologists, in a way similar to that first introduced by Kurt Lewin. The words are used differently by geneticists, with *genotype* referring only to genetic forces.)

Genotype refers to the similarity in background forces that produce behavior. One young man steals an automobile. Another holds down two jobs to pay for an automobile. Both are motivated chiefly by a desire to impress some young woman. They are genotypically alike in this specific aspect of their motivation even though their outward behavior differs. *Phenotype*, on the other hand, concerns the phenomenal or observable world. Phenotypically, or observably, these young men differ greatly.

Psychologists, and social scientists in general, have dwelt on phenotypes rather than genotypes and, further, have not done as good a job as they might on distinguishing between phenotypes. Consider the problem as it relates to the diagnosis and treatment of physical and psychological disorders. A physical disorder entailing an increase in temperature is called a fever. Although various fevers differ in a number of secondary aspects, their major phenotypical or observable feature is the heightened temperature they all share. If physicians had paid attention only to the temperature, no effective methods of treatment would have been developed, since a therapeutic aid for reducing one fever, such as quinine for malarial fever, is utterly useless in the treatment of many other fevers. Astute physicians managed, however, through keen observation, to distinguish several *sub*phenotypes within the general phenotype *fever*. These subphenotypes differed in genotype—or cause—and, once separated from one another, also differed in the treatment effective for each of them. This knowledge enabled development of individual treatments. By carefully examining subjects manifesting a common genotype, one can often discern systematic variations in their observable characteristics. Though superficially resembling one another, subjects in each group actually fall into distinct subgroups, each a result of another genotype. This distinction will be discussed at some length in Chapter 16.

How successful is this approach in psychology? Individuals with severe mental defects—say, below IQ 50—are phenotypically alike in being defective. Yet there are several rather easily observable distinctions among them. Some of these individuals have clearly suffered brain damage during prenatal development, in a difficult birth process, or after birth itself. Others form the low end of the normal distribution of intelligence. For every IQ of 160, presumably, there is another of 40, and its possessor is defective as a result of multiple genetic variation. Still others are defective from the effects of a single gene or of a chromosomal abnormality rather than the multiple-genetic deficiency responsible for the IQ of 40. More careful scrutiny divides these individuals into additional subphenotypes, suggesting the existence of still more genotypes than are casually perceived. One variety of defectiveness resembles any other *until* the individual's urine is subjected to chemical analysis. This particular disorder with the formidable name of *phenylpyruvic oligophrenia* or *phenylketonuria* has an observable symptom in the excretion of phenylpyruvic acid in the urine when phenylalanine, an amino acid, is incompletely oxidized. When this acid is found in the urine, the individual is nearly always defective, presumably because of the unmetabolized amino acid in the system. The condition results from a double recessive genetic characteristic. Anyone may be a carrier of the disorder, although the probabilities are slight. The carrier who transmits the disorder has one recessive and one dominant gene, whereas the defective child has a double recessive pair of genes. If married, by chance, to another carrier, the original carrier has one chance in four of having a child with this affliction, two chances in four of having children who do not have it but who are carriers, and one chance in four of having a child who is neither defective nor a carrier. Since any one of us may be carriers (though the odds are slim), it is worth noting that Hsia, Driscoll, Troll, and Knox (1956) developed a means by which carriers can be identified. Hsia (1968) provides further information on more recent developments in the study of phenylketonuria, including refinements on tests identifying heterozygote carriers.

Here is an instance in which careful phenotypical observation led to the discovery of a specific genotype. Once the genotype was found, effective treatment was soon developed. With a phenylalanine-free diet, especially during the first year of life, a child generally could overcome the hereditary disposition toward idiocy (Armstrong & Tyler, 1955; Woolf, Griffiths, & Moncrieff, 1955) and be, on the average, dull normal in ability. Without doubt, there are a number of genotypes of this sort hidden within the larger phenotypical category severely mentally defective, as there are in such widely inclusive phenotypes as juvenile delinquency, schizophrenia, or even shyness. But as long as psychologists continue to study individuals on the basis of broad phenotypes, there is scant likelihood for additional success in diagnosis, prediction of outcome, and treatment. A shift in interest to genotypes may very well improve the predictive powers of the child psychologist.

Control

A basic purpose of prediction is control. However, prediction and control are separate aspects of science. In fact, control is not a necessary part of science, since some sciences exist for which control is clearly impossible. Many sciences such as astronomy, cosmology, volcanology, and seismology, for example, are reasonably adequate at predicting events, but they obviously have not control over the phenomena to which they attend. Predicting an eclipse is a simple matter for an astronomer, whereas causing or controlling one is indeed beyond human capability.

One might contend that ability to predict without ability to control is essentially useless. The argument depends on the definition of utility. If immediate, demonstrable usefulness is necessary, then, as Bugelski (1960, p. 20) said, "Such a viewpoint might limit the work of astronomers to observations of the moon and the navigational stars since outside of these might be little of an immediately practical nature in astronomy." Most scientists, however, are unconcerned with practical utility. For them, knowledge that does not have immediate utility might be of value in the future. Bugelski (1960) noted that Faraday once demonstrated an elementary form of a dynamo to Disraeli. "What good is it?" Disraeli asked. Faraday retorted, "Someday you may tax it." The practical and concrete fact often arises from the impractical and abstract theory. From an interesting set of ideas proposed by a young man named Einstein evolved the atomic bomb. The justification for seeking knowledge clearly does not depend on the practical utility of the knowledge for controlling the surrounding world.

In certain areas of psychology, notably clinical psychology, control of behavior is often considered to be a major aim. As used in this sense, control does not mean forcing the individual to act in a desired manner. It rather means increasing the frequency of certain behaviors and decreasing the frequency of other behaviors through a manipulation of the environment. Suppose it is believed that a boy who sets fires does so because of neurotic difficulties stemming from his acceptance of the masculine sex role. The clinical psychologist, using some form of therapy, tries to bring these problems into the open where they can be treated. If given some insight into the roots of his problems, plus, perhaps, some form of training and support, the boy may indeed cease his arsonous activities. If successful, the clinician has controlled behavior. Certain behaviors, such as setting fires, decrease in frequency whereas other behaviors, such as dating, increase. Even if the boy now starts stealing cars to provide himself and his young lady friend with transportation, the therapy quite likely has been successful. It has discovered the sources of the arsonous conduct, and certain hypotheses have been formed regarding the efficacy of various treatment techniques. Behavior has been controlled.

Very often the child psychologist is asked questions pertaining to control. How does one increase a behavior such as eating everything on the plate, or decrease a behavior such as having temper tantrums? Psychology has some answers to these questions, and this book attempts to deal with them. The scientist may not be sure that control should be attempted because he is not certain that control is desirable for human beings. The parent, on the other hand, controls his children's present and attempts to control their future through manipulating the environment. Good or bad, this is parenthood. All any parent can do is to try to increase those behaviors that he values as "good" in a child and decrease those deemed "bad." Like the clinician and the parent, the teacher, too, must act. Since these acts have far-reaching consequences, parent and teacher, again like the clinician, should use what scientific understanding is available. Although much remains to be known, this book endeavors to discuss what is understood, what is predictable, and what forms control may take.

A good deal of emotion recently has been directed against behavior therapy (see pp. 530–536), a form of therapy that typically is explicitly directed toward increasing the frequency with which some behaviors occur, and reducing the frequency of other behaviors; therefore, most explicitly directed toward the control of behavior. The founder of modern behaviorism, B. F. Skinner, wrote a book, *Beyond Freedom and Dignity* (1971), that even evoked a negative response from Spiro Agnew, apparently as a consequence of Skinner's well-documented view that reinforcement histories, not free will, determine the behavior of organisms, and that the best way to change (control) the behavior of an individual is to change the kinds of reinforcements he receives.

RESEARCH METHODS IN CHILD PSYCHOLOGY

There are several reasons why knowledge of research methods is important for the beginning student in child development. Like other areas of the social sciences, child psychology is imprecise as compared with the more exact physical sciences. Yet in a relatively brief interval of time the precision of research and hence the reliability and validity of conclusions have shown a remarkable advance.

The volume dealing with research methods in child development (Mussen, 1960) illustrates the tremendous concern with research methodology in a wide range of areas including physical growth, intellectual development, language and communication, personality development, and social behavior.

The study of research methods tends to foster a critical faculty in a student; he is better able to judge the value of research data and the conclusions by examining the methods that produce them. This ability is perhaps more necessary in the field of child psychology than in any other scientific area. Here every layman considers himself an expert and is quite willing to proffer advice in such matters as child discipline, juvenile delinquency, and child growth. It is therefore of particular importance that the student of child psychology be well grounded in scientific methods. Only then can he judge, not on the basis of apparent meaningfulness and plausibility of statements, but by examining the source of the data, the correctness and appropriateness of the techniques employed, and the justifiability of the conclusion drawn.

Four main questions will guide the inquiry into research methods in child psychology: (1) When is the particular method applicable? (2) What are its advantages? (3) What are its disadvantages? (4) What does the method tell, and what kinds of information can it not provide?

Naturalistic Observation

The scientist, like the novelist, can gain his raw data from observing organisms in nature—that is, in their natural habitat—and not in any controlled or experimentally manipulated environment. Many psychologists believe that such naturalistic observation, which is relatively objective, will ultimately yield more information than better controlled but more limited techniques—limited in the sense of the amount of behavior observed—such as experimentation.

Baby Biographies. Among the types of naturalistic observation, the early diary accounts describing child behavior have been of both historical and methodological importance. The biographer, usually an interested parent or relative, has observed the behavior of a single child and recorded the observations in diary style. Often the biographers have been scientists in fields other than child behavior. Charles Darwin, for example, was a biologist. Thus an individual of scientific bent, curious, yearning to know, to understand, to find out, approaches each new, unexplored area with a desire to observe and record the phenomena under study. Many criticisms may be voiced over the trustworthiness of the information contained in these early biographies. The following excerpt from Darwin's biography of his infant son illustrates several points.

> It was difficult to decide at how early an age anger was felt; on his eighth day he frowned and wrinkled the skin round his eyes before a crying fit, but this may have been due to pain or distress, and not to anger. When about ten weeks old, he was given some rather cold milk and he kept a slight frown on his forehead all the time that he was sucking, so that he looked like a grown-up person made cross from being compelled to do something which he did not like. When nearly four months old, and perhaps much earlier, there could be no doubt, from the manner in which the blood gushed into his whole face and scalp, that he easily got into a violent passion. A small cause sufficed; thus, when a little over seven months old, he screamed with rage because a lemon slipped away and he could not seize it with his hands. When eleven months old, if a wrong plaything was given him, he would push it away and beat it; I presume that the beating was an instinctive sign of anger, like the snapping of the jaws by a young crocodile just out of the egg, and not that he imagined he could hurt the plaything. When two years and three months old, he became a great adept at throwing books and sticks, and the like at anyone who offended him; and so it was with some of my other sons. On the other hand, I could never see a trace of such aptitude in my infant daughters (Darwin, 1881).

Darwin's attempts to separate the facts of observation from an interpretation of them were not always successful. A common weakness of such observations is the tendency to project onto the child the emotions, motives, and attitudes of the adult. Besides, there are other disadvantages and limitations to the biographical approach. First, the relevance of the observations depends in part on the adequacy of the observer's background and training. Since such observations are highly subjective, the biases of the observer may very well influence the types of behavior recorded and the interpretations of these behaviors. Second, it is immediately apparent that the child cannot be considered truly representative of all children of his age and sex. This limits the extent to which the data can apply to other children. Third, the type of parent who would engage in such painstaking observation and recording would not be likely to represent parents in general.

So much for the observer and the observed. Several things may also be said about the information itself. Since the baby biographies were usually initiated with no specific purpose in mind, no single type of behavior was examined systematically. How representative any of these sampled behaviors might be is a matter for debate. Representativeness is imperative in research if the investigator attempts to conclude from his observations that a certain behavior is typical or characteristic of a particular child. As a final caution, the observer must remain alert to the danger of the observation itself interfering with the behavior of the child under observation. More recent research, to be discussed in the next section, has dealt with this problem through a similar observational method.

Case-Study Method. A modern approach that shows much similarity to the baby biography is the case study. This technique collects a great variety of information about a single child, usually to help a professional person understand the child's behavior. Delinquency, school failure, problem behavior are common subjects studied through the case method. School records, accounts obtained from parents, relatives, other interested adults, and the child himself, as well as the results of psychological examinations are among the sources of information consulted. The following case study was undertaken to obtain clinical evaluation of one child's behavior problems.

CASE-STUDY REPORT

Name:	ANDREWS, James	
Age:	10 years, 6 months	*Examined by:* L. S. Martin, Ph.D.

Reason for Referral

Mr. and Mrs. Andrews requested an evaluation of their son, James, because they have become increasingly upset by his behavior and have been unable to handle him at times. They are especially frightened of his rage reactions and are concerned about his lack of self-discipline and his inability to accept limits.

Interview with Parents

The parents describe Jim as an intelligent boy who is overweight, has a quick temper, and is a chronic "tease." They believe that he is sensitive about his obesity and that this prevents him from taking an active part in sports. They also noted that his rudeness, his unwillingness to cooperate, and his inability to accept criticism help to prevent his participation in organized sports.

The Andrews feel that Jim hates to be frustrated, is rebellious, disorderly, and that he refuses to dress up. He likes to work with mechanical things and is very interested in "hot rods." Jim shows a great deal of animosity toward his eight-year-old sister. He becomes profane when angry and constantly threatens to leave home.

The parents remember Jim to have been a relaxed and happy baby. They are rather vague about developmental history, but believe that he did everything early. Mrs. Andrews holds certain beliefs about food which do not have their basis in religious ideas. Hence, she has raised Jim as a vegetarian and he was fed soy-bean milk for approximately the first three years of life. Mrs. Andrews could not recall when he stopped taking the bottle, nor could she describe how weaning occurred. She thought that Jim walked at nine months and talked at one year, but she could not recall his first words. She thought she began toilet training at about a year and a half and that Jim was easy to train.

Jim fell out of a crib before age two, fell off a tricycle and hurt his chin at age four or five and he fell out of a car when he was four or five years old. His ears bother him; he feels as if there is wax in them and has had X-ray treatment for this irritation. He does not report hearing difficulties, however, nor does he hear peculiar sounds.

Jim never sucked his fingers or showed evidence of masturbatory activity. Nightmares, sleepwalking, or enuresis were not present according to the parents. Sexual information has been obtained largely from other boys, although he is able to talk with his father about sexual matters.

The Andrews have moved around a good deal; hence, Jim has attended a variety of schools. There were no apparent difficulties about starting to school and no academic problems until recently. He attended Broadhurst Elementary School, beginning two years ago, but was about to be expelled when his parent contacted the clinic. They transferred him to Edgewater Elementary School but Jim does not like this school. His recent school history indicates that he constantly disrupts the classroom with various kinds of attention-getting behavior.

The parents also described Jim as being somewhat belligerent toward younger children and as somewhat blustering in his approach to other children. He has to have his own way, and at times it seems that he deliberately antagonizes his playmates.

Mr. Andrews feels that he has always been "too indulgent" toward Jim. He has always found it difficult to set limits on Jim's behavior or to attempt to discipline him. Mrs. Andrews, on the other hand, feels that Jim should be made to conform to certain standards; she keeps after him to see that he does.

Psychological Evaluation

TESTS ADMINISTERED. (1) Wechsler Intelligence Scale for Children (WISC); (2) Rorschach Inkblot Test; (3) Thematic Apperception Test (TAT).

BEHAVIOR AND APPEARANCE. Jim is an obese ten-and-a-half-year-old boy who was quite belligerent toward the interviewer when first seen. At the same time, he seemed frightened about coming. On his first visit, he ran out of the building and across the street, and on his second visit, he sat in the car refusing to come into the building. On the third and last visit, however, he was able to talk about his anger toward the clinician, including his feelings that "what he was like was his business," and that he couldn't be helped anyway. He denied any fears about coming to the clinic, although he was able to talk about his concern with what his friends would think if they knew he was coming to see a "head shrinker." Initially, he denied having any problems, but as the session progressed, he was able to admit that he was not very satisfied with his family. He claimed that his mother always nags him, especially about eating and about getting his hair cut. He said he likes his father and that they get along fine together when they are away from the rest of the family. He describes his sister as a pest who always gets her own way.

In general, Jim's behavior was quite ambivalent. He vacillated between ingratiation and direct criticism and between joviality and hostility. He seemed to utilize blandness and denial in attempts to handle his anger and fear.

TEST RESULTS AND IMPRESSIONS. On the Wechsler Intelligence Scale for Children, Jim attained the following scores:

Verbal Scale IQ	= 123 (Superior)
Performance Scale IQ	= 114 (Bright-Normal)
Full Scale IQ	= 120 (Superior)

Despite Jim's superior intellectual abilities, he frequently does not function at this level because of his negativistic approach to tasks and his tendencies to put forth minimally adequate efforts. Such tendencies reflect a lack of stamina and of enduring goals and are sufficient to prevent constructive planning for the future.

Jim is able to see things as most people do; he is aware of conventionally approved standards of behavior. However, he maintains an active independence of thought and a stubborn insistence on the right to make up his own mind. Hence he finds it difficult to accept many conventional standards as being the appropriate ones for him to follow. Instead, his behavior is most apt to be governed by his needs for immediate gratification.

Jim has a great deal of anxiety about dealing with people and is unable to satisfy his needs by manipulating his environment in a socially acceptable manner. Hence he tends to avoid situations which require social conformity, despite his interest in achieving social adequacy. Furthermore, he has difficulties in forming close emotional relationships, and seems to vacillate between superficial emotional responsiveness and uncontrolled explosive outbursts.

The test protocols suggest rather intense feelings of hostility which are not very well defended. It appears that Jim's hostility stems largely from concerns about frustration of impulse gratification and particularly about frustration of oral-dependent needs. He is resentful of restrictions in general, and feels that social rules and regulations are unfair for the most part. For example, he told TAT stories about people who were put in jail or kicked out of school because they did not conform to certain standards, e.g., getting a license for a bicycle or getting a haircut.

These attitudes appear to be related to Jim's attitudes toward parental figures. He sees mother figures as depriving, restricting, and making demands upon their children. He sees father figures as intervening in such situations, siding with the child and talking the mother into giving in to the child's wishes. At the same time, he maintains strong underlying feelings of hostility toward father figures. For example, to TAT Card 8BM he told a story about a "foolish" boy who shot a man accidentally and the man died; then the boy wasn't foolish anymore and lived happily ever after. Then, too, in the story to Card 12M, the Lilliputians kill the giant. Jim's ambivalent feelings toward father figures as well as his apprehensiveness toward them is probably best illustrated in his story to TAT Card 13MF: "This guy came in drunk, and he's wipin' his eyes, 'cause he can't see. And he's an alcoholic and a dope fiend. And he's a teacher (laughs), and well–he started all his pupils out on the dope and the alcohol and the principal found that out, so he shot him and then he shot himself and everybody laughed–no–that's not a good ending. They died happily ever after." It appears that Jim is confused about the motivations of father figures and views them as destructive.

Jim's sexual identification is primarily a passive, feminine one. However, he struggles diligently to maintain a façade of masculine assertiveness and becomes very anxious if others think of him as feminine or refer to him as a "sissy."

Summary Impression

Jim is an emotionally disturbed boy who is currently functioning at a superior level of intelligence. However, his motivation for achievement is sporadic and his behavior is governed strongly by his needs for immediate gratification and his apprehensiveness about forming close attachments to others. Hence consistent intellectual efforts and effective achievement are minimal. The test records contain evidence of a passive, dependent orientation with hostility stemming largely from feelings of frustration. Ambivalent feelings toward parental figures are pronounced. Although reality awareness is adequate, there appears to be a lack of integration of conventional standards as guides for his own behavior.

Diagnostic Impression

This appears to be the record of a primary behavior disorder, passive-aggressive type. Although the test record is not suggestive of brain damage, in view of the history of falls, etc., as well as the uncontrolled outbursts of rage, neurological and electroencephalographic studies would seem warranted.

Some branches of child psychology have used the case study more frequently than others. Clinically oriented child psychologists employ it to a great extent.

Although the case study helps to understand a single child, the method unfortunately suffers from some of the same defects as the early baby biographies. For example, the reliability of the information gained from informants may be questioned. Does the informant's relationship to the child color his report? Do biases and emotional involvement cloud his memory of past events? Furthermore, how reliable are the test results in the case study? Often the very factors contributing to a child's failure at school also prevent him from scoring at his *true* level in an intellectual examination. The IQ score on the test tells very little about his intellectual potential; it does not contribute to an understanding of the child's school difficulty. Perhaps an even more important consideration in evaluating the case study is the professional who interprets and assesses the data. His experience, theoretical biases, knowledge of research findings, and psychological understanding and skill all influence the value of the study.

Finally, caution has to be exercised whenever one attempts to identify causes and effects. Was a child's rejection by his father the reason for his delinquent behavior? Is rivalry with a year-older sister the basis for a young girl's underachievement in school? Sweeping generalizations and explanations are often made and conclusions drawn from unreliable, sketchy information. *A child's past can never be completely reconstructed.* Rigorous safeguards are required in interpretation, and the person using case-study material must view his conclusions as *tentative* and subject to modification. Since the case study lacks many of the controls present in the experimental method (to be discussed shortly), generalization of the data tends to be hazardous. No child's heredity or environment is identical to another child's. For this reason, factors causing a certain type of behavior in one case may or may not produce the same result in others.

Psychological Ecology. Two psychologists, Robert Barker and Herbert Wright, have organized a Midwest Field Station in a small Kansas community, which they liken to a weather outpost or a biological field station. It has the purpose of collecting data about children and their daily lives, where they go, what they do, what they say, and with whom they interact. These two men argue that psychology, unlike many other sciences, began early and perhaps somewhat prematurely to gather data in laboratory situations. Psychologists manipulate and experiment with small isolated units of behavior and with specific behavior variables without first describing in detail some of the basic information of human life. They ignore such things as the frequency with which certain behaviors occur and the settings in which these take place.

> It is different in other sciences. Geolgists, biologists, chemists, and physicists know in considerable detail about the distribution in nature of the materials and processes with which they deal. Chemists know something about the laws governing the interaction of oxygen and hydrogen, and they also know how the elements are distributed in nature. Entomologists know the biological vectors of malaria, and they also know about the occurrence of these vectors over the earth. In contrast, psychologists know little more than laymen about the frequency and degree of occurrence of their basic phenomena in the lives of men—of deprivation, of hostility, of freedom, of friendliness, of social pressure, of rewards and punishments. Although we have daily records of the behavior of volcanoes, of the tides, of sun spots, and of rats and monkeys, there have been few scientific records of how a human mother cared for her young, how a particular teacher behaved in the classroom and how

> the children responded, what a family actually did and said during a mealtime, or how any boy lived his life from the time he awoke in the morning until he went to sleep at night (Barker & Wright, 1954, p. 2).

The study of behavior in natural situations is given the name *psychological ecology.* This distinguishes it, say Barker and Wright, from experimental psychology which studies behavior in artificially planned situations. Tests, interviews, questionnaires, and experiments distort and destroy the natural stream of behavior (Barker, 1963). Unlike experiments that impose conditions upon the phenomena investigated, ecological methods reveal and discover natural occurrences (Willems, 1965). The Kansas work involves primarily observation and recording of everyday behavior. To maintain some scientific precision and give some purpose to the observations, the psychological ecologists developed several categories. They call the stable parts of the physical and social milieu of a community, which by their very nature lead to standard and distinctive patterns of behavior, *behavior settings.* In their community, Midwest, U.S.A., these settings include the drug store, second-grade classroom, tavern, Methodist Regular Worship Service, cemetery, library, and Brownie's Regular Meeting (Wright & Barker, 1949). They designate the part of a stream of behavior that describes a separate action and the situation in which it occurs a *behavior episode.* Such episodes might include "painting the lips," "wiping paint off face," "moving crate across pit" (Wright & Barker, 1949, 1950). A third category, the *specimen record,* is a collection of behavior episodes. It is "a detailed, sequential, narrative account by skilled observers of an individual child's behavior through a more or less extended time" (Wright & Barker, 1949). A book entitled *One Boy's Day* describes a day in the life of seven-year-old Raymond Birch. Eight observers took turns throughout the day observing and recording the boy's activities. Their objective was to include everything he did. The following paragraphs typify their report.

> *Some cars were resting on a ledge part way up the sloping side of the pit. The ledge consisted of an old shingle and resembled a bridge, supported at each end by dirt. Stewart started undermining the ledge to make the cars fall into the pit. It seemed to me that his action copied Raymond's very closely, although his purpose differed.*
>
> Raymond suddenly stood up and brushed off the dirt which he had carelessly flipped upon his legs and lap.
>
> He knelt down and smoothed the dirt from the rock.
>
> Then he started chopping rhythmically. Time after time he shoved the stick into the damp dirt, and pulled sideways, flipping the dirt away. The stick bent under his vigorous efforts.
>
> *Inadvertently and unnoticed by Raymond, one of the flying clods of dirt happened to hit Clifford. Clifford didn't complain; he was too busy watching what Stewart was doing.*
>
> Finally a car fell off the ledge which Stewart was tearing down. Stewart shouted, "Look at it roll on down below in the canyon."
>
> Raymond looked over and watched the rolling car with mild interest.
>
> He returned immediately to his own digging, not even looking up to see the second car roll down (Barker & Wright, 1951, pp. 356–357).

With some exceptions, the advantages, disadvantages, and usefulness of psychological ecology are the same as those of the baby biographies. One is impressed by the ability of a specimen record to capture the richness and complexity of the environment, the multitude of interactions that influence and shape a child's approach to people and situations, and the repetitiveness but apparent randomness of child behavior. Moreover, the psychological ecologists seem to have avoided some of the shortcomings of the baby biographies. Well trained in observation and well grounded in the basic notions of psychology, the ecologists have deliberately attempted to separate the content of observation from interpretation; in fact, interpretation is indented and set off from observed data in a specimen record. There is also the question of the extent to which the observer, as a result of his observation, changes or influences the individual being observed. Wright and Barker hold that children under the age of nine show neither sensitivity nor self-consciousness when being observed and soon adjust or adapt to the presence of an observer. This view seems to be supported by the relatively small effect an observer has on those being observed, especially when the observation continues over an extended period. Children tend not to act very long in ways differing from their usual behavior. Finally, how representative is the group of children investigated? Although the community chosen was small enough to include all its children in the study, and its environment was undoubtedly less complex than that of a large urban area, it remains to be shown whether environmental complexity has psychological significance in the lives of children.

Controlled Approaches to Observation

Although observation lies at the base of all scientific research, "uncontrolled" observation, as we have seen, has many disadvantages. There is clearly a need for "controlled" observation of phenomena if meaningful comparisons and determinations are to be made. Scientists have developed many techniques for a controlled approach to observation, and in the following several pages we shall examine some of them.

Time Sampling. Arrington (1943) has defined time sampling as a method of observing the behavior of human beings "under the ordinary conditions of everyday life in which observations are made in a series of short time periods so distributed as to afford a representative sampling of the behavior under observation." The method was developed in order to overcome many of the weaknesses in the anecdotal descriptions of child behavior. It was first used by Willard Olson (1929) to record the incidence of "nervous habits" in school children. Briefly, Olson marked off a record blank into five-minute intervals and entered a check whenever a designated behavior occurred within each time interval among a classroom of children he was observing. As originally conceived, time sampling yielded a score indicating *the number of time intervals* in which a specific behavior manifested itself.

Over the years the technique has undergone a great number of modifications. Most of them have resulted from a desire for finer precision in the sampling and recording of behavior. The time interval has been shortened, often consisting of periods from 30 seconds to 1 minute. Only one child is observed at a time, with the observations distributed at random throughout the day as well as over a term of a week to several months. Symbols have been developed to record continuous behavior instead of the occurrence or nonoccurrence of specific acts. For example, an elaborate set of such symbols has been devised to facilitate the objective description and recording of interaction between adults and children (Moustakas, Sigel, & Schalock, 1956). This set uses 5-second time intervals and enters a series of category code letters on a prepared scoring sheet covering 16 minutes of continuous recording. Each square on the sheet represents 5 seconds of time, and the main categories symbolized by the code letters in this particular recording system include: nonattention, attentive observation, recognition, statement of condition or action, joint participation in activity, offering information, giving help, reassurance, seeking information, restricting, forbidding, disciplinary action, affection, compliance.

Most of the time-sampling studies have been concerned with the social behavior and social interactions of the young child. Among the specific behaviors studied have been language frequency or content, ascendant behavior, physical contacts, quarrels, conflict, resistance, friendship patterns, cooperative and competitive behavior, rivalry, and aggression. The principal advantages of this technique are the reliability and objectivity of recording. Attention is centered on a specific well-defined behavior so that agreement about it among different observers can be achieved. Since scores are obtained usually in terms of frequency, the results can be treated statistically. For example, the frequency of quarrels can be related to age, sex, IQ, ratings of adjustment, and many similar factors.

Time sampling will not work when the behavior under study is neither overt nor readily observable. It is not feasible, either, for observing infrequent behavior, such as the display of sympathy, compliance, or rare, private child behaviors like fire setting. Because time-sampling studies are restricted to the investigation of a specific behavior, much of the richness and meaningfulness of child interaction goes unrecorded. Precision may be obtained at the cost of understanding. Moreover, data thus obtained can never of themselves yield information about cause and effect. If it were found that one child quarreled more frequently than others, it would be necessary to draw on methods other than time sampling to determine the cause.

Although time sampling, as a tool of developmental psychology, is about half a century old, it recently has come to be associated much more with behavioristic approaches to psychotherapy (see pp. 534) and with applied social psychology than with traditional developmental psychological concerns. The behavior modification approach to intervention into problem behavior requires, first, highly accurate time sampling measures of the base rate (frequency prior to intervention) of the behavior as well as equally careful monitoring of the effects of intervention (through changes in rewards, punishments, nonreinforcement) on the rate at which the behavior occurs. For examples of the use of time sampling in the behavioristic tradition, see Watson and Tharp (1972) and Ackerman (1972).

Psychometric Instruments. Although intelligence and personality tests are not customarily considered as vehicles for observation, they are, in fact, very short samples of behavior and are extremely important in terms of their ability to disclose useful information. Knowledge of the results of an intelligence test provides insights into a child's ability in comparison with other children and into his level of intellectual performance. It also permits one to make predictions about how the child will cope with other tasks and other situations. The usefulness of a score on such *psychometric* tests —tests that measure the speed and precision of mental processes—depends on the meaningfulness of the theory on which the test is based, on the rigor of the procedure, and on the appropriateness of what is measured.

The object of a psychometric test is to provide in a brief interval of time information that would otherwise require hours of intimate contact to obtain. Tests, therefore, are shorthand observational techniques that enable us to make inferences about a larger body of data. For example, in administering a standard intelligence test to a five-year-old, we are not interested in his ability to answer the specific questions as such but in how these questions sample his general intelligence. Specific intelligence and personality tests will be discussed in subsequent chapters.

Questionnaires. Like intelligence and personality tests, the questionnaire is a shorthand method for gaining a considerable amount of information on a specific problem in a brief interval of time. Its use, either written or oral, to obtain information about children has a long history. G. Stanley-Hall is often credited with being the first to use this approach in child psychology. Under his supervision school-teachers in the Boston area administered a general information questionnaire to beginning first-grade children. Although such a procedure seems commonplace today, it was a marked contribution at a time when unscientific speculation often substituted for the collection of data.

One result of Hall's study was the realization that children's thinking did indeed differ from that of adults in terms not only of the quantity of information but also of its quality. The following excerpt from Hall's original paper gives the content of the children's responses to certain questions included in the questionnaire.

> The chief field for such fond and often secret childish fancies is the sky. About three-fourths of all questioned thought the world a plain, and many described it as round like a dollar, while the sky is like a flattened bowl turned over it. The sky is often thin, one might easily break through; half the moon may be seen through it, while the other half is this side; it may be made of snow, but is so large that there is much floor-sweeping to be done in heaven. Some thought the sun went down at night into the ground or just behind certain houses, and went across on or under the ground to go up out of or off the water in the morning, but 48 per cent of all thought that at night it goes or rolls or flies, is blown or walks, or God pulls it up higher out of sight. He takes it into heaven, and perhaps puts it to bed, and even takes off its clothes and puts them on in the morning, or again it lies under the trees where the angels mind it, or goes through and shines on the upper side of the sky, or goes into or behind the moon, as the moon is behind it in the day. It may stay where it is, only we cannot see it, for it is dark, or the dark rains down so, and it comes out when it gets light so it can see. More than half the children questioned conceived the sun as never more than 40 degrees from the zenith, and, naturally enough, city children knew little of the horizon. So the moon comes around when it is a bright night and people want to walk, or forget to light some lamps; it follows us about and has nose and eyes, while it calls the stars into, under, or behind it at night, and they may be made of bits of it. Sometimes the moon is round a month or two, then it is a rim, or a piece is cut off, or it is half stuck or half buttoned into the sky. The stars may be sparks from fire-engines or houses, or, with higher intelligence, they are silver, or God lights them with matches and blows them out or opens the door and calls them in in the morning. Only in a single case were any of the heavenly bodies conceived as openings in the sky to let light or glory through, or as eyes of supernatural beings—a fancy so often ascribed to children and so often found in juvenile literature. Thunder, which anthropologists tell us is or represents the highest

God to most savage races, was apperceived as God groaning or kicking, or rolling barrels about, or turning a big handle, or grinding snow, walking loud, breaking something, throwing logs, having coal run in, pounding about with a big hammer, rattling houses, hitting the clouds, or clouds bumping or clapping together or bursting, or else it was merely ice sliding off lots of houses or cannon in the city or sky, hard rain down the chimney, or big rocks pounding, or piles of boards falling down, or very hard rain, hail, or wind. Lightning is God putting out his finger or opening a door, or turning on gas quick, or (very common) striking many matches at once, throwing stones and iron for sparks, setting paper afire, or it is light going outside and inside the sky, or stars falling. God keeps rain in heaven in a big sink, rows of buckets, a big tub or barrels, and they run over or he lets it down with a water hose through a sieve, a dipper with holes, or sprinkles or tips it down or turns a faucet. God makes it in heaven out of nothing or out of water, or it gets up by splashing up, or he dips it up off the roof, or it rains up off the ground when we don't see it. The clouds are close to the sky; they move because the earth moves and makes them. They are dirty, muddy things, or blankets, or doors of heaven, and are made of fog, of steam that makes the sun go, of smoke, of white wool or feathers and birds, or lace or cloth. In their changing forms very many children, whose very life is fancy, think they see veritable men, or more commonly, because they have so many more forms, animals, faces, and very often God, Santa Claus, angels, etc., are also seen. Closely connected with the above are the religious concepts so common with children. God is a big, perhaps blue, man, very often seen in the sky on or in clouds, in the church, or even street. He came in our gate, comes to see us sometimes. He lives in a big palace or a big brick or stone house on the sky. He makes lamps, babies, dogs, trees, money, etc., and the angels work for him. He looks like the priest, Frobel, papa, etc., and they like to look at him, and a few would like to be God. He lights the stars so he can see to go on the sidewalk or into the church. Birds, children, Santa Claus, live with him, and most but not all like him better than they do the latter. When people die they just go, or are put in a hole, or a box or a black wagon that goes to heaven, or they fly up or are drawn or slung up into the sky where God catches them. They never can get out of the hole, and yet all good people somehow get where God is. He lifts them up, they go up on a ladder or rope, or they carry them up, but keep their eyes shut so they do not know the way, or they are shoved up through a hole. When children get there they have candy, rocking-horses, guns, and everything in the toy-shop or picture-book, play marbles, top, ball, cards, hookey, hear brass bands, have nice clothes, gold watches, and pets, ice-cream and soda-water, and no school. There are men there who died in the war made into angels, and dolls with broken heads go there. Some think they must go through the church to get there, a few thought the horse-cars run there, and one said that the birds that grow on apple-trees are drawn up there by the moon. The bad place is like an oven or a police-station, where it burns, yet is all dark, and folks want to get back, and God kills people or beats them with a cane. God makes babies in heaven, tho the holy mother and even Santa Claus makes some. He lets them down or drops them, and the women or doctors catch them, or he leaves them on the sidewalk, or brings them down a wooden ladder backwards and pulls it up again, or mamma or the doctor or the nurse go up and fetch them sometimes in a balloon, or they fly down and lose off their wings in some place or other and forget it, or jump down to Jesus, who gives them around. They were also often said to be found in flourbarrels, and the flour sticks ever so long, you know, or they grow in cabbages, or God puts them in water, perhaps in the sewer, and the doctors gets them out and takes them to sick folks that want them, or the milkman brings them early in the morning, they are dug out of

> the ground, or bought at the baby-store. Sometimes God puts on a few things or else sends them along if he don't forget it; this shows that no one since Basedow believes in telling children the truth in all things (Hall, in Dennis, 1948, pp. 267–269).

The questionnaire has several methodological advantages over the earlier baby biographies. Since questionnaires are designed to obtain information for specific purposes, their questions concentrate on a well-defined area. Besides, the researcher who uses them can obtain data from a large and representative sample in a relatively short time as compared with the baby biographies, which were concerned with an individual child. These data can be related to several variables. For example, several researchers have administered Hall's questionnaire, with modifications, to children of various ages, and related the subjects' scores to chronological age, mental age, IQ, socioeconomic class, and sex, noting the differences in total scores as well as in answers to specific questions.

A wide variety of questionnaires has been employed with children and their parents, but one further example will suffice. This questionnaire is directed to parents because knowledge of their attitudes and values is often essential to understanding the child's behavior and personality. Questionnaires of this type may deal with statements of fact, such as the age of weaning the child, or with statements that tap attitudes and values that often relate to child-rearing procedures. In the following items excerpted from the Parent Attitude Research Instrument developed at the National Institute of Mental Health, the parent is asked to check the response that best represents his point of view for each statement.

Complete reliance on questionnaire responses has its weaknesses. Both "truthfulness" and unconscious falsification have to be considered. Some questionnaires contain a "lie scale" designed to assess the respondent's willingness to falsify his replies. There are researchers who believe that in assessing a parent's attitude toward certain topics, falsification as such becomes unimportant. Moreover, parents differ in willingness to divulge various kinds of information. Whether the parent comprehends the question as it was intended by the creator of the questionnaire is another matter of concern. In evaluating the findings emerging from a questionnaire, critical note must be taken of all these points.

	Strongly Agree	Mildly Agree	Mildly Disagree	Strongly Disagree
Children should be allowed to disagree with their parents if they feel their own ideas are better.	A	a	d	D
It is frequently necessary to drive the mischief out of a child before he will behave.	A	a	d	D
A wise parent knows better than to pick up the baby whenever he cries.	A	a	d	D
The experience of being on their own is often good for children.	A	a	d	D
Most parents prefer a quiet child to a "scrappy" one.	A	a	d	D

(Schaefer & Bell, 1958)

Experimental Method. One of the outstanding characteristics of this method is its control over the phenomena under investigation and the variables being observed. Scientific experiments are often called "questions put to nature," and the more precisely the questions are stated—that is, the more carefully the experiment is designed—the more exact and unambiguous the answers will be. Tracing a hypothetical problem of the kind a child-development researcher might face may clarify various points.

Shortly before World War II, the effect of nursery-school experience on intelligence provoked an important controversy. Some say that more heat than light was generated over the issue; if so, the fault lay with the methods used to examine it. Suppose we consider this problem. To begin with, the problem must be stated clearly and precisely or else the research will be neither well defined nor definitive. The problem is usually presented in the form of a hypothesis: nurseryschool experience raises the IQ. Now the hypothesis needs to be tested.

First, the IQs are tested of a group of children who have had a year of nursery school. If their IQs are above 100 (average) the hypothesis would seem confirmed. But the group chosen might have been well above average intelligence before going to nursery school. It might have been a *biased sample.* Therefore the above-average IQs cannot be attributed to the nursery-school experience. Something has been learned, but it is necessary to test again.

This time the children to be tested are selected at random from a large group of five-year-olds to ensure an *un*biased sample. The children are tested for intelligence and then retested after a year of nursery school. If the measure of intelligence increases after the second test, the hypothesis would again seem confirmed. However, other factors than nursery-school experience might have improved the children's intelligence; in other words, the effects of other variables have not been controlled. The need is apparent for testing a similar group of children who are *not* exposed to nursery school.

This leads to selection of a *control group,* which does not undergo special treatment. The group accorded special treatment is called the *experimental group.* Subjects for both groups are drawn from a large pool of children and assigned at random to either one. Often, to ensure that no features are present that differentiate the two groups, both are matched on relevant variables, that is, other factors that might influence the results. These might include such things as initial level of ability, sex of the child, or occupational status of the parent. Thus only the one variable under investigation, the *independent variable* (in this illustration, nursery-school experience), is left to be systematically altered. Its effect on the *dependent variable* (intelligence scores) is then measured.

To return to the problem at hand, the intellectual level of both control and experimental groups is measured by administration of a standard intelligence test. The experimental group is then given nursery-school training while the control group is not. Once again, intelligence tests are administered after a period of time. If the scores in the experimental group are significantly higher than those in the control group, the hypothesis is accepted. If no difference in scores exists, the hypothesis is presumably invalid.

This method, then, holds all possibly relevant variables constant while identifying *the effects of the systematic manipulation of the single variable under investigation.* Although it is the most valuable method for research, this technique does not always apply in child development. In many important problems the researcher cannot manipulate the independent variable. For example, rejection or acceptance by parents is thought to have important bearing on child personality and adjustment. Yet it is mainifestly impossible to manipulate this variable for research purposes. Under the circumstances, researches turn to "experiments in nature." They assess the adjustment of children who are thought to have suffered from parental rejection in the past and contrast this with the adjustment of a group of children thought to be accepted. Even so, they can never be sure that the two groups do not differ in other variables that perhaps help to account for the difference in adjustments. Nor can they ever be sure that parental rejection or acceptance does, in fact, affect adjustment, because they are unable to set up an "experimental control," that is, a control group in distinction to an experimental group. The same criticism may be made of any studies that attempt to tie parental attitudes to a type of behavior in the child when the parental attitudes are sought *after* the behavior has appeared.

Experimenter Influences. The relationship between the experimenter and his subjects is an aspect of the experimental method that has received a great deal of attention only recently. Although much effort is made in any experiment to standardize and objectify the procedure employed, there is evidence that the experimenter influences the outcome of the research through his own expectations concerning the organism's behavior (Rosenthal, 1963, 1966) either through experimenter behavior toward the organism or through errors in observation.

In conducting an experiment, the researcher begins with certain hypotheses, expectancies, or biases concerning the results. These are communicated to the subject through various visual and auditory cues such as gestures and tone of voice.

Research has identified a number of characteristics of experimenter and subject that affect the results of an investigation. These include sex, race, need for social approval, status of the experimenter, and prior acquaintance between the experimenter and the subject. Two examples drawn from research with children will serve to illustrate this general phenomenon.

A methodological study (Cowan, Weber, Hoddinott, & Klein, 1967) was designed to examine the effects on mean length of response (MLR) of the stimulus used, the socioeconomic status, age, and sex of the child, and the sex of the experimenter. Approximately 250 children, aged 5, 7, 9, and 11, were shown 10 colored pictures with the request that they tell a story about each picture. An MLR score was computed for each story. In general the results showed an increase in MLR with age, and highly significant differences in MLR were obtained depending upon the pictures used to elicit the response. Further, one experimenter elicited longer responses from the 5- and 7-year-olds, whereas the 7- and 9-year-olds performed better with the other experimenter. Similar differences were found to depend on the sex of the child; one experimenter elicited higher MLR scores from males and the other from females.

In the second study (Allen, Dubanoski, & Stevenson, 1966), the effects of race of experimenter were examined, comparing praise and criticism in a simple marble-dropping task. In agreement with earlier findings, which suggested that a familiar person is less effective as a social reinforcer than a more remote person, those subjects (all white) who received praise from a Negro experimenter showed an increase in rate of response whereas those receiving praise from a white adult showed a decrease in rate of response. Interestingly, Rosenthal, specializing in the investigation of the distortion of reality by experimenters' biases was co-author of the well-publicized but severely defective research report *Pygmalion in the Classroom* (Rosenthal & Jacobson, 1968); (see Thorndike, 1968, for a discussion of the lethal errors in this research effort); defective, probably as a result of experimenter bias. We can hope to, and try to, guard against experimenter effects—but are not always successful.

Two points concerning the interaction between experimenter and subject require emphasis. First, results of research should be interpreted with some caution because they may be affected by experimenter biases and by various experimenter and subject characteristics. Second, the fact that the experimenter influences the subject in subtle and covert ways, even in a situation that is standardized, controlled, and arranged to eliminate such influences as much as possible, should give us pause for thought. How much greater are the mutual influences in parent-child and teacher-child interactions, in which one of the established goals of the relationship is the modification by the adult of child behavior and attitudes. No human interaction leaves the participants unaffected.

Interview Method. Although the interview has been used most frequently as a clinical tool for understanding an individual case, it is now being employed increasingly as a research device for gaining information about a specific question under investigation. An interview is made up of several questions designed to elicit certain kinds of information. Often the questions are tested beforehand to find out if they do, in fact, obtain the information desired. Frequently the interview is tape-recorded so that the interviewer need not rely on memory or sketchily written notes. The information acquired from the interview is evaluated in various ways on a rating scale, with ratings usually made independently by two persons to check on inter-rater agreement. In the following replies of two mothers to the question: "Some people feel that it is very important for a child to learn not to fight with other children; and others feel that there are times when a child has to learn to fight. How do you feel about this?" the first reply was rated as indicating no demand for the child to be aggressive toward her peers, whereas the second reply was considered a high demand to have the child fight.

A

Mother. I go out and ask other mothers what happened and when I find out, I say "All right come in the house now." Sooner than go to their mothers and fight with them, I bring her in the house and keep her in for a while and talk it all over with her and tell her where she's wrong or where the other child is wrong and then after a while I let her out again and tell her to go—either she'll end up probably playing with the same child again, anyway—to go play with somebody else.

B

Mother. Well, I believe that a child has to fight and to stick up for his own rights. I hate to see a kid that is always—well—I think if they don't they are whining babies and are always home with their mothers; and we have always taught Bill to hit them right back and to give them one better than what he got. And there are a few children, in this neighborhood, that Bill is afraid of and he will come home and tell me what they have done to him–but the only satisfaction that he has ever got was that, "We have told you if he hits you to hit him back, and until then don't tell me your stories" (Sears, Maccoby, & Levin, 1957, pp. 246–247).

Some of the disadvantages of the questionnaire pervade the interview technique, but others are eliminated. A mother's need to portray herself in a certain way affects her report. Moreover, the success of the interview depends on her willingness to divulge various sorts of information and on her memory. Several studies have found many inaccuracies in mother's recall of earlier events related to child-rearing attitudes and practices. One investigation compared information obtained in three interviews with mothers with data from a final interview (Haggard, Brekstad, & Skard, 1960). The interviews spread over a period beginning about a month before delivery and ending when the child was between seven and eight years of age. As a rule, the final interviews were more a reflection of the mother's current recollections of the past than of accurate accounts of past events themselves. The accuracy of recall was related to the type of information requested. Specific facts, such as the length of the child at birth, were recalled best, whereas information on general wishes and attitudes was recalled next best. Data based on earlier anxieties of mothers were recalled least accurately. Furthermore, the lack of independence of the data poses another problem in interviews, especially when the person interviewed is a mother or someone else who is not the actual subject of the investigation. The information so gathered may reflect the personality of the mother rather than the actual facts.

On the other side of the ledger, the face-to-face relationship between interviewer and interviewee enables a skilled interviewer to gauge the earnestness and sincerity of the respondent. This is not possible in a questionnaire.

Diffusion and Application of Research Findings

The beginning of research in child development in this country can be traced to the late 1920s and early 1930s. Our previous discussion has described some of the principal research methods which have been employed to gain information about children in the past 40–50 years. To what extent has this information been disseminated to the public, specifically to parents and to teachers, the two main groups whose job it is to socialize and instruct children? A quote from Toffler's (1970) brilliant book, *Future Shock*, will illustrate the situation in the technical field with regard to the recent acceleration in rate of change and in transmission and diffusion of ideas.

> Whether we examine distances traveled, altitudes reached, minerals mined, or explosive power harnessed, the same accelerative trend is obvious. The pattern, here and in a thousand other statistical series, is absolutely clear and unmistakable. Millennia or centuries go by, and then, in our own times, a sudden bursting of the limits, a fantastic spurt forward.
>
> The reason for this is that technology feeds on itself. Technology makes more technology possible, as we can see if we look for a moment at the process of innovation. Technological innovation consists of three stages, linked together into a self-reinforcing cycle. First, there is the creative, feasible idea. Second, its practical application. Third, its diffusion through society.
>
> The process is completed, the loop closed, when the diffusion of technology embodying the new idea, in turn, helps generate new creative ideas. Today there is evidence that the time between each of the steps in this cycle has been shortened.

Thus it is not merely true, as frequently noted, that 90 percent of all the scientists who ever lived are now alive, and that new scientific discoveries are being made every day. These new ideas are put to work much more quickly than ever before. The time between original concept and practical use has been radically reduced. This is a striking difference between ourselves and our ancestors. Appollonius of Perga discovered conic sections, but it was 2000 years before they were applied to engineering problems. It was literally centuries between the time Paracelsus discovered that ether could be used as an anaesthetic and the time it began to be used for that purpose.

Even in more recent times the same pattern of delay was present. In 1836 a machine was invented that mowed, threshed, tied straw into sheaves and poured grain into sacks. This machine was itself based on technology at least twenty years old at the time. Yet it was not until a century later, in the 1930's, that such a combine was actually marketed. The first English patent for a typewriter was issued in 1714. But a century and a half elapsed before typewriters became commercially available. A full century passed between the time Nicholas Appert discovered how to can food and the time canning became important in the food industry.

Today such delays between idea and application are almost unthinkable. It is not that we are more eager or less lazy than our ancestors, but we have, with the passage of time, invented all sorts of social devices to hasten the process. Thus we find that the time between the first and second stages of the innovative cycle—between idea and application—has been cut radically. Frank Lynn, for example, in studying twenty major innovations, such as frozen food, antibiotics, integrated circuits and synthetic leather, found that since the beginning of this century more than sixty percent has been slashed from the average time needed for a major scientific discovery to be translated into a useful technological form. Today a vast and growing research and development industry is consciously working to reduce the lag still further.

But if it takes less time to bring a new idea to the marketplace, it also takes less time for it to sweep through the society. Thus the interval between the second and third stages of the cycle—between application and diffusion—has likewise been sliced, and the pace of diffusion is rising with astonishing speed. This is borne out by the history of several familiar household appliances. Robert B. Young at the Stanford Research Institute has studied the span of time between the first commercial appearance of a new electrical applicance and the time the industry manufacturing it reaches peak production of the item.

Young found that for a group of appliances introduced in the United States before 1920—including the vacuum cleaner, the electric range, and the refrigerator—the average span between introduction and peak production was thirty-four years. But for a group that appeared in the 1939–1959 period—including the electric frying pan, television, and washer-dryer combination—the span was only eight years. The lag had shrunk by more than 76 percent. "The post-war group," Young declared, "demonstrated vividly the rapidly accelerating nature of the modern cycle."

The stepped-up pace of invention, exploitation, and diffusion, in turn, accelerates the whole cycle still further. For new machines or techniques are not merely a product, but a source, of fresh creative ideas.

Each new machine or technique, in a sense, changes all existing machines and techniques, by permitting us to put them together into new combinations. The number of possible combinations rises exponentially as the number of new machines or techniques rises arithmetically. Indeed, each new combination may, itself, be regarded as a new super-machine.

The computer, for example, made possible a sophisticated space effort. Linked with sensing devices, communica-

> tions equipment, and power sources, the computer became part of a configuration that in aggregate forms a single new supermachine—a machine for reaching into and probing outer space. But for machines or techniques to be combined in new ways, they have to be altered, adapted, refined or otherwise changed. So that the very effort to integrate machines into supermachines compels us to make still further technological innovations.
>
> It is vital to understand, moreover, that technological innovation does not merely combine and recombine machines and techniques. Important new machines do more than suggest or compel changes in other machines—they suggest novel solutions to social, philosophical, even personal problems. They alter man's total intellectual environment—the way he thinks and looks at the world.

Is this accelerated rate of the cycle of discovery, application, and diffusion true in the field of child psychology? Before attempting to answer this question, several related considerations will be discussed.

At the outset it must be noted that our thinking about children, about child rearing, and about teaching children has been marked by fads and by cyclical changes. While this does not in itself indicate that the "experts" have been either wrong or fickle, it does suggest an inadequate scientific basis for our thinking regarding human behavior. It would be only fair to add, however, that scientific evidence may not be sufficient for decision-making in the area of values. For example, even if research were able to tell us the specific child-rearing techniques which would produce a given type of individual, the final decision would rest upon our values regarding the preferred and desirable adult personality, behavior, and conduct. Perhaps this situation may help to explain the cyclical nature of child-rearing advice in this country. Advice in favor of a rigid approach in the thirties gave way to the permissiveness of the forties and fifties which in turn has been replaced by a middle-of-the-road position in the sixties and seventies. Similarly, the early phonics approach to the teaching of reading was spurned in favor of a "look-say" method which, for a variety of reasons, was superseded by a return to an emphasis on phonetics coupled with many other techniques. Is it any wonder that professionals in these areas are viewed with suspicion by the average layman.

To summarize, while there may be an inadequate scientific basis for understanding human behavior, the values held by a given individual in a given society largely determine his decisions concerning behavior and conduct.

Now to return to the original question regarding the dissemination of scientific information in child psychology. In a recent questionnaire administered to a group of college students by one of the present authors, they were asked to name those persons whom they felt had most influenced parents and teachers in their dealings with children. Perhaps not surprisingly, Spock was mentioned most frequently, and yet he cannot be considered a scientific researcher. To be sure, some of the advice included in the many editions (1946–1968) of his baby and child care manual may have been based on scientific evidence. *The fact remains, however, that professional researchers have written largely for professional audiences with little concern for the application of their research findings.* Consequently, the interpretation, application, and dissemination of the results of research have been left to others. Such dissemination has not been given priority in professional circles. Thus, the American parent has few places to turn to for sound advice and counseling concerning the daily problems he encounters in child rearing.

Some of the most popular topics in child research either have little relevance for understanding the child's behavior at home or at school, or it has not been translated into terms meaningful to parents and teachers. For example, conscience development has been the subject of a great many research investigations in the past 10–15 years, and yet little has emerged from this body of research which is useful to parents in understanding this extremely important area of child behavior. Many other such topics can be listed: form versus color preference, children's learning, infant conditioning, altruistic behavior, birth order effects, achievement motivation, aggression, anxiety, and Piaget's notion of conservation in children.

We must conclude that the accelerated rate of the cycle of discovery, application, and diffusion which characterizes the technological fields in this country is not true in child psychology. New, important, and useful ideas have not been generated. Old notions, some of which are sound and others not, still prevail. Researchers, as well as granting agencies which support research, must develop a deeper sense of responsibility and accountability in terms of the relevance of research problems to the human condition.

The findings of a great many research investigations are mentioned throughout this book; a great many others receive no mention. The authors based their selection, in part, on the extent to which the research data appeared relevant and meaningful to an understanding of the child's day-to-day behavior. It is hoped that the student will maintain a critical point of view towards the studies described, attempting always to examine the material in terms of individual children, their development, their problems, and the long range goal of achieving a balanced and productive adulthood.

Longitudinal versus Cross-Sectional Approaches

Although there is a multitude of "facts" one might wish to learn about child behavior, probably one of the most persistent objectives of child research is the study of development. This is the emphasis in child psychology: the changes that take place over time in the behavior and characteristics of children. Thus, if we know enough about development in general and about a particular child's past development, we can predict his future development, his adult personality, his adult adjustment, and the values and purpose he will have as an adult.

Because of this concern of child psychology with development, much research has been devoted to the description of children at various ages. Data are available in the areas of motor development, language development, intellectual development, social development, emotional development, and physical development. These have been acquired through two approaches, the longitudinal and the cross-sectional.

Longitudinal Method. This approach is suited to the study of development because the same children are studied over a period of time. Munn (1955, p. 8) has likened it to time-lapse photography, in which a single object is photographed at periodic intervals, providing a picture of continuous growth. Longitudinal study provides a knowledge of the patterns and processes of change over the long run; thus individual growth curves can be plotted in such areas as language and physical development. With this knowledge of changes in a single individual, one can relate them to the presence or absence of other factors. For example, the changes in IQ in an individual case can be shown to relate to various environmental circumstances (Honzik, Macfarlane, & Allen, 1948). But this does not necessarily mean there is a cause-and-effect relationship.

The early baby biographies discussed above used a longitudinal approach to record and describe the behavior of a single child over a certain time period. The first such study was that by Buffon, in which the height measurements of a child were reported for the 17-year period from 1759 to 1776.

Some research topics require use of the longitudinal approach. It is essential in investigating the effects on development of instituted procedures. It is also useful for gathering data on generational differences and consistency in child-rearing practices. A number of longitudinal studies have been conducted; for a report of them until 1954, see Stone and Onque (1959). More recently, a description of 10 long-term longitudinal studies has been presented by Kagan (1964). The sample, methods, and goals of each project are discussed and bibliographies of published research are included. The longitudinal studies described are the Oakland Growth Study (Adolescent Study), the Berkeley Growth Study, and the Guidance Study at the University of California, Berkeley; the Child Research Council's Study in Human Development at the University of Colorado Medical School; the Study of Human Development at the Fels Research Institute; the Child-to-Adult Study, University of Minnesota; the Longitudinal Study of Child Health and Development, Harvard School of Public Health; the Study of Gifted Children, Stanford University; the Infancy, Coping, and Mental Health Studies, Menninger Foundation; and the Study of Behavioral Development, New York University. Before considering some of the obstacles to this kind of research, let us briefly examine three longitudinal studies.

One of the first of its kind was the short-term longitudinal study by Shirley (1931, 1933a, b) of motor, intellectual, and personality development, which followed 25 infants from birth to two years of age. During the first week in the hospital, the infants were examined daily. During the second week they were examined every other day. For the remainder of their first year, they were seen at weekly intervals in their homes, and throughout their second year at biweekly intervals. All this time the infants' responses to simple tests were recorded in descriptive, qualitative terms, and mothers' records supplemented the examination data. With respect to motor development, Shirley concentrated on the sequence of development and concluded: (1) there is a consistency in the sequence, with few reversals in the appearance of such items as chest up, sit alone, stand with help, and creep; and (2) motor development is in line with the anatomical law of the direction of growth, which states that growth proceeds from the head to the feet (*cephalocaudal*). The data collected in the intensive study of the 25 infants have been of considerable interest and value in laying the basis for certain areas of developmental research and in providing information obtained by careful, scientific methods.

The second study deals with the long-term prediction of adjustment. In 1950 a wide variety of information was obtained from the entire school population —3200 children—in the fourth grade and above in Nobles County, Minnesota.

> There were scales measuring the child's attitudes toward his family, his sense of responsibility, his work and attitudes toward work based on his experience in home duties and chores, his interests and

> play activities, and his favorable attitudes toward experience. There was also a scale made up of items that in previous studies had been answered differently by delinquent and by nondelinquent children. The items had to do with personal-social attitudes, and with the child's fears and worries. From school records, we obtained the Intelligence Quotients of the children. In addition to information about the education and occupation of each parent, we also had several measures of socioeconomic or cultural status. On the basis of a check against the current adjustment of the children, five scores were selected from the inventories given the children to be combined into a Pupil Index, which is used as a general score to predict future adjustment.
>
> Because we wished to see how well ratings made by teachers would predict future adjustment of children, three rating forms were filled out by the teachers in 1950. These ratings concerned the child's responsibility, his personality traits, and his adjustment in the classroom or home room. Scores on these were combined to form the 1950 Teacher Index (Anderson, 1959, pp. 8–9).

Several follow-up studies were conducted and the final assessment of adjustment was made seven years later, in 1957. Again various kinds of information were obtained to measure the adjustment.

> In designing measures of outcomes in terms of later adjustment, the type of information that can be secured about a person's relation to the demands of life must be considered. There is first the record made by the person in school, community, and on the job, which is the most obvious sign of his success. Such information may be regarded as the objective aspect of the person's life and can be obtained from various records. Next, there are the person's own feelings about himself and his view of his relation to others. Does he feel happy and satisfied with his life? Does he think he gets along well? Such information may be regarded as more subjective evidence of the person's life adjustment and is obtained from the person himself. Last, there are the impressions made by the person upon other people. How is he seen by others who know him? Some who know him very well are likely to balance his traits and feelings against his objective record. Finally, an interview with the person himself secures information about his accomplishments and feelings. The psychologically trained interviewer may thus balance the objective and the subjective aspects of the process of adjustment. In our follow-up studies we attempted to secure information about the person for each aspect of his life, such as work, recreation, education, and family life, from each of the sources, that is, from the records, the person's own statement about himself, the impressions others had of him, and the judgment of skilled psychological interviewers with psychological training (Anderson, 1959, pp. 9–10).

In general, the investigators predicted good adjustment more readily and more accurately than poor adjustment. Although separate criteria proved useful for predicting adjustment by sex, IQ predicted equally well for boys and girls. The investigators concluded that "it seems unlikely that a very short screening instrument that will predict well into the future can be developed from our personality measures on the children" (Anderson, 1959, pp. 36).

The Berkeley Growth Study was initiated in 1928 (Bayley, 1965). Sixty-one infants were enrolled in the study within their first two months of life. Intelligence tests, anthropometric measures, physical examinations, and X-rays were administered to the subjects at periodic intervals. Assessment was made of manual skills and gross motor performance, and data were collected from projective tests, interest questionnaires, and incidental records. In addition, maternal behaviors toward the child were observed and rated. Data are still being gathered from the original subjects, who are entering their fifth decade of life.

Findings with regard to sex differences will illustrate some of the interesting results obtained in this longitudinal study. The correlations between IQ and several scioeconomic measures (family income, father's occupation, education of parents, and a rating of the home and neighborhood) were established earlier for girls than for boys. This was true also for the relation between the height of parent and child. These trends reflect sex differences in rate of maturing as well as differential effects of maternal behavior. The latter is suggested by the pattern of correlations between various maternal behaviors and the children's IQ level through adolescence. Boys with democratic, loving mothers in infancy scored higher on IQ measures than boys with hostile, rejecting mothers. However, few such relationships were obtained for girls. Bayley concluded that girls' IQs tend to be related to parental ability, whereas IQs of boys are more closely related to early maternal behaviors.

Several characteristics of the longitudinal approach make it costly in terms of time and effort as well as difficult to carry out. First is the matter of turnover in research personnel. Much time is lost if it becomes necessary to change research directors or other personnel during the investigation. Next is the problem of subjects dropping out. Often the data cannot be analyzed until the very end of the investigation; consequently, if a subject drops out during the study, considerable information involving many hours of research effort is lost. Moreover, the final sample may depart from the original group of subjects so markedly that it may affect the results of the research. Often, too, new insights are achieved and new measuring instruments are developed in the course of a longitudinal study, yet it is never possible to "go back" and obtain previously unsolicited information. Once the plan of research has been established and the subjects and procedure have been selected it is difficult if not hazardous to attempt to alter them without jeopardizing the entire investigation.

Cross-Sectional Method. Because of the foregoing disadvantages of the longitudinal approach, researchers have predominantly used the cross-sectional method in child-development research. This method consists of studying children of different ages. For example, to study language development in the young child, Templin (1957) selected 60 children at each of the following age levels: three, three-and-a-half, four, four-and-a-half, five, six, seven, and eight. This selection furnished norms for four measures of language: speech sound articulation, sound discrimination ability, sentence structure, and vocabulary. Obviously this approach is easier to pursue and saves more time than the longitudinal. The investigator does not have to wait for subjects to pass through various age periods; 8-year-olds, 9-year-olds, and 10-year-olds can all be studied simultaneously. A large number of subjects representative of the population is readily available in the public schools. Furthermore, the plan of research can be modified without a necessary loss of time.

Yet there are some types of information that cross-sectional studies, by their very nature, cannot provide. They teach very little about causation: why does a certain behavior appear at a certain age level? Why are there individual differences at every level? These cross-sectional data do not explain. Nor do they reveal the effect on personality of deviations in development: what effect does retardation in language development have on a child's social adjustment at school? How does an infant's accelerated motor development influence his father's attitude toward him? Finally, the cross-sectional approach does not illuminate the patterning of behavior over the long run for any single child because it studies different children at different age levels at one time.

Some of the advantages of both longitudinal and cross-sectional methods are incorporated in the accelerated longitudinal or convergence approach (Bell, 1953, 1954). Subjects of different ages are retested with some overlapping of age level for younger and older children. For example, four groups of children, ages 6, 8, 10, and 12, are each measured yearly over a three-year term. This provides data for twelve points in time rather than only three, and since there is an overlapping of ages tested rather than only three, and since there is an overlapping of ages tested during the three-year interval, information is obtained that permits the comparison of different groups at the same ages. Note the overlaps in the following illustration.

Group	Ages Tested
A	6, 7, 8
B	8, 9, 10
C	10, 11, 12
D	12, 13, 14

Normative Studies

A brief mention of normative studies or surveys should be made. Although these may be longitudinal, normative data are usually obtained from cross-sectional investigations. In this sense norms are stages related to the ages at which various skills or characteristics "normally" appear, or the ages at which they appear among "normal" children. *Norms do not, however, tell what is "normal" for an individual child.* Many aspects of development are related only loosely to chronological age. For example, at one time only norms of weight were listed for various ages. Then, as the importance of other variables affecting weight was recognized, weight norms began taking height into account also; and more recently, body build and structure have been added.

However, there has been an overemphasis on norms, especially in books and periodicals available to laymen. Such norms are misunderstood and have been the source of much unnecessary worry and concern, on the part of mothers particularly. Arnold Gesell, an early worker in child growth and development, has published norms for many aspects of development. Table 1-1 contains schedules describing the behavior characteristic of an 18-month-old child. Many of these items are presented pictorially in Figure 1-1. Such books by Gesell as *Infant and Child in the Culture of Today* (Gesell & Ilg, 1943), *The Child from Five to Ten* (Gesell, & Ilg, 1946), and *Youth: the Years from Ten to Sixteen* (Gesell, Ilg, & Ames, 1956) have been criticized for stressing ages and stages of normal development. Entire chapters of these books are devoted to descriptions of the "one-year-old," "two-year-old," and so forth. Perhaps the fault lies not so much with the books as with those who seek too eagerly for early indications of normality or precocity in their children. Additional sets of norms for selected behaviors are provided in Tables 1-2, 1-3, and 1-4.

Misconceptions about norms have also arisen because of the emphasis on the mean or "average" time of appearance of a certain skill or behavior. Too often, however, the age *range* at which the skill

TABLE 1-1 Developmental Schedules†

	15 Months	KEY AGE: 18 Months	21 Months
Motor	Walks: few steps, starts, stops Walks: falls by collapse (*18m) Walks: creeping discarded Stairs: creeps up (*18m) M. Cubes: tower of 2 Pellets: (no dem.) places in bottle Book: helps turn pages (*18m)	Walks: seldom falls Walks: fast, runs stiffly (*24m) Stairs: walks up, 1 hand held (*21m) Small chair: seats self Adult chair: climbs into (*. . .) Ball: hurls (*48m) Large ball: walks into (*21m) Book: turns pages, 2–3 at once (*24m)	Walks: squats in play (*. . .) Stairs: walks down, 1 hand held (*24m) Stairs: walks up, holds rail (*24m) Large ball: (dem.) kicks (*24m) M. Cubes: tower of 5–6
Adaptive	M. Cubes: tower of 2 Cup-cu: 6 in & out cup (*18m) Drawing: incip. imitation stroke (*18m) Formbd: (no dem.) places round block Formbd: adapts round block promptly	M. Cubes: tower of 3–4 Cup-cu: 10 into cup Pellet & bo: dumps responsively Drawing: scribbles spontan. (*36m) Drawing: makes stroke imitatively Formbd: piles 3 blocks (*24m)	M. Cubes: tower of 5–6 M. Cubes: imitates pushing train (*24m) Formbd: places 2–3 blocks Perf. box: inserts corner of sq. (*24m) Perf. box: retrieves ball
Language	Vo: 4–5 words includ. names Vo: uses jargon (*24m) Book: pats pictures (*18m)	Book: looks selectively Vo: 10 words includ. names Picture cd: names or points 1 Test obj: names ball Ball: 2 directions	Vo: 20 words Speech: combines 2–3 words spontan. (*24m) Ball: 3 directions
Personal-Social	Feeding: bottle discarded Feeding: inhib. grasp of dish Toilet: partial regulation (*24m) Toilet: bowel control Toilet: indicates wet pants (*18m) Commun: says "ta-ta" or equiv. Commun: points, voc. wants (*21m) Play: shows or offers toy (*21m) Play: casts obj. in play or refus. (*18m)	Feeding: hands empty dish (*. . .) Feeding: feeds self in part, spills (*36m) Toilet: regulated daytime (*24m) Play: pulls a toy (*30m) Play: carries or hugs doll (*24m)	Feeding: handles cup well Commun: asks for food, toilet, drink Commun: echoes 2 or more last words (*24m) Commun: pulls person to show (*24m)

*Temporary patterns are indicated on the schedules by an asterisk followed by the age at which the pattern is replaced by a more mature pattern of the same nature.
†Gesell & Amatruda, 1941, p. 24.

1. Walks alone; seldom falls

4. Builds tower of three

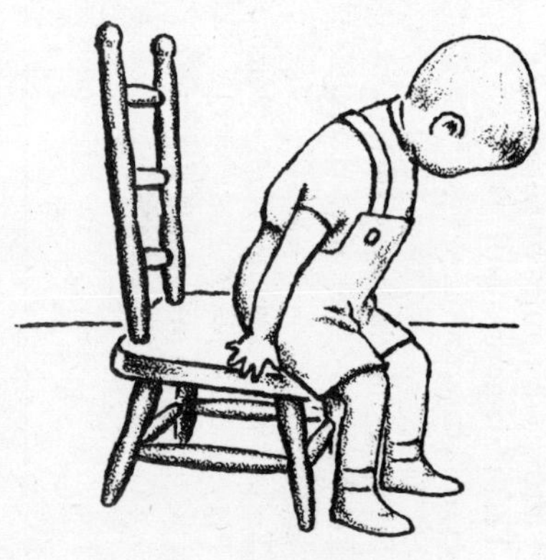
2. Seats self in small chair

5. Fills cup with cubes

3. Turns pages two or three at a time

6. Dumps pellet from bottle

FIGURE 1-1 Behavior characteristics of an 18-month-old child (adapted from Gesell & Amatruda, 1941).

7. Imitates stroke

8. Identifies one picture

9. Hurls ball

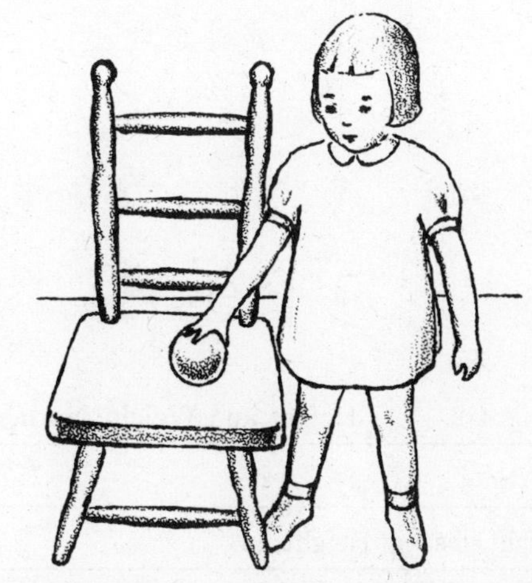

10. On command puts ball on chair

11. Walks into ball

12. Pulls toy

FIGURE 1-1 (*Continued*)

TABLE 1-2. Height and Weight Norms for American Children*†

BOYS			GIRLS	
Weight, lbs.	Height, in.	Age	Weight, lbs.	Height, in.
7.5	19.9	Birth	7.4	19.8
12.6	23.8	3 mo.	12.4	23.4
16.7	26.1	6 mo.	16.0	25.7
20.0	28.0	9 mo.	19.2	27.6
22.2	29.6	12 mo.	21.5	29.2
23.7	30.9	15 mo.	23.0	30.5
25.2	32.2	18 mo.	24.5	31.8
27.7	34.4	2 yrs.	27.1	34.1
30.0	36.3	2½ yrs.	29.6	36.0
32.2	37.9	3 yrs.	31.8	37.7
34.3	39.3	3½ yrs.	33.9	39.2
36.4	40.7	4 yrs.	36.2	40.6
38.4	42.0	4½ yrs.	38.5	42.0
40.5	42.8	5 yrs.	40.5	42.9
45.6	45.0	5½ yrs.	44.0	44.4
48.3	46.3	6 yrs.	46.5	45.6

*Nelson, et al., 1969, pp. 42–44.

†The following are useful "signposts" for American children (Weech, 1954):

Weight: (1) Average birth W, both sexes is 7 lb., 6 oz; (2) From 3 to 12 months W (lb.)—age in months plus 11; (3) At 30 months W = 30 lb; (4) At 3.5 years W = 35 lb; (5) From 4 to 8 years W (lb.) = 6 times age in years plus 12; (6) From 8 to 12 years W (lb.) = 6 times age in years plus 5.

Height: (1) Average birth length, both sexes, is 20 in; (2) At 12 months H is 30 in; (3) From 2 to 14 years H (in.) = 2½ times age in years plus 30.

TABLE 1-3. Developmental Sequences in Four Areas of Behavior*

Age Level	Developmental Area			
	Motor Behavior	Adaptive Behavior	Language Behavior	Personal-Social Behavior
5 years	Skips on alternate feet.	Counts 10 pennies.	Speaks without infantile articulation. Asks "Why?"	Dresses without assistance. Asks meanings of words.
4 years	Skips on one foot.	Builds gate of 5 cubes. Draws "man."	Uses conjunctions. Understands prepositions.	Can wash and dry face. Goes on errands. Plays cooperatively.
3 years	Stands on one foot. Builds tower of 10 cubes.	Builds bridge of 3 cubes. Imitates cross.	Talks in sentences. Answers simple questions.	Uses spoon well. Puts on shoes. Takes turns.
2 years	Runs. Builds tower of 6 cubes.	Builds tower of 6 cubes. Imitates circular stroke.	Uses phrases. Understands simple directions.	Verbalizes toilet needs. Plays with dolls.
18 months	Walks without falling. Seats self. Tower of 3 cubes.	Dumps pellet from bottle. Imitates crayon strokes.	Jargons. Names pictures.	Uses spoon with moderate spilling. Toilet regulated.
12 months	Walks with help. Cruises. Prehends pellet with precision.	Releases cube in cup.	Says two or more words.	Cooperates in dressing. Gives toy. Finger feeds.
40 weeks	Sits alone. Creeps. Pulls to feet. Crude prehensory release.	Combines two cubes.	Says one word. Heeds his name.	Plays simple nursery games. Feeds self cracker.
28 weeks	Sits leaning forward on hands. Grasps cube. Rakes at pellet.	Transfers cube from hand to hand.	Crows. Vocalizes eagerness. Listens to own vocalizations.	Plays with feet and toys. Expectant in feeding situations.
16 weeks	Head steady. Symmetrical postures. Hands open.	Competent eye following. Regards rattle in hand.	Coos. Laughs. Vocalizes socially.	Plays with hands and dress. Recognizes bottle. Poises mouth for food.
4 weeks	Head sags. Tonic neck reflex. Hands fisted.	Stares at surroundings. Restricted eye following.	Small throaty sounds. Heeds bell.	Regards faces.

*Gesell & Amatruda, 1941.

TABLE 1-4. Inventory of Developmental Tasks, Santa Clara, California, Unified School District

Developmental Ability Areas	Age Levels			
	Preschool	5–5½ years	6–6½ years	7 years
Motor Coordination	Creep Walk Run Jump Hop Balance on one foot	Skip Balance on walking beam	Demonstrate right and left Jump rope assisted	Jump rope alone
Visual Motor	Follow target with eyes String beads Copy circle Use scissors Copy cross	Copy square Tie shoes	Copy letters Copy sentences	Copy diamond
Visual Perception	Match color objects Match form objects Match size objects Match size and form on paper	Match numbers Match letters	Match direction on design Isolate visual images	Match words
Visual Memory	Recall of animal pictures Name objects from memory Recall of a three-color sequence	Recall of a two-picture sequence Reproduce design from memory	Recall of a three-picture sequence Recall of a three-part design	Recall of word forms
Auditory Perception	Discrimination between common sounds Identify common sounds	Locate source of sound Match beginning sounds	Hear fine differences between similar sounds Match rhyming sounds	Match ending sounds
Auditory Memory	Perform three commands	Repeat a sentence Repeat tapping sequence	Repeat four numbers Recall story facts	Repeat five numbers
Language		Give personal information Describe simple objects	Relate words and pictures Define words	Uses correct grammar
Conceptual		Assign number value	Identify positions Tell how two items are alike	Sort objects two ways

appears in the subjects sampled has not been described. Although the norm for walking alone may be 59 weeks, the *normal range* may be from 8 to 18 months. Few if any developmental skills can be considered to suggest a pathological condition if they do not appear at a *precise* age. Norms do provide some basis for comparison, however, and aid in understanding normal behavior and development.

SUMMARY

In this chapter we have explored techniques of observation, prediction, and control and have described various ways for obtaining information about children. Noting some of the advantages and disadvantages of each, we have seen the research areas in which each method of gaining information is most appropriate. In addition, we have stressed the cautions that must be observed in making statements about cause and effect. The identification of cause-and-effect relationships is most valuable, for it permits predictions about behavior, and predictability is the aim of all scientific research. Only through carefully designed and carefully controlled scientific experiments can safe statements about causation perhaps be made. Yet the basis for formulating "fruitful" experimental hypotheses—that is, hypotheses leading to new hypotheses—may be the use of other research methods.

Much has been learned and much else remains to be learned from use of case studies, questionnaires, broad observational techniques, and psychometric tests. Only when students and researchers recognize the safeguards that must be taken and the shortcomings and weaknesses of a given research method can they show adequate caution in accepting the findings and claims of research. How information is obtained determines the extent to which we can rely on its validity.

REFERENCES

Ackerman, J. M. *Operant conditioning techniques for the classroom teacher.* Scott, Foresman, Chicago, 1972.

Allen, S., Dubanoski, R., & Stevenson, H. Children's performance as a function of race of E, race of S, and type of verbal reinforcement. *Journal of Experimental Child Psychology*, 1966, **4**, 248–256.

Allport, G. W. *Personality; a psychological interpretation.* New York: Holt, 1937.

Anderson, J. E. *A survey of children's adjustment over time.* Minneapolis: Institute of Child Development, 1959.

Armstrong, M. D., & Tyler, F. H. Studies in phenylketonuria. I. Restricted phenylalanine intake in phenylketonuria. *Journal of Clinical Investigation*, 1955, **34**, 565–580.

Arrington, R. Time sampling in studies of social behavior: A critical review of techniques and results with research suggestions. *Psychological Bulletin*, 1943, **40**, 81–124.

Baller, W. R. A study of the present social status of a group of adults who, when they were in elementary schools, were classified as mentally deficient. *Genetic Psychology Monographs*, 1936, **18**, No. 3.

Barker, R. G. The stream of behavior as an empirical problem. In R. G. Barker (Ed.), *The stream of behavior.* New York: Appleton-Century-Crofts, 1963.

Barker, R. G., & Wright, H. F. *One boy's day.* New York: Harper, 1951.

Barker, R. G., & Wright, H. F. *Midwest and its children.* Evanston, Ill.: Row, Peterson, 1954.

Bayley, N. Research in child development: A longitudinal perspective. *Merrill-Palmer Quarterly,* 1965, **11**, 183–208.

Bell, R. Q. Convergence: An accelerated longitudinal approach. *Child Development,* 1953, **24**, 145–152.

Bell, R. Q. An experimental test of the accelerated longitudinal approach. *Child Development,* 1954, **25**, 281–286.

Bugelski, B. R. *An introduction to the principles of psychology.* New York: Rinehart, 1960.

Cohen, M. R. *Studies in philosophy and science.* New York: Holt, 1949.

Cowan, P., Weber, J., Hoddinott, B., & Klein, J. Mean length of spoken response as a function of stimulus, experimenter, and subject. *Child Development,* 1967, **38**, 191–203.

Darwin, C. A biographical sketch of an infant. *Mind,* 1881, **6**, 104–107. In W. Dennis (Ed.), *Readings in child psychology.* New York: Prentice-Hall, 1951.

Festinger, L. *A theory of cognitive dissonance.* Evanston, Ill.: Row, Peterson, 1957.

Gesell, A., & Amatruda, C. *Developmental diagnosis.* New York: Hoeber, 1941.

Gesell, A., & Ilg, F. L. *Infant and child in the culture of today.* New York: Harper, 1943.

Gesell, A., & Ilg, F. L. *The child from five to ten.* New York: Harper, 1946.

Gesell, A., Ilg, F. L., & Ames, L. B. *Youth: The years from ten to sixteen.* New York: Harper, 1956.

Haggard, E. A., Brekstad, A., & Skard, A. On the reliability of the anamnestic interview. *Journal of Abnormal and Social Psychology,* 1960, **61**, 311–318.

Hall, G. S. The contents of children's minds. *Princeton Review,* 1883, 249–272. Reprinted in W. Dennis (Ed.), *Readings in the history of psychology.* New York: Appleton, 1948. Pp. 255–256.

Honzik, M. P., Macfarlane, J. W., & Allen, L. The stability of mental test performance between two and eighteen years. *Journal of Experimental Education,* 1948, **17**, 320.

Hsia, D. Y-Y. *Human developmental genetics.* Yearbook Medical Publishers, Chicago, 1968.

Hsia, D. Y-Y., Driscoll, K. W., Troll, W., & Knox, W. E. Detection by phenylalinine tolerance tests of heterozygous carriers of phenylketonuria. *Nature,* 1956, **178**, 1239–1240.

Inventory of developmental tasks. Santa Clara, Calif.: Santa Clara Unified School District.

Kagan, J. American longitudinal research on psychological development. *Child Development,* 1964, **35**, 1–32.

Moustakas, C. E., Sigel, I. E., & Schalock, H. D. An objective method for the measurement and analysis of child-adult interaction. *Child Development,* 1956, **27**, 109–134.

Munn, N. L. *The evolution and growth of human behavior.* Cambridge, Mass.: Riverside, 1955.

Mussen, P. H. (Ed.). *Handbook of research methods in child development.* New York: Wiley, 1960.

Nelson, W. E. (Ed.), *Textbook of pediatrics.* Philadelphia: Saunders, 1969.

Olson, W. C. *The measurement of nervous habits in normal children.* Minneapolis: University of Minnesota Press, 1929.

Rapaport, D. *Emotions and memory.* Baltimore: Williams & Wilkins, 1942.

Rosenthal, R. On the social psychology of the psychological experiment. *American Scientist,* 1963, **51**, 268–283.

Rosenthal, R. *Experimenter effects in behavioral research.* New York: Appleton–Century–Crofts, 1966.

Rosenthal, R., & Jacobson, L. *Pygmalion in the classroom.* New York: Holt, Rinehart, & Winston, 1968.

Schaefer, E. S., & Bell, R. Q. Development of a parental attitude research instrument. *Child Development,* 1958, **29**, 339–361.

Sears, R. R., Maccoby, E. E., & Levin, H. *Patterns of child rearing.* Evanston, Ill.: Row, Peterson, 1957.

Shirley, M. M. *The first two years: A study of twenty-five babies, Vol. I. Postural and locomotor development.* Institute of Child Welfare Monograph Series, No. 6. Minneapolis: University of Minnesota Press, 1931.

Shirley, M. M. *The first two years: A study of twenty-five babies, Vol. II. Intellectual development.* Institute of Child Welfare Monograph Series, No. 7. Minneapolis: University of Minnesota Press, 1933. (a)

Shirley, M. M. *The first two years: A study of twenty-five babies, Vol. III. Personality manifestations.* Institute of Child Welfare Monograph Series, No. 8. Minneapolis: University of Minnesota Press, 1933. (b)

Skinner, B. F. *Beyond freedom and dignity.* New York, Knopf, 1971.

Stone, A. A., & Onque, G. C. *Longitudinal studies of child personality.* Cambridge, Mass.: Harvard University Press, 1959.

Templin, M. C. *Certain language skills in children.* Institute of Child Welfare Monograph Series, No. 26. Minneapolis: University of Minnesota Press, 1957.

Thorndike, R. L. Review of *Pygmalion in the Classroom. American Educational Research Journal,* 1968, **5**, 708–711.

Toffler, A. *Future shock.* New York: Bantam, 1970.

Watson, D. C. & Tharp. R. G. *Self directed behavior: Self modification for personal adjustment.* Monterey, Ca.: Brooks/Cole, 1972.

Weech, A. Signposts on the road of growth. *American Journal of Disturbed Children,* 1954, **88**, 452–457.

Willems, E. P. An ecological orientation in psychology. *Merrill–Palmer Quarterly,* 1965, **11**, 317–343.

Woolf, L. I., Griffiths, R., & Moncrieff, A. Treatment of phenylketonuria with a diet low in phenylalanine. *British Medical Journal,* 1955 (**4905**), 57–64.

Wright, H. Psychological development in Midwest. *Child Development,* 1956, **27**, 265–286.

Wright, H., & Barker, R. Psychological ecology and the problem of psychosocial development. *Child Development,* 1949, **20**, 131–143.

Wright, H., & Barker, R. *Methods in psychological ecology.* Lawrence, Kan.: Department of Psychology, University of Kansas, 1950.

section II

basic factors in development

For the most part, five areas of development provide a basis for the common qualities of human beings. These five—heredity, growth and maturation, learning and motivation, language, and intelligence—each explored in an individual chapter, form the substance of this section.

Heredity serves all species in the same way, providing human beings with a basic similarity. Regardless of individual differences, all human beings are moderately large primates who manipulate the environment with well-developed hands, who show much curiosity, and who seek experience and variation in their surroundings. All human beings follow a similar pattern of growth and maturation. Although human learning capacities and responses to various motivating forces in the environment in many ways resemble those of all other animals, in some forms of learning, especially those involving formation of concepts, solving of problems, and creativity, man excels. This is because of man's high intellectual capacity as a species; and although individual differences are marked, these differences conceal the basic similarity of one human being to another as compared with other species.

Superiority in learning ability and in retaining information appears largely to result from the fact that man is unique in being able to communicate symbolically. Mediated by common capacities, individual differences, whether hereditary or based on environmental forces, come into being. The hereditary forces producing these differences occupy attention in this section, whereas the environmental influences are discussed later in the book.

chapter 2

heredity

chapter 2

heredity

chapter 2

heredity

How mutable or changeable is human nature? To paraphrase a distinguished exponent of environmentalism, John B. Watson (1919), "Give me a dozen children and full control of the environment, and I will make of them what I wish–atomic scientists, commissars, professors, or hippies." If this assertion is correct, human nature is indeed changeable and future generations of mankind can be made to differ in basic character from the present generation. Yet the hereditarian insists that man is what he is, and that no amount of manipulation of the environment, unless it is accompanied by some form of selective breeding, can change him greatly.

Following World War II, the science of genetics–the study of heredity–received a setback in the U.S.S.R. The Soviets felt that a belief in genetics implied that human character was determined, in part, by biological inheritance; to that extent, human nature was immutable (Zirkle, 1949). Legislating out of existence one set of views about the nature of the world, the Soviets supported another (Lysenkoism–Michurianism), which holds that changes in the environment of an organism alter the genetic characteristics transmitted to the organism's offspring. This belief, known to the Western world long ago as Lamarckianism, was accepted in the West as a means of explaining variation among offspring (see Darwin, 1890), but was fairly well disproved by the 1920's. As a scientific theory it has little to recommend it, although it is most useful as a scientific rationalization for those who believe they can change the basic character of mankind. Yet even now, Soviet scientists are attempting to restore Soviet genetics to a Western point of view.

The belief espoused by the Soviets in the inheritance of acquired characteristics may seem, at first sight, an optimistic one. It holds that any efforts at self-improvement live on in one's offspring. But Herman Muller (1948), America's Nobel Prize-winning geneticist, suggested that this concept might not be as optimistic as it first seemed. If it were true, he noted, then individuals in a backward environment–an environment that allowed little growth in intellect or development of potentialities–should become *genetically inferior*. As Muller pointed out, this is not so. It certainly is not true, for example, of Chinese peasants. Assuming the same form of breeding in two different environments, individuals from environments that have been depressed for generations display, as a group, when placed in an adequate setting, the same level of abilities as any other group. Those who stress that heredity–as defined in Western culture–is the significant determinant of human capacities would maintain that just as a fine environment cannot make men into angels so a degraded one cannot make them like beasts.

These, then, are issues involved in the study of heredity and environment as they affect human nature. Although a lengthy discussion of the mechanisms of heredity may belong more appropriately in a course in genetics, the foregoing philosophical considerations are clearly a part of child psychology. How they are regarded determines to a considerable degree the way the child is viewed.

THE HEREDITARY PROCESS

The mechanisms of heredity are essentially the same for all species of plants and animals, although they may be more easily investigated in an ear of corn or a fruit fly than in humans. What is discovered about hereditary transmission in one species can apply, with few qualifications, to all others.

Among humans a sperm cell of the male penetrates the ovum (egg) of the female and thus fertilizes the ovum. Each normal male and female cell has 46 chromosomes. As a result of cell division, any single sperm or ovum contains approximately half the number of chromosomes of its parent cell—usually one-half of 46, or 23. In the fertilized egg, known as a *zygote*, the chromosomes of sperm and ovum combine to give the fertile egg 23 *pairs* of chromosomes; this restores the normal complement of 46, with half inherited from each parent. Each of these chromosomes is composed, in turn, of many genes.

The sperm and the ovum are *germ cells*. Their substance, the chains of genes formed into chromosomes, is called *germ plasm*, which is quite distinct from the plasm of the body, called *somatoplasm*. Through the germ plasm parents transmit their genes to their children. The offspring in turn pass on these genes to their progeny. In a sense, germ plasm, transmitting characteristics as it does across generations and generally unaltered by environmental influences, is immortal. Genetic inheritance determines in large part the physical structure and behavioral potentialities of human organisms. Gene changes occur in the case of mutations caused by factors in the environment. These mutations are sudden changes in the gene structure that result from X-ray, cosmic ray, or fallout irradiation, or from exposure to mustard gas.

What any individual is genetically is determined largely by chance. Half of his genes come from the one sperm cell, among millions of possible sperm cells, that penetrates one of the hundreds of egg cells produced by a female during her reproductive life. Each parent contributes one member of each pair of the many thousands of pairs of genes that affect human inheritance. Each sperm cell and each egg cell differs in the genes it contains from all other sperm and egg cells produced by the same individual. By the random combination of the genes from a particular sperm with the genes of a particular ovum, a human is formed. This human is unique from other humans and yet like fellow men in many respects.

Every individual, as we now know, contains thousands of genes. In some cases one gene is dominant and another is recessive. Those who receive one of each kind from their parents manifest the dominant characteristic, but stand an even chance of passing along the recessive gene to their offspring. Since genes are acquired from parents, it is very likely that individuals are more like their parents genetically, and hence in observable characteristics, than like people in general. However, many characteristics that are recessive in both parents, and therefore not visible, may turn up in the individual. This is one reason why children do not always resemble their parents as closely as might be expected.

Although some characteristics are determined by a single pair of genes, many more characteristics result from the interactive effect of a large number of gene pairs. Suppose that intellectual ability were determined by nine pairs of genes, which is certainly far less than the actual number. Suppose further that there could be only two possible genes in each pair—one that disposed toward "brightness" and the other toward "dullness." Now suppose that the genes disposing toward brightness were dominant in two particular parents, whereas those disposing toward dullness were recessive. Since brightness is dominant in this case any of the nine pairs of genes containing one or both bright genes would dispose the offspring toward being intelligent. Table 2-1 presents several possibilities.

TABLE 2-1 A Hypothetical Case of Multiple Gene Determination of a Trait*

Gene Pair	Father's Genes	Mother's Genes
1	bright-bright	bright-dull
2	bright-bright	bright-bright
3	bright-dull	dull-dull
4	bright-dull	dull-dull
5	bright-dull	bright-dull
6	dull-dull	bright-bright
7	bright-dull	dull-dull
8	dull-dull	bright-dull
9	dull-dull	bright-dull

Each parent can contribute only one gene out of any gene pair. Possible contributions include the following combinations.

Offspring No. 1		Offspring No. 2	
Offspring Gene Pair	Father-Mother	Offspring Gene Pair	Father-Mother
1	bright-dull	1	bright-dull
2	bright-bright	2	bright-bright
3	bright-dull	3	dull-dull
4	bright-dull	4	dull-dull
5	bright-bright	5	dull-dull
6	dull-bright	6	dull-bright
7	bright-dull	7	dull-dull
8	dull-bright	8	dull-dull
9	dull-bright	9	dull-dull
This offspring has nine of nine pairs of genes with one or more bright genes in the pair. The offspring, then, is brighter than either parent.		This offspring, on the other hand, has only three gene pairs disposing toward brightness and six double recessive pairs of genes disposing him toward dullness. He is less able than his parents.	

*We have decided to call bright genes dominant.

Because of the many potential combinations, numerous differences may result. Dull parents, for example, might produce a genius, and vice versa; this is not impossible but highly improbable.

INHERITED SIMILARITIES

Most psychological research into the influence of heredity has been directed toward determining its role in producing differences among humans. But the overwhelming significance of heredity is not really in this area; rather it is in the area of achieving similarities between individuals.

Humanness is the result of a number of genetically determined characteristics that, interacting with one another, produce the portion of behavior that is not common with other species. La Barre (1954) argued that the characteristics that made humans unique, except for resemblance to other higher primates, were bipedal locomotion, stereoptic vision, hands, and a fairly high capacity for learning.

> When man, heir of four limbs, uses only two of them for walking, his clever primate hands are then finally freed from use in any kind of locomotion whatever. They can now be used for purely exploratory grasping. The advantages of this are not to be underestimated.
>
> Emancipated hands are not enough: many dinosaurs had them, but they lacked sufficient brains. Intelligence is not enough: elephants have a great deal of intelligence behind their trunks, but they do not have stereoscopic sight; the prehensile-tailed monkeys are intelligent too, and they have stereoscopic vision as well, but they do not ordinarily see their tails. Stereoscopic eyes are not enough either: for the intelligent, tree-living apes have them, with color vision and the yellow spot in the retina to boot. It is the combination that counts. Man has paired grasping organs, fully in his field of vision and wholly freed from locomotor duties, in a stereoscopic-sighted, big-brained mammal—and these add up to the answer (La Barre, 1954, pp. 86–87).

La Barre's views were supported by Butler (1953, 1954) and others working with Harlow at the University of Wisconsin on experiments dealing with curiosity drive. Butler described his work as follows.

> . . . I was testing monkeys on a food-rewarded problem. The monkey worked behind a screen where it could not see the experimenter. By the same token, the experimenter could not see the monkey, and there was a great temptation to peek to find out what the animal was doing. I first made a small peephole in the panel, but the monkey quickly discovered it and thereafter spied on me as often as I did on him. I next tried placing a small mirror in a position that enabled me to watch the animal constantly. The monkey turned the tables by dropping its work and watching me through the mirror!
>
> Taking advantage of this lead, we designed an experiment to investigate monkey's visual exploratory behavior. The apparatus was essentially an enclosure with a built-in color discrimination problem. Monkeys were rewarded by a view of the surroundings outside the enclosure, provided they responded correctly on the problem.
>
> The results of the experiment left no doubt about the strength of the monkey's curiosity or its power in promoting learning. Throughout the 20 days of testing the animals worked away eagerly at the problem. . . . Without tiring of the game, they went on pushing the doors enthusiastically to get a look at the people working in the laboratory outside the box. In a second study that ran for 57 days and presented various color-discrimination problems, the subjects worked just as unflaggingly.
>
> These data strongly suggest that the drive to explore visually is indeed a fundamental drive in monkeys. To measure its strength and persistence further, two monkeys were tested for four continuous hours each day for five days. The animals worked as fast on Day Five as they did on Day One. A second experiment yielded still more surprising results. Three monkeys were put to the door-opening test hour after hour, with 30 seconds between trials, until they quit. One monkey performed for nine continuous hours, another worked for 11 and the third for more than 19 hours! The response time of this marathon performer was actually shortest during the final hour of the test. That the monkeys would work as long and as persistently for a food reward is highly unlikely . . . (Butler, 1954).

Through producing a better understanding of the environment, this primate trait, curiosity, has so much value for survival that natural selection has made it a human characteristic inherited in much the same manner as the opposable thumb. The existence of the curiosity drive and the need it may arouse for stimulation probably produces fundamental differences in learning between primates and nonprimates. This is shown, for example, in the work of Harlow and others who have found that primates attack problems involving manipulation, such as unlocking doors and solving problems, without any special reward. If such a reward is introduced, the primate does *less* in these tasks (Harlow, 1950). Yet there seems to be little doubt that intrinsic reward hastens learning. Since all responses that satisfy curiosity are rewarding to primates, it seems reasonable to believe that the primate will learn a wide variety of behaviors, some of which will have survival value. In contrast, the learning of nonprimates seems largely restricted to techniques to reduce such drives as hunger and thirst.

Curiosity is one of our primate traits. Perhaps much of human society and culture can be explained in terms of our simian background. Clarence Day, in *This Simian World*, argued this point with great wit and insight. In the excerpt below he imagines the world as it would have been if man had evolved from the great cats.

> A race of civilized beings descended from these great cats would have been rich in hermits and solitary thinkers. The recluse would not have been stigmatized as peculiar, as he is by us simians. They would not have been a credulous people, or easily religious. False prophets and swindlers would have found few dupes. And what generals they would have made! What consummate politicians!
>
> Don't imagine them as a collection of tigers walking around on their hind-legs. They would have only been like tigers in the sense that we men are like monkeys. Their development in appearance and character would have been quite transforming.
>
> Instead of the small flat head of the tiger, they would have had clear smooth brows; and those who were not bald would have had neatly parted hair—perhaps striped.
>
> Their mouths would have been smaller and more sensitive; their faces most dignified. Where now they express chiefly savageness, they would have expressed fire and grace.
>
> They would have been courteous and suave. No vulgar crowding would have occurred on the streets of their cities. No mobs. No ignominious subway-jams.
>
> Imagine a cultivated coterie of such men and women, at a ball, dancing. How few of us humans are graceful. They would have all been Pavlowas. (Day, 1936, pp. 17–18.)

A number of books have been published in recent years emphasizing another supposedly built-in characteristic of humans; aggression. Ardrey (1961), Lorenz (1966), Morris (1967), and others have taken up this basic theme. Since the above-mentioned works are basically popular or "trade" books, they inevitably are poorly documented at points, oversimplified, and tend to give short shrift to data contrary to the positions taken therein. Critics who argue that man is what he is because of his social environment, and that his biological heritage is of no present consequence, have been most severe in judgments of these books, chiefly as a result of these flaws. Critics of these writers to the contrary, humans have had a bloody history. Man went into the last ice age along with the cave bears, fighting for the use of caves. The cave bears stood about 18 feet tall and were well-equipped with claws and fangs. By the end of the last glacial period, humans had killed them all. As Bibby (1956) shows, man worshipped them, but did manage to kill them all. Perhaps it is to man's credit as a human that he did this deed, along with doing in the dodo, the great auk, and the passenger pigeon. Man was bloody enough to make extinct the most fearsome creatures in his environment as well as those without defenses. His encounter with the cave bears suggests that Ardrey may be correct in his major premise; if so, the future success of man, as a species, seems problematical. It is clear that he is sufficiently malleable that he can learn not to be curious, or to be aggressive; however, man's propensities may be in those directions.

Other aspects of human behavior that seem, to a substantial degree, to be built-in are discussed in Chapter 3.

Through an interplay of environment and biological inheritance, the primate—and especially man—has developed physical characteristics that enable an active, manipulative approach to the environment. As a consequence, genetically determined structure and behavior produce a basic similarity among all men. Within this similarity heredity helps to establish variations, or individual differences.

INHERITANCE OF INDIVIDUAL DIFFERENCES

All humans differ from one another. How much of these differences may be imputed to heredity? Although this is not an easy question to answer, since heredity and environment interact, data are available that can tell something about the relative contribution of each to human variability.

The idea that abilities are inherited certainly is not new. Long before there was a science of behavior, the belief in the inheritance of traits formed the basis for class distinction. A knight, no matter how impoverished, could not marry a merchant's daughter, no matter how substantial her dowry, without feeling he had married beneath his station. During the late Middle Ages people believed that there were vast differences between the nobility and the merchant class and between the merchant class and the peasantry. Those in superior positions considered themselves somehow transcendentally different, and held that this superiority was transmitted to their progeny. Even though such ideas, like subsequent notions of racial purity, rested on value judgments about the relative worth of individuals and on dubious principles, they indicate that man long has believed in heredity as a determinant of personality.

The first scientific study of the inheritance of ability was undertaken by Sir Francis Galton in *English Men of Science* (1874), *Hereditary Genius* (1869), and *Inquiries into Human Faculty* (1883). The first of these books had to do with the inheritance of scientific ability. A cousin of Darwin and a member of the brilliant but eccentric Darwin–Wedgewood-Galton family, Sir Francis may have been drawn to this area of research by his ponderings over his extensive family and its rich contribution to English science and industry. His discovery that a relatively small number of English families produced most of England's scientists suggested to him that genius was inherited. The difficulty in interpreting his work is the same one encountered in interpreting much of the research into the inheritance of characteristics conducted since his time. Some English families certainly produced many scientific geniuses—but can this be attributed to heredity? The child of a genius may inherit genius or, just as likely, may acquire it through association with a dedicated, brilliant parent—or both. This same contamination of heredity by environment pervades more recent studies, which nevertheless have some bearing on the inheritance of individual differences. *Hereditary Genius* was broader in scope, dealing with such diverse talents as mathematics, poetry, and wrestling, and concluding, on the basis of the same flawed type of evidence that the majority of these talents were inherited. The third book, *Inquiries into Human Faculty*, includes a chapter that opens a new approach to the inheritance of temperament and ability—the twin study, which is discussed later in this chapter.

The United States has an open class society, within which individuals of great ability may rise and those of lesser ability may descend in occupational level. Although there is considerable variation in ability within any social class, marked IQ differences are still found to exist among various classes when large samples of individuals are measured in each. If intelligence is inherited, these differences, though attenuated, should also appear in the children of tested individuals. Table 2–2 shows results of studies aimed at testing this hypothesis.

Individual differences do exist. Although superior environment in upper occupational levels probably plays a part in producing them, the similarity in the size of the gaps over a 20-year span during which class distinctions have markedly decreased suggests that heredity figures strongly in intelligence. Herrnstein (1971) has been taken to task for citing these and other data in support of his thesis that socioeconomic groups presently form somewhat separate breeding populations (since we tend to marry people like ourselves in terms of ability and background; see Vandenberg, 1972, for a discussion of assortive mating), that there are differences in mean or average ability between these breeding populations, and that these differences will increase so long as the tendency toward meritocracy persists. The data strongly support Herrnstein. However, the variability within a given socioeconomic group is great, as compared to the differences between groups. The role of "chance" factors (as opposed to individual ability scores, education, family background) in determining one's occupational level is very large (see Jencks, 1972). Therefore, the tendency for differing economic groups to increasingly differentiate as breeding populations is a relatively weak one. As in the case of Galton's work, however, the relative influence of heredity and environment and the effects of their interaction with one another are difficult, although not impossible, to disentangle (Falconer, 1960; Loehlin & Vandenberg, 1966).

Family Resemblances

Many studies have measured family resemblances in intelligence. Figure 2–1

TABLE 2-2 Mean IQs of Preschool Children Classified by Father's Occupation According to the Minnesota Occupational Scale*

	Study		
Father's Occupation	Goodenough (1928)	Terman & Merrill (1937)	Johnson (1948)
Professional	116	116	116
Semiprofessional and managerial	112	112	112
Clerical and skilled trades	108	108	107
Rural owners, farmers		99	95
Semiskilled, minor clerical	105	104	105
Slightly skilled	104	95	98
Unskilled	96	94	96

*Goodenough & Anderson, 1931.

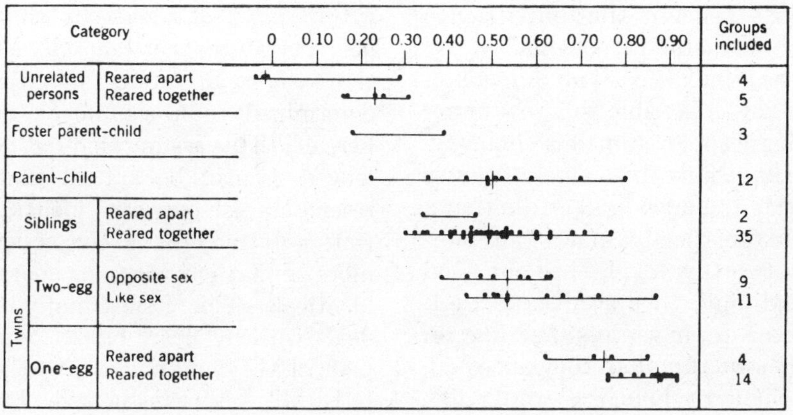

Category			Groups included
Unrelated persons		Reared apart	4
		Reared together	5
Foster parent-child			3
Parent-child			12
Siblings		Reared apart	2
		Reared together	35
Twins	Two-egg	Opposite sex	9
		Like sex	11
	One-egg	Reared apart	4
		Reared together	14

Scale: 0 0.10 0.20 0.30 0.40 0.50 0.60 0.70 0.80 0.90

FIGURE 2-1 Correlation coefficients for "intelligence" test scores from 52 studies. Some studies reported data for more than one relationship category; some included more than one sample per category, giving a total of 99 groups. Over two-thirds of the correlation were derived from IQs, the remainder from special tests (e.g., Primary Mental Abilities). Mid-parent-child was used when available, otherwise mother-child correlation. Correlation coefficients obtained in each study are indicated by dark circles; medians are shown by vertical lines intersecting the horizontal lines, which represent the ranges (Erlenmeyer-Kimling & Jarvik, 1963).

presents typical results of such studies. Even though higher correlations among identical (one-egg, monozygotic, or MZ) than fraternal (two-egg, dizygotic, or DZ) twins suggest the impact of heredity on similarity of intelligence, the correlation of fraternal twins in contrast to ordinary siblings or to parents and children implies that similarity of environment increases the degree of resemblance, since fraternal twins are no more alike, genetically, than the other two groups.

Mother-child as opposed to father-child correlations are not shown in Figure 2-1. Ausubel and Sullivan (1970) review this literature and point out that the correlations of father and of mother with their offspring are exactly the same—a somewhat surprising finding, since mothers, on the average, have substantially more contact with their offspring than do fathers. As Ausubel and Sullivan point out, the lack of difference in the magnitude of the correlations does not support the strongly environmentalist position.

The foregoing studies of family resemblances in intelligence shed some light on the inheritance of characteristics. However, these studies do not provide adequate controls for testing similarity of environment. Other experimental procedures are needed if we wish to identify more accurately the relative contributions of heredity and environment. Procedures employed to accomplish this task include comparisons of identical and fraternal twins, studies of separated identical twins, investigations of adopted children, selective breeding, and inbreeding.

What evidence about human characteristics has been produced by each of these approaches? Most research by psychologists into the role of heredity has concentrated on the influence of heredity and environment on scores in intelligence tests. This is partly the result of a historical accident. Soon after the turn of the century psychologists had developed an adequate test of intelligence, but there is still no comparable measure of personality. Moreover, an older generation of psychologists believed that intelligence was a central factor in personality. By knowing the intelligence of an individual, they held, it was possible to know many other things about him—his honesty, his leadership ability, his values. Today's psychologists are much less certain that a high IQ automatically makes an individual trustworthy, loyal, obedient, God fearing, and kind; thus studies of intelligence seem to have less bearing on personality structure than they once had. And although psychologists would like to know more about hereditary influences on personality characteristics, this is an area in which they are least knowledgeable. Research is, however, increasing, in number and in quality of studies, as may be seen in McClearn's (1964), McClearn's and Meredith's (1966), and McClearn's (1970) reviews of the literature. We know much of what we need to know and soon will know more.

Intra-Pair Resemblances between Identical and Fraternal Twins

About 100 years ago Galton realized the importance of twin studies in the investigation of hereditary influences on behavior. Once it became known that there were two varieties of twin, and once techniques were developed by means of which MZs and DZs could be differentiated reliably (see Sutton, Clark, & Schull, 1955; and Nichols, 1965, for discussions of recent developments in diagnostic techniques), the comparison of MZ and DZ pairs became an important approach in the study of heredity. (See Vandenberg, 1966b, for a comprehensive review of twin research.)

Whether identical or fraternal, twin pairs share a common environment. Identical twins also are alike genetically, whereas fraternals share no more genetic similarity than any other pair of siblings. Therefore, if greater resemblance is found within pairs of identicals than within pairs of fraternals, it generally is assumed that the trait under investigation is determined to a significant degree by heredity. This assumption has been challenged. It can be argued that greater resemblances between identicals than fraternals may be a consequence of a more similar environment shared by the identicals. This issue finally has been dealt with by Scarr (1968). She studied pairs of MZ twins believed by the parents to be MZ; MZ twins believed by the parents to be DZ; DZ twins believed by the parents to be DZ; DZ twins believed by the parents to be MZ. If MZ twins resemble one another more than DZs because of greater genetic similarity, they should show this resemblance whether the parents believe they are MZ or DZ. If environmental similarity is the key factor, and if MZs have greater intra-pair resemblances than DZs because they are reared in a more similar environment, pairs believed to be identical by the parents should resemble one another more closely, regardless of actual zygosity. Scarr's data suggest that, although parental belief concerning zygosity does influence similarities, actual zygosity is more important; that is, MZ twins, whether treated by their parents as MZ or DZ, resembled one another more than did DZ twins, even when DZ pairs were believed to be MZ. Thus her data indicate that greater resemblances between MZ as compared with DZ pairs cannot be attributed, to any large extent, to differences between identicals and fraternals in the degree of environmental similarity within pairs.

Another approach to the problem of determining whether the greater resemblance of MZ than DZ twins results from more similar parental treatment of MZ pairs would be to establish the degree of MZ and DZ resemblance on subtle as opposed to culturally obvious psychological traits. The term *subtle* is used here to denote traits about which few of us know our ability, and for which we seldom receive training in the schools or at home. For example, we generally do not know our short-term memory span, our ability to perceive and recall stimuli shown us for very short time intervals, or our relative learning ability under conditions of massed versus distributed practice. Despite the fact that these capacities are centrally involved in learning and memory, we have no formal training in these areas. On the other hand, parents often expend considerable efforts to train their offspring in such culturally obvious areas as mathematics and language (especially in vocabulary). If the greater degree of resemblance of MZ as compared with DZ twins is of the same magnitude for subtle, untrained traits as for culturally important and obvious traits, it would appear that differences in the treatment and training of MZs and DZs are not the cause of the observedly greater intro-pair similarity of MZ pairs.

As noted in Table 2-3, identicals (MZs) show a much stronger intra-pair resemblance in tested intelligence than do fraternals (DZs). This repeatedly obtained finding shows that heredity plays a considerable role in producing individual differences in tested intelligence. However, most studies of MZ-DZ pair differences make use of such tests as the Stanford–Binet or one of Wechsler's tests, and these tests are a conglomeration of items measuring many different intellectual domains. Probably of more theoretical and also more practical value are MZ-DZ comparisons making use of tests in which the different factors that make up intelligence are measured. A number of these "Primary Mental Ability" tests have been used by various investigators in tests of MZ and DZ twins, in order to determine the degree to which each distinct ability resulted from hereditary influences. The results of four separate studies are shown in Table 2-3.

These studies indicate that *some* intellectual abilities, and especially spatial ability—the ability to visualize objects in three-dimensional space have a substantial genetic component, while other abilities, such as reasoning ability and memory, are influenced little, if at all, by hereditary factors. Certain questions can be raised regarding these results. For example, the low amount of hereditary

TABLE 2-3 Ratio of DZ to MZ Within-Pair Differences for the Six Scores of the Chicago Primary Mental Abilities Test

Name of Score	Blewett 1953	Thurstone et al. 1955	Vandenberg 1962	Vandenberg 1966a
Verbal	3.13*	2.81*	2.65*	1.74*
Space	2.04*	4.19*	1.77*	3.51*
Number	1.07	1.52	2.58*	2.25*
Reasoning	2.78*	1.35	1.40	1.10
Word fluency	2.78*	2.47*	2.57*	2.24*
Memory	not used	1.62*	1.26	not used
Number				
DZ pairs	26	53	37	36
MZ pairs	26	45	45	76

*Hereditability differences between MZ and DZ pairs are statistically significant (from Vandenberg, 1967a).

influence shown in the memory test may be a result of the kind of task presented the persons tested—there seem to be at least two distinct kinds of memory, short-term and long-term (and there may be more)—or of the low reliability of the PMA test.

On the Mental and Motor Scales of the Bayley Infant Behavior Profile, Freedman and Keller (1963) compared sets of identical and fraternal twins within the first year of life, when the effects of differential treatment between types of twin could be expected to be minimal, if not nonexistent (especially since a number of twin pairs were misdiagnosed with regard to zygosity). The differences in scores, shown in Figure 2-2, were found to be significantly smaller between identical twins than between fraternal twins. This closer resemblance at such an early age supports the notion that hereditary influences produce variations in scores in these tests.

Wilson (1972), as part of the continuing Louisville twin study initiated by Vandenberg, reports data on the mental development of twins in the first two years of life, as measured by the Bayley scales of mental and motor development. Not only do identical twins resemble one another more closely than do fraternals, but the spurts and lags of development, across the period of 3–24 months, were much more similar for identical twins. Wilson (1972, p. 214) summarizes his findings by stating that infant mental development is primarily determined by the twins' genetic blueprint; except in unusual cases, other factors served mainly a supportive function.

Using the same MZ-DZ comparison techniques, Gardner has begun a still-continuing investigation of cognitive styles (1965). This study is intended to determine the contributions of heredity and of environment in the ways in which persons organize their thought processes. Gardner (1966) has already established that the ability to block out overlearned old habits in a new learning situation is determined in large part by heredity. Other valuable data concerning complex intellectual processes may be obtained from this continued investigation.

Just as MZ and DZ intra-pair resemblances can be compared on different intellectual or motor factors, they can be compared on different dimensions of personality. Gottesman (1963) studied 34 pairs each of MZ and DZ high-school-age twins in Minnesota and, later (1965), a larger number of MZ and DZ twin pairs in the Boston area. The results of the two studies differed somewhat but, as in other studies (see Vandenberg, 1967b), it appears that introversion-extroversion—the tendency to approach or withdraw from environmental stimulation—contains a very strong hereditary component. Psychopathic deviancy, a measure of tendencies toward antisocial behavior, seems second most strongly influenced by heredity. This may be because it is at least in part a result of emotionality and activity levels, and these have significant hereditary components (Scarr, 1966). Freedman's and Keller's (1963) research on infant MZ and DZ twins also supports the position that approach-withdrawal tendencies, measured in this case by *social orientation* and *fear of strangers*, has a hereditary base. Koch's (1966) data also support this position, since the study indicates that MZ twins are more often equal in dominance than are DZ twins. It may be that a strong hereditary component in approach-withdrawal tendencies is the reason individual differences in this area are highly stable over time, as shown in longitudinal studies (Tuddenham, 1959; Schaefer & Bayley, 1963).

Comparisons of MZ and DZ twins not only tell us that motor, mental, and personality characteristics result, in part from hereditary factors, but also tell us

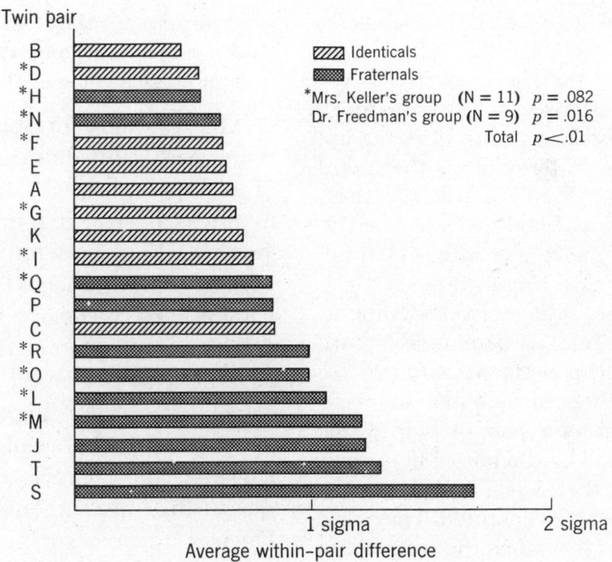

FIGURE 2-2 The Bayley Mental and Motor Scales averaged to form a single distribution. Average within-pair differences in the first year, based on 8–12 monthly administrations (Freedman & Keller, 1963, p. 197).

the degree to which particular characteristics are (as are spatial ability and introversion-extroversion) or are not (as reasoning and a number of personality traits appear not to be) inherited.

Separated Identical Twin Studies

Genetically, identical twins are exactly alike. By separating two individuals identical in heredity and raising them in quite disparate environments, thus holding heredity constant while varying the environment, it becomes possible to discern the relative influences of each.

The group of twins discussed most intensively were those studied by Newman, Freeman, and Holzinger (1937). These men investigated 50 sets of fraternal twins, a like number of sets of identical twins raised together, and 19 sets of identical twins raised apart from one another. The 19 pairs of identical twins raised separately are of present concern. Some rather startling resemblances were discovered among them. For example, consider these findings about Ed and Fred.

> The most interesting feature of this story is the remarkable parallelism in the lives of these twins in spite of the fact that they lived without knowledge of each other's existence for twenty-five years. They were both reared as only children by childless foster-parents, both being led to understand that they were own children. Though they lived a thousand miles apart, they had about the same educational experience, and both found employment as repair men in branches of the same great telephone company. They were married in the same year and each had a baby son. Each owned a fox terrier dog named Trixie. According to their statements, both of them from early boyhood on were obsessed with the idea that they had a brother who died and often stated this to their playmates.
>
> The story of their discovery of each other's existence is almost stranger than fiction. When Ed was twenty-two he was accosted by a jovial fellow who had just come from a distant city to work at Ed's

department. "Hello, Fred! How's tricks?" he inquired. Ed explained that he was not Fred and denied that he knew the newcomer, but the latter was hard to convince, declaring that Ed was trying to cover up his identity. Soon afterward another man accosted him as "Fred" and stated that if he was not Fred Blank he was exactly like a fellow of that name with whom he had recently worked in a distant city. Ed was by this time rather disturbed about the matter and told his parents about it. Reluctantly, the parents were forced to admit that Ed was an adopted son and that he was one of a pair of twins; the other of them had been adopted by a couple who lived in their home town but with whom they were not acquainted. They also revealed the fact that when the twins were small boys they had attended school together for a short time and that the other children often noticed their close resemblance. It occurs to us that this early association of the twins may have led to the above-mentioned mutual feeling about a brother who had died.

Needless to say, Ed lost no time in getting in touch with Fred. The latter was out of work at the time and came to visit Ed. It was during this time that we succeeded in inducing them to come to Chicago to see the Fair and, incidentally, to be examined. Their visit with us was made even more interesting to them and to us by reason of a confusion of dates which resulted in their coming to us at the same time as a pair of young women twins, Ethel and Esther, whose story comes next in this series. The two pairs of twins became great friends and were much impressed by similarity in the circumstances that led to their discovery that they were twins. The visits to the Fair were made together, each young man taking one of the young women. When they walked about people were startled to see one couple walking ahead and a duplicate couple following behind. Everywhere they went they attracted attention and enjoyed the sensation they created. On one occasion they attended a side show featuring a pair of Siamese twins and, according to their statement, stole the show, attracting more attention than the exhibits (Newman et al., 1937, pp. 147–148).

The 19 pairs of separated identical twins were studied at maturity. Members of each pair showed a close resemblance in physical size and in other phases of growth. They resembled one another closely in IQ and less closely in personality. Perhaps the degree to which heredity determines development diminishes from size to IQ to personality. Or perhaps the correlations were highest on concrete physical growth because here is where the best, most exact, and most reliable measuring instruments are available. Devices for measuring intelligence are less precise and reliable than devices used to check physical dimensions. The reliability of measures for personality is low even at the present time and was certainly a good deal lower at the time of the Newman et al. study in the 1930's. Actually, the reliability of most tests was so low in the 1930's that it was surprising to find any resemblance at all between twins.

Since the measures of intelligence were most central to the matters that concerned psychologists at the time, these tests have been the most widely discussed. Woodworth (1941) offered both IQ and environmental data for the 19 sets of twins studied by Newman and his associates, and for three other sets as well. As he noted:

> Taken without regard to sign, the average IQ difference between separated identicals is 7.6 points. Correction for chance errors of observation would bring this difference down to 6 points net, a figure to be compared with the estimated net difference of 3 points between identicals reared together, and of 15 points or more between children paired at random from the same community. It is probable, then, that environment did make these sepa-

rated twins differ in tested intelligence, though not to any such extent as obtains among the children of a community (Woodworth, 1941, p. 357).

The correlation obtained between identical twins reared in *separate* environments was +0.767. This was a more substantial relation than was obtained between fraternal twins raised in the *same* environment. Although Newman et al. considered their data to support an environmentalist view, heredity seemed to have played an important part in determining the level of intelligence. A more recent study of variations in intelligence among a comparable sample of identical twins who were raised separately (Burt & Howard, 1956) has turned up similar results. In this case it seems clear that some variability can be attributed to environmental circumstances, even though the heredity factor is quite strong.

One other intensive study of a single pair of identical twins (Burks, 1942) supplies considerable information about the interests and personalities of the twins, as well as the more customary measurements of intelligence and physical size. The twins were girls, who had been separated before they were two weeks old. At the age of 12, personality ratings showed them to be quite similar to one another, despite a variability in certain areas of adjustment, which was produced by familial and environmental influences. The girls differed markedly in Strong Interest Test scores. At 18 they seemed even more similar to each other than at 12 and their interest profiles showed a distinct increase in comparability. Moreover, Rorschach tests at age 18 indicated a high degree of likeness; the patterns of response were more alike than might have been anticipated even from previous studies of identical twins who had been reared together. The greater likeness at 18 suggested that as one grew older, hence freer from parental dominance, innate predispositions became more apparent. This study, one of the few to have measured separately raised identical twins with adequate devices for assessing personality, suggested that the extent to which individuals displayed *certain* personality traits was in large part the consequence of genetic inheritance.

Enrichment. Studies of identical twins who have been separated also have bearing on one controversial area of the subject of heredity and environment: the question of how "enrichment" affects intelligence-test scores and, presumably, intelligence. This dispute has centered around the value of the kindergarten experience in developing children's general abilities and around the variation in closeness and richness of mothering in the determination of children's level of intellectual performance.

The latest phase of enrichment to be explored is that of very early enrichment. This is the area of enrichment to which the study of identical twins is most relevant, although so far most of the experimental work has been conducted with laboratory rats. Hebb (1949, pp. 298–299) reported that rats from an ordinary strain of laboratory species who were reared as home "pets" performed in significantly superior manner on a learning task to rats from the same strain who were reared in a normal environment. Other well-controlled experiments have extended these findings. In a representative study of this sort conducted by Forgus (1956), infant rats were exposed to visual forms from the time they first opened their eyes at the age of 16 days until they reached 41 days of age. A second group of rats was exposed to these same forms during the interval from 41 to 66 days of age. In both cases control groups of littermates were reared without the visual experience. Tests of both enriched and both control groups showed that the two enriched groups learned more rapidly than the control groups, and that the group that had been enriched early learned more rapidly than the late-enrichment group. Several similar studies (Cooper & Zubek, 1958; Gibson & Walk, 1956; and Luchins & Forgus, 1955) concurred in this finding. These indicate that deprivation retards later learning, whereas early enrichment increases the rate of learning.

Studies in the early enrichment of lower organisms contain implications for problems of human development. This has been suggested by Hunt (1961), McCandless (1961, pp. 261–262), Smith and Stone (1962, pp. 6–7), and Thompson (1959, p. 33). Perhaps, for example, the enrichment or deprivation of problem-solving experience to which a human is exposed before the age of two or three may be related to later ability.

If early enrichment or deprivation bears on the intellectual ability of humans, then identical twins who are exposed to a common early environment and share the stimulation it offers should resemble each other more closely on IQ tests than identical twins who have not shared a common environment for any length of time. Johnson (1963) tested this proposition using data from 23 pairs of separated identical twins reported in the literature. Vandenberg and Johnson (1968) obtained data on 14 more pairs of twins tested on conventional intelligence tests, making a total of 37 pairs. These data, bearing on the relation between age of separation and similarity in IQ, are presented in Table 2-4.

Pairs of twins in the early (before one year) separation group differ by an average of 5.50 IQ points; in the late (one year or later) separation group by 9.59 points. The mean within-pair difference for the entire 37 pairs is 7.64 points.

Thus the similarity in IQ between identical twins, significantly, is *inversely* related to the time spent in the same environment. Since the two groups did not differ significantly in the age at which they were tested, in duration of separation, or in degree of environmental difference, it is hard to explain why the twins in the early separation groups were more similar. The fact that twins who spend more time in a common environment are more dissimilar in IQ appears to run counter to the animal research literature on environment and deprivation discussed above. Jensen (1970) conducted a further analysis of already published twin data. Working with a far larger number of twin pairs than did Woodworth (see p. 58), his data demonstrate that the amount of environmental difference between members of given twin pairs had little to do with the degree of difference in IQ within twin pairs.

Adopted-Child Studies

Something about the influence of heredity and environment may also be learned by investigating the intelligence of a number of adopted children, of their true parents, and of their foster parents. Inferences may be drawn about the role played by heredity (true parent) and by environment (foster parent) in shaping the child's ability level from correlations between true parent and child ability and between foster parent and child ability. Yet for several reasons the results of this kind of investigation are not as clear-cut as those of the studies of identical twins. Even when children are raised by their true parents, the correlation of parent-child IQ is only about +0.50. Moreover, as a result of the placement policies of adoption agencies, foster parents are somewhat similar to the true parents in ability and in appearance.

The most widely cited studies on adopted children were done years ago.

TABLE 2-4 Age at Separation, Source of Data, and Differences in IQ for 37 Pairs of MZ Twins from Various Studies*

Age	Source	Difference	Age	Source	Difference
1 day	(S & T)	4			
1 day	(J-N)	6	1 yr.	(J-N)	9
9 days	(B)	1	1 yr.	(J-N)	14
½ mo.	(M)	4	1 yr.	(NFH)	19
3 wk.	(J-N)	1	1 yr.	(NFH)	5
3 wk.	(J-N)	1	1 yr.	(NFH)	1
1 mo.	(S)	4	14 mo.	(NFH)	4
1 mo.	(G & N)	3	18 mo.	(NFH)	12
1 mo.	(NFH)	1	18 mo.	(NFH)	12
1 mo.	(NFH)	6	18 mo.	(NFH)	24
1 mo.	(NFH)	1	18 mo.	(NFH)	7
6 wk.	(J-N)	11	2 yr.	(NFH)	10
2 mo.	(NFH)	2	2½ yr.	(NFH)	2
3 mo.	(NFH)	15	3 yr.	(NFH)	8
3 mo.	(G & B)	19			
5 mo.	(NFH)	17	3½ yr.	(J-N)	8
6 mo.	(NFH)	1	3½ yr.	(J-N)	6
7 mo.	(J-N)	4	5¾ yr.	(J-N)	13
9 mo.	(J-N)	6	6 yr.	(NFH)	9
10 mo.	(J-N)	3			

*The following abbreviations are used for sources:
J-N = Juel-Nielsen (1964) S & T = Stephens & Thompson (1943)
B = Burks (1942) G & N = Gardner & Newman (1940)
M = Muller (1925) G & B = Gates & Brash (1941)
S = Saudek (1934) NFH = Newman, Freeman, & Holzinger (1937)

They were conducted by Burks (1928), Leahy (1935), Skodak (1939), and Skeels (1936). Burks's and Leahy's studies argued for the hereditarian point of view. The opposite position was taken by Skodak and Skeels.

Together, Skodak and Skeels (1945, 1949) followed up 154 children, their true mothers, and foster parents after having independently studied the true mothers and the children some years earlier. They found that according to test results the true mothers were retarded in mental ability, whereas the foster parents were above average. Examining 100 of these children longitudinally, they discovered that they did not resemble their true mothers in test scores, but instead resembled the foster parents in tests given over a period of years. At various test ages their mean IQs ranged from 104 to 118 (Skodak & Skeels, 1949). These means were more than 20 points higher than the true-mother mean. Although mean scores resembled the foster parents by the age of eight, the correlation between the IQ of a given child and the ability of its true mother, as estimated from her level of education, ranged from +0.33 to +0.38 (see Goodenough, 1940), whereas correlations with the ability of its foster parents, estimated from their educational level, were only +0.16 to +0.19. How can this be explained? These children, separated from their true mothers soon after birth, obtained mean IQs higher than their mothers', yet, by middle childhood, resembled them almost as closely, in a correlational sense, as children raised by their own mothers. This may be seen in Figure 2-3. Quite likely the IQs obtained from the true

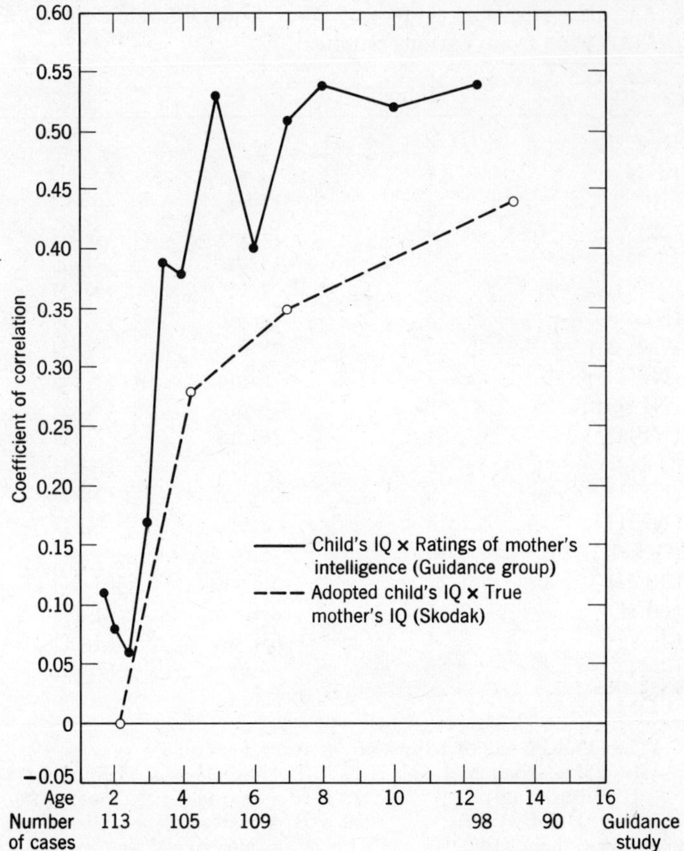

FIGURE 2-3 The correlation, at different ages, between true mother-offspring ability for children reared by biological parents (guidance groups) and for children reared by adoptive parents (Skodak's group) (Honzik, 1957).

mothers were not truly representative of ability. Many of them were tested shortly after having given birth, a rather inopportune time to test any woman—and especially a woman who had given birth to an illegitimate child in Iowa in the 1930's!

As a group, therefore, the adopted-child studies again point to the importance of heredity as a producer of individual differences.

A variant research approach half way between the parent-child pedigree type of study discussed on pp. 52–57 and the adopted-child study, discussed immediately above, has been reintroduced to the research literature. This is the half-sib approach used by Schuckit and his associates (Schuckit, Goodwin, and Winocur, 1971). Through studying half-sibs one can move in a rather simple way to disentangle the effects of heredity and environment. For example, Schuckit, et al. began by finding institutionalized alcoholics who had half-siblings and then investigated the rate of alcoholism of these half-sibs. Their data are presented in Table 2-5.

Evidence from Selective Breeding

Selective breeding is the breeding of organisms for the presence or absence of some particular trait. If the breeding is successful, the trait must necessarily

TABLE 2-5 Nature and Nurture—Alcoholism Among Half-Siblings of Alcoholics

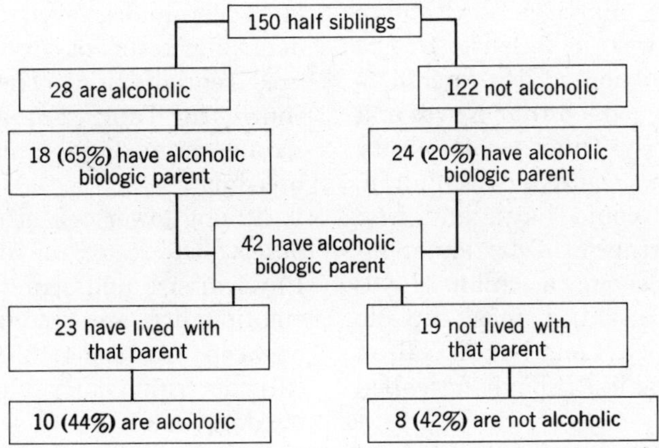

have some hereditary base. The speed at which selective breeding progresses indicates, in part, the importance of heredity in determining how much of the trait is present in any organism. Galton's study persuaded him that humans should engage in selective breeding. The able person should seek an equally able mate in order to improve the human race. This process of selective breeding Galton called *eugenics*. Although eugenics societies still exist, human beings have not taken Galton's ideas very seriously. They continue to fall in love without giving the slightest consideration to what the eugenicist might think of their choice. Yet even if people turned about and suddenly adhered to Galton's formula, problems would remain. What should be the goal of the breeders—vigor, beauty, intelligence? Often these are not found in the same individual, as the well-known story about George Bernard Shaw, the playwright, and Ellen Terry, the beautiful actress, illustrates. Miss Terry suggested to Shaw that they could produce a true *wunderkind* with her beauty and his brains. Shaw rejected the proposal, replying things might turn out the other way around; the child might inherit *his* beauty and *her* brains. The difficulty in any sort of selective breeding is thus the matter of choosing the objective of the process.

The few situations in which humans have bred selectively are indeed odd, since only eccentric people could and would indulge in such experiments. Frederick the Great is said to have married off a large number of his tallest guards to a group of strapping peasant girls and provided them with villages in which to live so as to ensure future rulers of Prussia a ready source of tall soldiers for honor-guard usage. Hitler attempted to breed "Aryan Supermen." The most interesting example of selective breeding among humans stemmed from the ideas of an American religious sect. John Noyes (see Holbrook, 1957) believed that the violent, antisocial emotions, such as jealousy and anger, resulted primarily from the existence of the *nuclear* family—the family composed of father, mother, and children formed into a tightly knit unit. Doing away with this family, Noyes held, also does away with possessiveness and hence with greed, jealousy, and anger. In its place he advocated a utopian scheme as part of a religion he called *Perfectionism*.

At Oneida, New York, Noyes and his followers maintained themselves for years in a communistic community. They practiced what outsiders called "free love" but what they themselves considered "complex marriage." Although sexual behavior was, in a sense, free, a substantial proportion of the members of the community agreed that Noyes and other leaders of the Oneida community would decide who could have children, how many they could have, and who would be the partner of a particular individual in conceiving a child. Noyes desired only the brightest, most capable adults to reproduce. Long before Galton he practiced eugenics, though he called it *stirpiculture*.

The community flourished but federal prosecution of Mormon polygamy in the 1880's spilled over into Oneida, and, along with internal dissention forced the end of the experiment, the only one in which humans were bred for general physical and intellectual excellence. Two descendants of the community (Noyes & Noyes, 1923; reprinted 1967) compared members of the community with the population at large and demonstrated that this self-selected group was a superior one; those involved in the stirpiculture experiment were more fit than members of the community as a whole. The offspring of stirpiculture were markedly more fit, in terms of survival than the population at large, and their children even more fit ("fitness" defined in terms of survival and, to a degree, reproduction). The summary data, shown in Table 2-6, demonstrate the strong, immediate impact of selective breeding.

Among lower organisms it is easier to observe the results of selective breeding. Physical size and structure, ability, and emotionality are among the variations between organisms that can be genetically determined. By selecting and breeding dogs for smallness, as well as for other characteristics, one obtains the Chihuahua, whereas for largeness, one obtains the Great Dane. Moreover, dogs of different breeds vary in temperament and in ability almost as widely as they do in size. Since the ancestry of pedigreed dogs is known for generations, the researcher has purer strains at his disposal than he can obtain among humans.

Scott (1958, pp. 117–125) has reported studies conducted by Fuller and himself which disclose the effect on temperament of hereditary differences produced by selective breeding. In several of these studies, they compared cocker spaniels with *basenjis* (African barkless dogs).

TABLE 2-6 Summary: Comparison of Actual and Expected Number* of Deaths in Various Oneida Community Groups

Group	Actual Deaths	Expected Deaths According to Contemporary Tables	Actual Percentage of Expected Number of Deaths
44 Prestirpicultural births	27	32.7	82.6
225 Oneida Community members, 16 years of age and over on September 15, 1880	166	227.2	73.1
Parents of the stirpicultural children	52	102.7	50.6
Children, one or both of whose parents were stirpicultural	5	21.2	23.6
The stirpicultural children	6	45.2	13.3
Children both of whose parents were stirpicultural	–	6.2	–

Basenjis proved considerably shier and more fearful than cockers, even when they were reared by cocker mothers. As a result of breeding cockers to basenjis, the hybrid progeny were as shy as fullblooded basenjis, suggesting that shyness was a dominant genetic trait in dogs. Breeds of dogs, which differ in parental stock and in the traits for which they are bred, also differ widely in other respects.

By shifting from dogs to rats, we move from the domain generally inhabited by the animal fancier to the domain of the animal scientist. Many rats have been bred by investigators to study the influence of genetic inheritance on a variety of animal characteristics. The most famous rat-breeding experiment was conducted by Tryon (1940). Krech and Crutchfield (1958) have succinctly summarized Tryon's work.

> Tryon started with a "parental" generation of 142 male and female rats. Each animal was run for 19 trials through a 17-unit maze. The brightest animals made a total of approximately 14 errors in learning the maze, the dullest, about 174. The bright females were then mated with the bright males, the dull females with the dull males—the other animals being discarded. Then the offspring of these matings were tested on the same maze. On the basis of their performance, the brightest rats within each of the bright litters were mated, and the dullest within each of the dullest litters were mated. This testing and selective breeding procedure was followed for 18 generations. The results are summarized in the distribution curves of [Figure 2-4] showing the errors made by the parental group, the third generation (F_2), the seventh generation (F_6) and the ninth generation (F_8). With successive generations the two strains of rats pull apart, until by the F_8 generations the dullest of the bright rats are about as bright or brighter than the brightest of the dulls (p. 572).

The Tryon experiment is itself of considerable significance and has led to further work in the biochemical aspects of brightness and dullness (see Chapter 6, pp. 169–170). Conceivably, this might be a key to the treatment of certain kinds of mental defect.

If, in eight generations, one can produce differences so great that strains of organisms do not overlap in a trait such as maze brightness, then genetic factors are indeed powerful in establishing individual differences. The many studies in selective breeding, although dealing for the most part with lower organisms, strongly support the notion that human beings do not enter the world as a *tabula rasa*—a blank tablet. Instead they are born with certain abilities and propensities that are further accentuated by the environment. In fact, it might be said that any characteristic that has a structural base, such as activity level, tendency toward schizophrenia, emotionality, or intelligence, is inheritable.

Inbred Strains

The student of heritability of individual differences who uses lower organisms as his subjects probably will study inbred strains that may or may not have been originally bred for a given characteristic. An inbred strain that fully meets standards involves 20 generations of brother-sister mating. Clearly, this line of research has no application to the study of humans. However, one can study inbreeding, to at least some extent, with human subjects. At the least degree of inbreeding, one can study groups of people who differ in the proportion of all marriages that are consanguinous (involve persons from related stocks—usually operationally defined as cousin marriages). Sutter and Goux (1962) report on degree of inbreeding in various *departments* (roughly equivalent to states in the United States) of France. Schreiber (1969) found a correlation of −0.32 between the height, and of −0.52 between the intelligence of

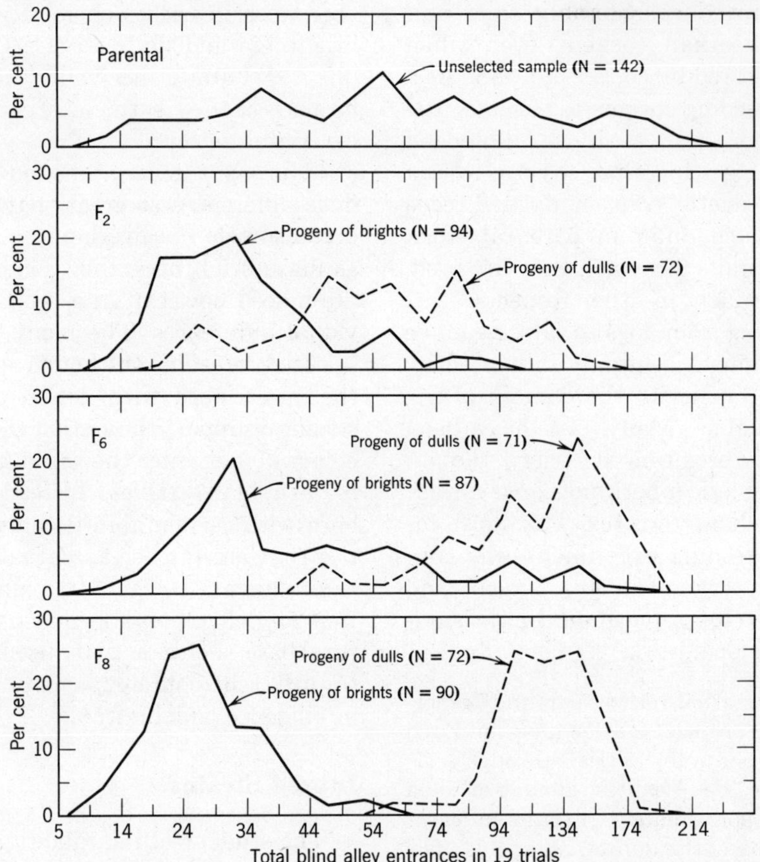

FIGURE 2-4 Error scores made by animals of successive generations. On the vertical axis is indicated the percent of the total group of rats of any one generation making the number of errors indicated on the horizontal axis (Krech & Crutchfield, 1958, p. 572).

recruits into the armed forces from various *departments* and the amount of inbreeding in the *departments*. Ferak, Lichardova, and Bojnova (1968) report similar findings with regard to height in Czechoslovakia (these studies cited in Vandenburg, 1972).

A somewhat greater degree of inbreeding is found in studies of cousin marriages than in the kind of inbreeding study reported above. Schull and Neel (1965) studied offspring of second cousins, of first cousins, and of first cousins once removed, comparing the mean IQs of these groups as compared with children of unrelated parents. The inbred groups were inferior in ability to the outbred groups as shown in Figure 2-5. These data (Weschler IQ scores) reveal the deletoriousness of inbreeding even in a culture, such as Japan, where cousin marriages are viewed favorably, so that the negative self-selection among those who marry cousins that probably is found in the United States is not a factor. That is, in the U.S., it seems reasonably safe to assume that the majority of persons that marry cousins are less able and/or less well educated than the population at large; the reverse seems true in Japan;

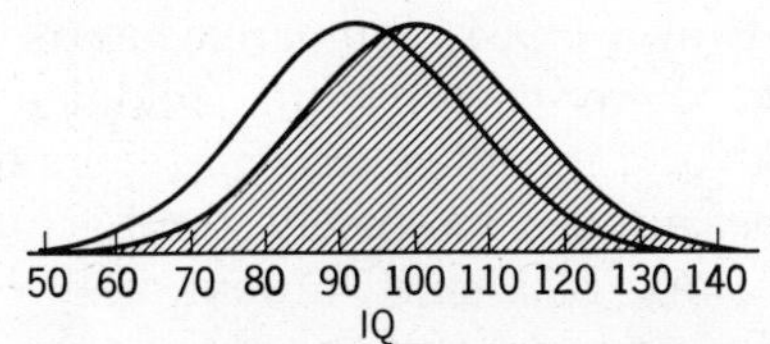

FIGURE 2-5 The average effect of inbreeding to the degree of first, one-and-a-half, and second cousin matings on the IQ distribution of offspring (heavy line). Shaded curve is the IQ distribution of the offspring of nonconsanguineous matings. (Schull & Neel, 1965, figure by Jensen, 1969, p. 57).

yet even in Japan the offspring of cousin marriages are less able than the offspring of unrelated couples.

An even greater degree of inbreeding occurs in incest, defined in our culture as a mating of parent and child or of brother and sister. One of the few empirical studies of the offspring of incestuous unions (Adams and Neel, 1967; Adams, Davidson, & Cornell, 1967) involved a comparison of children of incestuous unions with a control group of children, with mothers of both groups of children being matched in economic status, education, age, and ethnicity, and all children in both groups being either in foster homes or adopted. These results as shown in Table 2-7. It should be noted that incest is by no means a phenomenon found only among dull, disorganized, and deprived families; a good portion of the cases are from upper economic and educational strata.

These data, as well as data from other studies, are arrived at from a human analog of the inbred strain approach to obtaining behavioral genetic information.

A Special Problem Presented by the Results of Studies of Heredity

All the studies described here demonstrate that heredity rather strongly influences certain dimensions of intelligence, as measured by the most frequently used intelligence tests, and

TABLE 2-7 IQs of Children of Incestuous and Normal Matings*

Number	Incest	Controls
1	Died after 2 months	101
2	Died after 15 hours	100
3	Died after 6 hours	104
4	Severely retarded, seizures	107
5	Severely retarded, deaf, blind	93
6	64	100
7	64	133
8	64	109
9	85	103
10	92 (68 at age 3)	81
11	92	108
12	98	108
13	110	91
14	112	105
15	113	91
16	114	85
17	118	121
18	119	95

*Adams, Davidson, & Cornell, 1967.

important domains of cognitive style and of personality.

It sometimes is assumed—although it should not be—that an acceptance of the belief that certain of our intellectual and personality characteristics have strong hereditary components also implies an acceptance of the belief that racial differences in IQ are hereditarily determined. The question of whether blacks and whites are equal in intelligence is a complicated one. The controversy between Garrett (e.g., see Garrett, 1961), who believed in innate (hereditary) racial differences in intelligence, and Klineberg (1935, 1954), who did not, has continued for decades. Shuey (1966), in her review of the literature on racial differences in intelligence, concluded that a genetic intellectual difference exists separating whites and blacks. The evidence that Shuey presented is sufficiently compelling that Dreger (1967), who takes the position that races are equal in ability, reviewed her book favorably. The basic problem in studies of black-white intelligence is whether one can assume that the environments of the two groups are equal; there is ample evidence (e.g., the fraternal-twin-versus-sibling data presented in this chapter and the cross-generational studies and studies of socially isolated groups discussed in Chapter 6) that the nature of the environment substantially influences tested intelligence. Further, as will be discussed below and on pp. 000, it seems likely that intrauterine environmental differences, usually not controlled for, are far more important than previously believed. Dreger and Miller (1960) comment on the many problems involved in actually matching blacks and whites, even on such objectively defined variables such as place of residence, parental education, and years of education. Even in studies where these variables supposedly are controlled, subtle yet potent influences are not controlled. For example, Deutsch and Brown (1964) compared lower-class black, lower-class white, middle-class black, and middle-class white children on measures of intelligence and achievement. As is almost always the case, middle-class youngsters performed more adequately than those from lower-class groups; and within economic groups whites performed more adequately than blacks. Deutsch and Brown were aware, perhaps as a result of having encountered Mischel's (1961) research in this area, that father absence from the home has a number of deleterious consequences on behavior and on intellectual performance. They controlled for frequency of father absence in the four groups. Not surprisingly, lower-class children were reared in father-absent homes more often than middle-class children, and, within each social class, blacks were reared in father-absent homes more often than whites. When father absence was controlled among the four groups, differences in intelligence and achievement were markedly reduced. Since the studies that claim to demonstrate racial differences in ability have not controlled for such important sociopsychological factors as father absence, they cannot be accepted as having demonstrated what they claim. Studies like that of Deutsch and Brown, as well as data such as those presented in Chapter 8, suggest that programs such as Operation Head Start might gain at least as much from employing male teachers as from attempting to enrich the environment. Changing the affective-emotional environment in positive ways may well be more important than intellectual enrichment in producing positive change in intellectual performance. The data cited in Chapter 3, p. 80, on nutrition and uterine adequacy, though not necessarily in opposition to a genetic interpretation of race differences in ability test scores, suggests that increased nutritional aid and increased medical care of low-income mothers, whether black or white, also might be expected to have a greater pay-off value than the kind of enrichment provided by such programs as Head Start.

Cross-cultural data (Gay & Cole, 1967) obtained from white Americans and from westernized and tribal Africans suggests that African blacks are superior to American whites on tasks that are important to them and are not experienced by Americans, and that the reverse is equally true. Finally, it should be mentioned that whites, as compared with nonwhites, appear to be more likely to carry genes, such as the recessive gene causing phenylketonuria, that produce a severe amount of mental defect (Johnson, 1967). The data on racial differences in ability generally are uninterpretable because key variables are uncontrolled. When interpretable, they generally support racial equality or, in single gene effects, support the notion of white *inferiority*, perhaps as a result of a longer period of relaxation of natural selection (see Post, 1962) among the white group. Acceptance of the influence of heredity on intelligence and personality does not imply a belief in race differences in ability.

The position taken above is in contradiction to that taken by Jensen (1969), who has argued that black-white differences in tested IQ are substantial in magnitude and are almost entirely the result of genetic differences between blacks and whites. Since Jensen's position has led to substantial public controversy, some of the major problems of Jensen's position will be noted and evaluated, below.

Jensen assumed in his 1969 paper (though he since has acknowledged the incorrectness of his assumption; see Jensen, 1971) that an estimate, derived from one group, of the degree to which an attribute is under genetic control is generalizable to other groups. Nearly all of the data cited by Jensen were obtained from middle-class white populations. Scarr-Salapatek (1971) has demonstrated that blacks, for as yet unknown reasons, show substantially less evidence of genetic determination of tested ability than is found in the data obtained from middle-class whites. Far less of the variability *within* the black group can be accounted for by genetic analyses. Therefore, far more of the *between* group (black vs. white) differences in scores may be a result of the usual, presently measurable (e.g., socioeconomic status, income, education) environmental forces than Jensen believed. As noted above, more subtle differences, such as family structure, may play a role, as well.

Jensen assumed that, to the degree a given attribute is under genetic control, it is, essentially, impervious to environmental influence. As Hirsch (1970) first pointed out, there is no evidence to support this position. It sounds, on the surface, as though it should be correct. However, one of the present authors, following Hirsch's paper, asked agricultural geneticists for information. They mentioned such things as butterfat production of cows. Butterfat production is a trait showing a heritability of well over 0.90; one can predict the butterfat production of a given cow with almost perfect accuracy, *so long as environment is held constant*, if one knows the butterfat production of the cows in the cow's maternal and paternal ancestral lines. *But*, changes in the environment drastically and quickly influence butterfat production. Here is an attribute highly heritable, yet highly influenced by the environment. There are many others in the area of animal husbandry showing the same results. Jensen's assumption of high heritability = low environmental influences seems to be incorrect.

The two major published criticisms of Jensen, discussed above, are sufficient to lead one to question the validity of Jensen's conclusions that obtained differences in mean or average scores between blacks and whites are genetic in origin. The present writers have a third major criticism of Jensen. Jensen, at least in later work (Jensen, 1971) has seriously considered the possibility that pre- and postnatal nutritional factors may negatively influence black children's development *vis-à-vis* whites. He demonstrates, to the satisfaction of these writers, that the amount and the quality of food intake is not sufficiently different across races or socioeconomic groups to account for the differences in ability tests scores that are his central concern. However, he does not consider the idea that there may be differences within, and possibly across, groups in susceptibility to dietary inadequacies when they do occur. It is known that within-group differences in susceptibility exist (Ahern & Johnson, 1973); between-group differences also may exist, but whether they do or not, the fact that within-group differences exist indicates that the deleterious effects of malnourishment (and nonwhites are more often malnourished than whites), interacting with susceptibility, are greater than generally is believed. Several papers, starting from very different theoretical frameworks (Ahern & Johnson, 1973; Bessman, 1972) conclude that those mothers of any ethnic group who are most susceptible—most "at risk"—can be identified. Once identified, they can be provided with special prenatal care, so that their offspring are not disadvantaged by this susceptibility interacting, to a degree, with malnourishment. Much is known regarding the influence of nutrition on development, and of effective intervention techniques (Kaplan, 1972). If what now is known was brought to bear on society, it would seem highly probable to these writers that all groups would be benefited, but particularly those groups, such as blacks, consisting of individuals who are more frequently economically deprived.

As the foregoing material indicates, we do not accept the belief that obtained differences in ability test scores between groups are demonstrated to be a result of fixed genetic differences between groups. The actual basis of the obtained differences seems to us to be far more likely to be a result of intrauterine conditions than of any other kinds of gene-environment interaction. The problems with which we humans have had to cope seem sufficiently universal, especially since 99 percent of the history of all humanity was spent in similar preagricultural hunting-fishing-gathering societies, that it seems highly improbable that any major differences exist between groups in ability to function adaptively in the environment.

SUMMARY AND CONCLUSIONS

In many ways humans resemble lower organisms; in many ways humans resemble one another. These basic resemblances result from the hereditary process. These effects of biological inheritance, although of great significance, are often overlooked, since they are universal. Besides similarities, heredity produces individual differences in such matters as size, intelligence, and temperament. The role of heredity is more apparent in shaping these differences than in determining similarities. People who differ genetically in some way, as in intelligence, are also treated differently; thus environmental forces magnify the original hereditary distinctions. Some aspects of intelligence and personality appear to have a substantial hereditary component (e.g., spatial ability, approach-withdrawal) while other aspects of the same general domains of individual difference do not. Further, even when aspects of the self result largely from heredity, for example, physical size and appearance, how we view these qualities and respond to them results from environmental influences.

The study of genetic similarities helps to develop a point of view about how far human character can be modified. The human is a medium-sized omnivorous animal. He lacks specialized weapons of offense or defense, but possesses native curiosity, hands free for exploring and manipulating the environment and for carrying weapons, moderately high aggressiveness, and communicative skills that make cooperation possible. It is doubtful whether a tendency to respond bred in by thousands of years of natural selection—for example, a quick and aggressive response to threats from the environment—can be eliminated unless natural selection takes a new course. Veblen (1911) maintained that such a new course began at the time of the industrial revolution. Actually, there is hope for humanity, since built-in responses are susceptible to some modification as the social environment shifts.

It may seem pessimistic to hold that much of the variation between human beings in physique, intelligence, and some aspects of personality results from genetic factors. Yet, for various reasons, this is not a pessimistic view. First, if this view is correct, humans are what they are and no environment, however deprived, can wipe out those aspects of human beings that are most endearing: the forming of close attachments, the need for one another, curiosity, and the sense of wonder. Second, although heredity imposes limits on individual achievement, one cannot tell whether the limit has been reached for any individual unless that individual has been exposed to the best possible social and intellectual environment. Each child and each adult differs from all others. Unless opportunities for expression are made available, potential abilities cannot be judged. However, one should not be surprised to find that some individuals gain more than others from any single environmental opportunity.

Through the study of individual differences in general, and genetically determined individual differences in particular, people become aware of the vast range of these distinctions. We humans are even more different from each other than we seem and in more ways than was once realized. Although these differences at times impede communication between individuals and make the human being a baffling subject for scientific study, they do add richness to human interaction.

One specific result of the study of individual difference is apparent in child psychology. As we shall see in later chapters, child psychology was once "formula happy"—if you do *this* to the child, you will get *that* result. This approach to child-rearing, however, has never proved effective because humans vary so much from one another in their reactions to any treatment. Through increased awareness of the fact that individual differences exist, that they are of great magnitude, and that, to a fair degree, they are hereditary in nature, child psychology has progressed beyond oversimplified approaches to child-rearing practices and philosophies. This is the most important way that the study of individual differences has influenced child development.

REFERENCES

Adams, M. S., Davidson, R. T., and Cornell, P. Adoption risk of the children of incest: a preliminary report. *Child Welfare*, 1967, **47**, 137–143.

Adams, M. S. and Neel, J. V. Children of incest. *Pediatrics*, 1967, **40**, 55–62.

Ahern, F. M. & Johnson, R. C. Inherited uterine inadequacy: An alternate explanation for a portion of cases of defect. *Behavior Genetics*, 1973, **3**, 1–12.

Ardrey, R. *African genesis.* New York: Atheneum, 1961.

Ausubel, D. P. and Sullivan, E. V. *Theory and problems of child development* (2nd ed.). New York: Grune & Stratton, 1970.

Bessman, S. P. Genetic failure of fetal amino acid "justification." A common basis for many forms of metabolic, nutritional, and "nonspecific" mental retardation. *Journal of Pediatrics*, 1972, **81**, 834–842.

Bibby, G. *The testimony of the spade.* New York: Knopf, 1956.

Blewett, D. B. An experimental study of the inheritance of intelligence. *Journal of Mental Science*, 1954, **100**, 922–933.

Burks, B. S. The relative influence of nature and nurture on mental development: A comparative study of foster parent-foster child resemblance. *Yearbook of the National Society for the Study of Education*, 1928, **27 (I)**, 219–316.

Burks, B. S. A study of identical twins reared apart under differing types of family relationships. In Q. McNemar & M. A. Merrill (Eds.), *Studies of personality.* New York: McGraw-Hill, 1942.

Burt, C., & Howard, M. A multiple factorial theory of inheritance and its application to intelligence. *British Journal of Statistical Psychology*, 1956, **9**, 95–131.

Butler, R. A. Discrimination learning by rhesus monkeys to visual-exploration motivation. *Journal of Comparative and Physiological Psychology*, 1953, **46**, 95–98.

Butler, R. A. Curiosity in monkeys. *Scientific American*, 1954, **190**, 7–75.

Cooper, R. M., & Zubek, J. P. Effects of enriched and restricted early environments on the learning ability of bright and dull rats. *Canadian Journal of Psychology*, 1958, **12**, 159, 164.

Darwin, C. R. *The variation of animals and plants under domestication.* New York: Appleton, 1890.

Day, C. *This simian world.* New York: Knopf, 1936 (orig. publ. 1920).

Deutsch, M., & Brown, B. Social influences in Negro-White intelligence differences. *Journal of Social Issues*, 1964, **10**, 24–35.

Dreger, R. M. Review of *The testing of Negro intelligence* by Audrey M. Shuey. *Contemporary Psychology*, 1967, **12**, 49–51.

Dreger, R. M., & Miller, K. S. Comparative psychological studies of Negroes and Whites in the United States. *Psychological Bulletin*, 1960, **57**, 361–402.

Erlenmeyer-Kimling, L., & Jarvik, L. F. Genetics and intelligence: A review. *Science*, 1963, **142**, 1477–1479.

Falconer, D. S. *Introduction to quantitative genetics.* New York: Ronald, 1960.

Ferak, V., Lichardova, Z., and Bojnova, V. Endogamy, exogamy, and stature. (1968).

Forgus, R. H. Advantage of early over late perceptual experience in improving form discrimination. *Canadian Journal of Psychology*, 1956, **10**, 147–155.

Freedman, D. G., & Keller, B. Inheritance of behavior in infants. *Science*, 1963, **140**, 196–198.

Galton, F. *English men of science: Their nature and nurture.* London: MacMillan, 1874.

Galton, F. *Hereditary genius.* London: Clay and Sons, 1869.

Galton, F. *Inquiries into human faculty and its development.* New York: MacMillan, 1883.

Gardner, I. C., & Newman, H. H. Mental and physical traits of identical twins reared apart, Case XX. *Journal of Heredity*, 1940, **31**, 119–126.

Gardner, R. W. Genetics and personality theory. In S. G. Vandenberg (Ed.), *Methods and goals in human behavior genetics.* New York: Academic, 1965. Pp. 223–229.

Gardner, R. W. *The Menninger Foundation study of twins and their parents.* Topeka, Kan.: Menninger Foundation, 1966.

Garrett, H. E. The equalitarian dogma. *Mankind Quarterly*, 1961, **1**, 253–257.

Gates, N., & Brash, H. An investigation of the physical and mental characteristics of a pair of like twins reared apart from infancy. *Annals of Eugenics*, 1941, **11**, 89–101.

Gay, F., & Cole, M. *The new mathematics and an old culture.* New York: Holt, Rinehart and Winston, 1967.

Gibson, E. J., & Walk, R. D. The effect of prolonged exposure to visually presented patterns on learning to discriminate them. *Journal of Comparative and Physiological Psychology*, 1956, **49**, 239–242.

Goodenough, F. L. The Kuhlman–Binet tests of preschool age: A critical study and evaluation. *Institute of Child Welfare Monographs Series,* **No. 2**, 1928.

Goodenough, F. L. New evidence on environmental influence on intelligence. *Yearbook of the National Society for the Study of Education*, 1940, **39**, (I), 367–384.

Goodenough, F. L., & Anderson, J. E. *Experimental child study.* New York: Century, 1931.

Gottesman, I. I. Heritability of personality: A demonstration. *Psychological Monographs*, 1963, **77**, No. 9.

Gottesman, I. I. Personality and natural selection. In S. G. Vandenberg (Ed.), *Methods and goals in human behavior genetics.* New York: Academic, 1965. Pp. 63–74.

Harlow, H. Learning motivated by a manipulative drive. *Journal of Experimental Psychology*, 1950, **40**, 228–234.

Hebb, D. O. *The organization of behavior.* New York: Wiley, 1949.

Herrnstein, R. I.Q. *Atlantic*, 1971, **228**, No. 3, 44–64.

Hirsch, J. Behavior-genetic analysis and its biosocial consequences. *Seminars in Psychiatry*, 1970, **2**, 89–105.

Holbrook, S. H. *Dreamers of the American dream.* Garden City, N.Y.: Doubleday, 1957.

Honzik, M. P. Developmental studies of parent-child resemblance in intelligence. *Child Development*, 1957, **28**, 215–228.

Hunt, J. McV. *Intelligence and experience.* New York: Ronald, 1961.

Jencks, C. (*et al.*) *Inequality: A reassessment of the effect of family and schooling in America.* New York: Basic Books, 1972.

Jensen, A. R. How much can we boost IQ and scholastic achievement? *Harvard Educational Review*, 1969, **39**, 1–23.

Jensen, A. R. *Genetics, educability, and subpopulation differences.* University of California, Berkeley, California, Mimeo. (385 pp.), 1971.

Johnson, D. M. Application of the standard score IQ to social statistics. *Journal of Social Psychology*, 1948, **27**, 217–227.

Johnson, R. C. Similarity in IQ of separated identical twins as related to length of time spent in the same environment. *Child Development*, 1963, **34**, 745–749.

Johnson, R. C. Demographic characteristics of institutionalized phenylketonuries. Boulder, Colo.: Western Interstate Commission on Higher Education, 1967.

Juel-Nielsen, N. Individual and environment. A psychiatric-psychological investigation of monozygotic twins reared apart. *Acta Psychiatrica Scandinavia*, 1964 (Supplement 40), **183**, 152–292.

Kaplan, B. J., Malnutrition and mental retardation. *Psychological Bulletin*, 1972, **78**, 321–334.

Klineberg, O. *Negro intelligence and selective migration.* New York: Columbia University Press, 1935.

Klineberg, O. *Social psychology.* (Rev. ed.) New York: Holt, 1954.

Koch, H. *Twins and twin relations.* Chicago: University of Chicago Press, 1966.

Krech, D., & Crutchfield, R. S. *Elements of psychology.* New York: Knopf, 1958.

La Barre, W. *The human animal.* Chicago: University of Chicago Press, 1954. Pp. 86–87.

Leahy, A. M. Nature-nurture and intelligence. *Genetic Psychology Monographs*, 1935, **17**, 236–308.

Loehlin, J. C., & Vandenberg, S. G. Genetic and environmental components in the covariation of cognitive abilities: An additive model. Report 14, Louisville Twin Study, Louisville, Ky., 1966.

Lorenz, K. *On aggression* (translated by M. K. Wilson). New York: Harcourt, Brace, and World, 1966.

Luchins, A. S., & Forgus, R. H. The effect of differential post-weaning environments on the rigidity of an animal's behavior. *Journal of Genetic Psychology*, 1955, **86**, 51–58.

McCandless, B. R. *Children and adolescents: Behavior and development.* New York: Holt, Rinehart & Winston, 1961.

McClearn, G. E. Genetics and behavior development. In M. L. Hoffman & L. W. Hoffman (Eds.), *Review of child development research.* (Vol. 1) New York: Russell Sage Foundation, 1964. Pp. 433–480.

McClearn, G. E. Behavioral genetics. *Annual Review of Genetics*, 1970.

McClearn, G. E., & Meredith, W. Behavior genetics. *Annual Review of Psychology*, 1966, **17**, 515–550.

Mischel, W. Father-absence and delay of gratification. *Journal of Abnormal and Social Psychology*, 1961, **63**, 116–124.

Morris, D. *The naked ape.* New York: McGraw–Hill, 1967.

Muller, H. J. Mental traits and heredity. *Journal of Heredity*, 1925, **16**, 433–448.

Muller, H. J. The crushing of genetics in the U.S.S.R. *Bulletin of the Atomic Scientists*, 1948, **12**, 369–371.

Newman, H. H., Freeman, F. N., & Holzinger, K. J. *Twins: A study of heredity and environment.* Chicago: University of Chicago Press, 1937.

Nichols, R. C. *The National Merit twin study.* In S. G. Vandenberg (Ed.), *Methods and goals in human behavior genetics.* New York: Academic, 1965. Pp. 231–243.

Noyes, P. B. *My father's house: An Oneida boyhood.* New York: Farrar & Rinehart, 1937.

Post, R. H. Population differences in red and green color vision deficiency: A review and a query on selection relaxation. *Eugenics Quarterly*, 1962, **9**, 131–146.

Saudek, R. A British pair of identical twins reared apart. *Character and Personality*, 1934, **3**, 17–39.

Scarr, S. Genetic factors in activity motivation. *Child Development*, 1966, **37**, 663–673.

Scarr, S. Environmental bias in twin studies. In S. G. Vandenberg (Ed.), *Progress in human genetics.* Baltimore, Md.: Johns Hopkins Press, 1968. Pp. 205–213.

Scarr-Salapatek S. Race, class, and IQ. *Science*, 1971, **174**, 1285–1295.

Schaefer, E. S., & Bayley, N. Maternal behavior, child behavior, and their intercorrelations from infancy through adolescence. *Monographs of the Society for Research in Child Development*, 1963, **28** (3, Whole No. 87).

Schreider, E. Inbreeding, biological and mental variation, in France. *American Journal of Physical Anthropology*, 1969, **30**, 215–220.

Schuckit, M., Goodwin, D., and Winocur, G. Genetic investigation in alcoholism—the half sibling approach. In O. Forsander, & K. Eriksson (Eds.) *International Symposium: Biological aspects of alcohol consumption.* Helsinki: Finnish Foundation for Alcohol Studies, 1971, **20**, 163–167.

Schull, W. F. and Neel, F. V. *The effects of inbreeding on Japanese children.* New York: Harper & Row, 1965.

Scott, J. P. *Animal behavior.* Chicago: University of Chicago Press, 1958.

Shuey, A. M. *The testing of Negro intelligence.* New York: Social Science Press, 1966.

Skeels, H. M. Mental development of children in foster homes. *Journal of Genetic Psychology*, 1936, **49**, 91–106.

Skodak, M. Children in foster homes: A study of mental development. *University of Iowa Study in Child Welfare*, 1939, **16**, No. 1.

Skodak, M., & Skeels, H. M. A follow-up study of children in adoptive homes. *Journal of Genetic Psychology*, 1945, **66**, 21–58.

Skodak, M., & Skeels, H. M. A final follow-up study of one hundred adopted children. *Journal of Genetic Psychology*, 1949, **75**, 85–125.

Smith, H. T., & Stone, L. J. Developmental psychology. *Annual Review of Psychology*, 1961, **12**, 1–26.

Stephens, F. E., & Thompson, R. B. The case of Millan and George. *Journal of Heredity*, 1943, **34**, 108–114.

Sutter, T. and Goux, J. M. Evolution de la consanguinite in France of 1926–1958 avec des donnees recentes detaillees. *Population*, 1962, **17**, 683–702.

Sutton, H. E., Clark, P. J., & Schull, W. J. The use of multiallele genetic characters in the diagnosis of twin zygosity. *American Journal of Human Genetics*, 1955, **7**, 180–188.

Terman, L. M., & Merrill, M. A. *Measuring intelligence.* Boston: Houghton Mifflin, 1937.

Thompson, G. G. Developmental psychology. *Annual Review of Psychology*, 1959, **10**, 1–42.

Thurstone, L. L. *The Primary Mental Abilities Tests.* Chicago: Science Research Associates, 1941.

Thurstone, T. G., Thurstone, L. L., & Strandskov, H. H. A psychological study of twins. Report No. 4 from the Psychometric Laboratory, University of North Carolina, Chapel Hill, N.C., 1955.

Tryon, R. C. Genetic differences in maze learning in rats. *Yearbook of the National Society for the Study of Education*, 1940, **39**, (1), 111–119.

Tuddenham, R. D. The constancy of personality ratings over two decades.

Genetic Psychology Monographs, 1959, **60**, 3–29.

Vandenberg, S. G. The hereditary abilities study. *Eugenics Quarterly*, 1956, **3**, 94–96.

Vandenberg, S. G. The hereditary abilities study: Hereditary components in a psychological test battery. *American Journal of Human Genetics*. 1962, **14**, 22–237.

Vandenberg, S. G. The nature and nurture of intelligence. Report No. 20, Louisville Twin Study, University of Louisville, Ky., 1966. (a)

Vandenberg, S. G. Contributions of twin research to psychology. *Psychological Bulletin*, 1966, **66**, 327–352. (b)

Vandenberg, S. G. Genetic factors in poverty, a psychologist's point of view. Report No. 27, Louisville Twin Study, University of Louisville, Louisville, Ky., 1967(a).

Vandenberg, S. G. Heredity factors in normal personality traits (as measured by inventories). In *Recent advances in biological psychiatry*. (Vol. 9) New York: Plenum, 1967. (b) Pp. 65–104.

Vandenberg, S. G. Assertative mating or who marries whom? *Behavior Genetics*, 1972.

Vandenberg, S. G., & Johnson, R. C. Further evidence on the relation between age of separation and similarity in IQ among pairs of separated identical twins. In S. G. Vandenberg (Ed.), *Progress in behavior genetics*. Baltimore: Johns Hopkins Press, 1968. Pp. 215–219.

Veblen, T. *The theory of the leisure class*. New York: MacMillan, 1911.

Watson, J. B. *Psychology from the standpoint of a behaviorist*. Philadelphia: Lippincott, 1919.

Wilson, R. S. Twins: Early mental development. *Science*, 1972, **175**, 914–917.

Woodworth, R. S. *Heredity and environment*. New York: Social Science Research Council, 1941.

Zirkle, C. *Death of a science in Russia*. Philadelphia: University of Pennsylvania Press, 1949.

chapter 3

growth and maturation

chapter 3

growth and maturation

chapter 3

growth and maturation

Anything that lives grows. Among the higher species, growth proceeds along specific lines producing physical changes in the organism. At the same time, changes in behavior occur, which are believed to be direct consequences of growth. These behaviors, attributable principally or entirely to structural development, are called *maturational.* Many such behaviors occur in orderly fashion in young organisms, often appearing for the first time during the prenatal period. Their sequence of development is similar among widely divergent species. By their origins they illustrate the substantial role played by biological inheritance in the development of behavior.

PRENATAL GROWTH AND BEHAVIOR

After the egg is fertilized, it receives nurture from surrounding tissues and starts to grow. The mass of the cell increases more rapidly than its surface area, thus limiting the size of any cell while permitting sufficient nourishment to penetrate its walls. Perhaps because of this, the cell divides. This division continues as cells grow and split, until a ball-like cluster of cells emerges.

Up to this point in development, all cells are presumably the same and interchangeable. Now the cells begin to separate into layers according to their position in the cluster. The outer layer—*ectoderm*—becomes, for the most part, the sense organs and nervous system of the growing new organism. The middle layer—*mesoderm*—is the primary source of the skeleton and muscles, and the inner layer—*endoderm*—leads to the viscera and glands of later development.

Once these three layers have formed, specialized development overtakes the new organism. Development advances faster in the head than in the tail region of the embryo and in the central areas before the peripheral areas. These courses of development are called *cephalocaudal* —from head to tail—and *proximodistal*—from central to peripheral. In the embryo, and later in the newborn infant, many of the early behaviors are massive in approach because of this uneven nature of growth, whereas later movement becomes more specific. The young child, owing to less adequate distal development, uses his whole body in reaching and grasping, employing many distinct muscle groups. As he ages and as distal development improves, he is eventually able to use his fingers alone; this is a change from mass to specific movement.

Many behaviors become apparent before birth. These include a large number of reflexes, such as breathing, swimming, or sucking, as well as behaviors like flexing the leg, which occur as a direct response to stimulation. As a result, the infant is born with a large repertoire of unlearned behaviors in addition to some that may have been acquired through learning.

PRENATAL DEVELOPMENT AND INDIVIDUAL DIFFERENCES

The newborn infant is born with certain characteristics and capacities. It is difficult to determine whether these characteristics and capacities are a result of hereditary or of prenatal influences. For example, the form of mental deficiency called Down's syndrome (mongolism) results from several different kinds of chromosomal abnormality. The most frequent kind of Down's syndrome, trisomy 21, which is caused by the presence of an extra chromosome 21, is also closely associated with maternal age; that is, older mothers produce most cases of trisomy 21. This fact led researchers to believe for a long time that maternal aging produced an inadequate intrauterine environment that in turn caused Down's syndrome. In this case a genetically caused defect was incorrectly believed to result from an adverse prenatal environment. In the opposite direction, studies of maternal nutrition during pregnancy, such as those carried out by Pasamanick and his associates (discussed below), suggest that many instances of mild mental retardation believed to show polygenic type of familial inheritance actually may be a result of maternal malnutrition and inadequate prenatal care across generations. Thus errors in the attribution of causes occur in both directions: defects in the newborn are sometimes believed to be caused by prenatal conditions when they actually result from genetic factors, and are sometimes believed to be caused by genetic factors when they actually result from prenatal influences.

Our present state of knowledge suggests most strongly that inadequate maternal nutrition and inadequate prenatal care produce many kinds of defect in offspring. Improvement of maternal nutrition (and care) seems certain to markedly reduce certain varieties of problem behavior.

The most thorough study so far of the connection between maternal health and problem behavior was undertaken by Pasamanick and his associates. In one study, the subjects were 363 white and 108 Negro children who had been referred to a division of special services in the Baltimore Department of Education because of behavioral disturbances (Pasamanick, Rogers, & Lilienfeld, 1956). Their disorders were described as hyperactivity, confusion, and disorganization. During their pregnancies, the mothers of these children had had a higher proportion of complications than mothers of a corresponding group of white and Negro control children. The pregnancy complications most closely associated with behavioral disorders were maternal *toxemia*, a pathological condition resulting from poison in the blood, and maternal hypertension. It seemed likely that these complications produced *anoxia*, a shortage of oxygen supply for the tissues, and that this, in turn, gave rise to brain injury. As Kawi and Pasamanick (1959) noted, there was within the uterus a continuum of maldevelopment "with a lethal component consisting of abortions, still births, and neonatal deaths, and a sublethal component consisting of cerebral palsy, epilepsy, mental deficiency, and behavior disorders in children."

Since inadequate maternal diet and care is more frequent in lower economic groups, and is particularly frequent among Negroes (as noted in the Pasamanick studies), many social class and racial differences in the frequency of problem behavior probably can be traced back to this prenatal period.

There is evidence that there are genetic differences between women in the adequacy of the uterine environment they provide their offspring, with environment held constant (Robson, 1955; Ahern & Johnson, 1973). It may be that differences in susceptibility to inadequate nutrition (or to other forces influencing the uterine environment), as well as differing frequencies of inadequate nutrition, are involved in the race differences in pregnancy complications found in the set of researches carried out by Pasamanick and others (see above; see also Knobloch & Pasamanick, 1966; Pasamanick & Knobloch, 1966, for reviews of this literature). Bessman (1972), looking at amino acid metabolism of mothers interacting with the metabolism of the fetus, suggests that an interactive amino acid imbalance exists far more frequently than now is believed, and may have substantial deleterious effects on the offspring.

He discusses means of diagnosis and of treatment, as noted previously. These writers believe that this area is the most promising in terms of reducing stillbirths, neonatal deaths, congenital malformations and some varieties of mental retardation.

POSTNATAL NUTRITION AND DEVELOPMENT

Prenatal nutrition has substantial influence on later development. So does postnatal nutrition, especially during the first few years of life. Two recent reviews of the literature (Eichenwald & Fry, 1969; Kaplan 1972) deal with the effects of malnutrition on later development. Eichenwald and Fry point out that not only physical maturation (e.g., decreased rate of growth) but biochemical maturation, such as the ability to metabolize certain amino acids, is retarded by malnutrition. Severe protein-calorie malnourishment, in infancy, leads to the disorders of *marasmus* and *kwashiorkor*. These disorders probably are one and the same—called marasmus if occurring immediately after weaning; kwashiorkor if somewhat later. This kind of severe malnourishment result in apathy and mental slowness. Further, it results in there being fewer brain cells and lower brain weight. The introduction of an adequate diet results in gains, but some permanent deficit in height, weight, head circumference, as well as in resistance to stress and in intellectual functioning results. Ordinary undernourishment, the frequency of which is closely associated with social class, has similar though less striking effects as those found in kwashiorkor. There may be an association between susceptibility to malnourishment and social class as well as the well-established relationship between nutritional level and social class.

POSTNATAL MATURATIONAL GROWTH

Since many prenatal behaviors develop at a time and in a sequence that do not vary from child to child, occurring as the result of the growth of the embryo, we may naturally wonder about the development of postnatal behaviors. Are these, too, the result of growth?

Developmental Norms

Sequences of postnatal development common to all members of a species are readily observable. If any of these sequences is orderly, it may possibly stem from physiological maturation. Table 3-1 contains four sets of norms for stages of development, each obtained from a different sample of children. Figure 3-1 illustrates one of these sets. As both Table 3-1 and Figure 3-1 indicate, postnatal development is essentially cephalocaudal and proximodistal, thus suggesting that prenatal growth trends continue into the postnatal period. Reisen and Kinder (1952) believe that an increasingly large number of muscle groups is engaged in each successive behavior and that the pattern progresses from simple to more complex responses. Perhaps it is this passage from simplicity to complexity rather than gradients of inner growth that accounts for the apparent continuation of prenatal growth sequences. Either way, the order of development seems similar to all four studies cited in the table; the sequences of behavioral change are lawful and predictable even though the mean ages at which any behavior occurs vary somewhat among the four sets of norms.

As may be seen in Table 3-1, certain behaviors of infants of six months or more seem to occur earlier now than they did in the 1930's, perhaps as a result of better nutrition. Indeed, the whole course

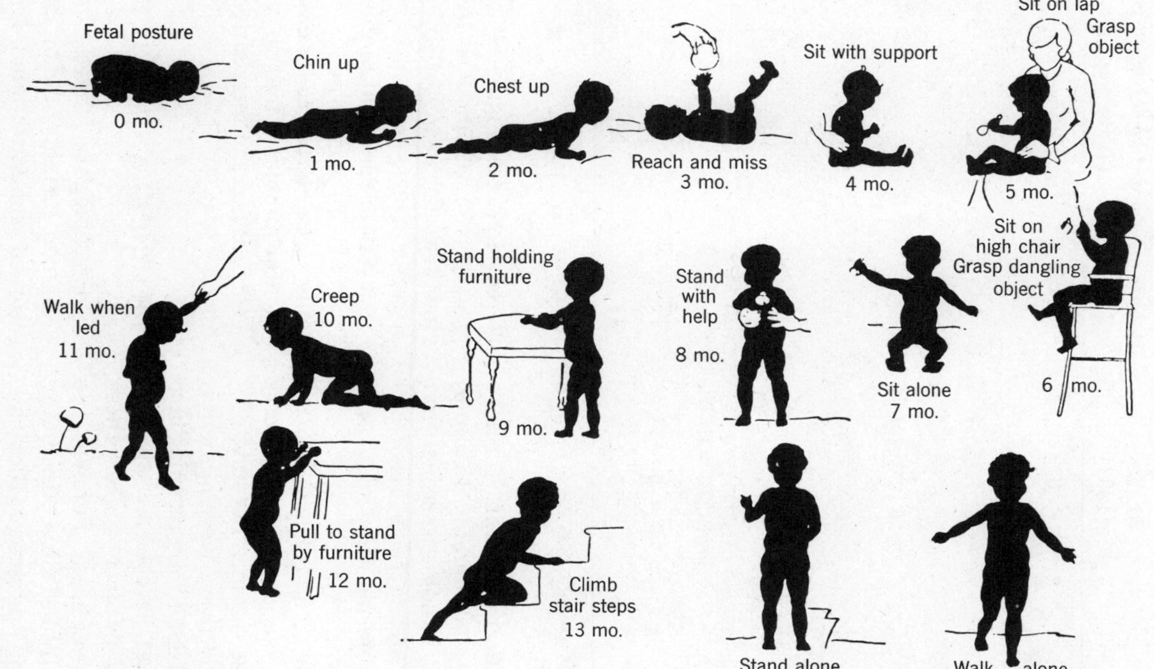

FIGURE 3-1 The motor sequence (Shirley, 1933, frontispiece).

TABLE 3-1 Four Sets of Developmental Norms

Test Items	Mean Age in Months (to Nearest Full Month)			
	Shirley (1933)	Baley (1935)	Aldrich & Norval (1946)	Frankenberg & Dodds (1965, 1967)
Fetal position	0			
Chin up (can raise chin when prone)	1			0–1*
Head erect		2		2
Chest up (can raise chest when prone)	2			3
Head control when sitting			3	3
Head erect and steady		3		3
Sits with support	4	4		
Sits alone	7	6	6	6
Crawls	9	9	7	7
Creeps	10			
Walks with help	11	12	10	
Stands alone	14	13	11	11
Walks alone	15	13	12	11

*90 percent pass item by one month.

of physical maturation seems to have been speeded up considerably (Tanner, 1968), so that it is not surprising that behaviors that are more a result of growth and maturation than of experience now occur earlier.

The Frankenberg and Dodds norms cited in Table 3-1 merit special consideration. First, these norms, obtained by means of the Denver Developmental Screening Test (DDST), are recent. Since the developmental process has speeded up, this recency in itself makes these norms the most accurate. Further, the norms were established on a reasonably representative and quite large (1036 children) sample. Norms for subgroups (e.g., low-income children) also are available. Along with the mean or average age at which an item is passed, one has data in the age at which 25 percent, 75 percent, and 90 percent of the children pass the item. There are a large number of different items (see Figure 14-1, Chapter 14,) and the items themselves are divided into four areas—gross motor, fine motor-adaptive, language and personal-social—so that a developmental profile can be constructed allowing the investigator not only to be alerted to a possible developmental problem, but to establish the generality of the retardation in development.

LEARNING AND MATURATION

Psychologists have often asked whether certain human behaviors are learned or maturational. In a sense this is another version of the question regarding heredity and environment. Maturation is hereditary; it is an orderly sequence of events determined by changing physical structure, which in turn is governed by heredity. Learning, on the other hand, results from environmental stimulation. If the behaviors of a young child, whether physical, emotional, or social, are largely the result of maturation, the role of parents is largely to let children grow by themselves, since development and change come from within rather than from without. Under these circumstances, whatever adults do to children, good or bad, will not change children drastically. If, however, early behaviors are learned, what children are taught, how they are taught, and when they are taught are of prime significance. We return to the question posed at the outset of Chapter 2: How mutable is the human organism?

If humans actually vary because of changes in the environment, the study of learning and maturation may shed some light on the extent to which they do. For example, one of two similar groups of subjects is exposed to environmental stimulation, while this stimulation is withheld from the other group. The two groups should differ in behavior if learning is a product of such stimulation and if learning really influences the development of that behavior. On the other hand, if innate maturational mechanisms occasion the behavior, the environmental difference between the two groups should be of no consequence. In another situation the experimental group may be stimulated excessively while the control group is limited to the ordinary amount of environmental stimulation. Both situations may use identical twins; this is called the co-twin method. From studies of this kind, it becomes possible to establish roughly the relative influences of hereditary, maturational factors on the one hand, and of learning, which is dependent on the environment, on the other.

Experiments in Nature

The first area of maturation studied by psychologists was that of physical maturation. One repeatedly hears the assertion, "We are teaching Johnny to walk." Is this true, or will the child learn without training–in fact, without having much opportunity to attempt to perfect his walking? Since withholding to walk from a group of children merely to test an idea would hardly be ethical, researchers turn to "experiments in nature" in the hope of finding the information they desire. Among various cultures for example, there are many that restrict–sometimes very severely–the movement of a child. The practice of *swaddling*–that is, wrapping and binding an infant in long, narrow bands of cloth–was and is an accepted cultural practice in the Near East, the Balkans, Poland, and Russia.

> In the great Russian peasant population, and to a varying degree in all the regions and classes which shared and continue to share the common cultural heritage of the great central plains of Russia, the item of child care called swaddling was developed to an extreme. While the custom of bandaging newborn infants is widespread, the ancient Russian extreme insists that the baby be swaddled up to the neck, tightly enough to make a handy "log of wood" out of the whole bundle, and that swaddling be continued for nine months, for the greater part of the day and throughout the night (Erikson, 1950, p. 344).

The effect of this kind of deprivation of motor experience on the rate of motor development is of importance to the study of maturation. Danziger and Frankl, as reported in Orlansky (1949), ventured into Albania to test swaddled children and compare their development with that of Viennese infants. This is what they found:

> Until they are one year old, the Albanian children are bound securely to a wooden cradle customarily placed in the darkest corner of the room, often with a cloth

thrown over their heads so that no light is visible. These children displayed poor muscular coordination, but once given an opportunity to practice, their performance improved rapidly so that it was clear no permanent retardation had been effected. Their social behavior, as measured by response to the experimenters in a series of standardized tests, was equal or superior to the norms for Viennese children of the same age. Identical observations could undoubtedly be made on the children of many primitive peoples who, tied securely to cradleboards during their first year of life, may experience comparatively little bodily contact or fondling by the mother (Orlansky, 1949, p. 16).

Most American Indian tribes believe—or once believed—that infants should be reared on some type of cradleboard. A cradleboard usually consists of a straight board for a back. The child, covered with skins or blankets, is bound to the board so that, as the Indians believe, its posture will be good.

In studying various groups of Hopi Indians, Dennis and Dennis (1940) noted that in most villages infants were placed on a cradleboard shortly after birth and remained on it almost continuously for the first 3 months of their lives. Then they spent less time on the board but were attached to it at least for some periods until reaching about 14 months of age. Compared with other Hopi infants reared in the same general fashion but without cradleboards, these children showed no difference in the age of walking.

Co-Twin Studies

In another study by Dennis and Dennis (Dennis, 1935, 1938, and 1941), a pair of fraternal female twins was raised under restricted opportunites to practice motor or special responses. These conditions prevailed from the thirty-sixth day to the fourteenth month in the lives of the twins. Writing years later to summarize their research, the Dennises gave the following description of the environmental background.

Throughout the experiment the twins lived in our home but they were confined to the nursery. This was a second-floor room, so situated that from the infants' position only sky and tree tops were visible through the windows. The room itself contained the subjects' cribs, a bureau, a table, two chairs, and a screen near the door. No picture or decoration of any sort was permitted in the nursery. The door of the room was kept closed, and we entered the room only to care for the subjects, to observe them, and to experiment with them. . . .

The subjects were placed in individual cribs, of the trade name "Kiddie Koop." The cribs were placed side by side with a screen equal in height to the cribs between the two, so that the twins could see each other only when taken from their beds. During the first nine months the subjects were taken from the cribs only for feeding and bathing or when removal from the cribs was demanded for the purposes of experimentation.

With the exception of a few occasions during the latter part of the experiment the sole care of the twins was supplied by the experimenters. This means that we bathed and fed the infants, changed the diapers and bed clothing, and cleaned the room. The infants seldom saw other people, and when they did it was with our knowledge and supervision. Visitors were required to adhere to the same practices which we imposed upon ourselves. . . .

With a few exceptions, we never encouraged or discouraged any act of the twins. The exceptions to this rule, and to other such general rules, occurred in the last month of the investigation, when the experimental conditions were partially suspended. . . .

We not only avoided reward and punishment but we avoided acts which might have provided examples for imitation. With certain exceptions to be noted later our behavior in the nursery was limited to changing diapers, bathing, feeding, etc. We carefully refrained from baby talk and from babbling, as we wanted to know whether such vocalizations would occur without example. Likewise, we never performed for the twins such acts as patting their hands or playing with their toes.

Thus far we have spoken only of the conditions which remained relatively constant until the last few weeks of the experiment. We turn now to more stringent restrictions in the environment of the subjects, which, in the main, were applied only for the first half-year. The conditions to be described were designed to provide answers to specific questions and were abandoned when the answers were obtained.

We wished to determine whether or not the infants would smile upon hearing the voice of the adult, if speech were not associated with the care and attention which the adult supplied. For this reason, until the twins were 26 weeks of age, we never announced our entry into the nursery and never spoke to the subjects. We were not totally silent, for we occasionally commented to each other while in the nursery, but we were careful not to make comments while we were feeding or otherwise caring for the twins. Our speech when we were outside the nursery could be heard by the infants, but it had no more relation to their behavior than did traffic noises or other common sounds (Dennis & Dennis, 1951, pp. 106–109).

From this description, it is clear that the twins were raised in an environment as cold and as unstimulating as the Dennises could make it. Yet it was the Dennises and not the children who found the routine trying, so trying that they ended it before they had planned in order to respond in a normal way to the infants. Figure 3-2 illustrates the age at which certain behaviors appeared in each of the twins as compared with a normally raised sample of children also studied by the Dennises. In the figure the symbol ○ represents one of the twins and the symbol △ the other. The vertical bar represents the mean; the horizontal bar indicates the normal range. Although somewhat retarded in motor skills but less retarded in social responses, the twins' sequences of development seemed normal and their retardation slight. It should be noted, however, that the twin symbolized by △ suffered from moderate brain injury during birth and that some, if not all, of her slowness can be attributed to this.

Another method of testing whether walking is inherent or taught is to compare the performances of a set of identical twins in which one twin T is trained and the other C is not. In the first experiment to use this approach (Gesell & Thompson, 1929) the experimental twin T was trained to climb stairs while the control twin C was given no such training. Once T had learned to climb stairs both twins were tested on stair-climbing ability. In several studies of essentially maturational phenomena, it was found that C, merely by growing older and becoming more developed—as well as receiving normal environmental stimulation—was immediately the equal of T as soon as confronted by a test of behavior—in this case, stair climbing. Other studies of the same sort, such as McGraw's study of Johnny and Jimmy, discussed below, found C's ability inferior but "ready" for learning. Since C was now older than T was when trained, C could be trained to the same proficiency as T in far fewer sessions.

Several similar studies all have led to the same conclusion. So far as *phylogenetic* skills are concerned—those abilities, such as walking or toilet performance, that are common to all humans—early training consumes valuable time and does not often achieve more than a transitory improvement in skills. However, if one is willing to invest the enormous amount of time and effort required, one might find, as evidence suggests, that early training of motor behaviors

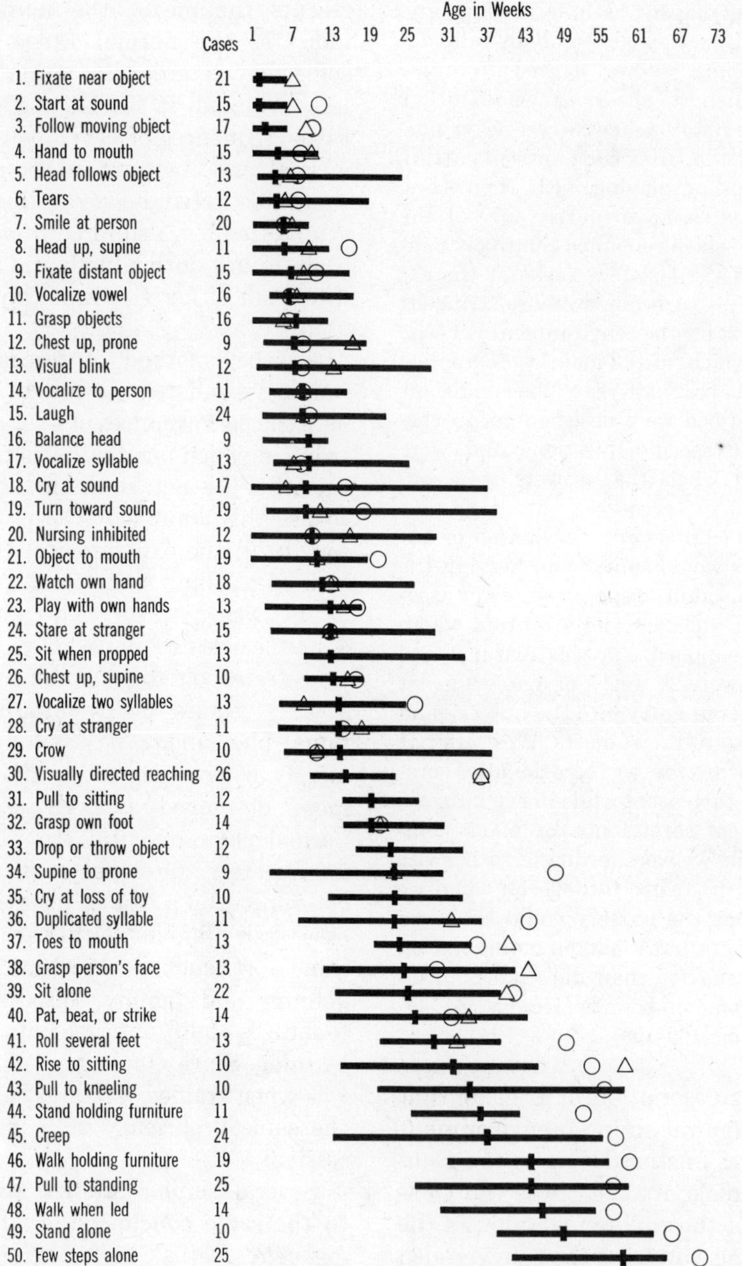

FIGURE 3-2 Age-related behavior occurrence (Dennis & Dennis, 1951, p. 112).

results in increased expertness in such behaviors in later life. An earlier McGraw study of maturation (1935; both the book and a film entitled *Growth: A Study of Johnny and Jimmy* are available) supports this view. In this study twin T was trained in various motor skills from the age of 21 days to 22 months. The training was extremely extensive and may be seen in the book or film. The control twin received no special training, except for regular tests of motor ability, which might, in themselves, have constituted some training. As a result of his training the experimental twin advanced greatly in some ways; for example, he was an accomplished roller skater before he was two. His greatest superiority turned up in *ontogenetic* skills—that is, individual or uncommon skills—whereas he showed little superiority in phylogenetic skills such as walking. Among skills like climbing, which are probably phylogenetic but only slightly exercised in normal child development, the experimental twin also disclosed a considerable degree of superiority. The value of this experiment is decreased, however, by the fact that although these twins at first seemed identical, they were actually fraternal. Yet the great differences between them seem unlikely to result from genetic distinction. Of greater interest is the knowledge that twin T, in tests conducted years after the differential training had ceased (McGraw, 1939), retained his motor advantages over twin C.

The co-twin approach is an excellent experimental procedure that has told us much of what we need to know regarding the effects of maturation on the development of skills. Although it has many advantages (see Vandenberg, 1966), it has not been used often in the last two decades. In recent years, however, both Fowler (1965) and Naeslund (1956) have used the co-twin approach on the very important problem of determining the most effective time and way of teaching children to read. Hopefully, this procedure may again become popular.

Readiness

Ontogenetic skills apparently can be acquired through training, as we have seen. Phylogenetic skills, in contrast, turn up in their own good time as a result of growth; neither training nor deprivation, within wide limits, has marked effect on their development. This suggests that an age of readiness exists for the appearance of many behaviors and that before this age these behaviors can be learned only with difficulty, if at all.

Readiness is discussed most frequently in relation to such academic skills as reading. The idea of reading readiness is of some utility; reading depends, for example, on the ability to discriminate symbols. This facility may be maturational. Nevertheless, some children learn to read much earlier than the age at which they are considered ready; according to Gates (1937) and others, this age is six and one-half years.[1]

If reading readiness is a common maturational skill, the variation in the age at which it is reached is far wider than in other areas of maturational development. It would thus seem that a number of unique factors contribute to the ability to read, only some of which contain maturational elements.

Let us consider some other research that seems to support the position that maturation may not be of as great importance in reading as the reading-readiness concept would imply. The length of time that a child will concentrate on a specific task is called the child's *attention span*. Attention span increases systematically with age. Van Alstyne (1932), for example, obtained mean attention spans of 7.0 minutes for two-year-olds, 8.9 minutes for three-year-olds, 12.4 for four-year-olds, and 13.6 for five-year-olds. This increase might be assumed to be maturational. Perhaps it is. Highly relevant, however, are the findings of Moyer and Gilmer (1955), who used one simple toy, a red plastic automobile, and

[1]For a discussion of children who learned to read at considerably earlier ages, see Fowler (1962).

six carefully designed, relatively intricate toys as stimuli in a study of attention span. Some of their results appear in Table 3-2.

Two things may be noted. First, there is no age progression in length of attention span among the complex toys. Second, all of the spans are very high compared with those of many previous studies of this sort, of which many are reviewed by Moyer and Gilmer, or as compared with the attention span evoked by the toy automobile. Attention span is governed primarily by the type of stimulus—in this case, the type of toy—not by age. The results make it clear that the cliché about young children having too short an attention span to tackle a specific task is so much nonsense. If the task can be made challenging and interesting enough, even very young children have extremely long attention spans.

How does attention span apply to reading? It applies both directly and indirectly. In a direct sense, teaching a child to read requires continued attention; indirectly, attention span is similar to reading readiness, for it purportedly shows a progression of age produced by maturation. Like attention span, reading readiness seems conditioned more by the amount of interest stimulated by the reading materials than by any development of phylogenetic skills. That is, reading readiness is more a matter of stimulation than maturation.

Now that Fowler (1965) and Moore (1966) have demonstrated that average children can learn to read by age three or four, the maturational point of view regarding readiness appears clearly incorrect. Presumably, in conventional methods of teaching reading, six-and-a-half may be the cutoff point; but conventional methods of teaching reading are analogous to the red auto in Table 3-2; they do not appear to make use of potential that is present. We see no particular reason why three-year-olds should learn to read, but they can, if proper teaching procedures and materials are used—maturational concepts to the contrary.

Although evidence supports the tremendous importance of maturation in the development of simple motor behaviors such as walking, it seems evident that the concept of maturation has been extended too far when carried into more complex areas such as attention span or reading. Saying that a child has an "inadequate maturational level" (as shown by a limited attention span or by seeming inability to learn how to read) often is used by a teacher as an explanation for that child's limited gains. The explana-

TABLE 3-2 Mean Attention Span for Toys, in Minutes

	Mean Attention Span by Age						
Toy	1½	2	3	4	5	6	7
Red automobile			3.1	4.9	5.4		
Complex toy No. 1*	24.3	26.5	21.2	22.7	18.5		
Complex toy No. 2		34.0	32.9	32.4	28.9		
Complex toy No. 3			30.3	33.0	30.7		
Complex toy No. 4			15.6	22.2	26.7	31.9	
Complex toy No. 5				29.0	29.4	33.0	
Complex toy No. 6				39.2	35.0	39.7	28.5

*Each complex toy was not presented at each age level because they were designed to arouse interest within a limited age range.

tion can be only partial, at best. Proper stimulus materials markedly increase attention span; innovative teaching techniques, such as those developed by Moore, dramatically increase rate of gain in reading ability.

Extreme Deprivation of Stimulation

Within a rather wide range, the deprivation of experience may result in nothing more than a temporary slowing down of the development of phylogenetic behaviors. Although moderate deprivation has no appreciable effect on the development of motor behaviors, severe deprivation has a profound influence. Moreover, there may be a *critical period* for the learning of certain common developmental skills. During this period any exposure to learning, even if brief, brings out behavior at a normal pace. Any exposure before this period has only a small, transient impact. But a lack of exposure, that is, a deprivation until the period has passed, results in permanent injury, leaving a lasting inferiority.

In the first study pertaining to this area, Von Senden (1932) examined medical reports written about people who were born nearly blind as a result of congenital cataracts. These individuals were often able to distinguish light from darkness but could not differentiate forms. Since some patients who have cataracts removed do achieve approximately normal vision (Von Senden, 1932; London, 1960), these people presumably should have been capable of making adequate visual discriminations after undergoing appropriate surgery. Yet interestingly and surprisingly, when their cataracts were removed, some of them remained unable to make certain types of visual distinction. They could tell that the visual field was varied, but could not identify objects or describe their shapes from visual cues. When allowed to feel the objects, they were able to identify them immediately. Colors were perceived and named accurately as soon as color names were learned; color mazes were learned quickly. Nevertheless, it took many trials for an individual to learn even so simple a difference as that between a square and a triangle. After learning, if required to make this discrimination in a new setting or under new conditions of illumination, the individual was again unable to differentiate. Despite an apparently adequate, although somewhat abnormal, visual mechanism (see Riesen, 1960), many who were studied remained unable to distinguish between different persons on a purely visual basis even after years of visual experience. Furthermore, some of them could not learn to discriminate between objects on the basis of their shapes, despite seemingly normal vision. Others learned, but very slowly. Von Senden's findings suggested strongly that many aspects of vision were permanently impaired by lack of visual experience during a critical period ending somewhere above the age of four.

These data were based on individual patients, one physician reporting on a single patient. Such accounts do not constitute the best scientific data. Besides, these patients had learned to cope with the world through other sensory means, such as touch, so that the motivation to make full use of their newly acquired vision might not have been great. However, other studies of humans who have not had early visual experience also support the critical period view. Dennis (1934), although finding the data to be equivocal, reached many of the same conclusions as Von Senden. London (1960), reporting on recent cataract patients in the U.S.S.R. whose cases were followed with more adequate scientific controls, fully supports Von Senden. From all this, it seems likely that even innate behaviors cannot be at all adequate in later development unless they undergo at least some exercise during a critical period. In the same vein, a commonly held (but, so far as we are aware, never experimentally tested) belief of ophthalmologists and optometrists is that if crossed eyes are corrected before about age eight, the child will develop adequate binocular vision. If corrected after this time, a cosmetic effect will result, but each eye will be used in a monocular fashion, so that binocular cues to depth will not be of use to the individual.

Early Environmental Enrichment

Burton White and associates at Harvard University have conducted a series of studies designed to explore the effect on infant development of various environmental enrichment procedures (see White, 1971). A number of aspects of vision and prehension were studied including visually directed reaching, visual exploration, hand regard, visual pursuit, visual convergence, and the blink response to approaching targets.

Following some of the animal research concerned with the effects of handling on subsequent development, one of White's early studies examined the effects of handling on infant development (White & Castle, 1964). Beginning with the sixth day of life and continuing for the next 30 days, a small group of institutionalized infants were given 20 minutes of extra handling daily. Following the 30-day period, a number of developmental tests were administered to the experimental infants and to a control group of infants who had not received the extra stimulation. The only difference between the two groups was in visual attention. The infants who received the extra handling were more visually attentive. The results of this initial study suggested that slight modifications of the environment are capable of facilitating development in one of the most important areas of early development—visual attention.

In a second study (White, 1967), a group of 19 institutionalized infants were given a variety of enrichment including 20 minutes of extra handling per day from day 6 through day 36; the crib liners were removed so that the activities in the ward were visible to the infants; the infants were placed in a prone position for 45 minutes each day from day 37 through day 124; a special stabile (see Figure 3-3) of contrasting colors and numerous forms were suspended over the infants' cribs from day 37 through 124; finally, the standard white crib sheets and bumpers were replaced by multicolored print ones. The results of this study were as follows: (1) Hand regard was somewhat delayed, presumably because of the availability of other interesting objects. (2) The most mature form of reaching behavior appeared at 98 days of age which was 45 days ahead of a control group of infants. (3) Amount of visual attentiveness was increased markedly. White interpreted results as showing the plasticity of early visual-motor development. Various features of the environment, including added stimulation and handling, facilitate development.

In a further study, red and white golfers mitts were worn by a group of infants from 21 to 105 days of age. This added visual enrichment served to enhance hand regard markedly. Hand regard occurred in the second month of life while such behavior was not present until nearly the third month in a control group.

White notes that visual control over the hand is the major sensorimotor acquisition of the first half year of life. That development in this area can be facilitated by various environmental modifications suggests the intimate interrelationship between maturation and learning, between growth and experience. A great deal remains to be learned about the

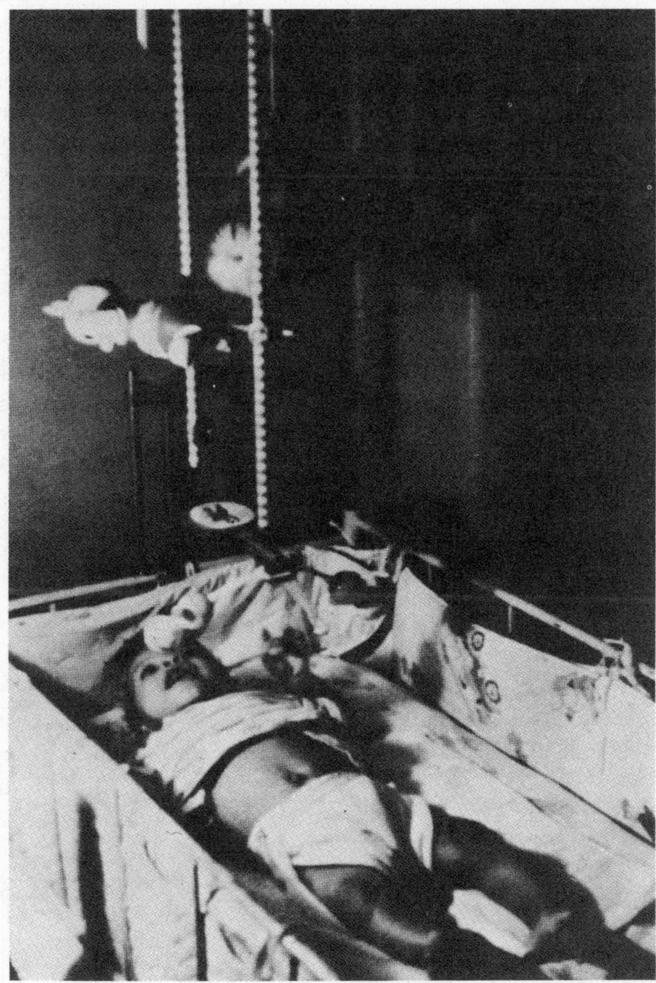

FIGURE 3-3 The massive enrichment condition.

kinds of experiences which will facilitate development, and the appropriate timing of these experiences. For optimal development, there must be a "match" of a "synchrony" between environmental learning experiences and the child's maturational readiness to profit from these experiences.

MATURATION RELATED TO SOCIAL AND EMOTIONAL BEHAVIOR

So far, this chapter has dwelt entirely on the maturation of motor behaviors. More interesting and less well settled, however, is the influence of maturation on social and emotional behavior. One may well ask: to what extent are social and emotional responses maturational in character? How does deprivation affect these responses? Are there critical periods for learning them?

In an early and thorough investigation of emotion conducted by Darwin (1881; present reprint edition, 1955), the noted scientist presented several main arguments. If human emotional expressions evoked by a certain kind of stimulus were shared by animals lower than humans, he maintained, then evolutionary linkage to these lower orders would be proved. Second, if all humans, irrespective of age or culture, responded in the same way when expressing a given emotion, one would have to concede that specific emotional expressions arose as a result of natural selection and were inherited and innate in the human.

The following quotation from Darwin's writings pertains to the first hypothesis.

> . . . Young chimpanzees make a kind of barking noise, when pleased by the return of any one to whom they are attached. When this noise, which the keepers call a laugh, is uttered, the lips are protruded; but so they are under various other emotions. Nevertheless I could perceive that when they were pleased the form of the lips differed a little from that assumed when they were angered. If a young chimpanzee be tickled—and the armpits are particularly sensitive to tickling, as in the case of our children, —a more decided chuckling or laughing sound is uttered; though the laughter is sometimes noiseless. The corners of the mouth are then drawn backwards; and this sometimes causes the lower eyelids to be slightly wrinkled. But this wrinkling, which is so characteristic of our own laughter, is more plainly seen in some other monkeys. The teeth in the upper jaw in the chimpanzee are not exposed when they utter their laughing noise, in which respect they differ from us (Darwin, 1955, p. 131).

In another quotation, Darwin deals with both hypotheses:

> . . . That the chief expressive actions, exhibited by man and by the lower animals, are now innate or inherited,—that is, have not been learnt by the individual—is admitted by everyone. So little has learning or imitation to do with several of them that they are from the earliest days and throughout life quite beyond our control; for instance the relaxation of the arteries of the skin in blushing, and the increased action of the heart in anger. We may see children, only two or three years old, and even those born blind, blushing from shame; and the naked scalp of a very young infant reddens from passion. Infants scream from pain directly after birth, and all their features then assume the same form as during subsequent years. These facts alone suffice to show that many of our most important expressions have not been learnt; but it is remarkable that some, which are certainly innate, require practice in the individual, before they are performed in a full and perfect manner; for instance, weeping and laughing. The inheritance of most of our expressive actions explains the fact that those born blind display them, as I hear from Rev. R. H. Blair, equally well with those gifted with sight. We can thus also understand the fact that the young and the old of widely different races, both with man and animals, express the same state of mind by the same movements (Darwin, 1955, pp. 350–351).

Darwin concluded that specific emotional expressions in response to particular emotional stimuli showed so great a degree of commonness that they had to be innate, inherited, and unlearned. On the other hand, certain emotions required practice before they could appear in their fullest form. Darwin was referring here to changes occurring with age which seemed likely to be the result of maturation rather than learning.

With its emphasis on innate characteristics, Darwinism was one of the forces that brought forth, in psychology, an environmentalist reaction led by John B. Watson (1919). Watson and others who shared his point of view believed that little human behavior was innate or unlearned; to the contrary, they held that a vast majority of behavior was learned. These "behaviorists" did much to make psychology a science by causing it to concern itself with observable, measurable behavior. Let us note that it was against such presumably innate characteristics as *instinctive motives,* rather than against phenomena now called maturational, that Watson's main criticism was directed.

The first experimental study of emotions by Watson and Morgan (1917) was undertaken to test the hypothesis that a large number of human emotions, such as fear of snakes or darkness, were innate to the species. By studying infants during the first months of life, they concluded that three basic, innate emotions were discernible. These emotions were fear, rage, and love. Fear, they maintained, was aroused chiefly by loss of support and by loud noises; it was *not* occasioned by experiences previously thought to be innately productive of fear, such as exposure to snakes or darkness. Rage emerged from restriction of movement, and love was the response to fondling and stroking.

This investigation inspired other psychologists to study the emotional development of infants. Some of these found reason to question parts of the Watson and Morgan conclusions. For example, Sherman (1927), in studying the responses of infants less than 12 days of age, noted that judges were unable to agree on the character of specific infant reactions *unless they saw the stimulus that preceded the response*. This suggests that adults read into the responses of the young infant the emotion that they themselves would feel if stimulated in the same way. As Watson and Morgan knew the stimulus preceding the response of their subjects, their observations were contaminated by this knowledge. They, too, may have read into the infant's responses the way that they would have felt under the same circumstances.

Another study to refute a portion of the Watson and Morgan findings was Dennis's (1940). This showed that infants habituated to restricted movement as a result of being reared on a cradleboard did not manifest any signs of anger because of the restrictions on their movements. Thus, it is possible that learning might have been involved in the responses of rage observed by Watson and Morgan, or else that the responses were provoked by "rough handling" rather than by restriction itself.

Other studies indicate, however, that specific forms of emotional responses to particular stimuli are unlearned. Again we turn to the fraternal twins raised by the Dennises. These twins were restricted in physical movement and also in exposure to the emotional responses of others. The Dennises, for example, did not smile at them. Having had no experience at seeing others smile, did the twins nevertheless respond with smiles?

> We wished also to know whether positive responses toward us would develop if we refrained from smiling at the twins and from petting, cuddling, and fondling them. In order to determine the answer to this question we avoided these expressions during the first 26 weeks. Withholding of demonstration of affections of this sort was not an easy task to impose upon ourselves, particularly as the subjects themselves were very expressive. From the 15th week onward they almost invariably greeted us with a smile and a vocalization. After this fact was thoroughly established, we decided in Week 27 to return their smile of greeting, and to speak to them as we approached (Dennis & Dennis, 1951, p. 109).

Clearly, smiling is a response to pleasurable events or experiences and is not the result of exposure to the smiling of others. As shown in Figure 3-2, even without social stimulation or opportunity for imitation, emotional responses such as smiling still occur at a normal time.

Similarly, a blind and deaf girl, who obviously had no opportunity to see others express emotions (Goodenough, 1932), displayed essentially the same responses to various forms of stimulation as children not subjected to such environmental deprivation. A more thorough and complex recent study and literature review of the emotional expressions of blind infants (Freedman, 1964) is in essential support of Goodenough. However, the *frequency* of emotional responsiveness such as smiling appears to depend on reinforcement from the environment (Brackbill, 1958; Freedman, 1964). Therefore, to the degree that reinforcement through visual experiences plays a role, we may expect blind infants and children to show a diminishing frequency of smiling behavior as compared with children who can see. As in most other maturational phenomena, experience facilitates and increases the frequency with which the behavior occurs.

Another study by Goodenough (1931) returns us to the problem of judges' ability to agree on the nature of infant responses. In her study, judges viewed pictures of a 10-month-old infant accompanied by captions describing various emotional states—dissatisfaction, astonishment, anger, pleasure, fear. The judges showed substantial agreement with the descriptions, indicating that the emotional expressions of a child of 10 months can be categorized with a fair amount of success. This, of course, counters Sherman's findings and supports Watson's and Morgan's position.

One further study pulls together the apparently contradictory findings into a unified whole. This is the frequently cited study by Bridges (1932), who observed for periods up to four months groups of children ranging in age from birth to slightly over two years. During the interval shortly after birth the only differentiation that could be made was between quietude and excitement. By six months a number of emotions might be distinguished from one another, whereas by two years even more emotional patterns might be reliably noted. The contradictory findings of Watson, Sherman, and Goodenough become understandable since each studied infants of markedly different ages.

The Bridges study suggests that Darwin was right. What is observed as a response associated with a specific emotion, such as blushing with shame, appears to be innate, that is, a result of maturation. In other words, emotional behaviors appear in a rather stable sequence, very much like motor behaviors. However, the frequency and intensity of emotional expression is largely learned. The feeling or emotion evoked by a stimulus has an element that is learned, and this phase of emotional development will be explored in later chapters. But once an emotion is felt the physical demonstration of the feeling seems largely *un*learned and indeed, as in the case of blushing, almost entirely beyond conscious control. Darwin was right, but it seems that his correctness needs repeated demonstration, possibly because the dominant tendency in American psychology is to ascribe behavior to learning rather than to any built-in response tendencies on the part of humans. Within the past few years the two explicit points made by Darwin in the citations above—that there are shared evolutionary links in emotion between humans and lower species, and that the form of an emotional response (once a given emotion is felt) is pan-cultural—have had to again be demonstrated, the first by Ellsworth, Carlsmith, and Henson (1972); the second by Ekman, Sorenson, and Friesen (1969) and by Eibl-Eibesfeldt (1970, pp. 408–431).

Critical Periods

Several students of emotions have suggested that the response of love depends on having received love during infancy, especially in the last half of the first year of life (see, for example, Ribble, 1943; Bowlby, 1952). Perhaps there is also a critical period in social and emotional development. In Chapter 9 we shall consider at length studies relating to the deprivation in infancy of love and other forms of stimulation. Those who believe that deprivation of contact with a single mother symbol during infancy causes a lasting emotional deficit, especially in the area of being able to give love, are often called the *maternal deprivation school.* Although this school is open to many criticisms, certain experiments support its view. However, not many of these are easily conducted among humans. Researchers are therefore obliged to search for analogous findings in the animal kingdom.

The ability of dogs (Melzack & Scott, 1957) and chimpanzees (Nissen, Chow, & Semmes, 1951) to adapt to pain stimuli requires early exposure to pain. Later exposure apparently produces little or no learning. A dog lacking early experience of pain will do such things as putting his nose into the flame of a paper match, thus extinguishing the flame; he will repeat this behavior, as badly adaptive as it may be, over many days of testing. Here, then, is a physical-emotional response that requires some exercise during a critical period if it is to develop at all.

In a most interesting book, *King Solomon's Ring* (1952), Lorenz presents much of the pioneering work on *imprinting* which he conducted concurrently with Tinbergen (see also Tinbergen, 1953). Imprinting is a type of learning that must occur within an innately determined period of time—within a critical period. It may be seen in the response of a young graylag gosling to objects in its environment, which was described by Heinroth and described by Lorenz (1957, pp. 103–104). The first object to enter the gosling's world during a fixed, quite short interval and which fits certain specifications, such as having movement, becomes "mother" to the bird. The gosling that does not have the opportunity to imprint during its critical period never identifies itself with a mother.

The length of time during which imprinting may occur varies for different species. Among jackdaws, the period for imprinting lasts up to 20 days of age (Lorenz, 1957, p. 106), whereas for certain types of ducks, it is successful only between 11 and 18 hours after hatching.

Imprinting appears to become less rigid, time-bound, and irreversible as the order of mammals ascends. Yet certain patterns of imprinting are evident in higher mammals; bottle-reared lambs, for example, identify with humans, not with sheep (Scott, 1958, p. 179). Even so, it is perhaps unsound to generalize too widely from the experiences of other species to humans because even such closely related species as the goose, duck, and jackdaw differ considerably from one another in length of critical periods and in the irreversibility of imprinting. Among humans, imprinting certainly seems possible but has never been shown to occur. Showing interesting parallels in the patterns of socialization of canine and human infants, Scott (1963) subscribes to the view of a critical period in human maturation during which something closely akin to imprinting presumably takes place.

Moreover, the work of Harlow (1958) on various types of mothering of monkeys and their after effects also bears on any discussion of this sort. Harlow reared young monkeys with artificial substitute (*surrogate*) mothers. His artificial mothers fell into two major groups, as may be seen from his description of them and from Figure 3-4.

> . . . In devising this surrogate mother we were dependent neither upon the capriciousness of evolutionary processes nor upon mutations produced by chance radioactive fallout. Instead, we designed the mother surrogate in terms of modern

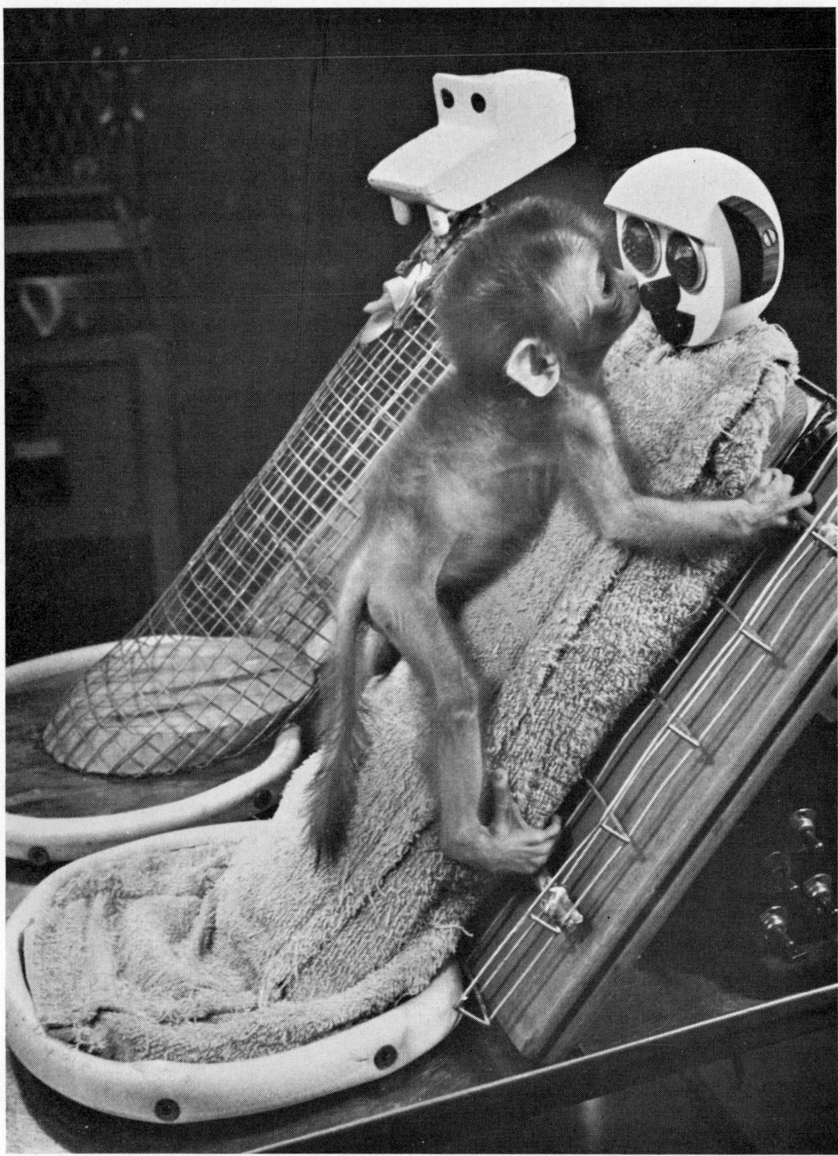

FIGURE 3-4 Cloth and wire mother surrogates were used to test the affection of infant monkeys. The infants spent most of their time clinging to the soft cloth "mother" (foreground), even when nursing bottles were attached to the wire mother (background) (Harlow, Scientific American, 1959, 200, p. 69; photograph by Gordon Coster).

human-engineering principles. . . . We produced a perfectly proportioned, streamlined body stripped of unnecessary bulges and appendages. Redundancy in the surrogate mother's system was avoided by reducing the number of breasts from two to one and placing this unibreast in any upper-thoracic, sagittal position, thus maximizing the natural and known perceptual-motor capabilities of the infant operator. The surrogate was made from a block of wood, covered with sponge rubber, and sheathed in tan cotton terry cloth. A light bulb behind her radiated heat. The result was a mother, soft, warm, and tender, a mother with infinite patience, a mother available twenty-four hours a day, a mother that never scolded her infant and never struck or bit her baby in anger. Furthermore, we designed a mother-machine with maximal maintenance efficiency since failure of any system or function could be resolved by the simple substitution of black boxes and new component parts. It is our opinion that we engineered a very superior monkey mother, although this position is not held universally by the monkey fathers.

Before beginning our initial experiment we also designed and constructed a second mother surrogate, a surrogate in which we deliberately built less than the maximal capability for contact comfort. This surrogate mother . . . is made of wire-mesh, a substance entirely adequate to provide postural support and nursing capability, and she is warmed by radiant heat. Her body differs in no essential way from that of the cloth mother surrogate other than in the quality of the contact comfort which we can supply . . . (Harlow, 1958, pp. 675–676).

A feeding bottle was attached to one of the mothers of each pair of monkeys. Even when fed by the wire-mesh mother, the young monkey spent a majority of its time clinging to the terry-cloth mother (see Figure 3-4). This suggests that body contact, not the primary reward of food when hungry, is the dominant factor that produces the young mammal's affection for its mother; terry-cloth mothers were good mothers, always there, never rejecting. The young monkey was not harmed by being reared by a terry-cloth mother; it was, in fact, more secure and emotionally stable than infant monkeys reared by their biological mothers (Harlow, 1958). *However,* monkeys reared by artificial mothers have been generally unable to mate (Harlow & Harlow 1961).

The majority of cloth-mothered animals are sexually mature. Yet none of the males has achieved any semblance of normal sex behavior, even though they show sexual excitement during mating opportunities. The females have been slightly more responsive, no doubt because their role is relatively passive compared with the male's, although success has been achieved only with three and only after numerous exposures to selected breeding males. . . .

At the present time, we have very limited data on the effect of early mothering experience on the child's maternal affectional pattern, but we have discovered enough to present some fairly suggestive findings. As already stated, through the use of patient measures, one cage-raised and three cloth-mothered females were successfully bred. All are now raising their babies in a playpen situation. . . .

The first mother paid no attention whatsoever to her baby after it was born but, instead, would sit in her cage staring vacantly into space. She gave no evidence of protective maternal responses either when her infant was threatened or when the experimenter took the baby away several times a day for artificial feeding. As soon as the baby could locomote, it struggled desperately to establish a normal contactual relationship with its mother. It would climb on its mother's back only to be brushed away by the mother as if she were brushing off flies. When the baby persisted, the mother would crush the baby's face or body down on the floor of the cage with her hand or foot while either looking at the infant or staring blankly into open space . . . (Harlow & Harlow, 1961, pp. 54–55).

The other three mothers, themselves reared without a real monkey mother, were also quite inadequate as mothers with regard to their first offspring. However, when mated again, they were completely normal in their responses to second offspring. Deficiencies were reversible, as a result of experience in raising the first offspring (Seay, Alexander, & Harlow, 1964). These data, as well as a comparison of the offspring of normal monkey mothers that have had one, as opposed to more than one offspring (Mitchell, Ruppenthal, Raymond & Harlow, 1966), suggest that human firstborns are not unique in having more than their share of problems.

Cleland and Swartz (1970) have pointed out one unexamined variable in the terry-cloth mother experiments. They suggest that a most important sense, in developing attachment, is that of smell. The cloth mothers' terry covering was changed each day. How would the offspring of terry-cloth mothers have fared if the coverings had not been changed; if a constant odor (resulting from the young monkey clinging to the artificial mother) had been present? Data presented by Cleland and Swartz suggest that a control for degree of scent present might very well influence the behavior of the young monkeys.

Festinger (1961) has suggested "that rats and people come to love things for which they have suffered." Perhaps punishment as well as reward is a necessary part of the mother-child relationship; hence, the young mammal that does not receive both during early immaturity—and conceivably within a specific critical period—may not make a normal social adjustment as an adult. In support of this statement, Rosenblum and Harlow (Harlow (1963) found that surrogate mothers that were punishing as well as always loving and accessible evoked more affection from offspring than nonpunishing mothers of the same sort. The source of love and of punishment need not be the mother, however. Young monkeys reared with artificial mothers, who otherwise would be abnormal, are completely normal if allowed contact with agemates (Harlow, 1963). Like the work of students of imprinting, the work of Harlow is merely suggestive with respect to human infancy. It may, however, provide the key to understanding the crucial elements of early socialization, the timing of the development of emotional responses, and the consequences of inadequate rearing among humans, in terms of when stimulation should be applied or the type of stimulation to be used. In short, it may supply the clue to handling the critical period in the social and emotional development of children.

When we consider the human, some evidence, although no conclusive, exists having to do with built-in mechanisms by which primary ties are established. The infant establishes eye contact with the mother by about one month of age; eye contact is followed by a smiling response (Robson, 1967). Robson (1967, p. 15) notes,

> "The human mother is subject to an extended, exceedingly trying and often unrewarding period of caring for her infant. Her neonate has a remarkably limited repertoire with which to sustain her. Indeed, his total helplessness, crying, elimination behavior, and physical appearance, frequently elicit aversive reactions. Thus, in dealing with the human species, nature has been wise in making both eye-to-eye contact and the social smile, that often releases in these early months, behaviors that at this stage of development generally foster positive maternal feelings and a sense of payment for services rendered. . . . Hence, though a mother's response to these achievements may be an illusion, from an evolutionary point of view it is an illusion with survival value" (p. 15).

Physical attributes of the infant also may imprint the mother to the infant and evoke maternal love and care. Eibl-Eibesfeldt (1970, pp. 431–434) reviews the literature, especially the work of Lorenz (1943), and conclude that humans have a strong pan-cultural tendency to feel affection for "fetalized" or "baby" organisms, as shown in Figure 3-5.

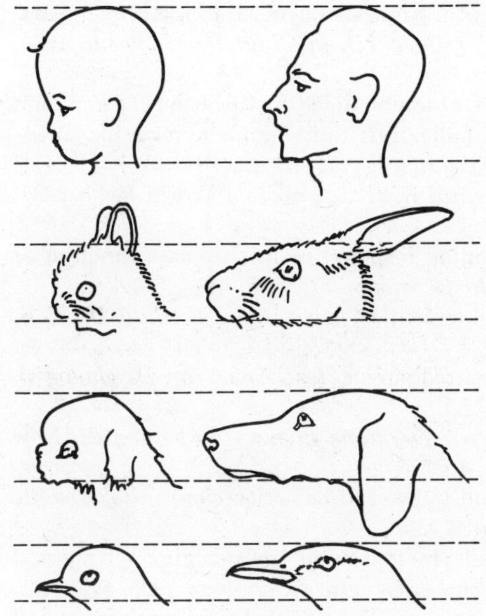

FIGURE 3-5 "Baby schema" of man. *Left*; head proportions that are generally considered to be "cute"; *right*, adult forms, which do not activate the drive to care for the young (brood care) (Lorenz, 1943).

Once this tendency has been developed in a species to select, prefer, or more adequately care for members of a given species with a large head in proportion to the body and a large forehead in proportion to the rest of the face, one can see that natural selection would be in favor of an increasing cranial capacity in the course of evolution.

SUMMARY

Several human motor behaviors seem to result largely from genetically determined patterns of growth rather than from learning. Because of this, the sequence in which the behaviors occur does not differ appreciably between individuals. Neither special stimulation nor deprivation of experience, within fairly wide limits, appears to influence the development of those behaviors that are phylogenetic or common to all members of the species. However, special training of ontogenetic skills seems to benefit performance. Phylogenetic behaviors, although not affected by moderate deprivation, require at least some exercise during a critical period if permanent or near-permanent deficiencies are to be avoided.

The motor accompaniments of many emotional states seem to be unlearned and innate, yet require the individual to have reached a certain level of maturation before they can appear. Certain social and emotional responses *may* also require exercise during critical periods if they are to be present in the individual's repertoire of behaviors.

Least influential in the child's motor development, of only moderate importance in the development of emotional expression, but probably of prime importance in the development of social responsiveness, is the role of the parent.

REFERENCES

Ahern, F. M. & Johnson, R. C. Inherited uterine inadequacy: An explanation for a portion of cases of object. *Behavior Genetics*, 1973, **3**, 1–12.

Aldrich, C. A., & Norval, M. A. A developmental graph for the first year. *Journal of Pediatrics*, 1946, **29**, 304–308.

Bayley, N. The development of motor abilities during the first three years. *Monographs of the Society for Research in Child Development*, 1935, **1**, 1, 3.

Bessman, S. P. Genetic failure of fetal amino acid "justification": a common basis for many forms of metabolic, nutritional, and "nonspecific" mental retardation. *Journal of Pediatrics*, 1972, **81**, 834–842.

Bowlby, J. *Maternal care and mental health.* Geneva : World Health Organization, 1952.

Brackbill, Y. Extinction of the smiling response in infants as a function of reinforcement schedule. *Child Development,* 1958, **29**, 115–124.

Bridges, K. H. B. Emotional development in early infancy. *Child Development,* 1932, **3**, 324–341.

Cleland, C. C. & Swartz, J. D. Scented surrogates? *American Psychologist,* 1970, **25**, 877–878.

Darwin, C. R. *The expression of the emotions in man and animals.* New York: Philosophical Library, 1955.

Dennis, W. Congenital cataract and unlearned behavior. *Journal of Genetic Psychology*, 1934, **44**, 340–351.

Dennis, W. The effect of restricted practice upon the reaching, sitting and standing of two infants. *Journal of Genetic Psychology*, 1935, **47**, 17–32.

Dennis, W. Infant development under conditions of restricted practice and of minimal social stimulation: A preliminary report. *Journal of Genetic Psychology*, 1938, **53**, 149–157.

Dennis, W. Infant reactions to restraint. *Transactions of the New York Academy of Science*, 1940, Series II, **2**, 202–217.

Dennis, W. Infant development under conditions of restricted practice and of minimal social stimulation. *Genetic Psychology Monographs,* 1941, **23**, 143–189.

Dennis, W., & Dennis, M. G. The effect of cradling practice upon the onset of walking in Hopi children. *Journal of Genetic Psychology,* 1940, **56**, 77–86.

Dennis, W., & Dennis, M. G. Development under controlled conditions. In W. Dennis (Ed.), *Readings in child psychology.* New York: Prentice-Hall, 1951.

Eibl-Eibesfeldt, I. *Ethology: The biology of behavior* (translated by Erich Klinghammer). New York: Holt, Rinehart, & Winston, 1970.

Eichenwald, H. F., & Fry, P. C. Nutrition and learning. *Science*, 1969, **163**; 644–648.

Ekman, P., Sorenson, E. R., & Friesen, W. V. Pan-cultural elements in facial displays of emotion. *Science*, 1969, **164**, 86–88.

Ellsworth, P. C., Carlsmith, J. M., & Henson, A. The stare as a stimulus to flight in human subject: A series of field experiments. *Journal of Personality and Social Psychology*, 1972, **21**, 302–311.

Erikson, E. H. *Childhood and society.* New York: Norton, 1950.

Festinger, L. The psychological effects of insufficient rewards. *American Psychologist,* 1961, **61**, 1–11.

Fowler, W. Cognitive learning in infancy and early childhood. *Psychological Bulletin*, 1962, **59**, 116–152.

Fowler, W. A study of process and method in three-year-old twins and triplets learning to read. *Genetic Psychology Monographs,* 1965, **72**, 3–90.

Frankenberg, W. K., & Dodds, J. B. (with J. F. Carland, E. G. Gloster, S. C. Hess, & S. R. Meachman). *Denver Developmental Screening Test.* Denver, Colo.: University of Colorado Medical Center, 1965.

Frankenberg, W. K., & Dodds, J. B. The Denver Developmental Screening Test. *Journal of Pediatrics*, 1967, **71**, 181–191.

Freedman, D. G. Smiling in blind babies and the issue of innate vs. acquired. *Journal of Child Psychology and Psychiatry*, 1964, **5**, 171–184.

Gates, A. I. The necessary mental age for beginning reading. *Elementary School Journal*, 1937, **37**, 497–508.

Gesell, A., & Thompson, II. Learning and growth in identical infant twins. *Genetic Psychology Monographs*, 1929, **6**, 1–124.

Goodenough, F. L. The expression of emotions in infancy. *Child Development*, 1931, **2**, 96–101.

Goodenough, F. L. Expressions of the emotions in a blind-deaf child. *Journal of Abnormal and Social Psychology*, 1932, **27**, 328–333.

Harlow, H. F. The nature of love. *American Psychologist*, 1958, **13**, 673–685.

Harlow, H. F. Love in Infant monkeys. *Scientific American*, 1959, **200**, 68–74.

Harlow, H. F. Effects of early experiences on personal-social, sexual, and maternal behavior. Paper read to the Society for Research in Child Development, Berkeley, California, April 11, 1963.

Harlow, H. F., & Harlow, M. K. A study of animal affection. *Natural History*, 1961, **70**, 48–55.

Harlow, H. F., & Harlow, M. K. Effects de la privation precose de contacts sociaux chez les primates. *Revue de Medecine Psychosomatique*, 1966, **8**, 11–24.

Kaplan, B. J., Malnutrition and mental retardation, *Psychological Bulletin*, 1972, **78**, 321–334.

Kawi, A. A., & Pasamanick, B. Prenatal and paranatal factors in the development of childhood reading disorders. *Monographs of the Society for Research in Child Development,* 1959, **24**, No. 4.

Knoblock, H., & Pasamanick, B. Prospective studies on the epidemiology of reproductive casualty: Methods, findings, and some implications. *Merrill–Palmer Quarterly of Behavior and Development*, 1966, **12**, 27–43.

London, I. D. A Russian report on the postoperative newly seeing. *American Journal of Psychology*, 1960, **73**, 478–482.

Lorenz, K. Die angeborenen Formen moglicher Erfahrung. *Zeitschrift Tierpsychologie*, 1943, **5**, 235–409.

Lorenz, K. *King Solomon's ring: New light on animal ways*. New York: Crowell, 1952.

Lorenz, K. Companionship in bird life. In C. H. Schiller (Ed.), *Instinctive behavior*. New York: International Universities Press, 1957.

McGraw, M. B. *Growth: a study of Johnny and Jimmy*. New York: Appleton, 1935.

McGraw, M. B. Later development of children specially trained during infancy. Johnny and Jimmy at school age. *Child Development*, 1939, **10**, 1–19.

McGraw, M. B. Neural maturation as exemplified in achievement of bladder control. *Journal of Pediatrics*, 1940, **16**, 580–590.

Melzack, R., & Scott, T. H. The effects of early experience on the response to pain. *Journal of Comparative and Physiological Psychology*, 1957, **50**, 151–161.

Mitchell, G. D., Ruppenthal, G. C., Raymond, E. J., & Harlow, H. F. Long term effects of multiparous and primiparous monkey mother rearing, *Child Development*, 1966, **37**, 781–791.

Montagu, M. F. A. *Prenatal influence*. Springfield, Ill.: Thomas, 1962.

Moore, O. K. Autotelic responsive environments and exceptional children. In O. J. Harvey (Ed.), *Experience, structure and adaptability*, New York: Springer, 1966. Pp. 169–216.

Moyer, K. E., & Gilmer, B. H. Attention spans of children for experimentally designed toys. *Journal of Genetic Psychology*, 1955, **87**, 187–201.

Naeslund, J. *Metodiken vid den forsta lasundervisningen.* Stockholm: Norstedts, 1956.

Nissen, H. W., Chow, K. L., & Semmes, J. Effects of restricted opportunity for tactual, kinesthetic and manipulative experience in the behavior of a chimpanzee. *American Journal of Psychology*, 1951, **64**, 485–507.

Orlansky, H. Infant care and personality. *Psychological Bulletin*, 1949, **46**, 1–48.

Pasamanick, B., & Knobloch, H. Retrospective studies on the epidemiology of reproductive loss: Old and new. *Merrill–Palmer Quarterly of Behavior and Development*, 1966, **12**, 7–26.

Pasamanick, B., Rogers, M., & Lilienfeld, A. Pregnancy experience and the development of behavior disorder in children. *American Journal of Psychiatry*, 1956, **112**, 613–617.

Ribble, M. A. *The right of infants.* New York: Columbia University Press, 1943.

Riesen, A. H. Effects of stimulus deprivation on the development and atrophy of the visual sensory system. *American Journal of Orthopsychiatry*, 1960, **30**, 23–36.

Riesen, A. H., & Kinder, E. F. *Postural development of infant chimpanzees: A comparative and normative study based on the Gesell Behavioral Examination.* New Haven, Conn.: Yale University Press, 1952.

Robbins, M. P. A study of the validity of Delacato's theory of neurological organization. *Exceptional Children*, 1966, **32**, 517–523.

Robbins, M. P. Test of the Doman–Delacato rationale with retarded readers. *Journal of the American Medical Association*, 1967, **202**, 389–393.

Robson, E. B. Birth weight in cousins. *Annals of Human Genetics*, 1955, **19**, 262–268.

Robson, K. S. The role of eye-to-eye contact in maternal-infant attachment. *Journal of Child Psychology*, 1967, **8**, 13–25.

Rosenblum, L. A., & Harlow, H. F. Approach-avoidance conflict, in the mother-surrogate situation. *Psychological Reports*, 1963, **12**, 83–85.

Scott, J. P. *Animal behavior.* Chicago: University of Chicago Press, 1958.

Scott, J. P. The process of primary socialization in canine and human infants. *Monographs of the Society for Research in Child Development*, 1963, **28**, No. 1.

Seay, B., Alexander, B. K., & Harlow, H. F. Maternal behavior of socially deprived Rhesus, monkeys. *Journal of Abnormal and Social Psychology*, 1964, **69**, 345–354.

Sherman, M. The differentiation of emotional responses in infants: I. Judgments of emotional responses from motion picture views and from actual observation. *Journal of Comparative Psychology*, 1927, **7**, 265–284.

Shirley, M. M. *The first two years of life.* (Vol. 2). Minneapolis: University of Minnesota Press, 1933.

Tanner, J. M. Earlier maturation in man. *Scientific American*, 1968, **218**, 21–27.

Tinbergen, N. *Social behavior in animals.* New York: Wiley, 1953.

Van Alstyne, D. *Play behavior and choice of play materials of preschool children.* Chicago: University of Chicago Press, 1932.

Vandenberg, S. G. Contributions of twin research to psychology. *Psychological Bulletin*, 1966, **66**, 327–352.

Von Senden, M. Space and sight: The perception of space and shape in the congenitally blind before and after operation (translated by P. Heath). New York: Free Press of Glencoe, 1960. (Original German edition, Leipzig: Barth, 1932).

Watson, J. B. *Psychology from the standpoint of a behaviorist.* Philadelphia: Lippincott, 1919.

Watson, J. B., & Morgan, J. J. B. Emotional reactions and psychological experimentation. *American Journal of Psychology*, 1917, **28**, 163–174.

White, B. L. An experimental approach to the effects of experience on early human behavior. In J. P. Hill (Ed.), *Minnesota symposium on child psychology.* Minneapolis,: University of Minnesota Press, 1967, **1**, 201–225.

White, B. L. Human infants: *Experience and psychological development.* Englewood Cliffs, N. J.: Prentice-Hall, 1971.

White, B. L., & Castle, P. W. Visual exploratory behavior following postnatal handling of human infants. *Perceptual and Motor Skills*, 1964, **18**, 497–502.

chapter 4

learning and motivation

chapter 4

learning and motivation

chapter 4

learning and motivation

Although some human behaviors appear to have larger unlearned than learned components, most human behavior is learned. The behaviors we learn come about through a pattern of reacting to stimuli and to the reward accompanying such reaction; the response may either be initiated by the human organism itself or copied from the responses of some other organism. Either way, the human differs in this respect from lower orders of the plant and animal worlds, which inherit their major patterns of response, even though these behaviors may be inspired by specific conditions in the environment. Learning, of course, takes many forms, which gradually become more complex from childhood to adulthood or from simple to more intricate organisms. In this chapter we shall explore these various forms and then the forces that motivate learning.

LEARNING

Essentially, there are two kinds of learning–simple and complex. Setting aside for the present the latter category, let us consider the two techniques through which simple learning occurs. Simple learning is either *respondent* or *operant*. Respondent learning is the classical method of conditioning often called *Pavlovian* after the Russian physiologist Pavlov (1927). In this type of learning the organism remains relatively passive as it learns; all that is required of it is to respond. Operant learning, on the other hand, engages the active participation of the organism seeking to learn. It is a trial-and-error process, sometimes called *instrumental* learning, in which the organism acts and in so doing generates results.

Both forms of simple learning blend together at times, so that in some cases it may be difficult to say whether a given behavior is learned in an operant or respondent way. However, the two forms generally can be distinguished from one another. Ardent followers of the learning theorist, B. F. Skinner, would argue that respondent learning is a rare phenomenon, and that a number of the studies referred to, herein, as examples of respondent learning actually are operant. This fact, in itself, indicates that the two forms of learning merge, and that the point of merging varies with one's set of definitions. Our definitions are presented above.

Respondent Learning

Pavlov had already won a Nobel Prize for his work on gastric secretions by the time he turned his attention to his now famous experiments on conditioned reflexes. Noting that the dogs he used in his experiments salivated before food entered their mouths, he saw that the mere presence of food or even the sound of the keeper's footsteps was enough to bring on salivation. Pavlov was so taken by this phenomenon that he dedicated the latter part of his life to pursuing it and its implications.

An organism instinctively responds to a stimulus in some concrete manner. The dog salivates, for example, on the presentation of food. This salivation is assumed to be innate and not learned. The dog is exposed to the sound of a bell and is then given food in the form of meat powder. After several repetitions of this pattern, the dog salivates at the sound of the bell even before the food arrives. The meat powder is called the *unconditioned stimulus* and the salivation it engenders, the unconditioned response or *unconditioned reflex*. The bell is the *conditioned stimulus* and the salivation occasioned by its sound, in the absence of the meat powder, is the conditioned response or *conditioned reflex*.

Besides the conditioned stimulus itself, other stimuli resembling it also produce the same effect. Thus, if an organism is conditioned to respond to a medium tone of bell, it will also react to a high or a low tone, although to a lesser degree. This phenomenon is known as *stimulus generalization* because it extends the power of the stimulus to other objects and events. The spread of effect from the positive stimulus to all stimuli like it was believed by Pavlov to be a powerful influence in learning. As we shall see when we consider complex learning later in the chapter, stimulus generalization contributes significantly to the concepts human organisms form.

The conditioned reflex diminishes and eventually ceases if the conditioned stimulus is presented repeatedly without the accompanying unconditioned stimulus. The conditioned reflex is then said to have been *extinguished.* Yet, curiously enough, this cessation may not be final. An environmental change can revive the reflex. Even a small change in the surroundings, such as slamming a door, is sometimes enough to reawaken an extinguished response for a time.

Several well-known examples of conditioning in humans illustrate the process. The first is the case of "Little Albert" who was conditioned by Watson and Rayner (1920). As remarked in Chapter 3, Watson believed that the young child was innately afraid of sudden, loud noises. In an experiment that demonstrated the fear of sudden loud noises, Watson and Morgan (1917) also found that infants showed no fear of darkness, snakes, or other stimuli which to that time had been thought to be innately or instinctively productive of fear. Watson therefore concluded that all fears, except for those involving sudden loud noises or loss of support, were learned—and further, were learned through conditioning. His experiment with Rayner around a nine-month-old boy, "Little Albert," demonstrated the conditioning of the fear response.

The infant was presented with a white rat. He was not afraid of it. Thereafter, whenever the rat was presented to the boy, a steel bar was struck, producing a sudden loud noise. Following relatively few conditioning trials, Little Albert responded to the rat with reactions of fear. In addition, he was also afraid of a fur coat, a rabbit, a Santa Claus mask, and a wad of absorbent cotton. Rather wide stimulus generalization had occurred, apparently among soft, white, hairy substances.

The Watson and Rayner study of "Little Albert" may well have influenced the plot of Aldous Huxley's *Brave New World* (1932). In this imaginary society of the future, ability is determined by the amount of oxygen allowed to enter the bloodstream of a fetus, which is grown in an artificial uterus. Each intelligence group is so adapted as to be best able to perform a given level of job. Problems of overproduction are solved by conditioning individuals to consume, whereas such nonconsumptive behaviors as enjoying books or nature are extinguished. This conditioning process is described in the following passage from the book and illustrated in Figure 4-1.

> Turned, the babies at once fell silent, then began to crawl towards those clusters of sleek colours, those shapes so gay and brilliant on the white pages. As they approached, the sun came out of a momentary eclipse behind a cloud. The roses flamed up as though with a sudden passion from within, a new and profound significance seemed to suffuse the shining pages of the books. From the ranks of the crawling babies came little squeals of excitement, gurgles and twitterings of pleasure.
>
> The Director rubbed his hands. "Excellent!" he said. "It might almost have been done on purpose."

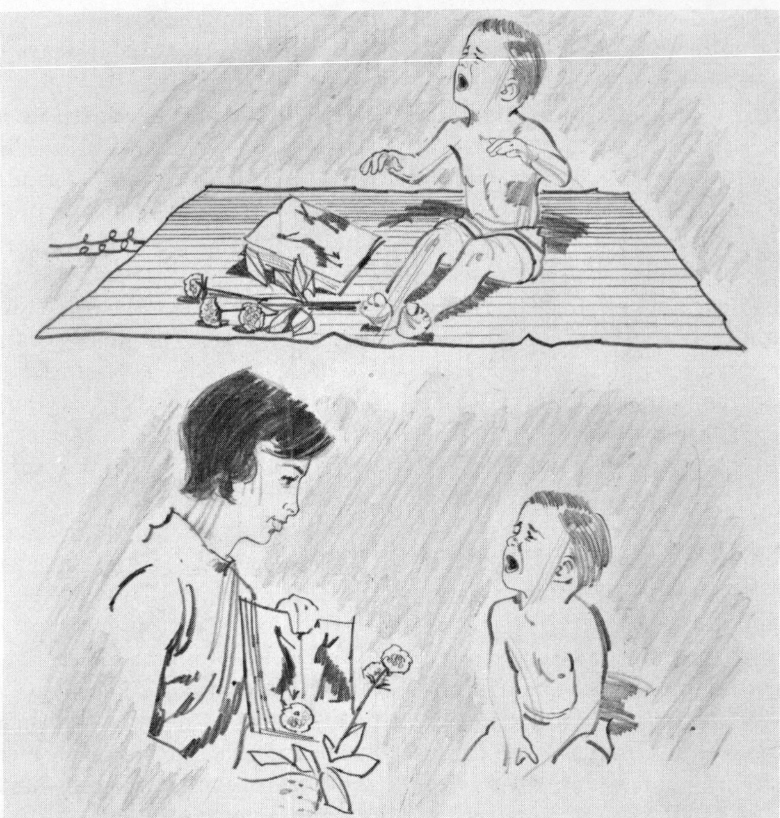

FIGURE 4-1 Conditioning in *Brave New World.*

The swiftest crawlers were already at their goal. Small hands reached out uncertainly, touched, grasped, unpetaling the transfigured roses, crumpling the illuminated pages of the books. The Director waited until all were happily busy. Then, "Watch carefully," he said. And, lifting his hand, he gave the signal.

The Head Nurse, who was standing by a switchboard at the other end of the room, pressed down a little lever.

There was a violent explosion. Shriller and even shriller, a siren shrieked. Alarm bells maddeningly sounded.

The children started, screamed, their faces were distorted with terror.

"And now," the Director shouted (for the noise was deafening), "now we proceed to rub in the lesson with a mild electric shock."

He waved his hand again, and the Head Nurse pressed a second lever. The screaming of the babies suddenly changed its tone. There was something desperate, almost insane, about the sharp spasmodic yelps to which they now gave utterance. Their little bodies twitched and stiffened; their limbs moved jerkily as if to the tug of unseen wires.

"We can electrify that whole strip of floor," bawled the Director in explanation. "But that's enough," he signalled to the nurse.

The explosions ceased, the bells stopped rining, the shriek of the siren died down fron tone to tone into silence. The stifly twitching bodies relaxed, and what had become the sob and yelp of infant maniacs broadened out once more into a normal howl of ordinary terror.

"Offer them the flowers and the books again."

The nurses obeyed; but at the approach of the roses, at the mere sight of those

> gaily-coloured images of pussy and cock-a-doodle-doo and baa-baa black sheep, the infants shrank away in horror; the volume of their howling suddenly increased.
>
> "Observe," said the Director triumphantly, "observe."
>
> Books and loud noises, flowers and electric shocks—already in the infant mind these couples were compromisingly linked; and after two hundred repetitions of the same or a similar lesson would be wedded indissolubly. What man has joined, nature is powerless to put asunder.
>
> "They'll grow up with what the psychologists used to call an instinctive hatred of books and flowers. Reflexes unalterably conditioned. They'll be safe from books and botany all their lives." The Director turned to his nurses. "Take them away again" (Huxley, 1932, pp. 21–22).

Despite the potentially negative use, described above, classical conditioning has many practical applications with infants and young children. For example, conditioning involving sound often has been used in testing infants for deafness when they still are so young that other procedures are not feasible (Glorig, 1965). Classical conditioning procedures have been used most effectively for decades in such areas as toilet training (Mowrer & Mowrer, 1938) and, as discussed in Chapter 16, have now been used in the treatment of many other types of problem behavior. In the Mowrer and Mowrer treatment of bed wetting, the child sleeps on a pad. The pad is electrically wired, so that the voiding of the bladder causes a circuit to be completed, which rings a bell. The bell, in this case, is the unconditioned stimulus, and the unconditioned response is waking. Since bladder tension is paired with the bell, it becomes the conditioned stimulus, evoking the conditioned response of waking. So now the child wakes up and *then* wets the bed. The conditioning procedure described above must be combined with the building in of a set of operant behaviors leading to a trip to the bathroom, resulting in an effective treatment of bed wetting.

Much learning is respondent, in adults as well as in infants. Simple enough in principle, it may be used to account for most, if not all, human learning. Watson (1919) thought so, and the Soviets continue to think so (Razran, 1961). Russian acceptance of classical conditioning as the only form of learning, although quite foreign to American way of thinking, has, as Brackbill (1960) has noted, produced research of both practical and theoretical importance. However, most American psychologists, unlike their Soviet colleagues, believe also in a second way of learning—the operant way.

Operant Learning

One of the foremost early students of learning was E. L. Thorndike. Concentrating his investigations on lower organisms rather than on humans, he placed his subjects in mazes and puzzle boxes where they were neither required to show sudden understanding of a problem at hand nor called on to solve it. Instead they had to learn a set of motor responses that had essentially no pattern, that is, no right-left-right-left turns. Thorndike (1913) noted, not surprisingly, that much like illiterates learning to find their way about a strange city without assistance, his organisms decreased their errors of entering blind alleys only slowly. Correspondingly, the amount of time they required to get from the start of the maze to the goal decreased slowly. From this, Thorndike concluded that learning in lower organisms was slow and lacked insight. He further believed that human learning was also of this trial-and-error sort.

Consider the acquisition of the ability to ride a bicycle. Complex operant or trial-and-error behaviors, as Skinner

(1958, 1960) has shown, can be learned by organisms. Such learning occurs most rapidly when the "method of approximations" is used in the training process and the learner tries to approximate or imitate the behavior of others. There is no magic way of learning to ride a bicycle; learning must take place by a simple, trial-and-error procedure. The beginner falls frequently, whenever he leans too far to one side to retain his balance at the speed at which he is then moving. But as he is highly impelled to ride, even crude approximations of bicycle-riding behavior bring him gratification; to be able to move even a few feet without falling is at first rewarding, indeed, a victory. Behaviors that lead to this victory tend to be repeated as a result of *positive reinforcement.* Meanwhile, the behaviors that precede falling begin to diminish in frequency. As the rewarding behaviors gradually increase, the child ultimately reaches the point at which he rides off alone, tipsy, insecure, and not really inspiring confidence in either himself or anyone watching. Eventually, of course, he makes it.

There is nothing intrinsically different between a child learning to ride a bicycle and a rat learning to run a maze. For both, learning is a slow, gradual, trial-and-error process in which rewarded responses are retained while those that do not bring reward are eliminated. Most likely, a substantial proportion of learning in infancy and childhood, such as the acquisition of motor skills consists largely of simple operant activity, common to all organisms. As discussed in Chapter 16, many forms of psychotherapy now make use of these simple, operant procedures, usually to good effect. Though respondent and operant learning may decrease in relative significance for the human with increasing age, they always are important forms of learning that may be used to change or modify behavior.

Learning Sets

It is a mark of progress to pass from the simple to the complex. But such transitions are not always easily made. Often they require some extra effort or some intermediate step. In learning, many believe that one connecting link is an understanding of *learning sets,* a concept that was developed by Harlow (1949) in the course of his experiments with monkeys. Learning sets, in substance, are groups of habits employed by organisms in the process of learning. Subjects in experiments on learning sets are presented with a series of problems. Each of these problems has its own stimuli, which are entirely different from those of the remaining problems, yet each must be solved by application of the same learning habits. If the organism learns the habits rather than the simple, operant solution to a particular problem, it can then apply them to any succeeding problem. The organism has learned to learn; it can extend its responses to other situations, transfer its habits of problem solving from one problem to the next. The organism has thus developed a *learning set,* by which it can cope with even unusual situations. Indeed, the learning set leads directly, as we shall soon see, to the formation of concepts, one of the principal forms of complex learning.

There are wide differences in the speed at which various species establish learning sets. Although it may take 100 or more trials for a monkey to acquire a learning set (Harlow, 1949), very young humans (Koch & Meyer, 1959) or severely retarded humans of below 50 IQ (Fehmi, 1960) develop them quite rapidly, often in fewer than 10 series of problems. As a rule primates are markedly superior to nonprimates in this form of learning, even when previous learning has been controlled. Moreover, there are great differences even among members of a primate order in the development of learning sets. That humans surpass other primates and primates surpass nonprimates suggests a distinct superiority among primates—and especially humans—in the transfer of old learning to new problems. It is this ability to transfer that contributes substantially to the formation of concepts.

Concept Formation

In simple learning adults are not always superior to young children, nor do humans invariably surpass other organisms. But in complex learning, to which we now shift attention, wide chasms separate all these groups. Except in rare instances, the human excels all others in the various forms of complex learning—concept formation, thinking, and creativity.

It is quite possible that from coping with problems that develop in a learning situation, a subject may evolve a concept for solving them all. Yet this is not necessarily so. The subject might actually solve each problem independently without ever becoming aware of a common principle or concept applicable to the entire series. Concept formation requires an organism to develop an understanding, which can be measured by the organism's behavior, that certain objects, events, or characteristics of a stimulus have a common element. On the basis of this element the organism then classifies the phenomena. The actual source of the concept lies in respondent or operant learning. It is the transfer—or generalization—of what is learned to other situations sharing common elements that constitutes the formation of a concept.

Humans generalize more adequately than other organisms. In large measure they succeed more widely than others in transferring learning because they have the facility of language. *Transposition*, in learning, involves learning to make a relational choice. In the example below, transposition means learning to choose the higher of two tones, no matter to what particular pair of tones the subject is exposed. Subjects are exposed to two musical tones, *do* and *re*, and are rewarded for choosing *re*. Once they learn to choose *re*, they are exposed to succeeding pairs such as *re-mi, mi-fa, fa-sol,* and so on. Lower organisms will choose the higher of the two tones only when it is one step removed from the learned tone. Beyond this point they tend to choose the stimulus most similar to the one rewarded in the original training session. For example, they would choose *mi* in a *mi-fa* choice situation. However, human children able to use words to describe the learning principle involved seem capable of transposing and generalizing responses to new stimuli no matter how far removed these may be from the original learning stimuli (Alberts & Ehrenfreund, 1951; Kuenne, 1946). Problems of transposition, such as establishing the conditions under which it will occur, are among the most intriguing that psychology has to offer (see Hebert & Krantz, 1965), partly because transposition is an area in which humans and nonhumans, or verbal as opposed to nonverbal humans, differ greatly in the way that they respond to a task.

Discrimination learning occurs whenever an organism learns to choose one stimulus rather than other stimuli because he is rewarded for making the particular choice. *Discrimination reversal*, or *cue reversal*, is another type of task that appears to produce substantial differences between children who can as opposed to those who cannot use verbal mediators in dealing with a learning task. The typical discrimination-reversal task goes something like this: The child is presented with a red circle and a white square, with the position of the two objects varying randomly between trials. He is rewarded for choosing the red circle. Then, after the habit has been learned thoroughly (i.e., the subject has chosen the red circle on 14 out of 15 successive trials), the ground rules are changed; the white square now is rewarded. Young children generally find this second task, overcoming a learned preference for the red circle and responding to the white square, more difficult than an entirely new task, while older children learn the new set of reward contingencies associated with the circle and square very rapidly (Kendler, Kendler, & Wells, 1960). Results in discrimination reversal are similar to those in transposition, in which children may have the verbal terms needed but will not transpose in tests of far transposition unless they not only know, but also *use* verbal cues in learning (Kuenne, 1946; Cole, Dent, Eguchi, Fujii, & Johnson, 1964). In the same sense, children may have the necessary verbal labels in a discrimination reversal situation, yet discrimination reversal is a most difficult task unless the labels are *both* available and used in learning (Kendler, et al., 1960). These areas of research suggest that the use of verbal mediators produces a rather abrupt change in the manner in which learning takes place, and in the generalization of this learning to comparable new learning tasks.

The learning of both concrete and abstract concepts seems to gain from language. Words provide additional, constant cues for the distinguishing of different "concrete" objects. Spoons, for example, vary in size and shape; nevertheless, they have enough common elements to fall into a single perceptual grouping. Despite their variations, they are identical in name, which facilitates development of the concept of "spoon." The mere presence of a name imposes limits on the concept more simply and perhaps more accurately for the young child than would a variety of stimuli lacking a name. Language simplifies the formation of concepts and also reduces the differences between individuals in the content of their concepts.

Language also enables the adequate development of "abstract" concepts that are independent of specific concrete physical stimuli or physical reference. Since specific objects cannot serve as cues in these cases, learning tends to be slower than for concrete concepts. Those concepts with few or misleading—sometimes both—verbal designations are generally considered abstract and are learned slowly and often erroneously (Johnson, 1962b; Voeks, 1954). This may be seen in the study of animism, the belief that certain important objects in the environment are living, or that they have some conscious purpose. Whether children (see Piaget, 1930) or college students (see Dennis, 1953), subjects have an inadequate concept of life, of what is alive. They attribute animacy to many nonliving things, such as the sun, the ocean, and a lighted match. The inadequacy of the concept appears to result from the sparseness and at times misleading nature of the verbal terms used to define life. The attribute of life most commonly mentioned is movement. But this is actually a characteristic shared by the animate and the inanimate, such as the railroad engine, the automobile, or the sun; hence an accurate demarcation between living and nonliving, and therefore an adequate concept of life, is difficult to obtain as long as movement remains life's chief criterion. Probably because of this, children have more difficulty in determining whether moving objects are alive than they do in determining whether things that do not move are alive (Laurendeau & Pinard, 1962).

Concept formation, then, rests on the bases of generalizing and transferring learning across stimuli, processes that are common to man and lower organisms.

Man's supermacy over other organisms stems from the ability to organize in a wide variety of ways, through the use of symbols, a greater amount of experience, only some of which is sensory. Although not unique to humans, concept formation is an area of learning in which human capacity far exceeds that of other organisms.

Thinking

The leading theories on children's thinking come from the European psychological tradition and are intimately tied to theories of concept formation. Best represented in American circles by Werner (1957), they have also been given attention in several critiques published in the United States (Fowler, 1962; Johnson, 1962b). These theories maintain that the thought processes of children differ in quality from those of adults.

The best known and most comprehensive of these theories was developed by the Swiss psychologist Jean Piaget (see Flavell, 1963, for a most comprehensive summary and evaluation of Piaget's research). In his view, a child passes through three stages of mental activity en route to maturity. First, there is a *sensorimotor* stage in which action is governed by sensations; simple learning occurs, but the child does not think. Next, the child moves into a phase of egocentricity; by *egocentricity* Piaget means neither selfishness nor self-centeredness, but more likely the inability to put oneself in the place of another. The major portion of this period, also termed *concrete operational*, lasts from the age of 7 or 8 to the age of 11 or 12; during it, the child is concerned with concrete ideas. In this stage the formation of concepts is felt to involve "operational groupings concerning subjects that can be manipulated or known through the senses" (Piaget, 1952, p. 123). Finally, the child advances to the stage of abstract concepts; "from 11 to 12 years and during adolescence, formal thought is projected and its groupings characterize the completion of reflective thought" (p. 123). By "reflective thought" Piaget refers to the ability to form adequate abstract concepts.

Piaget's theory might well be included in the chapter on growth and maturation; it is in many ways a maturational theory, in the sense that a child progresses through a set of stages of intellectual development in an orderly and invariant fashion. Environment does enter in, since experiences help the child to move from one stage of development to another.

Piaget's research has touched on many areas, but all of his investigations have had as a central aim the discovery of the nature of intelligence—its function, structure, and content—as well as the means by which it changes with age and experience. To Piaget, a biologist, the purpose of intelligence is to enable an organism to make adaptations of the environment that increase the probability of survival. Behavior is the action taken by the organism to establish and maintain states of equilibrium with the environment (Piaget, 1960). The organism attains this equilibrium by adaptation to the environment through *assimilation*, the influence of the organism on environment, and *accommodation,* the influence of the environment on the organism. Thus, by actively manipulating the environment (assimilation), and, somewhat more passively, being acted on by the environment (accommodation), a child comes, over time, to have an accurate understanding of reality. Piaget's position to this point is environmentalistic. However, his sequence of development through sensorimotor, concrete operational, and formal operational (abstract) thought must be invariant and maturational.

Every new experience is understood by a child on the basis of all relevant previous experiences. A given new experience is often misperceived because the child's inadequate understanding of the event is based on his previously held incorrect interpretations of reality. Yet each new experience brings him new information, and this new information finally leads to a modification of his understanding of the world. If the child is presented with an experience he cannot understand, he will transform it into something that he can understand. He himself is changed by the new experience, however, so that he may arrive at a more adequate understanding of the experience as a result of the experience itself. An example of this kind of development is seen in Piaget's work on the development in children of the *concept of conservation of substance*.

The concept of conservation is a general rule that the shape of an object can be changed, but, so long as nothing is added to or taken away from the object, its substance remains the same. For example, if two clay balls are of equal size, and one of them is made into a sausage shape, there is still the same amount of clay in both. An experimenter and a child agree that the two balls are of the same size; the experimenter then changes the shape of one of them and asks the child whether there is as much clay in the sausage as in the ball. The child has attained the concept of conservation if he says yes, and can explain why it is so (nothing added, nothing taken away, just changed shape).

A young child has a tendency to believe that things that change in shape change in quantity as well. Often, of course, this is true; a half-gone ice cream cone has changed in shape *and* quantity, and it is difficult for a young child to separate these effects. Given sufficient experience, however, he may come to see that changes in shape need not necessarily indicate changes in quantity. Testing a child on a number of conservation tasks in the manner described above frequently causes him to move rapidly toward an understanding of conservation of substance (Randall, 1967). Apparently the mere fact that he is required to make judgments of this sort produces sufficient dissonance, or, to use Piaget's term, "disequilibrium" that he is forced to re-evaluate his beliefs. Further, if the child himself makes the transformation, a sufficiently greater disequilibrium leads him to more frequently manifest conservation of substance (Johnson & Developmental Seminar, 1967). Finally, if a child manipulates the stimuli (e.g., makes the clay ball into a sausage) and, further, manipulates the stimuli in two directions (from a ball into a sausage; from a sausage into a ball), conservation responses are markedly increased over those shown in child-manipulated, one-way transformations, so that even four-year-olds frequently show a grasp of conservation of substance (Simmons & Johnson, 1968), though conservation is relatively rare even in five-year-olds when conventional procedures (experimenter manipulates stimuli, one-way transformations) are used. The increasingly obvious dissonance between previously held beliefs and experience appears to account for the obtained increase in conservation responses.

Piaget's work holds up remarkably well in some ways. For example, despite the fact that children are suggestible (in the sense that if they are asked whether two clay objects are the same they will probably say yes; if, instead, they are asked whether the two objects are different they are also likely to agree), in this instance it makes little difference how the question is phrased, as long as it is in simple and unambiguous language. If they have attained a grasp of conservation they will say that the ball and the sausage are the same; if they have not, they will say the two are different (Pratoomraj & Johnson, 1966).

Despite his concern for experience, Piaget states in nearly all of his writings that changes in the nature of the thought process occur at given ages without consideration for differences in experiences that might confirm or disconfirm previously held beliefs. He says, in effect (though he does not always mean to), that thought processes change with advances in age by sudden (saltatory) jumps. Thus any given 5-year-old would differ qualitatively from any given 12-year-old in the way he thinks.

Piagetan theory really does not rest on the idea that given changes in capacity occur at given ages, but rather on the proposition that these changes are sequential, with absolute rate of change through the sequence resulting from experience. Piaget has confused the issue by emphasizing age of change in both his early and his recent work. But the real task of the psychologist is not to investigate further the age at which certain abilities come into existence, but to determine the kinds of child-environment interaction that cause the change to occur. An even greater problem is to evaluate fully the main thrust of Piaget's theorizing—that qualitative differences exist between the thought processes of young children and older ones. One attempt to deal with this latter problem was that of Mehler and Bever (1967), in their study of the conservation of number. The basic Piagetan test of conservation of number is to have two sets of objects, with the objects equal in number —e.g. two sets of 5 M & M's each. The five objects in one set are placed in a closely spaced row—say, each object one-half inch apart from the next, while the five objects in the other set are spaced more widely—say, two inches apart. From Piaget's point of view, the child will recognize that the two arrays are equal in number only at about age 6, while younger children will believe that the longer row has more objects in it. What Mehler and Bever appear to have demonstrated (see Beilin, 1968; Bever, Mehler, & Epstein, 1968; Mehler & Bever, 1968; Piaget, 1968, for additional data and for conflicting interpretations of results) is that young (age 2 to 2½) children show conservation of numbers and that by age 4 the child no longer shows conservation. Then at some time following age 4 the child again shows conservation. It would appear reasonable to believe that the very young child attends to actual numerosity and is capable of responding correctly in a conservation experiment, that the lack of conservation shown by the 4-year-old results from his reinforcement history, not from some change in level of cognitive organization (after all, long rows of objects usually do contain more objects than do short rows of these objects), and that finally, by age 6 or so, the child realizes that this lawful generalization (longer row = more objects) is not a perfect one and again attends directly to number, and not to the spatial arrangement of the objects.

Opposed to the Piagetan view that children's thinking differs in quality from that of adults is the position, expressed less often, that children think in the same way as adults, only on the basis of less adequate information. Presumably, abstract concepts should be formed only after about 12 years of age. However, research on children shows clearly that such concepts are formed rather early, but with inaccurate or insufficient content. The three-year-old has a concept of life; adults just happen to believe that the *content of his concept* is wrong if he attributes life to a racing locomotive. But to be wrong in terms of concept content is far different from being incapable of dealing with the concept at all.

Examination of intelligence tests shows that items do not appear to change appreciably in character from middle

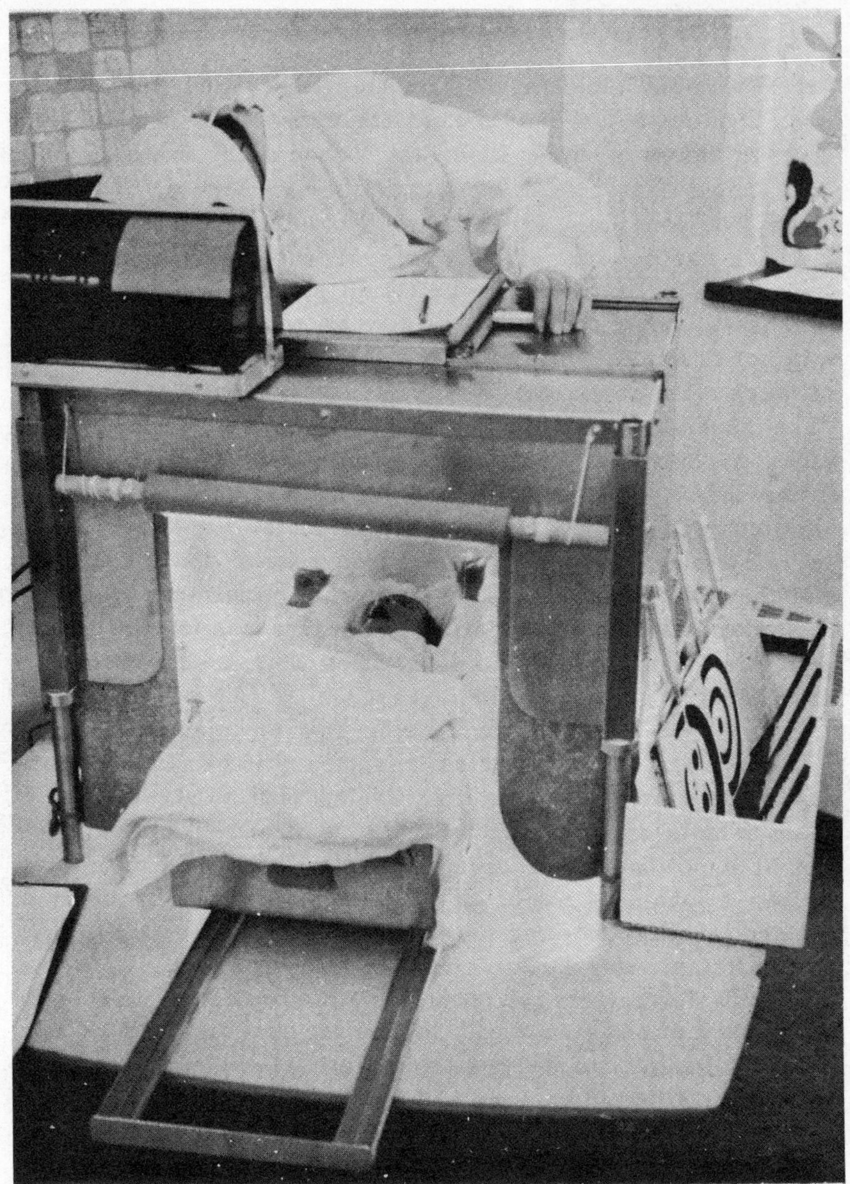

FIGURE 4-2 Newborn infant "looking chamber" in which stimulus targets were exposed one at a time over the infant by inserting a card with a handle in a stimulus holder and sliding it into the recessed portion of the chamber ceiling. Observer looks through a tiny hole in the ceiling to one side of the target. The peephole is obscured by the timers which record fixations and indicate end of exposure (Fantz, 1963).

childhood on to adulthood. The correlations between a given individual's test scores across time—for example, the correlations between IQ at age 11 and at age 18 for a group of subjects—are quite high (Honzik, McFarlane & Allen, 1948), and factor analyses reveal that the same basic factors (e.g., numerical ability, spatial ability, word fluency) make up tested intelligence in childhood, adolescence, and young adulthood (Thurstone & Thurstone, 1941). While it is true that intelligence tests do not measure all domains of thought and cognition, the results described above suggest that although a gradual accretion of knowledge occurs in the interval between age seven and adulthood, no qualitative changes in the nature of intelligence occur during this time interval. Further, studies interpreted as supporting Piaget's developmental stages in cognition show no more than a gradual increase to occur with age in ability to deal with various presumably abstract problems (e.g., see Elkind, 1961).

So much for the way behavior and knowledge are acquired. Through these various techniques organisms learn the things they need to know in order to survive. Indeed, learning is crucial to survival. But how does the necessity to survive make organisms learn? How do forces in the environment and in the organisms themselves activate the many techniques of learning? They do so by stimulating the organism, by supplying it with motivation to learn, and by reinforcing or not reinforcing the things that are learned. Because learning and motivation are almost two fitting pieces of the same jigsaw puzzle, the rest of this chapter deals with the second piece, motivation—including the effects of reinforcement and nonreinforcement on learning and behavior.

Development of Attention and Perception in Infants

Since attention and perception are prerequisites to learning, it is important to understand the development of these two processes in the infant. One cannot learn about an object unless he perceives it, and he cannot perceive it unless he attends to it. Knowledge concerning those features of an object or of the environment which attract the infant's attention should aid in the development of enrichment techniques for facilitating the development of attention and subsequent learning. What properties or characteristics of visual stimuli enhance attention? Are there developmental stages through which the infant passes with regard to preference for visual stimuli? In what way is attention in infancy related to later intellectual development? Answers to these questions will lead to the identification of optimal learning environments for infants. Clearly, learning begins at birth and we now realize that the early years play a vital role in laying the foundation for later learning.

Much of the extensive work currently being carried on regarding attention and learning in infants was stimulated by the pioneer studies of Fantz (1956, 1958a, b, 1961, 1963, 1965). He designed a relatively simple procedure for studying infant preferences for various visual patterns (see Figure 4-2). Infants were placed in a form-fitting crib in order to control the orientation of their head. The crib was placed in a test chamber which standardized the infant's field of vision. Stimuli varying along many different dimensions were presented in pairs to the infant. A small peephole in the top of the test chamber between the two visual stimuli permitted the investigator to observe which of the two stimuli the infant fixated. Finger switches were depressed by the observer to provide a record of the duration of the infant's fixation on a particular target.

Several highly interesting findings emerged from the early studies by Fantz. First, the very young infant is capable of making fairly fine visual discriminations, far more so than had been thought previously. Second, infants respond selectively to various visual stimuli, showing a preference, for example, for patterned over plain surfaces. The importance of this fact is summarized nicely as follows:

> It has long been known that the newborn infant can respond to light stimulation and probably to color. But it is patterned visual stimulation for which the vertebrate eye evolved, and from which derives almost all of the useful information taken in through the eye. Spatial orientation, object recognition, and social responsiveness in the child and adult are based largely on the perception of subtle variations in form and texture. Without pattern vision a person is blind for most practical purposes, even though light and color are received. Pattern vision is therefore of critical importance in studying perceptual development in the infant. (Fantz & Nevis, 1967, pp. 77–78)

Hunt (1961) has argued that for optimal perceptual stimulation there must be a "match" between the infant's developmental level with respect to his ability to process various kinds of information and the properties of the stimulus itself. For example, if a stimulus is more complex than the infant is able to assimilate, he will not attend to it. Likewise, if it is not complex enough, it will not maintain his attention. Two main areas of research have emerged from the notion that the infant's developmental maturity helps to determine those visual stimuli which will attract and maintain his attention.

First, the infant's looking preference for increasingly complex stimuli suggests intellectual development since he is able to process more complex kinds of information. Second, an infant's perference for a novel (new) stimulus over one he has been exposed to a number of times (that is, a familiar one) indicates several aspects of perceptual learning. Clearly, the ability to recognize a stimulus as new requires a "mental record" of old stimuli and the ability to "retrieve" that record and to compare it with the new stimulus. This process can be described as follows using the visual stimuli shown in Figure 4-3. Let us assume that previous research has shown that the two visual stimuli, A (horizontal stripes) and B (vertical stripes) are equal in their power to attract infants' attention. That is, they will look for the same amount of time (duration) at each. In the experiment for testing memory, an infant is shown stimulus B a certain number of times (familiarization trials). Now, if when shown stimulus A, he looks longer at it than he did for the last trials with stimulus B, one may conclude that the infant remembers the previously shown stimulus (B) and that he detects the difference.

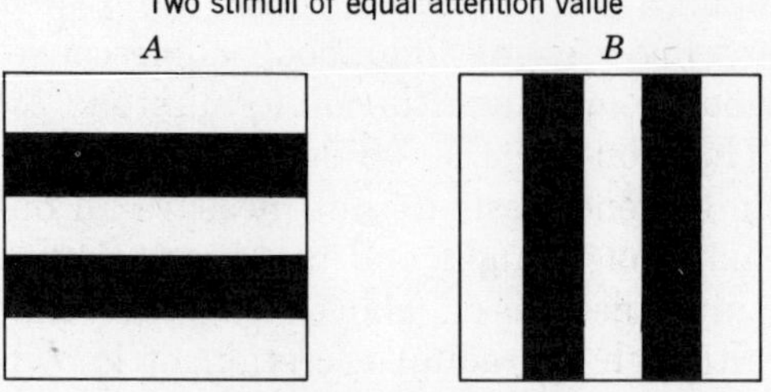

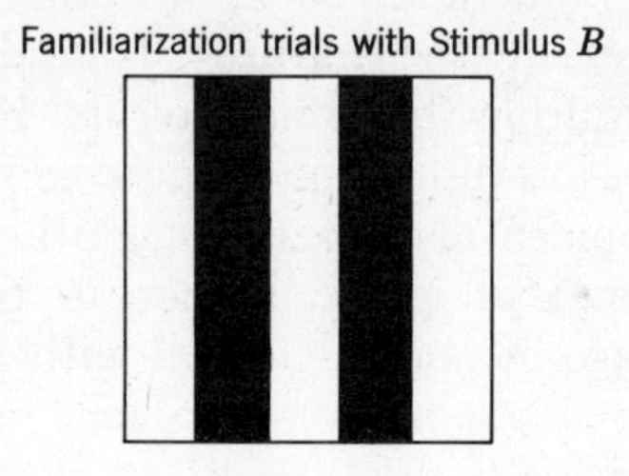

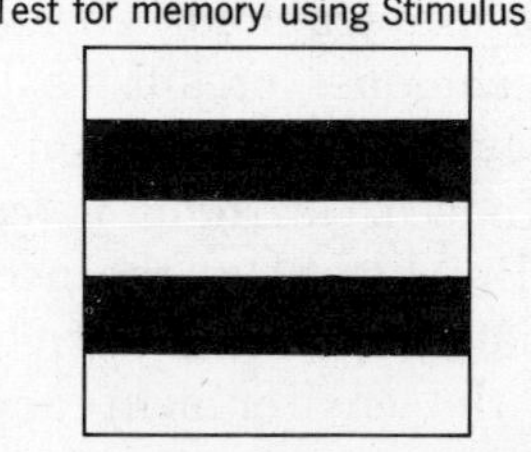

FIGURE 4-3 Procedure used in testing for perceptual learning.

This technique can be used to get at speed of perceptual learning. The number of times a stimulus must be shown to an infant before he is able to detect a new stimulus as different is used as a measure of the rate at which the infant acquires a mental picture or image or a "memory engram" for a stimulus. For example, returning to the technique described above, Infants X and Y are both given 10 trials or exposures to stimulus B. They both show the typical pattern of decreased duration of fixation to the stimulus upon repeated exposure to it so that at trial 10 they attend to it for 5 seconds. Now they are shown the new stimulus, A, which they have not previously seen. The duration of fixation for Infant X increases to 15 seconds, while Infant Y looks at it for 5 seconds or less. It is concluded that Infant X has developed a "memory engram" for stimulus B and thus identifies stimulus A as new, while Infant Y is unable to recognize the difference between the two stimuli. Further research might show that Infant Y requires 20 exposures to stimulus B before he shows increased attention to the new stimulus. Thus, the rate of perceptual learning is slower for Infant Y than for Infant X.

The recent research on infants has confirmed and extended the earlier findings by Fantz. During the early weeks of life infants can see relatively fine patterns and they can discriminate among patterns on the basis of form and complexity. Moreover, infants as young as eight weeks of age prefer complex and novel over simple and familiar stimuli (Weizmann, Cohen, & Pratt, 1971). That such preferences are related to intellectual development was demonstrated in a study by Fantz and Nevis (1967) comparing a group of home-reared and orphanage infants. More of the home-reared infants, children of University faculty members, preferred the novel rather than the familiar stimulis and they showed this preference at a consistently earlier age than the orphanage infants. It is interesting to note here that while differences between the two groups of infants in preference for novel stimuli appeared within the first 2 months of life, no difference was found between them on a standard infant intelligence test until 15 months. It appears that age at which preference for novel over familiar stimuli occurs is a better indicator of intellectual development than the traditional infant tests which include many motor items, such as age at sitting up and crawling.

While Fantz and Nevis did not experimentally manipulate the richness of the infants' perceptual environment, a study of Greenberg (1971) elicited the cooperation of a group of mothers in placing their infants in a crib with a pattern stabile attached for two 20–30 minute periods each day for 12 weeks. The results indicated that the infants' preference for increasingly complex patterns was accelerated by this visual enrichment experience. These findings have implications for the development of home-based programs designed to stimulate early perceptual learning.

Sex differences. While the nature of sex differences in attention is not entirely clear, most studies agree that such differences do exist. A relatively early study of attention (Kagan & Lewis, 1965) concluded that, as compared with boys, girls show more sustained attention to visual stimuli and 6 and 13 months; they attend longer to novel auditory stimuli; and they show greater stability in various measures of attention from 6 to 13 months. There is some evidence that auditory stimuli are more salient for girls while boys attend longer to visual stimuli. This suggests that different techniques may be required in stimulating early learning in boys as compared with girls, with boys profiting most from the use of actual objects and pictures, while talking and verbal descriptions may be more effective with girls.

In summary, research on attention in infants holds promise in furnishing information about (1) the prediction of later intellectual ability, and (2) the development of techniques for facilitating early intellectual development by enhancing attention, the basic element in learning.

MOTIVATION

Motivation is the force or condition within the organism that impels it to act or respond. Presumably organisms are motivated by physiological needs, such as hunger or thirst. These needs generate drives, that is, tendencies to behave in a manner likely to reduce the needs. Indeed, there is widespread belief that behaviors will be learned only if they can reduce an organism's needs or tensions.

The primary needs of an organism are biological—hunger, thirst, and, to a lesser degree, sex. In a society of plenty, such as American civilization, it is not often likely for drives engendered by primary needs to produce behavior among children or adults. Rather *secondary* drives, derived from primary drives, are considered to be more significant. The infant's affection for its mother comes from her feeding it; she reduces its primary drive of hunger. Not only is the feeding rewarding to the infant, but so is the mother, because she is always associated with reduction of the hunger. She becomes rewarding in her own right, if only on a secondary basis; this secondary reward, or *reinforcement,* is taken to be the basis for human socialization. The infant now needs the mother as well as the food and expands this need to encompass human beings in general. Although plausible, this explanation of the relationship between mother and child may not be correct. In Chapter 3, it will be recalled, Harlow's data (1958) regarding monkeys indicated that the development of infantile affection had nothing to do with feeding.

Perhaps, then, the mainspring for human motivation, and especially the motivation of the very young human, lies in other needs not tied to immediate biological necessity. Because of their value for survival, these other needs have become, through natural selection, part of the human condition. In their specific forms, they have been described as constituting curiosity and manipulative drives, which quite likely fit under the heading of *arousal* (see Hebb, 1955).

Arousal refers to the capacity of various sensory stimuli to excite the organism. It covers both primary and secondary drives, since all drives and all stimuli have the power to arouse. Actually, stimulation by the environment serves two purposes. The first of these, which is rather obvious, is to provide the organism with *cues* or hints on how to respond. The second, far less apparent, is highly significant: it is to *arouse* the organism and keep it actively engaged in dealing with the environment. This second function of stimulation may very well explain why primates seek stimulation for its own sake. Be that as it may, the amount of cueing supplied by a stimulus depends on when the organism is aroused. Figure 4-4 illustrates a cue-arousal curve, showing the quantity of cueing at various levels of arousal.

The validity of this curve is demonstrable. The organism that is overaroused because it is subjected to a large number of highly relevant stimuli receives very little cueing or information from the stimuli and is thus often wrong in its responses. In extreme cases, this may bring on panic. More typically, several studies (e.g., Birch, 1945; Johnson & Thomson, 1962) disclose that both high and low motivation are less effective in producing learning than moderate

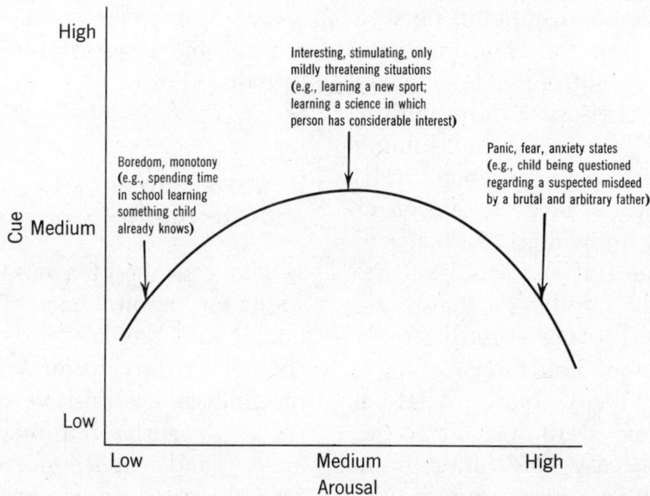

FIGURE 4-4 The amount of behavioral cues offered by a given stimulus at different levels of arousal.

amounts. In fact, there appears to be a point of diminishing return beyond which any increase in the amount of motivation results in a deterioration rather than an enhancement of learning. This point occurs at different places in different age groups and also varies among individuals within any given age bracket. Results of experiments in motivation indeed indicate the necessity for parent and teacher to show as much concern over learning situations in which motivation is very high as those in which motivation is very low.

In one study that appears to measure the effect of high arousal on children, Leitch and Escalona (1949) produced overstimulation in infants by presenting them with a succession of toys—all enjoyable, but too many and for too long. Behavior deteriorated rapidly. Although the children were highly alert or aroused, their behavior began to resemble that of an earlier stage of development; in other words, the children regressed. In fact, the case, observed rather frequently, of the child who has too many toys, too many experiences, too much contact with an excessively directive mother, and who becomes "difficult" might be explained as an instance of overarousal.

At the opposite extreme, monotony develops (see McBain, 1961). In this condition so few stimuli are present in the environment that the organism does not respond accurately to those at hand. The most striking example of this among children is found in the institutional care of infants. Institutionalization during infancy is said by many to inflict permanent psychic damage on those involved. But as we shall see in Chapter 9, this is a dubious view; the effects that are found tend to be temporary. Generally they consist of an apparent mental retardation, frequent tics, and peculiarities in affect. According to Casler (1961) lack of variation in the environment is a major factor in the generation of these deviant behaviors. Some of them, such as head banging, may stem from the child's own efforts to increase the environmental stimulation.

Although human behavior is motivated by the necessity to reduce tensions or arousal when biological needs grow too strong, far more behavior is engendered by the necessity to increase tension or arousal when the environment fails to provide enough variation. The most obvious thing about children, said Anderson (1948), is that they seek stimulation. There seems to be a need for maintaining arousal, and for increasing it when it falls too low. The optimal level of tension or arousal for any individual is likely to increase with maturation; this level lies somewhere in the middle, as Figure 4-4 shows, for that is where stimuli supply the most cues to guide behavior.

Rosenzweig (1945) found that if younger children were permitted to choose between easy and difficult—in this case, insoluble—tasks, they would, as a rule, choose the easy one. Older children, on the other hand, chose the difficult one. From this and other studies like it, one can conclude that young children, although they seek a wide variety of stimulation, are more easily overaroused than older children. Yet individual differences at any single level of maturation are probably influenced by inherited differences in emotional instability, emotionality, learned tolerance of frustration, capacity to reduce tensions, and a number of other variables.

Seeking stimulation, or being curious, certainly is almost synonymous with seeking arousal. We see, in this area, that less anxious (McReynolds, 1958; Penny, 1965) and more mentally healthy people (Howard, 1961; Sidle, Acker, & McReynolds, 1963) seek stimulation and apparently have a higher level of optimal arousal than more anxious, sick people. Degree of arousal seeking may be a major dimension of mental health.

The motivation to behave and to learn, then, may come from primary and secondary needs. The goal of the behavior may be the reduction of tensions produced by these needs. However, in primates, and particularly in young humans, such tension-*producing* behavior as curiosity or manipulation seems so marked that it may be sounder scientifically to accept the probable need to increase arousal and generate tension as well as to reduce both.

Reward, Punishment, and Nonreinforcement

The concept of arousal helps to account for the influence of three possible outcomes of any act on the probability of the act's recurring in the future. These possibilities are positive reinforcement—*reward*, negative reinforcement—*punishment*, and *nonreinforcement*—neither reward nor punishment. Thorndike (1913) in his "Law of Effect" stated that reward stamped in a behavior and punishment stamped it out. If things were this simple, life would also be simple, since most problem behaviors would vanish. The child who is a behavior problem has undergone considerable punishment through rejection by those around him, yet remains a problem. If punishment worked, then prisons—at least harsh prisons—should be 100 percent effective. The matter of reward and punishment, and especially punishment, is much more complicated than might be expected from the original law of effect. Moreover, questions regarding the influence of reward, punishment, and nonreinforcement are, of course, closely related to the very practical subject of disciplining children.

Reward. Before we can consider the influence of reward or positive reinforcement on learning, we must decide what constitutes reinforcement. All behaviors that lead to the reduction of primary and secondary drives must be regarded as positively reinforcing. Any behavior that decreases the probability of overarousal may also be included in this category. Since pain, for example, is usually overarousing, behaviors that lead to its avoidance are positively reinforcing. Even the painful consequences of behavior *can* be positively reinforcing. When they are, they increase the tendency for the behavior to recur. The head banging of institutionalized infants noted earlier may be viewed as positively reinforcing merely because it increases arousal. The daydreams and fantasies commonly reported by individuals in monotonous industrial, school, or prison situations are rewarding in the same sense.

There seems little doubt that positive reinforcement following a response increases the probability of the response's recurring. Thus, if a behavior is rewarded but does not increase in frequency, the positive value of the reinforcement may very well be open to question. On the other hand, if an act is rewarded every time it occurs—that is, if there is 100 percent reinforcement—the organism ultimately ceases to perform it (Hovland, 1936; Calvin, Clifford, Clifford, Bolden, & Harvey, 1956). Although this process has been interpreted in various ways, it may merely indicate that 100 percent reinforcement becomes monotonous. In other words, it decreases arousal, and the negative reinforcement associated with this decrease overtakes the positive reinforcement resulting from the reduction of specific needs.

Although full reinforcement may bring about the halting of a rewarded behavior, a program of reinforcement composed of smaller proportions of reward proves quite effective in impelling a behavior to recur. Skinner (1938, 1960) experimented with reinforcing organisms both at fixed intervals and at fixed ratios. In the first instance, he supplied reinforcement only once per time interval—once every five minutes in his original studies. In the other, he conferred a reward for every so many occurrences of behavior, such as one reward for every tenth appearance. He found that behaviors are learned best under 100 percent positive reinforcement. However, once learned, they are maintained best (show most resistance to extinction; recur most frequently), when there is far less than full reinforcement.

Anyone working with children does not need to be too concerned about reinforcing a child excessively. Even those behaviors that adults most desire to inculcate are usually not rewarded at anywhere near the 100 percent level, since children often perform them even when adults are not at hand. And often, when present, the parent or teacher may be too busy with other things to provide reinforcement. Moreover, it is as important to make certain that the same behavior is not rewarded on some occasions and punished on others as it is natural and good from the standpoint of learning neither to reward desirable behaviors nor to punish undesirable ones all the time.

Behavior, then, is likely to recur when rewarded. That intermittent reward is more effective than constant reinforcement suggests that other factors, perhaps related to arousal, may be significant aspects of the reinforcement, quite apart from its specific capacities to reduce needs and drives.

Punishment. The effects of punishment seem to be more varied than those of reward. If it is severe enough, punishment effectively reduces the frequency of a behavior's occurrence. In research with animals, Masserman (1943) exposed cats to severe punishment. A single, very painful exposure was often sufficient to bring about a permanent cessation of the behavior that led to the punishment. Bettelheim (1943), in describing his own experiences in a Nazi concentration camp, reported an analogous situation among humans. The harsh punishment of the concentration camp, along with other features of camp life, successfully broke the will of the inmates and made them innocuous. However, in such situations far more is changed than the behavior that originally occasioned the punishment. Severe punishment is capable of producing catatonic types of psychotic-like behavior, responses of extreme rage often directed toward the self, and a number of other bizarre symptoms, in addition to extinguishing more commonly accepted behaviors.

Azrin and Holz (1961), varying the intensity of punishment, have demonstrated that punishment may serve as a cue that increases the punished behavior (at the lowest level of punishment); may cause the behavior to cease temporarily; may cause a permanent but partial cessation; or may cause a permanent and complete end of the punished behavior, as the severity of punishment increases. But, as noted, severe punishment seems likely to have undesirable side effects, especially with humans.

Even relatively mild punishment produces a temporary decline in the frequency of a behavior's appearance. Skinner (1938) first demonstrated this phenomenon in an experiment with rats. Rewarded by food, the animals had learned to press a lever. Then the reward was withdrawn. Some rats were never punished; merely no longer rewarded. Some were punished by having their paws slapped during the first 10 extinction tests. For a while, the lever-pressing responses of the punished rat stopped. However, by the time the responses of the unpunished rat were extinguished, the punished rat had made as many lever-pressing responses as the unpunished; responses are not eliminated, they merely are postponed. Not long after this study, Estes (1944) discovered that punishment continued for a sufficient time did produce some decrease in the frequency of a response, but that Skinner was essentially right in his belief that the main function of punishment was to delay, not to extinguish or do away with the occurrence of undesired behavior.

During the temporary period of inhibition following punishment, the organism is more variable in behavior. Thus the chance of accidentally hitting upon the desired response and being rewarded for it increases. For example, Lovaas, Schaeffer, and Simmons (1965) punished rather severely "schizoid" or "autistic" (self-directed) types of children *until* they sought contact with an adult. Then punishment (shock) ceased, and they were rewarded in other ways as well. Learning of a valuable characteristic, that of being aware of and attracted to other humans, came as a result of punishment that disrupted well-learned but maladaptive modes of behavior. Clearly, punishment is helpful in producing changes in behavior. It is effective among humans for another reason as well. Humans tend to "internalize" punishment; they accept it as valid and punish themselves when performing the response that has led to punishment in the past. The toddler who has been punished for turning on the TV set at full volume may be seen to slap himself when approaching the console. He has become self-punishing.

> Mothers who punished toilet accidents severely ended up with bedwetting children. Mothers who punished dependency to rid of it had more dependent children than mothers who did not punish. Harsh physical punishment was associated with childhood aggressiveness and with the development of feeding problems. Our evaluation of punishment is that it is ineffectual over the long term as a technique for eliminating the kind of behavior toward which it is directed (Sears et al., p. 484).

Apparently the forms of punishment to which their findings allude were most often physical in character.

Sears, Maccoby, and Levin (1957) indicated that punishment does not eliminate the behavior toward which the punishment is directed. Others who have studied authoritarianism (e.g., Adorno, Frenkel-Brunswik, Levinson, & Sanford, 1950; Block, 1955) and creativity (e.g., MacKinnon, 1962) have suggested that an overly controlling parent reduces a child's curiosity, creative bent, and problem-solving ability. In many cases, the punished child is timider and less counteractive toward adults—although generally more aggressive toward peers. Thus he may be easier for parents to deal with and control even further. Punishment also helps to establish conflicts of approach and avoidance. Although punishment does not reduce motivation, the fear of it throws the organism into conflict; it still desires the goal at which the punished behavior is aimed, yet is afraid of pursuing it. Conflict of this sort, of course, disrupts behavior.

It should be noted that Solomon (1964), an astute student of punishment and its effectiveness, believes punishment to be very effective in changing behavior. Other reviews by Baumrind (1966) (see a discussion of Baumrind's conclusions in Chapter 10) and Marshall (1965) suggest that most forms of punishment are not as damaging as indicated in the earlier literature and that, under some circumstances, punishment is effective in producing the desired behavioral changes.

Even after considering these reviews, however, we still must conclude, from the evidence we have discussed above, that punishment has only limited utility in extinguishing a punished act that has been relatively well learned, and is far more likely than either reward or nonreinforcement to produce unexpected and often undesirable side effects.

Nonreinforcement. "A response can be permanently weakened only by a sufficient number of unreinforced elicitations . . ." (Estes, 1944). If it is neither rewarded nor punished, it is not reinforced. As both Skinner and Estes point out, the way to extinguish a behavior permanently is neither to punish nor reward it. Sometimes this is a slow technique. One of the authors spent considerable time among Eskimos, who generally frown on any punishment of children, and believes that at ages two to six, or thereabouts, Eskimo children are quite troublesome. But nonreinforcement, though slow, is effective, and by about age nine Eskimo children appear remarkably well adjusted *and* well behaved.

Nonreinforcement is thus more efficient than punishment, if one has the necessary patience and is dealing with behaviors for which a lesser speed of learning to inhibit responses is not dangerous to the learner or to others.

Reward, Punishment, Nonreinforcement, and the Problem of What Is Learned

Organisms do learn. The question remains, what do they learn? Do they learn to express behaviors that are rewarded, to inhibit behaviors that are not rewarded, or both? The earliest position regarding the effect of reinforcement on learning was that of Pavlov, who believed that organisms learned to respond to the stimulus that had previously led to reward. Spence (1937) resolved many contradictions among research findings (especially in the area of transposition) by suggesting that the learning process involves both increasing the organism's tendency to make rewarded behaviors and decreasing the tendency to perform behaviors that are not rewarded. Harlow and Hicks (see Harlow, 1959) later claimed that organisms, in learning, for the most part do not learn what to do; rather, they learn what not to do. Recent evidence suggests that organisms, whether pigeons (Terrace,

1963, 1964) or human children (Cole et al., 1964), learn far more from being rewarded for correct responses than for being punished (or nonreinforced) for making incorrect responses. The old folklore saying that we learn best by mistakes does not appear to be true. The best procedure, so far as learning an act is concerned (and probably more so in training dull than bright children), is to structure the learning event so that chances of failure are reduced to a minimum and success probability is maximized so that it can be rewarded. However, errorless learning has been shown to limit the range of generalization of learning (Terrace, 1964; Gollin & Savoy, 1968). The utility of punishment and nonreinforcement may be greater in situations requiring the generalization of what is learned than in situations when such generalization is not required. Perhaps the relatively slight importance of learning what not to do, as compared with what to do, in many learning situations, accounts for the fact that the effects of punishment are less strong and less predictable than those of reward.

SUMMARY

Simple learning may be either respondent or operant. Humans and lower organisms do not differ appreciably in the way they approach learning problems of this kind, nor do they show substantial differences in rates of learning. It is with the introduction of learning sets that wide distinctions may be noted across species, with humans showing considerable superiority. The learning set is a bridge to complex learning and in particular to concept formation at which humans excel. Humans are best at concept formation because of their wider experience, greater ability to transfer training, and language skills. Thinking is another form of complex learning that is considered unique to humans. The most comprehensive theory concerning the development of the thought process is that of Piaget, who believes that qualitative differences in thinking occur with age. Piaget to the contrary, we believe that evidence suggests that children probably think much the same way as do adults, although children's thought processes are handicapped chiefly by their smaller stores of information.

All these aspects of behavior, from simple respondent learning to complex problem solving, are part of the learning functions of humans. After years of concentrating on those phases of learning common to all organisms and the motivations for learning, researchers are finally acquiring information about the phases that are uniquely human. Although much remains to be learned, psychology has begun to develop considerable understanding of the forces that motivate higher levels of human functioning.

The learning of a response presumably depends on the reduction of a need and its related drive. Whereas nonprimates more often tend to act in order to reduce tension or arousal, primates need to maintain arousal. For this reason the latter engage in many learning experiences that are difficult to explain in terms of reducing the tensions produced by the more conventional primary biological needs or the secondary needs stemming from them.

A behavior may be either rewarded, punished, or nonreinforced. In most cases reward causes behavior to increase. Punishment *sometimes* decreases the frequency of a response, but also has a number of side effects. Nonreinforcement seems most effective in reducing the probability of response but is not likely to be widely used in Western society.

REFERENCES

Adorno, T. W., Frenkel-Brunswik, E., Levinson, D. J., & Sanford, R. W. *The authoritarian personality.* New York: Harper, 1950.

Alberts, E., & Ehrenfreund, D. Transposition in children as a function of age. *Journal of Experimental Psychology,* 1951, **41**, 30–38.

Anderson, J. E. Personality organization in children. *American Psychologist,* 1948, **3**, 409–416.

Azrin, N. H., & Holz, W. C. Punishment during fixed internal reinforcement. *Journal for the Experimental Analysis of Behavior,* 1961, **4**, 343–347.

Baumrind, D. Effects of authoritative control on child behavior. *Child Development,* 1966, **37**, 887–907.

Beilin, H. Cognitive capacities of young children. *Science,* 1968, **162**, 920–921.

Bettelheim, B. Individual and mass behavior in extreme situations. *Journal of Abnormal and Social Psychology,* 1943, **38**, 417–452.

Bever, T. G., Mehler, J., & Epstein, J. What children do in spite of what they know. *Science,* 1968, **162**, 921–925.

Birch, H. G. The role of motivational factors in insightful problem solving. *Journal of Comparative Psychology,* 1945, **43**, 259–278.

Block, J. Personality characteristics associated with fathers' attitudes toward child rearing. *Child Development,* 1955, **26**, 41–48.

Brackbill, Y. Experimental research with children in the Soviet Union. *American Psychologist,* 1960, **15**, 226–233.

Bronfenbrenner, U. The role of age, sex, class, and culture in studies of moral development, *Religious Education, Research Supplement,* 1962, **57**, S3–S17.

Bruner, J. S., Oliver, R., & Greenfield, P., et al., *Studies in cognitive growth.* New York: Wiley, 1966.

Calvin, A. D., Clifford, L. T., Clifford, B., Bolden, L., & Harvey, J. Experimental validation of conditioned inhibition. *Psychological Reports,* 1955, **2**, 51–56.

Casler, L. Maternal deprivation: A critical review of the literature. *Monographs of the Society for Research in Child Development,* 1961, **26**, Serial No. 80, No. 2.

Colre, R. E., Dent, H. E., Eguchi, P. E., Fujii, K. K., & Johnson, R. C. Transposition with minimal errors during training trials. *Journal of Experimental Child Psychology,* 1964, **1**, 355–359.

Dennis, W. Animistic thinking among college and university students. *Science Monthly,* 1953, **76**, 247–250.

Elkind, D. Quantity concepts in junior and senior high school students. *Child Development,* 1961, **32**, 551–560.

Estes, W. K. An experimental study of punishment. *Psychological Monographs,* 1944, **57**, No. 263.

Fantz, R. L. A method for studying early visual development. *Perceptual and motor skills,* 1956, **6**, 13–15.

Fantz, R. L. Visual discrimination in a neonate chimpanzee. *Perceptual and motor skills,* 1958, **8**, 59–60. (a)

Fantz, R. L. Pattern vision in young infants. *Psychological Record,* 1958, **8**, 43–47. (b)

Fantz, R. L. The origin of form perception. *Scientific American,* 1961, **204**, 66–72.

Fantz, R. L. Pattern vision in newborn infants. *Science*, 1963, **140**, 296–297.

Fantz, R. L. Visual perception from birth as shown by pattern selectivity. *Annals of the New York Academy of Sciences*, 1965, **118**, 793–814.

Fantz, R. L., & Nevis, S. Pattern preferences and perceptual-cognitive development in early infancy. *Merrill–Palmer Quarterly*, 1967, **13**, 77–108.

Fehmi, L. G. The formation of learning sets in severely retarded brain injured and familial children. Paper presented at the Spartan Psychological Association, San Jose, Calif., 1960.

Flavell, J. H. *The developmental psychology of Jean Piaget.* Princeton, N.J.: Nostrand, 1963.

Fowler, W. Cognitive learning in infancy and early childhood. *Psychological Bulletin*, 1962, **59**, 116–152.

Glorig, A. *Audiometry: Principles and practices.* Baltimore: Williams & Wilkins, 1965.

Gollin, E. S., & Savoy, P. Fading procedures and conditional discrimination in children. *Journal of Experimental Analysis of Behavior*, 1968, **11**, 443–451.

Greenberg, D. Accelerating visual complexity levels in the human infant. *Child Development*, 1971, **42**, 905–918.

Harlow, H. F. The formation of learning sets, *Psychological Review*, 1949, **56**, 51–56.

Harlow, H. F. The nature of love. *American Psychologist*, 1958, **13**, 673–685.

Harlow, H. F. Discrimination learning theory: Uniprocess vs. duoprocess. *Psychological Review*, 1959, **64**, 104–109.

Hebb, D. O. Drives and the C.N.S. (conceptual nervous system). *Psychological Review*, 1955, **62**, 243–253.

Herbert, J. A., & Krantz, D. L. Transposition: A re-evaluation. *Psychological Bulletin*, 1965, **63**, 244–257.

Honzik, M. P., McFarlane, J. W., & Allen, L. The stability of mental test performance between two and eighteen years. *Journal of Experimental Education*, 1948, **17**, 309–324.

Hovland, C. I. "Inhibition of reinforcement" and phenomena of experimental extinction. *Proceedings of the National Academy of Science* (Washington, D.C.), 1936, **22**, 430–433.

Howard, K. I. A test of stimulus seeking behavior. *Perceptual and Motor Skills*, 1961, **13**, 416.

Hunt, J. McV. Intelligence and experience. New York: Ronald, 1961.

Huxley, A. L. *Brave new world.* Garden City, N.Y.: Doubleday, Doran, 1932.

Johnson, R. C. A study of children's moral judgments. *Child Development*, 1962, **33**, 327–354. (a)

Johnson, R. C. Linguistic structure as a variable in concept formation and concept content. *Psychological Bulletin*, 1962, **59**, 468–476. (b)

Johnson, R. C., & Developmental Seminar. Manipulation of test stimuli social class, and the attainment of conservation. Paper presented at the meetings of the Society for Research in Child Development, New York, New York, March 30, 1967.

Johnson, R. C., & Thomson, C. W. Incidental and intentional learning under three conditions of motivation. *American Journal of Psychology*, 1962, **75**, 284–288.

Kagan, J., & Lewis, M. Studies of attention in the human infant. *Merrill–Palmer Quarterly*, 1965, **11**, 95–127.

Kendler, H. H., Kendler, T. S., & Wells, D. Reversal and non-reversal shifts in nursery school children. *Journal of Comparative and Physiological Psychology*, 1960, **53**, 83–87.

Koch, M. B., & Meyer, D. R. A relationship of age to learning set formation in the preschool child. *Journal of Comparative and Physiological Psychology,* 1959, **52**, 387–389.

Kuenne, M. R. Experimental investigation of the relation of language to transposition behavior in young children. *Journal of Experimental Psychology*, 1946, **36**, 471–490.

Laurendeau, M., & Pinard, A. *Causal thinking in the child.* New York: International Universities Press, 1962.

Leitch, M., & Escalona, S. The reactions of infants to stress. *Psychoanalytic Study of the Child.* **5**, New York: International Universities Press, 1949.

Lovaas, O. I., Schaeffer, B., & Simmons, J. Q. Building social behavior in autistic children by use of electric shock. *Journal of Experimental Research in Personality*, 1965, **1**, 99–109.

McBain, W. N. Noise, the "arousal hypothesis," and monotonous work. *Journal of Applied Psychology*, 1961, **45**, 309–317.

MacKinnon, D. W. The nature and nurture of creative talent. *American Psychologist*, 1962, **17**, 484–495.

McReynolds, P. Exploratory behavior as related to anxiety in psychiatric patients. *Psychological Reports*, 1958, **4**, 321–322.

Marshall, H. H. The effect of punishment on children: A review of the literature and a suggested hypothesis. *Journal of Genetic Psychology*, 1965, **106**, 23–33.

Masserman, J. H. *Behavior and Neurosis.* Chicago: University of Chicago Press, 1943.

Mehler, J. & Bever, T. G. Reply. *Science*, 1968, **162**, 979–981.

Mehler, J. & Bever, R. G. *Science*, 1967, **158**, 141.

Mowrer, O. H., & Mowrer, W. M. Enuresis—A method for its study and treatment. *American Journal of Orthopsychiatry*, 1938, **8**, 436–459.

Pavlov, I. P. *Conditioned reflexes* (translated by G. V. Anrep). London: Oxford University Press, 1927.

Penny, R. K. Reactive curiosity and manifest anxiety in children. *Child Development*, 1965, **36**, 697–702.

Piaget, J. *The child's conception of the world.* New York: Harcourt, Brace, 1930.

Piaget, J. *The origins of intelligence in children.* New York: International Universities Press, 1952.

Piaget, J. How children form mathematical concepts. *Scientific American*, 1953, **189**, 74–79.

Piaget, J. *Psychology of intelligence.* Totwa, N.J.: Littlefield, Adams, 1960. (Originally published in translation in 1947.)

Piaget, J. Quantification, conservation, and nativism. *Science*, 1968, **162**, 976–979.

Pratoomraj, S., & Johnson, R. C. Kinds of questions and types of conservation tasks as related to children's conservation responses. *Child Development,* 1966, **37**, 343–353.

Randall, D. L. *Examination of the hereditary assumptions underlying Piaget's theory of the development of intellectual structure.* Unpublished doctoral dissertation, University of Colorado, 1967.

Razran, G. The observable unconscious and the inferable conscious in current Soviet psychophysiology: Interoceptive conditioning, semantic conditioning, and the orienting reflex. *Psychological Review*, 1961, **68**, 81–147.

Rosenzweig, S. Further comparative data on repetition-choice after success and failure as related to frustration tolerance. *Journal of Genetic Psychology*, 1945, **66**, 75–81.

Sears, R. R., Maccoby, E., & Levin, H. *Patterns of child rearing*. Evanston, Ill.: Row, Peterson, 1957.

Sidle, A., Acker, M., & McReynolds, P. "Stimulus-seeking" behavior in schizophrenics and nonschizophrenics. *Perceptual and Motor Skills*, 1963, **17**, 811–816.

Simmons, C., & Johnson, R. C. Conditions influencing the learning transfer of conservation of substance. Unpublished manuscript, University of Colorado, 1968.

Skinner, B. F. *The behavior of organisms*. New York: Appleton–Century-Crofts, 1938.

Skinner, B. F. Are theories of learning necessary? *Psychological Review*, 1950, **57**, 193–216.

Skinner, B. F. Reinforcement today. *American Psychologist*, 1958, **13**, 94–99.

Skinner, B. F. Pigeons in a pelican. *American Psychologist*, 1960, **15**, 28–37.

Solomon, R. L. Punishment. *American Psychologist*, 1964, **19**, 239–253.

Spelt, D. K. The conditioning of the human fetus in utero. *Journal of Experimental Psychology*, 1948, **38**, 338–346.

Spence, K. W. The differential response in animals to stimuli varying within a single dimension. *Psychological Review*, 1937, **44**, 430–444.

Terrace, H. S. Discrimination learning with and without errors. *Journal of the Experimental Analysis of Behavior*, 1963, **6**, 1–27.

Terrace, H. S. Wavelength generalization after discrimination learning with and without errors. *Science*, 1964, **144**, 78–80.

Thorndike, E. L. *Educational psychology*. New York: Teachers College, 1913.

Thurstone, L. L., & Thurstone, T. G. *The Primary Mental Abilities Tests*. Chicago: Science Research Associates, 1941.

Voeks, V. Sources of apparent animism in students. *Science Monthly*, 1954, **79**, 406–407.

Watson, J. B. *Psychology from the standpoint of a behaviorist*. Philadelphia: Lippincott, 1919.

Watson, J. B., & Morgan J. J. B. Emotional reactions and psychological experimentation. *American Journal of Psychology*, 1917, **28**, 163–174.

Watson, J. B., & Rayner, R. Conditioned emotional reactions. *Journal of Experimental Psychology*, 1920, **3**, 1–14.

Weizmann, F., Cohen, L., & Pratt, R. Novelty, familiarity, and the development of infant attention. *Developmental Psychology*, 1971, **4**, 149–154.

Werner, H. *Comparative psychology of mental development*. (Rev. ed.) New York: International Universities Press, 1957.

chapter 5

language

chapter 5

language

chapter 5

language

The tools of communication are of two kinds. All organisms use signs and signals, but symbols are unique to humans. Symbolic communication, or language, is so closely related to learning that any attempt to separate them, even for purposes of discussion, is doomed to failure because of the tightness of their bond. Equally allied, as we shall see eventually, are language and memory. Since human achievement rests on both learning and memory, language, their common kin, is the central force in man's dominance over his environment.

Animals make a variety of sounds; in fact, a sound count published by Yerkes and Learned (1925) renders it possible to determine the relative frequency of different sounds uttered by chimpanzees. These utterances are specific and occur only in a single context. One cry may signify "food," another, "danger," but none is used in a new sense. Nor are two sounds combined to form a third sound distinct from the original two. These vocalizations refer to immediate situations, to the present danger and not to the danger of five minutes ago or to the danger yet to be discerned. Thus only objects or events that have been sensed can give rise to utterances. These sounds and other sign or signal types of communication in lower organisms are often compelling, for the animal exposed to a stimulus *must* respond to it. An exception to this statement may occur in the communication of porpoises, which are believed by some researchers to communicate symbolically.

In contrast, human symbolic behavior is highly varied. Humans are capable of emitting many sounds, each of which can be used in any combination with a large number of other sounds. Any single sound or group of sounds may have several meanings that are based on mutual agreement rather than on some innate response mechanism. Human speech can deal with the abstract or nonphysical and with the past and future as effectively as the present. It can also handle objects out of visual range as well as those sensed at the moment of vocalization. Sign-signal behavior appears to be oriented toward the communication of feeling or affect; symbolic communication contains a lesser proportion of affect and generally conveys more information. Although highly informative, human communication is not compelling in the same way that communication of lower organisms is. An extended discussion of these points may be found in Lorenz's (1952) and Tinbergen's (1953) work on animal communication.

Language permits the communication of information from one generation to the next. Since the wisdom as well as the errors of the past are thus available to the present generation without the necessity of having to learn by direct imitation, a fuller mastery of the environment is possible. Moreover, symbolic behavior through its intricacies enables individuals to understand one another better. With this understanding comes an increased prospect for cooperation and for the development of feelings. It is language that separates humans most clearly from all other organisms. In this chapter we shall first consider the normal development of language in childhood, then individual differences in language development, and, finally, the impact of language on thought, learning, and memory.

Most discussions of the acquisition of language in children begin when the child is able to utter simple words with appropriate meaning attached, some time before the end of the first year. In other words, most discussions have focused on language *production*. Even casual observation of the very young infant reveals that he is able to understand or comprehend speech long before he is able to produce it. This early *receptive* aspect of language, and the part it plays in later language development, have been largely ignored.

Recent research on auditory sensitivity and auditory discrimination in the young infant has produced some rather startling findings concerning his auditory capabilities. Work by Eisenberg, Griffin, Coursin, & Hunter (1964) and Butterfield (1968) has shown that newborns are able to differentiate between different auditory signals and to respond selectively to them. For example, Butterfield conditioned day-old infants to suck on a pacifier nipple which operated the playing of selections of classical, popular, and vocal music. The infants learned to control the onset and the offset of the tape-recorded music.

Other laboratory research has investigated infants' ability to discriminate between isolated speech sounds. Moffitt (1971), testing 30 infants between 20 and 24 weeks of age, found that they were able to differentiate between the syllables "bah" and "gah." Other research has shown that infants as young as 1 month of age are able to discriminate between the "bah" and "pah" sounds even though they differ only in that, in the former, voicing begins immediately, while in "pah" voicing begins 20 milliseconds later. This suggests the presence of built-in mechanisms for analyzing various aspects of speech.

Another investigator (Friedlander, 1970), attempting to study infants' auditory discrimination capabilities and their auditory preferences, has developed a "Playtest" machine which is attached to the infant's playpen or crib. Shown in Figure 5-7, the machine consists of a pair of large switches which the infant can operate, a loudspeaker, and a stereo tape player with a preprogrammed selection of two-channel audio tapes. Whenever

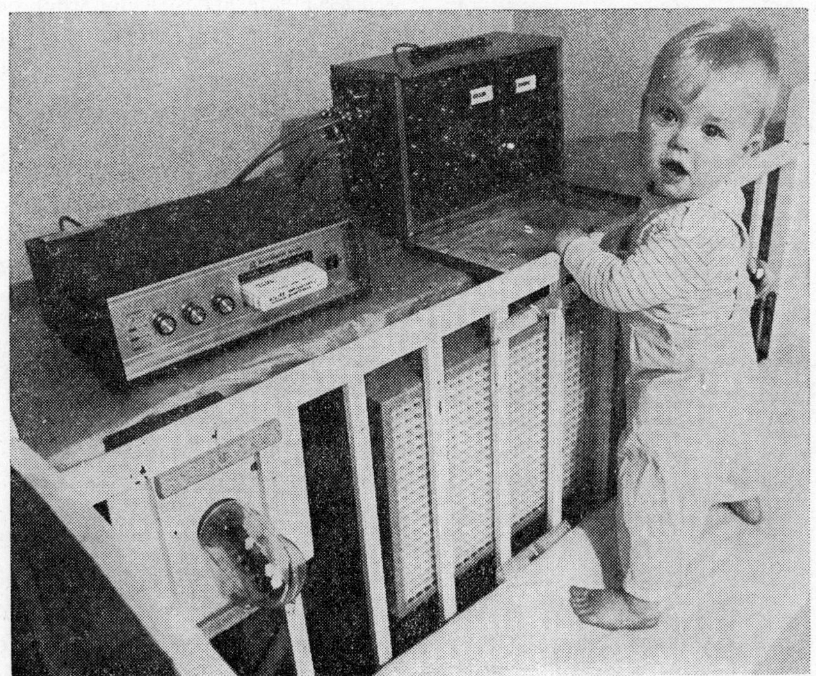

FIGURE 5-1 Twelve-month-old boy with PLAYTEST mounted on crib at home. Control units are normally placed below crib, out of reach.

the baby operates either switch, he turns on one of the two audio tape channels which are programmed separately with different stimulus materials, and a record is made of the frequency and duration of listening time.

In the following discussion Friedlander describes several interesting findings with individual infants:

> In a series of three long-term, single case studies, babies in the 11–15 month age range showed significant preferences in comparisons based on the variables of speaker identity, voice intonation, vocabulary, and message redundancy. The babies *did not* uniformly prefer their own mothers' natural voices. One 12-month infant preferred to listen to a stranger speaking in a voice with bright intonation when this voice was paired with his own mother speaking in flat monotone. This child, one of the younger infants studied, apparently was guided more by the intonation than by the identity of the speaker in making his selection. A 14-month baby, whose language development was informally judged to be more advanced, first showed great uncertainty when offered this choice. After several days he made an enormous burst of listening activity for the monotonous mother's voice and thereafter virtually ignored the switch that turned on the stranger's voice with the bright intonation. This was interpreted as as an "aha experience," or to use a more contemporary term, a discovery of recognitive familiarity (Hunt & Uzgiris, 1969) at having recognized the invariant properties of the mother's voice despite the disguise.
>
> Another baby showed an especially interesting pattern of selections when he was offered progressive comparisons between non-familiar, familiar, and disguised familiar voices. This baby initially demonstrated a clear preference for his mother's voice with normally bright intonation and familiar vocabulary when it was paired with a stranger's voice speaking with flat intonation and an unfamiliar vocabulary. He then made a significant selection of his mother's voice with the flat intonation and unfamiliar vocabulary when it was paired with a stranger's voice speaking with bright intonation and familiar vocabulary. This pattern of selection replicated the comparable choice made by the infant cited, but the next phase carried the problem one step further. The baby was offered a choice between two different modes of the mother's voice: one with bright intonation and familiar vocabulary, the other with flat intonation and unfamiliar vocabulary.
>
> We had no hypothesis when we offered the baby this choice, because we could not predict whether he would prefer the familiarity of the normal voice or the incongruity of the disguised voice. As it turned out, we could have hypothesized either preference and the data would have confirmed our prediction: the baby first made a decisive selection for the natural, familiar mode of his mother's voice, then shifted to a preference for the incongruous version. Apparently the baby first sought to assimilate an aspect of what he already knew, and then he preferred to listen to a variant form of the known values in which some of the stimulus characteristics remained unresolved—or were resolved in a different way.
>
> This crossover from the familiar to the unfamiliar anticipated what is perhaps the most provocative set of findings thus far encountered in all the PLAYTEST listening studies. Like the crossover effect from familiar to unfamiliar voice patterns, this other effect also seems to have significant implications for the role of receptive language processing in the organization of babies' schemata of auditory and linguistic experience. (Friedlander, 1970, pp. 16–17)

In a follow-up study, Friedlander used a larger sample of infants in order to verify this "crossover effect" from the familiar to the unfamiliar. On one tape the selection repeated itself every 20 seconds and on the other, every 240 seconds. Initially the infants preferred the highly repetitive (familiar) recording, but later showed a preference for the less repetitive one. This finding ties in nicely with the discussion in Chapter 4 regarding the shift in preference from familiar to novel and incongruous stimuli.

A second finding concerns the tremendous amount of listening the infants chose to engage in. One 19-month-old girl spent 65,000 seconds listening to the taped material over a period of 20 days. A 12-month-old boy spent an average time of 5000 seconds per day listening to tapes of nursery songs.

Clearly, auditory stimuli, voices, music, sounds, are highly attractive to young children beginning at a very early age. Moreover, this receptive ability matures long before the ability to produce meaningful words. Thus, the first year of life is important in developing *readiness* for speech.

A great deal of research has been conducted in recent years on the development of language comprehension. How much and what particular aspects of the language the child hears does he understand? Some of the methods used include giving young children various commands and observing to see if they are able to follow them; showing children pairs of pictures and asking them to choose the one that is represented by a sentence, such as "Show me the picture of the girl pushing the boy," or "Show me the picture of the girl being pushed by the boy"; and by observing the child's imitation of sentences spoken by an adult. This latter method assumes that a child imitates or repeats those parts of a sentence that have meaning for him, that he comprehends. The following are examples of imitation by a two-and-a-half year old (Slobin & Welsh, 1967). Although the child altered somewhat the first two sentences, his imitation indicated that he comprehended their meaning. However, in the last two, the meaning was changed, suggesting lack of comprehension.

Adult: Here is a brown brush and here is a comb.
Child: Here's a brown brush an' a comb.

Adult: John who cried came to my party.
Child: John cried and he came to my party.

Adult: The batman got burned and the big shoe is there.
Child: Big shoe is here and big shoe is here.

Adult: The boy the book hit was crying.
Child: Boy the book was crying.

In their imitations, children drop out those parts of speech and those grammatical constructions they do not understand.

It is apparent that even very young infants are highly attentive to intonation patterns, inflections, and pitch. For example, young infants lower their pitch when they are babbling back and forth with their mother; they lower it even further when they vocalize with their father. This clearly indicates that infants discriminate pitch and that their own pitch is altered by what they hear. Further, in "scanning" adult speech, children are able to segment the speech into words fairly easily even though they are no reliable acoustical measures of word boundaries. Research has shown that in listening to moderately incomprehensible adult speech, the young child first picks out and attends to those words with which he is familiar, and, second, he attends to those words that come after the familiar words (Slobin, 1972). Apparently the child's "auditory scanner" or "analyzer" is quite sophisticated.

While a great deal remains to be learned concerning the development of language comprehension, it is clear that the process begins very early. The development of techniques for facilitating language comprehension should also facilitate language production—speech.

THE COURSE OF LANGUAGE DEVELOPMENT

Sounds

The first sound uttered by a child is its cry at birth. Most of its vocalizing of the next few months falls under the heading of crying. Early crying consists of vowel sounds, Lewis (1959) has pointed out, especially a-a-a-a as in *fat*. Some of the sounds of the English language are difficult, if not impossible, to make before one has teeth, since several of them depend on the action of the tongue against the teeth. Other sounds are difficult for other reasons. But soon after birth the change from vowel cries to consonant-vowel combinations commences. Some sounds involving oral movements like those occurring in sucking—for example, *ba-ba*—come to be associated with comfort whereas others—for example, *na-na* with a nasal *a*—are linked to states of discomfort (Lewis, 1959). Consonants then increase in proportion to vowels (Irwin & Chen, 1946). Within a few months after birth, the child makes a wide assortment of sounds and by about a year of age is capable of uttering most of the different sounds used in the various languages of mankind (Irwin, 1947a, 1947b, 1948a).

Theories abound as to how humans progress from babbling to speaking meaningful words. Primates are noisy creatures as a rule, but it seems probable that the association of sounds with comfort, as in a mother's conversation when changing, feeding, and bathing an infant, causes sounds to become somewhat rewarding in themselves. The child receives pleasure through his own production of sounds. Sound making is thus reinforced and increases in frequency. In somewhat different ways both Mowrer (1950) and Miller and Dollard (1941) emphasize the emotive quality of early sound making. It is very pleasant for a parent to lie abed in the morning, soon after the sun comes up, and listen to a baby babbling in his crib. Although part of the pleasure comes from not having to get up, some of it comes from sharing the apparent joy of the infant as he works through his storehouse of sounds. It is this joy that is considered the first step in meaningful communication.

The English language does not contain all the sounds made by humans in communication. The French rolling *r*, the German umlauts, the Zulu or Bushman tongue-clicks, and some of the sounds the Swede must make to pronounce the name *Skjellbjörn* are foreign to the English-speaking adult. Yet infants in any culture can make them all, although those not found in English disappear quite rapidly in American and other English-speaking children. When an infant or young child in the English-speaking orbit utters foreign sounds, his parents more often look baffled and do not reinforce the sound-making behavior. The parents do, however, directly reinforce the sounds germane to English by parental attention and also by making the sounds themselves. This provides the sounds with an indirect or secondary rewarding quality. Through reward of sounds found in a language and nonreinforcement of others alien to it, infants begin to utter more often those sounds to be used later by them in forming words.

The emotive and affective aspects of sound making appear first in infants' awareness; the value of speech as a means to convey more specific information comes later. Although the two components of speech are associated with one another, the affective-feeling component may remain relatively distinct from the informational-cognitive component even into adulthood. Some support for this position may be found in the investigation of *aphasia*, a disorder in communication resulting from some forms of brain injury. If the speech capacity of the aphasic is impaired, as is often the case, the ability to express emotions (e.g., to swear) usually remains intact, even when the capacity to communicate information is totally or at least partially lost.

Intonation. As we shall discuss later, the investigation of the factors involved in the young (e.g., two-year-old) child's ability to form sentences is vigorously being pursued. One aspect of saying a sentence is changing the pitch of sounds as the speaker progresses from beginning to end. English-speaking peoples typically begin sentences at a rather high pitch, and lower them at the end. Scandinavians, on the other hand, generally reverse the procedure. No matter what means we use, changes in tone, like characteristic pauses, serve to break up a continued discourse into smaller, more easily digested elements. To learn intonation, then, is to learn one aspect of sentence construction. This particular aspect of sentence construction appears to be learned in the babbling stage—the child frequently makes a long succession of babbling sounds, none of which have meaning to the adult listener, yet which in intonation have a sentence-like sound to them. This is particularly noteworthy because when children finally begin to use real words in sentences, these sentences are usually of two words, far less complex in terms of number of sounds than the babbling "sentences" that have preceded them by about a year. It appears that this aspect (intonation) of what it takes to make a sentence in a given language is learned earlier than the constituent elements of sentences (words) and also earlier than the ordering of words within sentences.

Use of Words

Some sounds occur more frequently than others in infant vocalization, and it is to these that adults attach meaning. Since infants in all cultures often make the same sounds, the basic infant vocabulary of all languages is common, even though cultures differ in the association of specific sounds with specific meanings. In English-speaking homes, the child utters the sound *ma-ma* and the meaning *mother* is attached to it. But in other cultures *ama* is mother, and in still others, *da-da*. In some languages *ama* means grandmother; elsewhere it is nurse. To Americans *baba* signifies baby but to many Slavic peoples it means grandmother. And so on. Adults grasp at the sounds uttered frequently by children in babbling and invest them with meanings according to the cultures in which they live. This process hastens the learning of language, for the child now makes sounds denoted as words and reinforced as words.

Parents are well known for their understanding of their children's utterances. Although they doubtless find meanings even where none is intended, they also understand the approximations employed by one- and two-year-olds that are incomprehensible to strangers. One little boy living in a wet climate, for example, said "Ne-Ne-Lah-Lah." This is a relatively difficult sound pattern to decipher. So far as the boy was concerned, it appears that what the child meant was "Roni's (his sister's) umbrella." Actually, the syllables had a number of meanings. They could mean "It is raining," "Roni has her umbrella," "I want her umbrella," or "Here comes Roni with her umbrella," depending on the inflection of the sounds. From such slender roots, consisting of primitive sound groups that only in a very limited sense approximate the words they are intended to signify, yet that *have meaning for both speaker and listener,* stems symbolic communication.

Infants utter words such as da-da even before it is likely that they attribute sense to them or even know that words have meaning. Quite possibly infants may have their own meanings for words that adults cannot apprehend. Yet symbolic communication requires agreement in meaning between speaker and listener. Symbolic communication is a two-way affair; it cannot occur in a vacuum, nor can it take place unless the listener understands the speaker's utterances. Because understanding is essential, it is hard to ascertain when the first word appears in infant speech.

Available data suggest that a child's first word is uttered at about one year of age (McCarthy, 1946). Averages, however, are not always reliable. Gifted children are advanced in developing speech (Terman, 1925), whereas retarded children are slow in developing it. In fact, retarded children are infantile in speech, using fewer consonants and more vowels than normal children of the same age (Irwin, 1942). Nevertheless, although early speech is a reasonably good indication of general precocity, delayed speech is not, of itself, a portent of later deficiency. Some children are slow in developing speech merely because they have received little reinforcement and others because their mothers are so solicitous that their demands are met without having to speak. Some, of course, are behind in speech development owing to sensory or intellectual weaknesses, whereas others are retarded for no discernible reason at all.

Once a child has begun to speak, there are two ways to determine the number of words in his vocabulary. The first is to spend enough time with a child to hear every word he knows. Leopold (1937–1949) kept an accurate diary of the speech development of his daughter from the eighth week to the seventh year of her life. Although word counting was quite incidental to his major purpose, this diary is an excellent example of the approach in which *all* words the child says become part of a vocabulary score. The more common method for studying language growth is to select a sample of words and then present a child with pictures or other stimuli capable of leading him to say the word if he knows it. From the child's responses to this sample of words, his total vocabularly can be estimated. Figure 5-2 presents data presented by Lenneberg (1966) in a study of vocabulary growth.

Although these figures indicate the rapid increase in verbal comprehension, especially between two-and-a-half and three years, they do not say anything by themselves about the range of individual differences. Among the 25 children Shirley (1933) studied from birth to two years of age, the number of words spoken in the presence of examiners just prior to their second birthdays varied from 6 to 126. This was a tremendous range for a normal population.

Construction of Sentences

Granted that a young child (e.g., age 15–18 months) knows the meaning of a number of words, how does the child learn to put these words into understandable, syntactically correct sentences? Syntax, in English, consists largely of ordering words. "No say mama" is not an unusual construction for a child just turned two, who means that "Mama says no." The correct ordering of words

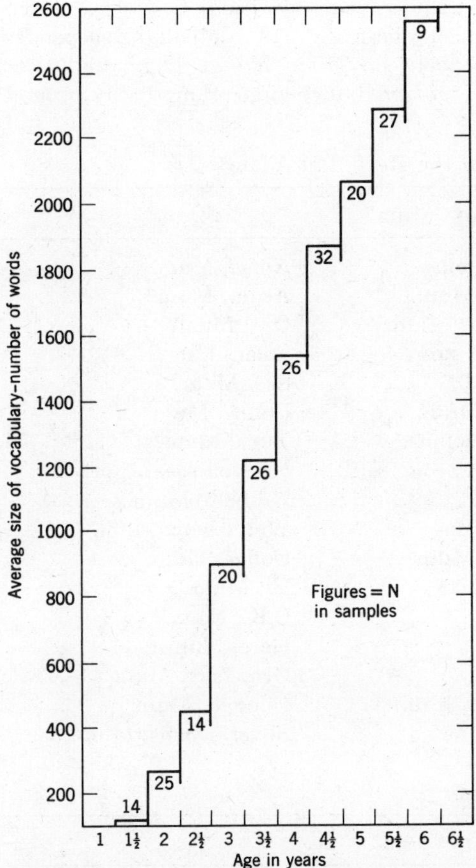

FIGURE 5-2 Average vocabulary size of 10 samples of children at various ages (data from Smith, as presented by Lenneberg, 1966).

within a sentence so as to follow the conventions of the language is learned rather early by the child. This is so whether word order is important, as in English, or relatively unimportant, as in Russian (Slobin, 1966).

Further, the child must learn, from the way words are used in sentences, what class the words belong to, so that they can be transformed and used in contexts other than those in which they were learned. Clearly, the young child just learning to make sentences does not know the formal names of various word classes, such as "nouns" and "verbs," but once he understands syntax so that he can use word position and connective terms as clues, he can begin to make adequate transformations. Berko (1958) developed a test using stimuli such as those shown in Figure 5-3. The general approach of using nonsense words within a sentence such as "The mog wibbled the gomp," has been used by other researchers as well (e.g., Bellugi, 1965).

Children show early skill in learning inflections. For example, children usually call the two creatures in Figure 5-3 wug/z, not wug/s. Adults usually do not notice that they pronounce plural nouns ending in "s" either with a "z," as in wug/z or dog/z, or with an "s" as in cat/s or bik/s (another of Berko's figures), and many foreign-born speakers of English never learn this distinction. Yet children know it early.

Berko tested out other propositions of this same sort, using possessive endings of nouns, the simple past tense, and so on, and tested children from preschool through grade 3. As Brown and Fraser (1964) note,

> The productivity of the regular inflections of children seems to be greater than

This is a wug.

Now there is another one.
There are two of them.
There are two ____.

FIGURE 5-3 Illustration of Berko's method for eliciting inflections.

it is for adults. Both kinds of subjects were shown a picture of a man swinging something about his head and told: "This is a man who knows how to gling. He glings every day. Today he glings. Yesterday he ________." Adults hang suspended between *gling, glang, glung,* and even *glought* but children promptly say *glinged.*

TABLE 5-1 Total Contexts of Four Words in the Record of Adam**

Total Contexts of "Mum"		
Here it is, Mum.	(The) pan, Mum.	Apple, Mum.
Here, Mum.	I want apple, Mum.	Again, Mum?
Here (the) coffee pot broken, Mum.	I want blanket, Mum.	Out, Mum?
More sugar, Mum.	I want blanket now, Mum.	Salad, Mum?
There it is, Mum.	I want juice, Mum.	See, Mum?*
What's that, Mum?	Mum, I want some, Mum.	Coffee, Mum?
Mum, (where is the cards)?	Popeye, Mum?	Turn, Mum?
Mum, (where's the rags)?	I wanta do, Mum.	No, you see, Mum?
Want coffee, Mum.*	I wanta help, Mum.	No help, Mum.
Want apple, Mum.	I found, Mum.	Won't help, Mum.
Want blanket, Mum.	I do, Mum.	Coffee, Mum.
Want more juice, Mum.	I don't, Mum.	Hi, Mum.*
I want blanket, Mum.	I get it, Mum.	O.K., Mum.
I want (it), Mum.	(Gonna) dump, Mum.	Here, Mum.
I want paper away, Mum.	Fall down, Mum.	Over here, Mum.
	Fall, Mum.	Enough, Mum.
	An apple, Mum.	Silver spoons, Mum.
Total Contexts of "Dad"		
See paper, Dad.	See, Dad?*	Work, Dad?
Want coffee, Dad.*	Dad, want coffee?	Hi, Dad.*
I want cream, Dad.	Some more, Dad?	
Total Contexts of "Here"		
Here (a car).	Here more bricks.	Here (we go).
Here all gone.	Here more blocks.	See the bolt here, see?
Here (block).	Here more firetruck.	That block here.
Here brick.	Here more toys.	That one here.
Here chairs.	Here more truck.†	That one right here.
Here coffee is.	Here Mum.†	I put bucket here.
Here comes Daddy.	Here Mummy.	Come here.
Here flowers.	Here my bricks.	Do here.
Here goes.†	Here not a house.	Leave that block here.
Here is.†	Here stars.	Put it here.
Here it goes.†	Here (the) coffee pot broken, Mum.	Here not a house.
Here it is.†	Here the card.	Right here.†
Here it is, Mum.†	Here the cards.	Over here.
Here's it here.	Here the cheese.	Over here, Mum.
Here light.	Here (the) flowers.	Now here.
Here (mail) more paper.	Here the paper.	
Here more.		

TABLE 5-1 (*Continued*)

Total Contexts of "There"		
There goes.†	There more block.	I wanta put (it) right there . . . (under) the couch.
There (he) goes.	There more truck.	Me see (in there).
There is.†	There more nails.	Blanket in there.
There it goes.†	There Mum.†	In there.
There it is.†	There my house.	Right there.†
There it is, Mum.†	There my nails.	
There kitty.	There Noah.	

*Identifies contexts common to "Mum" and "Dad."
†Identifies contexts common to "Here" and "There."
**From Brown & Fraser, 1964, p. 55.

Berko also tested to see whether children who generalize the regular inflection would correctly imitate irregular forms or would assimilate them to the rules. She showed a picture and said, for instance, "Here is a goose and here are two geese. There are two ________." Most of her subjects said *gooses* and performed similarly with other irregular forms. These observations suggest that rules of great generality may survive and override a number of counter instances (Brown & Fraser, 1964, pp. 46–47).

In Berko's study of syntax, nonsense syllables were placed in sentences in such a way that they were identifiable as various parts of speech. For example:

Where *wug* was to be identified as a transitive verb, the investigator said: "This is a little girl who wants to wug something." As the intransitive verb the same sentence was used with the omission of *something*. With *wug* as a mass noun the little girl would be "thinking about some wug." *Wug* became an adjective by having the girl think of "something wuggy" and an adverb by having her think of "doing something *wuggily*." Children in the first, second, and third grades all went on to make up sentences using their new words, but they did not always use them correctly. They did better as they got older and better at all ages with the count noun, adjective, transitive and intransitive verbs than with the mass nouns and adverbs. For the purposes of the present argument the important result is that children showed an ability, increasing with age, to construct grammatically correct sentences using new words (p. 48).

At an early age (e.g., four–five) most children know the proper transformational rules of English, as in changing from singular to plural. They know how to handle tenses, although, as noted above, the general rule (e.g., add "ed" for past tense—"want" to "wanted"; "went" to "wented") overrides the specific rule, for a time, perhaps as a result of far greater experience with the general than the specific rule (Palermo & Eberhart, 1968). And they know how to handle different parts of speech, as shown in Berko's experiment.

Such things as knowledge of word meaning, intonation, word order, transformational rules, even if combined together, do not, in their totality, comprise the art of making sentences; they are merely elements that may be required before sentence construction occurs. Yet all of these, plus other aspects of sentence making, must form a gestalt or whole before the art of sentence construction is fully learned.

Young (two- to three-year-old) children's sentences are by no means complete sentences, when compared with those of adults. Table 5-1 shows the sentences spoken by Adam, a 28½-month-old boy, in which he used the words "Mum," "Dad," "Here," and "There." Few of these sentences would have been spoken by adults. It seems unlikely that direct imitation (resulting from reinforcement of imitative efforts) of adult speech can explain the character of early sentence making, as is claimed, for example, by Skinner (1957, p. 31). The idea that children imitate adults, and thus learn to combine words into sentences, also appears invalid; young children make less adequate sentences when directly imitating adults than when making their own sentences (Ervin, 1964, p. 171).

It may be true, as Chomsky (1959) claims, that grammatical speech is a built-in human propensity. Even if built-in, it requires exercise to come into being. Until Weir's (1962) research, during which she taperecorded her young son's speech while he was lying in his crib, no one knew how much conscious, conscientious effort went into learning words and sentences. Weir's little boy would lie in the crib, going through monologues of this sort:

"Fiss"
"Fiss"
"Fiss"
"No Fiss! Fiss"
"No Fiss! Fiss"
"Fish"
"Fish"
"Fish"

Word making and sentence making are, in a way, innately determined human propensities, since we humans are unique in this respect; yet these activities also require practice. The use of words and sentences is so rewarding, in the sense that one can make his needs and ideas known to and responded to by others, that this general reinforcing quality of speech itself appears to be a much stronger motivational force than specific parental rewards for such things as imitation of adult sentences. Learning to speak sentences probably requires more than learning the rules of sentence construction; it also requires, probably before any specific rule learning, awareness on the part of the child that communication pays off in terms of obtaining desired ends. Once provided with speech models, but in a process different from direct imitation and reward for direct imitation, the child—still really an infant—expends a great deal of time on drilling himself in speech in order to gain these desired ends.

Short-Term Memory and Sentence Construction. Young children face one special problem in learning to make sentences. Even if they have highly adequate models, they have a very short memory span. The adult says to the child, "There's a funny little brown doggie playing in the grass." This is too much for the child to handle, and if responding, he might say "Funny doggie play grass." Many students of children's speech call this type of sentence "telegraphic speech." It certainly is common among young children. Adults can retain and use about seven units of information at a time. (Miller, 1956); at age two, when sentence construction begins, two units is about average; three units is superior. Being able to hold only a few things in the mind at any one time probably leads to the telegraphic sentences that children emit. The child copes with this problem in several ways. First of all, he does do away with unimportant (so far as conveying meaning) aspects of the sentence, as in the example above. Secondly, he may "chunk" or put together separate elements of meaning, so that they are held in memory as though they were a single unit. "Itsa" may be a convenient chunking or combining of the words "it is a" into a single unit, so far as memory is concerned. Through such tactics as telegraphic speech and chunking, the child attempts to produce meaningful, hopefully correct sentences even though he is severely handicapped in short-term memory span.

Children's defects in short-term memory lead to interesting questions regarding the effects of language structure, within a given culture, on the child's language development. Yngve (1960) hypothesized that (at least to the speaker) languages are right-branching; that is, that the first word determines, to a degree, what the second word could be, and so on, through the sentence (for example, with a first word of "A," we could say "cat" but could not properly say "cats").

For us, left-branching structures are difficult and sound ill-constructed (see McNeill, 1966, for examples of left-branchingness developed in rocketry). In English, for the most part a right-branching language, we need only to keep a few words ahead of ourselves in our thoughts. We do not need to know how a sentence is going to end before we begin it, since, so long as syntax is correct, each new word involves many different choices, as shown in Figure 5-4.

Left-branching languages do exist, although they are in the minority. Japanese, most American Indian languages, and Turkish are examples of largely left-branching languages. In these languages the speaker must know the end of a sentence before he can construct the beginning of the sentence correctly. Rather than moving from beginning to end, as in English and other right-branching languages, he must construct each of the preceding portions of the sentence to fit the end word or phrase. Clearly, left-branching sentences demand a great deal more from memory than do right-branching sentences, and are difficult even for adults to handle—especially if they have been raised in a right-branching language group, but even if they have been raised in a left-branching language group (Forster, 1966). Imagine the problems of a two-year-old attempting to learn sentence construction of a left-to-right-branching sentence. The limits of short-term memory are such that sentence construction would present a tremendous problem and be learned very late, as compared with the same kind of learning in a right-to-left-branching system. Comparisons of how children from these two kinds of language system learn to make sentences could tell us much about the relative role of each of a number of aspects of language (e.g., syntax, inflection) and of the forces influencing sentence construction (e.g., short-term memory). German youngsters would be especially interesting to study in this respect. Most

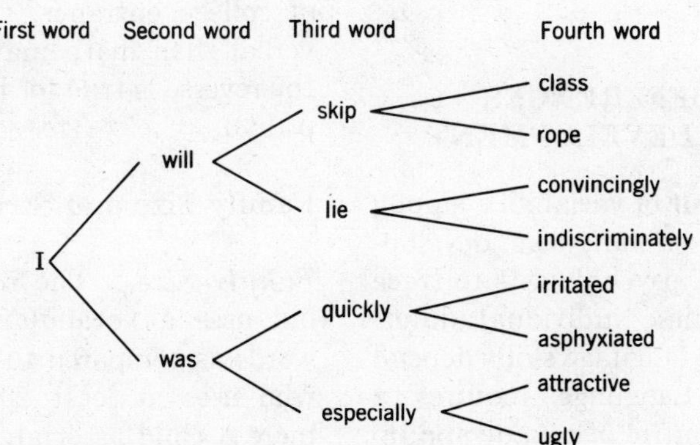

FIGURE 5-4 Some of the possible alternatives of sentence construction of a right-branching sentence starting with "I."

German sentences, like those in English, are right-branching; however, certain types of sentence[1] make German more left-branching than other existing European languages, for example: (1) dependent and relative clauses in which the main verb of the clause is the last element of the clause (the boy, who to the store went); (2) compound tenses in which the participle or the infinitive is the last element of the sentence (the boy has to the store gone); and (3) the so-called separable-prefix verbs in which the prefix is the last element of the sentence in the present and simple past tenses (no English equivalent). In these structures the final element or elements (in the case of compound verbs) must be retained in the temporary or short-term memory until the rest of the structure has been produced.

There are many problems to be solved by the child if he is to construct sentences in right-branching languages, such as English. Children learning left-branching have still more problems, and should differ markedly in the rate of language development, being retarded in at least some aspects of sentence construction unless parents provide a "baby syntax" similar to our "baby talk." But somehow we all manage to do it. Maybe we are innately grammarians, as Chomsky (1959) and Lenneberg (1966) have suggested.

INDIVIDUAL DIFFERENCES IN LANGUAGE DEVELOPMENT

The high amount of variability among children in rates of language development has impelled psychologists to trace the sources of these individual differences. To a degree language skills depend on maturation. Language requires a highly accurate control of tongue and lip movements; like most motor behaviors, this control is largely maturational in its development.

Sex differences

One would naturally expect girls to excel boys in language skills because females mature more rapidly than males. Most of the earlier studies of sex differences in language development show female superiority in vocabulary, articulation, length of sentences, complexity, and grammatical correctness up through the age of about 10 (see McCarthy, 1946, pp. 551–555). As to sheer number of words spoken, girls again lead (Jersild & Ritzman, 1938). Reasonable as it may seem to attribute this feminine superiority to maturational factors, this may not be the case. Most early students of sex differences in language development were women. It now is known that the characteristics of the tester markedly influence the response level of the child (Cowan, Weber, Hoddinott, & Klein, 1967). It may be that girls respond best to female testers, boys to male testers; therefore, some of the reported sex differences favoring girls in early language development may result from the fact that most of the testers were female. However, at least some of the difference appears to be real, since even at the age of college entrance, girls are higher in verbal than mathematical ability which the reverse is true for boys (Brown, 1965, p. 163).

Family Size and Structure

Family Size. The average three-year-old uses a vocabulary of nearly 1000 words as compared to the average adult who uses at least 20,000. Clearly, the more a child associates with adults, the

[1]Mrs. Linda Klank provided these examples.

more words he is exposed to and may learn. The only child is superior in nearly all forms of verbal ability to children with siblings; twins are more retarded than children with siblings (Davis, 1937); and triplets have less verbal facility than twins (Howard, 1934). The Dionne quintuplets were markedly slow in language development (Blatz, 1937). How could the five girls learn to speak at a normal rate when a great deal of their time was spent with one another? There is not much that a toddler can learn from four other, equally naive toddlers. Doubtless the amount of contact a child has with conversation of adult complexity is directly related to the rate of language growth.

Deprived Children. Studies over the years of neglected children (Bühler, 1931; Pringle & Bossio, 1958) and of institutionalized children (Skeels, Updegraff, Wellman, & Williams, 1938; Haggerty, 1959) concur that the lack of adult contact and speech reinforcement occasions considerable retardation of speech among children thus deprived. These four studies found among the children they tested a greater backwardness in language than in any other area of development. To the extent that communication is limited, all other aspects of development are handicapped. Nevertheless, the effect of severe language retardation can be transitory. Tutoring and enrichment of the environment are capable of producing marked, rapid, and permanent language gains in previously retarded youngsters (Dawe, 1942; Luria & Yudovich, 1959; Skeels et al., 1938).

The Bilingual Child. Great numbers of Americans in the past grew up knowing the language of their immigrant parents as well as English. Now again as the nation's isolation dissolves in a shrinking, contemporary world, a growing proportion of young Americans are learning two languages. Working in Hawaii, Smith (1939) observed that bilingual children were distinctly retarded in speech development. The deficiency was so pronounced that at school-entrance age the bilinqual child was about equal in language skills to a *haole* (how-lee = Caucasian) monoglot three years old. Smith noted that both bilingualism and pidgin English might be involved in this retardation. The bilingual children were probably not exposed to standard English to any marked degree, but instead learned pidgin, the *lingua franca* of Hawaii. This tongue of limited vocabulary that could be easily learned by all evolved from an admixture of many races and languages.

At the other extreme is the upper-class European tradition of ordering the environment in a manner that produces bilingual, trilingual, or even polylingual children. Although empirical data are largely lacking, the learning of several languages, when each of them is used at high level by adults in the environment, appears to have no harmful effects. In Leopold's four-volume description (1937–1949) of his daughter's language development, he told of how she was brought up as a bilingual in German and English. His account is an argument for the assertion that learning two languages need not retard language development.

Several factors enter into the successful rearing of a bilingual child who is fully competent in both tongues. The languages themselves must be bona fide languages, not simple dialects. Each language should be learned from a different source [(Smith, 1939); for example, each parent might communicate with the child in only one of the two languages], since it seems important for the child to become aware, as soon as possible, that the two languages are distinct from one another. Having separate speakers for each tongue is one way of handling this problem. Using the languages at different times or in different contexts might also serve this purpose. Finally, to produce a truly bilingual child, it would seem imperative to maintain situations in which each of the languages must be used. Most bilingual children have bilingual parents; if the parents respond to one language more than the other, the child will gradually cease using the less established one in the interest of communicating with as little effort as necessary. This is another argument for the position taken above, that knowledge of words and of sentence construction is *intrinsically* rewarding, and does not depend entirely on such things as parental reward of correct language behavior.

It has been argued, of late, that black children are handicapped in school for two different reasons associated with language: first, that black language, at least in urban slums and the rural south, differs from middle-class white language in being impoverished in conveying concepts (the *deficit* hypothesis); second, that black and middle-class white languages differ, and, since the teacher talks middle-class white language, the black child is handicapped (the *difference* hypothesis). A recent review of the literature (Williams, 1971) supports the second position more strongly. As Palermo (1972, p. 270) succinctly puts it, "In brief, not only is language fully available to the lower-class Negro child but it is a language at least as capable as that of the middle-class child in dealing with abstract, logically complex, and hypothetical questions." The problems in communication between the black lower-class child and the teacher appear to result from differences in language. While neither language is, *ipso facto,* superior to the other, it would seem likely to be of benefit to the black child to learn standard English, at least so far as success in school is concerned. This probably is best done through the procedures developed by persons who teach English as a second language (e.g., as an alternate to pidgin; to black-ghetto English; as a second language to persons from the non-English speaking world).

Recent Changes

As we have seen, it was believed years ago that in language skills children with many adult and few child associations excelled those with few adult and many child associations, 'and children from lower-economic backgrounds lagged behind children from upper-economic homes. This is no longer entirely so. Signs of decrease in the differences in some of these areas are evident. Templin (1957) noted that children in her study of language development were generally more talkative and used a more mature level and organization of speech than children studied 25 years earlier. Sex differences seemed substantially diminished, and although socioeconomic differences continued to be significant, they had apparently decreased in magnitude.

Television may be a very important factor in this change. It produces a general improvement in the language skill of young children at the same time that it narrows the variations between children exposed to different environmental circumstances. Two of the most intensive studies of television's impact on the child (Himmelweit, Oppenheim, & Vince, 1958; Schramm, Lyle, & Parker, 1961) agree that television increases the information —and presumably, the vocabulary—of all children, but that children of lesser ability and from lower-economic backgrounds receive more benefit for a longer time. Although television does narrow the differences in the way of life between families of separate regions and classes, it has not been able to eliminate individual differences between children in areas so influenced by environment as language.

Language in the Disadvantaged Child

Social-class differences in children's language have long been recognized.[2] In McCarthy's (1930) study, consistent differences were found in favor of upper-social-class children in terms of general language maturity. Similar findings were obtained by Templin (1957) in a replication of the McCarthy study. Again, lower-class children performed less well on nearly all of the language measures used, including accuracy of articulation, speech sound discrimination, vocabulary, and amount of verbalization. These social-class differences apparently emerge, or are apparent, by the end of the second year of life (Irwin, 1948b, c).

A number of factors have been described to account for social-class differences in language development. Less verbal interaction between parent and child occurs in the lower-class as compared with the middle-class home. Lower-class parents do not encourage verbalization and they do not stimulate the child linguistically by reading to him, discussing events with him, or reasoning with him. Further, the parents themselves are handicapped linguistically, and thus provide poor speech models for the child. In a study of maternal language in four social-class levels (Hess & Shipman, 1965), taped samples of the mothers' language were analyzed on a number of different measures. The total amount of verbal output was found to be greater for the middle-class as compared with the lower-class mothers. With respect to quality of the language used, middle-class mothers were more likely to use abstract words and they used more complex sentences.

Martin Deutsch (1963) has argued that a lower-class child is handicapped by a general restriction in the variety of stimulation to which he is exposed. This is true in language as well as in other areas (M. Deutsch, 1964). Further, the "signal-to-noise ratio" may be very low in a crowded lower-class home. Although there is a great deal of language (television, yelling, etc.), the young child has difficulty sorting out of this "noise" meaningful language, which, indeed, is seldom directed specifically to him. Moreover, John and Goldstein (1964) maintain that language development is retarded if it is learned only through receptive exposure (hearing). Corrective feedback in which the parent expands the child's utterance and corrects word usage is extremely important. Thus when the child says, "Johnny eat," the parent responds, "Yes, Johnny is eating his lunch." This provides the child with additional information regarding sentence structure, verb form, and vocabulary.

In an analysis of social-class differences in language usage, Bernstein (1961) has identified two styles of communication: *restricted* and *elaborated.* Working-class speech is characterized by a restricted style that is stereotyped and condensed; it is lacking in precision and composed of clichés that are readily understood by the listener. Elaborated style, employed by the better-educated middle class, is more specific, precise, individualized, and flexible. Bernstein's approach views language as part of larger social behavior in terms of organizing and structuring experience. The lower-class child exposed

[2]For a review of social-class differences in language development, see Cazden, 1966. Subcultural differences in child language: An inter-disciplinary review. *Merrill-Palmer Quarterly,* 1966, **12**, 185–219.

to limited and restricted language usage is handicapped in his ability to deal with his environment at an abstract and conceptual level.

The lower-class child has been found to be handicapped in auditory discrimination of speech sounds, which is related to reading ability (C. Deutsch, 1964). The important role played by language in concept formation, problem solving, and in communication of ideas is apparent. It is not surprising, therefore, to find the lower-class child retarded in the various skills required for school success. This strongly suggests that a remedial program for the disadvantaged child must place great emphasis on the language area.

The structured-language approach developed by Bereiter and Englemann (1966) is designed to facilitate in the disadvantaged child the acquisition of knowledge concerning pronunciation, sentence structure, and vocabulary. The learning of polar opposites, prepositions, connectives, and classes or categories of objects is stressed. While the social-emotional aspects of language are important, the disadvantaged child is most deficient in the use of language as a cognitive tool—a tool required for logical thinking.

In summary, the early concern with describing social-class differences in language development has given way to attempts to identify the reasons for such differences. In turn, remedial programs have been developed, based upon a careful analysis of the significant aspects of language required for conceptual thinking.

THE IMPACT OF LANGUAGE ON THOUGHT, LEARNING, AND MEMORY

Language and Thought

Many of the early psychologists conceived of thought as a stream of mental images. To understand the thought process, they believed, one had to look inward, to *introspect*, to discern this flow of images. The "Würzburg school" of psychologists (see Humphrey, 1951, pp. 30–131) demonstrated, however, that thought could occur without any conscious awareness of imagery. As a result, the Würzburgers and descendants of the imagery school of thought, led by Titchener, emphasized the relation of muscle tensions and other kinesthetic- proprioceptive responses to thought. This idea, that thought is primarily a set of motor behaviors, was brought to fruition by Watson (1914), who believed that human thought was nothing but subvocal speech. It was at this point that language reached its peak as an explanatory device: to many psychologists of this era language was not merely associated with thought, it *was* thought.

This view is not without support. Young children do speak without the intent of communicating to others and appear to be overtly verbalizing their thoughts, just as adults may covertly verbalize them. This observable phenomenon is the basis of Piaget's (1926) notion of children's egocentric speech—speech not based on the idea of social communication. Even as adults, people "think out loud," talking to themselves especially when confronted with complicated problems. Further, lip, tongue, and laryngeal movement increases among individuals as they silently solve problems of an increasing challenge (Jacobson, 1932). Yet despite this supporting evidence, the notion that language and thought are synonymous is generally rejected. It seems more likely that the movement of lip, tongue, and larynx accompanying thought are incidental consequences having no more significance than the snapping of fingers or the scratching of the head has when attempting to recollect a forgotten event. Several studies, beginning with Thorson's (1925), suggest that the motor accompaniments of thought are a nervous discharge rather than necessary substrata of thought. Although not synonymous with thought, language seems to be intimately related to learning and memory, as we shall discover in the remainder of this chapter.

Language and Learning

The relation of language to learning was mentioned in Chapter 4. There we said that language benefited learning by allowing a higher degree of—and more rapid—vicarious trial-and-error than occurred in other species. Language facilitates the formation of concrete concepts, providing a common name—for example, spoon—to link together a class of objects with a variety of physical characteristics despite their external variations. Because verbal terms are available, they govern the dimensions along which categories form and set the limits for the generalizing of stimuli. This leads to concept formation. Moreover, language enables the formation of abstract concepts as well.

Words and Memory. Although memory exists without language, language evidently facilitates memory. To use James's term, language provides "fish hooks." As James wrote before the turn of the century,

> In mental terms, *the more facts a fact is associated with in the mind, the better possession of it our memory retains.* Each of its associates becomes a hook to which it hangs, a means to fish it up by when sunk beneath the surface. Together, they form a network of attachments by which it is woven into the entire tissue of our thought (James, 1892, p. 294).

The more fish hooks or associations a word or an event has, the more likely it is to be recalled. Thus as the child's vocabulary grows, learning and retention increase. In view of this, children's textbooks are written with a concern for word frequency. Words are selected from those most frequently used in the English language for two reasons. First, if they occur often enough it is assumed that they have many associations and can thus be learned more readily. Second, once learned, they will be met often in the future and have a greater positive transfer value. Although word frequency and the number of associations evoked by words are correlated, there are many low-frequency words, such as *zoo* or *circus,* with many associations and many high-frequency words, like *the, when,* or *where,* that awaken few associations. Johnson, Frincke, and Martin (1961) have suggested that the choice of words for textbooks might better be based on a large number of associations rather than on word frequency per se, as is now done.

Words vary in the number of associations they evoke. Developmental differences exist as well. As children gain in vocabulary, more "fish hooks" come into existence. Further, the kind of "fish hooks," that is, the kind of associative net, changes with age. In word-association tests, the subject is presented with a stimulus word such as "table" and then responds with the first word he thinks of when he hears "table." Adults most frequently respond with "chair." Children show far less agreement in their associations than do adults, and also differ from adults in the class of associations that they make. For example, at grade 4 or 6, a child presented with the word "robin" would be more likely than would an adult to say "bird"—a superordinate class to which robins belong—while the adult would be more likely than the child to say "worm," a contrast or opposite association (Palermo, 1965). Both number and kind of associations change with age. Part of the variance in rates of learning and in memory between age groups may be due, basically, to differences in association. Thus, although language is not thought, as was once believed, it is closely linked with both learning and memory.

SUMMARY

Humans are a noisy bunch. Infants make many sounds and make them often. From their sound-making activity emerges language. Sound making becomes emotionally rewarding to the infant, thus increasing the amount of vocalization. Parents selectively reward or reinforce the sounds that are like those of words, thus causing the frequency of certain sounds to increase even more. Certain sounds come to have mutual meaning for the infant and the parent; at this point sound making has become symbolic communication.

Vocabulary growth is slow for a time, and then shows rapid increase at about age three–four. The child learns, beginning at about age two, to construct sentences. These sentences become longer and more grammatically correct as age and abilities associated with age, such as short-term memory, increase. The child learns the ground rules of communication. By about age four, errors in word usage result from the failure of the English language to follow the rules very closely.

Wide individual differences in communicative skills, especially vocabulary, have been shown to exist between children. The sex of the child, his family's size, his parents' occupational and educational levels, the number of languages spoken in the home, and parental attitudes toward their children's speech are among the factors associated with individual differences. Since IQ, on most intelligence tests, depends largely on language ability, children from lower-occupational groups and large families may be unfairly handicapped on such tests. Some presumed handicaps to adequate language development, such as bilingualism, may have been greatly exaggerated in their influence. Apparently increasing homogeneity of the environment is decreasing the individual differences between children in rate of language development.

Although it was once held that the entire thought process was merely subvocal speech, this view is not supported by the majority of research findings. Language does seem to alter and enhance learning and to strengthen memory. All said and done, language is the uniquely human characteristic that sets humanity apart from all other organisms.

REFERENCES

Bellugi, U. The development of interrogative structures in children's speech. In K. Riegel (Ed.), *The development of language functions.* Ann Arbor, Michigan: University of Michigan Center for Human Growth and Development, 1965. Pp. 103–137.

Bereiter, C., & Englemann, S. *Teaching disadvantaged children in the preschool.* Englewood Cliffs, N.J.: Prentice-Hall, 1966.

Berko, J. The child's learning of English morphology. *Word,* 1958, **14**, 150–177.

Bernstein, B. Language and social class. *British Journal of Sociology,* 1961, **11**, 271–276.

Blatz, W. E., et al. *Collected studies on the Dionne quintuplets.* Toronto: University of Toronto Press, 1937.

Brown, R. *Social psychology.* New York: Free Press, 1965.

Brown, R., & Fraser, C. The acquisition of syntax. In U. Bellugi & R. Brown (Eds.), The acquisition of language. *Monographs of the Society for Research in Child Development,* 1964, **29**, Serial No. 92, No. 1, 43–79.

Bühler, C. *Kindheit and Jugend.* (3rd ed.) Leipzig: Hirzel, 1931.

Butterfield, E. C. An extended version of modification of sucking with auditory feedback. Working paper No. 43, Bureau of Child Research Laboratory, University of Kansas Medical Center, October, 1968.

Cazden, C. Subcultural differences in child language: An inter-disciplinary view. *Merrill–Palmer Quarterly,* 1966, **12**, 185–219.

Chomsky, N. Review of B. F. Skinner, *Verbal Behavior. Language,* 1959, **35**, 26–58.

Cowan, P. A., Weber, J., Hoddinott, B. A., & Klein, T. Mean length of a spoken response as a function of stimulus, experimenter, and subject. *Child Development,* 1967, **38**, 191–203.

Davis, E. A. The development of linguistic skill in twins, singletons with siblings, and only children from age five to ten years. Minneapolis: University of Minnesota Press, *Institute of Child Welfare Series,* No. 14, 1937.

Dawe, H. C. A study of the effect of an educational program upon language development and related mental functions in young children. *Journal of Experimental Education,* 1942, **2**, 200–209.

Deutsch, C. Auditory discrimination and learning: Social factors. *Merrill–Palmer Quarterly,* 1964, **10**, 277–296.

Deutsch, M. The disadvantaged child and the learning process. In A. H. Passow (Ed.), *Education in depressed areas.* New York: Bureau of Publication, Teachers College, 1963. Pp. 163–179.

Deutsch, M. Facilitating development in the pre-school child: Social and psychological perspectives. *Merrill–Palmer Quarterly,* 1964, **10**, 249–263.

Eisenberg, R., Griffin, E., Coursin, D., & Hunter, A. Auditory behavior in the human neonate: A preliminary report. *Journal of Speech and Hearing Research,* 1964, **7**, 245–269.

Ervin, S. M. Imitation and structural change in children's language. In E. H. Lenneberg (Ed.), *New directions in the study of language.* Cambridge, Mass.: M.I.T. Press, 1964. Pp. 163–189.

Forster, K. I. Left to right processes in the construction of sentences. *Journal of Verbal Learning and Verbal Behavior*, 1966, **5**, 285–291.

Friedlander, B. Receptive language development in infancy. *Merrill–Palmer Quarterly,* 1970, **16**, 7–51.

Haggerty, A. D. The effects of long term hospitalization or institutionalization upon the language development of children. *Journal of Genetic Psychology,* 1959, **94**, 205–209.

Hess, R., & Shipman, V. Early experience and socialization of cognitive modes in children. *Child Development,* 1965, **36**, 869–866.

Himmelweit, H. T., Oppenheim, A. N., & Vince, P. *Television and the child.* London: Oxford University Press, 1958.

Howard, R. *A developmental study of triplets.* Unpublished doctoral dissertation, University of Minnesota, 1934.

Humphrey, G. *Thinking*. London: Methuen, 1951.

Irwin, O. C. The developmental status of speech sounds of ten feeble-minded children. *Child Development,* 1942, **13**, 29–39.

Irwin, O. C. Infant speech: Consonantal sounds according to place of articulation. *Journal of Speech and Hearing Disorders,* 1947, **12**, 391–401. (a)

Irwin, O. C. Infant speech: Consonantal sounds according to manner of articulation. *Journal of Speech and Hearing Disorders,* 1947, **12**, 402–404. (b)

Irwin, O. C. Infant speech: Development of vowel sounds. *Journal of Speech and Hearing Disorders,* 1948, **13**, 31–34. (a)

Irwin, O. C. Infant speech: The effect of family occupational status and of age on use of speech sounds. *Journal of Speech and Hearing Disorders,* 1948, **13**, 224–226. (b)

Irwin, O. C. Infant speech: The effect of family occupational status and of age on sound frequency. *Journal of Speech and Hearing Disorders,* 1948, **13**, 320–323. (c)

Irwin, O. C., & Chen, H. P. Infant speech: Vowel and consonant frequency. *Journal of Speech and Hearing Disorders,* 1949, **II**, 123–125.

Jacobson, E. Electrophysiology of mental activities. *American Journal of Psychology,* 1932, **44**, 677–694.

James, W. *Psychology: briefer course.* New York: Holt, 1892.

Jersild, A. T., & Ritzman, R. Aspects of language development: The growth of loquacity and vocabulary. *Child Development,* 1938, **9**, 243–259.

John, V., & Goldstein, L. The social context of language acquisition. *Merrill–Palmer Quarterly,* 1964, **10**, 265–275.

Johnson, R. C., Frincke, G., & Martin, L. Meaningfulness, frequency, and affective character of words as related to visual duration threshold. *Canadian Journal of Psychology,* 1961, **15**, 199–204.

Lenneberg, E. H. The natural history of language. In F. Smith & G. A. Miller (Eds.), *The genesis of language.* Cambridge, Mass.: M.I.T. Press, 1966. Pp. 219–252.

Leopold, W. F. *Speech development of a bilingual child,* Vols. I–IV, Evanston, Ill.: Northwestern University Press, 1937–1949.

Lewis, M. M. *How children learn to speak.* New York: Basic Books, 1959.

Lorenz, K. *King Solomon's Ring.* New York: Crowell, 1952.

McCarthy, D. *The language development of the preschool child.* Institute of Child Welfare Monographs Series, 4. Minneapolis: University of Minn. Press, 1930.

McCarthy, D. Language development in children. In L. Carmichael (Ed.), *Manual of child psychology.* (2nd ed.) New York: Wiley, 1946.

McNeill, D. Speaking of space. *Science,* 1966, **152**, 875–880.

Miller, G. A. The magic number seven, plus or minus two: Some limits on our capacity for processing information. *Psychological Review,* 1956, **63**, 81–97.

Miller, N. E., & Dollard, J. *Social learning and imitation.* New Haven: Yale University Press, 1941.

Moffitt, A. Consonant cue perception by twenty- to twenty-four-week-old infants. *Child Development,* 1971, **42**, 717–731.

Mowrer, O. II. *Learning theory and personality dynamics.* New York: Ronald, 1950.

Palermo, D. S. Word associations as related to children's verbal habits. In K. Riegel (Ed.), *The development of language functions.* Ann Arbor,

Michigan: University of Michigan Center for Human Growth and Development, 1965. Pp. 53–64.

Palermo, D. S. Review of "Language and poverty." *Science,* 1972, **176**, 270–271.

Palermo, D. S., & Eberhardt, V. L. On the learning of morphological rules: An experimental analogy. *Journal of Verbal Learning and Verbal Behavior,* 1968, **7**, 337–344.

Piaget, J. *The language and thought of the child.* New York: Harcourt, Brace, 1926.

Pringle, M. L., & Bossio, V. A study of deprived children. II. Language development and reading attainment. *Vita Humana,* 1958, **I**, 142–170.

Schramm, W. L., Lyle, J., & Parker, E. B. *Television in the lives of our children.* Stanford, Calif.: Stanford University Press, 1961.

Shirley, M. M. *The first two years of life: A study of twenty-five babies,* Vols. I and II. Minneapolis: University of Minnesota Press, *Institute of Child Welfare Monographs Series,* No. 7, 1933.

Skeels, H. M., Updegraff, R., Wellman, B. L. & Williams, H. M. A study of environmental stimulation: An orphanage preschool project. *University of Iowa Study in Child Welfare,* 1938, **15**, No. 4.

Skinner, B. F. *Verbal behavior.* New York: Appleton-Century-Crofts, 1957.

Slobin, D. I. Acquisition of Russian as a native language. In F. Smith & G. A. Miller (Eds.), *The genesis of language.* Cambridge, Mass.: M.I.T. Press, 1966. Pp. 129–148.

Slobin, D. I. Cognitive prerequisites to grammatical development in children. Paper presented to Merrill-Palmer Conference on Research and Teaching of Infant Development, Detroit, 1972.

Slobin, D. I., & Welsh, C. Elicited imitation as a research tool in developmental psycholinguistics. Unpublished manuscript, Department of Psychology, University of California, Berkeley, 1967.

Smith, M. E. An investigation of the development of the sentence and the extent of vocabulary in young children. *University of Iowa Study in Child Welfare,* 1926, **3**, No. 5.

Smith, M. E. Some light on the problem of bilingualism as found from a study of the progress in mastery of English among preschool children of non-American ancestry in Hawaii. *Genetic Psychology Monographs,* 1939, **21**, 121–284.

Templin, M. C. *Certain language skills in children: Their development and interrelationships.* Minneapolis: University of Minnesota Press, 1957.

Terman, L. M., et al. *Genetic studies of genius: Vol. I. Mental and physical traits of a thousand gifted children.* Stanford, Calif.: Stanford University Press, 1925.

Thorson, A. M. The relation of tongue movements to internal speech. *Journal of Experimental Psychology,* 1925, **8**, 1–32.

Tinbergen, N. *Social behavior in animals.* New York: Wiley, 1953.

Weir, R. H. *Language in the crib.* The Hague: Mouton, 1962.

Williams, R. (Ed.) *Language and poverty.* Chicago: Markham, 1971.

Yerkes, R. M., & Learned, B. *Chimpanzee intelligence and its vocal expression.* Baltimore: Williams & Wilkins, 1925.

Yngve, V. H. A model and a hypothesis for language structure. *Proceedings of the American Philosophical Society,* 1960. **104**, 444–466.

chapter 6

intelligence

chapter 6

intelligence

chapter 6

intelligence

Certainly one of the most basic factors in human development is intelligence. Although intelligence is intimately related to both learning and language, psychologists are still of two minds as to whether it is a single trait of the individual or the sum of many abilities to cope with all sorts of situations. This chapter deals with intelligence from various vantage points. It beings with a review of various definitions of intelligence and ideas about its nature, then considers the growth of intellectual ability, the constancy of that ability, and the relation of individual differences in intelligence, as it is ordinarily measured, to learning capacities and social skills. Specific intelligence tests are noted here only as they pertain to the topics under examination. A more comprehensive discussion of them has been reserved for Chapter 14, which treats individual appraisal.

DEFINITIONS

In the first useful intelligence test (see Binet & Simon, 1916), Binet maintained that intelligence consisted of comprehension, invention, direction, and censorship. This definition contains several interesting elements. One interesting aspect of Binet's definition is its inclusion of direction; this is really a measure of purposiveness and perseverance rather than ability. Also, Binet includes censorship, that is, self-censorship; this is an aspect of intelligence not included in any other definition, yet is clearly one of considerable significance.

In designating invention as a mark of intellectual ability, Binet foreshadowed Guilford (1950, 1959), who emphasized creativity in his definition of intelligence. Because of this position, Guilford has expressed dissatisfaction with conventional intelligence tests, developing in his own research tests of divergent thinking that he believes allow the prediction of creativity more than conventional intelligence tests, which measure "convergent" thinking for the most part.

Another who attacked such conventional tests was Cattell (1957), who held that there were two types of intelligence, which he labeled *fluid* and *crystallized.* Fluid intelligence solves novel or "culture-free" problems; it is the more general of the two types and is largely innate. Any decline in fluid ability from, say, brain injury will influence a wide variety of intelligence-test scores. Crystallized intelligence, on the other hand, is seen in acquired, complex, familiar cultural activities and skills—for example, reading or mathematics; it is composed of quite specific factors, such as verbal fluency and mechanical ability, and is dependent largely on environmental forces. For the most part, conventional intelligence tests measure crystallized intelligence while neglecting the fluid kind of ability most closely allied with the creative talent stressed by Guilford. Studies of the nature of crystallized and fluid intelligence are discussed later in this chapter.

A distinction similar to Cattell's had been made earlier by Hebb (1949, pp. 294–303). In Hebb's view, intelligence tests tapped far more than they should, namely, those aspects of intelligence influenced substantially by forces in the environment. Even if one does not agree completely with Hebb and Cattell on the role of environment in conventional intelligence-test scores, he must concede that such tests leave much to be desired as instruments for measuring high levels of intellectual ability, such as skills in solving problems and creativity.

How one defines intelligence determines and is determined by the kind of behavior he wishes to tap by intelligence tests and also his satisfaction with the testing apparatuses available. Porteus

(1941, 1959, 1965) waged a long and lonely fight to emphasize planfulness, the capacity to use a long-term perspective, as a measure of ability. Another view (Goddard, 1946) defined intelligence as the amount of experience available for the solution of immediate problems and the anticipation of future ones. Addressing a seminar, John E. Anderson, long the director of the Institute of Child Welfare at the University of Minnesota, once said he believed that intelligence could be defined as the ability to maintain a high level of response under stress. This definition may be synonymous with another based on the maintenance of an optimal level of arousal in the face of variations in the environment. Finally, the one definition of intelligence that has had the most influence on intelligence-test construction, although it may not be the most adequate definition, was Terman's (1916), which said that intelligence was the individual's capacity to think abstractly and use abstract symbols.

Since Terman and his associates produced all of the more widely accepted revisions of the Binet test, which have received extensive use both as a test and as a criterion for other tests, Terman's definition has had a marked impact on test construction and on theories about the nature of intelligence. Perhaps most conventional intelligence tests measure too much verbal but too little performance ability, too much crystallized but too little fluid intelligence, and too much abstract material slanted to the middle class. This essentially results from the pervasive influence of Terman's belief that intelligence consists of the talent to deal with abstract symbols, which is another way of saying verbal skill. One thing that may be said on behalf of Terman's definition is that the sort of facility he wished to measure was apparently the kind of intelligence most closely correlated with success in formal academic undertakings. Although Terman's definition did not lead to the construction of a test that could measure with accuracy such personal characteristics as perseverance, planfulness, and creativity, it did give rise to a device apparently well suited to its most frequent task, that of predicting success in academic endeavors.

It should be noted that whether viewed in terms of one (IQ), two (verbal and performance IQs), or more (factor scores; see immediately below) measures, "intelligence," as defined herein, has to do chiefly with how one scores on various measuring devices. These measures certainly are not the ultimate measures, in terms of excellence, so far as determining how people organize their perceptual world and respond to it.

Nature of Intelligence

Quite special in their approach to the nature of intelligence are the factor analysts. Factor analysis is a technique for determining the number of basically unrelated capacities that by their total impact produce individual differences in some observable characteristic. For example, athletic ability seems to depend on three unrelated factors—weight, intelligence, and reaction time. The relation of each of these to athletic success differs with the sport concerned. Weight would be expected to count in success as a football tackle but would be negatively related to prowess at ping pong. However, a major part of the variance between individuals in any type of athletic competition could be explained if measures of each of these three factors were available for every competitor.

The scientist seeking to measure the factors that constitute intelligence is in a much more difficult position. No simple, directly observable criterion exists for intelligence as for athletic success. In fact, if Cattell, Hebb, and others are correct in their analysis, there appears to be more than one kind of intelligence. In the view of Spearman (1904), there seems to be a *g* or general factor present in all forms of intellectual behavior. His conclusions were based on students' examination scores in such things as classics and mathematics, on rated capacities—that is, on cleverness and common sense—and on responses in laboratory tasks such as weight discrimination. As he put it: "All branches of intellectual activity have in common one fundamental function." Yet promptly after this statement Spearman noted that the "one fundamental function" might actually consist of a group of functions. His data, discussed in both his 1904 and 1927 studies, suggested, in addition to the *g* factor, the presence of specific or *s* factors whose importance varied from subject area to subject area, with *s* factors being of least significance in the study of the classics and of highest significance in musical accomplishment.

The findings of other factor analysts who have studied intelligence have depended largely on the tests used to measure intelligence. The Binet test, a conglomeration of diverse test items with an emphasis on verbal skills, implies that intelligence is composed of a *g* factor plus certain *s* factors, especially *v* or verbal ability (McNemar, 1942). The Wechsler Intelligence Scale for Children (WISC) measures both verbal and performance capacity and consists of fewer and more disparate test items. Probably because of this difference in structure, a different set of factors emerges, with *g* having much less significance (Digman, 1962).

Since the results of factorial studies are conditioned, to a considerable extent, by the instruments used to acquire the raw data, current views may be outmoded by the emergence of a new and radically different test of ability. At the time of this writing, the long-term trend seems to depart clearly from the emphasis on *g* toward a belief that intelligence comprises a large number of distinct factors, facets, or dimensions (Guilford, 1956; Humphreys, 1962; Thurstone, 1946). What Thurstone (1946) called the "primary mental abilities" are: S (space), N (number), V (verbal comprehension), W (word fluency), and M (memory), in addition to induction, deduction, flexibility, and speed of closure. Others have posited a different number of factors, perhaps containing the same elements designated by different names. Indeed, the great number of rather specific factors discovered since Spearman's time leads to a far different notion of intelligence than might be obtained from a thorough-going acceptance of his *g*.

Factor analytic studies of young children, and of retarded individuals (Meyers, Dingman, Orpet, Sitkei, & Watts, 1964) show essentially the same factors to be present from mental age two to six, though their emergence is not as full at two as it is at six. Other studies suggest that the number and type of factors found from middle childhood on through to adulthood are remarkably similar. These data also suggest that the organization of intellectual factors is relatively constant across the developmental span, but that the factors become more distinct and independent with increasing age.

In the same line of factor analytic approach, the constituent elements of crystallized and fluid intelligence have been determined by Horn and Cattell (Horn & Cattell, 1966a, 1966b, 1967). Although the same types of ability (e.g., perceiving relations, educing correlates) seem to be involved in both types of intelligence, differences (1) in amount of pretraining involved in fluid versus crystallized tasks (Horn & Cattell, 1966b);

(2) in age trends in ability (Horn & Cattell, 1966a, 1967); (3) in the importance of visualization skills (Horn, 1968), with fluid intelligence being closely associated with imagery [this last finding bodes ill for the social sciences, including psychology, since social scientists are notoriously deficient in visual imagery (Roe, 1951)], all indicate that these two types of intelligence are clearly distinct from one another.

Those who believe that intelligence is composed of many separate and unrelated specific factors should also believe that most individuals are good at *something* and can be greatly benefited vocationally if the area in which they manifest high ability is exploited. On the other hand, those who consider intelligence as consisting largely of a *g* factor would expect individuals to show a good deal of consistency in their level of functioning in many widely diverse areas of behavior. They would look for "common level traits"—that is, the individual who is academically able should also score high in such other areas as social and mechanical intelligence. Since there seems to be evidence for believing in at least a moderate amount of similarity in performance across a wide array of intellectual domains [e.g., the high-level performance of individual members of Terman's (1925; Terman & Oden, 1947, 1959) gifted group in diverse areas of behavior] the authors of this book are inclined to believe that a fairly strong *g* factor is present. Nevertheless, the variability in performance of different types of activity is certainly great enough to suggest that highly specific factors also exist. The whole of vocational and academic counseling rests on the premise that any individual has areas of relative strength and relative weakness; that is, that there are specific factors present. Intelligence, as usually measured, seems to consist of a moderately strong *g* factor and a number of specific factors. There seems also to be another *g* factor, usually not adequately measured at present, that taps fluid intelligence.

Piaget's Theory of Cognitive Development

As already discussed in Chapter 4 one of the most comprehensive theories of children's cognitive development is that by Jean Piaget, a Swiss psychologist.[1] Stemming from his original work and interest in biology (his first paper dealing with the albino sparrow was published when he was 11 years old), he has adapted many of the terms and concepts of biology in his explanations of intellectual growth: structure, adaptation, equilibrium, and many others. Piaget views intelligence as a type of biological adaptation to the environment which enables an individual to deal effectively with environmental demands. Two major processes are used to describe the individual's approach to coping with the environment. *Assimilation* involves the organism incorporating into its existing mental framework new elements from its environment. *Accomodation* involves a modification of existing mental structures to fit new perceptions of the environment. The following example will illustrate these two complementary processes:

> Suppose an infant of 4 months is presented with a rattle. He has never before had the opportunity to play with rattles or similar toys. The rattle, then, is a feature of the environment to which he needs to adapt. His subsequent behavior reveals the tendencies of assimilation and accommodation. The infant tries to grasp the rattle. In order to do this successfully he

[1]See footnote on page 163.

> must accommodate in more ways than are immediately apparent. First, he must accommodate his visual activities to perceive the rattle correctly; then he must reach out and accommodate his movements to the distance between himself and the rattle; in grasping the rattle he must adjust his fingers to its shape; in lifting the rattle he must accommodate his muscular exertion to its weight. In sum, the grasping of the rattle involves a series of acts of accommodation, or modification of the infant's behavioral structures to suit the demands of the environment.
>
> Grasping the rattle also involves assimilation. In the past the infant has already grasped things; for him, grasping is a well-formed structure of behavior. When he sees the rattle for the first time he tries to deal with the novel object by incorporating it into a habitual pattern of behavior. In a sense he tries to transform the novel object into something that he is familiar with; namely, a thing to be grasped. We can say, therefore, that he assimilates the object into his framework. (Ginsburg & Opper, 1969, p. 19)

Four major periods are described in Piaget's theory of intellectual development: sensorimotor (birth to 2 years); preoperational (2 to 7 years); concrete operational (7 to 11 years); and formal operational (11 years and above). Each of these will be discussed in turn.

Sensorimotor. Initially the infant possesses a number of built-in reflexes. These may be viewed as organized patterns of behavior which enable the infant to act upon and interact with his environment. Thus, for example, sucking movements will be made when any object touches the lips. Additionally, the infant will spend a great deal of time looking at objects in his environment; this clearly serves an adaptive function. These simple patterns of behavior are called *schemas*. According to Piaget, an important aspect of intellectual development is the tying together of various schemas, permitting the individual to deal in an increasingly effective manner with his environment.

Following the early reflexive period, the infant tends to repeat behaviors which have produced certain results. Piaget calls this *primary circular reaction*. For example, the young infant exhibits sucking movements in the absence of any object on which he can suck since such behavior has, in the past, provided him with nourishment. Subsequently, the infant directs behavior toward objects and events in the environment and, through manipulating objects and observing the result, he develops a sense of "cause-and-effect" or "means-ends relationships." Ultimately during this period the infant begins to experiment with new ways to solve problems and he shows a high level of curiosity and enjoyment of novelty. Further, as a result of his interaction with the environment, the infant comes to differentiate himself from his environment which marks the beginning of a sense of self. Related to this process in the development of object concept. Bound initially by his immediate sense experiences, the infant is unaware that objects have permanence. Thus when an object disappears from his sight, he makes no attempt to search for it because it no longer exists. Later, he understands that objects have an independent and permanent status separate from his own actions and perceptions. Thus, the infant becomes aware that an object exists even though he cannot see or feel it.

Nearing the end of the sensorimotor period, the beginning of representational thought appears. The infant imitates the behavior of another individual in the absence of that person and after a delay period. This deferred imitation is illustrated by the following behavior:

> At 1;4(3) Jacqueline had a visit from a little boy of 1;6 whom she used to see from time to time, and who, in the course of the afternoon got into a terrible temper. He screamed as he tried to get out of a playpen and pushed it backward, stamping his feet. Jacqueline stood watching him in amazement, never having witnessed such a scene before. The next day, she herself screamed in her playpen and tried to move it, stamping her foot lightly several times in succession. (Piaget, 1951, p. 63)

Preoperational Thought. During this period the child becomes increasingly able to deal with his environment in an abstract or symbolic manner. He is able to visualize solutions to problems rather than solving them through physical manipulation and a trial-and-error approach. However, the child's conceptualizations are still dominated by his immediate perceptions. A clear illustration of this occurs in the case of *conservation,* a term denoting the realization of the invariant nature of objects despite changes in certain features. Consider the following example: a piece of clay is divided into two equal halves. Each is rolled into a ball, with the child agreeing that they are equal in quantity. Then one of the balls is rolled into a long sausage shape and the child is asked whether the two pieces have the same amount. Now he asserts that the long one has more clay because it is longer. The young child does not realize the invariant nature of quantity. Weight, volume, and number are other invariant physical properties which the child in the preoperational period does not comprehend.

Piaget has stressed several other aspects of the child's thought during this period. First, the child's thinking and his point of view is *egocentric,* that is, it is centered about himself. He lacks the kind of perspective which would permit him to view objects and events in the world from another's point of view. His communication does not consider the listener. *Moral realism* also characterizes the thought of the child under the age of seven or eight. This is defined as "the tendency which the child has to regard duty and the value attaching to it as self-subsistent and independent of the mind, as imposing itself regardless of the circumstances in which the individual may find himself" (Piaget, 1948, p. 106). In other words, moral rules are regarded as right in themselves and they are applied in a relatively rigid manner. Moral realism possesses three principal features: (a) Duty is essentially heteronomous. Obedience to adult commands is good, and any act which does not conform to adult rules is bad. (b) Because of the externality of the adult-imposed rules, moral realism demands that the letter rather than the spirit of the law be observed. (c) Objective responsibility, in which an act is evaluated in accordance with its conformity to rules rather than in terms of its motive and in which consequences rather than intentions are stressed, arises from features (a) and (b). According to Piaget, moral realism is due to the conjunction of two series of causes, the spontaneous realism and egocentricity of the thought of the child and the constraint exercised by adults.

Concrete Operational Period. With age, the child's thought becomes increasingly logical. He comes to understand the operations involved in number concepts (e.g., $5 \times 6 = 30$ and $30 \div 5 = 6$). He is able to comprehend hierarchical classification of objects; in other words, objects can be classified into larger broader, and more general categories.

Further, he understands that objects can be classified along various continua, such as length; this is called *seriation*. Because of his comprehension of the nature of the physical properties of objects, the child in this period is aware of *conservation*. Conservation reflects the child's ability to deal with a number of different aspects simultaneously.

In the area of moral judgment and reasoning, objective responsibility is gradually eliminated as the child passes from a status which requires obedience to one characterized by mutual respect and cooperation. Taking intention into account is made possible only when the child is able to go beyond his own immediate point of view; his thinking becomes less absolute and more relativistic in nature and he is able to ascribe motives to other persons' behavior. Around the age of seven-eight years, the child's changing relationship with adults and with his peers is reflected in his moral judgment. Unilateral respect is gradually changing to mutual respect; cooperation is taking the place of constraint; autonomy is replacing heteronomy. Peer solidarity leads to the priority of equality over authority.

In general, during the concrete operational period, the child's thought becomes increasingly logical and coherent; he is able to consider broad categories of objects and events. Further, through changes in his thought processes and in his relations with others, his thought becomes *decentered*—that is, it is freed from a personal or self reference which permits him to consider the points of view of those around him.

Formal Operational Period. In his thought, the adolescent is liberated from the immediate and the concrete. By thinking in abstract terms and by manipulating abstract symbols, he is able to solve problems and to reason in an abstract manner. He considers alternative solutions without going through concrete trial-and-error procedures. The adolescent is able to draw logical conclusions from a set of observations. Hypotheses are formed, considered, and substantiated or discarded. Formal operational thought is characterized by adaptability and flexibility. Abstract, theoretical, and philosophical matters are considered, partly because the adolescent discovers his ability to deal with these. Contradictions in the world can be dealt with and resolved, at least in the sense of arriving at a balance or a perspective.

Summary. To summarize briefly, Piaget has outlined a theory of intellectual development, drawing on his earlier interest in biology. He views intelligence as involving a progressively organized and integrated adaptation to the environment which permits an equilibrium between the individual and his environment. This adaptation passes through various stages which result from alterations in the individual's mental structures and in his relations with others. Early sensorimotor functioning gives way to concrete modes of thought which in turn are replaced by abstract thinking. The developmental process involves initially a decentration—that is, the early egocentricity is followed by an ability to take the point of view of others and to view events and objects in a broader perspective. Later, as the child moves from concrete to abstract thinking, he is not bound by his immediate perceptions but is able

[2]The reader is referred to the following two volumes by Piaget: *The origins of intelligence in children* (translated by M. Cook.) New York: International University Press, 1952, and *The construction of reality in the child* (translated by M. Cook). New York: Basic Books, 1954.

to deal with his environment in an abstract manner.

THE CURVE OF INTELLECTUAL GROWTH

Although the nonparent may not recognize it, a one-year-old child has gained tremendously in ability as compared to his capacity at birth. In any year of infancy or early childhood the changes in symbolic and problem-solving skills are profound. Yet we do not expect any marked gain in native wit to occur between the ages of 20 and 21. Casual observation leads to the belief that there are unequal increments in mental growth during various stages of development. This belief is reinforced by the postulation of several possible curves of mental growth.

Many intelligence tests are designed to show that the average person gains one year in mental age for each year of chronological age, usually up through the age of 15. In the 1937 Stanford–Binet test, this curve of mental growth—actually a straight-line function—is a built-in feature. Tests of this kind are constructed to display an equal gain in mentality for each year of gain in chronological age. In the Stanford–Binet, this holds through 15. At that point the growth curve breaks down because no items can be presented beyond 15 to indicate a significant increase with age in percentage of subjects able to pass them. From the structure of the test, therefore, it need not follow that any intellectual growth will take place beyond this age. This particular growth curve is represented by curve A in Figure 6-1.

Thurstone and Ackerson (1929) established, statistically, an absolute zero of intelligence shortly before birth, a point where there is no variation in ability between individuals. By equating mental growth units of various ages, they obtained curve B in Figure 6-1. From this curve, it may be seen that growth is slow at first, but then positively accelerates for about the first 10 years of life. After 10 it slows down and is negatively accelerated by 11. According to Thurstone and Ackerson growth continues at least through 18.

Using data from the Berkeley Growth Study, from studies by Owens (1953), and from Terman's work on intellectual

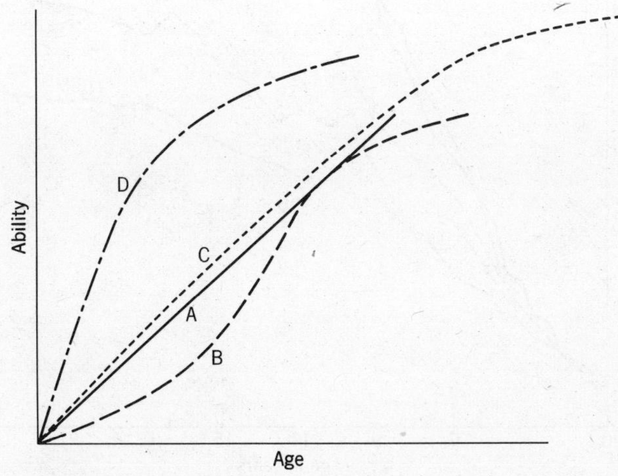

FIGURE 6-1 Hypothetical curves of intellectual growth (see the text for a description of the basis of these curves).

growth during maturity, Bayley (1955) developed curve C. This curve shown intellectual growth to continue at least to age 50. Terman and Oden (1959) indicate this to be true for gifted individuals. Owens (1953) shows it applies to a bright, but not remarkably talented, sample of subjects. And Bradway, Thompson, and Cravens (1958) demonstrate that essentially the same growth curve exists for a random sample of the population.

The final type of mental growth curve is suggested by the work of Gesell (1928) and to an even greater degree by data provided by Goodenough (1954, p. 479). This kind of curve, represented by curve D, implies a far higher proportion of mental growth occurring very early in life than do any of the other curves. Consider the newborn infant, his conceptual skills, and his ability to cope with his environment. Now consider an average adult in the same way. At what point in development does the individual come halfway from the almost "absolute zero" intelligence of the newborn child to the capacities of the adult? Goodenough posed this general question to experts in the field of developmental psychology. The mean age of their responses was three. A fair amount of experience with young children tempts one to agree with Goodenough's view and to believe that curve D most accurately represents mental growth. Bloom (1964), after a thorough review of the literature, reaches essentially the same conclusion as that of Goodenough.

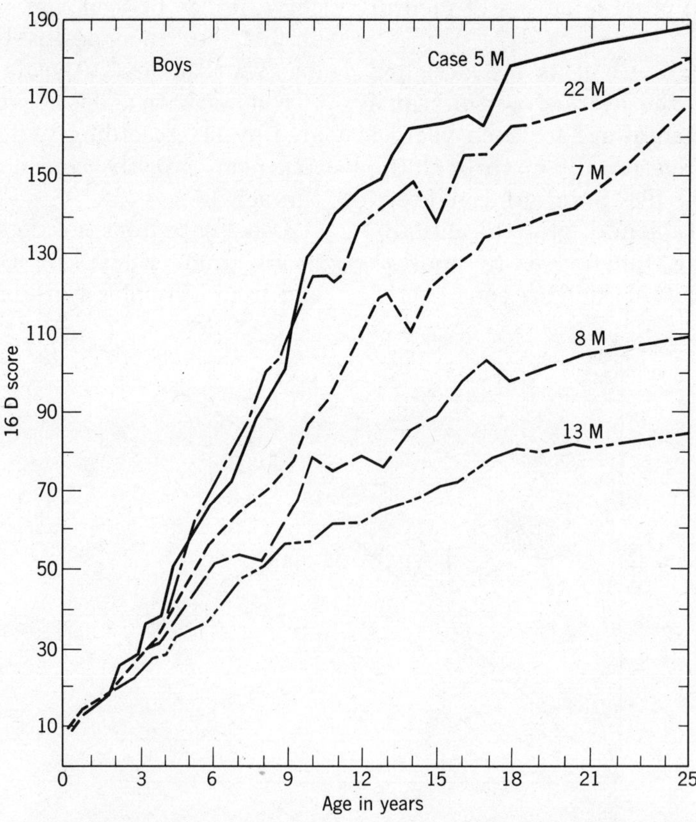

FIGURE 6-2 Individual curves of intelligence (16 D units) for five boys, 1 month to 25 years, Berkeley Growth Study (Bayley, 1955, p. 815).

Individual Differences

The curves of mental growth contained in Figure 6-1 represent various hypotheses on general patterns of intellectual development. In charting the intellectual growth of any single individual, it becomes necessary to switch to his actual intelligence-test scores. For the Stanford-Binet test, the mental growth curve should resemble curve A in Figure 6-1, as the test is designed to show this type of development. However, the variations from this curve are numerous in individual cases, even when using the Stanford-Binet test. Figure 6-2 illustrates this variability.

The figure shows two kinds of variation. First, the differences in ability become increasingly apparent with age. Cases 5M and 13M differ enormously in ability, and since 13M is not too capable, his growth is slow as compared with more intelligent individuals. This should not surprise anyone who believes that individuals vary in ability. Second, there is the irregularity found in the growth curves of specific individuals. For instance, Honzik, McFarlane, and Allen (1948) analyzed the data from the Berkeley Growth Study, from which Bayley also acquired her information, and found that many of the 252 individuals studied longitudinally from shortly after birth through the age of 18 varied widely in intelligence-test scores. Take the extreme case presented in Figure 6-3. Although few young people vary as greatly as this boy, several studies (Honzik et al., 1948; Sontag, Baker, & Nelson,

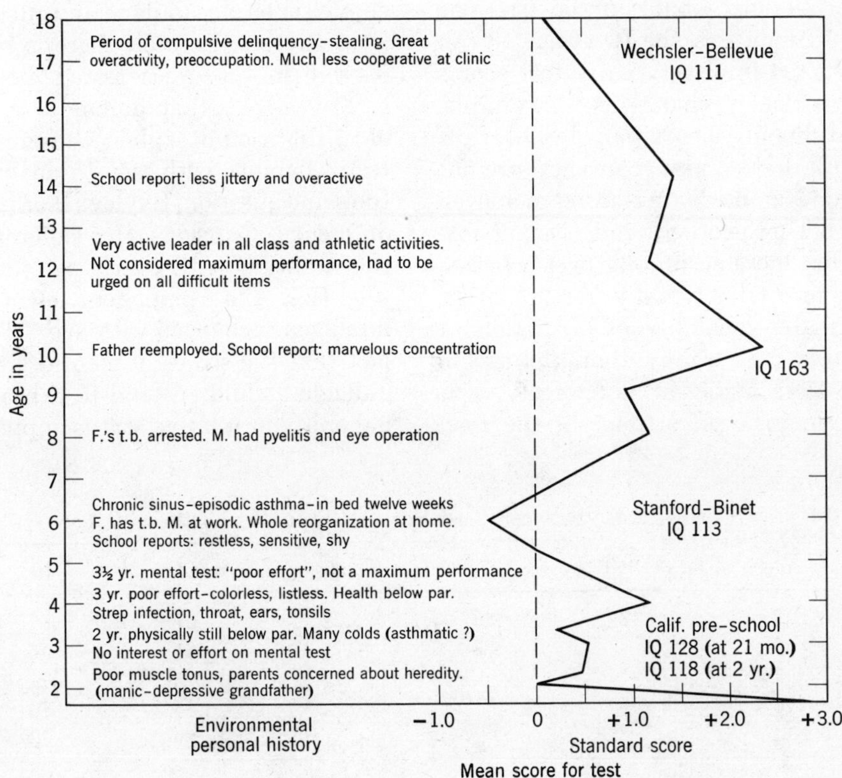

FIGURE 6-3 Variation over time in one subject's intelligence-test scores (Honzik et al., 1948, p. 320).

1958) demonstrate that the *average* amount of deviation from the highest to the lowest scores among children followed from early childhood to early adulthood is at least 15 points. Thus there could be a change in intellectual rank from being fiftieth among 100 to being one of the lowest 25 or the highest 25 in test score.

Table 6-1, adapted from Honzik et al. (1948), shows the amount of variation in individual test scores over a period of time. The table contains correlations between test scores of individuals at different ages. If individual scores remained constant, if each individual maintained the same position in the group from the first to the final test, the correlations would all be +1.00. Were there no connection between an individual's score on one test and his score on any other test, the correlations would all be 0.00. As Table 6-1 indicates, the IQ at age 18 can be predicted from very early test scores no better than by chance, as, for example, by coin flipping: heads he is bright, tails he is dull. Indeed, test scores at 2 are not very good at predicting scores achieved at 5 or 6. On the other hand, it is possible to predict more accurately over a period of time at a later age, say from 14 to 18. This greater reliability of prediction at later ages may signify that ability becomes more stable at later ages, or it simply may be an artifact of the test.

The data in the table disclose that intelligence-test scores vary much more than is commonly supposed. This may be explained in a number of ways. First, the variation may stem from the changing amounts of intellectual enrichment in the child's environment at various times. Differences in enrichment may indeed contribute to the variance, yet even those who most believe that intelligence test scores are influenced by such enrichment probably would not hold that it produces so much variation. Second, Anderson (1939) argued that intelligence tests tapped quite different abilities at different ages and therefore should not be expected to yield identical scores, even if the actual level of ability remained constant. Early tests, for example, contain several sensorimotor items and the Binet tests place greater emphasis on vocabulary and memory as age increases. Because there is far more overlap in the areas tested among 14- to 18-year-olds than among 2- to 6-year-olds, this would explain the increase in test reliability with age. In dealing with the same question, Bayley (1955) reached different conclusions. Her explanation of the variation in IQ over a period of time was that the component elements of intelligence changed with age: "The very fact that the scores of mental growth in individual children tend to exhibit gradual shifts in relative status supports the

TABLE 6-1 Correlations* between Test Scores Obtained at Different Ages

Age	5	7	10	14	18
2	.32	.46	.22	.07	.07
5		.73	.75	.61	.56
7			.77	.73	.71
10				.85	.70
14					.73

*The tests from which these correlations are derived are the California Pre-School Schedule through age five, the Stanford–Binet (Form L) from 7 through 14, and the Wechsler–Bellevue at age 18. (Data from Honzik et al., 1948.)

theory that a changing organization of factors is in process." Is change in intelligence-test score due, then, largely to the changing character of the items in the tests, as Anderson contended, or to the changing character of intelligence, as Bayley said? Pinneau (1961), in analyzing the Berkeley longitudinal data, noted some of both. Part of the variation in test scores results from the characteristics of the test, he concluded, and part from actual changes in intelligence with age.

Honzik et al. (1948) imputed individual deviations in test scores to persisting social and emotional factors. Their findings showed that these factors, when more than mere day-to-day fluctuations in feeling, bore a substantial relation to test-score variation.

Bayley and Schaeffer (1964), again working with the Berkeley data, found that the emotional atmosphere of the home had considerable influence on IQ level in boys, with loving and warm mothering being associated with high ability and maternal hostility being associated with low ability. Girls appear far more influenced by parental ability level. The influence of home atmosphere also is shown in the Fels studies (Baldwin, Kalhorn, & Breese, 1945), which demonstrated that children reared in warm, democratic homes gained eight points in mean IQ over a three-year interval, whereas the mean IQ of children from rejecting, indulgent, and less emotionally gratifying homes either fell or remained constant. Personality factors that appear to be mediated by the home environment also play a considerable role. The children within the Fels sample who showed the most gain in IQ also were more independent, competitive, and "self-initiating" in activities (Sontag, Baker, & Nelson, 1958) and showed higher need for achievement (Kagan, Sontag, Baker, & Nelson, 1958). Far more boys than girls show gains in ability, possibly because independence and achievement are more often valued and rewarded for boys than for girls. It may be that parents, regardless of their own ability and educational level, generally reinforce these traits in boys, but that only parents of relatively high ability and educational attainment reward independence and high achievement motivation in girls. If so, this might explain Bayley's and Schaeffer's finding, noted above, that IQ gain in girls, but not in boys, is most adequately predicted by parental ability, while IQ gain in boys, but not in girls, is predictable from maternal characteristics regarding the use of positive reinforcement that are only minimally related to parental ability and educational level.

Although all these explanations of variation in tested intelligence have some merit, the one regarding social and emotional influences, advanced by Honzik et al. (1948) and supported in various ways by Bayley and Schaeffer and by the Fels studies, apparently accounts for the largest proportion of the IQ changes found in longitudinal studies. Certain hypotheses may be derived from it. If this explanation is correct, changes in tested intelligence should occur in direct proportion to improvements in adjustment resulting from psychotherapy. Furthermore, class differences in tested ability may be narrowed by matching children in adjustment across class lines, since children from various social classes generally differ in adjustment, with those from lower economic groups manifesting a larger number of social and emotional problems.

Generational Differences

Nearly a hundred years ago, Galton was worried. He felt that human ability would decline because the least able members of the population produced the most children. This worry, supported by a fair amount of data (e.g., Maxwell, 1954), persists to the present day. Maxwell has shown that duller individuals have more children; the correlation between IQ and number of children is approximately −0.30.

However, Higgins, Reed, and Reed (1962) demonstrate that in following up the siblings of individuals of varying intellectual ability, there is a higher and higher proportion of childless siblings as one moves down in the ability scale. In other words, a dull individual may have many children, if he has any at all, but his brothers and sisters are less likely to have any children. Once this correction is made, there is a slight positive correlation between IQ and family size. Since people of low ability have a remarkably high death rate (Baller, Charles, & Miller, 1967)—particularly as a result of accidents that might have been avoided with a bit of forethought—the positive correlation between parental IQ and number of offspring who in turn reproduce would undoubtedly be larger if one looked only at those offspring who themselves managed to survive to childbearing age. Bajema (1963) has examined data having to do with this question and found that the reproductive rates of persons of IQ 69–79 is approximately 58 percent of that of persons of above IQ 120. Bajema (1971), in another study, found the reproductive rates shown in Table 6-2, for individuals of differing ability who were subjects in the Third Harvard Growth Study. Galton need not have worried; natural selection, both in terms of individual survival and in terms of mating and having offspring still seems to be at work, and still favors the more able.

TABLE 6-2 Mean Number of Children by IQ Range for 1533 Persons Studied in the Third Harvard Growth Study

IQ Range	Number of Persons	Mean Number of Offspring
120+	206	2.17
105–119	421	2.24
95–104	392	2.14
80–94	420	2.08
79−	94	1.87

Average level of ability, as measured by conventional intelligence tests, is rising as time moves onward (Tuddenham, 1948; Wheeler, 1942), judging from tests of succeeding generations. While some of this gain may be a result of natural selection, it seems almost certain that the most likely explanation for the majority of the gains is that many intelligence tests, assumed to be relatively "culture free," are heavily influenced by educational and cultural factors. American culture has grown so much richer and the term of formal education has been so greatly extended over the last several generations that these forces have raised performance levels.

THE CONSTANCY OF ABILITY

Although an individual's IQ does vary over the long run, the cause of the variance is not yet clear. Some of this may be due to test construction, some to the fact that intelligence tests are not entirely culture free, and some to long-term variations in the emotional healthfulness of the environments of those being tested. But how much can be attributed to a deliberate manipulation of the intellectual richness of the environment? This is the major question and its wide implications have yet to be satisfactorily resolved.

If a rich early environment produces lasting changes in ability, these changes must have some physiological base. Among lower organisms this has been shown to be so. Rats reared in an enriched environment differ in brain chemistry from rats not exposed to the same conditions (Krech, Rosenzweig, & Bennett, 1960). In addition, enrichment produces an increase in brain weight (Rosenzweig, Krech, Bennett, & Diamond, 1962). And as noted in an earlier chapter, enrichment or deprivation by the environment influences the later learning capacities of lower organisms, quite possibly because of the effects of these factors on brain structure and function.

Presumably these findings should apply across species. If enrichment occasions lasting physiological and behavioral change in lower organisms, it should have the same impact on humans. Yet, paradoxically, the evidence suggests something else. Analyses of data pertaining to separated identical twins (Johnson, 1963; Vandenberg & Johnson, 1968), the slight and ephemeral effects of special nursery-school training (see Chapter 12), and the inability of Honzik et al. (1948) to find a discernible consistent relation between amount of environmental enrichment and IQ variation, as well as many other studies, all run counter to the hypothesis.

At least two explanations are possible for the differing results of research on humans and subhumans. To begin with, laboratory rats reared in cages are far more severely deprived than even the most deprived humans. Thus, by starting from a far lower base, the effects of enrighment may be much more apparent for subhumans. Put another way, the influence of enrichment among humans within the normal range of environmental variation may not be enough to produce an appreciable change in IQ. The nursery-school studies noted above were studies of middle-class children, for the most part. Since these children had been exposed to the "built-in curriculum" of the middle-class home, it is not surprising that gains were relatively slight. As noted in Chapter 12, it may well be that starting from a lower base—that is, from a more deprived environment—the beneficial effects of environmental stimulation may become more sizable and more apparent. Skeel's (1966) follow-up study of the later careers of individuals reared under conditions of deprivation (orphanage) or of relative stimulation (lovingly cared for by older retardants) appears to support the position that performance can be changed by enrichment, so long as one is dealing with truly deprived youngsters.

The second explanation maintains that bright and dull organisms differ more pronouncedly in learning ability when learning is *massed*, that is, when learning events follow one another in rapid succession, than when learning is *distributed*, when there is a longer interval of time between them. This applies alike to rats (Jennings, 1960; McGaugh, 1961; McGaugh, Westbrook, & Burt, 1961) and children (Madsen, 1963; Dent & Johnson, 1964; Shapiro, 1964). Among rats, changes in the internal or external environment of the organisms effect a greater impact on massed than on distributed learning (Breen & McGaugh, 1961; McGaugh, 1961; McGaugh, Westbrook, & Thomson, 1962). Thus massed learning appears to be far more susceptible to various hereditary and environmental forces. Perhaps humans, like rats, are greatly benefited by enrichment, but this has not been evident to researchers because they have tried to measure the influence of enrichment on tasks that are *not* highly responsive to such influence. Or it may be that enrichment has more impact if one moves away from the study of IQ change to investigate the influence of environment on proficiency at tasks that involve massed learning techniques, such as maze learning or the verbal learning of paired associates.

Early Intellectual Enrichment Programs

Several aspects of preschool programs for disadvantaged children are discussed in Chapter 12. In that discussion it is pointed out that a great surge of interest was shown in the early 1960s for preschool educational enrichment for children from disadvantaged backgrounds. A great deal of data have been available for many years showing that such children are not ready for school learning when they enter the school situation. They lack many of the skills required for school readiness. Concern for the educational progress of these children led to the initiation of Project Head Start, a program focusing on medical, nutritional, and educational development of low-income preschoolers. The results of attempts to evaluate the effectiveness of Head Start in terms of the child's subsequent educational progress have been mixed. Some studies have shown that children who received a year of Head Start training were no more advanced in later school achievement than comparable children without this experience. Perhaps for this reason, coupled with new theoretical points of view and new evidence, interest in the late 1960s shifted downward to the infancy level. In an exciting little volume entitled *Stability and Change in Human Characteristics*, Bloom (1964) presented evidence to indicate that ". . . in terms of intelligence measured at age 17, at least 20% is developed by age 1, 50% by age 4, 80% by age 8, and 92% by age 13" (p. 68). Bloom argues convincingly that when any human characteristic is developing most rapidly, it is most susceptible to environmental effects. Thus, environmental enrichment or environmental deprivation will exert their most marked effects in the early years.

A number of early intervention programs have been attempted involving stimulation of infants either in day care or institutional settings or in their own homes. The general goals of the Syracuse infant care program are described in Chapter 9. The home-tutoring programs have utilized either professional staff (Painter, 1968; Schaefer, 1969; Weikart & Lambie, 1970), such as elementary school teachers, or trained paraprofessional aides (Gordon, 1969; Giesy, 1970). Some of these programs have emphasized the involvement of the mother in the tutoring program while others have not. It would seem that the long-term goal in all such programs would be to train the mother to become the child's teacher. After all, it is only the mother who is in a position to provide continuity in the learning process throughout the preschool years. Moreover, the mother can use these teaching skills with her other children. Numerous problems have been encountered, however, in attempts to involve and train the mother in the teaching process. For example, Gordon reported that many mothers were uninterested in the training and failed to continue with the learning exercises in the absence of the home visitor. Weikart and Lambie found that mothers could be placed into the following categories:

> 1) A few mothers have a good understanding, usually intuitive, of their children's needs and have already established a growth-encouraging relationship. These mothers receive extensive teacher support in what they are doing. 2) Most of the mothers want to do what is best for their infants but they do not know how to go about it. These mothers receive specific

> consultation from the teacher including ideas, demonstrations, and information. 3) Some mothers are not involved with their infants and see their children as "slow" or different in some way. A mother from this group demands to know what is wrong; then, if the problem can't be easily solved, she prefers to ignore the child. 4) Some mothers seem to provide detrimental assistance to their children, as everything they do with the baby seems to go wrong. These mothers react to these difficulties by becoming punitive, treating the infant with detachment, or showing overwhelming concern. These last two groups of mothers need considerable assistance in developing an equilibrium in child rearing. The teacher constructs, through carefully related educational activities, a responsive relationship between mother and child. She supports the vital interest the mother has in the child by helping her achieve success in some activity with the baby. (Lambie & Weikart, 1970, p. 365)

The various programs have used a variety of curricula with emphasis in most cases on the language, intellectual, and motor development areas. The general areas as well as specific activities employed in the Peabody program in Nashville are listed in Table 6-3.

The following developmental categories, together with some of the activities, were emphasized in the Painter study:

Language Development

Beginning Language

- A. Initiating speech
- B. Naming objects
- C. Picture representation (the identification, differentiation, labeling, and demonstration of usage of pictured objects)
- D. Pictures in books
- E. Verbalizing needs or wants
- F. Carrying out simple verbal instruction

Elaborative Language

- A. Extended speech and spontaneous speech in dramatic play, rhymes, and songs
- B. Action pictures
- C. Adjectives and adverbs
- D. Prepositions
- E. Antonyms

Conceptual Development

Concept of Body Image

- A. Mirror training
- B. Doll, paper doll, puppets
- C. Identifying pictures
- D. Tracing an outline of hand and foot
- E. Tracing an outline of the child
- F. Drawing a face
- G. Teaching drawing (with errors for child to detect)
- H. Making a clay or play dough human figure
- I. Placing body parts on a felt figure
- J. Putting together a home-made puzzle
- K. Finger plays
- L. Songs stressing parts of the body or size of child
- M. Gross motor movements

Concept of Space

- A. Form perception
- B. Size perception
- C. Spatial relationships
- D. Seriation

Concept of Number

- A. Differentiating "one" from "many" or "more"
- B. One for me, and one for you
- C. Placing one penny in each of two, three, or five boxes
- D. Counting to 10 by rote
- E. Counting the fingers on each hand
- F. Asking the child, "How old are you?"
- G. Counting songs
- H. Counting fingers plays

TABLE 6-3 Home Teaching Assignments for the Mother*

Gross-Motor	Fine-Motor	Cognitive	Language	Personal-Social	Specific Assignments* for Mothers
Pull or push the toy. Encourage infant to roll over from flat of back to upright position to obtain toy. Allow infant opportunity to sit alone. Encourage infant to pull up, crawl and walk. Practice: throwing, rolling, and bouncing ball.	Scribbling (weekly). Putting in, taking out objects from can. Use cups and spoon. Look at picture book, turning pages. Substitute old magazines for picture book when infant wants to tear pages. Practice putting spools in correct hole in can. Practice stacking bowls—cans of varying size usually found in home. Practice fitting tube in hole in egg carton. Practice stacking blocks.	Allow opportunity for free play with blocks. Shake bell blocks. Practice fitting snap beads together. Stack blocks: tower 2–3. Use action verbs when playing with ball: "Get the ball." "Roll the ball." "Throw the ball." "Catch the ball." "Give me the ball." Present action song and game for imitation in which infant can participate. Look at picture book; name objects. Look at "Baby's Book to Touch" and label sensory experiences. Stack blocks: tower 4–6.	Use words while looking in mirror: "See baby." "Pat baby." Wave to baby." "Kiss baby." Use one word when naming objects on picture cards. Sing nursery rhymes. Talk about objects in pictures. Imitate sounds of animals in picture book, also cars, airplanes, music. Name objects when infant is exploring. Use action verbs with a ball: "Roll," "Catch," "Go get," "Give me," "Throw" etc. Encourage infant to follow simple directions and respond to requests.	Hold mirror so infant can see himself. Play with doll. Cuddle terry cloth animal. Have pictures of members of family available for the next home visit. Name parts of body (use doll). Handle cup and spoon at mealtime.	Read all available information pertaining to infant and child development. Make picture cards. Cover foam blocks with terry cloth. Make tagboard blocks putting bells inside blocks. Make terry cloth animal. Record new sounds or words, and behavior of infant. Cut out pictures and make picture book. Make pull toy (shoe box wagon). Make doll. Present action song and game for imitation in which infant can participate. Practice nursery rhyme on xylophone.

*Forrester, Hardge, Outlaw, Brooks, & Bois meir, 1971, p. 61.

I. Counting cookies
J. Stacking blocks
K. Counting objects in pictures
L. Identifying numerals

Concept of Time

A. Progression of tutoring session
B. Progression of the day
C. Relating today to yesterday and tomorrow
D. Looking at watch or clock

Concept of Categorical Classification

A. Colors
B. Same and different
C. Classification of pictures

Sensory-Motor Training

Sensory input through the following channels

A. Visual
B. Auditory
C. Haptic (tactile and kinesthetic)

(Painter, 1968, pp. 69–93)

With regard to the effectiveness of the various attempts at early enrichment, one can conclude that the infants receiving such enrichment have shown gains in intellectual development beyond that shown by comparable infants who did not receive the enrichment experience. Thus, early development can be facilitated by a tutoring program which focuses on specific learning activities.

In a thorough review of infant intervention studies, Starr (1971) posed six main questions, with tentative answers based on existing information furnished by research studies.

> First, one can ask whether day care programs which serve to place the infant in an environment which is structured for learning but in which he is removed from his familiar home environment are more effective in fostering cognitive development than home intervention studies. (Starr, 1971, p. 178)

Starr concluded that both types are effective, and, ideally, they should be used to complement each other in a community.

> Second, one can ask whether professionals or paraprofessionals are more effective intervention agents. (p. 178)

Both professionals and paraprofessionals have been shown to be effective; however, both require careful and specific training in the skills required to work with mothers in their homes. An apprenticeship under an experienced home tutor is desirable.

> Third, should intervention procedures emphasize training the mother to interact with her child or should the home tutor intervene directly with the child? (p. 179)

As mentioned previously, the most practical approach is to train the mothers, recognizing that problems will be encountered. Mothers should be encouraged to become actively involved with their infant's developmental progress, but they require training just as the professional or paraprofessional tutor.

> Fourth, when should intervention start? (p. 179)

Since research has shown that social-class differences in intellectual development appear between 15–18 months of age, this would seem to be an appropriate time for beginning intervention. Furthermore, infants younger than this present problems of attention and cooperation.

> Fifth, are the effects of early intervention lasting? (p. 180)

There is insufficient research evidence on this point at the present time. It seems likely, however, that in order for intellectual gains to be maintained, training should be continued for several years.

> Sixth, we need to consider whether or not curricula make a difference in the attainments of the infant. (p. 180)

Data from the Weikart and Lambie (1969) study suggest that the committment of the individuals involved in the program is more important than the specific curriculum. This assumes, of course, that the learning goals are spelled out, and that specific activities and materials to achieve these goals are developed.

Evidence for the current emphasis on early infant development is provided by the number of available books and pamphlets which describe techniques and procedures for mothers to employ with their infants. Included among these are the following:

Engelmann, S., & Engelmann, T. *Give your child a superior mind.* New York: Simon & Schuster, 1966.

Gordon, I., & Lally, R. *Intellectual stimulation for infant and toddlers.* Florida: Institute the Development of Human Resources, 1967.

John Tracy Clinic. *Getting your baby ready to talk. A home study plan for infant language development.*

Lejon, E., Barber, L., & Williams, H. *Let me introduce myself. A guide for parents of infant children.* Schenectady, N.Y.: Union College Character Research Project, 1971.

Painter, G. *Teach your baby.* New York: Simon & Schuster, 1971.

Segner, L., & Patterson, C. *Ways to help babies grow and learn: Activities for infant education.*

In conclusion, the late 1960s witnessed a tremendous surge of interest in infant development in general as well as in approaches for stimulating that development. A wide variety of techniques have been explored, with many questions remaining unanswered. It does seem plausible that since development is most rapid in the very early years, intervention at that time will prove to be most effective.

Intelligence and Creativity

Creativity might well be discussed as an area of problem solving, yet might also be considered an aspect of intelligence. Relatively high formal intelligence, as measured by intelligence tests, seems to be a necessary but not in itself sufficient cause for creativity to be manifested, while the form of intelligence that might be termed fluid and divergent seems a central element to creativity.

Creativity has been described by Drevdahl as follows.

> Creativity is the capacity of persons to produce compositions, products, or ideas of any sort which are essentially new or novel, and previously unknown to the producer. It can be imaginative activity, or thought synthesis, where the product is not a mere summation. It may involve the forming of new patterns and combinations of information derived from past experience, and the transplanting of old relationships to new situations and may involve the generation of new correlates. It must be purposeful or goal directed, not mere idle fantasy—although it need not have immediate practical application or be a perfect and complete product. It may take the form of an artistic, literary or scientific production or may be of a procedural or methodological nature (Drevdahl, 1956, p. 22).

Originality and creativity are probably present in all individuals—adults and children—but clearly in quite different degrees (Wilson, Guilford, & Christensen,

1953). The measures used most frequently to test creativity are those developed by Guilford and his colleagues.

The basic components of creativity, Guilford (1950) maintained, are a sensitivity to problems, an ability to produce many novel ideas or solutions, a flexible approach to solving problems, and the capacity to analyze and synthesize a complex collection of ideas. The tests he and his colleagues devised (see Wilson et. al., 1953) were aimed at measuring these qualities. On these tests, adult subjects are asked to do such things as describe how the United States might have developed if there had been no Mississippi-Missouri river system or think up a title for a movie scenario presented to them. Their responses can be rated on the basis of quantity and quality, since most studies show the two to be closely related, and then compared with criteria of creativity in real life. Responses to the Barron–Welsh Art Scale (Barron & Welsh, 1952) or the Welsh Figure Preference Test (Welsh, 1959) predict creativity in real life among both adults and children fairly well (MacKinnon, 1962). Creative individuals prefer nonrepresentative art and complex and asymmetrical figures to representative art or the simple and symmetrical figures. They also produce a very high proportion of unusual word associations (MacKinnon, 1962); hence tests for such associations also may help to judge creativity.

In following up these findings, Houston and Mednick (1963) discovered creative adults to be far less tolerant of the banal or the commonplace. And Jacobsen and Asher (1963) have remarkably predicted creativity in real life from the way individuals reacted to a perceptual task. The task in question consisted of a series of 21 pictures during which the silhouette of a dog gradually changed into one of a cat. The more flexible subjects caught the change early in the series; these individuals generally proved the most creative in the actual life task which, in this experiment, was to design a desk. Thus these various tests in their different forms were able to measure the presence in an individual of the basic components of creativity.

Presumably these components relate to a manner of intellectual functioning, but they are at least somewhat independent of intelligence as it usually is measured through IQ. In most creative endeavors, a minimal IQ (somewhere around IQ 115–120) may exist below which an individual cannot function. However, above this level, IQ has little significance (MacKinnon, 1962). If one compares, for example, the 150 least creative and productive males with the 150 most creative and productive from Terman's study of gifted children (Terman, 1954) there is little difference in IQ between the two groups. Other studies (Drevdahl, 1956; MacKinnon, 1962; Torrance, 1960) contain similar findings. Among individuals selected to form an above-average group in terms of creativity, the specific preformance of any one of them on a conventional intelligence test is no indication of creativity. Creativity may involve divergent thinking—described by Guilford as "thinking different, new, or unusual directions"—fluid but not crystallized intelligence. Formal IQ, on the other hand, may depend on memory and on convergent thinking—an awareness of the recognized best or conventional answer (Guilford, 1959).

Writers who value creativity and sometimes appear to downgrade the kinds of ability measured by formal intelligence tests (e.g., Getzels & Jackson, 1962; Wallach & Kogan, 1965) may well be correcting past errors of psychology, since creativity generally has been undervalued. Yet creativity must be coupled with at least a minimal and probably a considerable amount of intelligence in IQ terms, or else it is so idiosyncratic that it cannot be evaluated or made use of; after all, schizophrenia, the most serious mental disorder of our time, also has as a symptom extremely divergent thinking—sometimes interesting, it is true, but certainly maladaptive.

Besides intellectual traits such as fluency of ideas and flexibility, certain personality characteristics differentiate the creative from the noncreative individual. There are those who say that creative persons are less anxious (Reid, King, & Wickwire, 1959), less defensive, and more willing to concede faults (MacKinnon, 1962). They are by no means problem-free, but have sufficient ego strength that they can cope adequately with their problems (Cattell & Drevdahl, 1955; Barron, 1963). Creative individuals tend to be radical, unconventional, and sensitive to the feelings of others (Drevdahl, 1956). On tests of masculinity versus femininity they score more toward the feminine end of the scale (MacKinnon, 1962). This does not signify any sexual aberration, but merely indicates a higher number of cultural interests. Creative persons are also independent and self-sufficient, not overly concerned with maintaining close ties with social groups or with receiving the approval of others (MacKinnon, 1962). The data cited above indicate that creative people are highly aware of, yet unconcerned with, the evaluations of others—a combination of traits that suggests a realistically high level of self-esteem.

Since highly creative individuals share all these traits that are believed to be shaped by environment, creative individuals should also have common elements in their backgrounds. Abundant evidence shows they tend to have close ties with parents. McCurdy (1957) demonstrated that historic geniuses had very little contact with their peers, but had intensive, generally warm relations with parents and siblings. Both Greenacre (1958) and MacKinnon (1962) also found this to be true. The family of a genius is a tightly knit unit, often estranged from its neighbors because of different values or cultural aspirations, and the creative individual himself is often alienated from his mates during childhood (MacKinnon, 1962; Torrance, 1960). The family, therefore, has a more profound influence on him than on most of his peers, since the peers, the neighborhood, and probably the school have less opportunity to induce behavioral change.

Possessed of the necessary formal intelligence (IQ), the creative individual benefits most by growing up in a home that is hospitable and sympathetic to creative interests. In such a home there is marital harmony. This intimate, closely knit family relationship is marked by warmth and by mild discipline of a psychological turn rather than severe and physical discipline. The child is presented with a clear set of parental standards but is given much freedom of expression, which he is encouraged to exercise (MacKinnon, 1962). Parental democracy also stimulates creativity and imaginativeness among children (Baldwin, 1949). The emphasis is on achievement and independent action, with parents establishing conditions that allow the child to meet these expectations. Moreover, Terman's (1954) comparison of creative as opposed to noncreative gifted children showed that the noncreative came from homes having more stress, more conflict, and less interest in achievement than the homes of the creative subjects among his sample.

These data indeed suggest that parents have a great deal of influence in developing the ability of their children to cope creatively with tasks requiring the solution of problems. If a parent wishes his child to be creative, to be a productive artist, scientist, or innovator, his parental behavior must follow directions that are fairly well marked. Yet it is possible that many parents are unwilling to accept these conditions for having a creative, self-directed child (since this kind of child will question any parental claim to omniscience) despite their lip service to the idea that creativity is good.

It sometimes is suggested that all young children are creative, and that it is the school situation that destroys creativity. Torrance (1962) demonstrated that both teachers and peers show some disapproval of highly creative children, believing them to have "silly" or "wild" ideas. Teachers, as usual, take the rap quite willingly. Yet of all the forces that most of us encounter, teachers may well be the group that do most to promote creativity. Most people who get through college can remember at least a few teachers who did more than anyone else did to encourage their creativity and originality, even in opposition to parents and to school boards.

It seems more likely that pervasive cultural influences, rather than specific teacher behaviors, are the chief forces producing the sometimes observed diminution of creativity that accompanies getting older. For example, as cited in various portions of this book, girls are expected to be dependent, unambitious, and unoriginal. Although there are creative women (see Helson, 1967, for a description of creative women), they are few in number, probably because of sex differences in pressures toward conformity. If the general tone of the culture does so much that is negative for girls, it is likely that it has the chief role in producing a similar but less deleterious effect in males.

High Intellectual Ability

Once it was believed that highly intelligent young people were physically weak, of questionable moral character, rejected by their agemates, antisocial, prone to psychotic or neurotic disturbances, and likely to become mentally defective in later years. Although unsupported by acceptable evidence, these notions were widely held. Possibly the reason for this acceptance is that it is only fair to have "compensatory traits." It would be manifestly unfair for one individual to have everything—brains and brawn, and beauty, too. If this latter idea were buttressed by empirical evidence, the gifted would certainly suffer.

Shortly after World War I, Terman and his associates undertook their extensive study of gifted children in order to test currently prevalent ideas on the exceptional. Starting in 1921, Terman gathered data on more than 1000 children with IQs of over 140, except for a few cases in which a sibling of an exceptional child, whose IQ fell between 135 and 140, was included. Thus the children in Terman's sample constituted the top 1 percent of the population as judged by tested ability. These younsters differed completely from popular belief. They were physically superior, highly acceptable socially, of good character, and in excellent health—a superior group *generally;* most superior in intellectual pursuits, but superior in other ways as well.

This group was followed from 1921, when its mean age was 10, to 1956 and a mean age of 45 (Terman et al., 1925; Burks, Jensen, & Terman, 1930; Terman & Oden, 1947, 1959). Almost all performed well in academic pursuits. Most entered college and received bachelor degrees. Many went on to obtain graduate degrees. Those who did not achieve as well as might have been expected from their IQ scores seemed handicapped by little emphasis on scholarly accomplishment and many tensions at home. These particular individuals, however, gained considerably over their young adult days. At last check (1959), many of them seemed finally to have overcome the adverse effects of their childhood environment and to have begun at last to achieve. Far from "burning out" or becoming mentally defective, the entire group seemed to grow progressively more superior in accomplishment as well as in tested ability at least through the age of 45. During these 35 years, the group had a low death rate, a low divorce rate, a low crime rate, and a low rate of psychological disturbance. The findings about this group indeed demonstrated the falsity of many beliefs about the gifted.

However, the optimal level of IQ in relation to adjustment is believed to lie between 125 and 155 (Hollingworth, 1942). In her book, *Children Above 180 IQ*, Hollingworth described a number of children far above this level. Although high achievers, the young people studied by Hollingworth were not well-adjusted members of the age group to which they belonged. They were neither antisocial nor actively maladjusted; rather they were largely asocial, uninterested in their agemates and their activities, and apparently living in a different world from their classmates, teachers, and sometimes their parents. They did not interact easily with agemates; in fact, children of this high a level of ability might benefit from isolation from peers.

Perhaps the most interesting personal account of childhood experiences of a genius, not merely genius in IQ terms, but a genius in the sense of changing the world around him, is that of Norbert Wiener. His two books, *Ex-Prodigy* (1953), dealing with his childhood and college years, and *I Am a Mathematician* (1956), dealing with his professional career, describe the joys and sorrows of being of such high ability that an entirely normal childhood is impossible. As is frequently the case with highly intelligent and highly creative individuals, Wiener's family ties were close. His father played the largest role in his education, and his books provide an interesting example of the emotional ambivalence that often results from this close yet demanding father-son relationship that is a highly frequent aspect of the boyhood of genius. Wiener's description of some aspects of his first year in college provides an interesting picture of the problems involved in living in two worlds, that of a child and that of an adult, at the same time.

> With my high school days over, my father had decided to send me to Tufts College rather than to risk the strain of the Harvard entrance examinations and the inordinate publicity which could have been caused by sending an eleven-year-old boy to Harvard. . . .
>
> I began to get acquainted with the children of the neighborhood. In my early reading I had learned something about hypnotism and decided to try it out myself. I succeeded in nothing, except in offending and terrifying the parents of my playmates. I played a good deal with children of my own age, but without any great community of interest. I found the clerk at the corner drugstore an interesting medical student, who was prepared to discuss my scientific reading with me and who seemed to be acquainted with the whole of the writings of Herbert Spencer. I have since found Herbert Spencer to be one of the most colossal bores of the nineteenth century, but at that time I held him in esteem. . . .
>
> I had not yet reached the proper stage of social maturity for my English courses. Moreover, the mere mechanics of writing were a serious hurdle to take. My mechanical clumsiness in writing tended to make me omit any word that I could eliminate, and to force me into a great crabbedness of style.
>
> I was already beyond the normal freshman work in mathematics. There was no course which exactly fitted my requirements, so Professor Ransom took me on in a reading course on the Theory of Equations. . . .
>
> The course was really over my head, particularly in the parts concerning Galois' theory, but with a great deal of

help from Professor Ransom I was able to get through. I had started my mathematics at the hard end. Never again at Tufts did I have a mathematics course that demanded so much of me. . . .

I had several . . . extracurricular adventures in physics and engineering, more especially in the study of electricity. I shared electrical experiments with a Medford neighbor. We used to generate electricity by turning a hand-run dynamo for the making of colloidal gold and colloidal silver. Whether we actually made these substances I cannot remember, but we thought we did. We also made attempts to realize in practice two physical ideas of mine. One of them was an electromagnetic coherer for radio messages different from the electrostatic coherer of Branly. It depended on the effect of a magnetic field independently of its direction, in compressing a mass of iron filings and powdered carbon, and thus in changing its resistance. There were times when we thought we had obtained a positive effect, but we were not certain whether it was due to this magnetic cohesion or to something quite different. Nevertheless, the idea was sound and if the day of all such devices had not passed with the invention of the vacuum tube, I should be interested to undertake these experiments over again from the beginning.

The other piece of apparatus we tried out was an electrostatic transformer. It depended on the fact that the energy or charge of a condenser is carried as a dielectric strain. The trick was to charge a rotating glass disk or series of disks through electrodes arranged in parallel and to discharge them through electrodes arranged in series. It differed from the electromagnetic transformer in acting on direct currents, and also in the fact that it was essential to the apparatus that the disks should be revolved. We broke an indefinite number of panes of glass in trying to make the machine, and we never quite got it to work. Unbeknown to us, the idea was already in the literature and had been there for a long time. In fact, I have seen a very similar piece of apparatus within the last two years in the laboratories of the School of Engineering of the University of Mexico. It functioned very well. Two successive stages of this machine multiplied the potential by several thousand (Wiener, 1964, pp. 102–106).

The adjustment of the gifted depends, to a large extent, on the criterion used for giftedness. With Terman's criterion of a 140 IQ, adjustment is indeed superior. With the criterion of Hollingworth (1942) or of McCurdy (1957), adjustment most likely could not be considered optimal. In any case, with respect to intellectual performance, *achievement* is high.

The Mentally Deficient

At the other end of the intelligence curve are those individuals who are regarded as mentally deficient. It is not entirely fair, as is often done, to designate individuals below IQ 70 as "mentally defective." An IQ score alone is not enough to justify this diagnosis. Social competence is a better standard of measurement. If an individual with an IQ of 50 makes his own way in the world without supervision and manages to keep employed, out of trouble, and even marry and successfully raise a family, it would be very unfair to label him defective. The most recent set of diagnostic criteria for mental deficiency or mental retardation includes criteria involving both intelligence and socially adaptive behavior (Heber, 1959).

The earliest studies of social competence, some of them undertaken long before the introduction of intelligence tests, were actually investigations of families that displayed social incompetence for several generations. The best known of these probably is Goddard's (1912) study of the "good" and the "bad" Kallikaks, in which one family line generally evinced social competence and the other social incompetence, presumably because of the inheritance of these characteristics.

Because of these studies and their findings, it once was believed that all mental defects, except for clear instances of anomalies of development, were hereditary. Nowadays it seems apparent that although some defective individuals may inherit general low ability as a result of the influence of many different gene pairs, a large number of persons are called defective because of brain injury, inherited biochemical factors such as phenylketonuria (the incomplete oxidation of certain amino acids), deprived backgrounds, or a number of other reasons. There are many sources for a low IQ, and individuals of the same low level of ability differ substantially from one another, depending on the specific etiology (cause) of their low scores. Some of these persons will show considerable social competence and will benefit greatly from training, whereas others will not. In other words, only *some* individuals with low IQs are mentally defective within the customary definition. Persons diagnosed as retarded, even when matched in IQ, show substantial differences in adaptive and maladaptive problem behavior across diagnostic categories (Johnson, 1969; Johnson & Abelson, 1969a, 1969b), demonstrating the heterogeneity underlying the label "retarded."

Most individuals with low IQs seem to do poorly in school. A low intelligence-test score was once thought to be an almost certain indication of social and scholastic incompetence. This is not the case. During the depths of the Depression, Baller (1936) studied 206 individuals, most of whom were in their middle twenties, whose IQs fell below 70 and who, in grade school, had attended "opportunity classes" for extremely slow learners. Of these 206, 33 had completed elementary school, three had finished high school, and one had entered college. Despite the challenging economic conditions of the time, 84 percent were partially or wholly self-supporting. Only 8 percent were confined in institutions. Following up Baller's subjects in the late 1940's and early 1950's, Charles (1953, 1957) found 80 percent of them to be employed and self-supporting. Their mean age at the time he began studying them was 42. Their types of home and percentage of home ownership closely resembled the general population's. Those who had married did not have "herds of children" as is sometimes the case with persons of low ability; the average number of children was actually a little under the national norms. The children on the whole fell into the range of low-average ability.

The most recent follow-up of this group of individuals (Baller et al., 1967) plus two control groups, one dull but not retarded and one normal, demonstrates that while the group diagnosed as defective made few highly positive contributions to their community, they generally become normal, noncriminal, self-supporting people. The most startling difference among the three ability groups was death rate, with the mentally defective group having a remarkably high rate. Of the three groups, the retarded individuals gained most in IQ over the approximately 40 years since they had been in school, moving from an average IQ of 60 to an average of 80. It may be that, with age, retarded individuals are more likely to encounter learning situations under conditions of distributed practice from which they can benefit, and, as a result, more closely approximate normal functioning.

These data are not isolated. Other studies have supplied similar results. Kennedy (1948) also demonstrated that most individuals who were below IQ 70 while in school did reasonably well on the job once they got out of school. Muench (1944), like Baller, et al. showed that many who scored in the defective range in childhood and early adolescence scored within the normal range as adults.

The Binet test seems to be a good forecaster of school success so long as no special intervention is introduced to the learning situation. However, if the learning situation is structured so that conditions of practice are controlled (Shapiro, 1964), the correct response is made highly salient (Cole, Dent, Eguchi, Fujii, & Johnson, 1964) and correct responses, when made, are immediately positively reinforced, then even children quite low in ability can learn relatively adequately. We believe that bright children can learn under almost any condition, but that dull children's learning experiences must be very carefully structured if learning is to occur at a proper rate.

Since little is done to make the learning of retarded and dull children more comparable to that of normal and bright children, they generally suffer through the school years. After this period of frustration and low esteem during school years, many persons of low ability (in terms of IQ) come into their own when finally employed. More important, they not only perform well on the job, but also often do relatively well as adults on intelligence tests. This may be explained in various ways. First, the low-ability individual has "regression toward the mean" operating on his side. If he scores low on his first test, he has nowhere to go but up on his second one. Second, many individuals with a low tested IQ may score low because of emotional problems (Honzik et al., 1948) or because of a deprived environment. Age and independence from parents may cure both these ills. Third, as noted above, they may encounter learning situations under optimal learning conditions.

Since the diagnosis of mental deficiency depends largely on social competence, many persons with low IQs are not mentally defective as children but are merely academically inept—and even fewer can be legitimately termed mentally defective as adults. While the gifted stay gifted, the retarded or defective frequently do not remain retarded.

SUMMARY

There are many definitions of intelligence. Different definitions accent such distinctive aspects of intelligence as comprehension, direction, invention or creativity, censorship, availability of past experience, ability to operate at a high level under stress, and ability to use abstract symbols. Terman emphasized the capacity to deal with abstract problems and to use abstract symbols. Since he devised the most widely used intelligence test and shaped the format of most others, his definition appears to have been most influential. As a result, conventional intelligence tests, as usually interpreted, provide an adequate measure of abstract symbolic skills, but are far from satisfactory at checking the kind of *fluid* intelligence involved in creativity or the abilities central to other definitions of intelligence. Factorial studies differ in their conclusions at least partly because different tests, or even the same test at different age levels, seem to measure other aspects of intelligence. The evidence suggests strongly that intelligence consists of a *g* factor of moderate strength plus a number of specific factors.

Various theories try to account for the shape of the curve of intellectual growth. It seems reasonable to believe that the average growth curve accelerates sharply during infancy and early childhood, slows down after this point, but continues to rise at least into middle maturity. Individual growth curves of persons reared in typical American environments show much irregularity. Differences in the kinds of material tapped by intelligence tests at various ages and differences in the emotional well-being or intellectual stimulation of those being tested might be responsible for this variation. A comparison of generations discloses that the present generation demonstrates greater intellectual growth than its forebears, as measured by scores on conventional group intelligence tests. The mental growth curves of individuals raised outside the mainstream of American culture indicate a deceleration that apparently results from the intellectual impoverishment of their environment.

Individual differences in intelligence-test scores do not relate substantially to most laboratory measures of learning, nor do they always predict creative capacities. Intelligence-test scores, however, do permit prediction of academic success with a fairly high amount of accuracy. Individuals who score high on such tests, when compared to the general population, are not only superior in accomplishment, but also are better physical specimens and seem better able to withstand psychic stresses. Individuals found in the ranks of the genius category as children maintain their superiority at least through the mid-forties. Individuals on the low end of the intelligence curve do poorly in school but perform better on the job. In many cases they also test within the normal range of intelligence as adults.

Although measures of intelligence are far from perfect, thus preventing an understanding of the nature of intelligence and of intellectual growth from being complete, psychologists have come a long way toward achieving accuracy in predicting performance in a highly complex area of behavior.

REFERENCES

Anderson, J. E. The limitations of infant and preschool test in the measurement of intelligence. *Journal of Psychology*, 1939, **8**, 351–379.

Bajema, C. F. Estimation of the direction and intensity of natural selection in relation to human intelligence by means of the intrinsic rate of natural increase. *Eugenics Quarterly*, 1963, **10**, 175–187.

Bajema, C. F. The relationship between intelligence and completed fertility among Third Harvard Growth Study participants. Annual meeting, American Association of Physical Anthropologists, 1971.

Baldwin, A. L. The effect of home environment on nursery school behavior. *Child Development*, 1949, **20**, 49–62.

Baldwin, A. L., Kalhorn, J., & Breese, F. H. Patterns of parent behavior. *Psychological Monographs*, 1945, **58**, No. 268.

Baller, W. R. A study of the present social status of a group of adults, who, when they were in the elementary schools, were classified as mentally deficient. *Genetic Psychology Monographs*, 1936, **18**, No. 3.

Baller, W. R., Charles, D. C., & Miller, E. L. Mid-life attainment of the mentally retarded: a longitudinal study. *Genetic Psychology Monographs*, 1967, **75**, 235–329.

Barron, F. The needs for order and disorder as motives in creative act activity. In C. W. Taylor & F. Barron (Eds.), *Scientific creativity*. New York: Wiley, 1963.

Barron, F., & Welsh, G. S. Artistic perception as a possible factor in personality style: Its measurement by a figure preference test. *Journal of Psychology*, 1952, **33**, 199–203.

Bayley, N. On the growth of intelligence. *American Psychologist*, 1955, **10**, 805–818.

Bayley, N., & Schaeffer, E. S. Correlates of maternal and child behaviors with the development of mental abilities: Data from the Berkeley growth study. *Monographs of the Society for Research in Child Development*, 1964, **29**, No. 6, Serial No. 97.

Binet, A., & Simmon, T. *The development of intelligence in children* (translated by E. S. Kite). Vineland, N.J.: Vineland Training School, 1916.

Bloom, B. *Stability and change in human characteristics.* New York: Wiley, 1964.

Bradway, K. P., Thompson, C. W., & Cravens, R. B. Preschools IQs after twenty-five years. *Journal of Educational Psychology.* 1958, **49**, 278–281.

Breen, R. A., & McGaugh, J. L. Facilitation of maze learning with posttrial infections of picrotoxin. *Journal of Comparative and Physiological Psychology*, 1961, **54**, 498–501.

Burks, B. S., Jensen, D. W., & Terman, L. M. *Genetic studies of genius: III. The promise of youth: Follow up studies of a thousand gifted children.* Stanford, Calif.: Stanford University Press, 1930.

Cattell, R. B. *Personality and motivation structure and measurement.* New York: Harcourt, Brace & World, 1957.

Cattell, R. B., & Drevdahl, J. E. A comparison of the personality profile of eminent researchers with that of eminent teachers and administrators and that of the general population. *British Journal of Psychology,* 1955, **46**, 248–261.

Charles, D. C. Ability and accomplishment of persons earlier judged mentally deficient. *Genetic Psychology Monographs,* 1953, **47**, 3–271.

Charles, D. C. Adult adjustment of some deficient American children. *American Journal of Mental Deficiency,* 1957, **62**, 300–304.

Cole, R. E., Dent, H. E., Eguchi, P. E., Fujii, K. K., & Johnson, R. C. Transposition with minimal errors during training trials. *Journal of Experimental Child Psychology,* 1964, **1**, 355–359.

Dent, H. E., & Johnson, R. C. The effects of massed vs. distributed practice in the learning of organic and familial defectives. *American Journal of Mental Deficiency,* 1964, **68**, 533–536.

Digman, J. M. A factor analysis of WISC IQ test scores. Unpublished manuscript, University of Hawaii, 1962.

Drevdahl, J. E. Factors of importance for creativity. *Journal of Clinical Psychology,* 1956, **12**, 21–26.

Forrester, B., Hardge, B., Outlaw, D., Brooks, G., & Boismier, J. *Home visiting with mothers and infants.* Nashville: George Peabody College for Teachers, 1971.

Gesell, A. *Infancy and human growth.* New York: Macmillan, 1928.

Getzels, J. W., & Jackson, W. *Creativity and Intelligence.* New York: Wiley, 1962.

Ginsburg, H., & Opper, S. *Piaget's theory of intellectual development.* Englewood Cliffs, N.J.: Prentice-Hall, 1969.

Goddard, H. H. *The Kallikak family.* New York: Macmillan, 1912.

Goddard, H. H. What is intelligence? *Journal of Social Psychology,* 1946, **24**, 51–69.

Goodenough, F. L. The measurement of mental growth in childhood. In L. Carmichael (Ed.), *Manual of child psychology.* (2nd ed.) New York: Wiley, 1954.

Gordon, I. Early child stimulation through parent education. Final report.

Greenacre, P. The family romance of the artist. *Psychoanalytic Study of the Child,* 1958, **13**, 9–43.

Guilford, J. P. Creativity. *American Psychologist,* 1950, **5**, 444–454.

Guilford, J. P. The structure of intelligence. *Psychological Bulletin,* 1956, **53**, 267–293.

Guilford, J. P. Three faces of intellect. *American Psychologist,* 1959, **14**, 469–479.

Hebb, D. O. *The organization of behavior.* New York: Wiley, 1949.

Heber, R. A manual on terminology and classification in mental retardation. *Monograph Supplement to the American Journal of Mental Deficiency,* 1959, **64**, No. 2.

Helson, R. Personality characteristics and developmental history of creative women. *Genetic Psychology Monographs,* 1969, **76**, 205–256.

Higgins, J. V., Reed, E. W., & Reed, S. C. Intelligence and family size: A paradox resolved. *Eugenics Quarterly,* 1962, **9**, 84–90.

Hollingworth, L. S. *Children above 180 IQ.* Yonkers, N.Y.: World Book, 1942.

Honzik, M. P., McFarlane, J. W., & Allen, L. The stability of mental test performance between two and eighteen years. *Journal of Experimental Education,* 1948, **17**, 309–324.

Horn, J. L. Organization of abilities and the development of intelligence. *Psychological Review,* 1968, **75**, 242–259.

Horn, J. L., & Cattell, R. B. Age differences in primary mental ability factors. *Journal of Gerontology,* 1966, **21**, 210–220. (a)

Horn, J. L., & Cattell, R. B. Refinement and test of the theory of fluid and crystallized intelligence. *Journal of Educational Psychology,* 1966, **57**, 253–270. (b)

Horn, J. L., & Cattell, R. B. Age differences in fluid and crystallized intelligence. *Acta Psychologica,* 1967, **26**, 1–23.

Houston, J. P., & Mednick, S. A. Creativity and the need for novelty. *Journal of Abnormal and Social Psychology,* 1963, **66**, 137–141.

Humphreys, L. G. The organization of human abilities. *American Psychologist,* 1962, **17**, 475–483.

Jacobsen, T. L., & Asher, J. J. Validity of the concept constancy measure of creative problem solving. *Journal of Genetic Psychology,* 1963, **68**, 9–20.

Jennings, R. D. Strain differences in the effects of distribution of practice on maze learning. Unpublished master's thesis, San Jose State College, 1960.

Johnson, R. C. Similarity in IQ of separated identical twins as related to length of time spent in the same environment. *Child Development,* 1963, **34**, 745–749.

Johnson, R. C. Behavioral characteristics of phenylketonurics and matched controls. *American Journal of Mental Deficiency,* 1969, **74**, 17–19.

Johnson, R. C. & Abelson, R. B. Intellectual, behavioral, and physical characteristics associated with trisomy, translocation, and mosaic types of Downs syndrome. *American Journal of Mental Deficiency,* 1969, **73**, 852–855. (a)

Johnson, R. C. & Abelson, R. B. The behavioral competence of mongoloid and non-mongoloid retardates. *American Journal of Mental Deficiency,* 1969, **73**, 856–857. (b)

Kagan, J., Sontag, L. W., Baker, C. T., & Nelson, V. L. Personality and IQ change. *Journal of Abnormal and Social Psychology,* 1958, **56**, 261–266.

Kennedy, R. J. R. *The social adjustment of morons in a Connecticut city.* Hartford, Conn.: Mansfield–Southberry Training Schools, 1948.

Krech, D., Rosenzweig, M. R., & Bennett, E. L. Effects of environmental complexity and training on brain chemistry. *Journal of Comparative and Physiological Psychology,* 1960, **53**, 509–519.

Lambie, D., & Weikart, D. Ypsilanti Carnegie Infant Education Project. In J. Hellmuth (Ed.), *Disadvantaged Child. Vol. 3. Compensatory education: A national debate.* New York: Brunner/Mazel, 1970.

MacKinnon, D. W. The nature and nurture of creative talent. *American Psychologist,* 1962, **17**, 484–495.

McCurdy, H. G. The childhood pattern of genius. *Journal of the Elisha Mitchell Scientific Society,* 1957, **73**, 448–462. [Also in R. A. King (Ed.), *Readings for an introduction to psychology.* New York: McGraw–Hill, 1961.

McGaugh, J. L. Facilitative and disruptive effects of strychnine sulphate on maze learning. *Psychological Reports,* 1961, **8**, 99–104.

McGaugh, J. L., Westbrook, W. H., & Burt, G. Strain differences in the facilitative effects of 5-7-diphenyl-1-3-diazadamantan-6-OL (1757I.S) on maze learning. *Journal of Comparative and Physiological Psychology,* 1961, **54**, 502–505.

McGaugh, J. L., Westbrook, W. H., & Thomson, C. L. Facilitation of maze learning with posttrial injections of 5-7-diphenyl-1-3-diazadamantan-6-OL (1757I.S.). *Journal of Comparative and Physiological Psychology,* 1962, **55**, 710–713.

McNemar, Q. *The revision of the Stanford–Binet Scale: An analysis of the standardization data.* Boston: Houghton Mifflin, 1942.

Madsen, M. C. Distribution of practice and level of intelligence. *Psychological Reports,* 1963, **13**, 39–42.

Maxwell, J. Intelligence, fertility, and the future. *Eugenics Quarterly,* 1954, **1**, 244–247.

Meyers, C. E., Dingman, H. F., Orpet, R. E., Sitkei, E. G., & Watts, C. A. Four ability factor hypotheses at three preliterate levels in normal and retarded children. *Monographs of the Society of Research in Child Development,* 1964, **29**, No. 5, Serial No. 96.

Muench, G. A. A follow-up of mental defectives after eighteen years. *Journal of Abnormal and Social Psychology,* 1944, **39**, 407–418.

Owens, W. A. Age and mental abilities: A longitudinal study. *Genetic Psychology Monographs,* 1953, **48**, 3–54.

Painter, G. *Infant education.* San Rafael, Calif.: Dimensions, 1968.

Piaget, J. *The moral judgment of the child* (translated by M. Gabain). Glencoe, Ill.: The Free Press, 1948.

Piaget, J. *Play, dreams, and imitation in childhood* (translated by C. Gattegno and F. M. Hodgson). New York: Norton, 1951.

Pinneau, S. R. *Changes in intelligence quotient–infancy to maturity.* Boston: Houghton Mifflin, 1961.

Porteus, S. D. *The practice of clinical psychology.* New York: American Book, 1941.

Porteus, S. D. *The maze test and clinical psychology.* Palo Alto, Calif.: Pacific Books, 1959.

Porteus, S. D. *Porteus Maze Tests: Fifty years' application.* Palo Alto, Calif.: Pacific Books, 1965.

Reid, J. B., King, F. J., & Wickwire, P. Cognitive and other personality characteristics of creative children. *Psychological Reports,* 1959, **5**, 729–737.

Roe, A. A study of imagery in research scientists. *Journal of Personality,* 1951, **19**, 459–470.

Rosenzweig, M. R., Krech, D., Bennett, E. L., & Diamond, M. C. Effects of environmental complexity and training on brain chemistry and anatomy: A replication and extension. *Journal of Comparative and Physiological Psychology,* 1962, **55**, 429–437.

Schaefer, E. Need for early and continuing education. Paper presented at the meeting of the American Association for the Advancement of Science, Boston, December, 1969.

Scott, W. A. Structure of natural cognitions. *Journal of Personality and Social Psychology,* 1969, **12**, 261–278.

Shapiro, G. M. The effects of massed and distributed practice on the learning ability of bright, average, and dull children, matched in mental age. Unpublished master's thesis, University of Hawaii, 1964.

Skeels, H. M. Adult status of children with contrasting early life experiences. *Monographs of the Society for Research in Child Development,* 1966, **31**, No. 3, Serial No. 105.

Sontag, L. W., Baker, C. T., & Nelson, V. L. Mental growth and personality development: A longitudinal study. *Monographs of the Society for Research in Child Development,* 1958, **23**, No. 2. Whole No. 68.

Spearman, C. "General intelligence," objectively determined and measured. *American Journal of Psychology,* 1904, **15**, 201–292.

Spearman, C. *The abilities of man.* London: MacMillan, 1927.

Starr, R. Cognitive development in infancy: Assessment, acceleration, and actualization. *Merrill–Palmer Quarterly,* 1971, **17**, 153–186.

Terman, L. M. *The measurement of intelligence: An explanation of and a complete guide for the Stanford Revision and Extension of the Binet–Simon Intelligence Scale.* Boston: Houghton Mifflin, 1916.

Terman, L. M. The discovery and encouragement of exceptional talent. *American Psychologist,* 1954, **9**, 221–230.

Terman, L. M., et al. *Genetic studies of genius: I. Mental and physical traits of a thousand gifted children.* Stanford, Calif.: Stanford University Press, 1925.

Terman, L. M., & Oden, M. H. *Genetic studies of genius:* IV. *The gifted child grows up.* Stanford, Calif.: Stanford University Press, 1947.

Terman, L. M., & Oden, M. H. *The gifted group at mid-life: Thirty-five years' follow-up of the superior child.* Stanford, Calif.: Stanford University Press, 1959.

Thurstone, L. L. Theories of intelligence. *Science Monthly,* 1946, **62**, 101–112.

Thurstone, L. L., & Ackerson, L. The mental growth curve for the Binet tests. *Journal of Educational Psychology,* 1929, **20**, 569–583.

Torrance, E. P. Explorations in creative thinking. *Education,* 1960, **81**, 216–220.

Torrance, E. P. *Guiding creative talent.* Englewood, N.J.: Prentice–Hall, 1962.

Tuddenham, R. D. Soldiers in World Wars I and II. *American Psychologist,* 1948, **3**, 54–56.

Vandenberg, S. G., & Johnson, R. C. Further evidence in the relation between age of separation and similarity in IQ among pairs of separated identical twins. In S. G. Vandenberg (Ed.), *Progress in human genetics.* Baltimore: Johns Hopkins, 1968.

Wallach, M. A., & Kogan, N. *Modes of thinking in young children.* New York: Holt, Rinehart & Winston, 1965.

Weikart, D., & Lambie, D. Ypsilanti–Carnegie infant education project progress report. Department of Research and Development, Ypsilanti, Michigan Public Schools, 1969.

Welsh, G. S. *Welsh Figure Preference Test: Preliminary manual.* Palo Alto, Calif.: Consulting Psychologists Press, 1959.

Wiener, N. *Ex-prodigy.* Cambridge, Mass.: M.I.T. Press, 1964 (originally published in 1953).

Wiener, N. *I am a mathematician.* Cambridge, Mass.: M.I.T. Press, 1964 (originally published in 1956).

Wilson, R. C., Guilford, J. P., & Christensen, P. R. The measurement of individual differences in originality. *Psychological Bulletin,* 1953, **50**, 362–370.

section III

the family and its influence on development

This section, composed of the next four chapters, concerns the child in his family setting. Such forces as heredity and maturation impose limits on the influence that parents and other social groups may bring to bear. At the present time this subject of the influence of family on the behavior and personality of the child is a matter of lively interest among researchers, and much effort is being expended in its investigation.

Chapter 7 considers the anthropological, sociological, and historical forces that have made the family in America what it is today and that determine, in part, the way in which the family influences development. Chapter 8 examines various aspects of the family and of the child's place within it. Such matters as "onliness," sibling position, physical or mental defects of siblings, maternal employment, and divorce are discussed.

Chapter 9 covers the interaction of the child with parents during infancy. Among the topics explored are Freudian concepts; the relation of early parent practices, such as toilet training and weaning, to personality and behavior;

and the effects of maternal deprivation. Chapter 10, the final chapter of the section, pertains to parental influences during the period of childhood following infancy. It concludes such matters as the impact of parent personality, parent attitudes, and parent behavior on child personality and behavior.

All told, the cultural, psychological, and social forces in the family situation, together with the personalities, attitudes, and behaviors of each parent and other members of the family, affect the child. Born with certain characteristics that form the core of his uniqueness, the child finds this uniqueness increased by these many influences. Their interplay within the family renders accurate prediction of the effect of any single force on any single child difficult. As this section indicates, however, child psychology is developing predictive skills, notwithstanding the complexity of the problem.

chapter 7

the influence of culture on child-rearing practices

chapter 7

the influence of culture on child-rearing practices

chapter 7

the influence of culture on child-rearing practices

Individuals who share a set of values, beliefs, practices, and information, and who pass these views from one generation to the next, constitute a culture. Americans are part of Western culture, a broad grouping of individuals in North America, Europe, the British Commonwealth, and other areas of the earth. Western culture, an amalgam of Judeo-Christian, Greco-Roman, and other influences, differs from other cultures in the "world view" it builds into people. Although philosophers since Hume have argued that it is improper to talk of "cause" and "effect," Westerners at a very early age accept the ideas that present conditions have their roots in the past, that the future can be predicted from the present, and that the future, moreover, can be changed. Yet the implied notion that there is lawfulness and predictability in the world, based on orderly cause and effect, is far from universally held. Further, the idea that we determine the nature of the future by our own actions is very much of a minority opinion, viewed cross-culturally.

Other ideas common to the West also are not accepted by all cultures. Such value judgments as that life in this world is "good," that progress is possible and desirable, that individuality should be developed to as high a degree as it can, or that the individual human is of considerable worth are not necessarily shared by others. Nor are the values prized by others always acceptable to the West. We cannot imagine many Americans believing that the goal of existence is to lead such a good life that once dead reincarnation is no longer necessary and instead one again becomes nothing. Few within Western culture take the position that if an individual develops a skill more than others do, he is disturbing the equilibrium of the group and thus making supernatural beings unhappy. Americans do not believe that the old way is necessarily the best way. Instead they welcome change for its own sake.

Beliefs shape patterns of child-rearing in various subtle ways. But since all within a culture are subjected to the same influences, these factors and their effect of making people similar to one another in basic approach are often overlooked. Frequently it is necessary to be thrown suddenly into another culture to recognize the essential oneness underlying the apparent diversity of the West. Although part of the same Western culture, Americans have produced within it their own adaptation of it, the *American* culture. This chapter begins with an examination of various cultural considerations that bear on the social environment of the child. This will be followed by discussion of the forces, both past and present, that have produced current child-rearing practices, and by an attempt to show the impact of these forces on various groups in their approaches to child-rearing.

A sufficient number of students are familiar with the idea that there are feral or wild children, reared apart from humans, so that this topic deserves mention. There are two kinds of environmental circumstance found in the feral child literature.

First, there are children who appear to have been in some way isolated from contact with other humans. To these writers, the most believable and instructive case of this sort of upbringing is that of Victor, "the wild boy of Aveyron." He was seen by hunters while, apparently, living in a forest with no human or animal companions. He was captured and exhibited in a cage until rescued by Itard, who made great efforts to "humanize" Victor (Itard, 1932; orig. publ. 1894). One really knows nothing about Victor's precapture experiences–it is impossible to determine the degree to which Victor was "feral" and unfamiliar with humans prior to capture but certainly he must have been cared for in some way for a number of years of his life. The chief value of Itard's description of his wild boy is in the techniques developed by Itard in the process of socializing Victor. These techniques still are of substantial value in the training of the retarded. While Itard himself viewed his efforts as having failed, readers of his book are impressed with his high degree of success, as well as by Itard's brilliant and humane character.

The second—and much more sensational—kind of circumstance in which feral children reportedly are found is that in which they are reared by wild animals. The most famous children in the literature are the two girls, Amala and Kamala, supposedly reared by wolves in India, described by Gesell (1941) and by Singh and Zingg (1943). Singh claimed to have rescued these children from a wolf den. Gesell's book is based on Singh's diary, while the first portion of the Singh and Zingg book contains the diary. Both internal evidence from the diary (in which the girls act as wolves are believed to act, but not as wolves do act) and an investigation conducted in India (Ogburn & Bose, 1959) suggests that the level of accuracy of Singh's account falls well below the usual criteria for acceptance as scientific evidence.

DIMENSIONS OF CULTURE

Cultures can be variously divided into distinct groups, but all such dichotomies have a certain inherent falsity. Things seldom are "either-or." More likely they are blends of various sorts, shading toward one or the other of the types that form the dichotomy. Such is the case with the dimensions of culture to be discussed. Cultures probably do not differ from one another in kind, but rather in the degree to which certain characteristics are present.

Child-Rearing Practices of Primary versus Secondary Groups

This distinction is mentioned first for several reasons. First, having formed an important aspect of sociological theory since the 1860's, it has a certain historical priority. More important, considerable evidence suggests that the development of the *self concept*—an individual's attitudes and beliefs about himself—is an extremely significant phenomenon. The concept of self comes largely from a person's ideas about his social roles, and the type, consistency, and clarity of the roles played seem to depend on whether he grows up in a primary- or a secondary-group society. *Primary groups* are characterized by intimate, face-to-face contact, by the mutual society support of the individuals who belong, and by the group's ability to proscribe, constrain, or order a considerable proportion of the behavior of its individual members. Family and peers, two such primary groups, have considerable influence in American society. Such groups as the typical urban community or neighborhood, or a trade union or professional association are *secondary groups*. These are not characterized by close or continual contact or by a concern in any but a limited segment of a member's behavior. They do not offer any great deal of support, nor generally can they exert any great degree of pressure, except perhaps within rigidly limited areas, toward conformity to group standards of behavior.

Historically, according to many social theorists (Durkheim, 1947; Tonnies, 1940; Becker, 1948), societies composed solely of primary groups reigned supreme. In a primitive culture or even in a contemporary rural one, all individuals know one another. Although not much happens, everyone knows everything that does happen. These social groups are primary groups; little conflict of value systems occurs among them, since everyone holds much the same values. A high proportion of behaviors are "public" behaviors, known to all members of the group and judged by them in terms of propriety.

One of the authors of this book recalls, for example, coming home in a newly acquired 1939 Buick phaeton to the rural community in which he grew up. Everyone in the community asked him, at first encounter, how much he paid for it. They told him that going to college must have made him foolish—that no one in northern Minnesota should buy a convertible. Had they been reprimanded, "None of your business," they would have been surprised as well as hurt. In their opinion it *was* their business to pass judgment on the behavior of members of the group, just as it was to take up a collection and have a building bee if someone's house or barn burned down, or to do the farm chores for a neighbor with a broken leg. It is their business to help members of the group. This combination of inquisitiveness and psychological support found in a primary-group society makes the majority of people escape as soon as possible and then remember the society with nostalgia for the rest of their lives.

A city, on the other hand, is largely a secondary-group society. The individual is exposed to a wide variety of groups, most of which are not characterized by intimate, face-to-face contact across a broad range of behavioral settings. Multiple-group membership is the rule. Since urban groupings, such as trade unions, church organizations, P.T.A.s, and fraternal organizations, differ in composition and often in values and goals, an individual can easily encounter conflict between two antagonistic social roles. Further, the roles prescribed by any one group generally do not deal with wide varieties of behavior, but only with that narrow range of public behaviors of concern to the group. Because no universal consensus exists regarding the "goodness" or "badness" of a given behavior, all values are relative, and none is held as strongly as in a primary-group society (Durkheim, 1915).

Some segments of American culture are still dominated by primary-group associations. This is true of isolated farm groups, members of pietist religous sects (see Francis, 1955; also Kaplan & Plaut, 1956), and probably the very rich. An ever-increasing proportion of Americans, however, lives in urban areas. U.S. Census figures show that well over three-fourths of the population now, as opposed to one-half in 1890, are city dwellers or suburbanites. This majority does not often have such ties as those of religious zealots or of the very rich and thus is not as subject to the influence of primary codes.

Children reared in these two types of environment are subjected to discernibly different forms of parental training. The parent within that part of society still composed largely of primary groups takes a stand toward behavior based on the one traditional set of values to which he has been exposed. There is only one acceptable way for him to respond to any given situation; his whole group agrees on the matter. Once he *knows* what is right, it becomes his duty to teach this to his children and to extirpate any tendencies they may disclose to respond in other manners. Social roles are clearly defined and strengthened by the views of the group. If the child learns to play his allotted share of roles correctly so that they do not conflict with the group and so that he fulfills its expectations, the parent's task is essentially complete. If none of the few available roles seems desirable to the child, he must be induced to make do with them. The function of the parent is to hammer home "self-evident, universally held truths" and to defend the group against the youngster's tendency toward change. Small wonder that parents in primary-group societies are believed to be highly conservative (Spencer, 1912; Durkheim, 1951) and authoritarian (Jaensch, 1938).

The child-rearing practices of a secondary-group society vary to an ever-increasing degree from those of a primary-group environment. An urban culture is dynamic and rapidly changing. Traditional behaviors are of little utility in preparing a child for adulthood, since the adulthood of any child will differ greatly from that of his parents. As a result the parent is quite uncertain as to what to teach the child (Riesman, 1953; Boehm, 1957). Despite the desire to rear children with values consonant with their own, parents often must grant their children autonomy in a number of decision-making areas quite early in the developmental process. This is because the differences in experiences are so great between generations. Moreover, because the parent is less certain that he knows the correct course of action, he delegates authority to other groups. The peer group and the schools take over and thus influence the development of conscience, as shall be discussed presently. The American urban child as opposed to the Swiss, Boehm (1957) has shown, is far more autonomous and far less guilt ridden, presumably because of this weakened parental and increased peer influence.

Owing to economic changes accompanying the development of an industrial, urban, secondary-group society, the parent is warmer and more permissive. Equalitarian treatment of the child follows both from the viewing of the child primarily as a love object and from the parent's own lack of certainty as to what the child should be like. The child is exposed to many differing social groups with diverse values; none of these groups has a high degree of dominance in its influence. No group, not even the family, can keep a constant check on the child in all areas of activity as in a less complex social setting. The child, as a result, knows many sets of conflicting values and probably accepts none of them wholeheartedly until he must select from them as well as from diverse social roles those that he finds best. Then he must adapt them to form a self-consistent set of roles, often referred to as the major component of the *self concept*.

The historical changes in child-rearing practices apparent in American culture may result largely from the continuing shift from a relatively uniform, rural, agrarian society to a variegated, urban, industrial one.

Child-Rearing Techniques in Cultures of Want and of Plenty

Urbanization requires the development of technology and the division of labor. These, in turn, are necessary for a materially rich culture. The American culture is presumably the richest the world has yet known. Certain aspects of child-rearing within it appear to relate to economic circumstances.

Because of advanced scientific technology, the death rate among children is very low. A grandmother stressed the significance of this fact, with respect to child-rearing. In discussing the changes that occurred in the 80 years she could remember, she commented on one quite noticeable development, the greater amount of love that parents lavish nowadays on children. "Back in the old days," she said, "parents couldn't get involved with younger children as greatly. They were afraid that deep love would lead only to deep sorrow, for so many children died before reaching maturity." Although other factors undoubtedly enter into this increased parental involvement and love, mortality figures indicate that a parent at the turn of the century could not *assume* that his children would live to maturity.

Advanced technical achievements appear likely to have contributed in other ways to increased parental love and involvement. Children of a few generations ago were viewed primarily as economic assets. The farmer with a crop of growing boys knew that if he could only hold on for a few more years, he would have plenty of help. Moreover, this help would be of the very best sort, since wages would not be required nor would there by any complaints about a 12-hour day, 7-day work week. No longer can children be viewed in this fashion. There are fewer and fewer things a child is useful for, even on the farm. It is easier, cheaper, quicker, and more efficient to buy a new hay baler or harvesting machine than to breed a crop of farm hands. Since another function of children is that of receiving and giving love, this role has come to the fore, no longer overshadowed by economic necessity. Children are to be loved.

Not only are children loved more, but they are also loved as children far longer. The closer a culture is to a subsistence economy, the shorter the period of childhood, one writer has suggested (Landis, 1945). Hunting or fishing cultures, nearly always only a few days away from starvation, have the shortest childhoods, whereas agrarian cultures are intermediate, and industrial societies are longest in the period they term childhood.

Continuous versus Discontinuous Cultures

Anthropologists such as Ruth Benedict make a distinction between continuous cultures. In a continuous culture, the child begins learning adult roles as soon as he begins to understand the world about him. A discontinuous culture, on the other hand, does not prepare the young child for adulthood through a continuous inculcation of social roles. Discontinuous cultures teach children roles that are in opposition to those they will assume later. For example, the mainstream of American culture (see Haimowitz, 1960, p. 2), like the American Indian subculture, places high value on courage. The Indians, who desire this attribute more than any other, are continuous in their training for it. A bold act, such as that of a two-year-old boy physically attacking his father, is applauded. The prevailing American culture, on the contrary, is truly discontinuous; it expects the individual to be submissive while young and then magically to become dominant at maturity.

American society is clearly discontinuous—not only in failing to provide training for certain adult functions, but also in establishing childhood roles that are antagonistic to the roles demanded by adulthood. It may not be as discontinuous, however, as is believed by many anthropologists. Nor is it certain that discontinuity is undesirable. Perhaps in a complex, rapidly changing, secondary-group society, a certain facility in taking new roles is necessary. Conceivably the ease in making these shifts and adjustments comes from the discontinuity of roles and from the conflicts among those roles faced and mastered during the growing-up process.

Guilt versus Shame Cultures

A traditional aim of a parent in urban industrial culture is to produce a child with what used to be called a well-developed conscience but is now more often termed a strong superego—in any case, a child who feels guilt following wrongdoing. Guilt comes from within. If cultural conditioning has been successful, many humans are self-regulating organisms who punish themselves without being caught. This is an explicitly stated goal in Western culture. It is not common to all cultures. Anthropologists say that the very notion of guilt is lacking in some cultures, and that social controls are based on shame. Shame results from an act being found out by others; as long as one is not caught, any action is acceptable.

It should be noted that there is no one-to-one relation between primary versus secondary groups and the guilt-shame dichotomy. Many primary groups use shame as a means of control, but others base social controls on guilt. Some secondary-group societies emphasize guilt; others shame.

Shame, as a technique for controlling behavior, is probably quite effective when used by a primary-group society, since most behaviors are public. Many primary-group societies do use shame as a major technique. For an urban industrial culture shame does not appear to be an effective technique, since it is so simple to maintain anonymity. Few group ties are strong enough to cause concern about the opinion of the group. Even if one belonged to groups before which one would feel shame, one would first have to be caught and then be forced to remain in the group that would be aware of the misdeed. Persons in urban societies are less likely to be caught, and if caught, can probably join another group that either does not know of the shameful deed or else does not care. Here guilt has the greater influence. Although irrational and excessive guilt may dispose one toward neurosis, members of a mass society may need at least a moderate sense of guilt to maintain the society.

It is believed, however, that urbanites are moving away from a guilt orientation (Riesman, 1953). This may result, in part, from the influence of psychoanalysis, as has recently been claimed (LaPiere, 1959). Other forces probably have contributed far more greatly to this shift. American culture is changing at so rapid a rate that parents are unsure of their own values, and as a result, abandon much of their function to other groups such as the school and the peers. The peers, unlike the usual parent, use shame as a major disciplinary technique. Parents also do a less adequate job of building a sense of guilt since, as already noted, children are more precious these days. Hence the parent is unwilling to withhold love for fear that it may lead to his own rejection by the child. Lessened parental influence, differing to some degree in type from that of a generation ago, appears to have resulted in a shift away from guilt and toward shame as a means of social control.

Persons such as LaPiere, concerned with "the subversion of the American character" as a result of the impact of the Freudian ethic, might view this secular change negatively, whereas the more frequently observed variety of clinical psychologist might view the same change with pleasure because, if the predominant clinical position is correct, this shift might be expected to result in a lowered proportion of neurosis and "withdrawn" behavior problems.

The basic proposition underlying the clinical position is that Freud was right, that adjustment is on a normal curve, as shown in Figure 7-1, with sociopaths and/or psychopaths (people unconcerned with and uninfluenced behaviorally by the disapproval of others) on one end of the normal curve, "normal" persons in the middle, and neurotic, that is, overly guilty, persons on the other extreme of the curve. Mowrer (1960, 1961, 1967), on the other hand, believes that the neurotic is disturbed because of real guilt, over real misdeeds, and that the curve of adjustment is that shown in Figure 7-2,

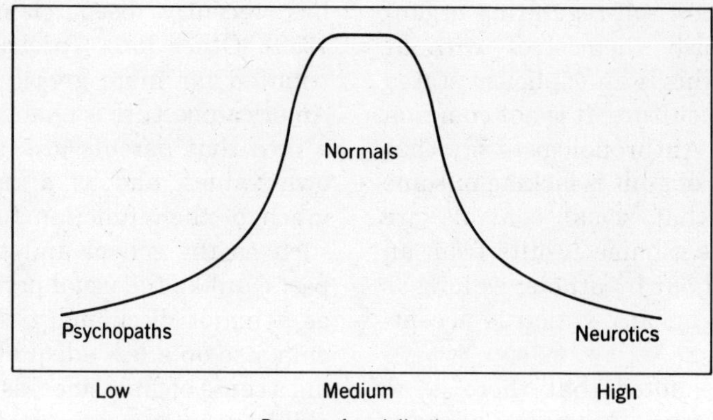

FIGURE 7-1 The usual clinical position concerning adjustment.

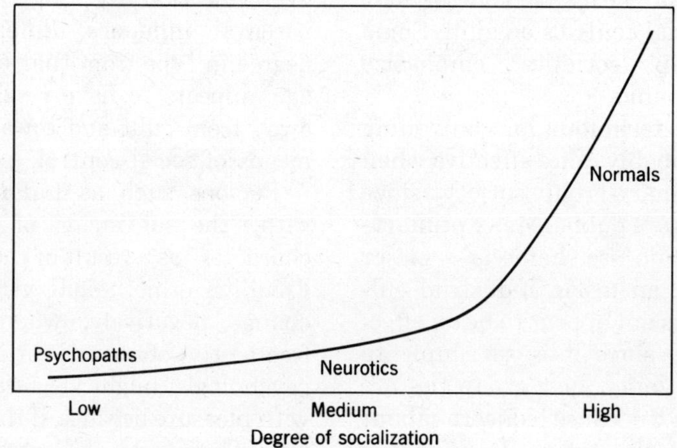

FIGURE 7-2 Mowrer's view of the adjustment of continuum (Peterson, 1967).

with the normal person being the most adequately socialized, the neurotic being intermediate, and the psychopath or sociopath least well socialized.

The majority of empirical research supports Mowrer's point of view (e.g., see Peterson, 1967), despite the fact that it is a somewhat unpopular position. However, Mowrer does not distinguish in his writings between two separate domains of conscience: resistance to temptation and guilt following yielding; further, he shows little concern regarding resistance and a great deal of concern with regard to guilt following yielding. Recent research (Johnson, Ackerman, Frank, & Fionda, 1968) indicates that although prevailing clinical theories associate excessive guilt with mental health problems, there may be no real relationship. However, there is a strong relationship between high resistance to temptation and mental health. These data suggest that both sides of the argument concerning the effects of the Freudian ethic on mental health in America are wrong, since amounts of guilt and/or shame may be unrelated to mental health. The data still support the view of Mowrer, LaPiere, and others that the commonly accepted popular position derived from psychiatry and clinical psychology (act out; express your impulse life; then you'll be mentally healthy) is incorrect, since the tendency to *resist* temptation tends to be positively associated with mental health.

Cultural Norms in Family Structure and Conscience Development

Mischel (1961) demonstrated that a male child reared without a father was less able to delay a small immediate reward in favor of a larger delayed reward. Seigman (1966) showed that even within a highly select group (medical students), those whose fathers had been absent while they were ages one–five were more psychopathic and criminal in their behavior than those whose fathers were not absent during this time period. These data suggest that cultural differences in family structure, resulting in differential amounts of father-son contact, should have highly important effects on conscience development and in other forms of behavior as well (see Deutsch & Brown, 1964). This proposition was put to the test by Bacon, Child, and Barry (1963). Their cross-cultural study shows quite clearly that the less the opportunity in a culture for a son to get to know, love, and identify with his father, the higher the crime rate of that culture will be. While father absence versus presence may have little or nothing to do with the amount of guilt a member of a given culture feels after he has committed a misdeed, it seems a strong determinant of whether a male member of that culture (males comprise the majority of offenders against society) will resist the temptation to violate cultural norms. Therefore it seems clear, both within and between cultures, that certain culturally or subculturally determined aspects of family structure have a marked influence on behavior. Growing up in a matriarchal, frequently father-absent subculture provides real handicaps in willingness and ability to achieve that perhaps can be overcome only if the culture provides other means of male identification for father-absent boys, for example, "Big Brothers," or more male elementary-school teachers.

Culture, Childhood Determinism, and the Freudian Variables

The Freudian variables (discussed in Chapter 9 as they apply to the American experience), having to do chiefly with such aspects of parent practices as toilet training and weaning, often have been studied by anthropologists in an attempt to determine a modal personality structure of a given culture, a structure that presumably results from certain childhood experiences. For example, the Japanese are said to be concerned with ritual, tidiness, and orderliness (Benedict, 1946; Gorer, 1943), and this concern is said to be a *consequence* of extremely early and rigid toilet training. This general position may be questioned from two points. First, are the Japanese overly compulsive and overcontrolled? One of the authors has heard an honored, elderly, and dignified Japanese scientist describe to a group of American and Japanese colleagues how he became so drunk at Maxim's of Paris that he could not walk, faked a heart attack, and was taken back to his hotel in an ambulance. This account, and a general Japanese permissiveness toward drunkenness, do not suggest an overly compulsive, rigid, or ritualistic approach to the world and suggests that certain stereotypes concerning the Japanese are incorrect. Second, even if we grant, for the moment, that Japanese are ritualistic and compulsive, could these behaviors be attributed to early toilet training, as Benedict and Gorer suggest? Both Benedict and Gorer assume that toilet training in Japan is early and harsh. Unfortunately, for their position, actual studies of Japanese toilet-training practices (Sikkema, 1949; Lanham, 1956; Norbeck & Norbeck, 1956) show Japanese to be no more early or rigid in training than are Americans. It may be that Japanese as a group are more ritualistic and compulsive than Americans (though there are no data demonstrating this) but even if they are, there appears to be no link between the supposed personality traits and toilet training. Anthropological data often can be questioned. Margaret Mead's (1935) gentle Arapesh tribe, within which both males and females were "maternal" in their interests in gardening and in child-rearing, and which was portrayed by Mead as a culture in which both male and female adult roles were kindly, nurturant, and "feminine," also was a group whose male members were among the most feared warriors and headhunters in New Guinea (Fortune, 1939). Kindly, motherly, cannibalistic headhunters! There appear to be contradictions in the description, just as there are contradictions in describing the tradition-oriented (yet highly adaptable), rigid and orderly (while condoning thoroughgoing intoxication and the complete chaos of Tokyo traffic) Japanese. As will be seen in Chapter 9, the Freudian variables do not hold up well within a culture as an explanation of adult behavior. These variables seem better able to predict behavior across cultures (e.g., see Whiting & Child, 1953), since the range of differences between cultures is greater than the range of differences in parental treatment within one culture, but even cross-culturally seem to be only partial and inadequate.

Crosscultural Variation in Parent Practices

The investigation of the Freudian variables as elements of parental treatment of children that determine the modal personality of members of a given culture appears to have produced a minimal payoff in terms of reliable information. There are other aspects of parenthood that do seem to influence personality development. As in our own culture (see Chapter 9), it is the more global aspects of parenthood that seem to be important. Such things as maternal warmth, emotional stability, the degree to which parents feel responsible for children, and the means by which children are trained to fulfill cultural norms regarding responsibility and aggression appear to be the significant determinants of the nature of the mother-child relationship, which, in turn, has profound influence on the behavior and personality of the child (Triandis & Lambert, 1961).

THE CHILD IN AMERICA

So much for cultural factors. Historical influences also appear to be significant in modes of child rearing. Some of these influences, such as the Protestant Ethic, operate in Europe as well as America. The effects of other influences, such as that of the frontier, are uniquely America's own.

The Frontier and American Child-Rearing Practices

The settler of the Atlantic seaboard was a transplanted European, generally an Englishman, still tied to Old World behavior patterns. Clad in homespun, he bowed to the squire and deacons, and still "knew his betters." Entering the Allegheny Mountains, he fought it out with the Indians. A generation later, clothed in the skins of wild animals, swinging strings of scalps, and refusing to admit any man to be their equal, much less their better, some of his descendants emerged on the western side of the Alleghenies. The frontiersmen were called, with considerable justice, "White Indians" by those who remained on the seaboard. They moved on to master the continent.

The frontier did much to shape American attitudes toward the world. Since the pervasive attitudes of a culture shape its child-rearing practices, the experience of the frontier necessarily contributed markedly to the differences in child-rearing between the American and the European branches of Western culture.[1] Frederick Jackson Turner in his classic study, *The Frontier in American History* (1921), described some of the changes in American attitudes and character wrought by the frontier. The frontiersman was optimistic: the promised land was always just over the next hill. Today may be bad but tomorrow will be better. This hopeful attitude, resulting from the fluidity of social position on the frontier, may have much to do with high levels of aspiration for oneself and one's children. The hope and belief, so widespread in America, that one's children can and should surpass oneself in accomplishment may well stem from this basically optimistic world view of the frontier.

Most European visitors to America such as the Trollopes, the mother in the 1830's and the son 30 years later (see F. Trollope, 1832, and A. Trollope, 1862), have remarked on the wilfulness, independence, and general orneriness of American children. This general feeling persists to the present time and probably has a certain basis in fact; it is attested to by anyone who has spent much time in Europe. Equalitarian treatment of children—equalitarian by European standards—was and is at least partially the result of the frontier experience.

The frontiersman, as a member of a relatively anarchistic hunting society, may have desired independence in his children in order to improve their chances of survival. Further, he apparently believed, with a fervor not understandable today, in the idea of equality in social relations. The frontiersman also may have been exposed sufficiently to American Indian child-rearing practices to have received social reinforcement for his beliefs from them; the Indians valued a fairly high degree of self-assertion on the part of children, especially male children, because they believed this to be indicative of later strength and determination. Whatever the relative influences of specific underlying causes may have been, American experience has resulted in the American parent granting to the child a greater degree of freedom and equality than is granted by his European counterpart at any given period of time. As the content of the American experience has changed, it is not surprising that different modes of child-rearing have appeared, as was evidenced in shifts associated with the decline of the Protestant Ethic and the rise of the Social Ethic.

Protestant Ethic, Social Ethic, Self-Reliance, and Child-Rearing Practices

Max Weber (1930) introduced the term *Protestant Ethic* to denote a set of ideas about man's relation to the natural and supernatural which gained prominence during the period of the Reformation. This new "world view" emphasized the development of the individual. The individual, within this framework, was without a mediator in his church and had to find salvation for himself. Self-reliance was emphasized as opposed to reliance

[1]Like the American branch of Western culture, the Australian branch underwent the same experiences and, similarly, differed from the Europeans.

on the social group. Further, the Protestant Ethic contained within itself the doctrine of "stewardship," the belief that God had made us the stewards or caretakers of His material world. The amount of possessions a person had was a good predictor of whether he would fall among the sheep or the goats, the elect or the damned. Thus hard work, self-sacrifice, and thrift, leading to the acquisition of funds, indirectly served as a measure of an individual's probability of being saved. Within the Protestant Ethic man became steward not only of his possessions, but of his time; God granted humans only a brief time to serve Him and this was not to be wasted on frivolous activities. The Protestant Ethic, in pure form, has as an ideal a pleasureless, hard-driven, and independent individual, ultimately responsible for his own affairs in both this and the next world.

It has been argued that the Protestant Ethic is being replaced in contemporary American society by the Social Ethic, an ethic that emphasizes adjustment to and dependence on others at the cost of independence and self-reliance; an ethic in which "other-direction," a concern for group approval, takes precedence over "inner-direction," the satisfaction of one's own standards and values (Riesman, 1953; LaPiere, 1959; Whyte, 1956). Adherents of this position believe that we have:

> . . . On the one hand, "the man of enterprise" of The Protestant Ethic, self-confident that through reason, integrity, industry, initiative, and faith in God he can bring into being the perfect social order, and, on the other hand, the delicate, womb-yearning individual of The Freudian Ethic, lacking self-reliance, at odds with "pathological society" from birth to death, chafing under its restraints, socially irresponsible, needing to be constantly nourished with love and pampered through such consideration as condones his offenses, delinquencies, and crimes, no matter what his age or status (Wescott, 1960).

This is an extreme view (not held, by the way, by Wescott). The changing structure of society forces people in some ways, as in decreased reliance on the support of primary groups, to be *more* independent. Yet it seems likely that dependency relations are increasing within the family at one extreme and toward the federal government at the other. This results from the weakening of extrafamilial primary group ties that used to sustain individuals.

With regard to child-rearing, it has been demonstrated that child-training practices differ between hunting and fishing as opposed to agricultural societies (Barry, Child, & Bacon, 1959). Achievement and independence are more highly prized by hunters and fishers than by agriculturalists, whereas the reverse holds true for obedience and responsibility. The aims of child-rearing differ according to the manner in which food is acquired. It may be that forces equally strong as those differentiating hunting and fishing from agricultural societies produce differences in child-rearing patterns in entrepreneurial, industrial societies, in contrast to bureaucratic, welfare-state societies. The independence, inner-directedness, and self-reliance that were the goals of the Protestant Ethic might have been a result of an adaptation to the industrial revolution, whereas the supposedly increasing emphasis on other-direction and reliance on, and conformity to, larger social groups may be a necessary adjustment to the new and growing welfare-state bureaucracy.[2]

[2]We should note that the words *welfare state* and *bureaucracy* have acquired negative connotations. We do not intend to use the words in either a positive or a negative sense, but merely to describe an existing phenomenon.

This explanation of the shift from Protestant Ethic to Social Ethic finds considerable support in contemporary psychological research. In a most interesting and important book entitled *The Changing American Parent,* Miller and Swanson (1958) differentiate between entrepreneurial and bureaucratic parents.

We discuss the distinction between entrepreneurial and bureaucratic attitudes later in this chapter. Here, however, let us point out that results of studies of occupational types, bureaucrat and entrepreneur, show considerable agreement in finding entrepreneurs to be more closely tied to the values of the Protestant Ethic. As a consequence, their goal is to produce independent children. To do so, they are more inclined to reject the child's impulse life—his responding to impulses rather than to reason—and to allow less variability in role playing than are bureaucrats. The bureaucrat, probably because his life is less demanding and his world more secure, it more optimistic. He appears to emphasize adjustment—the Social Ethic—rather than independence. The child is given wider areas of freedom, since mistakes, when made, do not bear as dire consequences. The bureaucrat generally is more permissive.

In the view of William H. Whyte (1956), the independent entrepreneur has abdicated in favor of the "organization man." Although the Protestant Ethic, and the parent attitudes and behaviors that went along with it, might have been admirably suited to an earlier economic era, the milder, more socially oriented Social Ethic has supplanted it, and parents have adapted their demands on children to newer circumstances. For better or worse, change has occurred in the basic orientation of Americans toward the world, and with it, changes in child-rearing practices. As the proportion of bureaucrats continues to increase in the future, present trends should become even more pronounced.

Contemporary Trends—Culture and Counter-Culture

A child grows up with his mother and father as well as with a number of other adults. These adults differ from one another, but one learns from all of them. The adults generally are interested in children learning their skills; learning from their experiences. The adults are with the children all day long training them in useful roles by example and by telling them interesting and instructive stories in front of the fireplace, cookstove, or campfire in the evenings. A child works and plays with the adults—learns how to farm, to cook, to be an adequate rough carpenter, to play the musical instrument that is needed for the family music sessions, to take part in amateur dramatic productions within the family circle. There are lots of other kids in the family. Not many playthings, except for homemade toys, but lots of playmates and a good deal of freedom—after having done the chores—for play. What does this family sound like? It sounds like the family of frontier America. It sounds like the old style extended family of rural and small town America that existed before our increasing mobility caused us to shift to the nuclear family structure. It also may be the wave of the future, the former flower children of Haight-Ashbury, along with many other "hippie" types, seem to be developing a "new" kind of family in the commune that really is a very old kind of family—the extended family.

Certainly there are many varieties of life-style that fall within the general rubric "counter-culture." The United States again, just as in the past (see Holloway, 1966), contains a variety of social experiments. It appears that more and more of these social experiments are moving toward rural environments and to the kind of rural self-sufficiency that once was part of the American frontier tradition (Hedgepeth, 1970). The counter-culture appears to be developing what may be a viable alternative to the dominant anomic, nuclear-family dominated, urban American life-style.

Is the Child Basically Good or Bad?

Until the middle of the 1950's it was often assumed that before the advent of psychology parents had led a relatively untroubled life in which each generation was reared in the same fashion as the one before. The father was a bearded, stern but fair judge, and the mother a subordinate, warm, loving, motherly, house-bound woman. Research has since shown that even that era of comparative calm was rocked with such controversies as those having to do with the morality of bottle feeding and with "breaking the will of the child" (Sunley, 1955). The golden age was less golden than had been believed.

One historical analysis of child-rearing in America demonstrated that religious orientation prompted certain assumptions about the nature of children. The major orthodox Christian point of view is that man is depraved. Adherents of the Calvinistic point of view, for example, believed the newborn to be damned as a result of Original Sin, and to be full of "the Old Adam." From this point of view, the young child was both evil and rebellious. The child's will had to be broken so that he would submit to parents and to God's will. This Calvinistic tradition was very strong in America in the 1800's, leading to episodes like the following:

> . . . One mother, writing in the Mother's Magazine in 1834, described how her sixteen-month-old girl refused to say "dear mama" upon the father's order. She was led into a room alone, where she screamed wildly for ten minutes; then she was commanded again, and again refused. She was then whipped, and asked again. This kept up for four hours until the child finally obeyed. Parents commonly reported that after one such trial the child became permanently submissive. But not all parents resorted to beatings to gain this end. One mother spoke of "constant though gentle drilling," which consisted partly of refusing to give the child an object just out of its reach, however much it cried. Another mother taught submission and self-denial at one and the same time by taking objects away from the child. Strictness in diet and daily routine was apparently frequently an accompaniment to obedience training. However, many mothers seemed to find it hard to follow out such prescriptions, and the Mother's Magazine carried many exhortations to mothers to do their duty toward their child (Sunley, 1955, p. 160).

This point of view was not without opposition, even in the 1700's. Jean Jacques Rousseau taught that natural man—man before he was socialized—was good, and that society produced evil. Rousseau's ideas about child-rearing are described in his book *Émile*. They consist in part of advocating that the child be let alone so that natural goodness can become manifest, and in part of hardening the child, through vigorous exercise, for a difficult and harsh world. A third point of view, held most fully and defended most ably by Froebel (1898), also was present in this early era. This maintained that the child was like an unfolding flower and needed love and nurture.

Benjamin Franklin, first in so many things, was one of the first to espouse the "tender loving care" point of view. In 1770 he wrote his friend Polly Henson, advising her how to care for her son (his godson). He said:

> . . . Pray let him have everything he likes, I think it of great consequence while

> the features of the face are forming; it gives them a pleasant air, and, that being once become natural and fixed by habit the face is everafter the handsomer for it; and on that much of a person's good fortune may depend. Had I been crossed as much in my infant likings and inclinations as you know I have been of late years, I should have been—I was going to say—not near so handsome, but as the vanity of that expression would offend other folks' vanity, I change it, out of regard for them and say a good deal more homely (Franklin, 1770, cited in Van Doren, 1952, p. 411).

It is this last set of beliefs that appears to have gained ascendancy, but only after long and bitter struggle.

Sunley (1955) suggested that the view of the child as evil had prevailed for a long time, and still has some adherents. This attitude has decreased in strength, as shown in analyses of the changes in the child-rearing practices advocated over the years by the U.S. Children's Bureau pamphlet, *Infant Care* (see Wolfenstein, 1951). We are becoming warmer and more lenient, largely as a result of the shifts occurring in the culture. Some of these shifts are material, such as greater wealth and higher technical level, but others have to do with the changing view of man—the increasing conviction that humans are not, by their nature, depraved.

Influence of "Experts" on Child-Rearing Practices

Evidence indicates that there have been two "revolutions" during the twentieth century in the definition of parental roles and practices. These definitions have been made by experts and accepted by individuals in the mass media of communication, who advise parents. Actually parents have not shifted in behavior as much as might have been expected from the written media, but the experts have influenced parental practices, with the amounts of any particular influence differing among social classes at various times.

Watsonianism. Tight scheduling of infant feeding was beginning to be advocated by 1900. The trends toward early weaning and toilet training, toward rigid scheduling, toward a rejection of play, rocking, fondling, and other forms of bodily contact between parent and child, and toward a prohibition of such devices as pacifiers that gave the child passive pleasure increased in force. This often is called Watsonianism, since John B. Watson culminated these trends in his book, *Psychological Care of Infant and Child,* published in 1928. It seems clear that Watson was merely riding the tide and did not himself produce the trends. Yet his book did add weight to the idea of how child-rearing should be conducted. Here are some of the typical passages from it.

> The behaviorists believe that there is nothing from within to develop. If you start with a healthy body, the right number of fingers and toes, eyes, and the few elementary movements that are present at birth, you do not need anything else in the way of raw material to make a man, be that man a genius, a cultured gentleman, a rowdy or a thug (Watson, 1928, p. 41).
>
> There is a sensible way of treating children. Treat them as though they were young adults. Dress them, bathe them with care and circumspection. Let your behavior always be objective and kindly firm. Never hug and kiss them, never let them sit in your lap. If you must, kiss them on the forehead when they say good night. Shake hands with them in the morning. Give them a pat on the head if they have made an extraordinarily good job of a difficult task. Try it out. In a week's time you will find how easy it is to be perfectly objective with your child

> and at the same time kindly. You will be utterly ashamed of the mawkish, sentimental way you have been handling it (pp. 81–82).

The aims of this system of child-rearing are described by Watson as follows.

> We have tried to sketch in the foregoing chapters a child as free as possible of sensitivities to people and one who, almost from birth, is relatively independent of the family situation. . . . Above all, we have tried to create a problem-solving child. We believe that a problem-solving technique (which can be trained) plus boundless absorption in activity (which can also be trained) are behavioristic factors which have worked in many civilizations of the past and which, so far as we can judge, will work equally well in most types of civilizations that are likely to confront us in the future (pp. 186–187).

Watson positively valued independence, a lack of concern for others, a controlled impulse life, and an active, manipulative, striving posture toward the world. He wished to rear children in a way consonant with the Protestant Ethic. Watsonianism, most fashionable in the entrepreneurial 1920's, may have begun losing its influence partially as a result of the accelerated growth of bureaucracy in the 1930's.

There are other reasons why Watsonianism was not destined for a long life. Its child-rearing technique appeared to be full of stress to parents. One still finds, occasionally, a Watsonian mother rearing her infant on a rigid, four-hour schedule. It is 3 hours and 55 minutes since the last feeding, the baby is howling as it has been for 15 minutes, and has turned red with rage. The mother's eye is on her wristwatch. The remaining 5 minutes seem like hours. The psychic wear-and-tear alone of such aspects of Watsonianism seemed sufficient to turn parents away from this philosophy of child-rearing. Many mothers of the era say that they reared the first child *a la* Watson; the later ones in terms of what seemed to be the most expedient procedure. Besides, as has been noted, the role of children is more and more that of being a love object. It is difficult to express this love when every kiss leads to future neurosis, and even such relatively innocuous activities as bouncing the baby on one's knee may produce sexual feelings in the young child and lead to later sexual abnormality.

Certain ideas ran counter to Watsonianism and helped its decline. Although Watson apparently accepted the reality and significance of the Oedipus complex, and for this reason advocated a "distant" relation with the child in order to reduce the Oedipal conflict, other interpreters of Freud used the same theory to defend the gratification of the child's impulse life. More important in bringing about the eventual decline of Watsonianism was the idea of *homeostasis,* or *internal equilibrium,* originated by Claud Bernard in the 1860's and developed by Walter B. Cannon in the early 1920's, culminating in his book *The Wisdom of the Body.* (1932). Cannon's thesis, in brief, was that the body adapted to environmental stresses and among other adaptive mechanisms often "told" the individual through cravings what the body needed. The tendency of pregnant women in some parts of the world to eat earth as the result of an "irresistible urge" really occurred because the women suffered mineral deficiencies that could be reduced through the eating of certain kinds of earth. Cannon's theory, buttressed with facts, suggested that if individuals craved something, the craving might be the result of actual physiological needs. Clara Davis (1931) operating from this same general point of view, allowed infants to self-select their diets. They chose the nourishment they desired from a rather wide variety of foods. Although any infant might go on short "food jags" during which he ate only one type of food, each infant over a long time interval chose a perfectly balanced diet. This fact showed that Cannon's theory was correct and also countered Watson's view that children almost necessarily liked what was bad for them.

People began to think that if infants thrived on self-selected diets, they also might thrive on self-regulated schedules, and also might "need," in a physical sense, the contact and cuddling they seemed to enjoy, despite Watson's belief that these behaviors led to later maladjustment. Their demands were probably because they needed the gratification, not because of perversity.

"Tender Loving Care." The first complete reversal of the Watsonian trend was by Margaret A. Ribble in her book *The Rights of Infants* (1943).[3] From the earlier position that fondling, hugging, kissing, rocking, and other forms of body contact between parent and child was *bad*, she demurred, maintaining that these activities were all important, and that the child denied them was deprived as significantly as one denied nourishment or sunshine. She held that the complex of treatments often lumped together as "tender loving care" was necessary for the physical, intellectual, and emotional growth and well-being of any child. Research data (Harlow, 1958) suggest that she might be basically correct regarding the need for body contact, even though certain of her hypotheses have shown to be incorrect (Hopper & Pinneau, 1957; Pinneau, 1951).

Support for Ribble's position came fast. A new, "easier," warmer approach gained ascendancy. Yet there have been suggestions that the field is being reversed again—that society is moving back to the tough approach (Wolfenstein, 1951). It seems doubtful, however, that parent practices will swing back completely to Watsonianism. If they should, they will be bucking a strong current of forces, such as increasing bureaucracy and greater involvement with children, which dispose parents toward increased mildness.

There is not much probability that expert opinion will intensify future changes in child-rearing practices. Naive acceptance of expert opinion has dwindled. The higher level of general education and the several rapid about-faces in advocated techniques have made the public wary about experts. Parents wonder whether the experts really know what they are talking about. Besides, the experts themselves are less likely to be certain of having *the* formula for perfect child-rearing as they grow aware of the wide range of innate individual differences in temperament and ability among humans. Watson and his followers explicitly rejected the notion of innate individual differences, and the "tender loving care" school has largely ignored them. If individual differences are great, then no single method of rearing can be expected to work for all. Nevertheless, as shown in Chapter 10, there are ways to increase the probability of rearing children with the virtues prized most highly by parents and the defects they find least offensive.

Class Variations in Child-Rearing Practices

Social class had continued to attract the interest of child psychologists. This variable, drawn from sociology, has had

[3]Other prominent adherents of this orientation were Spitz (1945) and Bowlby (1952).

considerable significance in child-psychology research because of the wide belief that parental practices vary among classes, which results in discernible differences in the personality and behavior of children in these classes. Education, occupation, area of residence, and income play major roles in the definition of social class. To the extent that children are reared differently by parents who vary in these respects and who respond in diverse ways to social institutions, class differences may be expected to produce variance in their upbringing.

Researchers once found that social classes differed substantially, but races only slightly, in child-rearing practices. The middle class showed greater harshness and an earlier and more general curbing of the child's impulse life than the lower class (Davis & Havighurst, 1946). These observations may have been entirely correct in describing the child-rearing patterns of the 1940's. But apparently what was true of the 1940's no longer applies. A study conducted, for example, in the Boston area in the early 1950's (Maccoby & Gibbs, 1954) obtained results markedly opposed to the Davis–Havighurst study. Although both studies found the middle class to have higher educational and occupational aspirations for its children, the Maccoby–Gibbs study noted that the middle, not the lower, class was more tolerant of aggression, sex play, and other expressions of impulse life. It was less demanding in toilet and cleanliness training, and it used less severe punishment. This reversal is probably due in part to the later researchers' inclusion in their lower-class sample of individuals who by other criteria of social class would perhaps fall in the lower-middle class. The shift in the opinion of experts, whose influence is likely to be greater among the middle class as a result of wider exposure to the mass media, may also have been a contributing factor. In addition, the reversal may have been prompted by other forces.

Still more recent and more psychologically important data (Miller & Swanson, 1958; Klatskin, 1952) lead to the conclusion that differences in classes decreased appreciably in the postwar years.

> As of 1957, there are suggestions that the cultural gap may be narrowing. Spock has joined the Bible on the working-class shelf. . . . Apparently "love" and "limits" are both watchwords for the coming generation of parents. As Mrs. Johnson, down in the flats, puts away the hairbrush and decides to have a talk with her unruly youngster "like the book says," Mrs. Thomas, on the hill, is dutifully striving to overcome her guilt at the thought of giving John the punishment she now admits he deserves (Bronfenbrenner, 1958, p. 423).

The differences in world view that once existed among classes must have had some basis in sociological, anthropological, and historical influences. Doubtless the differences in child-rearing and in child personality have dwindled substantially as a result of the increased homogeneity of the culture. One distinction often noted—the willingness of the middle, but not the lower, class to delay gratification—has been attributed to the uncertainty of lower-class life (Davis, 1946). It also may be accounted for by the fact that father absence reduces the ability to delay gratification (Mischel, 1961), and father absence is more frequent in lower-class families (Deutsch & Brown, 1964). This uncertainty led individuals to seize gratifications immediately; otherwise the opportunity would very likely vanish. As members of lower-economic groups acquired the greater security of relatively low but certain income, resulting from union protection on the job, unemployment compensation, and other features of a welfare state, their lives were likely to become more predictable. Hence they became more willing to postpone reward and develop long-range goals. Accompanying this kind of change comes what the sociologists call "upward mobility." There is an increased interest in education as a means of self-improvement, and a greater acceptance of the Protestant Ethic at the very time that it appears to be losing its appeal for the middle class.

A final force narrowing the differences between the classes is the mass media of communication. Middle-class patterns of democracy, consultation, and arbitration; of paternal involvement in household chores and child care; of parental permissiveness; and of delayed gratification, long-range planning, and high aspirations for children—all these are grist for the mills of producers of television family series. Exposure to any set of values should have some effect on exposed individuals. Although television and other mass media may present a distorted image of middle-class life, their picture is an intimate one that allows social learning to occur.

Though class differences in life experiences and in finances and housing have diminished, some value differences persist. Kohn (1963) suggests that working-class parents are more traditionally oriented and middle-class parents more positively oriented toward social change; and that for these reasons working-class parents have the goal of teaching children to conform to parental values, while middle-class parents continue to be interested in producing children more capable of self-determination of values and self-direction of behavior.

Class differences that persist in the area of maternal behavior more often are associated with maternal coerciveness (with lower-class mothers being more restrictive and severe) than with affection or nurturance (Waters & Crandall, 1964). It would seem that mothers love their children as much across social classes, and have roughly the same goals for them, but that there are class differences in the procedures used in attempting to help the children reach these goals.

Entrepreneur versus Bureaucrat. As previously noted, beyond the more conventional social-class differences considerable variation exists between entrepreneurial and bureaucratic individuals in the upper-occupational brackets, probably as a result of conflicting social demands. The entrepreneur, an independent individual, accepts the Protestant Ethic and feelings of guilt as a means of controlling behavior more than does the more socially minded bureaucrat. This difference is less discernible than the one concerning classes. Yet entrepreneurs and bureaucrats are faced with different sets of social pressures; this occasions a variance between them in their attitudes toward the world. Because they view the world differently, they raise their children differently; and the children have to adjust to the world as perceived by their parents.

According to Miller and Swanson (1958), the basic difference between the two groups appears in the area of risk taking, and their differentiation should be made in these terms. Such representative entrepreneurial occupations as physician or clinical psychologist in private practice, small businessman, door-to-door salesman on straight commission, or contract fruit picker, though differing widely in status and required skills, have in common the fact that they require the older ethic of self-reliance and independence. Income depends on hard work, individual initiative, and a fair degree of risk taking. In bureaucratic occupations, on the contrary, job security is high and risk taking minimal. A "womb-to-tomb" security is available to anyone who accepts the system and represses the once necessary trait of independence. Adjustment to the group and its norms becomes an important aspect of employment. Small wonder that bureaucrats and entrepreneurs differ in their attitudes toward the world, in what they believe their children should be like, and in how they go about obtaining the kind of behavior they seek from their children.

Entrepreneurs, as a group, believe the world to be harsher than do bureaucrats. They believe that children should be trained early to cope with this hostile environment. At least so far as early parent practices are concerned, the entrepreneur is more severe. Toilet training, weaning, and the completion of many other developmental tasks are demanded earlier of children by entrepreneurs than by bureaucrats (Miller & Swanson, 1958). As compared with bureaucrats, entrepreneurs are more authoritarian and lean toward a more rigid delineation of sex roles and a more traditionalistic orientation to family life (Johnson, Johnson, & Martin, 1961). These differences may result in part from the higher educational achievements of bureaucrats than of entrepreneurs of comparable social-class level.

Perhaps many conflicts regarding child-rearing practices, such as the question of the school being overly concerned with adjustment at the expense of achievement, have their roots in the entrepreneurial-bureaucratic antithesis. The bureaucratic orientation of educators, for example, may be at odds with the entrepreneurial orientation of school boards dominated by businessmen. The differences between these groups are substantial and, unlike some of the previously discussed social-class differences, may retain their significance for some time.

Race, Religion, Region

It is sometimes claimed (e.g., Davis & Havighurst, 1946) that race differences in child-rearing practices are slight, once racial groups are equated on social class. This may be so, with regard to such things as age of weaning and toilet training. However, differences in family structure may produce marked differences in child behavior. As noted in Chapter 2 the absence of a male figure in the home appears to produce a number of deleterious effects: reducing achievement and ability to delay gratification; increasing psychopathic tendencies. The black family is much more frequently characterized by father absence than is the white family (Deutsch & Brown, 1964; Frazier, 1966). This difference in family structure might be expected to have considerable social consequence regarding the behavior of the offspring—especially the male offspring. Ethnic differences in family structure may also differentially influence the offspring of Latin-American as opposed to Anglo-American families. Latin-American fathers (including many of the Latins in the United States) play a more patriarchal role than is common among the Anglos. The Latin father has, as an ideal, a highly dominant but somewhat distant role (e.g., see Lewis, 1959, 1964). Even when equated in social class, a father-absent Negro boy, frequently involved in gangs to learn the masculine role, has a problem very different from that of a Mexican-American boy, who usually has an adequate opportunity to learn the masculine role at home but joins gangs more often in an attempt to gain freedom from paternal dominance in order to exercise his masculine role.

The effects of religious orientation on patterns of child-rearing often have to do with such "unworldly" groups as the Hutterites (Kaplan & Plaut, 1956) and the Amish (Francis, 1955). Nunn (1964) discussed parents who attempt to control their children through a "coalition with God"—for example, "If you do what I told you not to do, then God will be angry." This approach to controlling children appears to be a maladaptive one, usually used by incompetent and ineffectual parents, and probably has deleterious influences on the children. Type of religious affiliation has a strong influence on the frequency with which this approach to child training is used. Democracy and mother-father equality in sharing of authority seems also to be associated with religion; Catholic children believe that authority is *not* shared in their homes more frequently than do children from other religious groups (Hess & Torney, 1962).

Another comparison of religiocultural groups is found in Kluckholn's and Strodtbeck's *Variations in Value Orientations* (1961), which compares, among other things, the child-rearing practices of Spanish Americans, Texans, Mormons (Latter Day Saints), Zuni, and Navajo (also see Hollenberg, 1952; and Vogt & Roberts, 1956, for other publications involving the study of certain of these groups). Despite the fact that these five groups live close together in an area of the American Southwest, they have very different views of their relations to the environment (e.g., does man attempt to master the physical environment, does he accept it fatalistically, or does he attempt to place himself in harmony with it?) and as a result vary in the values transmitted to offspring and in the manner in which these values are transmitted.

Even within America, race, religion, and regional subcultural differences produce some of the diversity in attitudes toward child-rearing, and the goals of child training.

CONCLUSION

Benjamin Lee Whorf (1956), whose studies of language have played a significant role in contemporary psychology, concluded from a study of Indo-European tongues that the differences among them are very minor—so minor, in fact, that he lumped them all together as "Standard Average European." This may be small consolation to a student learning a language. Yet German, Classic Greek, French, Latin, and Latvian resemble one another so closely that the differences among them are slight in comparison with the distinction between all of them and non-Indo-European languages. The same might be said about variability within the Western culture. Although Westerners differ from each other, they nevertheless have been subjected to sufficiently similar experiences to show a strong resemblance. Since experiences within American society disclose a common quality even greater than that of its ties with Western culture, variability among Americans is reduced still further.

To draw another analogy from language, Americans speak a number of dialects. The differences among Down East Yankee, "Brooklynese," the dialects of the Midwest and Far West, and the drawl of the Southerner are easily discerned, but all Americans can understand each other without strain. So, too, with differences in child-rearing patterns. Differences certainly exist, but within a larger pattern of homogeneity.

This common bond in the socialization process is strong enough to produce an "American type," an individual different from all others yet patently similar to fellow Americans in basic orientation. Since all individuals are exposed to the various influences described in this chapter, if in somewhat varying degrees, the differences between parents in child-rearing practices and between children in personality and behavior are markedly narrowed. It is within this cultural homogeneity that the specific life situation of an individual child produces a unique person.

REFERENCES

Bacon, M. K., Child, I. L., & Barry, H. A cross cultural study of correlates of crime. *Journal of Abnormal and Social Psychology,* 1963, **66**, 291–300.

Barry, H., Child, I. L., & Bacon, M. K. Relation of child training to subsistency economy. *American Anthropologist,* 1959, **61**, 51–63.

Becker, H., & Meyers, R. C. Sacred and secular aspects of human socialization. *Sociometry,* 1948, **5**, Nos. 4 and 5.

Benedict, R. *The chrysanthemum and the sword: Patterns of Japanese culture.* Boston: Houghton Mifflin, 1946.

Benedict, R. Continuities and discontinuities in cultural conditioning. In P. Mullahy (Ed.), *A study of interpersonal relations.* New York: Hermitage, 1949.

Boehm, L. The development of independence: A comparative study. *Child Development,* 1957, **28**, 85–92.

Bowlby, J. *Maternal care and mental health.* Geneva: World Health Organization, 1952.

Bronfenbrenner, U. Socialization and social class through time and space. In E. E. Maccoby, T. M. Newcomb, & E. L. Hartley (Eds.), *Readings in social psychology.* (3rd ed.) New York: Holt, 1958. Pp. 400–425.

Cannon, W. B. *The wisdom of the body.* New York: Norton, 1932.

Davis, A. The motivation of the underprivileged worker. In W. F. Whyte (Ed.), *Industry and society.* New York: McGraw-Hill, 1946. Pp. 84–106.

Davis, A., & Havighurst, R. J. Social class and color differences in child rearing. *American Sociological Review,* 1946, **11**, 698–710.

Davis, C. M. Self-selection of diets: An experiment with infants. *The Trained Nurse and Hospital Review,* 1931, 629–634.

Deutsch, M., & Brown, B. Social influence in Negro-white intelligence differences. *Journal of Social Issues,* 1964, **10**, 24–35.

Durkheim, E. *The elementary forms of religious life* (translated by J. W. Swain). New York: Macmillan, 1915.

Durkheim, E. *The division of labor in society* (translated by G. Simpson). Glencoe, Ill.: Free Press, 1947 (originally published in 1902).

Durkheim, E. *Suicide* (translated by J. A. Spaulding and G. Simpson). Glencoe, Ill.: Free Press, 1951 (originally published in 1897).

Fortune, R. F. Arapesh warfare. *American Anthropologist,* 1939. **41**, 28.

Francis, E. K. *In search of Utopia.* Glencoe, Ill.: Free Press, 1955.

Frazier, E. F. *The Negro family in the United States.* (Revised and abridged edition) Chicago: University of Chicago Press, 1966.

Froebel, F. *Mother play* (translated by H. R. Eliot and S. E. Blow). New York: Appleton, 1898.

Gesell, A. L. *Wolf-child & human child.* New York: Harper, 1941.

Gorer, G. Themes in Japanese culture. *Transactions of the New York Academy of Sciences,* Series II, 1943, **5**, 106–124.

Haimowitz, M. L. What price virtue. In M. L. Haimowitz and N. R. Haimowitz (Eds.), *Human development: Selected readings.* New York: Crowell, 1960.

Harlow, H. The nature of love. *American Psychologist,* 1958, **13**, 673–685.

Hedgepeth, W. *The alternative: Communal life in new America* (photographs by D. Stock) New York, MacMillan, 1970.

Hess, R. D., & Torney, J. V. Religion, age, and sex in children's perceptions of family authority. *Child Development,* 1962; **33**, 781–789.

Hollenberg, E. Child training among the Zeepi. Unpublished doctoral dissertation, Harvard University, 1952.

Holloway, M. *Heavens on earth: Utopian communities in America 1680–1880.* New York: Dover, 1966.

Hopper, H. E., & Pinneau, S. R. Frequency of regurgitation as related to the amount of stimulation received from the mother. *Child Development,* 1957, **28**, 229–235.

Itard, F. M. G. *The wild boy of Aveyron* (translated by G. H. Humphrey). New York: Century, 1932 (originally published in 1894).

Jaensch, E. R. *Der Gegentypus.* Leipzig: Barth, 1938.

Johnson, R. C., Ackerman, J. M., Frank, H., & Fionda, A. J. Resistance to temptation, guilt following yielding, and psychopathology. *Journal of Consulting and Clinical Psychology,* 1968, **32**, 169–175.

Johnson, R. C., Johnson, C. M., & Martin, L. Authoritarianism, occupation, and sex role differentiation of children. *Child Development,* 1961, **32**, 271–276.

Kaplan, B., & Plaut, T. *Personality in a communal society: An analysis of the mental health of the Hutterites.* Lawrence, Kan.: University of Kansas, 1956.

Klatskin, E. H. Shifts in child care practices in three social classes under an infant care program of flexible methodology. *American Journal of Orthopsychiatry,* 1952, **22**, 52–61.

Kluckhohn, F. R., & Strodtbeck, F. L. *Variations in value orientations.* Evanston, Ill.: Row, Peterson, 1961.

Kohn, M. L. Social class and parent-child relationships: An interpretation. *American Journal of Sociology,* 1963, **68**, 471–480.

Landis, P. H. *Adolescence and youth.* New York: McGraw-Hill, 1945.

Lanham, B. B. Aspects of child care in Japan: Preliminary report. In D. G. Haring (Ed.), *Personal character and cultural milieu. A book of readings.* (3rd ed.) Syracuse, N. Y.: Syracuse University Press, 1956.

LaPiere, R. *The Freudian ethic: An analysis of the subversion of American character.* New York: Duell, Sloan & Pearce, 1959.

Lewis, O. *Five families.* New York: Basic Books, 1959.

Lewis, O. *Pedro Martinez.* New York: Random House, 1964.

Life, 72, 16, April 28, 1972, pp. 72–73.

Maccoby, E. E., & Gibbs, P. K. Methods of child rearing in two social classes. In W. E. Martin and C. B. Stendler (Eds.), *Readings in child development.* New York: Harcourt, Brace, 1954.

Mead, M. *Sex and temperament in three primitive societies.* New York: Morrow, 1935.

Mead, M. *And keep your powder dry.* New York: Morrow, 1943.

Miller, D. R., & Swanson, G. D. *The changing American parent.* New York: Wiley, 1958.

Mischel, W. Father-absence and delay of gratification. *Journal of Abnormal and Social Psychology*, 1961, **63**, 116–124.

Mowrer, O. H. Psychotherapy and the problem of guilt, confession, and expiation. In W. Dennis (Ed.), *Current trends in psychology, X.* Pittsburgh: University of Pittsburgh Press, 1960.

Mowrer, O. H. *The crisis in psychiatry and religion.* Princeton, N. J.: Van Nostrand, 1961.

Mowrer, O. H. (Ed.), *Morality and mental health.* Chicago: Rand McNally, 1967.

Norbeck, E., & Norbeck, M. Child training in a Japanese fishing community. In D. G. Haring (Ed.), *Personal character and cultural milieu. A book of readings.* (3rd ed.) Syracuse, N. Y.: Syracuse University Press, 1956.

Nunn, C. Z. Child control through a "Coalition with God." *Child Development*, 1964, **35**, 417–432.

Ogburn, W. F., & Bose, N. K. On the trail of the wolf children. *Genetic Psychology Monographs*, 1959, **60**, 117–193.

Peterson, D. R. The insecure child: Over-socialized or undersocialized. In O. H. Mowrer (Ed.), *Morality and mental health.* Chicago: Rand McNally, 1967.

Pinneau, S. R. A critique on the articles by Margaret Ribble. *Child Development*, 1951, **21**, 203–228.

Riesman, D. (with N. Glazer & R. Denny). The lonely crowd: A study of the changing American character. New Haven: Yale University Press, 1953.

Ribble, M. A. *The rights of infants.* New York: Columbia University Press, 1943.

Seigman, A. W. Father absence during early childhood and antisocial behavior. *Journal of Abnormal Psychology*, 1966, **7**, 71–74.

Sikkema, M. Observations on Japanese early child training. In D. G. Haring (Ed.), *Personal character and cultural milieu.* (2nd ed.) Syracuse, N. Y.: Syracuse University Press, 1949.

Singh, J. A. L. & Zingg, R. M. *Wolf-children and feral man.* New York, Harper, 1943. [First half, diary on wolf children; second half, the acts of feral children by Zingg.]

Spencer, H. *The study of sociology.* New York: Appleton, 1912.

Spitz, R. Hospitalism. In O. Fenichel et al. (Eds.), *The psychoanalytic study of the child.* (Vol. 1) New York: International Universities Press, 1945.

Sunley, R. Early nineteenth century American literature on child rearing. In M. Mead and M. Wolfenstein (Eds.), *Childhood in contemporary cultures*, Chicago: University of Chicago Press, 1955.

Tonnies, F. *Fundamental concepts of sociology: Gemeinschaft and Gesellschaft* (translated by C. P. Loomis). New York: American Book, 1940.

Triandis, L. M., & Lanbert, W. W. Pancultural factor analysis of reported socialization practices. *Journal of Abnormal and Social Psychology*, 1961, **62**, 631–639.

Trollope, A. *North America.* New York: Harper, 1862.

Trollope, F. *Domestic manners of the Americans.* New York: Knopf, 1949 (originally published in 1832).

Turner, F. J. *The frontier in American history.* New York: 1921.

Van Doren, C. *Benjamin Franklin.* New York: Viking, 1952.

Vogt, E. Z., & Roberts, J. M. A study of values. *Scientific American*, 1956, **195**, 25–31.

Waters, E., & Crandall, V. J. Social class and observed maternal behavior from 1940 to 1960. *Child Development*, 1964, **35**, 1021–1032.

Watson, J. B. *Psychological care of infant and child.* New York: Norton, 1928.

Weber, M. *The Protestant Ethic and the spirit of capitalism* (translated by Talcott Parsons). London: Allen and Unwin, 1930.

Westcott, R. H. Man of enterprise: Whither bound? A review of LaPiere's "the Freudian ethic. . . ." *Contemporary Psychology*, 1960, **5**, 258–259.

Whiting, J. W. M., & Child, I. L. *Child training and personality: A cross cultural study.* New Haven: Yale University Press, 1953.

Whorf, B. L. *Language, thought and reality.* Cambridge, Mass.: Technology Press, 1956.

Whyte, W. H. *The organization man.* New York: Simon and Schuster, 1956.

Wolfenstein, M. The emergence of fun morality. *Journal of Social Issues*, 1951, **7**, 15–25.

chapter 8

psychosocial aspects of the family setting

chapter 8

psychosocial aspects of the family setting

chapter 8

psychosocial aspects of the family setting

What a child learns in the home is conditioned by a number of diverse influences. Such things as order of birth, position of siblings, family size, marital relations of parents, the presence of a handicapped child, whether the mother works, and whether the family belongs to a minority group all affect the social learning experiences of the child in his home. These factors might be called, as R. Sears (1950) designated them, "sociological variables." How much, if any, psychological bearing they have can be judged only through examining the research in existence, sparse as this may be in several of these areas. In some instances, little more than reports of clinical impressions are available; in others, the research undertaking has not been designed adequately enough, having neglected many controls. Thus, the precise *psychological* import of these *sociological* variables remains to be uncovered through research. Even so, there is sufficient evidence of some psychological content in these factors to warrant their close examination in order to understand the psychosocial nature of the family environment.

Later in this book we shall encounter some of the major psychological forces prevalent in the home, such as democracy and acceptance. As they affect the child these forces may outweigh the sociological variables to be considered here, even though the latter may well diminish the significance of the psychological influences. Often omitted in a psychological treatment of childhood, the sociological variables so contaminate and interact with the psychological that the result of their interaction, the child's behavior, is the product of both. The exact impact of each set of variables, however, is not easy to assess. For example, we might believe that democracy in the home is a pervasive influence on the child's behavior, yet it would be misleading to ignore the presence of one or more of the sociological variables. How does divorce, to cite one of them, affect parental use of democratic policy?

Psychology has been relatively unconcerned with the sociological variables. Ex post facto study based on retrospective reports has been the main source for investigating such matters as the effects of divorce on the child. Although some other procedure may pose greater difficulty, the pursuit of it may be worthwhile, if only because of the greater conclusiveness of the results likely to be obtained. As we shall see presently, the Koch investigation, which dealt with sibling position, exemplifies both the complexity of a well-designed study and the richness of findings yielded by a well-planned empirical exercise.

FAMILY COMPOSITION

Early in this century an unusual amount of time and effort was invested in discovering the effects of order of birth and ordinal position in the family—that is, family composition—on personality. Nearly every phase of behavior of any psychological import was studied in relation to the order in which the child was born. Many publications contained studies on the ties between birth order and "(a) genius and feeblemindedness, (b) suggestibility and aggressiveness, (c) dominance-feeling and sensitivity to pain, (d) sociability and ascendancy, (e) religious attitudes and political attitudes, (f) emotionality and stability, (g) neurotic make-up and psychotic trend, (h) happiness and jealousy, (i) school failure and fame" (Krout, 1939, pp. 5–6). In a handbook on child psychology, Murchison (1931) devoted an entire chapter to the "Order of Birth in Relation to the Development of the Child," mentioning 78 references.

Onliness

Before discussing birth order and sibling position, let us view the narrower topic of "onliness." Largely refuted by research findings, statements regarding the effect on personality of being an only child provide a lesson for child psychologists. Students of child psychology know that statements unsupported by research, even if made by so-called experts, are to be taken with caution. Scientific thinking differs from nonscientific thinking, as we saw in Chapter 1, in that ideas, hypotheses, or theories are abandoned whenever research proves them wrong. One can be truly critical of statements in the area of scientific endeavor only when aware of the research findings. In child psychology, the literature on onliness illustrates the point.

"Being an only child," said G. Stanley-Hall, "is a disease in itself." In an early book on child guidance, the Blantons (1927) asserted: "The only child is greatly handicapped. He cannot be expected to go through life with the same capacity for adjustment that the child reared in the family with other children has" (p. 175). And a book concerned with abnormal psychology (Maslow & Mittleman, 1951) maintained: "The only child is likely to be overprotected, and he is never dethroned by any later children. His parents may spoil him, make him dominating, egotistical, and, at the same time, essentially weak in his character structure. In that case he tends to be deeply hurt when he is not the center of interest and attention" (p. 147). All three statements were made in textbooks written by reputable practitioners of psychology.

But what does research show on the bearing of onliness on development and personality? Several studies have compared only with *non*only college students on standard behavior and adjustment tests as well as on achievement (Fenton, 1928; Campbell, 1933; Dyer, 1945), whereas other studies have employed teacher ratings of elementary school children (Fenton, 1928; Guilford & Worcester, 1930). In general, the findings have indicated no essential differences between only and other children. One researcher (Campbell, 1933) felt that his results suggested a more pronounced effect of onliness among girls than among boys. He attributed this to the fact that boys are given more freedom than are girls. This enables boys more than girls to associate with other children outside the home, which compensates for the absence of siblings at home.

Consistently in language development, as noted in Chapter 5, only children advance more rapidly than children with siblings (Davis, 1931). The superiority of only children in language facility is significant because it leads to the real psychological importance of onliness—the effect on the child of the undeniably greater contact he enjoys with his parents. What are the results of a comparatively intensive parent-child relationship? How does a greater amount of interaction with adults affect development and personality as compared with interaction with children of one's own age?

As we have seen, a child with adults as his primary speech models is advanced in language development. There are also indications that relative isolation from peers, including siblings, contributes to intellectual achievement and scientific eminence (Faris, 1940; McCurdy, 1957; West, 1960). Two related explanations support this hypothesis. One holds that an individual who finds great satisfaction in his social relationships has little motivation to partake of the intense effort required for high achievement. The other point of view, which is more attuned with this discussion, emphasizes the influence of close contact with interested adults who stimulate the child in intellectual spheres. Combined with isolation from children of one's own age, this influence encourages a rich fantasy life, independence, and originality.

As to the effects of onliness on personality, the research is inconclusive, and with good reason. Undoubtedly the significant factor is the quality of the relationship between child and parent. The adjustment, personality, child-rearing attitudes, and behavior of the parent need investigation before we can make assumptions about the impact of onliness on a child. When research lumps together all only children and investigates various aspects of personality, small wonder that the findings show few differences between only and *non*only children. Important as onliness may be in directing attention to the crucial importance of the parent-child relationship, the fact of wide differences among parents of only children suggests that onliness is phenotypical. Too often, as mentioned in Chapter 1, research in child psychology has investigated phenotypes with inconclusive results. It has failed to account for really important psychological characteristics and for wide differences among children and parents within any single group, differences which cancel each other out when subjects are bunched together for research purposes.

Birth Order and Sibling Position

For both birth order and sibling position the literature and findings are as contradictory as they are voluminous. This results, of course, from the importance of a child's "psychological position" in the family, which may bear no relation whatsoever to his order of birth.

> The question whether the child feels accepted and loved; his emotional relation with his parents; the competition or support which brothers and sisters bring to him; and the specific pressures or areas of freedom and stimulus that come along with one position in the family or another are probably more important than the objective fact of ordinal position (Murphy, Murphy, & Newcomb, 1937, p. 363).

No one would argue that the child's psychological environment is not significant, or that siblings are an unimportant part of this environment. Siblings, interacting with each other, create an ever-changing psychological environment in the family. Jealousies and hostilities, favoritism, the extent to which the child meets the unconscious needs of the parent—all these arise early in the family situation and may have intense emotional bearing on the child's personality and development.

It may be useful to note what Adler (1928) had to say on this subject.

> The oldest child feels dethroned by the coming of his brother and wants to restore his place by fighting. Unless he can overcome in the struggle for supremacy in his universe he is apt to become depressed, peevish, more or less hopeless, and will show his hopelessness later in life if confronted by problems. He is very likely to be conservative, to understand power and to agree with it. If he is strong enough he becomes a fighting child.
>
> As for the second child he is never alone, but is always confronted by the older child. This constant picture before him of an older and bigger child begets in him a sense of rivalry. If successful, he is an excellent type, but if defeated, for instance, if he is not able to compete successfully with the older child in word and in play, he loses hope, becomes depressed and has a bad time of it.
>
> The third child has to fight for a place in the sun, but he has no successor. This gives him a great sense of power, and if he is capable he often overcomes the older children in the family by his sense

of importance. If he is not capable, he perhaps hides behind the fact of being spoiled, and becomes lazy, escaping from tasks, wasting time and making excuses.

First-born and early-born children have been found to be inferior in size and weight to children born later. First-borns also show higher percentages of premature births and stillbirths. Findings regarding intelligence are contradictory but generally there seems to be no connection between order of birth and intelligence.

Although first-borns are sometimes thought to be handicapped in emotional adjustment, conclusive research is lacking. One early study found that first-borns were more likely than children born later to be given ratings of undesirable traits by their teachers (Goodenough & Leahy, 1927). It cited the comparative inexperience of parents in the case of first-borns, the imposition of tasks on the eldest child, and the difficulty of changing from only child to *non*only child as possible explanations for its findings. Another study (P. Sears, 1951) noted less doll-play aggression among older than among younger siblings. This would indicate that, at least in the family setting, the older sibling experiences fewer frustrations than the younger sibling. The older sibling has fewer more powerful frustrating agents in his environment. Moreover, in the doll play there was stronger identification with the mother among older brothers than among their younger siblings.

While a majority of the studies of birth-order effects have been concerned with either the young child or the college student, a study (Douvan & Adelson, 1966) involving interviews with 3050 adolescents produced a number of interesting findings. First-borns of both sexes exhibited strong drive and ambition; they were achievement oriented. Two areas distinguished middle from other birth-order positions: they tended to be downward mobile with regard to aspirations, a fact that was associated with faulty development of the process of internalization and behavior controls. While the oldest child showed close identification with parents, the youngest was more closely identified with the peer group. He relied less on the family for social interaction. This difference may reflect changes in parental needs and concerns. The youngest child is given greater freedom of social interaction because the parents do not need to form the close emotional attachment with him that they had with the first child. Moreover, by the time the youngest child reaches adolescence, the parents may be faced with various occupational and physiological concerns that reduce their involvement with any one child in the family.

The Koch Study. The extensive study by Helen Koch (1956a, b, c, d, and e; 1960) deserves special mention. It is one of the few relatively recent investigations of sibling influence on a child's psychological development. Its rarity and extensiveness both stress the great complexity of this zone of research, especially if a study is to be designed adequately, employing most of the necessary controls. This study covered 360 five- and six-year-old children from two-child, urban, native-born, white, intact families (Koch, 1956e, 1960). Investigated as independent variables were the sex of the child under study, the sex of the sibling, ordinal position, and three spacings between siblings —less than two years, two–four years, and four–six years. Each of 24 subgroups contained 15 children. Through analysis of the ratings assigned by teachers for a variety of traits, the impact of these variables on the characteristics of child behavior was discerned. The following are samples of Koch's findings.

1. In language development (Koch, 1956a), first-born children consistently spoke more articulately than second-born. The greater the gap in age between siblings, the better the articulation tended to be. In addition, there were indications that stuttering might be related to the sex of the sibling and the difference in age between the two children; the amount of stuttering was thought to stem from how much jealousy and conflict there was as a result of the sibling's sex and difference in age. Similarly, the degree to which the child was frustrated by its sibling as well as the extent to which the child was allowed to express these frustrations was felt to have some bearing on the amount of stuttering.
2. Identification with a sex role was studied through ratings of sissiness in boys and tomboyishness in girls (Koch, 1956b). Boys with a slightly older sister were rated as relatively sissified. This characteristic tended to decrease as the age differential between siblings widened. In parallel manner, girls with older brothers were considered more tomboyish than girls with sisters. Such findings provided evidence for the psychological impact of having a sibling.
3. In intellectual development, children with male siblings scored higher than those with female siblings on both verbal subtests and total scores of the Primary Mental Abilities Test (Koch, 1954). Possibly the broader experience of boys, a result of a higher level of activity, might have had some relevance. The greater competitiveness and aggressiveness associated with boys may create a more stimulating environment for the sibling.
4. Both ordinal position and spacing of siblings influenced range of interest. The wider the spacing, or age difference, the greater was the number of interests held by the child under study. Indeed, second-borns were noted to have more numerous interests than first-borns. Again, familiarity with an older sibling's preoccupations and association with his companions proved important influences on the later-born child.
5. Even when the gap in age was minimal, first-born children seemed better planners than second-born. To Koch this implied a greater responsibility as the lot of the first-born as well as a necessity to plan carefully in order to maintain his superior position.

In her findings, Koch proceeded beyond mere description to offer valuable clues and insights concerning the motivations for various traits and behaviors of children (Koch, 1956c). Her analysis of ratings of several emotional factors pointed to the existence of greater stimulation or strain when siblings belonged to opposite sexes than when they were of the same sex (Koch, 1956d). Perhaps this may be explained by sex rivalry, parental preference for one sex over the other, or other subtle factors in the family and sibling relationship.

Largely the data indicated that as spacing between siblings increased the tendency grew for each to go his own way. It might be said that the narrower the spacing, the more easily various emotional characteristics of the child could be imputed to sibling interaction, whereas the wider the gap, the greater were the influences of the child's interaction with his parents (Koch, 1956d).

Several studies have modified some of Koch's findings. While Koch's results that male siblings enhance the IQ scores of their siblings, Cicirelli (1967) found that children in three-child families who have brothers only score lower on IQ and reading achievement measures. This suggests that in such families boys turn the sibling's attention to nonintellectual types of activity, including sports. Cicirelli also found that children with a like-sex sibling close in age scored higher on measures of creativity and reading and arithmetic achievement than children with like-sex sibling separated in age or with an opposite-sex sibling. In a difficult-to-interpret finding Brittain (1966) showed that adolescent girls with an older sister were more peer oriented while girls with a younger brother were higher in parent conformity.

In a further analysis of the Koch data, Brim (1958) advanced several hypotheses from role interaction theory. Through interaction with others an individual learns something of the characteristics of other roles. Thus a boy learns a great deal about a girl's role (her behavior, attitudes) through daily contact with a female sibling. Moreover, this interaction results in a certain amount of assimilation of roles, the incorporation of aspects of another's behavior into one's own behavior repertoire. Related to this is the fact that an individual is more likely to adopt characteristics of a more powerful person than a less powerful one. The Koch findings reported above substantiated these hypotheses. Thus a girl with a male sibling was rated higher in masculine traits than a girl with a female sibling, thus showing the result of cross-sex interaction. Similarly, boys with sisters were rated as more feminine than boys with brothers. These findings were especially marked for the younger child, supporting the prediction that the more powerful figure (in this case, more powerful because of age) is more influential. An interesting secondary finding of the Brim analysis indicated that girls were rated more feminine than boys were masculine. Recent research has suggested that the effect of the sex of sibling on sex role adoption of the other child is a complex one. For example one study (Leventhal, 1970) found that men with older sisters often display more masculine behavior than men with older brothers. In a family with two male children, the younger boy may adopt behavior patterns opposite those of his older brother in order to avoid being compared unfavorably with him. Another investigator (Vroegh, 1971), finding no effect of sex of older sibling on sex-role identity of the younger child, argued that the actual extent of masculinity or femininity of the older sibling must be determined before attempting to assess the effect on the younger sibling. Clearly, it is not enough simply to note the sex of the older sibling; a variety of subtle aspects of his performance as a model are important.

The Koch findings illustrate the enormous complexity of both the research on sibling influence and the influence itself. While parents play the major role in influencing the child in a variety of areas (sex-role learning, attitudes, interests), the part played by siblings cannot be ignored. Sex and age of siblings, perceived parental favoritism toward a sibling, and the general interaction and relationship among siblings are important factors to be considered in understanding and interpreting an individual's behavior.

Studies of Maternal Behavior. Three studies in particular have probed the crucial area of maternal attitude. In the first of these Dean (1947) asked 20 mothers of pairs of children of the same sex to compare their youngsters with regard to a number of traits. The mothers reported their older child to be more fearful, dependent, worrisome, and anxious, whereas they described their younger one as more physically aggressive, negativistic, stubborn, affectionate, happy, and good-natured. Whether these children actually possessed the characteristics is less important than the fact that the differences in how the mothers perceived their first as compared with their second child were consistent. If expectations as to the behavior of first and second are uniform, they could well exert an influence on the outcome.

In the second study, Lasko (1954) compared the behavior of mothers toward first and second children. Mothers of 46 pairs of children were rated on the Fels Parent Behavior Rating Scales, based on interviews with the women and observations of mother and child interaction in the home. Because the families considered in this project had been participants in a longitudinal investigation lasting a number of years, ratings of the mother's behavior toward her two children at the same chronological age could be matched. In general, the mothers were less warm emotionally and were more restrictive and coercive toward their first child than toward their second. Moreover, they tended to baby and protect the second child more than the first. Analyzing the shifts in parent behavior as the two children grew older, Lasko concluded that the most important trend for the first child was a lessening of parent-child interaction. There seemed to be no parallel change for the second child. The first child was subjected to much verbal stimulation and attempts to speed up its development during the first two years of life, whereas no such regimen was imposed on the second child. There was also a tendency for disciplinary frictions to be exacerbated in dealing with the oldest child. As women had more children, they seemed to develop warmth combined with a sense of strictness.

In an interesting experimental study Hilton (1967) attempted to identify differences in maternal behavior toward first- and later-born children in such aspects as interference and inconsistency. Each child was given a series of puzzles to complete, with the mother instructed to remain unobtrusive while observing him. After five minutes the testing was interrupted and the mother was given either a success or failure induction; the child's performance was either complimented and praised or it was noted that he did not measure up to his age level. Subsequently the mother was observed interacting with her child for a five-minute period. First with regard to child behavior, first-borns, as compared with later-borns, were significantly more dependent. They were more likely to run to their mothers during the intermission period and to ask for help and reassurance. The mothers of the first-borns were more likely to interfere with and direct the child's behavior. They were more extreme and more inconsistent in their emotional responsiveness to the child. These mothers showed a significant decrease in their supportiveness following the "failure" comments by the examiner, whereas the mothers of the later-borns showed little change. It is clear from the results of this study that there is a higher level of interaction and greater emotional involvement between a mother and her first-born as compared with later-born children. The inconsistency and intemperateness of the mother's behavior may well serve to produce dependency in the first-born child.

In a similar experimental study (Rothbart, 1971) two groups of mothers were observed interacting with their five-year-old child. In one group the child was the first-born and in the other, the second-born. In all cases, the family consisted of two children of the same sex. Each mother was given five tasks to engage in with her child: (a) general conversation; (b) explaining a cartoon; (c) showing child twenty pictures, asking him to name them and then seeing how many he could remember; (d) explaining how a water tap works; and (e) supervising the child on a difficult geometric puzzle. In agreement with the Hilton study, Rothbart found greater pressure exerted by mothers of first-borns than by mothers of second-borns. Also, mothers of first-borns showed greater anxious intrusiveness. This greater interference with first-borns was particularly marked for girls.

That the differences in maternal attitudes and behavior pointed out by Lasko and Hilton could produce differences in the personalities of children is indeed plausible. The reduction in babying and protectiveness, the decreased contact with the mother, less parental solicitude, and the less child-centered home experienced by the first child could well influence his perception of the extent to which he is accepted by his parents. The first child, upon the birth of a sibling, must adjust to a change in the quality of his interaction and relationship with parents. The second child, on the other hand, enjoys a greater stability of parental policies. From all these considerations, we can see how position in the family may very well explain differences in personality and behavior among children.

Recent Research on Birth-Order Effects. As a result of Schacter's (1959) observation that birth order is a determinant of social affiliation, a number of brief studies have examined the relation between birth order and numerous other variables. The most consistent finding is that first-borns are over-represented in the college population (Altus, 1965). Interestingly enough, the rate of college attendance decreases regularly with each later birth-order position (Warren, 1966).

Although research results are not clear-cut, there is some evidence that, under stress, first-born women indicate a stronger need for companionship or social affiliation than later-borns. This suggests that first-born females are more vulnerable to stress; they require social support in order to cope with it. First-born females also show a higher need for social approval than later-borns (Moran, 1967). In addition, first-borns have been found to be more susceptible to social pressures (Arrowood & Amoroso, 1965); are more suggestible than later-borns in social situations; are more apprehensive in surroundings that arouse anxiety (Staples & Walters, 1961); exhibit higher need for achievement (Sampson & Hancock, 1967); and are more easily influenced (Carrigan & Julian, 1966) than later-borns. As compared with later-borns, first-borns tend to possess stronger and more demanding superegos (Palmer, 1966). They identify with and internalize parental prohibitions and parental patterns of authority and discipline. That first-borns may be more self-disciplined and inner-directed may account for their higher intellectual achievement. An interesting follow-up of the children involved in the earlier work by Koch found that, at age 18, first-borns showed a preference for intellectual activities and for directing others while second-borns manifested a preference for social activities (Oberlander, Frauenfelder, & Heath, 1970; 1971). These findings reflect the kinds of pressures and expectations held by parents as well as the notion of role specialization described in the next section. If the oldest child, for a variety of reasons, preempts the intellectual role, the second-born turns to the social sphere as his domain.

Interaction with a younger child, particularly in the early years, should provide the older sibling with knowledge about younger children, their comprehension level and their social skills. In an attempt to study this area, two groups of fifth- and sixth-grade children, one with younger siblings and one without, were asked to tell a story to a young child (Medinnus & Forsell, 1970). The stories were scored for the number of simplifications which was used as an index of the child's ability to modify his language in order to communicate effectively with a young child. No difference was found between girls with a younger sibling and those without; both groups simplified their language. However, boys with a younger sibling were much more likely to simplify their language than boys who did not have a younger sibling. This suggests that interaction with children of different age levels provides the child with information which causes him to modify his own behavior to be more compatible with other persons. Only children, or children who interact little with others, may be at a disadvantage in this respect.

The recent research concerning birth-order effects has not defined carefully all of the relevant variables. For example, first-borns must be differentiated from only children. Attention has not been paid to the fact that later-born status interacts with family size, age of parents, and pre- and postnatal health of the mother. Despite some of these methodological shortcomings, recent findings are provocative. Continued research in this area should lead to a fuller understanding of general family interaction and dynamics. It may well be that some birth-order effects are of long-term significance while others are transitory. Moreover, sibling position in the family may affect some attitude and personality dimensions while others are determined by such variables as the general psychological atmosphere of the home.

FAMILY SIZE

Like family composition, the size of the family is a sociological variable. This is an area scarcely touched by psychologists because of the problems of designing properly controlled studies of the effect of family size on personality and development. However, sociologists have dealt at length with the changing trends over the years in the size of American families.

The Small Family

Bossard and Sanger (1952) have contrasted the large and small family with respect to impact on the child. In the small family, most issues such as family size, spacing of children, and the main objectives of education and child-rearing are matters of general agreement. Parenthood is intensive rather than extensive. For the child the implications are many. Considerable emphasis is placed on individual development. Because of the parents' tremendous investment, emotional and otherwise, in each of the few children, the child is under relentless pressure to measure up to family expectations. His development and achievements are weighed against others in his neighborhood and social class. The primary disciplinarian is the mother, with little discipline issuing from siblings. In view of the identification of intimate relations with only a few people, mostly adults, the child's resentments, said Bossard, tend to be directed toward the same person or persons. The small family group enables a greater degree of democratic participation by all the children, something not possible in larger families.

> In summary, the small family rests upon the ideas of planning, individualization, democratic cooperation, social isolation and intensive pressures. The small family system is one of ambition, in an open class system; its social justification, if one may thus speak of it, is that it represents an adjustment to a rapidly changing society, with its train of attendant insecurities (Bossard & Sanger, 1952, p. 6).

The Large Family

Large families are different. They take many crises in stride, partly because so many of them, large and small, occur. In a large family one has to learn to make adjustments to all sorts of changes—changes in status, in responsibilities, in role. Emphasis on the group rather than on the individual is encouraged. Often economic necessity makes cooperation mandatory. Moreover, one's own actions and behavior inevitably depend on the conduct and attitudes of others. Because a large number of persons reside within a limited space, a greater degree of administration, organization, and authoritarian control is needed (Bossard & Sanger, 1952). This suggests that the authoritarian control exercised several generations back may have stemmed from the larger family size of that day. Although this authority usually rests with the dominant member of the family—one of the parents or an older sibling—it is often wielded by the siblings toward one another. Furthermore, there is less intimate contact in a large family between the parent and any individual child. Overprotectiveness, overindulgence, and intrusiveness seldom occur. And by the very nature of the family's size, problems of internal stress and strain are manifold.

Conditions in large families have been described in a book by Bossard and Boll (1956) covering a study of 100 families with at least six children. The data were obtained from interviews and questionnaires in which at least one member of each family responded. In evaluating the findings we must bear in mind the limitations and disadvantages of the interview and case-study techniques as these were explained in Chapter 1. Although several aspects of the Bossard and Boll study were beyond the pale of psychological significance, many of its points are worthy of consideration.

Through necessity, sibling sacrifice was often inevitable. Where death befell one of the parents, the burden of caring for the rest of the family descended generally on the older children.

> My sister was the oldest of a large family. After my father's death and my mother's remarriage, the entire responsibility of the large house became hers. Instead of going to dances, parties, and playing basketball, as her friends were doing, she was at home, keeping house, doing the laundry, and watching over her younger brothers and sisters. When mother went to the hospital, she and I were left in charge altogether. The baby cried routinely every night, but still we got up and saw that the family had breakfast and were ready for school. Often my sister would miss school (Bossard & Boll, 1956, p. 121).

The responsibilities assigned to the older children were mentioned frequently.

> "From the time that I was five," writes the oldest of eight, "I can remember taking care of the children. I used to lie on my mother's bed and push my little brother back and forth in his carriage until he fell asleep. Mother kept on having babies. Many problems beset us. By the time I was in the third grade, I was always helping mother while the others played with the neighboring children. This made me old beyond my years, serious, and quite responsible for all that went on in the household. . . . Each Saturday, my mother went into the city six miles away for the groceries and stayed for the day. In the evening she and dad visited friends and came home at about midnight. From age fifteen to nineteen, I found myself responsible for seeing that the housework was finished, cooking lunch and dinner for the children, and caring for the newest baby. At night, I bathed six children, washed their heads, and tucked them into bed. Saturday nights continued like this until I rebelled. I wanted to have time for dates like other girls had" (Bossard & Boll, 1956, pp. 159–160).

Discipline was often administered by siblings. Many of the responses received during the study considered this to be perhaps more satisfactory and effective than parental discipline. For one thing, children might understand each other and each other's problems better than parents do. Besides, the respondents felt that children were often better judges than parents of what constituted misbehavior. Finally, sibling discipline might be more effective because ostracism or disapproval by one's brothers and sisters might be more meaningful than a parental spanking.

Most of the respondents believed that a large family produced a sense of security in the individual. Support by siblings and cooperation helped to foster this belief. It would be interesting to see what carefully controlled research that compared large and small families might turn up here.

Bossard and Boll (1955, 1956) also discussed the various roles played by the members of a large family. To them specialization of role, specifically personality role, was characteristic of life in the large family unit. The following eight personality types were described.

1. The *responsible* type. This was most often the oldest child, especially the older or oldest daughter because of her responsibility in rearing the young children.
2. The *popular, sociable, well-liked* type. Frequently this was the second-born, or the one following the responsible sibling in order of birth.
3. The *socially ambitious* type, or "social butterfly." Most of these were usually third, fourth, or fifth in order of birth.
4. The *studious* type. This child withdrew from sibling activities to find satisfaction in books.
5. The *self-centered isolate*. This was the child affected by the pairing off of other siblings or the child who staged a general rebellion because of a rebellion against one of the parents.
6. The *irresponsible* type. This child withdrew from family life and family responsibility.
7. The *physically ill* child. In some cases, this child suffered from chronic illness, in others, he seemed hypochondriacal.
8. The *spoiled* sibling. Often this was the youngest child.

Since each child strives for recognition in the large family, as Bossard and Boll have emphasized, he adopts a specialized role for this purpose. Quite naturally, the older children preempt a number of these roles, leaving the younger ones to scramble for those that are left.

The reduced parent-child contact and the greater frustration encountered by children are two aspects of the large family that have been used to explain several differences found between children from large as compared with small families. Rosen (1964) found greater similarity in value orientation relative to achievement between mother and son in small- and medium-sized families than in large families. This suggests that value and attitude internalization is enhanced by an intensive amount of parent-child interaction. In large families, interaction among siblings reduces and dilutes the amount of contact each child experiences with the parents.

Dependency behavior among nursery school children (Waldrop & Bell, 1964) and alcoholism among adults (Smart, 1963) have been found to be related to family size. General deprivation in childhood and frustration of dependency needs may account for these findings. In the former study a measure of family density, in terms of family size and spacing, was also related to dependency. It appears that lack of maternal availability increases the dependency strivings of the young boy.

The effect of family size on behavior and values in adolescence was revealed in the extensive interviews with adolescents mentioned earlier in connection with birth-order effects (Douvan & Adelson, 1966).

> Children from small families have a higher activity level and seem to be more poised and self-confident with adults. They date earlier, and report a larger

> number of leisure activities and memberships in organized social groups. As a group, these children show most of the qualities we have seen earlier in our studies of the upward-aspiring. They show a longer time perspective; they are more preoccupied with educational plans; they refer to personal achievement more frequently in daydreams and in thinking about the most wonderful thing that could happen to them. They are more often upwardly mobile, and the boys, at least, use achievement criteria in judging future jobs more often than do boys from large families. Fundamentally, children from small families tend to be active, energetic, and future-oriented (Douvan & Adelson, 1966, p. 273).

Adolescents from small families were more strongly identified with parents. They reported a close relationship with parents that involved shared leisure time and reliance on parental advice. By contrast, the responses of adolescents from large families indicated a marked separation between parental interests and their own. Perhaps because of this, the adolescent from a large family is more peer-oriented than family-oriented. Related to this is his ambivalence toward parental authority, which indicates a mixture of dependency and resentment. Boys show more difference than girls between large and small families in internalization and attitudes toward authority. The adolescent from a small family does not rely too heavily on family authority; rather, his identification with parents leads to well-developed and autonomous internal controls. Undoubtedly many of these differences result in part from the greater strictness and authoritarian control of the large family.

Certainly these data pertaining to the size of the family suggest interesting and fruitful hypotheses about whether size is actually a psychological as well as a sociological variable. Nevertheless, on the basis of available evidence, we must side with Bonney (1942) who held that family size neither explained nor described adequately the personality of any particular child.

MARITAL RELATIONS OF PARENTS

Based on the conclusions of clinical studies that marital conflict and divorce affect the adjustment of children, many writers have attributed a number of child behaviors to domestic discord. Delinquency, stealing, truancy, lying, disciplinary difficulties, jealousy, hyperactivity, problems of speech, reading problems, poor social adjustment, and homosexuality are all said to result from marital strife. This list is far from inclusive. Yet not much adequately designed research is at hand to help in sorting out the effects of a variety of factors and in identifying true cause-and-effect relationships. It may seem "obvious," for example, that divorce in an adolescent's background is *the* cause of current poor social adjustment. When quizzed, in fact, an adolescent will recall a vast number of truamatic feelings associated with the divorce (Landis, 1960). However, one cannot be sure from after-the-fact recollections what the experience was like at the time of occurrence. A child's past can never be fully reconstructed, as was noted in Chapter 1. Motivated by all kinds of conscious and unconscious needs and feelings, a person may falsify in retrospect the memory of circumstances and events. Besides, it is impossible to single out one particular event as *the* source of all future behavior. Finally, the independent variable, in this case marital conflict or divorce, has not been systematically controlled: there is no control group matched with an experimental group on a number of variables, with only the factor of divorce or strife differentiating the two. With these limitations in mind, let us review the meager literature in existence on research into the effects of marital adjustment on the child.

Marital Adjustment and the Child

A number of studies have sought to identify the marital factors in the home that have contributed to the behavior of the young child in school (Hattwick, 1936; Baruch, 1937). Children from "happy, calm" homes tend to be less negative than youngsters from the opposite type of home (Hattwick, 1936). The latter showed more signs of emotional disturbance, such as jealousy, fear, grumbling, nervousness and sulking, and tenseness. Baruch and Wilcox (1944) named the following five main tensions in the home as influencing poor adjustment among preschool children: Tension over sex satisfaction, tension over lack of consideration, tension over insufficient expression of affection, tension over inability to talk things through, and tension over ascendance-submission relations. The first three were interpreted as indicating a lack of security in the marriage relationship. The fifth reflected on the child's feelings of adequacy. No doubt both parent security and adequacy exert important psychological influences on the adjustment and personality growth of the young child. But the primary significance of marital adjustment seems to be its reflection of a more basic adaptation of the two people involved in the relationship.

Divorce

That divorce hampers child adjustment cannot be denied. However, its precise effects are not easy to determine because most of the data come from clinical case studies. How much of a child's maladjustment may be charged to the divorce as such, or how much results from the long period of conflict, tension, and discord leading to divorce is hard to say. Then, too, how much may be attributed to the poor personality adjustments of the partners in the particular marriage? Whatever the case, many child behaviors stem from parental divorce, as several research studies have indicated.

As a group, adolescents from broken homes showed less psychosomatic illness, less delinquent behavior, and better adjustment to parents than those from unhappy, unbroken homes (Nye, 1957). This would suggest that in some cases separation and disruption of the home is desirable. Perhaps this might follow from the additional finding that the adjustments of parents individually and to their spouses were superior in broken homes than in the unhappy homes that remained intact.

To Landis (1960), the grouping together for research purposes all children of divorce and treating them as if they were a homogeneous group with respect to the effects of divorce seemed unsound. He found differences between adolescents who remembered their homes as happy before they had learned of the divorce, and those who considered their homes as unhappy and full of conflict. The former were especially likely to feel that their first knowledge of the divorce was a traumatic experience; they had been caught by surprise and had been unable to accept the fact. Asked to state how they believed the divorce had affected their feelings of security and personal happiness, they replied that they had experienced little change in these areas. Those who, on the other hand, had conceived of their homes as unhappy said they felt greater security and happiness after the divorce. The children from homes regarded as happy reported greater difficulty in adjusting to their peers as the children of divorced parents.

We must remember, however, that all these responses bear the disadvantages of any retrospective account.

Landis divided the respondents into three groups according to age at the time of divorce–5–8 years, 9–12, and 13–16. Fewer among the younger children said they felt a loss of security and were less happy because of the divorce. Memory may play tricks here, or the finding may suggest that divorce is less damaging to a young child's security than to the security of an older child. Landis thought there were certain potentially traumatic situations awaiting the child of divorcing parents.

> First, there is the necessity to adjust to the knowledge that divorce will probably take place; (2) there is the necessity to adjust to the fact of divorce; (3) there is the possibility that in the predivorce or postdivorce years one or both parents may "use" the child as a weapon against the other, with traumatic effects upon the child; (4) there is the necessity for a redefining of relationships with parents; (5) the new status of being the child of divorced parents may necessitate new adjustments with the peer group; (6) some trauma may result for children who recognize the implications of their parents' failure in marriage; and (7) there may be problems of adjustment for the child if the parents remarry (Landis, 1960, p. 7).

To gather data on the effects of divorce, Goode (1956, p. 317) interviewed 425 divorcées. That these mothers did worry about the possible impact of their divorces on their children was evident from comments made throughout the interviews. Table 8-1 reports the replies to a question on this matter.

The women were questioned as to the extent to which they believed that the divorce experience had been a traumatic one for them. A link clearly related the severity of this trauma to the women's reports of how "hard to handle" were the children. The greater the trauma, the higher was the proportion of mothers who stated that their children at some time had been difficult to manage. Although

TABLE 8-1 Replies of Divorcées Regarding Impact of Divorce on Their Children

Question: Now that the divorce is all over, would you try to tell me, in your own words, how you felt about the divorce and the children. What went through your mind when you thought of the possible effects of the divorce upon him/her/them?

Coded Answers	Respondents Giving Answer* (N = 425), Percent
Better for them; I was right	31
Worried about lack of parent; clear ambivalence with no explanation (child needs father, but not this one)	27
No effect, child too young, didn't worry	10
Didn't worry then, but negative items appeared later	3
Worried about possible effects of remarriage on child	2
Worried about social stigma for child	6
Religious difficulties: child in Catholic school; child might be rejected by congregation	1
Finances (other than education): support, clothes, etc.	8
Bad for child (answer not elaborated)	9
Miscellaneous, never thought of it, not sure	6

*Some respondents gave more than one answer.

half the women considered the children no harder to handle after the father's visits, 25 percent of them believed that the child became more of a problem in management following these occasions. It would seem clear that the whole matter of custody and visiting privileges might well prove a source of anxiety for the child.

Subtle Factors. In Western culture parents feel a responsibility to the child, not only for his physical welfare but also for his emotional welfare. Since divorce threatens the child's emotional stability, the parent contemplating such action often experiences strong feelings of guilt. These feelings may also arise from resenting the child who renders the divorce situation more difficult. To compensate for them, the parent may attempt to be overprotective of the child and to show excessive concern for its welfare. Yet, just as divorce may foster feelings of guilt in the parent, it may arouse similar sentiments in the child. To the youngster's mind, the separation may seem punishment for his own past "naughtiness" or for unconscious, hostile feelings toward his parent. More obvious, however, are the occasions when the child overhears parental controversy in which such statements as the following may be hurled at one another: "If it weren't for Jimmy we wouldn't have had all this trouble; I would have divorced you long ago." It is not too challenging to discern how the child may feel himself the cause of this discord, nor how he may view the subsequent divorce and loss of one parent as punishment (Despert, 1953).

Parents themselves in a predivorce situation are not sure of the course to be followed; their uncertainty and anxiety are communicated readily to the children. The tension and vague threat of change are hard for the child to cope with psychologically. Although the statement "the emotional stability of the child is dependent upon the emotional stability of the parent" lacks confirmation through research, it is quite evident that an unstable home environment, for whatever cause, may have harmful implications for the child's psychological adjustment.

Following divorce, moving often becomes necessary. This adds to the adjustment problems facing the child, especially if he is of school age. Furthermore, arrangements for substitute care for him may be required if the mother returns to employment outside the home.

In a later chapter we shall discuss the process of identification whereby the child patterns his behavior after that of the parent of his own sex. This process is impaired in many ways when there is only one parent present in the home. In approximately 90 percent of divorce cases the mother receives custody of the child. This certainly affects a boy's identification with a father figure, and a gap in learning certain aspects of future adult roles may well occur when there is one parent lacking in the home. The phrase "I am marrying again because Johnny needs a father" may be another way of expressing the need for a male figure with whom a young boy can identify. Additional complications may aggravate the divorce situation when the mother deliberately endeavors to subvert the child's loyalties to the father by derogatory comments. Recent research literature indicates clearly that paternal absence during childhood has the effect of feminizing the young boy, creating difficulties in his peer relationships, and producing initially blunted aggressiveness and greater maternal dependency. At adolescence the boy who lacks a male identification figure evidences problems in several areas (Douvan & Adelson, 1966). He has difficulty adjusting to the masculine sex role and in accepting authority, and he is deficient in the internalization of standards. The exaggerated masculinity of adolescent boys from divorced homes suggests their insecurity in this area. This insecurity is reflected also in their inability to accept and identify with any adult models. Exaggerated independence in these boys very likely involves a denial mechanism. In their interviews with adolescents, Douvan and Adelson found that those from divorced homes reported strict maternal control. While boys appeared to rebel against this authoritarianism, girls seemed to acquiesce to it. However, girls from divorced homes did not show the strength of identification with their mothers as those from intact homes. There was a psychological distance between these girls and their mothers; the girls developed strong and mature peer friendships and they sought other adult models. In general, boys suffer far more than girls from the effects of divorce. This is probably because of girls' greater resiliency and adaptability and the harmful effects of loss and devaluation of the like-sex model for the boy.

In the family, in general, the parents tend to serve as buffers or neutralizers in their mutual influences on the child. This is familiar in fiction and folk literature where the mother often is pictured as the intercessor between father and son, attempting to temper the severity of the father's punishment. When there is but a single parent in the home, the child's relation with that parent is unmitigated by the presence of another. Any conflicts and antagonisms already in existence may become accentuated.

Thus, even though research has yet to separate the effects of divorce from those of the marital strife that might have preceded it, factors present in the divorce situation are known to exert harmful influences on the child's psychological adjustment. Tensions, instabilities, lack of proper figures for identification, hostilities, guilt feelings—all these come to the fore when divorce occurs. To understand and identify the precise impact of divorce on any child one needs to know how much love and understanding will continue after the action and how much real concern and affection exists for the youngster. In other words, does the child perceive the divorce as punishment and rejection or has the situation been approached with maturity and insight so that the child's love for and confidence in the parents are not shaken?

HANDICAPPED CHILD IN THE FAMILY

Much has been written about the handicapped child, but the material is predominantly clinical in character. Few carefully designed research studies can be found, understandably. It is not easy to impose the controls necessary for effective research on investigations into the influence of a handicapped child on siblings. Left largely with clinical reports, therefore, one must beware of the pitfalls of acquiring information through these channels. Undoubtedly a host of considerations colors the parent's account. Certainly the extent of his own emotional involvement and his own needs and motivations, as noted in Chapter 1, affect his report. In addition, as we have already seen, caution must be exercised in seeking to attribute effects to specific causes. For example, many parents have ascribed marital discord to the presence in the family of a retarded child. However, one careful study (Farber, 1959) found a similarity between marital integration *before* the arrival of the handicapped child and marital integration some years after. Moreover, it may be easier for a parent to blame the presence of a handicapped child for sibling maladjustments than to impute these to disruptive factors within the parent-child relationship and within the family structure. Another very important consideration is that the presence of a handicapped child affects parent attitudes and outlook just as the reverse is true (Bell, 1964). The mutual impact of parent and child is discussed at the beginning of Chapter 9. While a number of pathogenic factors have been found to characterize parents of deviant children, the cause-and-effect relationship here is by no means clear. For example, although mothers of stutterers show signs of rejection (Kinstler, 1961), it is impossible to identify such rejection as causing the stuttering since the mother's attitude toward the child was not assessed prior to the onset of the stuttering.

Although a few studies supply direct evidence of the influence on siblings of a handicapped child in the family, most of the literature has dealt with the impact on parents and the whole family unit. Any upset such as mental illness, depression, or unemployment that affects the family structure or parental personality and adjustment may be said to concern the personalities, adjustments, and attitudes of that family's children. For this reason, we shall consider briefly some of the repercussions of the presence of a handicapped child.

Nonclinical Impact

Before examining the clinical aspects of having a handicapped child in the family, let us consider some of the other problems. First comes the obvious additional financial burden that specialized medical attention imposes. For both diagnosis and treatment, parents of a handicapped child often spend a considerable amount of money. Such outlays may directly affect the siblings and work more subtly through the worries and tensions they produce in the parents.

Family activity and the pattern of living may be curtailed, which may influence the siblings in a number of ways. Frequently parents of a mentally retarded child mention a gradual social isolation. Neighbors and the community do not understand mental retardation. They do not know its causes, or what can be expected from such a child, or how to handle the youngster. This ignorance leads to unfounded fears and apprehensions. One parent would not permit his child to play with a neighbor's mentally retarded youngster because of a fear that his child might be led "into all sorts of perversions." The isolations and withdrawals that occur certainly affect the social adjustment of the siblings. Adolescents often hesitate to invite friends into the home because of their feelings of shame and embarrassment over the appearance and behavior of the retarded child.

The extra toll levied on the parents of a retarded or handicapped child by the necessity to provide physical care and to plan for the youngster, together with the responsibility they assume, may easily produce an undue amount of anxiety and tension. The very nature of the child's limitations places more demands on a parent than would a normal child—and it is no secret that the demands of even the normal child often exhaust the parent! Any such increase in tension and anxiety in the household is likely to have profound influences on the siblings.

The possible theological conflicts (Murray, 1959) confronting the parent of a handicapped child could perhaps affect his outlook and philosophy of life. Although such problems may be resolved either with bitterness and disillusionment or with acceptance and constructive effort, the normal siblings cannot escape unscathed.

Clinical Findings

Parents of handicapped children vary considerably in the adequacy of their own personality adjustments on which the birth of such a child may impose a great strain. Many aspects and decisions stemming from the presence of a handicapped child in the family prove threatening to the parent and are capable of arousing anxiety within him. The question of whether to place the child in an institution, for example, may stir unconscious feelings in the parent; these may be repressed feelings of wishing to be rid of the child or feelings of rejection that he cannot resolve. Then, too, since the child is his own biological offspring, the parent may regard any injury, impairment, or disability in the child as an injury to himself. More important, perhaps, the parent may view the birth of a handicapped child as a reflection of his own inadequacy and incompetence. The parent may find it difficult to adjust to "this blow to the psychological self."

Often the presence of a handicapped child arouses a tremendous amount of guilt in the parent. He may interpret the birth of such a child as a punishment for real or imagined sins. Or perhaps the feeling of ambivalence, or often rejection, toward the handicapped child may generate strong sentiments of guilt. This can have unfortunate consequences of overconcern and of overprotection of the child. Such overprotection may result in neglect of the siblings as well as an intrusive behavior by the parent in the relationship between the handicapped child and his siblings.

While some parents respond to a congenitally handicapped child by creating psychological distance between themselves and the child, the more common response is intrusiveness and overprotection (Bell, 1964). This has been found to be true for mothers of children exhibiting cerebral palsy, mongoloidism, congenital heart defects, and blindness. Intrusiveness, characterized by domination, excessive vigilance, and restriction, may be the mother's reaction to actual or perceived limitations in the child's ability to cope with the environment.

All in all, self-blame is sometimes the outcome of guilt feelings. One mother, for example, expressed excessive concern that her handicapped child might fall into the family swimming pool. It developed from therapeutic consultation that her concern arose from a time when she deliberately tried to push the child into the water. The satisfactory solution of these various types of problems hinges upon the parent's own adjustment to himself and to life. How he succeeds or fails may indeed affect the personality growth of the siblings. Some parents, of course, use the handicapped child as a psychological scapegoat for their own shortcomings and inadequacies. Those who do are prevented from dealing realistically with their own problems.

A parent's disappointment at the birth of a handicapped child may have far-reaching implications for the siblings. Some children have reported increased parental pressure to achieve in academic and nonacademic pursuits—for example, athletics—to compensate for the nonachievement of the handicapped sibling. One study (Zuk, 1959), in fact, found mothers more willing to accept a young mentally retarded child than an older one. This might be taken to mean that dissatisfaction with the nonperformance and nonachievement of the child increases over the years.

What, then, do research studies have to say about all this? What do they find about the effects on families of the presence of a retarded child? In a study of the adjustment of parents and siblings of institutionalized and noninstitutionalized retarded children (Caldwell & Guze, 1960), which combined psychiatric interviews with several objective measures, including a family attitude scale and a children's anxiety scale, few differences were generally found between the two groups of siblings. Yet the study showed that although most siblings of the institutionalized mentally retarded thought institutionalization worked best, most of the siblings of the retarded who were not institutionalized felt that home care was preferable. Perhaps the demands of a handicapped child in the household produce a sense of responsibility and a certain amount of resourcefulness among the siblings. That such a situation may also result in increased sensitivity to the needs, misfortunes, and problems of others is a matter for speculation.

Farber's large-scale, well-designed study (Farber, 1959), which covered 240 families with a severely mentally retarded child, was based on interviews with both husband and wife and on results of a variety of measures. The study sought to check the effects on family integration of such a handicapped child in the home. These were the results obtained from two of the indices, an index of marital integration and another of sibling role tension: in general it was noted that the marital integration of parents of mentally retarded boys at home was lower than that of mentally retarded girls similarly at home. One possible explanation for this is the usually more disruptive effect of the boy; another is the thwarting of greater parental expectation for the boy than for the girl. Although the sex of the retarded child did not affect the integration of its siblings, a high degree of dependence on the part of the deficient youngster did do so adversely. The pressures on the mother of caring for the retarded child and the added responsibilities falling to the siblings had relevance here. Supporting this intepretation was a finding that the younger the retarded child was the more he influenced the adjustment of his siblings. Since the retarded child often assumes the role of the youngest child (even though there may be younger siblings), the effects of a handicapped child appear to be greater on the youngest children in the family. Girls appear to be affected more adversely than boys by the presence of a retarded sibling (Fowle, 1968). This may result in part from their greater responsibility in caring for the child.

Through interviews with parents, Kershner (1970) compared family functioning in two groups of homes; in one group the mentally retarded child was kept in the home, while in the other, the child was institutionalized. Follow-up interviews were conducted a year later to obtain an estimate of the effect on the two groups of families over time. The quality of family functioning was rated in a number of areas: home and household practices, economic practices, social activities, health and health practices, care and training of children, family relationships and family unity, and individual behavior and adjustment. As predicted, the level of family functioning increased over the year interval for the families that institutionalized the child and decreased for those that kept the child in the home. Since a mentally retarded child is a source of family stress, institutionalization is one way in which a family attempts to cope with that stress, and, according to the Kershner study, this solution is successful in alleviating some of the family tensions.

In an excellent summary of research on the handicapped child, Jordan (1962) has suggested that research on the significance of handicapped children in other cultures would be enlightening. Different cultures view children and childhood in various ways. Some cultures, such as our own, value and place great emphasis on independence. Thus the inability of the handicapped child to achieve independence may be particularly stressful to parents in our society. Several subgroups in our society show strong family cohesiveness. Might a handicapped child be less disruptive to family unity in these groups? Because of the group arrangement for child care in Israeli kibbutzim, it would seem that siblings would be less affected by a handicapped child. Also, some societies might accept institutionalization more readily than others.

There is evidence that a handicapped child in the family may affect the siblings in various ways. This seems to be fairly well established even though research in this area has been sparse. To recapitulate, a handicapped child in the family affects parental personality and adjustment. It also causes financial strain, curtailment of family activity, possible social isolation and withdrawal, anxiety, and tension in the parents, and an increase of expectations and pressures among normal siblings.

MATERNAL EMPLOYMENT

Since World War II, when women entered the labor force on an unprecedented scale, there has been increasing interest shown in the influence of a working mother on child adjustment. In fact, a large number of wartime and postwar juvenile problems have been charged to the absence of the mother from the home. But here, as with other family situations discussed in this chapter, early claims regarding the harmful consequences of maternal employment have not been confirmed by subsequent research.

The traditional view of the family pictures the mother, as the helpmate of the male breadwinner, standing in the doorway eagerly awaiting the children's return from school; but this is no longer an accurate portrayal of reality. In March, 1969, there were 11.6 million working mothers with children under 18. These working mothers constituted 39 percent of the total number of women in the labor force and 40 percent of all mothers in the population (as compared with 20 percent in 1950 and 10 percent in 1940). The age of the children is related to whether or not the mother is employed outside the home. Among families with children under 3 years of age, only 26 percent of the mothers were in the labor force in March, 1969. For mothers with children between 3 and 5 years of age, the proportion was 37 percent. Of mothers with children 6–17 years of age, 51 percent were in the labor force. Over the decade of the sixties, the percent of working wives with children under 6 increased from 18 to 33 percent, with the most rapid increase in the latter years of the decade (see Figure 8-1). The primary reason for mothers to work outside the home is economic need.

This need, in large measure, is determined by the husband's earnings and the regularity of his employment. The higher his earnings, and the greater the security

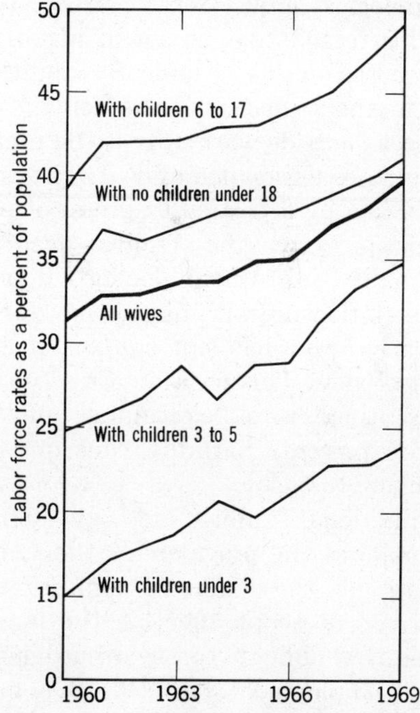

FIGURE 8-1 Labor force participation rates of married women by presence and age of children, March 1960 to March 1969.

> afforded by his job, the less likely the wife is to work. In homes left fatherless by death, divorce, or separation, the compulsion on a mother to seek work is obviously great. Her earnings are not supplementary; they are basic to the maintenance of her family. In this most affluent of nations, 32 percent of all families headed by a woman lived in poverty in 1968; many other such families had incomes barely above the poverty line. (U. S. Department of Labor, 1970)

As Nye and Hoffman (1963) have pointed out, "Few, if any, single changes in family life have as profoundly affected so many families in so few years as the movement of mothers into paid employment" (p. 3). As we shall see from the largely inconclusive research mentioned below, maternal employment has a greater impact on the family structure than on specific aspects of the children's psychological adjustment; perhaps it is for this reason that so much attention has focused on this variable. By tradition, "the mother's place is in the home," and she seeks outside work only if the family economic situation demands it. The position taken by a particular group of psychologists, that the child's eventual personality adjustment depends upon a close relationship with his mother during his early years, has lent support to this point of view. This position stresses that unless there is a "continuous mother figure" present, harmful consequences are likely to ensue.

Traditional family ideology defines the male as the provider for the family welfare and the dominant member with regard to decisions affecting the family. While it is difficult to say whether maternal employment had led to a more equalitarian conception of the family structure, or whether this conception has made maternal employment more acceptable, the fact remains that family organization has altered considerably in the past three decades. Limitation of family size and labor-saving devices resulting from technological advances have contributed to this change.

Research Findings

Discussion of the research concerning the effects of maternal employment is divided into three main areas: effect on the children, the husband-wife relationship, and the adjustment of the mother.

Effect on the Children. Early research investigations that compared children of working mothers with those of nonworking mothers ignored important variables that cut across this division. Some of these variables include age and sex of child, social class, full-time versus part-time maternal employment, provisions for substitute care, the consistency between mother and substitute in attitudes and behavior, the personality and personality needs of the particular child, the motivations for maternal employment, and the mother's attitude toward working and toward child care. Only if the fact of maternal employment were more pertinent to the well-being of the children than these other factors would one expect to find significant distinctions between the children of working and nonworking mothers.

While Douvan and Adelson (1966) found little relation between maternal employment and the adolescent boy's activities and psychological characteristics, several effects were noted for the adolescent girl. Daughters of working women are more likely to share in home responsibilities; they participate in fewer leisure activities. As compared with daughters of nonworking women, those whose mothers work admire and respect their mothers more. They enjoy a close relationship with their mothers and identify with them. In addition, maternal employment affects the daughter's conception of the female role. In Hartley's study (1960) more daughters of nonworking mothers said "housewife" when asked what they expected to do when they grew up, whereas more daughters of working mothers mentioned various professional aspirations. Also, more daughters of working mothers said they would continue to work after marriage. It seems likely that the more equal status of husband and wife in families where both are employed affects the children's perception of masculine and feminine roles. This was supported in a study (Vogel, Broverman, Broverman, Clarkson, & Rosenkrantz, 1970) in which college students were asked to rate the behavior of typical adult males and females on a number of adjectives. As compared with students whose mothers were primarily homemakers, those from homes where the mother was employed perceived smaller differences between masculine and feminine roles. This was especially true for the girls who were less extreme in their ratings of both male and female roles. Clearly, sex-role perceptions are affected by actual parental role behaviors to which children are exposed. One might speculate that the recent trends involving unisexual dress and the women's liberation movement resulted in part from the high rate of maternal employment beginning during World War II.

Although Douvan and Adelson found maternal employment (part- or full-time) affected adolescent girls in a positive fashion in several areas, the social class variable was an important consideration. As compared with middle-class girls whose mothers frequently choose employment for achievement reasons, working-class adolescent girls spend less time with their families and yet exhibit greater emotional dependency on them. This may be because their need for security within the family has not been met.

The variables of age and sex of child may interact in determining the effects of maternal employment. In early childhood, a boy may be adversely affected, showing dependency (Hoffman, 1961; Siegel, Stolz, Hitchcock, & Adamson, 1959), withdrawal (Rouman, 1956), and maladjustment (Hand, 1957). These findings may reflect an inadequate male model in families in which the mother is employed; or, as in our discussion of divorce, they may suggest that a young boy is more negatively affected than a girl by any deviation in the family structure that reduces his feelings of security.

Often listed as causes of delinquency are neglect and lack of supervision by the working mothers. Yet some investigations have failed to set up controls for the socioeconomic status of the family. Because both the employment status of the mother and juvenile delinquency are moderately related to the economic level of the home, the variable of socioeconomic status clearly must be controlled before valid comparisons can be made. In a study of 500 delinquent boys matched with an equal number of nondelinquents for age, ethnic and racial derivation, and general intelligence, the Gluecks (1957) observed no difference in the proportions of delinquents and nondelinquents whose mothers were regularly employed. However, a larger number of delinquents than nondelinquents had mothers who worked irregularly. Still, it does not follow that irregularity of employment is the cause of delinquency; the irregular worker may be the kind of mother who works to escape household tasks and maternal obligations. In other words, both the sporadic employment of the mother and the child's delinquency may be products of a more basic emotional maladjustment of the parents. In a further analysis of several studies yielding conflicting results concerning the effect of maternal employment on juvenile delinquency, Hoffman (1963) concluded that the two are positively related only in the middle class. While reasons for this are only speculative at this point, one factor may be that middle-class delinquency differs from lower-class delinquency in terms of its causes and its nature.

Hoffman (1961) found that the mother's attitude toward employment affected her relation with her children. Mothers holding positive attitudes toward work employ less severe discipline and less power-assertive techniques. They feel more sympathy, more affection, and less hostility in their interaction with their children. An interesting extension of Hoffman's findings was obtained in a study (Woods, 1972) that showed that children of mothers who held favorable attitudes toward their jobs scored high in measures of personal and social adjustment. This clearly indicates that a mother's attitude toward her life situation determines the kind of psychological atmosphere she establishes in the home as well as the kind of relationship she enjoys with her children. This is true, of course, whether or not the mother is employed outside the home.

Husband-Wife Relationship. It seems clear that the mother's employment outside the home alters the traditional structure of the family, including such aspects of the husband-wife relationship as participation in household tasks, decision-making, and power and dominance roles. Indeed, when the responses of children of working mothers were compared with those of nonworking mothers regarding parental performance of various household tasks, the former group reported that their mothers participate less and fathers participate more in all areas (Hoffman, 1960). Related to this is the fact that working mothers make fewer decisions about routine household matters while the fathers make more. However, with regard to general family decisions, especially in the economic area, the working wife plays a more powerful role than the nonworking one (Nye, 1963).

Although most studies show more quarreling and more marital conflict in families where the wife is employed, a number of other variables such as social class, reasons for the employment, and the husband's attitude toward his wife's employment, are important here. Powell (1961) found no difference in reported marital adjustment between working and nonworking mothers if the oldest child was of elementary or preschool age. However, if the oldest child was an adolescent, the working mothers reported a poorer adjustment. Further analysis of the data suggested that fathers of adolescents participated less in household tasks than fathers of younger children. This could account in part for the poorer marital adjustment of these mothers.

Adjustment of the Mother. A number of aspects of maternal adjustment in relation to employment have been examined. These include emotional adjustment, satisfaction or dissatisfaction with employment and with the maternal role, physical health, and community and recreational participation.

Most studies agree in showing a more favorable attitude toward children on the part of working mothers as compared with those not employed outside the home. Nye (1963), for example, found that nonemployed mothers were more likely to say that "children make me nervous." From the finding that "adjustment to children" improved the longer the mother worked, Nye concluded that although her employed status at first produced some conflict, these contentions began to disappear as the mother became reconciled to her new role in the family structure.

As compared with nonemployed mothers, employed ones express more satisfaction with their daily work and with the community in general. In addition, employed mothers express more positive self-attitudes, including higher self-esteem. Moreover, they report fewer physical symptoms, suggesting that their health is not impaired by the demands of home and employment.

In summary, maternal employment has not been found to exert marked effects on the behavior and adjustment of the children involved. It is the quality, not the quantity, of interaction between mother and child that is of psychological significance. In individual cases where the mother's employment seems to have adverse effects, it is likely that other disruptive factors in the home are responsible. The American family structure is changing markedly. It will continue to do so. Perhaps a more equalitarian approach is no less favorable to the mental health of children than the traditional one.

MINORITY GROUP MEMBERSHIP

Finally, there is the impact on the child of membership in a minority group. Although the country abounds with racial, religious, and political minorities, the present discussion deals largely with the Negro minority group; to a large extent what is said about Negroes applies equally to other minority groups. The Negro group is distinguishable from other minorities for several reasons. To cite two of the most obvious, Negroes are more readily identifiable by the color of their skin and they constitute the country's largest minority.

Awareness and Identification

At what age do racial awareness and accurate racial identification develop? The typical procedure for finding this out involves individual interviews with young children in which they are presented with dolls or drawings that include white and colored figures. The children are asked questions to elicit information concerning racial identification and racial preference. This is the set used by Clark and Clark (1947, p. 169):

1. Give me the doll that you like best.
2. Give me the doll that is a nice doll.
3. Give me the doll that looks bad.
4. Give me the doll that is a nice color.
5. Give me the doll that looks like a white child.
6. Give me the doll that looks like a colored child.
7. Give me the doll that looks like a Negro child.
8. Give me the doll that looks like you.

Table 8-2 (from data by Clark & Clark, 1947) lists the results obtained from 253 Negro children divided according to age levels. It is evident that in general there was an increase with age in the percentage of children who identified themselves accurately with the colored doll. There was also a marked tendency for the children to show a preference for the white doll. This tendency decreased with age, although most children at each level preferred the white to the colored doll.

That the extent or severity of discrimination affects the Negro child's rejection of his own race was shown in a study comparing race awareness and race attitudes of northern and southern preschoolers (Morland, 1966). As compared with northern Negroes, those from the South indicated a greater preference for whites, and indeed both groups showed a preference for whites over their own racial group. There is some recent

TABLE 8-2 Choices of Subjects at Each Age Level

	Age 3	Age 4	Age 5	Age 6	Age 7
Request 1 (play with)					
colored doll	42	24	26	29	40
white doll	55	76	74	71	60
Request 2 (nice doll)					
colored doll	36	24	28	46	44
white doll	58	76	72	53	52
Request 3 (looks bad)					
colored doll	68	52	78	63	43
white doll	19	24	11	15	17
Request 4 (nice color)					
colored doll	39	28	20	43	48
white doll	58	72	78	56	48
Request 5 (for white)					
colored doll	13	14	7	3	0
white doll	77	86	94	97	100
Request 6 (for colored)					
colored doll	77	83	94	96	100
white doll	13	17	7	4	0
Request 7 (for Negro)					
colored doll	55	59	61	78	85
white doll	29	35	30	17	7
Request 8 (for you)					
colored doll	36	66	48	68	87
white doll	61	31	52	32	13

evidence (Ogletree, 1969) that black children are more willing now, as compared with those in the Clark and Clark study, to identify themselves as black. Thus it appears that the black pride movement has had a positive effect on the self-acceptance of black children.

In attempts to identify various aspects of the self concept, investigators have posed the question "What are you?" to young children. As children increase in age, they shift from describing themselves by their own names or with reference to individuals in their specific environment to the use of ethnic designations (Hartley, Rosenbaum, & Schwartz, 1948). This vividly illustrates the increasingly important role played by ethnic membership in one's feelings and attitudes about oneself.

Accurate racial identification, of course, does not necessarily imply full awareness of racial prejudice and of the significance of racial membership. Yet several investigators have reported great emotionality among some of the Negro children asked to make a racial self-identification. That racial awareness itself has certain psychological implications is borne out by its earlier occurrence among Negro children than white children (Horowitz, 1939). Actually, psychological factors such as the effect of minority group membership on parents produce this earlier awareness in Negro youngsters.

Studying racial awareness in four-year-olds, Goodman (1952) discovered strong evidence for its presence among these children. The recognition of racial differences exceeded their capacity to express their feelings about them. One of the children interpreted the significance of membership in a minority group in these succinct terms: "The people that are white, they can go up. The people that are brown, they have to go down" (Goodman, 1952, p. 28). This is cut from the same cloth as the statement by a Negro adult: "You live in a city all your life, but you're never home. Maybe that's what it means to be a Negro" (Karon, 1958, p. 1). Goodman further noted a strong inclination for Negro children to refuse to identify, or to resent identification, with their own group.

> [Dianne] is a dark brown child, even darker than her mother, and she likes whiteness to a rather extreme degree. There are only a few colored children in her nursery school. She is conspicuous among the assorted whites, and conscious of the fact. She went home one day and asked her mother "am I colored?" The affirmative answer was followed by the explanation that "some people are black and some are white." Dianne, like most of our four-year-olds, was most concerned about herself. "I don't *want* to be colored," she declared. Back at nursery school again one day, Carol (w) took a good look at Dianne and asked her if she were colored. "Yes, I am. Don't touch me! Don't sit near me!" And Dianne sat away by herself looking unhappily at her arms. Then there were days when she vigorously lathered her arms and face with soap. After one of these efforts, she said triumphantly to Peter: "This morning I scrubbed and scrubbed and it came almost white." But she knew it had not really done so . . . (Goodman, 1952, pp. 37–38).
>
> There is a kind of desperation in Tony's cry of "Brown—brown—brown!!" as he throws down the picture about which we have been talking, and talking too long for his peace of mind. The matter is becoming more and more personal and personally threatening. He and others must have felt like Barbara, who was obviously unhappy. She did not enjoy being asked to tell which doll or picture looked most like herself, and her parents. And finally she said so, with intensity and exasperation: "Don't ask too many questions!—*I can't stand it*" (p. 42).
>
> Tony A. admits that his parents look like the pictured Negro couple, but finds it necessary to add, about his father and mother, "they're *good* people." Viola likes the white doll better " 'cause it's cuter than the other one" (the brown doll to which she has given scarcely a glance). Tony R. evades self-identification, as a good many of these children do occasionally. He says that he was like neither of the baby dolls, when he was a baby. But he adds wistfully: "I was called 'Butch' when I was a baby. Is that one (white) 'Butch'?" Joan G. says of the matching boy dolls that the brown one is nicer because "the white one is too heavy." But her resolution to like brown fails her when we come to the girl dolls. She fondles the white one, and then—briefly—the brown one. "This one," she says, "this one I'm holding (brown)—*it just gets on my nerves*" (p. 43).
>
> . . . "Then one night when he wasn't yet seven he did a queer thing. After he'd had his bath he put powder all over himself—he loves to do that—and he came out of the bathroom with this powder all over his face. I said to him 'you look awful—go wipe that stuff off your face.' He looked at himself in the mirror and said: 'No, I don't mummy. I look just like a little white boy now' " (p. 124).

Using ratings by the nursery-school teacher, Goodman unearthed evidence indicating that the personalities of the Negro children were affected by minority group membership even by the age of four. These youngsters were rated higher in activity, emotionality, sensitiveness, competitiveness, and aggressiveness than their white schoolmates. Greater aggressiveness among Negro children also showed in other studies. In a study by Hammer (1953), for example, the drawings of Negro children in a projective type of drawing test received higher ratings for the amount of hostility and aggression expressed.

Over half of the Negro youngsters in the Goodman study conveyed a sense of inferiority to whites through an assertion that whites were "nicer," "prettier," and "more desirable as playmates." This kind of acceptance of white standards leads not only to a depreciation of one's own group but also to a depreciation of oneself. "Though living in a democracy, many Negro citizens apparently learn by three years of age that skin color is important, that white is to be desired, dark to be regretted" (Landreth & Johnson, 1953). This same feeling is shared by members of other minority groups. At a Mexican baptismal party, the father was heard to utter the shocking imprecation, *"negro, negro; malo, malo"* (black, black; bad, bad). This was a terrible verdict to pronounce on one's own son at his baptism and seemed to be prophetic of the later life experiences of an unusually dark child (a "Black Mexican") in a light-skinned family. It pointed out the potentially dreadful consequences for self-acceptance in the minority group member's surrender to the majority group dictum that light is good and dark is bad. Several investigators (Williams & Edwards, 1969; Edwards & Williams, 1970) have been successful in weakening the negative stereotypes held by white children regarding black skin color through reinforcement techniques. The children were shown pictures with an accompanying story and were asked to choose either the white or black figure in the story to answer several questions. For example, "One of these rabbits is good. He helps mother rabbit care for all his little brothers and sisters. Which one is the good rabbit?" Six positive evaluation adjectives were used: clean, nice, good, pretty, smart, and kind; and six negative evaluation adjectives were used in the story questions: dirty, naughty, bad, ugly, stupid, and mean. The children were rewarded for selecting the positive adjectives as characterizing the black figure. Upon later testing with Negro and Caucasian human figures, the children were less likely to attribute negative adjectives to Negroes and positive adjectives to Caucasians than they were in the pretesting. These investigators argued that evaluation of color concepts as positive or negative tends to support similar racial evaluations and that by altering children's attitudes toward color, their racial stereotypes may be modified. There is no doubt that white is seen as good (pure, clean), and black as bad (dirty, sinister) in our society.

The minority group child's early acceptance of the prevailing prejudices of the white majority is illustrated in an interesting study of fifth-grade Negro children (Epstein & Komorita, 1966). The children were shown slides of a fictitious group labeled "Piraneans." Both race and social class were introduced by pictures depicting Negro and white Piraneans in middle-class and working-class environments. After viewing the slides, the children completed a seven-item social distance scale designed to elicit their attitudes toward the fictitious group. The items ranged from "would you want to marry these people when you grow up?" to "would you want these people to visit your country?" Results indicated that the children manifested greater social distance toward the Negro than toward the white Piraneans. The social-class variable was not related to social distance. This suggests that the Negro child perceives his skin color, rather than his typically lower socioeconomic status, to be the basis for the white person's hostility and prejudice. The reverse was found to be the case, however, when white children were tested using a similar technique. Social distance toward the Negro was related to his inferior social status rather than to skin color.

In an interesting study (Palmer & Masling, 1969) which asked children to sort 16 bubble gum pictures of Negro and white baseball players along a skin color continuum and to name the skin color, Negro children were found to have a relatively greater vocabulary for skin color than white children. We have known for a long time that the importance attached to a concept by a group of people is reflected in the number of words they use to describe that concept. The larger "language of skin color" possessed by Negro children is evidence of the importance they have been forced to attach to this concept.

In an experimental study of race and conformity in children (Mock & Tuddenham, 1971) small groups of fourth-, fifth-, and sixth-grade children were asked to make perceptual judgments regarding geometric relationships. False information concerning the judgments of the others in the group was fed back to the children in order to determine the extent of conformity to group norms. The results showed that Negro children tended to conform to the group norm established by white children. They were also less confident in their judgments than the white children. This investigation shows another aspect of the damaging effect on the Negro child of the prevailing attitude of white superiority.

That knowledge of the relative status of Negro and white is developed early is dramatically illustrated in the book *Children of Crisis* (Coles, 1967), which examines the reactions of Negro and white children in the South to school desegregation. Though initially unable or unwilling to verbalize their attitudes and feelings, the children revealed through drawings their profound understanding of the social context of race relations. Johnnie, a seven-year-old Negro child, described his drawing (Fig. 8-2) of a white and Negro boy as follows:

> Freddie wishes he were up top, like Billy, but he isn't, because there's not room for both of them up there, at least not now there isn't. They're not talking, they're just there. Freddie would be afraid to be on top. He wouldn't know what to do. He's used to where he is, just like Billy is. . . . When they talk it's real hard, because they are far from one another, so they have to shout (Coles, 1967, pp. 67–68).

Figures 8-3 and 8-5 are done by white children. In spite of an otherwise generally careful attention to detail, these children drew their Negro classmates in a very sketchy manner and often, as in Figures 8-2 and 8-4, assigned them to special sections of the picture. In Figure 8-4 the sunny, "white" side of the street, with its grass and trees and large, sturdy buildings, is very much in contrast with the "Negro" side. This boy carefully drew a red traffic light, which he said never turned green, as a reminder that the road was "a big highway, and you're not supposed to cross over" (p. 70).

Problems Encountered Later

Although much psychological theory relating to the development of personality has stressed the critical nature of the early years, it would be misleading to overlook forces that impinge on the individual during his growing-up years as well. In fact, particularly with reference to the Negro in the South, Davis (1943) suggested that the full impact of belonging to a minority group was not felt until the individual sought a job; at that time he became fully aware of the educational, social, and economic barriers in his path. Frustration, disillusion, and cynicism followed.

The responses of 150 preadolescent Negroes concerning their feelings and impulses when placed in unfortunate situations illustrated some of the emotional difficulties of Negro children because of their race (Goff, 1950). Disparagement, rude treatment, direct ridicule, and physical ill-treatment were some of the things they suffered.

> "One day the teacher told us she wouldn't take us on no trips because it would be a disgrace to be seen on the street with a bunch of monkeys and laughing hyenas. She said, 'What would my friends say?'"
>
> "I went to get on the street-car and a white man jerked me off, and let a white woman on and then he got on."
>
> "One day I was swinging in the park, and a white girl stuck out her tongue at me and wouldn't use the swing when I got through using it. She waited for a white girl to get through."
>
> "I was riding my bicycle and got a flat. I took it in the station to get it fixed. The man wouldn't let me have no air, and he said he couldn't fix things for colored people (Goff, 1950, pp. 154–155).

Material from the interviews indicated that ridicule alone had a marked effect on development of personality. There seemed to be a sex difference in reaction to the kinds of treatment related in the responses. More resentment was found among boys, whereas girls were more likely to express feelings of inferiority.

The discrepancies between the impulses of the Negro youngsters in response to mistreatment by whites and what actually occurred dramatically demonstrate the psychological impact of such mistreatment. Although a desire to fight or to argue was reported in 57 percent of the instances, withdrawal followed 82 percent of the time. No wonder that frustration and ill-concealed hostility are psychological earmarks in the personalities of many minority group members.

Some of the problems faced by the Negro child in the process of school desegregation are described in a moving account written by a high-school teacher in Clinton, Tennessee (Anderson, 1966). In the book entitled *The children of the South,* Mrs. Anderson comments on the long-term effects resulting from the atmosphere of tension and violence. This is not surprising in view of the persecution to which the Negro children were subjected.

> The Negro children had eggs smashed on their books, ink smeared on their clothes in the lockers, knives flourished in their presence, nails tossed in their faces, and spikes left on their seats. Obscene words were constantly whispered in their ears (Anderson, 1966, p. 62).

Some of the Negro children, though persisting in the face of almost insurmountable handicaps, felt at times that the price was far too great. Like any individual, the Negro child needs acceptance and approval in addition to the basic need for safety and physical well-being that the white child takes for granted.

> A teacher can rebuke students who mistreat a Negro child openly. If a fight breaks out, you can go into the corridor and separate the children and stop the fight. But the more subtle harassment is not so easily detected or stopped. You can see the effects it has on the children; you watch them struggle to adjust to this order, and you try to change it. You see how difficult the change is going to be for everybody and how long it is going to take, so that in a sense the Negro child of today is giving up some part of his childhood to bring about a social change.
>
> The struggle produces in the Negro child an anxiety, a deep fear which seems to be ever present. It is revealed in such questions as:
>
> "Will I be able to play ball with white boys?"

FIGURE 8-1 Johnnie draws a Negro friend and a white classmate.

FIGURE 8-2 Ruby in school, by Jimmy at age 7.

FIGURE 8-3 Ruby, by Jimmy at age 6.

FIGURE 8-4 Allen draws the difference between Negro and white. Draw ings are from Coles (1967).

> "Will there be a place for me when the class goes on an overnight field trip? Where will I eat and sleep?"
>
> "Will there be someone who will walk down the aisle with me on graduation night?"
>
> "What would happen if I sat down at the table with white students?"
>
> It is a kind of apprehension that makes the child wonder who he is and why. For, above all else, a child desires to be accepted by those around him. The Negro boy or girl worries about being accepted in the white school by the other students and by those in authority. He comes in frightened and insecure, concerned not only for his physical safety—will he be treated kindly?—but by something else which goes very deep: his need to be wanted and loved. And he knows, as do all children, who cares about his well-being and who does not (Anderson, 1966, pp. 67–68).

The full significance of membership in the Negro minority, of course, cannot be discussed apart from factors of social class. A spate of circumstances has relegated most Negroes to the lower socioeconomic group. Thus, they are members not only of the lower *caste* but also of the lower *class*. In this country lower-class families are characterized by two things: material deprivation and low standards of conduct (Dai, 1956). Broken homes, dominance of maternal authority, residence in impoverished and deteriorating neighborhoods, parent-child friction and antagonism accompanied by harsh and severe parental treatment, encouragement of delinquency by the environment—all these are the lot of Negro lower-class, lower-caste membership.

In a study of 25 Negroes through psychoanalytic interviews, Rorschach tests, and Thematic Apperception Tests, Kardiner and Ovesey (1951) maintained that the direct effects of discrimination were low self-esteem and anger. Low self-esteem might be manifested in unrealistically high aspirations, or in apathy, in living for the moment, in hedonism, or in criminal behavior. Denial of aggression and of hostility together with the anxiety-provoking feeling of being angry lead the Negro adult to contradictory behavior; he is good humored, affable, irritable, fearful, submissive, capable of explosive outbursts, and generally constricted in his emotional life. In the opinion of Kardiner and Ovesey, the failure of the Negro subjects to use their potential intelligence might be attributable to inner conflicts that rendered them incapable of focusing their attention.

Similar findings were reported by Karon (1958), who compared the personality characteristics of southern Negroes with those of northern whites and Negroes. Eleven characteristics differentiated the southern Negro from the latter two groups. Six of these were related to aggression, either with its denial or with the suppression of anger. The southern Negro was characterized also by "weakened affect," which may be interpreted as a "deadening of one's emotions" through the stifling of one's anger and hostility and through inability to express feelings of aggression and to solve frustrations.

Much variation exists among individuals in their reactions to membership in a minority group. This variation may be ascribed to psychological factors in the home. How does the parent respond to the situation: positively and constructively, or negatively and self-defeatingly? More important, to what extent is the child accepted by the parents? How far does the child, in consequence, develop feelings of self-worth, self-esteem, and self-acceptance? It has been noted that Negro children who are most self-accepting also tend to disclose more positive attitudes toward other Negro and white children (Trent, 1953). Moreover, the sense of powerlessness which comes from membership in a stigmatized minority group may be cushioned by a positive self-image (Epstein & Komorita, 1971). Unquestionably, the greater the child's sense of adequacy and security, the less need he has for counteraggression, and the less stinging, as a rule, the detrimental blows of prejudice and intolerance will be.

SUMMARY

In this chapter we have examined the psychological consequences of six sociological variables: family composition, family size, marital adjustment and divorce, handicapped child in the family, maternal employment, and minority group membership. Conclusions are difficult to draw because of the problems of conducting adequate research. Although most researchers would agree that these variables are of potential significance to the personality development of the child, they would have to concede that the precise influence remains to be clearly established.

Unfortunately, research follows the easiest course. Consider maternal employment. The research suggests that the quality of the interaction between mother and child is more pertinent to the child's behavior and adjustment than whether the mother is employed outside the home. But it is much easier to ascertain the employment status of the mother than to evaluate the psychological relation between mother and child. So it goes for the other variables considered in this chapter. Yet since the psychological factors in the home stem from a variety of circumstances, it would be unwise to ignore the possible influence on the parents and, in turn, on the child, of the variables discussed in these pages.

REFERENCES

Adler, A. Characteristics of the first, second, third child. *Children,* 1928, **3**, 14 and 52. Quoted in H. E. Jones, Order of birth in relation to the development of the child, in C. Murchison (Ed.), *A handbook of child psychology.* Worcester, Mass.: Clark University Press, 1931. Pp. 204–241.

Altus, W. Birth order and academic primogeniture. *Journal of Personality and Social Psychology,* 1965, **2**, 872–876.

Anderson, M. *The children of the South.* New York: Farrar, Straus & Giroux, 1966.

Arrowood, A., & Amoroso, D. Social comparison and ordinal position. *Journal of Personality and Social Psychology,* 1965, **2**, 101–104.

Baruch, D. W. A study of reported tension in interparental relationship as co-existent with behavior adjustment in young children. *Journal of Experimental Education,* 1937, **6**, 187-204.

Baruch, D. W., & Wilcox, J. A. A study of sex differences in preschool children's adjustment co-existent with interparental tensions. *Journal of Genetic Psychology,* 1944, **64**, 281–303.

Bell, R. Q. The effect on the family of a limitation in coping ability in the child: A research approach and a finding. *Merrill–Palmer Quarterly,*

1964, **10**, 129–142.

Blanton, S., & Blanton, M. G. *Child guidance.* New York: Century, 1927.

Bonney, M. E. A study of the relation of intelligence, family size, and sex differences with mutual friendships in the primary grades. *Child Development,* 1942, **13**, 79–100.

Bossard, J. H. S., & Boll, E. S. Personality roles in the large family. *Child Development,* 1955, **26**, 71–78.

Bossard, J. H. S., & Boll, E. S. *The large family system.* Philadelphia: University of Pennsylvania Press, 1956.

Bossard, J. H. S., & Sanger, W. P. The large family system—a research report. *American Sociological Review,* 1952, **17**, 3–9.

Brim, O. G., Jr. Family structure and sex role learning by children: A further analysis of Helen Koch's data. *Sociometry,* 1958, **21**, 1–16.

Brittain, C. Age and sex of siblings and conformity toward parents versus peers in adolescence. *Child Development,* 1966, **37**, 709–714.

Caldwell, B. M., & Guze, S. B. A study of the adjustment of parents and siblings of institutionalized and non-institutionalized retarded children. *American Journal of Mental Deficiency,* 1960, **64**, 845–861.

Campbell, A. A. Personality adjustment of only and intermediate children. *Journal of Genetic Psychology,* 1933, **43**, 197–205.

Carrigan, W., & Julian, J. Sex and birth-order differences in conformity as a function of need affiliation arousal. *Journal of Personality and Social Psychology,* 1966, **3**, 479–483.

Cicirelli, V. Sibling constellation, creativity, I.Q., and academic achievement. *Child Development,* 1967, **38**, 481–490.

Clark, K. B., & Clark, M. P. Racial identification and preference in Negro children. In T. M. Newcomb & E. I. Hartley (Eds.), *Readings in social psychology.* New York: Holt, 1947. Pp. 169–178.

Coles, R. *Children of crisis.* Boston: Little, Brown, 1967.

Dai, B. Some problems of personality development among Negro children. In C. Kluckholn & H. A. Murray (Eds.), *Personality in nature, society, and culture.* New York: Knopf, 1956.

Davis, A. Racial status and personality development. *Science Monthly,* 1943, **57**, 354–362.

Davis, E. A. The mental and linguistic superiority of only girls. *Child Development,* 1931, **8**, 139–143.

Dean, D. A. The relation of ordinal position to personality in young children. Master's thesis, State University of Iowa, 1947.

Despert, J. L. *Children of divorce.* Garden City, N.Y.: Country Life Press, 1953.

Douvan, E., & Adelson, J. *The adolescent experience.* New York: Wiley, 1966.

Dyer, D. T. Are only children different? *Journal of Educational Psychology,* 1945, **36**, 297–302.

Edwards, C., & Williams, J. Generalization between evaluative words associated with racial figures in preschool children. *Journal of Experimental Research in Personality,* 1970, **4**, 144–155.

Epstein, R., & Komorita, S. Prejudice among Negro children as related to parental ethnocentrism and punitiveness. *Journal of Personality and Social Psychology,* 1966, **4**, 643–647.

Epstein, R., & Komorita, S. Self-esteem, success-failure, and locus of control in Negro children. *Developmental Psychology,* 1971, **4**, 2–8.

Farber, B. Effects of s severely mentally retarded child on family integration. *Monographs of the Society for Research in Child Development,* 1959,

24, No. 2 (Serial No. 71).

Faris, R. E. L. Sociological causes of genius. *American Sociological Review,* 1940, **5**, 689–699.

Fenton, N. The only child. *Journal of Genetic Psychology,* 1928, **35**, 546–556.

Fowle, C. M. The effect of the severely mentally retarded child on his family. *American Journal of Mental Deficiency,* 1968, **73**, 468–473.

Glueck, S., & Glueck, E. Working mothers and delinquency. *Mental Hygiene,* 1957, **41**, 327–352.

Goff, R. M. Problems and emotional difficulties of Negro children due to race. *Journal of Negro Education,* 1950, **19**, 152–158.

Goode, W. J. *After divorce.* Glencoe, Ill.: Free Press, 1956.

Goodenough, F. L., & Leahy, A. M. The effect of certain family relationships upon the development of personality. *Journal of Genetic Psychology,* 1927, **34**, 45–71.

Goodman, M. E. *Race awareness in young children.* Cambridge, Mass.: Addison-Wesley, 1952.

Guilford, R. B., & Worcester, D. A. A comparative study of the only and non-only child. *Journal of Genetic Psychology,* 1930, **38**, 411–426.

Hammer, E. F. Frustration-aggression hypothesis extended to socio-racial areas: comparison of Negro and white children's H-T-P's. *Psychiatry Quarterly,* 1953, **27**, 596–607.

Hand, H. Working mothers and maladjusted children. *Journal of Educational Sociology,* 1957, **30**, 245–246.

Hartley, E. L., Rosenbaum, M., & Schwartz, S. Children's use of ethnic frames of reference: An exploratory study of children's conceptualization of multiple ethnic membership. *Journal of Psychology,* 1948, **26**, 367–386.

Hartley, R. E. Children's concepts of male and female roles. *Merrill–Palmer Quarterly,* 1960, **6**, 83–91.

Hattwick, B. W. Interrelations between the preschool child's behavior and certain factors in the home. *Child Development,* 1936, **7**, 200–226.

Hilton, I. Differences in the behavior of mothers toward first- and later-born children. *Journal of Personality and Social Psychology,* 1967, **7**, 282–290.

Hoffman, L. W. Parental power relations and the division of household tasks. *Marriage and Family Living,* 1960, **22**, 27–35.

Hoffman, L. W. Mother's enjoyment of work and effects on the child. *Child Development,* 1961, **32**, 187–197.

Hoffman, L. W. Effects on children: Summary and discussion. In F. I. Nye and L. W. Hoffman (Eds.), *The employed mother in America.* Chicago: Rand McNally, 1963. Pp. 190–212.

Horowitz, R. E. Racial aspects of self-identification in nursery school children, *Journal of Psychology,* 1930, **7**, 91–90.

Jordan, T. Research on the handicapped child and the family. *Merrill–Palmer Quarterly,* 1962, **8**, 243–260.

Kardiner, A., & Ovesey, L. *The mark of oppression.* New York: Norton, 1951.

Karon, B. P. *The Negro personality.* New York: Springer, 1958.

Kershner, J. R. Intellectual and social development in relation to family functioning: A longitudinal comparison of home vs. institutional effects. *American Journal of Mental Deficiency,* 1970, **75**, 276–284.

Kinstler, D. Covert and overt maternal rejection in stuttering. *Journal of Speech and Hearing Disorders,* 1961, **26**, 145–155.

Kock, H. L. The relation of "Primary Mental Abilities" in five- and six-year-olds to sex of child and characteristics of his sibling. *Child Development,* 1954, **25**, 209–223.

Koch, H. L. Sibling influence on children's speech. *Journal of Speech and Hearing Disorders,* 1956, **21**, 322–328. (a)

Koch, H. L. Sissiness and tomboyishness in relation to sibling characteristics. *Journal of Genetic Psychology,* 1956, **88**, 231–244. (b)

Koch, H. L. Children's work attitudes and sibling characteristics. *Child Development,* 1956, **27**, 289–310. (c)

Koch, H. L. Some emotional attitudes of the young child in relation to characteristics of his sibling. *Child Development,* 1956, **27**, 393–426. (d)

Koch, H. L. Attitudes of young children toward their peers as related to certain characteristics of their siblings. *Psychological Monographs: General and Applied,* 1956, **70**, No. 19 (Whole No. 323). (e)

Koch, H. L. The relation of certain formal attributes of siblings to attitudes held toward each other and toward their parents. *Monographs of the Society for Research in Child Development,* 1960, **25**, No. 4.

Krout, M. H. Typical behavior patterns in twenty-six ordinal positions. *Journal of Genetic Psychology,* 1939, **55**, 3–30.

Landis, J. T. The trauma of children when parents divorce. *Marriage and Family Living,* 1960, **22**, 7–13.

Landreth, C., & Johnson, B. C. Young children's responses to a picture and inset test designed to reveal reactions to persons of different skin color. *Child Development,* 1953, **24**, 63–79.

Lasko, J. K. Parent behavior toward first and second children. *Genetic Psychology Monographs,* 1954, **49**, 97–137.

Leventhal, G. Influence of brothers and sisters on sex-role behavior. *Journal of Personality and Social Psychology,* 1970, **16**, 452–465.

McCurdy, H. G. The childhood pattern of genius. *Journal of the Elisha Mitchell Scientific Society,* 1957, **73**, 448–462.

Maslow, A. H., & Mittleman, B. *Principles of abnormal psychology.* (Rev. ed.) New York: Harper, 1951.

Medinnus, G. R., & Forsell, E. The effect of interaction frequency on role-taking in children. Paper presented at Western Psychological Association meetings, Los Angeles, April, 1970.

Mock, R., & Tuddenham, R. Race and conformity among children. *Developmental Psychology,* 1971, **4**, 349–365.

Moran, G. Ordinal position and approval motivation. *Journal of Consulting Psychology,* 1967, **31**, 319–320.

Morland, J. A comparison of race awareness in northern and southern children. *American Journal of Orthopsychiatry,* 1966, **36**, 22–31.

Murchison, C. (Ed.). *A handbook of child psychology.* Worcester, Mass.: Clark University Press, 1931.

Murphy, G., Murphy, L. B., & Newcomb, T. M. *Experimental social psychology.* (Rev. ed.) New York: Harper, 1937.

Murrary, M. A. Mrs. Needs of parents of mentally retarded children. *American Journal of Mental Deficiency,* 1959, **63**, 1078–1088.

Nye, F. I. Child adjustment in broken and in unhappy unbroken homes. *Marriage and Family Living,* 1957, **19**, 356–361.

Nye, F. I. Marital interaction. In F. I. Nye and L. W. Hoffman (Eds.), *The employed mother in America.* Chicago: Rand McNally, 1963. Pp. 263–281.

Nye, F. I., & Hoffman, L. (Eds.). *The employed mother in America.* Chicago: Rand McNally, 1963.

Oberlander, M., Frauenfelder, K., & Health, H. Ordinal position, sex of sibling, sex, and personal preferences in a group of eighteen-year-olds.

Journal of Consulting and Clinical Psychology, 1970, **35**, 122–125.

Oberlander, M., Frauenfelder, K., & Heath, H. The relationship of ordinal position and sex to interest patterns. *Journal of Genetic Psychology,* 1971, **119**, 29–36.

Ogletree, E. Skin color preferences of the Negro child. *Journal of Social Psychology,* 1969, **79**, 143–144.

Palmer, R. Birth order and identification. *Journal of Consulting Psychology,* 1966, **30**, 129–135.

Palmer, R., & Masling, J. Vocabulary for skin color in Negro and white children. *Developmental Psychology,* 1969, **1**, 396–401.

Powell, K. S. Maternal employment in relation to family life. *Marriage and Family Living,* 1961, **23**, 350–355.

Rothbart, M.,Birth order and mother-child interaction in an achievement situation. *Journal of Personality and Social Psychology,* 1971, **17**, 113–120.

Rosen, B. Family structure and value transmission. *Merrill-Palmer Quarterly,* 1964, **10**, 59–76.

Rouman, J. School children's problems as related to parental factors. *Journal of Educational Research,* 1956, **50**, 105–112.

Sampson, E., & Hancock, F. T. An examination of the relationship between ordinal position, personality, and conformity. *Journal of Personality and Social Psychology,* 1967, **5**, 398–407.

Schachter, S. *The psychology of affiliation.* Stanford University Press, 1959.

Sears, P. S. Doll play aggression in normal young children. Influence of sex, age, sibling status, father's absence. *Psychological Monographs: General and Applied,* 1951, **65**, No. 6 (Whole No. 323).

Sears, R. R. Ordinal position in the family as a psychological variable. *American Sociological Review,* 1950, **15**, 397–401.

Siegel, A. E., Stolz, L. M. Hitchcock, E., & Adamson, J. Dependence and independence in the children of working mothers. *Child Development,* 1959, **30**, 533–546.

Smart, R. Alcoholism, birth order, and family size. *Journal of Abnormal and Social Psychology,* 1963, **66**, 17–23.

Staples, F. R., & Walters, R. H. Anxiety, birth order, and susceptibility to social influence. *Journal of Abnormal and Social Psychology,* 1961, **62**, 716–719.

Trent, R. Analysis of expressed self-acceptance among Negro children. Unpublished doctoral dissertation, Teachers College, Columbia University, 1953.

United States Department of Labor. Who Are the Working Mothers? Leaflet 37 (Rev.), October, 1970.

Vogel, S., Broverman, I., Broverman, D., Clarkson, F., & Rosenkrantz, P. Maternal employment and perception of sex roles among college students. *Developmental Psychology,* 1970, **3**, 384–391.

Vroegh, K. The relationship of birth order and sex of siblings to gender role identity. *Developmental Psychology,* 1971, **4**, 407–411.

Waldman, E. Marital and family characteristics of the labor force. *Monthly Labor Review,* 1970, **93**, 18–27.

Waldrop, M. F., & Bell, R. Relation of preschool dependency behavior to family size and density. *Child Development,* 1964, **35**, 1187–1195.

Warren, J. R. Birth order and social behavior. *Psychological Bulletin,* 1966, **65**, 38–49.

West, S. Sibling configurations of scientists. *American Journal of Sociology,* 1960, **66**, 268–274.

Williams, J., & Edwards, C. An exploratory study of the modification of color and racial concept attitudes in preschool children. *Child Development,* 1969, **40**, 737–750.

Woods, M. The unsupervised child of the working mother. *Developmental Psychology,* 1972, **6**, 14–25.

Zuk, G. H. The religious factor and the role of guilt in parental acceptance of the retarded child. *American Journal of Mental Deficiency,* 1959, **64**, 139–147.

chapter 9

family influences in infancy

chapter 9

family influences in infancy

chapter 9

family influences in infancy

Both sociologists and anthropologists have paid great attention to the family. Sociologists have dwelt at length on the functions served by the family in modern industrial society. Anthropologists have contrasted the role of the family in various cultures that differ widely in complexity and in their goals for socialization. Despite the vast differences in child-rearing practices from one culture to another, the family in most societies appears to serve three principal functions. First, it must be responsible for the physical care of the child, at least in infancy. Second, the parents must educate or train the child in certain areas that are essential to an adequate adjustment to the particular culture. Third, the family must accept the responsibility for the psychological and emotional welfare of the child. Although the first two functions have long been recognized, the third has been stressed only recently as a result of the growing body of psychological theory and research concerning the importance of the very early years and their influence on adult personality and adjustment.

The total physical helplessness of the human infant is immediately apparent. Although the newborn babe is capable of making a number of responses and enacting a number of behaviors, he is completely dependent on other human beings for his physical survival. Some of his responses actually elicit behaviors from the persons in his immediate environment; thus, from the very beginning, the infant plays some part in the continuing interaction between himself and other individuals. Most of this interaction, however, is initiated by others for the purpose of meeting the infant's physical needs. Whether this early environmental pattern of physical care affects the infant's psychological development will be considered presently.

It is the second main function of the family, the training and education of the child for adjustment to the culture, which has received the most attention from psychologists interested in the socialization process. This function can be broken down into two broad categories. The first is the training in the methods whereby the child gratifies his physical needs such as feeding and excreting. He is also trained in the development of such skills as self-help in dressing and tidiness, which seem to be important in Western culture. The second category is the inculcation of various attitudes and values that, although varying greatly among subcultures within the culture, deal with uniform aspects of socialization. The attitudes toward siblings, adults, and other persons in authority, and toward such social institutions as school and law-enforcement agencies all fall into place here. The child is also made aware of various cultural prohibitions, ranging all the way from sanctions against biting another individual to the taboos associated with incest. Since cultural values filter down to the child from the parent who colors the transmission with his own particular sense of them, the values held by one child may indeed vary in some respect from those possessed by any other child.

The third function of the family, responsibility for the child's psychological and emotional welfare, emphasizes the importance of the early psychological relation between parent and child. Although few psychologists would contend that the early years have no psychological significance, two related controversial issues are explored in this chapter. The first grows out of the notion that the child is most susceptible to psychological influences in the environment during the first year or two of life. The second concerns the extent to which very early experiences exert long-range influences on the child's personality.

MUTUAL INFLUENCE OF PARENT AND CHILD

Research into parent-child relations has by tradition viewed the parent as the independent variable and the child as the dependent one. In this light all of the child's characteristics, his behavior, his personality, and his adjustment, are seen as the direct product of various parental characteristics, namely, parental behavior, personality, and attitudes. Table 9-1A depicts this one-way relationship. Yet there are those who believe that, although parents exert a tremendous influence on a number of aspects of the child's development, the parent is affected reciprocally by various child characteristics that develop quite apart from parental actions. This results in the two-way, circular interaction represented by Table 9-1B. Under this process come the several listed characteristics, which vary from child to child and which appear so early in life that it would be misleading to attribute them to parental handling.

That there are marked differences among infants at birth has been documented in recent research dealing with the infancy period. In one study (Birns, 1965), infants from two to five days of age were presented with various stimuli including a loud and soft tone, a cold disk applied to the thigh, and a pacifier inserted in the baby's mouth. Ratings were made of the intensity of the infant's response to these stimuli. The major finding of the study was that there were consistent individual differences in response intensity. Further, the infants were consistent from one day to the next in their responsiveness; each responded in a way characteristic for him. Other studies have furnished additional evidence for the uniqueness and individuality of response capacity in early infancy. This is true for autonomic functions such as cardiac and respiratory rate and for the stability versus the lability of their responsiveness (Lipton & Steinschneider, 1964). Using fixation time, behavioral measures, and cardiac and respiratory rate as measures of attention, Kagan and Lewis (1965) noted early sex differences, with girls displaying more mature and more stable fixation patterns in the first year of life. Although the extent to which some of these early individual differences in physiological and behavioral functioning are related to later behavior is not clear, it is apparent

TABLE 9-1 Two Conceptions of Parent-Child System

A. All of child's characteristics attributed to parental treatment and handling

Parental characteristics ⟶ Child characteristics

B. Parent and child characteristics mutually interacting

Parental characteristics ⟷ Child characteristics:
- physical appearance
- health
- sex of child
- alertness
- activity level

that the environment acts upon an organism that possesses certain initial characteristics. Development is a function of the continuous interaction between innate and environmental factors.

Further support for the uniqueness of the human organism at birth is provided in a longitudinal study of over 200 infants (Chess, Thomas, & Birch, 1965). The infants were studied beginning during the first several months of life. Extensive interviews were conducted with the parents and the children were observed at various intervals. *Clear individual differences in a variety of temperamental and behavioral characteristics were evident in the very early months.* These individual characteristics were classified under the following nine headings:

1. Activity level.
2. Regularity of biological functioning.
3. Approach or withdrawal as a characteristic response to a new situation.
4. Adaptability to a change in routine.
5. Level of sensory threshold.
6. Positive or negative mood.
7. Intensity of response.
8. Distractibility.
9. Persistence and attention span.

The subsequent course which these initial characteristics took depended upon the parents' response to them. The following description of two highly active boys illustrates the continuous interaction between innate and environmental factors:

> The Highly Active Child
>
> Two children in our study shared a talent for moving more actively and quickly than most children. When Larry and David were little babies, their arms and legs seemed to be in constant motion. When they got to be toddlers, no corner of the house was safe from them. Their sudden darts in unanticipated directions when they were on the street kept their parents constantly on the alert. In view of their ability to climb to dizzying heights in two seconds, it was amazing how few accidents they had.
>
> At the playground they always made a beeline for the Jungle-gym. In a moment they would be hanging from the top rung. It was futile to put things on high shelves. Nothing was ever really out of their reach. Sharp objects seemed to hold a special fascination for them. No matter how carefully the kitchen knives were put away, these toddlers always seemed to find them. But for some unaccountable reason, minor burns, scratches, and an occasional scraped elbow or knee were the only pain their misadventures ever cost them.
>
> When the children were three years old, the arrival of a friend to play was a signal for shrieking activity. This meant wild running around and jumping from furniture. Later, standing on heads, cartwheels, and more daring acrobatics predominated during play sessions.
>
> Larry's parents labeled him "the monster" very early in life. But this was really a term of endearment. They seemed to enjoy him even when they were holding their breath for his safety. They reported his extraordinary physical exploits goodhumoredly and even with pride as he grew.
>
> On a nursery-school expedition Larry's teacher noticed that the youngster was missing just as the group was about to cross a street. The four-year-old had shinnied up a lamppost while the others were waiting for the light to change.
>
> When Larry was eight, his gym teacher had a similar experience with him. The teacher was showing the class how to climb a rope and then get down. Just as he was about to demonstrate how to get a foothold and take a few steps, he noticed that his class was missing one member. Larry was again on high, this time at the top of the rope.
>
> "What are you doing? You weren't supposed to go up there," the teacher said.

"Now he tells me," Larry replied as he slid to the floor.

Although Larry wasn't always the easiest child to be responsible for, he was pleasant and responsive. By the time he was two, his parents had accepted the fact that he would get into forbidden places, look with his hands, and think with his feet. Despite a number of frightening incidents, the youngster's father and mother were not alienated by his behavior. As Larry grew in understanding they were able to impress a few rules upon him, and he did his best to follow them. Of course, his best was not always very good. In active games he tended to be rough. Other children sometimes got hurt, but despite this, he was well liked and the doorbell and the phone rang frequently for Larry.

David's parents may have had less stamina, less humor, or more bric-a-brac. They would have been appalled at parents who called their child "the monster." No terms of opprobrium were ever applied to David. However, the parents were constantly annoyed at the streak of lightning they were harboring in their house. Admonitions like "Sit still," "Don't touch," "Put that down," and "Stop running" were constantly directed at the child from the time he could climb. Half of these commands were impossible for him to follow despite his good intentions. He just had to move.

In the welter of correction it became impossible for David to distinguish between important and unimportant admonitions, and between acceptable and forbidden activity. As a result, he began increasingly to ignore all attempts to curb his activity. By the time he was three, he developed into a negative child who got attention from his parents primarily by provocative teasing.

When he went to school at five, he was always blamed for any rough play that developed, not only by his mother and father, but also by the parents of his playmates. The more he was criticized, the bigger grew the chip on his shoulder. He began to play rough, pushed ahead in line, disregarded other people's comfort. By the age of eight, he made little or no effort to control his behavior, anywhere, at any time.

More and more desperate for ways to discipline him, his parents withheld privileges. He was deprived of television for week after week, put in his room on countless occasions, and not allowed to have friends in to play. Gradually he developed an I-don't-care attitude. His parents complained: "We can't find anything that matters to him to take away." As soon as he developed an interest his parents used it as a club. By the time he was ten he gave up *having* interests of which they could deprive him. (Chess *et al.*, 1965, pp. 41–43)

Harper (1971) has provided a number of convincing illustrations of the ways in which young mammals of many different species are a source of stimulation for the mother which affect her behavior. For example, adult rhesus monkeys do not play among themselves and yet they play with infants. Apparently certain properties of the infant "trigger" these play responses in the adult. Distress calls in the young elicit protective behavior in the adult. A beautiful example of the reciprocal relation between mother and infant at the human level and the way in which the behavior of each is affected by that of the other is provided in the following caretaking sequence:

Caretaking Sequence

The infant had been alone in his crib, awake and quiet for a 13-minute period in which there was no interaction. The interaction was initiated by a 3½-minute period in which he changed to an awake fussing state. This oriented the mother to the infant but did not at that time disrupt other ongoing activities or elicit approach. Presumably, the level of fussing was below a level which activates her soothing repertoire. This period was followed by 1½ minutes during which fussing progressed to full cyclic crying, and the latter did elicit the mother's approach. She looked and presumably saw grimacing and threshing—further stimuli from the infant which had the effect of keeping the mother in the immediate vicinity. The mother stood over him, since he continued to thresh and cry. She then talked. The crying continued. The mother then picked him up and cradled him in her arms. This part of her repertoire was reinforced by the infant, who reduced motor movement but continued crying. After about 8 seconds the mother again talked, but the crying continued, and another element was introduced from the maternal repertoire—she stressed his musculature by holding him so his weight was partially on his arms and legs. The crying was maintained, however, and the mother then showed another behavior: holding the infant up in the air in front of and above her. The crying continued. She then held him against her shoulder and relieved ingested air. This was followed by rather massive tactile stimulation, jiggling, rubbing, and patting, but, after a pause, the infant resumed crying. Continuation of the tactile stimulation by the mother was followed by a reduction of the crying to fussing. However, the infant started crying again. Then the infant opened his eyes and was quiet for several seconds. The mother talked again, and the infant provided reinforcement for this behavior by continuing to remain quietly awake for several seconds, then emitting a noncrying vocalization. This elicited responsive talking by the mother, who then placed her baby in an infant seat. He remained quiet and awake in his seat, smiled, and the mother left a few seconds later. The state of the infant apparently terminated the interaction sequence. The smile could have differentiated this unit into a reciprocal social interchange, but the mother at this time was apparently only set to quiet the infant. Eighteen minutes in which the infant remained quiet and awake elapsed before another unit of interaction. (Bell, 1971, p. 67)

In an interesting study of adult-child interaction in a nursery-school setting (Yarrow, Waxler, & Scott, 1971), two female adults were trained to play either a high- or a low-nurturant role with the children. The two adults were successful in showing clear differences in the following behaviors in the two conditions: attentive interest, praise, encouragement, helping, affection, control, and critical evaluation. Each child was to receive equal treatment from the adults. Actually, however, there were great differences among the children in the amount and kind of positive and negative behaviors directed toward them by the adults. The differences were determined by such child characteristics as dependency, friendly and aggressive interaction with peers, approach to the adult, and sex of child. For example, 3 percent of the children received 10 or fewer approaches initiated by one of the adults, while 15 percent received more than 70 such contacts. In the nurturant condition, the children's bids for attention were responded to positively most of the time, while in the nonnurturant conditions such attention-getting behavior was ignored or rebuffed. From this, the investigators speculated that perhaps children's dependent qualities intensify nurturance from a warm parent or teacher while magnifying nonnurturance from cold parent figures. Another finding showed that children with high-peer interaction, particularly of an aggressive nature, received more negative responses from the low-nurturant adult than children who interacted less frequently with peers. Finally, there were sex differences in the degree to which the child's behavior affected the adult's behavior. In general, various characteristics of boys had a stronger modifying effect on the adult's behavior than girls' characteristics. In summary, this experimental study furnished evidence that the behavior of nursery school teachers is affected by a number of different child characteristics. Interaction between any two individuals always involves mutual give-and-take.

In the course of research in which he analyzed the interaction between mother and infant, Yarrow (1963) became greatly impressed by the variability in a mother's behavior depending upon the characteristics of the infant. The following case example illustrates this point. The two infants, Jack and George, were placed in a foster home at the same time.

> The one infant, Jack, was, from early infancy, a passive baby, with a low activity level and a generally low level of responsiveness to environmental stimuli. He usually accepted environmental frustrations without overt protest. He tended to wait quietly if he was not fed immediately when hungry. Even at three months, much of his day was spent in sleeping. He was not much interested in food, ate without much zest. By three months, he could be encouraged to respond socially with a smile or a mild increase in activity, but only after very strong stimulation. At five months he still showed no initiative in social interaction. He did not reach out toward people or make approach responses. He enjoyed his thumb, and when awake spent much of his time in a state of passive contentment, sucking his fingers or thumb.
>
> In marked contrast to Jack, George was a vigorously active infant. He ate with great zest and sucked on the bottle with exceptional vigor. By three months, he was showing much initiative in attempting to handle and master his environment. He actively went after objects, expressed his needs directly, was very forceful in demanding what he wanted, and persisted in his demands until he was satisfied. By six months, he was showing a high degree of persistence in problem situations. George was highly responsive to social stimulation and took the initiative in seeking social response from others.
>
> On only one dimension of the maternal rating scale—routine physical care—was the home environment comparable for these two infants. To some extent, there may have been differences even in this aspect of the environment, inasmuch as George's greater forcefulness in making his needs known probably resulted in more immediate response. On most other dimensions, the environment was markedly different for these two infants. George received a great deal of physical stimulation, not only from the foster mother, but from all members of the foster family. He was very much a part of this family; they related to him as a family member. He was held and played with a great deal by the foster mother, the foster father, and all the children.
>
> On all aspects of physical contact, social stimulation, and relatedness to the family, Jack's environment was markedly different. He spent much of his time lying on the floor of the playpen. The playpen was in an isolated corner of the dining room, outside of the main stream of family traffic. The life of the family tended to flow on past him. He demanded very little and received very little stimulation. This pattern of isolation and stimulus-deprivation started very early. Even at seven weeks, the foster mother referred to him as "the other one," and talked about him as the "poor little thing." By three months, the foster mother came around to verbalizing basic feelings of rejection toward this infant. Her evaluations of him were consistently negative. It seemed as if he possessed no characteristics which were seen as desirable. He slept too much; he was not interested in anything. The one positive was that he had a nice smile—*when* he smiled. Whereas she spontaneously made many projections about George's future development, there was little investment in

> Jack's future. With regard to the quality of physical contact, the foster mother reported how the members of the family fought for the privilege of holding George for his feedings because they enjoyed his "cuddly" qualities. On the other hand, they were all reluctant to take care of Jack for his feedings because of his restlessness and apparent discomfort in being held. As a result, his bottle was often propped (Yarrow, 1963, pp. 109–110).

Yarrow and Goodwin (1965) have commented on the possible disturbances that may be produced by an incompatibility between mother and child in characteristics such as activity level if this incompatibility remains relatively stable over lengthy periods of time (Thomas, Chess, Birch, Hertzig & Korn, 1964). While it is, of course, impossible to match natural mother and infant on some of these characteristics, attention might be given to this matter when placing infants for adoption or in foster-homes. Schaffer and Emerson (1964) have used the term "mutual adaptation" to describe the interaction between mother and infant in the area of emotional attachment. The emotional needs or emotional responsiveness of the infant interact with the mother's ability to respond to these needs.

Psychological Environment at Birth

Although the principal concern of this chapter are the influences in infancy that affect personality development in later life, there are not many long-range studies capable of pinpointing them. Therefore, let us consider the broader area of the environmental differences that are potentially significant in this regard.

Among 38 of 46 couples, LeMasters (1957) found "extensive" or "severe" crises in adjusting to their first child. Most of them found the transition to parenthood hard to take. In another study (Sears, Maccoby, & Levin, 1957), a number of factors were seen to affect the mother's attitude toward pregnancy. Table 9-2 (Sears et al., 1957, p. 32) lists the attitudes of mothers covered in this investigation when they discovered they were with child.

By and large, the fewer the children the mother had, the more pleased she was to learn she was pregnant. Thus 64 percent of the mothers were judged "delighted" to find themselves pregnant if the child was their first, but only 34 percent of those who already had children fitted this description. In addition, the favorable response to the news increased as the gap between the expected child and the next older one widened. To some extent the mother's attitude was affected by the sex of the children already in the family. That mothers tended to be more pleased with their condition if their family consisted entirely of girls than if it was composed of only boys or of boys and girls may be interpreted in diverse ways. Either parents are more eager to have at least one boy than at least one girl, or they are more willing to take on the responsibility of another child if they have only girls, assuming that girls are easier to raise in the early years; having only boys, a mother may quickly become discouraged from inviting further burdens. Age did not seem to be an important factor affecting the mother's attitude toward her pregnancy.

Clearly the psychological atmospheres into which children are born vary greatly. A child may have been anticipated with some eagerness, with numerous favorable parental attitudes accompanying the birth. Or a pregnancy may have been unwanted, in which case the newborn infant is considered an unbearable burden. The harmful long-range impact of these early negative attitudes on eventual personality and adjustment has been

TABLE 9-2 How Mother Felt When She Discovered She Was Pregnant

Attitude	Percent
1. Delighted; very happy; had been waiting and hoping for this	50
2. Pleased, but no evidence of enthusiasm (includes: "This was a planned baby," said matter-of-factly)	18
3. Pleased generally; some reservations	6
4. Mixed feelings; advantages and disadvantages weighed about equally	9
5. Generally displeased, although some bright spots seen	9
6. Displeased; no reservations	7
7. Not ascertained	1
Total	100

pursued in clinical case studies, but regrettably these undertakings have lacked control groups. And since clinical reports are not the most reliable source of data for scientific endeavor, one must be careful in attributing long-term influences to experiences in early life, though differences in attitudes among parents with respect to a newborn infant must indeed exist.

Is there a kind of communion between mother and infant so that the child is able to perceive various emotional states of the mother and respond to them (Escalona, 1945)? Sullivan (1940) maintained there was, and gave to this emotional linkage the term *empathy*. Disturbances in the mother are often reflected in feeding upsets in the infant. At birth the child was seen as possessing innate tendencies that permitted him to "sense" disturbances in his relationship with his mother (Ribble, 1944). Since most of the literature regarding such emotional linkage has been based on clinical observation, there is little research to illuminate the situation. It becomes necessary to examine developmental characteristics of the newborn and infant as established through observational research. In the opinion of William James the world to the newborn was a "blooming, buzzing confusion." The newborn's perceptual and intellectual faculties are only immaturely developed. He can neither focus on nor follow a moving object until four weeks of age, and he does not smile in response to the human face until three months. The infant cannot distinguish between strange and familiar faces until he is 24 weeks old. And only at the age of four does the child begin to understand the meaning of sarcasm. From these various considerations it is difficult to conceive of the infant as able to interpret and fathom the significance of nuances or subtleties in its mother's feelings, moods, and motives. True, the infant responds with crying and restlessness to bodily tensions induced by unmet biological needs. But it is probably unscientific to regard this behavior as the infant's response to insensitivity on the part of its mother.

FAMILY INFLUENCES IN INFANCY

Attachment

Influences from several different sources has stimulated a tremendous interest in the early relationship between mother and infant. Ethologists have commented on the evolutionary survival function served by this relationship. In a provocative paper published in 1958, Bowlby introduced the term *attachment* to describe the tie between mother and infant. Largely in agreement with Bowlby, Ainsworth (1969) has defined attachment as "an affectional tie that one person or animal forms between himself and another specific one—a tie that binds them together in space and endures over time." Bowlby distinguished four main phases in the development of attachment behavior: Phase 1, orientation and signals without discrimination of figure; Phase 2, orientation and signals directed towards one or more discriminated figures; Phase 3, maintenance of proximity to a discriminated figure by means of locomotion as well as by signals; and Phase 4, formation of a reciprocal relationship. Bowlby focused on five main classes of behavior as reflecting attachment: (a) behavior that initiates interaction, such as greeting, approaching, touching, embracing, calling, reaching, and smiling; (b) behavior in response to the mother's interactional initiatives that maintains interaction (the above behaviors plus watching); (c) behavior aimed at avoiding separations, such as following, clinging, and crying; (d) exploratory behavior, as it is oriented with reference to the mother; and (e) withdrawal or fear behavior, especially as it is oriented to the mother.

In line with Harlow's study of infant monkeys, Ainsworth has argued for a reciprocal relation between attachment and exploration. Both serve a survival function; there is "a balance in infant behaviors (and in reciprocal maternal behaviors) between those which lead the infant away from the mother and promote exploration and acquisition of knowledge of the properties of the physical and social environment, and those which draw mother and infant together and promote the protection and nurturance that the mother can provide" (Ainsworth & Bell, 1970, p. 51).

In a large-scale study designed to investigate the relationships among mother-infant interaction the early feeding situation, attachment, and exploratory behavior (Ainsworth & Wittig, 1969), a group of 26 mothers and infants were observed over a period of time beginning when the infants were three weeks of age. Interviews with the mothers and observations of the feeding situation focused on four main aspects of the feeding interaction: (1) timing of feeding; (2) determination of the amount of food ingested and the termination of feeding; (3) mother's handling of the baby's food preferences; and (4) pacing of the rate of the baby's intake. Nine patterns of mother-infant interaction were identified:

I. *Demand: thoroughgoing and consistent.* Only one mother-infant pair in this sample was characterized by thoroughgoing and consistent demand feeding. This mother consistently fed her little girl when her signals suggested that she wished to go to the breast, and sometimes this was merely for comfort. No consideration was given to the lapse of time since the last feeding. Perhaps because breast fed, the baby did not get too much. She was allowed to drowse at the breast and then to resume sucking. By 6 weeks of age she could release the nipple voluntarily and find it again, and she was very active in her participation in feeding. Her mother was vague in her recall of timing, but by the end of the first quarter, her impression was that the baby usually signalled for the breast about every 4 hours.

II. *Schedule: flexible.* Six babies were fed according to a schedule flexibly regulated by mothers highly sensitive to their signals. All these mothers intended from the beginning to establish a schedule, but there were gentle nudgings towards regularity rather than rigid control. The least flexible of the group were mothers no. 19 and no. 21. While giving prime emphasis to gratifying the baby, mother no. 19 was striving for spacing that would suit her working hours, and mother no. 21 had been cautioned not to feed her baby more than every 3 hours because of a congenital gastric disorder in the baby.

These mothers sometimes woke their babies to feed them, and sometimes tried to stave them off. This staving-off was usually carried out in a sociable way intended to give the baby pleasure. If the baby could not be beguiled into happy activity, then he would be fed without further delay. Yet none of these mothers hesitated to let their babies fuss a little. They believed it to be good for the baby to wait long enough to be genuinely hungry so that he would enjoy his food. But none ever wittingly let tension mount until the baby was frantic.

The most conspicuous feature of the feeding interaction of these mother-infant pairs was the pacing of the feeding, especially the feeding of the solid food. These mothers had skilful techniques of spoon-feeding which presented the food so that the baby could take it easily and could show some initiative in sucking or gumming it from the spoon. All of them built up the feeding interaction into a smooth and harmonious process, and feeding was an occasion for reciprocal exchanges of smiling and vocalization.

Finally, it should be noted that three of the six mothers used some version of instalment feeding, in which an unfinished bottle of juice would be given if the baby seemed to want something between scheduled feedings. Without a statement of the mother's intent it would have been difficult to distinguish between flexible-schedule feeding and demand feeding.

III. *Demand: overfeeding to gratify the baby.* There were two feeding patterns, labelled "demand feeding" by the mothers, in which the babies were conspicuously overfed—pattern VII and this one. In pattern III the babies were overfed in an attempt to gratify them; in pattern VII the mothers undoubtedly intended to stuff the baby so full that he would sleep a long time and demand little attention. This distinction in intent seems important.

The two mothers showing pattern III wanted their babies to be happy, but tended to treat too broad a spectrum of cues as signals of hunger. Each mother held her baby for a long time after he seemed to have finished feeding, herself enjoying the contact, and occasionally she coaxed him to take more. If he failed to do so she played with him, and then came back to the feeding later—a kind of instalment feeding. If he did not finish his bottle even then, but later began to move his mouth or to fuss, his mother reheated the contents of the bottle and offered it again. Finally, when the baby was completely satiated, having taken a very large amount of food over an extended period, he slept for an excessively long time. Both mothers worried about these long sleeps, but neither ever woke the baby in an attempt to get his rhythms more regular. When the baby finally awoke after a marathon sleep he was ravenous, demanding, and protested at any delay in feeding. These babies fed fast at first and, probably because they ingested too much, both had considerable gastric discomfort and spitting up.

IV. *Schedule: overfeeding to gratify the baby.* The two babies of this pattern both seemed constitutionally to have a high threshold for arousal. Throughout most of the first 3 months they slept virtually all the time they were not being fed. Their spontaneous awakenings were so erratic and after such long intervals that their mothers abandoned demand feeding and woke them according to a schedule; but the schedule was a widely spaced one, for both babies were down to three meals a day in short order. Once awake, both were eager for food and fed fast. After solids had been begun the mothers complied with the babies' demands by fast spoon feeding. During bottle feeding, however, both babies tended to fall asleep before they had finished the bottle. The mother let the baby drowse for a while, but then repeatedly coaxed him to take more, interpreting any mouth movement as a sign of hunger. Consequently the babies were overfed, although both mother and baby seemed to enjoy the prolonged contact. It seems likely that the overfeeding interacted with the constitutional disposition towards oversleeping.

V. *Schedule: too much staving-off.* The three mothers who showed this pattern of interaction would have been delighted to get their babies down to three meals a day, and indeed strove constantly to do so, but their babies did not oblige them by oversleeping. On the contrary, these were alert babies who slept little and seemed hungry and fussy much of the time. These mothers all declared their intention to feed on demand—meaning they would not wake the baby to feed him, which seemed to be the chief criterion of demand feeding for the mothers in this sample. But they referred frequently enough to their hope that the baby would get onto a schedule that it is no real distortion to class this pattern as schedule feeding. They maintained the fiction of demand feeding by mechanisms of denial. They refused to recognize hunger signals when they occurred. Their staving-off activities often began within 2 hours of the previous feeding and lasted sometimes as long as 3 more hours; meanwhile the baby fussed intermittently. Saying "I can't imagine what he wants", the mother tried a series of interventions—pacifier, change of position, toys, nap, bath, and sometimes social interaction—and ended by feeling frustrated and irritable when the baby refused to co-operate in a sustained way. These were mothers who later proved themselves capable of delight in reciprocal exchanges of vocalization and smiling, and they would have been pleased to make feeding a happy time. But, probably because the babies were too hungry and upset when they were finally fed, feedings were tense and unhappy.

VI. *Pseudo-demand: mother impatient.* The mothers in the four pairs who showed this pattern used feeding practices which had some of the characteristics of demand feeding, but these departed enough from a sensitive responsiveness to the baby's signals for the pattern to be labelled "pseudo-demand"—as was pattern VII also.

The babies were fed when they were hungry and cried, after more or less delay, but the feedings were disorganized and inconsistent because of the mother's failure to satisfy the baby. None of the four women could tolerate pauses, and all discontinued the feeding far too soon. In truth, none of the four was sufficiently patient in any transactions with the baby to get sustained chains of interaction. The baby behaved as though the feeding situation was an occasion for social interaction—for the looking, smiling and vocalizing for which the mother otherwise had too little time. When the baby smiled and paused in feeding, his mother concluded that he had finished. The baby, having been put down half fed, soon fussed again, and if he was insistent enough, his mother would feed him in a second or even third instalment. Perhaps as an unconscious reflection of the mother's desire to have the feeding over quickly, all these babies had bottles with nipple holes so large that the milk came too fast. Unless the baby swallowed very quickly, he choked, coughed or gagged, and this, in itself, made for a pause and provided an excuse for the mother to discontinue. Spitting up was a great problem with all four babies, and three were underfed enough to cause the pediatrician concern.

VII. *Pseudo-demand: overfeeding to make the baby sleep long.* Two mothers, who also claimed to feed according to demand, deliberately stuffed their babies so full that they would sleep a long time and demand little attention. The feedings were very long. In one case the baby, aged 3 weeks was induced to ingest 7 ounces of formula over a period of 2 hours. Both babies were given cereal almost from the beginning, but neither accepted it well. They spat it out, struggled, and tried to avert their heads, but both mothers were determined to get the food in and they did. Needless to say, the feedings were tense and anxious. Neither baby was well regulated in rhythms by the end of the first 3 months, and neither was permitted to be an active participant in feeding.

VIII. *Schedule: rigid, by the clock.* Only one mother in this sample fed strictly by the clock. She adhered to a progressively more stringent and more widely spaced schedule of feedings, until by the time the baby was 10 weeks old he was on three meals a day. He adapted himself reasonably well to this regime during his first 3 months. On the face of it, it seemed a fairly harmonious partnership. But this pattern is placed low on the list because this mother was almost completely impervious to the baby's signals, and she fed him almost entirely at her own timing.

IX. *Arbitrary feeding.* Finally, there were five cases in which feeding was arbitrary either in the time of feedings or in the pacing of intake or both. In each case, the pattern of feeding stemmed directly from the mother's disturbed personality. The mother in pair no. 4 had a postpartum reaction; she was detached and very insensitive to the baby's signals, although she improved suddenly when the baby was about 12 weeks old. Mothers no. 5 and no. 12 were both very anxious and fragmented. They put their babies away for long periods and either "tuned out" the crying or failed to perceive it as a signal of hunger. Mother no. 18 was anxious, and the only way in which she could stem her anxiety was to control everything and everybody in a compulsive and sometimes sadistic way. She could not bear the way her baby defied her by refusing to sleep, wake, feed, and smile in accordance with her will. The timing of feedings was erratic, but the most conspicuous feature was the forced nature of the feeding—both of milk and of solids—which had to be seen to be believed. Mother no. 20 was less obviously disturbed, and less arbitrary in her feeding practices than the others. She treated her baby as a plaything—sometimes charming, but sometimes tiresome and to be put away and ignored. Her transactions with him were always at her own whim, and consequently, in her own way, she was as arbitrary as the other more disturbed mothers. (Ainsworth & Bell, 1969, pp. 144–148)

At the end of the first year of life all but one of the 26 babies were introduced to a standardized strange situation in order to assess the infant's reaction to separation from mother, and the amount of exploratory behavior displayed. The results of the study indicated that babies whose mothers were especially sensitive and responsive to them in the early feeding situation showed strong attachment to their mothers in the experimental situation at the end of the first year. They actively sought to regain contact with the mother after brief separation and they maintained contact with her by clinging and by resisting attempts at release. On the other hand, infants whose mothers were relatively insensitive and unresponsive to them in the earlier feeding situation showed little interest in regaining contact with their mothers following brief separation. Moreover, some of these infants showed an ambivalence toward their mothers by alternately attempting to maintain contact with her and by rejecting her efforts to approach them.

In a further study of the relation between attachment and exploratory behavior (Ainsworth & Bell, 1970), infants were found to use their mothers as a secure base from which to explore the novel and strange situation. However, when the mother left the room for a few minutes, attachment behaviors (crying and search) were aroused, with a marked decrease in exploratory behavior. When the mother returned, the attachment behaviors (proximity- and contact-seeking and contact-maintaining) remained strong. Crying frequently did not subside and the mothers were unable to interest their infants in resuming exploration of the novel toys.

Taken together, the studies by Ainsworth and co-workers suggest that the infant's early attachment to the mother results from a great many subtle aspects of relation between them beginning in the early months. Subsequently, this attachment facilitates the infant's exploration of his environment.

Another group of investigators have studied a sample of 54 mother-infant pairs over a period of time from pregnancy through the first year of life, with special attention to the amount of eye contact between mother and infant. Based on interviews with the mothers during pregnancy, ratings were made on two main variables. "Degree to which the baby is seen in a positive sense" was defined as the extent to which the mother viewed a baby as gratifying, pleasant, and nonburdensome. The amount of interest shown toward the prospect of holding, cuddling, and rocking the infant was labeled "Interest in affectionate contact with infants." Significant relations were found between these two variables and the frequency of mutual looking between one and three months of age (Moss & Robson, 1968). Moreover, this frequency of mutual regard predicted, for girls, the amount of time they spent looking at stimulus faces in the laboratory situation at three months. These investigators feel that interpersonal gazing or eye contact is a measure of the infant's sociability. Clinical reports of autistic and severally withdrawn children indicate their failure to establish eye contact with others. In a further study of the same group of mothers and infants (Moss, Robson, & Pedersen, 1969; Robson, Pedersen, & Moss, 1969), a relation was found between amount of mother-infant gazing at one month and the infant's gazing at a stranger and amount of spontaneous social behavior with a stranger at eight to nine-and-a-half months. Also, those infants who showed less mutual looking with mother at one month and who received less auditory and visual stimulation from mother at three months were more fearful of strangers at the later months. From these data it is impossible to say whether the early mother-infant visual interaction produced the later differences in social behavior or whether both are related to basic differences among infants in approach-withdrawal tendencies. Perhaps mothers are less likely to initiate social interactions with infants who tend to avoid such contacts. Certainly such interactions would not be highly rewarding for the mother.

While differences among mothers and infants in their social interactions in the early months and years are highly interesting, longitudinal studies are needed in order to show the possible long-range effects of these early differences. We are not justified in stressing the importance of the child's early relationship with his mother until we have much more long-term information. The child's interaction with other members of his family as well as his later social interactions with peers both play a part in influencing the course of his social development.

Age at Onset of Attachment. The age at which infants develop an attachment to a specific individual, usually the mother, has important implications for understanding the possible effects on the infant of separation from his mother, as in hospitalization. It seems likely that separation would be less harmful prior to the development of such attachment. In a large-scale study of 60 infants, Schaffer and Emerson (1964) explored three aspects of social attachment: (a) age at onset of attachment, (b) intensity of attachment, and (c) objects of attachment. The amount of protest shown upon separation from a familiar person was used as the index of attachment. The age at which fear of strangers appeared was determined by a procedure in which one of the investigators approached the infant. Fear reactions were specified as whimpering, crying, lip trembling, screwed-up face, looking or turning away, drawing back, running or crawling away, and hiding face.

First with regard to the onset of attachment to a specific individual, for a majority of the infants, this fell within the third quarter of the first year, with 7 months being the average age. Schaffer and Emerson argue that the attachment process is marked by two phases. In the first phase the infant cries and protests when he is separated from anyone, familiar or strange. This indiscriminate phase gives way to specific attachments at about 25–32 weeks of age. Fear of strangers appears approximately 1 month following the onset of specific attachment. Both of these developmental milestones appear to be related to the infant's ability to discriminate individuals in his environment.

While a majority of the infants showed an initial attachment to mother only, 29 percent manifested an attachment to several persons from the very beginning. Moreover, by 18 months of age only 13 percent showed attachment to just one person, and a third of the infants had five or more attachment figures. This certainly argues against the notion that the infant must have an initial continuous relation with a single mother figure.

Summary. The infant's early attachment to his mother may well stem from the long process of evolution in which it served a survival function. Such attachment provides the infant with a sense of security which, in turn, permits him to explore his environment, another form of behavior which made for evolutionary survival. Infant attachment to the mother is enhanced by certain aspects of their relationship. Infants whose mothers are sensitive to their needs and responsive to them show a high level of attachment. The amount of visual contact between mother and infant appears to be an index of early social development, including such behaviors as fear of strangers and responsiveness to others. The attachment process involves an initial indiscriminate phase in which separation from anyone produces some protest. Attachment to a specific individual appears around seven months of age, with the infant forming attachments to several people thereafter. The age at which specific attachments appear is related to the child's early interaction with his mother as well as to his level of cognitive development.

EFFECTS OF EARLY EXPERIENCE ON LATER BEHAVIOR

In one form or another the rest of this chapter pertains to the relationship between experiences in infancy and early childhood and subsequent behavior. For example, consider this passage:

> "That's not the point," replied Mrs. Overmeyer. "Did you see The Snake Pit?"
> "Yes."
> "Lady in the Dark? Spellbound? All those psychological things?"
> "Yes."
> "In every single one of those pictures, people go nuts because of something their parents did to them when they were kids."
> "But what has that to do with you?" I asked, "You and George would never treat a child unkindly or cruelly."
> "You don't get the idea at all," answered Mrs. Overmeyer. "In those movies the parents weren't unkind or cruel. They were perfect bricks to their children. And

yet they did some mild little thing—something so unimportant they didn't notice it—and twenty years later the kids end up in the laughing academy. Remember Lady in the Dark? Remember what knocked the heroine off her trolley? When she was a little girl, her mother was all dressed up to go to a party. The girl wanted to kiss the mother good night, but the mother wouldn't let her because she was afraid the girl would muss her hair. The next thing you know, the girl's got a neurosis as big as the Ritz."

Mrs. Overmeyer poured herself another brandy and continued. "Who knows what goes on in their goddam subconsciouses? Anything can be traumatic, and it's always the parents' fault. It doesn't matter what you do for a kid—you buy him toys and candy and clothes; you send him to camps, take him to shows, bring him on trips; you never say a hard word to him—and then one day you happen accidentally to scowl at him and—wham!—he thinks he's Napoleon."

She sighed mightily. "How do you cope with something like that? Take our daughter Linda—a mean little bastard if you ever saw one. A good clout in the chops is what she needs. But how can we risk it? We're scared even to raise our voices to her. How do we know what would happen? We yell at her today and ten years later she's exposing herself on streetcars" (Shulman, 1959, pp. 91–92).

One of the hazards arising from the emphasis on the long-term effects of early childhood experiences, a point so prevalent in recent and current psychological research among children, is depicted stunningly in this excerpt from a popular work of fiction. Modern parents are confronted by the problem in their handling of the child. "Common sense," a term grossly misapplied in parent-child relations, and child-rearing practices and attitudes learned from their own parents conflict with the idea that each and every childhood experience leaves an indelible mark on the child. Current points of view, however, argue against this notion. Since research here, as in many other phases of parent-child associations, is both sparse and inconclusive, how one regards the contribution of early experience to subsequent behavior depends inevitably on one's view of the infant and the young child.

Conceptions of Infancy and Early Childhood

Oversimplified, inaccurate, and unjust as it may be to separate points of view and writers into two camps, suppose we do so for purposes of discussion. On the one hand there is the *clinical* point of view, probably traceable back to Freud but given impetus more recently by Ribble. This view holds that infantile experiences are of primary importance because of the early age at which they occur and the impressionability of the infant at this time. The other point of view is the *developmental*; from it, the infant is seen as having tremendous capacity for adjustment, flexibility, and modifiability.

First, let us consider the Ribble position (Ribble, 1943, 1944). Her main thesis is the importance of mothering for the infant. This arises from her conception of the infant as inadequately developed at birth. Because of an immature nervous system, Ribble believed, the infant is dependent on maternal stimulation for the development of proper physiological functioning.

> All good science begins by defining its terms, so that it is essential to make clear first of all just what we mean by mothering. It is really a continuance of the closeness of the prenatal state, and the more clearly it imitates certain of the conditions before birth the more successful it is in the first weeks. The newborn baby still needs to be carried about at regular intervals until he can move and coordinate his own

> body. This helps to strengthen his sense of equilibrium and to give him reassurance. Also he must have frequent periods of actual contact with the mother because the warmth and the holding give him reassurance. Contact takes the place of the physical connection before birth when the child was like an organ of the mother's body. In addition, mothering includes the whole gamut of small acts by means of which an emotionally healthy mother consistently shows her love for her child, thus instinctively stimulating his psychic development. Obviously, feeding, bathing, and all the details of physical care come in, but in addition to these duties, which can easily become routine and perfunctory, we mean all of the small evidences of tender feeling–fondling, caressing, rocking, and singing or speaking to the baby. These activities have a deep significance (Ribble, 1943, p. 9).

From physiological functioning Ribble moved to psychological functioning. Lacking consistent mothering, she held, the infant feels tense, insecure, and frustrated. The infant's development of personality depends on this early relationship with one consistent mother figure.

> It is difficult to draw a clear line between the infant's physical and psychological needs, for the very act of making him more comfortable physically, if done by a kindly hand, may at the same time stimulate his sense of aliveness and his consciousness of personal contacts. Certainly we know now that the capacity for mature emotional relationships in adult life is a direct outgrowth of the parental care, more specifically the mothering, which an infant receives. It is the first relationship of life which activates the feelings of the baby and primes his dormant nervous system into full functional activity, giving to each individual personality its original slant. Social impulses are part of our primary equipment; emotional hunger is an urge as definite and compelling as the need for food. When we deny an infant fulfillment of these needs, we stifle his emotional and social life (13).

Ribble believed that deprivation of mothering not only definitely produces permanent psychological ill effects but also can bring on physical deterioration. Consistent mothering, on the other hand, facilitates speech development, intellectual development, and emotional development. Danger lurks in thwarting the infant's needs or desires. "The human infant in the first year of life should not have to meet frustration or privation, for these factors immediately cause exaggerated tension and stimulate latent defense activities" (Ribble, 1943, p. 72).

According to Ribble, then, the infant is characterized by immaturity and incompleteness, dependent on consistent maternal administrations for physiological and psychological welfare. The early relationship with the mother sets the pattern for all future emotional involvements. Thus any disturbance, even in the early months of life, has far-reaching implications for the child's development of personality.

The developmental view is represented most clearly by Anderson (1948). As the developmentalists see the infant, it is an active energy system that seeks stimulation, is able to withstand a variety of stresses and strains, and has a great capacity for self-repair and readjustment. Both as infant and young child, the youngster reacts to a large number of stimuli each day, of which only a few are retained in memory to affect later behavior. When trauma occurs it does not result from a single instance but from the repetition and reiteration of events in the child's life. This keeps the events alive to achieve their traumatic effect. Thus, sexual assault may have a long-range traumatic significance for the child only if his parents react to it in a highly emotional manner and continue to talk about it.

In this view the child is a persistent and consistent personality system that maintains its integrity and resists "deformation, stress, and trauma." Out of his environment the infant selects those stimuli or events that are congruent with his personality structure. He is not subject, willy-nilly, to all of the influences surrounding him, nor does he respond passively to the many stimuli in his environment. Instead, he is at least somewhat selective and reacts to the stimuli in a manner determined by his goals and attitudes toward himself. To Anderson, the child is a tough, resilient organism, capable of adapting to different environments and environmental pressures, and of responding actively to the world around him.

Evaluation of these two views is difficult. To begin with, research in the area is really not definitive. Once more, the controls required for clear-cut results are almost impossible to impose. For example, Anderson took the position that in order to have traumatic consequences for a child an event had to be repeated or reiterated in the child's experience. Quite obviously, it is not very easy to control a child's subsequent experiences so that the long-term impact of single traumatic events can be tested.

Yet somewhat stronger evidence seems to support the developmental rather than the clinical position. The following case report typifies the kind of data used to justify Ribble's "clinical" conception of the child.

> A man suffered from a phobia of being grasped from behind, the disturbance appearing early in childhood and persisting to his fifty-fifth year. When walking on the street he was under a compulsion to look back over his shoulder at intervals to see if he was closely followed. In social gatherings he arranged to have his chair against the wall. It was impossible for him to enter crowded places or to attend the theater.
>
> In his fifty-fifth year he returned to the town in which he had spent his childhood. After inspecting his old home, he went to the corner grocery and found that his old boyhood friend was still behind the counter. He introduced himself and they began to reminisce. Finally the grocerman said this, "I want to tell you something that occurred when you were a boy. You used to go by this store on errands, and when you passed you often took a handful of peanuts from the stand in front. One day I saw you coming and hid behind a barrel. Just as you put your hand in the pile of peanuts, I jumped out and grabbed you from behind. You screamed and fell fainting on the sidewalk."
>
> The episode was remembered and the phobia, after a period of readjustment, disappeared (Bagby, 1922, p. 17).

The issue is not whether experiences and relationships in childhood are important in shaping future attitudes and personalities. Rather, it revolves around the susceptibility of the infant to effects of single specific events and the extent to which these events in the long run are powerful determinants of personality. The balance hangs on how one approaches the subject and regards the emotional and mental nature of the infant.

A common weakness of the clinical view is its interpretation of the child's feelings in terms of adult attitudes, feelings, and responses. Thus, holding the infant tightly is said to give him feelings of security. It may do so for the adult, but can we validly project such feelings into the infant? Stevenson (1957) stressed the fact that experiences have one meaning for the infant and the child and another for the adult; this results from differences in memories, in the meaningfulness of the contexts of events, and in the nature of thought processes. "If you take a toy away from a child, he will probably cry, but if you tell him the mortgage has been foreclosed he will probably go on playing with the toy. We have no proof that within the world as he sees it, a stress is any harder to bear in infancy than in adulthood" (Stevenson, 1957, p. 158). Anderson similarly discussed the fallacy of interpreting children's feelings on the basis of adult behaviors.

> At a recent panel discussion another error was made. A participant talking on jealousy described the situation of the jealous child as like that in which a husband tells his wife that he is bringing a new wife into the home, expatiates on her desirability and asks his wife to assist in preparing for the new wife's coming. While this analogy has obvious dramatic qualities, it is far from a good description of child behavior. There is little evidence that marked jealousy on the arrival of a new member of the family is frequent. However, the evidence available has been played up in the practical writings and jealousy quite appropriately ascribed to an unwise distribution of affection.
>
> But a young child is not like an old wife who has a whole series of attitudes reinforced by memory and by experiences tied in with the moral, social, and institutional systems of a monogamous society. Nor are the neighbors' valuations of conduct—so essential in the situation faced by the wife—present in the young child who reacts more specifically to the situation and less to the complex of background factors. Which, then, is the more tender, the wife who has been socially sensitized or the young child who has not (Anderson, 1948, p. 478)?

Turning more directly to the developmental view of the child, the data support the idea that the child is resilient, adaptable, and flexible. Reports from the concentration camps of World War II (Kral, 1951) showed that children and adolescents adjusted to the inhumane regimen far more quickly and completely than adults. Moreover, one must agree with Anderson that, in view of the host of events and experiences impinging on the child, the crucial significance of any one of them seems doubtful. Just the same, the pattern of experiences in childhood does contribute to the determination of a variety of attitudes toward others and oneself. As illustrated in the Bagby excerpt, specific incidents exert long-range influences in individual cases. However, one may question the pervasiveness of such incidents on the individual's personality. In other words, particular events of childhood may affect only isolated aspects of a person's later personality unless intervening experiences embellish, generalize, and magnify the import of the original event.

Since infants evince wide differences in their responses to environmental stimuli and in their spontaneous behavior, it would be erroneous to impute all of an adult's personality characteristics to the manner in which he was treated by his parents in the very early years, or to his original relationship with his mother. Although this admittedly exaggerates the clinical view, there is a disposition to ignore those infant characteristics that play a part in molding his psychological environment and that cause him, in a sense, to cull from the environment those aspects to which he will respond. As Anderson asserted, the infant does not respond passively "to all the stimulation to which he is exposed without action or selection on his part" (p. 488).

The impression that individual personality is fixed or jelled permanently in childhood, Stevenson (1957) felt, stems from the fact that one's range of experience ordinarily becomes channelized and constricted. Because both infant and child depend on parents for their experiences, they are relatively unable to extend their own range; "their personalities fail to change, not because they have permanently jelled, but because they never have the new experiences which seem essential for any change."

Early parent-child relationships are indeed important. Their repetitiveness and the lack of corrective experiences to alter the attitudes, impressions, and conceptions gained from repeated parent-child contacts make them so. They do not, as some have held, gain their significance from the view of the child as a particularly impressionable individual during these early years. Later on, as we shall see when discussing the relationships of peers, one of the principal functions of interacting with one's own playmates becomes to balance out or normalize any deviant experience undergone in the home before entrance into the peer set. Thus the consequences of early parental rejection, for instance, may be countered to some extent for the child by acceptance among his agemates.

Freudian Influence

Turning now to the examination of specific maternal child-rearing practices, let us dwell on the part they play in the socialization process and on their long-range influence on adult personality. The practices that might be surveyed are legion. Those for which the most research is available, however, can be labeled the *Freudian variables,* namely, feeding, weaning, and toilet training. Let us deal primarily with these. To fit research findings into a suitable framework and understand why investigators have paid so much attention to these variables, it becomes necessary to review briefly the notions in Freud's "psychoanalytic" theory relevant to the discussion.[1]

To Freud it seemed apparent that many adult problems were traceable to parental frustration of the young child's basic biological drives. Because of this frustration, infantile strivings were repressed at the moment only to reappear in disguised form or as sources of unresolved conflicts that caused stress and anxiety in the adult. Thus we are able to understand the child-rearing advice emerging from psychoanalytic theory, which emphasizes the dangers of frustrating the infant's biological needs; immediate gratification is desirable in a sense —although Freud believed that the child had to and should ultimately come to terms with society and abandon immediate gratification.

Freud observed a basic energy, termed *libido,* in every individual at birth. This energy supplies the sexual drive; the goal of that drive is to gain pleasure for the organism. To Freud, therefore, any pleasurable impulse was an expression of sexuality. In various areas of the body are tissues that provide pleasurable feelings when stimulated; these areas, the mouth and lips, the anal region, and the genital organs, are called *erogenous zones.* In the course of psychosexual development, each of these zones becomes in turn the center of erotic pleasure. Frustration results if erotic impulses are denied gratification.

Sexuality in the infant, although not the same as adult sexuality, is a forerunner of it and is continuous with it because the same libidinal energy is released through the different erogenous zones throughout development. What are the stages of psychosexual activity related to these zones?

Oral Stage. Anyone who has observed an infant knows that much of its activity centers in the region of the mouth. Sucking, mouthing, and crying are important infantile behaviors. Fatty pads in the

[1]For clear expositions of Freud's theories, see: Munroe, 1955; Hall & Lindzey, 1957.

cheeks are present at birth to help the infant suck. A head-turning reflex also causes the infant to pivot toward sources of stimulation whereupon stimulation of the oral region elicits a response of sucking. No doubt the act of sucking to receive nutrients serves a survival function. Freud maintained that sucking was also a source of pleasure.

Two psychological phenomena are said to emerge during the oral stage: *fixation* and *regression*. These are the two phenomena most frequently used to explain child behavior. Should excessive frustration occur in any of the psychosexual stages, fixation may then develop. That is, the libidinal energy may remain locked in the erogenous zone from which the child obtained pleasure in that particular stage. In like manner, too much gratification, especially if it helps to relieve anxiety or tension, may also bring on fixation. This may be seen, for example, in giving an infant the breast or a bottle every time he shows signs of extreme upset or disturbance.

Regression refers to the tendency to return to an earlier mode of obtaining satisfaction when frustrated or anxious. A child of seven who has long since relinquished thumb sucking may resort to this behavior when faced with a new or strange situation or when tense and fatigued. Regression may occur in adults as well, according to Freudian psychology, but the method of gratification may be camouflaged. Instead of thumb sucking, the adult may smoke excessively or overeat. From the gratification comes momentary relief from tension and frustration.

The oral stage continues until some time in the second year of life as a rule, and then the center of libidinal energy shifts to the anal region. The various psychosexual stages, of course, are not distinct, nor do they inevitably occur at a fixed age in every child. Although they overlap, the sequence remains constant.

Anal Stage. The young child now obtains pleasure from expelling feces and urine. However, since toilet activity receives much attention in regard to the socialization process, conflict arises between the child's yearnings for satisfaction and parental sanctions. Parents teach the child to abhor feces, to view them with repulsion, and to eliminate at the proper time and place. These demands run counter to the child's desires; they impose limits on his impulse gratification.

Because the child learns ultimately to regulate elimination, he feels some sense of mastery over his environment. Nevertheless, too severe parental demands in toilet training may develop a fixation in the youngster at this point.

Phallic Stage. Sometime near the end of the third year the genital region displaces the anal as the area of libidinal energy. Erotic pleasure is obtained from stimulation of the genital organs. At this stage, both boys and girls show concern for the genitals; as a result, the beginnings of identification with the appropriate sex appear.

The phallic stage culminates in the Oedipal situation, a notion accorded a vast amount of attention by the Freudians. Drawing on the Greek tragedy in which Oedipus murders his father and marries his mother, Freud described the Oedipus complex as one in which the son experiences a sexual attachment to his mother, although an emotional or affectional relationship has already existed between them since it is the mother who is the principal caretaker for both sexes.

The Oedipal situation creates tensions and antagonisms between father and son, which are resolved because of several pressures. First, of course, there is the strong social taboo against incest; consequently, the mother rebuffs any sexual behavior directed toward her by the son. Second, because the father is superior to the boy in strength and authority, the son gives up or represses his desires for his mother in order to avoid retaliation by the father and to relieve the anxiety that develops from fear of loss of love of both parents. Identification with the father takes place; the child wants to be like him and models his behavior after his father's.

Latency Period. At about the age of six the child represses erotic impulses toward the parent of the opposite sex, thus resolving the Oedipus complex. This is the start of the latency period. The findings of the famed Kinsey survey show, however, that there is not a cessation of sexuality in this interval. Parental inhibiting of sexual behavior and the child's growing *superego*—his conscience—merely play a part in swinging his attention to the development of social relations with his peers. Interests stimulated by intellectual curiosity now assume importance. This state of affairs continues until just before adolescence, when a sharp rise in the production of hormones strongly reactivates the sexual impulses.

Genital Stage. At this stage increased sexual interests appear. The adolescent must now make adjustments to the opposite sex as well as to sexuality itself because of the prohibitions and sanctions relating to the sex drive in Western society. Satisfactory progress through the several psychosexual stages culminates in adequate adult heterosexual adaptation.

Feeding and Weaning

Having outlined Freud's ideas, we may now move along to the significance for personality of variation in maternal behavior in relation to the "Freudian variables"—first of all, to feeding and weaning. The earliest pressures of socialization are applied to the infant in the area of feeding. Regularity in gratifying the hunger drive is thought to be important, even when no rigid schedule is required; the method of acquiring sustenance changes from sucking to eating and chewing; and the nature of the diet shifts from a liquid base to one of solid foods. In each of these aspects of feeding, the mother intervenes to a greater or lesser degree.

As a consequence of Freud's emphasis on the dangers inherent in frustrating the infant, much attention has been paid to the implications for personality of self-demand versus rigid feeding schedules and gradual versus abrupt weaning practices. In the latter case the criteria for measurement have been the age at which weaning has occurred and the severity of the weaning process. There has also been interest in the mother's initial decision of whether to breast or bottle feed the infant. Somehow breast feeding is seen as the more desirable, perhaps because of Ribble's emphasis on the importance of close contact between mother and infant and on the need for "mothering."

Breast versus Bottle Feeding. The mother who breast feeds her infant is thought to be desirous and capable of establishing a warm, affectional relationship with her infant. In contrast, the mother who bottle feeds the infant is seen as a woman who shrugs off the psychological aspects of maternal responsibility. However, studies of differences between mothers who breast feed and those who bottle feed their infants have concluded that the principal difference revolves around attitudes concerning the psychosexual area (Adams, 1959; Sears et al., 1957). Mothers showing strong feelings of discomfort toward sexual matters are more likely to bottle feed. Nevertheless, it would be a mistake to overlook the fact that a decision to breast feed may be governed by a variety of reasons, some having slight psychological relevance. These may include pressures of time, scheduling convenience, and physical factors, to mention but a few. Moreover, as noted in an earlier chapter, many aspects of child care in Western culture are subject to cyclical fads which have no relation whatsoever to the personality pattern or attitudes of any particular mother. In rating mothers' feeding behavior, Brody (1956) concentrated on the sensitivity of the mother to the infant. Not all mothers who fed by the breast were rated as disclosing completely satisfactory responsiveness to the infant.

The findings of research into the effects of breast versus bottle feeding on the child's personality have been generally negative. In the Pattern Study, as the Sears et al. (1957) study is familiarly known, six aspects of child behavior such as aggressiveness, dependency, and development of conscience were examined in relation to whether the child was breast or bottle fed, and no broad links were found. Sewell and Mussen (1952), in an extensive study of some phases of infantile feeding, detected no tie between the type of feeding in infancy and various oral symptoms of general adjustment, such as thumb sucking, nail biting, and stuttering, among five- and six-year-olds. Evidently, the container from which the infant obtains his milk, whether breast or bottle, has no psychological import. Despite speculation that the quality of the child's feeding experience is significant, scientific data on the subject is meager and equivocal.

Duration of Breast Feeding. The duration of breast feeding has also been given weight as a factor affecting the child's later personality. Moreover, Levy (1943) suggested that the length of breast feeding related to maternal attitudes: "In general, all factors favoring rejection of the child tend to shorten, all factors favoring overprotection tend to lengthen, the breast feeding act" (p. 59). Although this may be true in individual cases, especially in certain ones seen in clinical settings, there is not much evidence to support the generalization among a normal population. In fact, one investigation found no relation between length of breast feeding and maternal rejection (Peterson & Spano, 1941). Likewise, no relation has been established between length of breast feeding and personality ratings of nursery-school children.

In an extensive analysis of data obtained in the California Guidance Study described in Chapter 1, Heinstein (1963) examined the relation between early nursing experience and subsequent behavioral adjustment. In addition to length of breast and bottle feeding, ratings were made of three psychological variables: warmth of the mother, nervous stability of the mother, and marital adjustment of the parents. The results indicated that "there were no apparent over-all advantages in behavioral adjustment associated with either breast or formula feeding as such" (p. 33). Fewer behavior problems were noted in those children whose mothers were rated as warm rather than cold in their interactions with them. For boys, the combination of length of nursing, and warmth of mother was particularly important. Those who experienced a long period of nursing by a cold mother were the most maladjusted group. Breast feeding by a cold mother was most conducive to problem behavior in girls. In both of these instances the mother's behavior appears to contradict her feelings with regard to the maternal role. The conflict between a cold attitude and behavior reflecting nurturance (breast feeding and long nursing periods) seems to produce harmful effects in the child. This strongly suggests that the adoption of approved maternal behavior cannot nullify a negative attitude toward the child or toward the maternal role.

Heinstein concluded that early feeding experience may be important only when considered in the context of the psychological relation between mother and child. Further, the sex of the child must be taken into account when examining the effect on the child of infant feeding practices.

Schedule versus Self-demand Feeding. Over the years there have been many variations in expert advice on this topic. Thus it seems fruitless to examine in detail the research that has endeavored to relate this aspect of early infant care to factors of maternal or child personality. In the Pattern Study an inverse relationship was noted between a mother's confidence in her ability to employ correct child-rearing procedures and the fidelity with which she followed her pediatrician's advice; the less confident the mother, the more she was likely to accept her doctor's recommendation of feeding techniques. This finding suggested once more that although a mother's methods of child-rearing might be related to other aspects of her general attitudes and personality, her procedures might not reflect her feelings toward the child or toward child-rearing itself.

A study by Durrett (1959) will serve to illustrate the inconclusive relationships typically obtained between measures of early infant scheduling and child behavior. Based on home interviews, a group of mothers of preschoolers were rated on a scale concerning feeding schedules, ranging from a strict schedule to complete self-regulation. The children were scored on the extent of verbal and physical aggression displayed in a doll play session. No significant relations were found between the mother and child variables, although according to the frustration-aggression hypothesis (see Chapter 15), one would expect more aggressive behavior in those children who had experienced a stricter, and therefore presumably more frustrating, feeding schedule.

Sucking and Thumb Sucking. Psychoanalytic theory contends that if an infant lacks sufficient oral gratification through his sucking to obtain food, he will indulge in sucking behavior unrelated to the feeding process. Learning theory, on the other hand, maintains that the greater the reinforcement received by the infant from sucking, the stronger his sucking drive will be. Each of these theories thus predicts different consequences for the infant's early sucking experience. Psychoanalytic theory would hold that an infant who is cup fed from birth or whose breast- or bottle-feeding experience is brief would exhibit more "nonnutritional" sucking than an infant who received much oral gratification through sucking. If it could be shown that sucking the thumb were caused by lack of oral gratification, a mother could be advised with some assurance as to the appropriate method for preventing this behavior. The controversy is indeed an interesting one.

Although here, too, the research findings are contradictory, we must conclude that there is a variety of reasons for prolonged thumb sucking, some of which bear absolutely no relation to gratification or deprivation in early sucking. For example, Simsarian (1947) observed five thumb suckers among a group of 26 children who had been breast fed on self-demand schedules and who had been permitted to nurse as long as they wished. In another study, Traisman and Traisman (1958), who interviewed mothers of more than 2000 infants and children, noted little difference in the occurrence of thumb sucking between children fed by bottle and those partially or completely fed by breast. They also found only slight differences of types of psychological problem between those who did and those who did not suck their thumbs.

As a clinical matter, thumb sucking is taken as one sign of maladjustment or personality disturbance in a child. The seriousness of thumb sucking would depend, of course, on the frequency and extent of the behavior and the age of the child. In a three- or four-year-old such conduct would not be considered unusual in the face of a new, strange, or challenging situation. In an elementary-school child it may, however, require prompt investigation by a person trained in psychology. Even if one does not adhere strictly to psychoanalytic explanations of behavior, sucking the thumb may be regarded as regression, in the broad psychological sense of the term; the child reverts to an earlier form of behavior, which assured gratification. In an older child, therefore, thumb sucking is sometimes interpreted as indicating strong feelings of insecurity.

Not much is known through definitive medical research about the effects of such behavior on the teeth. Current thinking generally holds that prolonged thumb sucking after the child's permanent teeth have appeared may very well affect the bite, especially where there is some tendency toward irregularity. Prior to this time, there is not much likelihood that sucking of the thumb would harm the dental structures. Nor is there any knowledge to speak of about the thumbs themselves becoming deformed through such activity!

Weaning. In the Pattern Study both the age at which weaning occurred and the severity of the process, that is, the amount of pressure exerted on the infant, were linked to a rating of the child's emotional upset during the procedure. Although nearly twice as many youngsters were rated as having shown some upset when weaning was initiated after 11 months of age as when it was stated before 5 months, the children weaned in the intervening period showed the fewest emotional reactions. Then, too, the less severe the procedure was, the fewer the emotional upsets. What was learned about the relation of age of weaning to the emotional reaction to it contradicted the idea implied in psychoanalytic theory that the longer the infant remained breast or bottle fed, the more emotionally healthful this would be. The Sewell and Mussen study detected no connection between the personality adjustment ratings of its five- and six-year-olds and the age at which they were weaned or the character of the weaning process, whether sharp or gradual.

More than one writer (Fries, 1941; Escalona, 1945) has stressed the importance of feeding as a particularly sensitive indicator of both the child's relationship with its mother and its general adjustment. However true this may be, the point of concern here is the difference between short- and long-range effects of various maternal practices. Conceivably the mother's behavior toward her infant with respect to feeding may influence the infant's responses during the infancy period. But there is little support for the view that her conduct in this one aspect of child rearing exerts long-range impacts on the child's personality. To anticipate the beginning of the next chapter, there may be shifts in maternal behavior and attitudes toward child-rearing over a period of time. Although a mother may employ a rigid, insensitive approach toward the young infant, she may revise her methods and attitudes as a result of both the child's changing developmental characteristics and capabilities and of her own learning about child care.

Another consideration is the interrelationships among the various practices a mother employs. One study (Klatskin, Jackson, & Wilkin, 1956) explored the tie between the flexibility of the mother's practices in feeding, sleeping, toilet training, and socialization, and evidences of disturbance in the child. Among its findings appeared a tendency for the relation between maternal flexibility and problem behavior in the child to be a discrete one; specific deviation from optimal handling by the mother led to problems in the child only in the one particular area. Thus, extreme rigidity in toilet training might lead to disturbances in toilet habits but leave unaffected the child's sleeping and eating behaviors. Second, the study uncovered no link between the mother's behavior in areas of feeding and socialization in the child's first year and his behavior then or in the year which followed.

In a study by Sewell, Mussen, and Harris (1955) mothers of a group of five- and six-year-olds were interviewed to try to ascertain the relationships among child-rearing practices during infancy and the years immediately following. Obtaining information on 38 items bearing on infant care, child-training procedures, and the handling of disciplinary problems, the study generally showed low and insignificant correlations. Apparently a mother's attitude in one area of child training was germane to that area alone and did not affect her behavior in others. Inconsistency *as to the favorableness of the practice* was the rule.

What, then, are the effects of feeding practices on the child? First, regarding the significance of the mother's decision to breast or bottle feed, a host of factors, some without much psychological relevance, influence it. Several studies even propose that breast feeding may have some sexual implications for the mother, which may be more important than her attitude toward the infant in deciding whether to breast feed. Second, no permanent effects of weaning activities on the child have been noted, although there is some evidence for a curvilinear relationship between age of weaning and emotional upset. Third, despite support for both deprivation and reinforcement of sucking as causes for thumb sucking, actually several causes exist. Finally, a child-rearing technique may exert immediate or short-range influence on child behavior but have no long-term significance; and the links among the various child-training practices employed by a mother are slight, so that it would seem hardly likely for one specific practice to have a general bearing on the child's development of personality.

Toilet Training

Every culture regulates toilet behavior. Cultures vary widely, however, in how much control and restrictiveness they impose. Presentday American society is relatively strict in this phase of child training. It is likely that the urban, crowded conditions of American life, which create an almost fanatical consciousness of germs and dirt, contribute to this strictness. Be that as it may, mothers express great amounts of concern over the toilet habits of their young children, frequently mentioning the development of bladder and bowel control as a "problem" area.

Notwithstanding Freud's heavy emphasis on the crucial importance of toilet training to the child's subsequent development of personality, research offers little corroborating evidence for a relationship between the two. In an ingenious study designed to test the relation predicted by Freudian theory between early maternal toilet training practices and the anal personality type characterized by obstinacy, orderliness, and parsimony, Hetherington and Brackbill (1963) found stronger evidence for identification theory. Significant correlations were found between boys and their fathers and between girls and their mothers in these three personality traits, suggesting that identification with like-sex parent is an important determinant of the child's personality characteristics. Inconclusive relations were obtained between ratings of age and severity of toilet training and the child's personality ratings. Abundant clinical reports, however, indicate the harmful consequences of overly severe toilet training. Examining case histories of children referred to a child-guidance clinic, for example, Huschka (1942) observed that in more than half of the children bladder and bowel training was started prematurely. The list of child behaviors seen to derive from coercive toilet training includes negativism, aggressiveness, fearfulness, compulsiveness, rigid behavior, rage, guilt, excessive cleanliness, and defiance. But as we shall presently see, the relationship between toilet training and behavior or personality is by no means simple. More influential than the mother's practices are her own personality and the factors prompting her behavior. Moreover, the greater permissiveness of child-rearing practices in America suggests that coercive toilet-training procedures are much less common today than formerly. The practices of most mothers in this respect, therefore, fall within the normal range and do not contribute to aberration.

Although there are some similarities between weaning and toilet training, the differences are more significant. In both procedures built-in reflexes help the child to perform these behaviors. The basic mechanisms involved exist and operate efficiently at birth. Toilet training differs from feeding behavior, however, by requiring the child to control the built-in reflexes and prevent their operation except at certain approved times and places.

At first the child has no desire to control the process of elimination. To develop control he must learn to recognize signs that indicate the imminent relaxation of the anal sphincter muscles. Besides inhibiting action, voluntary control also involves the ability to "let go." Such a relatively complicated process requires much learning. If anxiety, resulting from punishment, is introduced into the situation, learning becomes more difficult and the process prolonged. Take the analogy of the impatient husband who attempts to teach a hopeful but unsure wife to drive a car. Punishment takes the form of disapproval, which causes the wife to give up in despair. In both cases, toilet training and learning to drive, pressure and its resulting frustration so complicate and retard the learning process that negative attitudes may affect the whole "teacher-learner" relationship, whether between husband and wife or mother and child.

When does toilet training customarily begin? It should not begin before the child is ready to undertake the necessary learning. Because some amount of physiological maturation is probably required and children mature at different rates, it becomes impossible to state a precise age at which toilet training should be initiated. In the Pattern Study 87 percent of the mothers started bowel training before the child was 20 months old; 11 months represented the average age. In 80 percent of the cases the training was completed by the time the child reached 24 months of age, the average age of completion being 18 months. The data showed that the later training was undertaken, the quicker it succeeded.

A wide variety of reasons prompt a mother to undertake toilet training at a particular age, but the Pattern Study noted that maternal anxiety about the sexual sphere was an important element in her decision to begin training early and complete it as rapidly as possible. And this anxiety may indeed influence the restrictiveness with which she regards manifestations of sexuality in the child.

Severity of Training. From descriptions by mothers of their practices, ratings were made of the severity of toilet training. More important than the percentages listed in Table 9-3 (Sears, et al., 1957, p. 119) are the details of each of the five rating categories. As might be expected, the severity of the training was an influential factor in causing emotional upset in the child. But severity alone was not the full story. The attitudes of the mother also bore on the amount of upset. Severe toilet-training procedures became far more emotionally disturbing if accompanied by maternal coldness and undemonstrativeness than if presented in an atmosphere of maternal warmth that made the child feel emotionally secure. Thus the entire emotional context within which day-to-day child-rearing methods occur must be evaluated to ascertain the effect of child-care techniques on child development.

Many writers have said that coercive and insensitive toilet training damages the parent-child relationship, perhaps with long-range consequences. If so, this assertion is entirely speculative. No doubt, coercive techniques are unwise for several reasons, yet other considerations are worth restatement. That no over-all favorableness or unfavorableness characterizes child-rearing methods implies that although a mother may use ill-advised techniques in toilet training, some of her other procedures may be perfectly acceptable. Moreover, the basic attitudes of the mother may be more significant for the child's development than any single child-rearing practice.

Taken together, these points suggest the need to assess the pervasiveness of a mother's attitudes toward her child before trying to predict their bearing on his future personality. Then there is the possibility that maternal attitudes may change in time. A mother may pressure her child into early toilet control and may not seem to accept him until he has achieved it, but once he has attained this goal, she may grow relaxed and accepting in her relationship with him.

To summarize, various explanations may account for the failure of the Freud-

TABLE 9-3 Severity of Toilet Training

Degree of Severity	Percent
1. Not at all severe. Child more or less trained himself. Not his fault when he has accidents; they are considered natural. No punishment or scolding.	10
2. Slight pressure. Mild disapproval for some late accidents. Mother makes some efforts to show child where, when, and how to go to toilet.	42
3. Moderate pressure. Scolding for some late deviations; fairly frequent toileting.	29
4. Fairly severe training. Child scolded fairly often; mother clearly shows disapproval. Child may be left on toilet for fairly lengthy periods.	16
5. Very severe training. Child punished severely for deviations; mother angry and emotional over them.	2
Not ascertained	1
Total	100

ian variables–feeding, weaning, and toilet training–to yield many clues to the personality development of the child. First, the range of practice for mothers in Western culture is limited, with few mothers at either extreme. Part of this situation may be charged to the widespread expert advice available and the general trend toward permissive child-rearing. Second, the fact that a mother's child-training methods are often shaped by pediatric counsel or by current fads rather than by her own attitudes and personality makes them less pertinent psychologically than might otherwise be the case. Finally, since there is little connection among a mother's various child-rearing techniques, the general quality of the relationship between parents and child is more predictive of future personality than are the clearly observable effects of specific, short-term practices.

Other Infant Care Variables

Caldwell (1962, 1964) has noted that the tremendous concern with feeding and elimination practices has left a large number of psychological variables unexplored. For example, little attention has been paid to early intellectual and verbal stimulation or to early autonomy given the child in terms of physical activity and exploration. Was the child pressured to perform some of the early developmental tasks such as walking and talking? How early did the parents begin to read to the child? Was infant care consistent from one area to another? Was the infant cared for primarily by a single mother figure or was the caretaking shared by several individuals? In this section three studies are examined, each focusing on a somewhat different set of variables.

In the Yarrow study (Yarrow, 1963; Yarrow & Goodwin, 1965) mentioned earlier in this chapter the main maternal care categories were:

> (1) the amount and varieties of stimulation provided by the mother; (2) the activities of the mother primarily concerned with need gratification and tension reduction in the infant; (3) the conditions under which stimulation and need gratification are provided, broadly conceived as learning conditions; and (4) the underlying feelings and attitudes of the mother toward the infant (Yarrow & Goodwin, 1965, p. 475).

The relation between these maternal behaviors and a number of infant personality and developmental characteristics at six months of age were examined. The learning conditions were significantly correlated with the measure of IQ and moderately related to the infant's exploratory and manipulative behavior. Strong relations were found between the infant's ability to handle stress and the maternal affectional variables. While no longitudinal data are available showing the long-term stability of these early infant ratings, it is clear that Yarrow has identified important interactions between mother and infant characteristics during the infancy period.

Schaefer and Bayley (1963) have analyzed the longitudinal data collected in the Berkeley Growth Study in order to identify the effects of maternal behavior on the child's social and emotional development. Since data bearing on the relation between mother and child behavior in later childhood and adolescence are dealt with in the next chapter, the present discussion is confined to their study of the early age period. The infants were tested periodically during their first three years. Extensive written observations were made of the interactions of the mother with the examiners, the child, and any other persons present.

Later, behavior ratings scales were developed and the written records were evaluated on each of the 32 scales. A factor analysis of these scales revealed two main factors (Schaefer, 1959): love versus hostility and autonomy versus control. These broad dimensions are discussed in greater detail in the next chapter. Following each of the 12 testing sessions between the ages of 10–36 months the infants were rated on these seven-point rating scales:

Degree of strangeness: shy–unreserved
Speed of movements: slow–rapid
Amount of positive behavior: negative behavior–positive behavior
Emotional tone: unhappy–happy
Activity: inactive–vigorous
Responsiveness to persons: slight–marked
Irritability (or tendency to be sensitive to and react to stimulation): excitable–calm

Figure 9-1 illustrates the kinds of relationship that were established between maternal behaviors and child characteristics. In general, the love-hostility dimension showed strong correlations with happy, calm, and positive behaviors of both sons and daughters. Stronger correlations were found between mothers and sons than between mothers and daughters, suggesting that boys are more deeply influenced than girls by the interaction between them and their mothers.

While investigating infant behavior and personality development, Brody

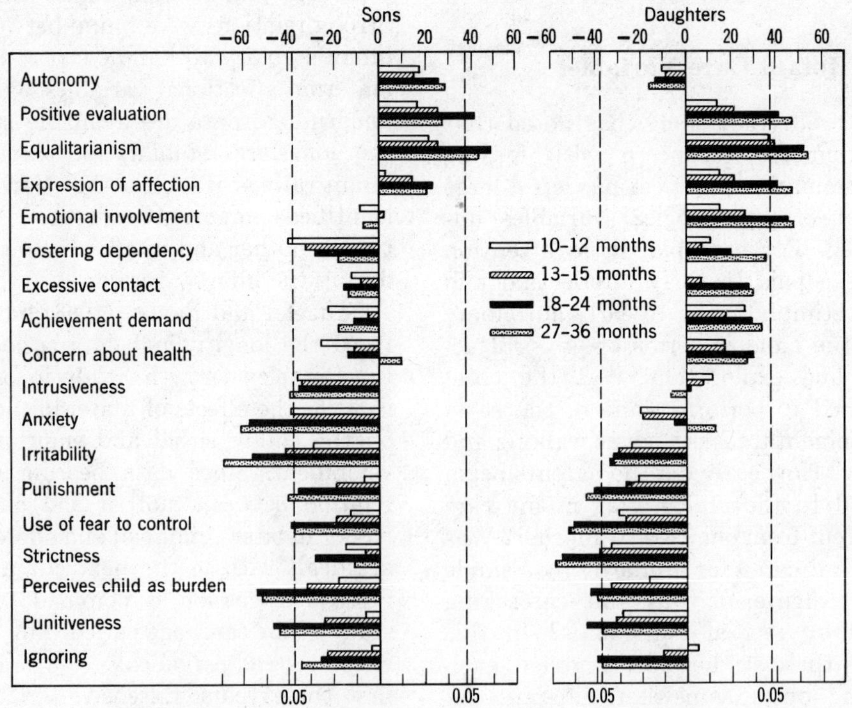

FIGURE 9-1 Correlations between maternal behavior (0–3 years) and children's happiness at four age levels (10–36 months) (Bayley, 1965, p. 205).

(1956) and her associates studied the conduct of mothers during a four-hour period in which they performed their normal functions of caring for the infant's needs. Their study had a great methodological advantage over the investigations dealing with feeding and toilet training. It actually observed the mothers caring for their infants, whereas the information acquired in the other studies came from retrospective verbal reports by the mothers.

The Brody team concentrated on 32 infants, 4 males and 4 females at each of four levels of age, 4, 12, 20, and 28 weeks. The mothers brought their children to a central location where rooms were expressly equipped with the supplies needed to care for infants. Although the ostensible purpose was to observe infant patterns of behavior, two researchers kept detailed records of each mother's behavior in relation to her child. They particularly attended to six maternal activities: feeding, cleaning, moving, touching, offering objects, and speaking. In each of these areas they rated behavior on a five-degree scale in terms of the sensitivity with which the mother responded to the needs or wishes of her infant. Three indices, each describing a particular quality of maternal behavior, were computed for each of the six activities. The first, *frequency,* measured the absolute amount of a mother's sensitivity in the specific activity. The second, *mean*, measured the average amount of her sensitivity. The third, *standard deviation,* measured the consistency of the sensitivity.

Judged by these measures, the mothers fell into four main groups or types.

> The mothers of group A were conspicuous for their ability to accommodate to the needs of their infants. By virtue of the kind of physical and emotional support they provided and the steadiness of their interest in and communicativeness toward their infants, they gave them freedom to move about, to vocalize, feed, rest or play with a minimum of interference. More regularly and with more ease than all the other mothers they recognized and tried to relieve passing discomforts in the infants. The mothers themselves were not without tension, but most of the time that tension appeared to heighten their intimacy with the infants.
>
> The mothers of group B were conspicuous for their conscious willingness to accommodate to their infants. At first glance some of their behavior resembled that of the A mothers, but on the whole they were more tense, less communicative and less steadily attentive. At times they tried more actively to stimulate their infants and at other times they were mildly distant or insensitive to the infants' immediate needs. The quality of satisfaction with the infant and of enjoyment of their mothering tasks, outstanding in the A mothers, was much less evident, although B mothers were generally positive toward their infants.
>
> The mothers of Group C were conspicuous for their lack of spontaneity and their intentions to be efficient above all else. Physically and socially they were detached from their infants. Some reduced their attention to the carrying out of a minimum of essential details of infant care, and showed a low degree of interest in any activity with the infant of a nonphysical nature.
>
> The mothers in group D were conspicuously active but also erratic in their attentiveness, efficiency and sensitivity. They quite sedulously governed their infants' actions by stimulating, restricting or instructing them, apparently hardly aware of the possible effects of their behavior on the infants' condition (Brody, 1956, pp. 265–266).

Thus, group A mothers were sensitive, consistent, and attentive. Group B mothers, as a rule, closely followed the group A pattern but fell short of the mark on each index; they were less sensitive, less consistent, and somewhat overactive or overattentive. Group C mothers were insufficiently sensitive, moderately inconsistent, but adequately attentive, whereas the mothers in group D were hypersensitive, very inconsistent, and hyperactive.

Besides probing aspects of maternal behavior, the study sought to relate the behavior and activity patterns of the infants to it. Few differences were found, generally speaking, among the four groups of infants either in level of activity or on scores obtained on Gesell Development Schedules. Although some correlation appeared between maternal behavior and the developmental status of the infant, Brody concluded that the relationship might not be causal. Innate differences among infants might easily have influenced the behaviors of the mothers.

Brody's study demonstrated, of course, that differences did exist among mothers in their behavior toward the infant. If these differences are based on or are related to fundamental characteristics of attitude and personality in the mother which persist over the years, they may actually affect the child's development in ways as yet unknown.

Maternal Deprivation

This is a subject that has aroused much current interest and much controversy.[2] Essentially, maternal deprivation is a circumstance in which an infant or young child does not have a relationship with his mother because of his separation from her. If its importance were to be judged by the number of infants suffering from maternal deprivation, the issue would be relegated to oblivion. However, both the issue itself and the findings on the effects of such deprivation on the child are relevant to many basic aspects of child development and the mother-child relationship.

Although few psychologists would argue against the useful and necessary functions performed by the mother in the infant's early years, the issue of maternal deprivation revolves about the long-range, debilitative repercussions on the infant separated from his mother. Granted that every infant may need tender loving care, will deprivation of it scar him permanently?

The appearance of Ribble's *The Rights of Infants* in 1943, together with an essay by the same author (1944) heralded a new conception of the mother-infant relationship. As was evident in the excerpts from Ribble's book quoted earlier in the chapter, she conceived of the infant as incomplete and immature physiologically at birth and totally dependent on the mother's ministrations for survival.

> When the umbilical cord is cut at birth, the child, as we have said, is far from being a complete and independent individual. The infant is peculiarly helpless, and it is not until after the faculties of speech and locomotion have developed that he can cope with any separation from the mother without danger. Mother and child after birth are psychologically still a unit, and close relationship is as important for early mental development as was the more primitive connection with the fetus for physiological development. As we have seen in the study of marasmus, interference with this natural relationship means that the infant starves for mothering, and as a result the vital activities, first of alimentation, then of breathing and circulation, get out of order, and we find the small body functioning much as it did before birth (Ribble, 1943, p. 12).

Having observed 600 infants, Ribble (1944) concluded that tension was seen to disappear when the infant was in phys-

[2]For comprehensive reviews of the subject, see: Casler, 1961; and Yarrow, 1961.

ical contact with the mother, whereas separation produced anxiety. Ribble imputed a wide variety of infant reactions to inadequate mothering: negativism, refusal to suck, hypertension, vomiting, wild screaming, a stuporous sleep, diarrhea, and finally, marasmus.[3]

Much interest was stimulated by Ribble's contentions. Her position was strengthened in a series of articles by Spitz (1945; Spitz & Wolf, 1946) which described the deleterious effects of institutionalization on infants separated from their mothers. A sharp drop in developmental quotient, a high mortality rate, and the appearance of disturbed behavior occurred in a group of foundling-home infants in the final third of their first year (Spitz, 1945). These phenomena were ascribed to the absence of a mother-child relationship; in the foundling home the ratio of nurses to infants was one to eight. Spitz asserted that impairment of the mother-child relation for more than a three-month interval during the first year of life inflicted irreparable damage on the infant.

The terms used to describe infant reaction to the loss of maternal love and maternal stimulation are *hospitalism* and *anaclitic depression*. The principal symptoms of these syndromes are weepiness, withdrawal and lack of contact with the environment, refusal to act, and stupor. Take this case reported by Spitz:

> White female. Intelligent, friendly child who smiles easily and ecstatically at the approaching observer. No notable event in the course of the first 7 months. At this time a change occurred in the child. The observers got the feeling that the child was apprehensive. A week or two later the change was accentuated. The temper of the child had become unequal. She still was mostly friendly to the observer, but as often as not broke out crying when the observer approached closer. After another two weeks she could no longer be approached. No amount of persuasion helped. Whenever approached she sat up and wailed. Two weeks later, she would lie on her face, indifferent to the outside world, not interested in the other children living in the same room. Only strong stimulation could get her out of her apathy. She would then sit up and stare at the observer wide-eyed, a tragic expression on her face, silent. She would not accept toys, in fact she withdrew from them into the farthest corner of her bed. If the approach was pressed she would break into tears. This went on until the child was 9 months old (Spitz & Wolf, 1946, p. 315).

Sharp criticism by Pinneau (1950, 1955) of the efforts of Ribble and Spitz induces one to question many of the effects of maternal deprivation which they postulated. To cite one example of this criticism, Pinneau pointed out that the drop in development quotient described by Spitz occurred before, not after, the infants were separated completely from their mothers; thus it could not possibly be charged to this circumstance.

It is not within the scope of this book to examine at length all the studies that have confirmed or invalidated the Ribble-Spitz belief. Yet certain lines of evidence of several key ideas help to clarify some of the basic matters at issue, of which the four main ones are consequences of institutionalization, the need for a single mother figure, deprivation of stimulation, and the contrast between long-range and short-range effects.

Institutionalization. Unfortunately, many of the investigations into the impact of institutionalization are weak methodologically. A number of important

[3]A disease, characterized by apathy and deterioration, said to be caused by an infant's separation from its mother.

variables have not been controlled. Some of those that must be considered are the age at which separation occurs, the nature of the mother-child relation prior to separation, the reason for the separation, and the quality and atmosphere of the institution. Individual characteristics of the child must be considered also. Schaffer (1966) has shown that inactive infants are affected more adversely than active ones by a deprivation experience. The reduced vulnerability of active infants is due to their ability to maintain a state of alertness and to avoid perceptual monotony by initiating contact with new environmental stimuli.

If a separation occurs after the infant's first six months of life, any ill effects upon the child may result from the separation itself and the breaking of an affectional relationship rather than from the subsequent deprivation of a mother. Thus, a distinction must be made between separation and deprivation. To which of these are the ill effects being specifically attributed? Besides, if the child is separated at the mother's own instigation, the possibility must not be overlooked that the later harmful effects may stem from the mother's earlier rejection and neglect, and not from the actual separation and consequent deprivation.

Although the ratio of adults to children is low in most institutions, the percentage can vary widely, as can the amount and quality of care. In a study comparing maternal care between institutionalized and home-reared infants, Rheingold (1960) found that the latter group received 4.5 times more "caretaking," although differences between the two groups varied depending on the specific caretaking activity. For example, the home infants were shown affection 18 times more frequently than the institutionalized infants.

In addition to the sheer number of children assigned to each adult for care, one must also assess the quality of the care. Is affection shown by the nurse or attendant? How much stimulation do the infants receive from the caretakers? How much consistency exists in the handling of the infants? Then there are the physical characteristics of the surroundings. Are they drab and colorless? Are the infants deprived of visual and aural stimulation as well as the social and emotional stimulation of an adult? Nor can the length of institutionalization nor the ages at which it occurs be ignored in investigating the consequences.

In sum, the effects of institutionalization may result as much from a lack of emotional involvement in relations with other persons as from an insufficient amount of sensory stimulation. Having conducted research among lower organisms, Scott (1962) argued that "the speed of formation of a social board is dependent upon the degree of emotional arousal, irrespective of that arousal" (p. 951). The emotional chill that often pervades the general psychological atmosphere of institutions as well as the relationship between caretaker and child may hinder the development of normal social, affectional ties.

Single Mother Figure. Various kinds of "multiple mothering" would certainly argue against Ribble's belief in the need for an infant to enjoy a relationship with a single mother figure. As Margaret Mead (1935) has reported, the extended family is the prevailing pattern in many South Seas cultures. The responsibilities of child-rearing are shared by many members of the community. Brothers, sisters, and other members of the larger family may assume several of the maternal functions. Yet no effects on personality adjustment and development comparable to those noted by Ribble and Spitz have been attributed to this type of child care.

In the communal nurseries established in many Israeli settlements today the children are cared for by more than one significant adult. Although the child spends most of his day in the nursery he often sees his parents for several hours each evening as well as on weekends. This is an example of what might be called "intermittent mothering." The *metapelet,* the trained caretaker of the children, performs most of the traditional functions of motherhood related to routine care and training of the child. Accounts of the daily contacts between the children and their natural mothers indicate a warm, permissive, and affectionate relationship. Perhaps such a separation of care and training from the "affectional" functions of the maternal role might reduce some of the ambivalent feelings of parents and children characteristic of traditional parent-child relationships.

Compared with Israeli children raised in their own homes, these children reared in the settlements, or kibbutzim, show few differences in personality and intellectual development. Either this sort of multiple mothering does not exert any deleterious influence on the development of personality or experiences occurring after early childhood nullify any potentially harmful effects. Possibly both are true.

One study (Rabin, 1958) found that 10-year-old boys reared in the kibbutzim showed less intense feelings of sibling rivalry than boys reared in another fashion. Although the topic at hand is maternal deprivation, this finding suggests that some of an individual's most intense, destructive emotional feelings emanate from the traditional family arrangement of Western culture. Sibling jealousies, parent-child hostilities, and other long-lasting conditions of like kind may emerge from this scheme. Support for this point comes from a fascinating report (Freud & Burlingame, 1943) on the nurseries provided for the children evacuated from war-gutted London. At one point artificial families were created in which four children were assigned to one nurse, or mother substitute, investing the relationship with some continuity and stability. Out of this arrangement flowered violent attachments, possessiveness, and anxiety resulting from fear of loss of the mother figure, and jealousies resembling sibling rivalry. There were also positive consequences in evidence. Thus the small family group, somewhat isolated, heavy on contact between its members, which symbolizes the family arrangement in Western society, may exert both negative and positive influence on the child's development of personality.

Stimulus Deprivation. Few controlled experiments pertaining to lack of sensory stimulation have been conducted among children. Several have used adults as subjects, and even more have involved lower organisms. A kinesthetic need or drive in infancy has been postulated by Kulka, Fry, and Goldstein (1960). It is a need for incoming stimulation through a variety of modalities related to the senses: light, touch, pressure, and temperature. The infant obtains gratification of this kinesthetic need when an adult cuddles him, rocks him, or supplies similar soothing services. Severe early deprivation of this need may lead to apathy and inactivity, or rocking, banging of the head, and other rhythmic movements by the infant that may represent an attempt to satisfy this yearning for stimulation. Could it be that the infant often stops crying when rocked because his need for such stimulation is fulfilled?

Although research concerning the importance of early sensory stimulation in animals is not conclusive, it is clear that the quality, the intensity, and the timing (age at which stimulation is provided) of such stimulation can affect later behaviors, such as activity level and emotionality. An interesting study (Korner & Grobstein, 1966) with newborn infants showed that crying stopped when they were picked up and put to the shoulder, and that the infants then showed signs of alertness and visual scanning of the environment. These investigators concluded that tactile stimulation may activate visual behavior, thus providing the infant with more opportunities to explore the environment and to become acquainted with it. This conclusion was supported in a study by White and Castle (1964), which indicated that extra handling of newborn institutionalized infants increased their visual interest in the environment later.

In a typical experiment involving adults (Goldberger & Holt, 1958), volunteer college students were placed in isolation in a specially designed chamber that admitted only a minimum amount of stimulation, whether visual, aural, or tactile. During an eight-hour period or less in the chamber, these students manifested anxiety, decreases in complex reasoning, and hallucinations. They reported disturbances in their awareness of time, unpleasant emotional feelings, and a sense of intellectual disorganization. Clearly, a certain level of sensory stimulation appears to be necessary for adequate intellectual performance. This notion is supported by the isolation included in the brainwashing of American prisoners by the Chinese communists, which has apparently resulted in a variety of psychological repercussions.

Long-Range versus Short-Range Effects. Most of a series of papers by Goldfarb (1943a,b,c; 1945a,b; 1947; 1949) on the harmful long-range effects of early institutionalization dealt with a set of 15 children who entered an institution at about four-and-a-half months of age and remained there a little more than three years before placement in foster homes. These children were compared with a control group reared wholly in foster homes. When tested, they ranged from 10 to 14 years of age. Subjected to a number of personality and intelligence measures, the group that had experienced institutionalization showed itself to be inferior to the control children in many respects. Its members were apathetic, passive, fearful, apprehensive, less persistent, withdrawn, retarded in social maturity, and inferior in intelligence, lanugage, vocabulary, and concept formation. Goldfarb concluded that the poorer adjustment of this group was caused by its early privation during institutionalization.

Although Goldfarb's studies have been criticized for their methodology, the possibility of some inferiority in language and on intelligence tests, insofar as the latter depend on language ability, seems reasonable. As observed in the chapter on language, the superiority of only children in this area stems from their extensive contact with adults. Whether the limited association of Goldfarb's institutionalized group with adults during the first three years of life could exert so long-range an effect on language development remains a matter of speculation. There is little in the literature to substantiate this view.

Two other studies take an opposite position. They suggest that any deleterious effects institutionalization may produce in children do not persist. Dennis and Najarian (1957) examined the development of infants and children in a Beirut, Lebanon, foundling home. At the institution a ratio of one to ten prevailed between the caretaking staff and the children. Swaddling was employed until the infants reached about four months of age. Except for feeding and bathing the infant had very little contact with adults and was seldom taken out of his crib. From one to three years, the children spent most of the day in play groups of about 20 youngsters, with play equipment quite limited. At four kindergarten was provided.

Through tests administered to infants between two and twelve months of age and children between four-and-a-half and six years old, as well as to comparable control groups of noninstitutionalized Lebanese children, the investigators found the experimental infants markedly inferior to the control infants in the two- to twelve-month range. However, among the four-and-a-half- to six-year-olds the institutionalized children were only slightly retarded in abilities measured. For the infants, the Cattell Infant Scale was used; for the children, the Goodenough Draw-A-Man Test, the Knox Cube Test, and the Porteus Maze Test were employed.

These investigators attribute the early retardation to lack of learning opportunities resulting from environmental restriction. But such privation did not seem to have lasting effects. It may be that the child gains from his peers the minimal amount of stimulation required for adequate development once he is able to behave actively toward his environment.

In a later study Sayegh and Dennis (1965) again found the institutionalized infants to be markedly retarded in early development. In order to test their earlier hypothesis that the retardation resulted from the insufficiency of learning opportunities provided the infants, a small group of infants was given an hour of supplementary experiences each day for a period of 15 days. The infants were placed in upright positions; their interest in objects was stimulated; and they were encouraged to develop skill in object manipulation. As compared with the controls, these experimental-group infants showed significant gains on the developmental test administered after the enrichment experience. These findings suggest that lack of appropriate stimulation retards early development, but this retardation can be remedied by providing enrichment experiences.

Experimental modification of the social environment of a group of institutionalized infants was tried by Rheingold (1956). For the typical institutional "multiple mothering" type of care, she substituted care by a single mother figure for a term of eight weeks, five days a week, seven-and-a-half hours per day. Each control and experimental group consisted of eight infants about six months old. Before the experiment, at weekly intervals during it, and for four weeks thereafter, a battery of tests, including a test of social responsiveness, tests of postural development and of cube manipulation, and the Cattell Infant Intelligence Scale, was administered to the infants. Because the experimental group of infants became more socially responsive than the control group, Rheingold concluded that the social behavior of infants could be modified by changes in their environment. Contrary to predictions, however, the experimental group did not perform significantly higher on the postural, cube, or Cattell tests.

A year later, 14 of the original 16 children were subjected to a similar set of tests (Rheingold & Bayley, 1959). Apart from the fact that more members of the experimental group engaged in vocal expression during the social tests, there were no statistically significant differences between the two groups. Although attentive mothering produced some differences in behavior during infancy, the differences did not endure, except perhaps in the area of verbal performance. One can only guess as to the effects of a longer period of "single mothering," in view of the failure of this study to show long-range consequences of a brief period during which social surroundings were modified.

Several writers have mentioned that taking a child away from its mother is most harmful in the second half of its first year; during the first six months of life the infant has not developed sufficiently in intellect to differentiate between strange and familiar faces or to be aware of changes of environment. In an extensive longitudinal study of the development of emotional attachment in infants, Schaffer and Emerson (1964) found that a phase of indiscriminate attachment is followed by a period of specific attachment in the third quarter of the first year. Fear of strangers was correlated with the onset of attachment behavior, suggesting that both are part of a developmental trend in emotional, intellectual, and perceptual behavior. Maternal deprivation after the first six months may be a matter of *separation* after an emotional bond has been established and as a result, harmful effects of perhaps long duration may appear in the emotional area.

Group Care for Infants

The maternal deprivation issue, with its emphasis on the harmful effects on the infant of separation from mother, has been a major deterrent to constructive and rational thinking about group day care for infants. A great deal of resistance to group infant care exists currently in the thinking of professionals (child psychologists, social workers, child welfare workers) and laymen alike. Two principal issues are involved: (1) the infant's need for stimulation, and (2) whether normal development requires that the infant identify with a single mother figure. Each of these will be dealt with briefly.

Much of the resistance to group care for infants probably stems from the inadequate care provided by the orphanages which were common in this country prior to the second world war. High adult-infant ratios were typical in these institutions with the result that the infants received little stimulation. Older children were able to seek out their own stimulation through interaction with the environment, including other children; consequently, they were affected less by such deprivation. We have learned a great deal in recent years about the need of the young infant for stimulation. An appropriate level of arousal is required in order to process and receive incoming stimuli, and a foundation for a "learning to learn" set may be established very early as a result of patterns of discimination made to objects and persons in the environment. There is no question but that this first issue can be taken care of readily in a group setting by providing adequate perceptual and social stimulation.

The second issue involving a single mother figure may be misleading at the outset for a variety of reasons. First, it seems likely that the issue evolved in part from the typical middle-class arrangement of child-rearing in which the mother devotes full-time caring for a small number of children. This arrangement exists neither in lower- nor upper-class homes. In the former, child care frequently is the responsibility of older siblings and other members of the extended family group such as aunts and grandmothers, while in the latter, most of the routine aspects of child care are assigned to a paid employee, such as a nanny. Further, a "multiple mothering" type of arrangement for child care is common in many countries, including Russia and Israel, with no apparent ill effects on personality development. Second, since much of the research evidence for the harmful effects of insufficient mothering has come from institutionalized infants, it is not clear whether these effects are due to the actual separation from mother, to lack of mothering, or to insufficient stimulation (tactile, visual, auditory, kinesthetic).

While a number of research studies have been conducted in recent years to

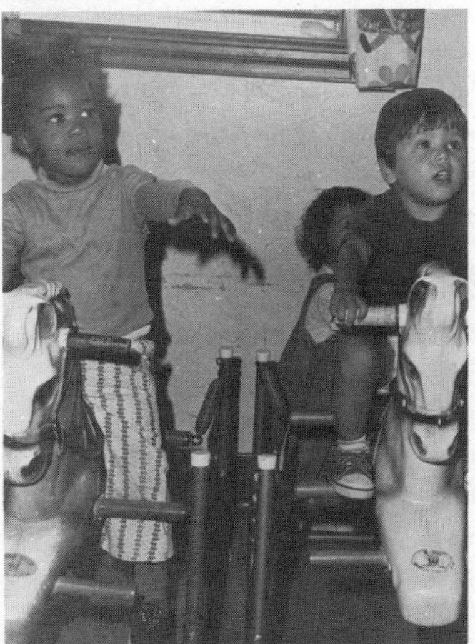

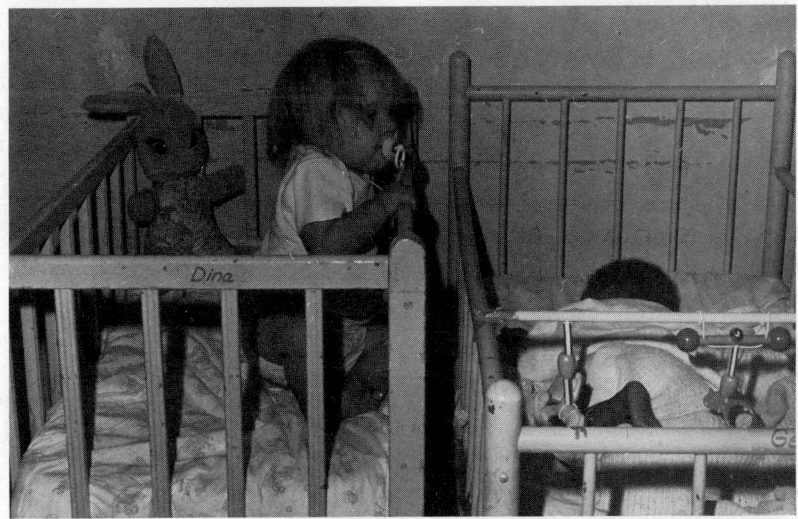

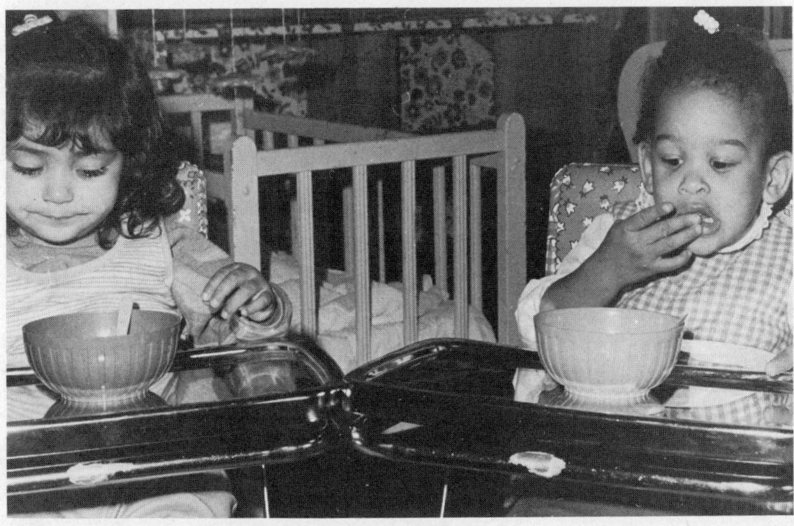

Photos courtesy of Don and Elaine White.

determine the effect of early enrichment on intellectual development in infancy (see discussion in Chapter 6), few day care programs for infants have been in operation. One of the earliest was the Children's Center at Syracuse University begun by Caldwell and Richmond (1964, 1968) in 1964. Initially the program involved 25 infants from six months to three years of age. One of their basic hypotheses was that "an appropriate environment can be created which can offset any developmental detriment associated with maternal separation and possibly add a degree of environmental enrichment frequently not available in families of limited social, economic, and cultural resources (Caldwell & Richmond, 1968, p. 327).

In addition to concern with health and nutrition, the Syracuse program attempted to develop an educational program for the infants. Included in the learning curriculum were such activities as reading books, labeling objects in the environment, art activities, and learning games involving sensory discrimination (e.g., big-little, rough-smooth). The teachers were taught principles of social reinforcement so that approved behavior was rewarded with attention, a smile, favorable comment, and physical contact. Table 9-4 shows the three main goal areas which were emphasized in the program.

In a follow-up study comparing a group of home-reared infants with a group who had spent an average of 18 months in the day care center, Caldwell and associates (Caldwell, Wright, Honig, & Tannenbaum, 1970) focused on the extent of mother and child attachment and the infants' developmental progress. The results indicated no differences between the two groups on the various measures used to assess attachment. With regard to developmental progress, the day care infants showed a slight rise in Developmental Quotient from 12 to 30 months, while the home infants showed the decline in DQ which has been consistently reported for disadvantaged children.

The pioneer efforts in the Syracuse infant-care program strongly suggests that group care for infants is eminently feasible. No marked health problems, such as numerous illnesses produced by early contact with others, were evident in the infants. Moreover, the group care arrangement had no harmful effects on the infant's attachment to his mother as one might have been led to expect by the earlier mother-infant separation literature. Finally, the group care infants showed normal developmental progress.

One of the present writers was instrumental in initiating one of the first licensed infant-care centers in California under the auspices of the Foundation for Research and Community Development, a nonprofit Mexican-American agency in San Jose, California. Guidelines for group care for infants were adopted in California in 1970. Prior to this time, the state-funded Children's Centers, a statewide program of child care for working mothers, were forbidden to enroll children below the age of two. While resistance to official sanctioning of group infant care came from many sources, the overwhelming need for adequate arrangements for infant care was obvious.

The Los Pequenitos Infant Care Center (see pictures on p. 293) was begun in December of 1970 in several rooms made available by a local church. Approximately 8 infants were enrolled initially, with the total number soon reaching 22, the maximum for which the facility was licensed. Through the year-and-a-half of operation the infants have ranged in age from 6 weeks to 24 months. Local monies received from the United Fund agency are matched on a three to one basis by federal funds under provisions of Title IIIA of the 1967 Social Security

TABLE 9-4 A Schematic Model for Describing Developmental Goals and Types of Environmental Influence*

Area of Influence	*Includes*	Involves programming
1. Personal-social attributes	A sense of trust Positive self-concept Curiosity about environment Tolerance of delay of gratification Sense of mastery and competence Self-acceptance Acceptance of differences Persistence toward goals Independent behavior Social skills Consideration for others Joy of living Self-expression	The interpersonal environment The total learning atmosphere
2. Motor, perceptual, and cognitive functions	Balance Coordination Agility Intersensory integration Listening and hearing Looking and seeing Classifying Evaluating (counting, ordering) Coordinating and relating Conceptualizing Forming learning sets Remembering Interpreting language Producing language Graphic communication	The interpersonal environment The experiential environment The physical-spatial environment
3. Culturally relevant knowledge	Words Ideas Reservoir of solutions to representative problems	Content of developmental milieu Sequential assimilation and integration of age-appropriate experiences

*Caldwell & Richmond, 1968, p. 348.

Act; these funds provide the monies for the operation of the center. The families of the infants are low income and are certified by the county Department of Social Services as either former, present, or potential welfare recipients. Many of the infants are from one-parent families.

Following the state guidelines, the infant to staff ratio is four to one. In addition, each semester between 20–40 students enrolled in child development courses at a nearby state college participate in the program. While the center is open from 7 a.m. to 6 p.m., few of the infants remain the entire 11 hours. The average daily stay at the center is 8–9 hours.

To the present time no formal assessment of the infants has been made with regard to intellectual and emotional development. However, feedback from mothers based on periodic interviews as well as observations by staff and students strongly indicate at least normal development in all areas. In several cases there is clear evidence that enrollment in the Center has facilitated developmental progress. For example, eight-month-old Anthony was unable to sit without support when he entered the Center. Discussions with the mother revealed that he had spent most of his time lying in his crib. He had not been encouraged to sit up and was never placed in a sitting position. After being placed daily in a highchair for brief periods of time at the Center, Anthony was able to sit normally within several weeks. While this is an extreme example, many of the mothers have commented on the marked progress they have observed in their infants in the areas of language, social behavior, and self-help and independence. Contrary to early research in child development regarding stages in social development, the infants interact with one another at very early ages. They show marked awareness of and interest in one another, and by 12–15 months of age, they interact in a meaningful reciprocal manner. Emotionally the infants appear happy in the Center. They react positively to the large number of student observers which certainly argues against the fear of exposing infants to too many adults.

Daily contact is maintained with each mother when she brings her child in the morning and returns in the late afternoon. Any marked changes in the child's home behavior can be ascertained and information regarding the mother's concerns and anxieties is obtained.

While there are undoubtedly wide individual differences among infants in their ability to thrive in a group care setting and to profit from it, federally funded infant care centers should be established to provide high quality care for infants of working mothers and for infants who presently are receiving far less than optimal nurturance. Our society can ill afford to continue to ignore and to neglect its necessary role in ensuring proper conditions for the optimal development of every child. A great variety of complementary and interlocking programs are required to achieve this goal. These include a large network of infant and child care centers, family day care homes, private and parent cooperative nursery schools, prekindergarten programs for low-income children, and community-based drop-in centers where a wide range of courses including some which focus on child development, nutrition, and family problems are available to the mothers while the young children are cared for by trained personnel.

SUMMARY

There are differences in the psychological environments into which infants are born. That such differences may not have long-range effects is because of the possibility that early parental attitudes toward the child may change in time, or because of the subsequent experiences of the child. From birth the various characteristics of the infant affect the mother's attitude toward him, so that from the very beginning the infant plays a part in creating his psychological environment. There is mutual interaction between parent and child.

The position one takes on the long-range effects of early experiences is determined in part by one's conception of the infant. Is he a passive recipient of environmental stimulation, impressionable, irreversibly affected by early events? Or does he react actively toward his environment, thus showing himself capable of resisting the long-term effects of traumatic experiences? Are single events crucial or is the repetitive pattern of events most influential?

Since Freudian theory emphasizes the importance of feeding and toilet training in affecting the child's development of personality, maternal practices in these areas were surveyed. The literature suggests that no long-range effects on the child's personality have resulted from the wide variation in maternal behavior in these two areas of early socialization. Since much maternal concern in the early years revolves about feeding and toilet training, these are important areas at the time, but their effects are of short-run significance for the child.

Maternal deprivation was examined at some length because of the light it casts on important elements in the early mother-child relation. Sensory deprivation seems to explain many of the harmful consequences of maternal deprivation. Attention from the mother is important because it provides the infant with a variety of stimuli.

REFERENCES

Adams, A. B. Choice of infant feeding technique as a function of maternal personality. *Journal of Consulting Psychology,* 1959, **23**, 143–146.

Ainsworth, M. D. S. Object relations, dependency and attachment: A theoretical review of the infant-mother relationship. *Child Development,* 1969, **40**, 969–1025.

Ainsworth, M. D. S., & Bell, S. M. Some contemporary patterns of mother-infant interaction in the feeding situation. In J. A. Ambrose (Ed.), *The functions of stimulation in early post-natal development.* London: Academic, 1969. Pp. 133–170.

Ainsworth, M. D. S., & Bell, S. Attachment, exploration, and separation: Illustrated by the behavior of one-year-olds in a strange situation. *Child Development,* 1970, **41**, 49–67.

Ainsworth, M. D. S., & Wittig, B. A. Attachment and exploratory behavior of one-year-olds in a strange situation. In B. M. Foss (Ed.), *Determinants of infant behavior IV.* London: Methuen, 1969. Pp. 111–136.

Anderson, J. E. Personality organization in children. *American Psychologist,* 1948, **3**, 409–416.

Bagby, E. The etiology of phobias. *Journal of Abnormal and Social Psychology,* 1922, **17**, 16–18.

Bayley, N. Research in child development: A longitudinal perspective. *Merrill-Palmer Quarterly,* 1965, **11**, 183–208.

Bell, R. Q. Stimulus control of parent or caretaker behavior by offspring. *Developmental Psychology,* 1971, **4**, 63–72.

Birns, B. Individual differences in human neonates' response to stimulation. *Child Development,* 1965, **30**, 249–256.

Bowlby, J. The nature of the child's tie to his mother. *International Journal of Psychoanalysis,* 1958, **39**, 350–373.

Brody, S. *Patterns of mothering: Maternal influences during infancy.* New York: International Universities Press, 1956.

Caldwell, B. M. Assessment of infant personality. *Merrill–Palmer Quarterly,* 1962, **8**, 71–81.

Caldwell, B. M. The effects of infant care. In M. L. Hoffman & L. W. Hoffman (Eds.), *Review of child development research.* Vol. I. New York: Russell Sage Foundation, 1964.

Caldwell, B. M., & Richmond, J. B. Programmed day care for the very young child—A preliminary report. *Journal of Marriage and the Family,* 1964, **26**, 481–488.

Caldwell, B. M., & Richmond, J. B. The Children's Center in Syracuse, N.Y. In L. L. Dittman (Ed.), *Early child care: The new perspective.* New York: Atherton, 1968. Pp. 326–358.

Caldwell, B., Wright, C., Honig, A., & Tannenbaum, J., Infant day care and attachment. *American Journal of Orthopsychiatry,* 1970, **40**, 397–412.

Casler, L. Maternal deprivation: A critical review of the literature. *Monographs of the Society for Research in Child Development,* 1961, **26**, No. 2.

Chess, S., Thomas, A., & Birch, H. *Your child is a person.* New York: Viking, 1965.

Dennis, W., & Najarian, P. Infant development under environmental handicap. *Psychological Monographs: General and Applied,* 1957, **71**, No. 7.

Durrett, M. Relationship of early infant regulation and later behavior in play interviews. *Child Development,* 1959, **30**, 211–216.

Escalona, S. K. Feeding disturbances in very young children. *American Journal of Orthopsychiatry,* 1945, **15**, 76–80.

Freud, A., & Burlingame, D. T. *War and children.* New York: Willard, 1943.

Fries, M. E. Mental hygiene in pregnancy, delivery, and the puerperium. *Mental Hygiene,* 1941, **25**, 221–236.

Goldberger, L., & Holt, R. R. Experimental interferences with reality contact (perceptual isolation): Method and group results. *Journal of Nervous and Mental Diseases,* 1958, **127**, 99–112.

Goldfarb, W. The effects of early institutional care on adolescent personality (graphic Rorschach data). *Child Development,* 1943, **14**, 213–223. (a)

Goldfarb, W. The effects of early institutional care on adolescent personality. *Journal of Experimental Education,* 1943, **12**, 106–129. (b)

Goldfarb, W. Infant rearing and problem behavior. *American Journal of Orthopsychiatry,* 1943, **13**, 249–265. (c)

Goldfarb, W. Effects of psychological deprivation in infancy and subsequent stimulation. *American Journal of Psychiatry,* 1945, **102**, 18–33. (a)

Goldfarb, W. Psychological privation in infancy and subsequent adjustment. *American Journal of Orthopsychiatry,* 1945, **15**, 247–255. (b)

Goldfarb, W. Variations in adolescent adjustment of institutionally-reared children. *American Journal of Orthopsychiatry,* 1947, **17**, 449–457.

Goldfarb, W. Rorschach test differences between family-reared, institution-reared, and schizophrenic children. *American Journal of Orthopsychiatry,* 1949, **19**, 624–633.

Hall, C., & Lindzey, G. *Theories of personality.* New York: Wiley, 1957.

Harper, L. The young as a source of stimuli controlling caretaker behavior. *Developmental Psychology,* 1971, **4**, 73–88.

Heinstein, M. Behavioral correlates of breast-bottle regimes under varying parent-infant relationships. *Monographs of the Society for Research in Child Development,* 1963, **28**, No. 4.

Hetherington, E., & Brackbill, Y. Etiology and covariation of obstinacy, orderliness, and parsimony in young children. *Child Development,* 1963, **34**, 919–943.

Huschka, M. The child's response to coercive bowel training. *Psychosomatic Medicine,* 1942, **4**, 301–308.

Kagan, J., & Lewis, M. Studies of attention in the human infant. *Merrill-Palmer Quarterly,* 1965, **11**, 95–127.

Klatskin, E. H., Jackson, E. B., & Wilkin, L. C. The influence of degree of flexibility in maternal child care practices on early child behavior. *American Journal of Orthopsychiatry,* 1956, **26**, 79–93.

Korner, A., & Grobstein, R. Visual alertness as related to soothing in neonates: Implications for maternal stimulation and early deprivation. *Child Development,* 1966, **37**, 867–876.

Kral, V. A. Psychiatric observations under severe chronic stress. *American Journal of Psychiatry,* 1951, **108**, 185–192.

Kulka, A., Fry, C., & Goldstein, F. J. Kinesthetic needs in infancy. *American Journal of Orthopsychiatry,* 1960, **30**, 562–571.

LeMasters, E. E. Parenthood as crisis. *Marriage and Family Living,* 1957, **19**, 352–355.

Levy, D. M. *Maternal overprotection.* New York: Columbia University Press, 1943.

Lipton, E., & Steinschneider, A. Studies on the psychophysiology of infancy. *Merrill-Palmer Quarterly,* 1964, **10**, 103–117.

Mead, M. *Sex and temperament in three primitive societies.* New York: Mentor, 1935.

Moss, H. A., & Robson, K. S. Maternal influences in early social-visual behavior. *Child Development,* 1968, **39**, 401–408.

Moss, H. A., Robson, K. S., & Pedersen, F. Determinants of maternal stimulation of infants and consequences of treatment for later reactions to strangers. *Developmental Psychology,* 1969, **1**, 239–246.

Munroe, R. *Schools of psychoanalytic thought.* New York: Dryden, 1955.

Peterson, C. H., & Spano, F. L. Breast feeding, maternal rejection, and child personality. *Character and Personality,* 1941, **10**, 62–66.

Pinneau, S. A critique on the articles by Margaret Ribble. *Child Development,* 1950, **21**, 203–228.

Pinneau, S. The infantile disorders of hospitalism and anaclitic depression. *Psychological Bulletin,* 1955, **52**, 429–452.

Rabin, A. I. Some psychosexual differences between kibbutz and nonkibbutz Israeli boys. *Journal of Projective Techniques,* 1958, **22**, 328–332.

Rheingold, H. L. The modification of social responsiveness in institutional babies. *Monographs of the Society for Research in Child Development,* 1956, **21**, No. 2.

Rheingold, H. L. The measurement of maternal care. *Child Development,* 1960, **31**, 565–575.

Rheingold, H. L., & Bayley, N. The later effects of an experimental modification of mothering. *Child Development,* 1959, **31**, 363–372.

Ribble, M. *The rights of infants.* New York: Columbia University Press, 1943.

Ribble, M. Infantile experience in relation to personality development. In J. McV. Hunt (Ed.), *Personality and behavior disorders.* New York: Ronald, 1944. Pp. 621–651.

Robson, K. S., Pedersen, F. A., Moss, H. A. Developmental observations of diadic gazing in relation to the fear of strangers and social approach behavior. *Child Development,* 1969, **40**, 619–627.

Sayegh, Y., & Dennis, W. The effect of supplementary experiences upon the behavioral development of infants in institutions. *Child Development,* 1965, **36**, 81–90.

Schaefer, E. A circumplex model for maternal behavior. *Journal of Abnormal and Social Psychology,* 1959, **59**, 226–235.

Schaefer, E., & Bayley, N. Maternal behavior, child behavior, and their intercorrelations from infancy through adolescence. *Monographs of the Society for Research in Child Development,* 1963, **28**, No. 3.

Schaffer, H. Activity level as a constitutional determinant of infantile reaction to deprivation. *Child Development,* 1966, **37**, 595–602.

Schaffer, H., & Emerson, P. The development of social attachments in infancy. *Monographs of the Society for Research in Child Development,* 1964, **29**, No. 3.

Scott, J. P. Critical periods in behavioral development. *Science,* 1962, **138**, 949–958.

Sears, R. R., Maccoby, E. E., & Levin, H. *Patterns of childrearing.* Evanston, Ill.: Row, Peterson, 1957.

Sewell, W. H., & Mussen, P. H. The effect of feeding, weaning, and scheduling procedures on childhood adjustment and the formation of oral symptoms. *Child Development,* 1952, **23**, 185–191.

Sewell, W. H., Mussen, P. H., & Harris, C. W. Relationship among child training practices. *American Sociological Review,* 1955, **20**, 137–148.

Shulman, M. *Sleep till noon.* New York: Bantam Books, 1959.

Simsarian, F. P. Case histories of five thumbsucking children breast fed on unscheduled regimes, without limitation of nursing time. *Child Development,* 1947, **18**, 180–184.

Spitz, R. A. Hospitalism: An inquiry into the genesis of psychiatric conditions in early childhood. *Psychoanalytic Study of the Child,* 1945, **1**, 53–74; 1946, **2**, 113–117.

Spitz, R. A., & Wolf, K. Anaclitic depression. *Psychoanalytic Study of the Child,* 1946, **2**, 313–342.

Stevenson, I. Is the human personality more plastic in infancy and childhood? *American Journal of Psychiatry,* 1957, **114**, 152–161.

Sullivan, H. S. Conceptions of modern psychiatry. *Psychiatry,* 1940, **3**, 1–117.

Thomas, A., Chess, S., Birch, H., Hertzig, M., & Korn, S. *Behavioral individuality in early childhood.* New York: Universities Press, 1964.

Traisman, A. S., & Traisman, H. S. Thumb- and finger-sucking: A study of 2650 infants and children. *Journal of Pediatrics,* 1958, **53**, 566–572.

White, B., & Castle, P. Visual exploratory behavior following postnatal handling of human infants. *Perceptual and Motor Skills,* 1964, **18**, 497–502.

Yarrow, L. J. Maternal deprivation: toward an empirical and conceptual re-evaluation. *Psychological Bulletin,* 1961, **58**, 459–490.

Yarrow, L. J. Research in dimensions of early maternal care. *Merrill–Palmer Quarterly,* 1963, **9**, 101–114.

Yarrow, L. J., & Goodwin, M. Some conceptual issues in the study of mother-infant interaction. *American Journal of Orthopsychiatry,* 1965, **35**, 473–481.

Yarrow, M., Waxler, C., & Scott, P. Child effects on adult behavior. *Developmental Psychology,* 1971, **5**, 300–311.

chapter 10

family influences on the growing child

chapter 10

family influences on the growing child

chapter 10

family influences on the growing child

The adult fills a variety of roles—father or mother, husband or wife, son or daughter, brother or sister, teacher, colleague, friend. For each of these roles, certain sets of behavior seem particularly appropriate. Thus the behaviors that characterize or typify any individual permit him to fulfill one role more suitably and more adequately than another. Similarly, an individual's personality fits him better for one role than for some other. To paraphrase Abraham Lincoln, all people can play some of these roles, some people can play all of these roles, but all people cannot play all of these roles with equal facility. How successfully any individual fills any one of them depends on the sum total of his characteristics and the requirements of the particular role.

Take parenthood. Western culture prescribes general requirements for the role of the parent. The father must provide food, clothing, and shelter for his children—that is, economic support. He is also responsible for the children's behavior in public. Increasingly it is thought that the role of father includes emotional and psychological support for the children, too. What are some of the specific behaviors demanded of the modern, urban father beyond his occupational pursuits? He may accompany his son to the weekly cub scout meeting, mend a broken bat, punish his daughter for misbehavior, change the baby's diapers while the mother is shopping, attend a meeting of the P.T.A. to hear another daughter recite some verse, watch a two-year-old try to catch a bird, rush a child to the doctor to set a broken arm, arbitrate a battle between siblings, teach a four-year-old the proper form for cartwheels, or drive the baby-sitter home at two o'clock in the morning. This is merely a smattering of the behaviors performed by the typical father.

What of the mother? Society dictates that she provide physical care for the children—feed them, keep them healthy and, if possible, clean. She must comfort and console them when necessary and in general nurture them and provide emotional support. Long extolled by novelist and bard, the role of mother has been made almost impossible to fulfill by the ordinary woman. Her feelings of inadequacy are matched only by her undying efforts. What, then, are some of the day-to-day behaviors demanded of her? A mother's typical day might begin—or end—with waking to give her infant a two o'clock feeding. Later she may urge a son to the breakfast table to spoonfeed him cereal or hurry him off to school, clean up spilled orange juice, diaper and bathe the baby, wipe a daughter's running nose, tend to another child's chicken pox, listen to a five-year-old's account of his day, drive another daughter to a music lesson, enjoy the two-year-old's mimicry of his mother's household activities, or soothe a seven-year-old's broken heart because her best friend pushed her into the mud.

The young child depends totally on these parents who must be capable of meeting his needs. As the child grows older, the dependency on the parent lessens, so that father and mother must be able to relinquish some of the earlier control. Different behaviors and attitudes are required at different times; this is the price of parenthood. To say that some adults find the parental role more satisfying than others is to belabor the obvious. But how acceptable a woman finds the maternal role may indeed influence how adequately she performs it. As an individual, a parent possesses many psychological needs, most of which must be met if he is to be moderately well adjusted. If the demands of the parental role conflict or are incompatible with the needs of the parent as an individual, difficulties almost invariably ensue.

THE NATURE OF PARENT-CHILD RELATIONS

Although all human relationships are unique, those existing between parents and child possess certain characteristics that explain the tremendous and permanent impact of one upon the other. The intimacy and intensity of contact and the everyday interaction and interchange exist in an emotionally charged atmosphere. A child serves as a mirror to the parent, who sees reflected there his own childhood, his own unresolved and frequently long-term conflicts, and his own needs and aspirations.

The mutual interplay of psychological needs among family members creates a dynamic system such that a breakdown of any member affects the entire system. Clinical reports suggest that the family member who seeks psychological treatment often may be the one least in need of it. This indicates that the psychological disturbance of that individual reflects a more basic disturbance in the family system. Further, family-therapy case studies show that when the psychological symptoms are relieved for one family member, they frequently reappear, though perhaps in different form, in another member.

The phenomenon of child abuse illustrates vividly the emotional intensity of parent-child interaction. Recent professional and public concern with the "battered child syndrome" has revealed the startling extent of its occurrence. A 1962 study by the American Humane Society found 662 cases of child abuse reported in newspapers—and many, of course, are not reported. Most of the victims were under four years of age; most of the parents were young. The legal aspects of child abuse are multiple, with 47 states adopting statutes similar to the model law proposed by the United States Children's Bureau (Paulsen, 1966). But whatever the legal solutions to the problem may be, the psychological implications are indisputable. Frustrated and disturbed parents, unable to cope with the psychological, economic, and social problems facing them, discharge their hostility onto the young child, who may be a partial cause of the hostility. More important, however, the young child is a part of an ailing family system. Although child abuse is hardly new, its extent may represent in part modern society's failure to create the kinds of conditions that are conducive to the mental health of the individual, and that permit him to function successfully within the family system—at once a demanding and rewarding interpersonal network.

HOW THE PARENT BECOMES AS HE IS

Does parenthood require a certain kind of person? Perhaps to some extent it does. Parenthood involves a number of demands and behaviors: sacrifice, relating emotionally to a child, intense emotional rewards and perhaps disappointments, willingness to let a child be a child—all these and more.

At the human level there is little evidence for the existence of a "parental instinct" or even a "maternal instinct." Although there is a connection between hormonal secretion and lactation, for example, this in no way implies that maternal behavior and the various activities and functions it involves are a direct outgrowth of hormonal activity. A mother cannot rely on innate, "built-in" mechanisms to guide her maternal behavior. How, then, does she become the kind of mother she is? To what sources may we attribute her maternal behavior and attitudes? As noted in the previous chapter, current fads and fashions in child-rearing and her individual personality structure influence her behavior as a parent. There is also *generational continuity,* the relationship between parent and offspring in the way in which each, in due turn, fills the parental role. An individual's own parents are probably the only persons he observes intimately in the parental role. Like it or not, they serve as the models for his own behavior as a parent, in addition to wielding an enormous influence on his personality development and adult character.

Several studies have looked into the similarity between parent and offspring in their handling of the parental role and into the influence of a person's own childhood and early attitudes toward parents on his own performance as a parent. In a study of four groups of parents—accepting, rejecting, dominating, and submissive—Symonds (1939) observed that the accepting type grew up in homes marked by good adjustment and acceptance. Dominating parents were dominated by their parents, whereas submissive parents enjoyed much freedom in their own childhood. A parent behaved just like his own parents and established a similar relation with his children; he repeated his early experiences in the home. More specifically, Symonds held, parents adopted an attitude toward their children that resembled the attitude taken toward them by the parent of the same sex.

Radke (1946) noted a tendency for parents to use disciplinary techniques similar to those remembered from their own childhood. And in Bronson, Kalten, and Livson's study (1959), mothers were inclined to exercise strong authority in their homes if they remembered their own mothers as having done so. A similar pattern was found among fathers; they emulated their paternal parent, but rather in the area of affectional relationship than of authority. Why in one area and not in others is a matter for speculation. Methodologically, both studies involved an individual's memory of his parents' practices and behaviors. Although an individual's perception and memory of parental treatment in childhood may have significance for his own behavior as a parent, it would be useful to have actual information of what happened years ago.

Attempting to trace the transmission of authority in the home from one generation to the next, Ingersoll (1948) defined the patterns in terms of leading or controlling the family activities. Four main patterns were discerned: *matricentric*—a pattern of authority in which the mother had the greater control; *patricentric*—the father exercised the greater control; *balanced*—fairly equal husband-wife control; and *intermediate*—lying midway between balance and control by either husband or wife. The parental backgrounds of second-generation couples were *homogamous* or *heterogamous.* In the former, husband and wife were reared in homes having the same prevailing pattern of authority, whether matricentric, patricentric, or balanced. In the heterogamous situation, husband and wife came from homes of opposing authority patterns. Among homogamous marriages, the patterns of parental authority tended to be reproduced. In heterogamous marriages, the patterns were modified to form a balanced compromise. Nevertheless, in all cases, the Ingersoll study found that there were exceptions to the dominant trends.

In a study of the backgrounds of a group of normal children, Harris (1959) noted that what had happened to the mothers "as children was happening to their own children; what happened to their parents was happening to them as parents" (p. 39). Four factors influenced this continuity. The first was the degree to which the mothers were aware of it: "Joan is just like I was at that age—flighty and unconcerned." The second was the degree to which they wished to see repeated the experiences of their own youth: "I want our children to enjoy the kind of summer outings which I loved as a child." The third was the degree to which the mothers were involved in the continuity of their childhood, wishing to assume similar roles of dependence or independence as adults, and the fourth was concern with their own unfulfilled childhood expectations: "I want to be a better mother to my children than my mother was to me."

The kind of continuity experienced by a mother with her own childhood affected the adjustment she made to the maternal role. Too rigid an adherence to the past or too much conflict with it created problems of dependability and understanding between a mother and her children. Three types of mothers were discerned: traditional mothers, rebellious mothers, and dependent mothers. The traditional mother was satisfied with her own mother's child-rearing tactics and attitudes, and used them as a reference point in raising her own family. The rebellious mother sought to be less controlling than her own mother, with whom she was dissatisfied because of excessive control, strictness, and interference. The children of such mothers tended to rebel against any rule interfering with their quest for pleasure. Indeed, there was some evidence that these mothers were endeavoring to work out their rebellious feelings against their own parent through their children. The third type, the dependent mother, was dissatisfied with her own mother because she thought she had not been accorded proper attention, love, or interest. Children of such mothers seemed to search for interpersonal warmth.

Not all the factors of continuity may operate at the conscious level, nor do they necessarily work directly on the child. Moreover, how a woman regards her husband may, in subtle ways, affect her children's attitude toward him. Thus, although parental behavior may not be inherited in a biological sense through the genes, it may be transmitted through the mechanisms of personality. Observations of mothers of problem children seen in clinics substantiate the notion that the "sins of the fathers are visited on the sons."

Parenthood by Choice. The current concern with overpopulation and with ways to deal with it by family planning and restricting family size may lead to a searching analysis of many aspects of parenthood: What role does parenthood play in an individual's life-style? Should parenthood be eliminated as a desirable goal in an overpopulated world? What are some of the meaningful alternatives to parenthood? How can young people best be prepared for making the decision whether to become parents? Should couples be paid for limiting their family size? If parenthood becomes entirely a matter of choice, what types of people will choose to be parents? Moreover, will these people be best qualified for the role of parenthood?

Some of the above questions have assumed major importance of late, since it now seems highly probable that Malthus was correct: resources increase arithmetically while population increases geometrically, and grim consequences may occur unless our rate of population increase is cut drastically. Psychologists concerned with population are interested in determining why people have children in the first place, and why they have as many as they do in the second place. Hoffman (1971) argues that the reasons people want children include: demonstrating one's adulthood, expanding the self, support religious and social norms, providing expanded primary group ties within which to develop affectional relations, seeking stimulation and novelty, seeking power, influence, and a life to influence, competition with others, and economic. Bogue (1967) outlines the arguments in favor of having many (high fertility) as opposed to none or few (low fertility) children as shown in Table 10-1.

The result of the relatively permissive policies regarding abortion adopted by a small number of states has yet to be determined in terms of the effect of the abortion on the woman's subsequent attitudes toward pregnancy and parenthood. Few studies have explored personality and attitudinal differences between girls who terminate their pregnancy by abortion and those who choose to give birth. Many writers have described various personality characteristics of unwed mothers. For example, Khlentzoes and Pagliaro (1965) have identified four major emotional states of rebelliousness, worthlessness, ambivalence, and loneliness, observing that

> when the unweds failed through self-destructive behavior to engage their parents in a more active and interested role with them, they acutely felt their loneliness. Hungry for affection, they became aggressively involved with almost the first boy who found them attractive, gave them interest and attention and in this way charmed them into re-enacting the family romance. If a pregnancy occurred the unweds treasured this experience as "putting something over on them" and rarely told parents voluntarily until they found out through their own or another's suspicions (Khlentzoes & Pagliaro, 1965, p. 783).

Butman (1965) found low self-image to differentiate between girls who later became pregnant and those who did not. Pollak and Friedman (1969) state that adolescent sexual behavior can best be understood in terms of family dynamics. Friedman (1969) specifies that sexual acting-out indicates "the breakdown of parental control and an acute disturbance in the parent-adolescent relationship" (p. 116). Giel and Kidd (1965), Jungreis (1969), and Pollak (1969) all support Friedman's hypothesis of disturbance in the parent-adolescent relationship. McCord, McCord, and Verden (1962) emphasize the particular influence of parental attitudes and behaviors upon the adolescent's sexual expression.

Much of the above discussion may be inaccurate and passé when we are approaching the time when parenthood may become a matter of choice. "Sexually acting-out behavior" may be an outdated phrase in an era of widespread premarital sexual activity. Transient cohabitation living arrangements with or without children and communal living styles may alter traditional views of the optimal family structure for child-rearing. It is too early to assess the long-range effects of some of these current trends on parenthood and child-rearing. It is certain, however, that behavioral scientists must turn their research efforts to an examination of the implications of these trends. In a review of such family variables as family size and spacing, birth-order effects, unwanted conceptions, sex education, and sterilization, Arasteh (1971) concluded that ". . . the whole spectrum of parenthood, its antecedents and consequences, deserve the greatest priority in both research and applied programs" (p. 198).

It remains to be seen whether parenthood by choice will eliminate such problems as child abuse, child neglect, and child emotional disturbances stemming from parent-child conflict.

THREE PRINCIPAL PARENT VARIABLES

More important than how individuals model their behavior after perceptions of

TABLE 10-1 Motives For and Against Birth Control*

High Fertility Motives	Low Fertility Motives
HEALTH Children often die. ECONOMIC CONDITION Children are an economic advantage. Social security in old age. FAMILY WELFARE Can help with work around house. Big families are happy families. Children from big families have better personalities. Continue the family name. Strength of the clan. MARRIAGE ADJUSTMENT Large families promote good marriage adjustment. PERSONALITY NEEDS Ego support, virility, manliness. COMMUNITY AND NATIONAL WELFARE Large families are good for the community or nation. MORAL AND CULTURAL Large families are God's will. Large families promote morality. Tradition. You have high status in the community. DISLIKE FOR CONTRACEPTION Dislikes use of contraception.	HEALTH Preserve health of mother. Assure healthy children. Lessen worry and overwork. ECONOMIC CONDITION Everyday, general expenses are less. Avoid worsening present (poor) economic condition. Gain a higher standard of living. Permit saving for future, for retirement. Desire to avoid subdividing property or savings. FAMILY WELFARE Improve children's lot in life, give them good education. Happier family life, more companionship, less tension. Opportunity to do a better job of rearing children. Avoid overcrowding of house. Easier to find a more desirable house or apartment. MARRIAGE ADJUSTMENT Provides husbands and wives more leisure opportunity. Improves the sexual adjustment by eliminating or reducing fear. PERSONALITY NEEDS Facilitates realization of ambitions. Facilitates self-development Facilitates realization of social needs. Reduces worry of the future. COMMUNITY AND NATIONAL WELFARE Helps avoid overpopulation. Helps community meet demands for education, other community services. Helps nations with economic development. Helps reduce welfare burden of the community.

*Bogue, 1967; in Fawcett, 1970.

their parents' behavior is the influence parents exert on the adjustment and personality of their children, which determines the kind of adults and, in turn, the kind of parents they will be. A mother spanks her five-year-old son if he flaunts her command to obey instantly when an order is given. Her choice of disciplinary tactic may be related to her belief or attitude that physical punishment is necessary when children do not submit readily to parental authority. This belief may emanate from her authoritarian personality structure, a vestige from her parents. It is one of three main parent variables—parent behavior, parent attitudes, and parent personality. Although it may seem obvious that the three variables are closely related—that is, a parent behaves toward his child in accord with his attitudes toward child-rearing, which are an aspect of his personality structure relatively little research has been undertaken to find the nature of their relationships. Several studies (Zunich, 1962; Brody, 1965) attempting to relate maternal attitude scores to actual maternal behavior with the child have met with little success, although some significant trends were observed. For example, Brody found that mothers scoring high in authoritarianism were more restrictive toward their children than mothers scoring low on this dimension. Although this is what we would expect, assuming a relation between parent attitudes and parent behavior, the problems involved in assessing parent attitudes make research in this area extremely difficult.

Parent Personality

If personality is the sum of an individual's character traits, attitudes, and values, the personality of a parent may be expected to influence the personality development of his child. Although not much is known about the precise operation of this influence, we can get some idea of how the parent's personality affects the atmosphere and emotional tone of the home and the child's development by categorizing parental personality as either healthy or neurotic. In addition, there are many other aspects of personality that psychologists have described.

Behrens (1954) assessed the adjustment of a small group of children and related their ratings to the feeding, weaning, and toilet-training practices of their mothers. Also, she rated each mother as a "total mother person," which signified the woman's character structure as reflected in how she fulfilled the maternal role. Behrens found little consistency among the three child-rearing practices and no tie between ratings of children's behavior and their mothers' procedures. There was, however, a close relation between child adjustment and "total mother person" ratings. Apparently what a mother *is* bears more on child adjustment than what she *does*. Actually, the Behrens study noted that the majority of mothers in the particular sample functioned reasonably well in specific child-rearing tasks, even though poorly adjusted themselves.

Clinical research has found that parents of children referred to child clinics score in a deviant direction on personality tests as compared with parents of normal children; however, attempts to differentiate parents of children in various diagnostic categories have been unsuccessful (Wolking, Dunteman, & Bailey, 1967).

Several studies (Morris & Nicholas, 1950; Phillips, 1951; Hanvik & Byrum, 1959) have noted similarities between parents and children in the nature of personality disturbances. One can only speculate about the origin of these similarities. Are they the result of the child's modeling his behavior after his parent's? Or is the parent's behavior toward the child dictated in part by his own unresolved psychological needs, which, in turn, produce like disturbances in the child? Parents, of course, are people whose own childhoods influence their adult personalities and behavior. Perhaps they project unmet needs and unsolved childhood problems onto their own children, as the following example illustrates.

> "Tom," age six, was referred because of enuresis, and this was the behavior which concerned the mother most. The interviews finally brought out that the mother had been enuretic until she began to menstruate, that ". . . people used to kid me about it." The mother recalled in this context that as a child she had been so afraid that she would wet the bed that she refused to go to bed at night, or when she did go to bed she would lie awake for long periods of time disturbed over possible bed-wetting (Phillips, 1951, p. 189).

Perhaps the personality of the parent is more influential than his child-rearing practices and his attitudes toward child-rearing in shaping the personality development of the child. However, as we mentioned earlier, much remains to be known concerning the relation among parent personality, parent attitudes, and parent practices. Recent work by Cattell and co-workers is based on the thesis that any aspect of interpersonal behavior satisfies some "need" of the individual. Thus, the attitudes held by a parent towards his family and towards family life reflect certain basic drive patterns. These investigators have identified six drives—pugnacity, aggressiveness, assertiveness, sex, gregariousness, and fear—and two "sentiment" patterns—toward the spouse and toward the child (Delhees, Cattell, & Sweney, 1970). The following items illustrate the kind of attitude statements included in this study of intrafamily attitudes:

> Parent to Child Relationship
> Pugnacity-Aggression
> 1. I want to punish my child more severely for irritating behavior.
> 2. I want my child to go away and stop annoying me.
>
> Gregariousness
> 1. I want to go out to places with my child.
> 2. I want my child to talk with me, sharing hobbies and roles.
>
> Fear
> 1. I want my child to be safe and watched over, not having accidents, and illnesses.
> 2. I want my child to keep me from loneliness and insecurity in my old age.
>
> Parent to Parent Relationship
> Sex
> 1. I want to have the most satisfactory sex life with my spouse.
> 2. I want to have a continuing playful courtship with my spouse.
>
> Fear
> 1. I want to feel secure in the faithfulness of my spouse.
> 2. I want my spouse to stand with me against all sources of danger.
>
> Hostility
> 1. I feel I should punish my spouse for various irritating shortcomings and neglects.
> 2. I feel the need to withhold my affection and show my resentment at times.
>
> (Delhees, *et al.,* 1970, p. 240)

The research by Cattell represents an attempt to establish linkages between parent personality and parent attitudes and to place this information in the larger framework of general personality theory and research.

Parent Attitudes

How the adult conceives of the parental role in relation to the child influences his attitudes as a parent. Does he see the parent's primary function as one of restricting and controlling child behavior? Does he view the socialization process as essentially a taming of the young child's uncivilized nature? Or does he regard the parental role as mainly one of guidance and setting the proper example for the child to emulate? The conception of the responsibilities, functions, and obligations of a role mold the individual's attitudes in the role which, in turn, presumably engender his behavior in it. The interest of the child psychologist in parental attitudes stems, therefore, from the notion that a basic, underlying attitude influences many behaviors of parenthood that are assumed to affect the personality development of the child.

"The essence of parent-child relations, it must be emphasized, lies more in how a parent *feels* than in what a parent *does*," Symonds (1949, p. xiii) remarked. In this respect Symond's concern lay with parental attitudes *toward the child*. Subsequent research has also been concerned with attitudes *toward child-rearing*.

The assessment of parent attitude poses a number of problems (Bell, 1958), most of them arising from attempts of psychologists to find a cause-and-effect relationship between these attitudes and child behavior. The first problem results from changes in parental attitudes. It is extremely hazardous to maintain in the assessment of parent attitudes that certain ones *cause* particular child behaviors when the measurement is made *after* the appearance of the behavior. One cannot know the attitude of the parent *before* the onset of the behavior, whether it be schizophrenia, stuttering, delinquency, or anything else. More important, one must be aware of the possibility of changes in parent attitudes. For example, a large percentage of parents can readily name the age level of children that they prefer and the level that they regard least endurable. Since one age level is more satisfying and rewarding than another, it might be assumed that the parent-child relationship is most conducive at that period to healthy personality development in the child. The following case study illuminates the point.

Billy was born after a labor of six and a half hours which Mrs. A experienced as being much less painful than she had anticipated from the stories she had heard from her older sisters and friends. From the very beginning in her handling of the baby—a boy—she was not only surprisingly technically skillful and competent but she seemed particularly responsive to clues from him related to his needs and had great success in making him comfortable and happy. For example, by the time he was four days of age she was noting that he had particular objections to being wet, was able to change his diaper competently and was exceedingly pleased that she was able to comfort him. In the first visit of the pediatrician to the home when Billy was three weeks of age a note was made that Mrs. A.'s way of comforting him, once she picked him up and once when she patted him in his bassinet seemed to be "all he needed and not more."

During the first nine to ten months she was described by all members of the research team who saw her as a particularly warm and skillful mother and the impression of unity and understanding between her and Billy was repeatedly commented upon. This came up not only in relation to her ability to persuade Billy to respond as she wished him to in the areas of eating, sleeping, and toileting, but also in the definite but indirect and subtle ways of prohibiting things of which she did not approve. It was noted, for example, that she interrupted the thumb sucking which she did not like not by pulling his thumb out, but by enticing him to become busy with something else—i.e., playing with her or with a toy. . . . She seemed to set limits in a way that aroused a minimum of protest from the baby. She anticipated no difficulty and seemed to feel perfectly sure that everything would go well between them. . .

Some time must here be given to a description of Billy who showed surprising adaptability and smoothness in many of his physiological and maturational patterns from the beginning. As a newborn he was described as well developed, moderately active and mature. There was a specificity about his way of expressing this discomfort or wishes which seemed to make comforting him quite easy (i.e., not just by his mother but by others as well). One might say he gave clues which could easily be interpreted. His parents found him attractive, entertaining and easy to live with.

Thus those first nine to ten months gave us the impression of such an untroubled, conflict-free, mutually satisfying and stimulating mother-child relationship that the period of the "crisis" which became apparent during the tenth month was impossible to overlook. The first indication of this came on the occasion of Mrs. A.'s and Billy's visit to the clinic for his regularly scheduled checkup. It was both reported by Mrs. A. and observed that Billy was more difficult to dress. He did not "co-operate" in this as he had before and it looked as if his mother's usual ways of restraining him by distraction or touch could no longer control his drive toward activity. At this time he was creeping and cruising. He walked with two hands held. When his mother tried to hold him on her lap, he tried to get down. He was reaching out and scratching at her neck or face in a now provocative way and she was scolding him with a new sharpness in her tone. She looked more harassed and tired at that visit than the pediatrician had ever seen her and said about Billy, "I really work up a sweat trying to figure out what he wants now." She reported that Billy was now so active that he seemed to want to be down on the floor, out of his crib, or chair, or the previously satisfactory laps of his elders. She spoke with much more feeling before about how much she wanted a "place of our own"–and added, "big families are nice in a way, but I'm tired of crowds." Such a move seemed impossible at that time as they had just bought a car which Mr. A. had to have for his work. At that point Billy would permit no one except his mother to feed him his meals and she was both pleased and irritated by this behavior. He also was making persistent grabs for the spoon during feeding and she found this annoying.

During the next three months she indicated her irritation at certain continuing aspects of her environment which had previously seemed less important to her. She complained about her husband's doing things for his mother. There was distinct displeasure expressed for the first time at Billy's enjoyment of his paternal grandmother, and the need to say, "but she [paternal grandmother] can't *really* take care of him" and an ever increasing determination to have a place of her own as soon as possible. She talked about Billy's behavior in a different way. For example, his activity and impatience with the lap were often spoken of as though they were primarily aimed at irritating her. His wish for certain objects to play with was seen as "everything he shouldn't have he wants." She was bothered by the fact that Billy could no longer be so easily persuaded to comply with her wishes. She summarized her difficulty in saying: "I can't figure him out any more."

Under the pressure of the dissatisfaction Mrs. A. returned to work and left the part-time care of the child to her sister. This does not mean that her relationship to B. had deteriorated, that she had become a "rejecting mother." The relationship has remained close, but has lost one impressive component–the full unity of mother and child. The relationship between mother and child now bears more resemblance to her relationship with other people. She is a woman who tries gently but firmly to dominate every situation. This is apparent in her relationship with her husband, and could be studied in some detail in her relationship with interviewer and pediatrician.

Retrospectively we find from this material that her reaction to the child's growing independence might have been anticipated, but we missed an even more significant clue. When the pediatrician discussed with her the giving of solid foods and in enumerating mentioned that he might not like the taste of some of them, Mrs. A. quickly responded, "Oh, he'll like spinach; I like it." What we saw in this was the unity; what we missed was the germ of discord since what she implied was that Billy was not thought of as having a taste of his own (Coleman, Kris, & Provence, 1953, pp. 30–33).

The above excerpt is an example of clinical or anecdotal evidence of changes in parental attitudes over time. However, little research documentation is available on this point. One study (Hurley & Hohn, 1971) was able to illuminate the nature of such changes. A child-rearing attitude scale consisting of the following three dimensions was administered to a group of college undergraduates:

> Manifest rejection was defined as the general tendency to assume a negative and punitive stance toward children. It was represented by items endorsing behaviors which minimize or restrict contact with children, inhibit the child's legitimate demands for attention and considerate care, or which would impose harsh disciplinary sanctions.
>
> Overprotection was defined as a pervasive overconcern and overattentiveness toward children, apparently rooted in the parental conviction that children will make many serious, perhaps catastrophic errors if permitted to explore the environment without painstaking parental supervision. It was represented by items endorsing attempts to make the child excessively dependent upon parental "babying," advice, guidance, and admonitions.
>
> The achievement pressure items were selected to represent a variety of ways in which children might be pushed toward the acquisition of social skills. They concerned a variety of specific topics, including walking, talking, weaning, eating, toilet training, care of clothing, orderliness, and school success in addition to related generalizations. (Hurley & John, 1971, p. 325)

A majority of the original sample filled out a similar questionnaire six years later. A comparison of the two sets of scores showed an increase in manifest rejection, a decrease in overprotection, and little change in achievement pressure. When the attitude shifts were analyzed according to the number of children in the family, those former students with three or more children showed a greater increase in manifest rejection.

The fathers in the sample were divided according to whether they were engaged in person-oriented occupations (psychologists, teachers, parole officers) or impersonally oriented occupations (insurance agents, salesmen, government workers). The latter group showed a greater shift toward manifest rejection, while those engaged in person-oriented occupations decreased more on overprotection, suggesting more relaxed and less controlling attitudes toward child-rearing. This interesting study revealed some of the factors producing shifts in parent attitudes. Much more information is needed, however, especially with regard to the ways in which various child behaviors and characteristics modify and influence child-rearing attitudes of parents.

The second problem relates to the first. It is the impact on the parent's attitudes of the feedback provided by a certain kind of child. That children at birth differ in many ways is obvious and that these differences affect the parent's attitudes toward a child must be considered. Since parental attitudes condition the child's further development of personality, the point is especially important in relation to the effect of such attitudes on the personality growth of the handicapped, the chronically ill, or the extremely sensitive child. This brings up the matter of the "vicious circle" phenomenon which has such dreadfully harmful consequences for the youngster. Two examples will suffice. That a child's intellectual capacities are below his parents' expectations may first come to parental attention when the youngster experiences some difficulty in learning to read in the first grade, or when he is placed in a reading group that the parents consider beneath his level. The child must thus face the frustrations flowing from reading difficulties as well as the equally bitter torment of parental rejection. At a time when the child most needs parental acceptance and reassurance to bolster his self-confidence and sense of security, he is met with criticism and disapproval. This change in parental attitude only serves to handicap the child further in his efforts to improve his reading. Or, to cite the other example, perhaps for deep-seated reasons rooted in his own psychological past, a parent may find himself unable to accept fully one of his children. From this nonacceptance may emerge undesirable school behavior such as attention seeking. When the teacher or other school officer expresses concern over this behavior, the nonacceptance may increase. Here again the change in parental attitude may aggravate rather than ameliorate the child's disturbance.

Third among these problems is the necessity for identifying the attitudes of the parent toward a particular child. It is well known that an individual views each of his children differently. Not only does a parent's attitudes vary according to the age of the child but also, undoubtedly, on the basis of such factors as sex, intelligence, personality, and appearance.

The fourth problem is that the emphasis in psychological literature on the crucial significance of parental attitudes for child adjustment has made parents highly sensitive and defensive about revealing their attitudes. Tapping a parent's attitudes directly is no simple task. How difficult this may be through a paper-and-pencil test may be judged from the failure of the Parent Attitude Research Instrument (PARI) to distinguish among the attitudes of various groups of mothers. For example, the PARI cannot differentiate significantly between the attitudes of parents of well-adjusted and poorly adjusted first-grade children (Medinnus, 1961), nor among the attitudes of mothers of children with speech articulation problems, delayed speech development, or lack of speech (Moll & Darley, 1960), nor among mothers of asthmatic, chronically ill, or healthy children (Margolis, 1961).

From the various attitude tests two dominant attitudes emerge. One is the pattern of authority in the home. The other is the acceptance of the child as an individual. This is what the findings of research have to say about each of them.

There is undoubtedly a wide margin of safety in parent attitudes (Ausubel, 1958, p. 362). Only when they deviate markedly from the typical do these attitudes exert harmful influences on child adjustment. In such cases, it is more likely the attitudes toward the child, relative to acceptance or rejection, rather than toward child-rearing that are significant.

The relation between maternal personality and maternal child-rearing attitudes was examined in a study of a group of mothers hospitalized because of emotional disturbance following child birth (Cohler, Weiss, & Grunebaum, 1970). These investigators argued that ". . . motherhood may be viewed as a series of developmental tasks, each of which represents, for the mother herself, a unique crisis or conflict which must be resolved in an adaptive manner in order for further maturation to take place" (p. 5).

A maternal attitude scale was developed consisting of the following five factors:

(1) Inappropriate versus Appropriate Control of the Child's Aggressive Impulses

> Mothers achieving a high positive score on this factor (a score indicating maladaptive attitudes) indicate overly permissive or, more frequently, overly rigid and restrictive attitudes regarding the control of the toddler's impulses, particularly those of aggression. (Cohler et al., 1970, p. 15)

(2) Discouragement versus Encouragement of Reciprocity

> Mothers earning a high positive score on this factor (maladaptive attitudes) believe that infants do not and cannot communicate with their mothers. (p. 17)

(3) Appropriate versus Inappropriate Closeness

> Mothers earning a high positive score on this factor are said to score in the direction of adaptive attitudes, while women scoring low on this factor are said to indicate maladaptive attitudes. Such women feel that all aspects of pregnancy and childbirth are depleting and destructive. They feel anxious about the prospect of delivery and are afraid of the possibility of injury to themselves resulting from delivery. At the same time, they wish to be the baby's sole caretaker, and worry both that the baby might develop an attachment to someone other than themselves, and also worry about leaving the baby alone with a babysitter or taking on activities outside the home. (p. 17)

(4) Acceptance versus Denial of Emotional Complexity in Child-Rearing

> Mothers with high positive scores on this factor indicate adaptive attitudes and are able to express a variety of concerns about how well they function as mothers. They admit to feeling that motherhood is sometimes far more work than pleasure and also a feeling that they sometimes do not know what is best for the child. (pp. 17–18)

(5) Comfort versus Discomfort in Perceiving and Meeting the Baby's Needs

> Mothers who attain a high positive score on this factor believe they can understand what babies want and that they can provide for this support. (p. 18)

The maternal attitude scale as well as several personality scales were administered to a group of hospitalized mothers and to a control group of normal mothers. Two significant relations were found between the mother's social adjustment prior to hospitalization and her child-rearing attitudes with respect to Failure of Reciprocity and Appropriate Closeness with the Child. The less well-adjusted mothers were unable to achieve reciprocity between themselves and their children, and they were likely to feel that the baby represented a narcissistic extension of themselves. Two of the five attitude factors differentiated between the normal and the hospitalized mothers: Failure of Reciprocity and Acceptance of Emotional Complexity. These differences were interpreted as indicating that the hospitalized mothers deny that the typical mother has concern regarding child-rearing; they are unable to admit to certain of the ambivalences and uncertainties present in most mothers. Further, they are not concerned with establishing a meaningful interpersonal relationship with their child.

In summary, these investigators concluded that emotional illness in a mother is related to her inability to resolve some of the crises and conflicts which are a normal part of parenthood. Parenthood, just as childhood, involves a series of developmental tasks which require resolution and adaptation in order for further growth and maturity to take place.

Parent Behavior

From what has been seen of parent behaviors in Chapter 9, it is apparent that an isolated examination of them is not likely to bear much fruit. At this point in man's knowledge more is to be learned from exploring the characteristics that describe the *general* behavioral atmosphere of the home. Table 10-1 contains some of the principal parent characteristics identified over several decades of research activity.

Two characteristics recur throughout the studies; these are acceptance versus rejection and autonomy versus control, depicted in Figure 10-1. In theory, the psychological atmosphere of a home may fall into any of the four quadrants, each of which represents one of four general combinations: acceptance-autonomy,

TABLE 10-1 Major Parent-Child Dimensions

Investigators		Psychological Dimensions
Symonds (1939)	Dimensions:	Acceptance-rejection Dominance-submission
Baldwin, Kalhorn, & Breese (1945)	Syndromes:	Democracy in the home Acceptance of child Indulgence
Baldwin, Kalhorn, & Breese (1949)	Clusters:	Warmth Adjustment Restrictiveness Clarity Interference
Roff* (1949)	Factors:	Concern for child Democratic guidance Permissiveness Parent-child harmony Sociability-adjustment of parents Activeness of home Nonreadiness of suggestion
Lorr & Jenkins† (1953)	Factors:	Dependence-encouraging Democracy of child training Organization and effectiveness of control
Milton‡ (1958)	Factors:	Strictness or nonpermissiveness of parent behavior General family interaction or adjustment Warmth of the mother-child relationship Responsible child-training orientation Parents' attitude toward aggressiveness and punitiveness
Schaefer (1959)	Dimensions:	Autonomy-control Love-hostility

*Based on the Baldwin et al. (1945) data.
†Based on the Baldwin et al. (1945) data and Roff's (1949) factor analysis.
‡Based on the Pattern data (Sears et al., 1957).

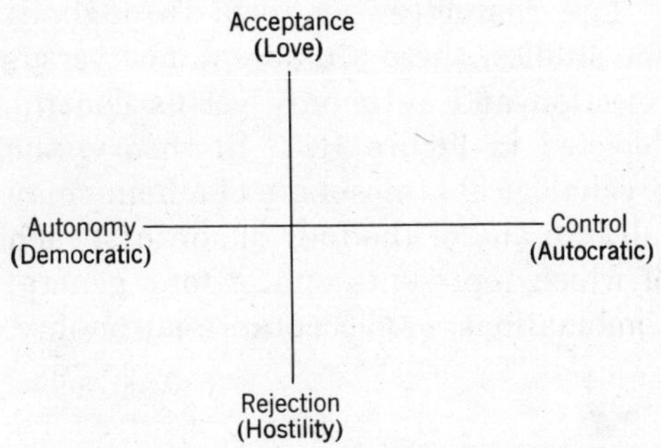

FIGURE 10-1 Two major psychological dimensions in the home.

acceptance-control, rejection-autonomy, rejection-control.

Acceptance versus Rejection. The most significant aspect of the home is the warmth of the relationship between parent and child. Both the Pattern Study (Sears, Maccoby, & Levin, 1957) and the Fels research have maintained that warmth is the most crucial and pervasive factor affecting the child.

Symonds' Studies. After a careful review of the literature, Symonds (1939) concluded that the matter of acceptance or rejection was one of the two most significant considerations in the home, the other being autonomy as opposed to control. Although it left much to be desired methodologically, since its findings were based on case histories compiled by Symonds' former students, the study was fruitful enough to warrant examination. These were some of the parent behaviors that served as evidence for acceptance or rejection according to the study:

Evidence for Acceptance

Participates with child in games, sports, hobbies, takes trips together, special vacations together, pals
Parents make rearing child their main job—devoted
Interested in child's plans and ambitions
Gives child loving care and protection
Interested in school progress
Demonstrative in affection
Speaks well of child
Wanted at birth
Child encouraged to bring friends home
Parents worry when child is ill
Accepted as individual rather than as child
Child trusted
Parents talk over plans with child
Parents do not expect too much of child
Parents give wise counseling and encouragement
(pp. 62–63)

Evidence for Rejection

No interest in child
No time for child—neglect
Unfavorable comparison with siblings
Verbal punishment—nagging, scolding
Failure to support child
Criticism or blame of child
Physical punishment or cruelty
Turned out of home or threaten to place in an institution
Does not speak well of child
Ridicule
Child unwanted at birth
Suspicious of child's behavior
Too much supervision
Neglect health, clothes, training, etc.
(pp. 60–61)

Symonds sought to find differences in behavior between accepted and rejected children in order to discover the causes of such differences in the marital relations of the parents and in the parents' own childhood. In general, he noted that accepted children engaged predominantly in socially acceptable behavior, whereas rejected children manifested a number of unacceptable behaviors. Specifically, the behaviors characteristic of accepted children included good-naturedness, consideration of others, cheerfulness, interest in work, friendliness, cooperativeness, and emotional stability. Among rejected children, on the other hand, attention-getting behavior, tendency toward delinquency, and problems in school were evident. More important, however, than descriptions of behavioral differences between accepted and rejected children is the need to understand how parental acceptance and rejection produce them.

Symonds (1949) observed that an individual's attitudes toward himself grew out of the attitudes displayed toward him by his parents during childhood. A child who was rejected developed feelings of insecurity and inferiority because it seemed to him that if he were unworthy of parental love, he was evidently worthless. A low conception of the self resulted from a low view of the child by his parents.

Such rejection brings on attempts by the child to win parental affection. These efforts may take the form of various attention-getting behaviors: refusal to eat, refusal to talk, temper tantrums, bed wetting, and whining. If these tactics prove futile, two general types of behavior often result: the child becomes hostile and aggressive or withdrawn and submissive. Symonds pointed out that whereas rejection might lead to good social adjustment outside the home and to close identification with and attachment to one's peers, it more frequently resulted in more negative consequences —feelings of insecurity, inferiority, inadequacy, worthlessness, isolation, humiliation, and anxiety. Even though a number of childhood experiences might not exert long-range influences on the child, a persistent pattern of rejection might very well prove pervasive in its effect on the child's adult personality and adjustment.

In a later study Symonds (1949) examined a number of factors, conscious as well as unconscious, contributing to the parent's rejection of the child. Among the more obvious were the economic burden imposed by the youngster, the invasion of the parents' privacy and activities, the strain of childbirth and child care on the mother, the child's failure to meet parental expectations, and parental disappointment in the sex of the child. Symonds maintained that some children are easier to accept than others; the child who is easiest to accept is the one most likely to be accepted by his parents. In this respect, the characteristics of the child definitely figure in the degree to which he receives parental acceptance.

Six elements, in particular, play an unconscious part in parental rejection, Symonds believed. First, the pattern of rejection adopted by a parent might be similar to the one experienced in his own childhood. Second, the parent might kindle in the child the hostility he felt toward his own parents. Third, one parent might show hostility toward the child as a means of injuring the other parent. Fourth, the parent might transfuse into the child the hostility he felt toward one of his own siblings. Fifth, he might implant in the child some of the feelings of hostility and rejection that he feels toward himself. Sixth, a mother—or a father, for that matter—might be so immature and narcissistic as to be unable to love another person wholeheartedly, and the resultant guilt might cause her to reject the child.

Maternal behavior toward the child on the love-hostility dimension has been found to be quite consistent over time (Schaefer & Bayley, 1963). This consistency may reflect a basic aspect of the mother's personality. Maternal hostility appears to be related to the woman's emotional maladjustment, to poor relations with her husband, and to environmental stresses and frustrations.

Erikson (1950) spoke of the necessity for a child to develop a sense of basic trust in his relationship with his parents; this is a requirement for development of a healthy personality. From this basic trust in parents stems a basic trust in the world, in the universe, in other people, and, most of all, in oneself. With this comes a sense of security, of self-acceptance, and it all goes back to early acceptance by parents. Much of the behavior of rejected children probably can be charged to a lack of a secure feeling and a lack of self-acceptance. Such children are hostile and aggressive, striking out at an unfriendly world. Seeking the affection and acceptance they need, they are often unsuccessful in their quest; a rejected child fails to understand others because he has never been understood himself.

Parental rejection, then, may have pervasive, long-range, harmful implications for the child's personality. Lack of parental acceptance seemed to constitute an important factor in the poor adjustment of certain first-grade children (Medinnus, 1961). Bandura and Walters (1959) maintained that the failure to satisfy the child's needs for dependency in early years contributed significantly to the development of aggressive behavior in adolescence.

Autonomy versus Control. The other important aspect of the psychological atmosphere in the home is the extent to which parents restrict the child's behavior or give him autonomy and freedom.

Symonds' Studies. Returning to Symonds' (1939) early study, these were some of the characteristics that described the behavior of dominant parents. They insisted on complete obedience. They supervised the child closely in the youngster's choice of activities. They provided too much supervision. They trained the child carefully. They expressed concern over trifles and criticized the child. Submissive parents, on the other hand, let the child have his own way. They could not control the child. They employed lax, inconsistent discipline and allowed the child to upset the home routine.

Although fathers satisfied many of their personality needs outside of the family, mothers were especially likely to fulfill their needs for dominance or submission by controlling or letting themselves be controlled by their children, Symonds noted. This finding supports the widespread notion that mothers exert a greater influence on the child than the father. The primary obligation of the mother's role is rearing the children, whereas occupational success and economic support of the family are important aspects of the father's role. Small wonder, therefore, that the mother may be more emotionally involved than the father in the end result of the child-rearing techniques used. Failure may cast a dark shadow over the mother's feelings of competence and adequacy. The father, however, can compensate for any deficiency as a parent with success in his job and the recognition it achieves. Whereas several recent investigations (Becker, Peterson, Hellmer, Shoemaker, & Quay, 1959; Peterson et al., 1959) suggested that the father's attitudes and behaviors were as intimately connected as those of the mother to the development of problem behavior in the child, this finding might reflect an increased paternal participation and involvement in child-rearing. It further signifies that the father's role is an important one in contemporary, urban, somewhat isolated psychologically, small-sized, child-oriented families.

Symonds found differentiation in a number of behaviors between children of dominating parents and those of submissive parents. The former were better socialized as a rule; their behavior was more acceptable, more conforming to the group. They seemed to be more interested in school work. Yet they tended to be sensitive, shy, self-conscious, seclusive, retiring, and submissive as compared with children who were given more freedom by their parents. The children of submissive parents inclined toward disobedience, irresponsibility, lack of interest in school, stubbornness, and defiance of authority. They were able, however, to express themselves effectively.

As to personality, the dominated children were more likely to be courteous, loyal, honest, polite, and dependable, albeit submissive and docile. The children of submissive parents were aggressive, disrespectful, and antagonistic, although independent and self-confident.

Present Status of Autonomy-Control Dimension. Traditionally couched in democratic-autocratic terms, this dimension has received far more attention than the love-hostility dimension. In part this is because this aspect of child-rearing is easier for parents to discuss on an intellectual level, whereas parental acceptance or rejection of a child is a deeply emotional area. Another reason for study of authoritarian approaches to child-rearing may be that such approaches are thought to reflect more general authoritarian attitudes, which have broad political overtones. The disproportionate attention given the autonomy-control dimension is particularly interesting in view of the Schaefer and Bayley data described above, which show much greater effect on the child of maternal acceptance or rejection.

Shifting trends in child-rearing advice by experts have been discussed in Chapter 7. The rigid, autocratic Watsonian approach of the 1930's gave way to the permissiveness of the 1940's and early 1950's. Anything smacking of authoritarianism or structure was derogated as alien to our democratic way of life and to the needs of the child. Excesses became apparent, and in some cases, total self-regulation on the part of the child was advocated.

Although it is difficult to determine the predominant philosophy of child-rearing in the United States today, there are many signs to indicate that the pendulum is swinging back in the direction of a firmer approach. Perhaps the most noteworthy indication of this trend is an exciting discussion by Baumrind (1966) in which, in addition to permissive and authoritarian, a third approach called "authoritative," is described:

> The authoritative parent attempts to direct the child's activities in a rational, issue-oriented manner. She encourages verbal give and take, shares with the child the reasoning behind her policy, and solicits his objections when he refuses to conform. Both autonomous self-will and disciplined conformity are valued by the authoritative parent. Therefore, she exerts firm control at points of parent-child divergence, but does not hem the child in with restrictions. She enforces her own perspective as an adult, but recognizes the child's individual interests and special ways. The authoritative parent affirms the child's present qualities, but also sets standards for future conduct. She uses reason, power, and shaping by regime and reinforcement to achieve her objectives and does not base her decisions on group consensus or the individual child's desires (Baumrind, 1966, p. 891).

Baumrind examined eight commonly held propositions with regard to authoritarianism versus permissiveness in the light of research evidence. Several of these will be dealt with briefly.

Much has been written about the harmful effects of punishment. However, most of this concern has been with severe punishment, frequently administered in a context of a poor parent-child relationship. Mild punishment, however, may have beneficial effects:

> (a) more rapid re-establishment of affectional involvement on both sides following emotional release, (b) high resistance to similar deviation by siblings who vicariously experience punishment, (c) emulation of the aggressive parent resulting in prosocial assertive behavior, (d) lessening of guilt reactions to transgression, and (e) increased ability of the child to endure punishment in the service of a desired end (p. 896).

Further, nonaction on the part of the parent may be interpreted by the child as approval for a given act, which, coupled with whatever reinforcement the child may receive from performing that act, tends to increase the likelihood that the child may repeat the behavior. Mild punishment may, indeed, be effective if properly timed and if accompanied by explanation.

Authoritarian control, but not authoritative control, is linked with rebelliousness in children. Placing demands upon children does not provoke hostility. Parental exercise of authority in complex situations is appropriate and beneficial for the child; such authority continually exerted in simple situations seems unwise. The effect of parent control depends upon the personality characteristics of the child. Moreover, the effect of parental restrictiveness depends upon the other parent behavior variables with which it appears. Restrictiveness combined with hostility may produce passivity and dependence, whereas restrictiveness and warm involvement with the child may be beneficial. Creativity, self-assertiveness, and responsibility may be facilitated by appropriate demands, realistic standards, and an authoritative model.

Baumrind (1971) observed an interesting pattern of parental control in eight families included in her large-scale study of the effect of parental authority on the behavior of preschool children. In these families, designated as harmonious, the parents seemed neither to exercise control nor to avoid it. They were more interested in developing principles for resolving differences than in forcing their dictates on the child. The following is an excerpt from an interview with one of these eight mothers regarding her four-year-old daughter.

Interviewer: Describe Nina.

Mother: She's strong-tempered, which comes up because she's always been taught that her opinions are valid. So if you disagree with her, she'll stand there and argue all day if she feels differently. But all of the things that make her hard to deal with are again the same things that make her very appealing. She's a very individualistic person. She tries very hard to please people and to communicate with people and to amuse them, but she's not a follower, really. And she doesn't need other people—she's not dependent, really. Psychologically she's not dependent on other people—I don't think she feels so, although she knows she couldn't do a number of things herself.

Interviewer: How do you feel when she disobeys?

Mother: If you use the term disobeys, that sort of conjures up a negative feeling. Oftentimes she just doesn't *think* the way I do. It's just a difference of opinion. But I figure to a certain amount that I've been here longer—walked around on the earth longer, so I know more. Which isn't particularly valid either.

Interviewer: Does Nina ever downright refuse to obey?

Mother: Oh yeah.

Interviewer: What do you do?

Mother: It depends on what is in question. If I really feel it's not all that important, I'll just give up—just walk off. Say forget it. If from my point of view it's important, I'll pursue it. . . . There have been times when we've sat for hours and hours and yelled at each other—just incredible—really stubborn, both of us. But most of the time, if I really feel it's not important, I'll drop it.

Interviewer: Do you reason with Nina?

Mother: Oh yeah. She tries to reason with me too, from her point of view. What I consider reasonable, I'll throw at her. We just had a big discussion of reason the other day. Reason—I'd never thought about it as much as the other night. It's a very charged word also—it only means that the person who's saying it thinks it fair, or, quote, 'reasonable.' But it doesn't mean that in some huge allover sense it's just or anything. As far as I'm concerned it doesn't mean that at all.

Interviewer: What do you do when Nina disobeys?

Mother: I don't know. I don't ask her to do a heck of a lot, really. Usually it gets done. We go and do it together, or—if she's really dead-set against it, she won't do it completely on her own. If she feels that from her standpoint it's not something she's required to do, whether it makes sense to me for her to do it, she won't do it. I really dislike punishing her. Punishing her comes down to—most of the time—doing physical things. And I have a strong distaste for that so I conk out. That's probably why she's so headstrong too.

Interviewer: What do you think about the importance of children obeying parents?

Mother: We discuss general philosophies. . . . There's a lot of discussion now. Terry [older sister] is exposed to a lot of my philosophy, but she's also been exposed to the fact that it's just the way *I* feel—that it's not particularly the way she has to feel, or the way she should feel. Or the way anybody else feels.

Interviewer: What do you think of respect for parents as a reason for obedience?

Mother: Being Japanese has a bearing on this. I've always felt that you owe a certain cognizance of the fact that your parents are your parents and they more than likely raised you and clothed you and fed you and saw that you didn't get sick and die. So the degree of respect would be how much they'd earned. There would be a certain amount of respect just because of the things I mentioned. But past that, it would be how much you earned as an individual.

Interviewer: Is it to her best interest in the long run that Nina learn to obey?

Mother: No.

Interviewer: Why not?

Mother: I only think that obedience is practical. I've taught my kids to do whatever you want to do, but you're responsible for your actions and therefore also suffer the consequences or whatever you want to say. For instance, in the sense of society, if you break a law and are cognizant of the fact, and you know that if you're going to go out and play the game, if you break the rules, you're going to have to take the consequences.

Interviewer: What decisions does Nina make for herself?

Mother: She makes all her own decisions and then we argue about them. She really does. She decides all her own things. She decides her clothes, what she'll eat; but they're sort of in the context of what's happening. She goes to the store and she decides what she'll wear by what she'll see. Or if she gets dressed in the morning, she'll decide what she'll wear by what she can see around her.

(Baumrind, 1971, pp. 101–102)

Interestingly enough, there were clear sex differences in the effect on the children of the harmonious family pattern. The six daughters were highly competent, achievement oriented, friendly, and independent, while the two boys were submissive, aimless, dependent, and not achievement oriented. Although the sample was small, the findings suggest that boys and girls are affected differently by various patterns of parental attitudes and behaviors. Perhaps boys profit less than girls from a rational child-rearing approach!

In the larger study by Baumrind mentioned above comparing the effects of authoritarian, authoritative, and permissive homes on the behavior of preschool children, she concluded that authoritative parent behavior was most likely to facilitate the development of competence involving independent and responsible behavior in children. This was particularly true for girls. Authoritarian parent behaviors, on the other hand, adversely affected independence in girls and social responsibility in boys. While Baumrind found few homes in her middle-class white sample which fit her definition of permissiveness, this approach affected girls and boys differently. The boys from permissive homes were less competent than those from the other types of homes, while the girls were somewhat more autonomous in both constructive and disruptive ways. It is readily apparent from Baumrind's study that the relation between parent behavior and child behavior is indeed a complex one. Certainly various initial characteristics possessed by a child will help to determine the manner in which his parents' behavior will affect him. For example, a passive, submissive child will react differently to a harsh, authoritarian approach than an active, aggressive child.

Summary of Parent Behavior Dimensions. Research attempting to identify the effects on children of various parent characteristics has received increasing attention in the last decade. Because of the complexity of this area, much remains to be done before we will be able to make precise statements, based on research evidence, regarding the nature of the interrelations. Research has become increasingly sophisticated in terms of methodology, with numerous attempts to conduct carefully controlled investigations in which parents and children are observed in the laboratory in standard situations (see Bell, 1964). Several points emerge from an examination of current research in this general area.

1. No longer is it possible to speak of the effect of parents on their children. The sex of the parent and the sex of the child must be specified. For example, a complicated study of mother-child interaction (Hatfield, Ferguson, & Alpert, 1967) found that mothers reward aggressiveness in their sons but not in their daughters, while the reverse is true for dependency. In an interesting study (Rothbart & Maccoby, 1966) in which parents gave their immediate reactions to taped statements made by a four-year-old, fathers showed greater permissiveness toward girls than boys for both dependency and aggression while mothers showed greater permissiveness toward boys. In a study relating the performance of two-year-olds on vocabulary and learning discrimination tasks with their parents' educational level (Reppucci, 1971), a strong relation was found for girls but none for boys. While there are several possible interpretations of this finding, it is plausible that educational level of parents influences the way they treat their daughters but their behavior toward their sons is influenced by other factors. Support for this interpretation was provided in a study which found that better educated mothers responded more than less well educated mothers to their four-month-old daughters' vocalizations. No differences were found between these two groups of mothers with regard to their verbal interactions with their sons (Levine, Fisherman, & Kagan, 1967). The old saw, "boys will be boys," may indicate a somewhat "hands off" parental attitude toward the development of boys as compared with girls. Bronfenbrenner (1961) has argued that there is a risk of oversocialization in girls because they receive a combination of high affection and love-oriented discipline. Boys, receiving less affection and more physical punishment (which is less effective than love-oriented discipline in inhibiting behavior) may be undersocialized. Bronfenbrenner maintains that an optimal balance between affection and control is different for boys and girls.
2. The effect of certain parent behaviors and attitudes may depend upon the age of the child. Encouragement or acceptance of dependency, for example, may be less harmful at one age (preschool) than at another (adolescence).

Schaefer and Bayley (1963) found the maternal dimension of love-hostility to be significantly correlated with sons' behavior up to the age of 12 years, but not thereafter, whereas the reverse was true of the autonomy-control dimension. In their report of longitudinal data from the Fels research, Kagan and Moss (1962) found that *early* maternal restrictiveness has a long-term effect in inhibiting behavior. Restrictiveness *later*, when the child is better able to judge the inappropriateness of this restrictiveness, is likely to generate hostility.

3. It has become apparent that it is not fruitful to attempt to establish relation between specific parent characteristics and specific child characteristics. Parent variables do not operate in isolation but in combination, so that effects upon the child can be predicted only by considering the patterning and interaction among the parent dimensions. In a study of child-care antecedents of several patterns of preschool children's behavior, Baumrind (1967) found parents of competent and mature boys and girls to be firm, loving, demanding, and understanding. Parents of children showing disaffiliative behavior were firm, punitive, and unaffectionate. Further, parent variables that we have thought to be related may not be. Baumrind and Black (1967) found firm, demanding behavior on the part of the parent not to be associated with punitiveness or lack of warmth. Undoubtedly there are a great many combinations and permutations of parent behavior.
4. Any particular type of home atmosphere gives rise to both desirable and undesirable child characteristics. Fearless, curious, and planful as children may be from homes in which a psychological climate of democracy and autonomy prevails, they are also inclined toward cruelty, rebellion, and nonconformity. On the other hand, the well-behaved child of a home characterized by strict control may show signs of a constricted personality.
5. In the past much of parent-child research has been concerned with the development of social-emotional behaviors in the child. As mentioned in Chapter 9, increased attention is being paid currently to parental antecedents of cognitive development and cognitive abilities in children. Although some of the parent dimensions examined in this area deal with the emotional relations between parent and child, most are directly related to intellectual stimulation of the child, such as amount of time spent reading to the child (Bing, 1963), the level (quality) of the mother's communication with the child (Hess & Shipman, 1965), and parental expectations for the child (Wolf, 1964). Freeberg and Payne (1967) have constructed a questionnaire to assess parental practices that previous research has shown to influence the child's cognitive development. Six factors emerged from a factor analysis of the responses to the questionnaire of a large group of parents of preschool children: willingness to devote time to the child, parental guidance, parental aspiration for achievement, rejection versus acceptance of the child's behavior, provisions for the child's intellectual needs, dependence upon external resources (toys, nursery school attendance).
6. The role of the father in affecting the child is receiving increased recognition (Nash, 1965). Although American society is considered a matricentric one, it is apparent that the father influences the children directly, and indirectly through the mother. The concept of identification, to be discussed shortly, has drawn attention to the importance of the father in affecting a boy's development. For example, the delinquent boy has been shown to hold strong feelings of paternal rejection and neglect (Medinnus, 1965b). Since in our culture the role of the father in the family structure is less clearly defined than the maternal role, one might speculate that there are wider differences among fathers than among

> mothers in their parent behavior, and that the way in which the father assumes the role more clearly reflects his personality needs than the mother's behavior reflects her personality needs.

A tremendous number of studies are available showing the effects on the child, particularly on the boy, of father absence. Sex-typing and sex-role identification is the general area of development about which the most concern has been shown. It certainly makes sense to assume that the lack of a male figure in the home would affect the boy's identification with the male role. And, indeed, studies (e.g., Hetherington, 1966; Biller & Bahm, 1971) have found that, as compared with boys from father-present homes, boys from father-absent homes are less masculine, hold less masculine self-concepts, are less assertive, and are more dependent on peers. Unfortunately, however, there is not high agreement in the research literature concerning the effects of father-absence. In fact, two reviews of this literature (Herzog & Suda, 1968; Hetherington & Deur, 1971) arrive at different conclusions. This is very likely due to the fact that a great many other family variables are important in increasing or in minimizing the effects of father-absence. For example, the age of the child at the time of father-absence is important. The age of five–six appears to be a critical one, with the most adverse effects resulting if the father is absent prior to that time (Hetherington, 1966; Biller & Bahm, 1971). Another significant factor is the child's relation with his mother. Biller (1971) has argued that ". . . mothers in father-absent homes and mothers in homes where the father is relatively ineffectual often undermine their sons' feelings of masculine adequacy and ability to function interpersonally" (p. 237). For the boy's appropriate masculine identification, it is important for the mother to have a positive attitude toward males and for her to encourage her son's active participation in masculine type of activities. Family composition is another significant variable. In father-absent homes, boys with a brother are less affected than boys without a male sibling (Sutton–Smith, Rosenberg, & Landy, 1968; Santrock, 1970). Interaction with another male in the family setting apparently encourages sex-appropriate behavior. Finally, the availability of substitute father figures is important. While father-absence has been shown to affect adversely boys' school achievement and IQ test scores, this appears not to be the case in homes where a stepfather is present (Lessing, Zagorin, & Nelson, 1970). Certainly a great deal can be learned about male and female roles from many sources including TV, the peer group, and adults outside the home. In summary, while it seems likely that a two-parent family has certain advantages with respect to family relations and child development, no single aspect of the home, such as father-absence, can be considered apart from many other variables. Moreover, with the increasing frequency of single-parent adoptions in this country, one-parent families should be recognized as a legitimate family form. "We need to take account of its strengths as well as its weaknesses; of the characteristics it shares with two-parent families as well as its differences; of ways in which it copes with its undeniable difficulties; and of ways in which the community supports or undermines its coping capacity" (Herzog & Sudia, 1968, p. 181).

THREE FACTORS IN PARENT-CHILD RELATIONSHIPS

For an understanding of the psychology of parent-child relationships, three topics are significant. These are the child's perception of his parents, the matter of identification, and the question of discipline. We conclude this chapter with a consideration of each of these.

Perception of Parents

As we saw earlier, attempts to link parent attitudes to various child behaviors have not proved fruitful. Sufficient research is now accumulating to indicate that a more profitable approach is to elicit the child's report of his relations with his parents. Perhaps more crucial than the parents' attitudes and behaviors is the child's perception and interpretation of them. Indeed, one study (Cox, 1970) explored the relation among the following three variables: (1) adolescents' perceptions of their parents; (2) parental reports of their child-rearing attitudes; and (3) teachers' ratings of the adolescents on 24 behavioral traits, including nonaggressive, considerate, responsible, popular, outgoing, and cooperative. Comparable items on three scales, loving, rejecting, and neglecting, drawn from the Roe–Siegelman scale mentioned below, were used in a questionnaire administered to the adolescents and to their parents. For example:

Adolescent Questionnaire
My mother
1. objected when I was late for meals.

Parent Questionnaire
In raising my son, I
1. objected when he was late for meals.

The results of the study showed that the teachers' ratings of the adolescents were more closely related to the adolescents' perceptions of their parents than to the parents' self-reports. Thus it appears that the adolescent's perception of his parents' affectional behavior towards him is particularly important in affecting a number of aspects of his behavior.

The approach using children's perceptions of their parents is not without problems, however. First, attempts to identify cause-and-effect relations are especially tenuous. Let us say that a poorly adjusted 15-year-old perceives his parents in a very unfavorable light. It is just as likely that his present poor adjustment causes him to view all of his interpersonal relations negatively, including his relationship with his parents, as it is that his negative perception of his parents has produced his poor adjustment. Second, the young child is not a very reliable informant, not through any desire to deceive, but through inability to express himself adequately in his early years.

Many techniques have been employed to study children's perceptions of their parents. Directly, children have been interviewed about their parents. Indirectly, they have been asked general questions about parents, such as "What do parents do that boys and girls don't like?" Indirect methods also include drawings to obtain an idea of parental preference and pictures portraying a variety of child situations. Several standardized questionnaires are available in which items are designed to tap the child's perception of the parent on a number of dimensions. The Bronfenbrenner Parent Behavior questionnaire includes the following 15 variables (statements illustrating each variable are provided):

1. Nurturance: I can talk with her (him) about everything. Comforts me and helps me when I have troubles. Is there for me when I need her (him).
2. Affective Reward: Says nice things about me to other people. Is very affectionate with me. Praises me when I have done something good.
3. Instrumental Companionship: Teaches me things which I want to learn. Helps me with hobbies or handiwork. Helps me with schoolwork when I don't understand something.

4. Affiliative Companionship: Goes on pleasant walks and outings with me. Is happy when with me. Enjoys talking with me.
5. Prescriptive: Expects me to help around the house. Wants me to run errands. Expects me to keep my own things in order.
6. Social Isolation: Punishes me by sending me out of the room. As punishment she (he) forbids me to play with other children. As punishment she (he) sends me to bed early.
7. Expressive Rejection: Holds it before me that other children behave better than I do. Nags at me. Scolds me and yells at me.
8. Physical Punishment: Threatens to spank me. Spanks me. Slaps me.
9. Deprivation of Privileges: Punishes me by making me do extra work. When I am bad she (he) forbids me to do things I especially enjoy. Punishes me by taking my favorite things away.
10. Protectiveness: Comes with me when I go someplace for the first time to make sure that everything goes well. Worries that I can't take care of myself. Won't let me roam around because something might happen to me.
11. Power: Insists that I get permission first before I go to a movie, a carnival or some other entertainment. Wants to know exactly how I spend my money when I want to buy some little things for myself. Tells me exactly when I should come home.
12. Achievement Demands: Insists I make a special effort in anything I do. Demands that I do better than other children. Insists that I get particularly good marks in school.
13. Affective Punishment: Appears disappointed and sad when I misbehave. Makes me feel ashamed or guilty when I misbehave. Tells me, "I don't want to have any more to do with you," when I misbehave.
14. Principled Discipline: Is just when punishing me. When I must do something, she (he) explains why. Finds it difficult to punish me.
15. Indulgence: I can talk her (him) into most anything. Lets me off easy when I misbehave. Finds it difficult to punish me.

(Siegelman, 1965a, p. 165)

Another scale, the Parent-Child Relations questionnaire (Roe & Siegelman, 1963) is composed of 10 dimensions: protective, demanding, rejecting, neglect, casual, loving, symbolic-love reward, direct-object reward, symbolic-love punishment, direct-object punishment. Factor analysis of these 10 scales yields three main factors: loving-rejecting, casual-demanding, and overt attention. Two separate factor analyses of another questionnaire dealing with children's perceptions of their parents (Schaefer, 1965) yielded three similar factors: acceptance versus rejection; psychological control versus psychological autonomy; and firm control versus lax control (Schludermann & Schludermann, 1970; Burger & Armentrout, 1971). Interestingly enough, these principal factors dealing with affection and control are similar to those obtained for parent behavior and attitude scales.

One consistent finding of research investigating the attitudes of children toward the parent role is that children of most ages choose the mother as the preferred parent (Gardner, 1947; Harris & Tseng, 1957). Generally the mother is seen in a more favorable light than the father. She is considered friendlier, less strict, less punitive, less threatening, and more nurturing (Kagan, 1956; Kagan, Hosken, & Watson, 1961; Eisenberg, Henderson, Kuhlmann, & Hill, 1967). The father and his role, in contrast, are regarded as more powerful, more interfering, more competent, and as the major source of punishment (Emmerich, 1959, 1961; Kagan & Lemkin, 1960). Both boys and girls report their mothers as using covert, indirect methods of control more frequently than fathers (Droppleman & Schaefer, 1963). In addition, children usually ascribe "high power" to the adult role and "low power" to their own (Emmerich, 1961).

Although children ordinarily perceive their parents in positive terms, they are willing to criticize and voice dissatisfactions with them. Preschool children in the Radke (1946) study frequently mentioned punishment in this connection. The fifth- and sixth-graders studied by Gardner (1947) enumerated the following dissatisfactions with their fathers: scolding, general irritability, poor adjustment with the mother, and absence from home. These children's preference for their mother was based on her greater understanding, better nature, and less domineering behavior.

As children age, a trend becomes discernible of preference for the parent of the same sex. Moreover, children incline to perceive themselves as more similar to the parent of the same sex (Gray, 1959). This will become more evident in the consideration presently of identification.

Several interesting sex differences are apparent in children's perceptions of their parents. First, for girls there is fairly high agreement in their perceptions of mother and father, while there is low agreement for boys (Heaps, 1970). This might suggest greater inconsistency between parents in their treatment of boys than of girls. Second, as a rule boys see their parents as stricter than do girls (Hawkes, Burchinal, & Gardner, 1957). Boys also seem to be more critical of their parents, especially of the father, and in general see them through their disciplinary function (Meltzer, 1943), with the father as a strong authority figure. Girls more than boys tend to perceive themselves as accepted by their parents (Ausubel, Balthazar, Rosenthal, Blackmore, Schpoont, & Welkowitz, 1954).

Although the data on differential treatment of boys and girls are inconclusive, the fact that boys more than girls believe there is disciplinary friction may account in part for the greater number of behavioral and disciplinary problems among sons than daughters. Possibly because of their higher level of activity and greater aggressiveness boys become more involved in situations requiring discipline both at home and at school. This view supports the *biosocial* explanation of human behavior, that biological differences at birth accentuated by differential environmental, or social, treatment produces substantial variation among the individuals of a society.

Identification

Even though the concept of identification has been used in many ways with a host of meanings (see Sanford, 1955), let us define it as *the process by which an individual incorporates certain aspects of someone else's behavior, attitudes, and characteristics.* The terms copying, modeling, and imitating are sometimes used synonymously with identification. However, these connote a conscious process, whereas identification may occur essentially at the unconscious level. Furthermore, these terms frequently are restricted to level of behavior, whereas identification may encompass even more. The discussion of identification in the young child primarily concerns his identification with sex role, that is, the process whereby he develops characteristics similar to those of the parent of the same sex. However, numerous other behavioral traits seem to emerge from this process. Aggressive behavior, behavior and attitudes toward others, leisure-time pursuits, and a host of other characteristics may sprout from the child's identification with another person—usually, in early years, the parent.

Why the need for such a notion as identification? Are not the principles of learning (see Chapter 4) sufficient to explain the reason for the child developing characteristics similar to those of the parent of the same sex? Parental approval should be reward enough for behaviors valued by the parent, and thus encourage their repetition. However, child behavior seems to go beyond what would be predictable from learning theory. A tremendous amount of learning occurs without any direct teaching as such. That children observe and are aware of their parents' behavior became evident to the father of a four-year-old when, after he had shouted at her, the child replied, "Don't yell at me. I'm not mommy."

The endless hours spent by a little girl playing house suggest some higher level of patterning or modeling of one's behavior after the behavior of someone else. But what is the motive for such behavior? Three main explanations have been advanced to explain the occurrence of identification. There is some research support for each of these positions.

Two types of identification have been described in psychoanalytic literature. *Anaclitic* or *developmental* identification is based on the young child's anxiety concerning the loss of love, usually from the mother, with whom a nurturant, affectionate relationship has been established. The child gains some measure of security by introjecting or incorporating the qualities of the mother. From this point of view one would predict that the warmer and more nurturant the adult figure, the stronger the identification. And, indeed, the findings of several studies have supported this. Payne and Mussen (1956) used as an operational measure of identification the actual similarity between father and son on several personality and attitude tests. A positive relation was found between identification and the boy's perception of the father as warm, helpful, and kind. Bandura and Huston (1961) found that nursery-school children were much more likely to imitate a model if they had experienced a nurturant and rewarding interaction with her than if the relation had been a distant and nonrewarding one.

The second psychoanalytically based type of identification is *defensive* or *aggressive* identification. According to the theory, this occurs in the boy at the time of the resolution of the Oedipal conflict. Fearful of punishment from the father because of incestuous wishes toward the mother, the boy identifies with the father, adopting his characteristics. While it is apparent that aggressive parents frequently have aggressive children, as is the case among delinquents, there is little evidence that this has arisen from defensive identification. Based on several research investigations, Bandura and Walters (1963) have argued that children will imitate the aggressive behavior of a model if that behavior has been successful in producing social and material reward. However, if such aggressive behavior is punished, children will not imitate it.

Whiting (1960) has proposed a status-envy theory of identification. The degree of identification with another person depends on the extent to which that individual controls desired resources. The parent, for example, may give reward, either social or material; he may withhold it; or he may deprive the child of such reward as he already has. "The more a child envies the status of another with respect to the control of a given resource, the more he will covertly practice that role" (Whiting, 1960, p. 119). In an experiment designed by Bandura, Ross, and Ross (1963), children more frequently imitated a model who possessed rewarding power than one with whom they competed for these rewards.

Thus it appears that children identify with the source of rewarding power, not with the competitor for the rewards, as a theory of defensive identification might suggest.

At what age does identification begin? No specific age seems identifiable, although it would appear that it could not occur until the child was able to put himself in the place of someone else, as in taking the role of the parent in play, to pretend, to "assume the role of another." Certainly by ages two to three there is evidence for the beginning of such behavior in the child.

Turning to the literature on sex-role identification, Lynn (1961) has hypothesized that marked differences exist between boys and girls in several aspects of the identification process. As he saw it, both sexes in the very early years identify with the mother. Later, however, the boy has to shift his identification to the father and to a masculine role. No such shift is required of the girl. Several factors in the boy's environment facilitate the switch, however, There are numerous pressures for the boy to behave like a "little man." Moreover, in American society, at least, the male role is more desirable for many reasons. Males enjoy positions of dominance and authority. And in so material-minded a society the occupation of the father is the major source of prestige for the family.

For the girl, of course, although she continues in her identification with her mother, she discovers that the female role is devaluated by society. She thus experiences some difficulty in identifying with the role appropriate to her sex. Moreover, her mother may feel some ambivalence about the female role because of society's downgrading of it. And there is less pressure on her to be girl-like in all behaviors than there is for boys to be manly. No punishment attaches to her wearing certain items of male apparel. Nor does tomboyishness in girls incur the stigma of sissified behavior in boys. Girls may play with boys without censure, but boys are ridiculed for playing with girls.

For these reasons, Lynn believed that with increasing age girls became less firmly tied to the female role, whereas boys who successfully make the transition from identifying with their mother to identifying with their father become more fully associated with the male role. Because of the importance in Western culture of an appropriate sex identification, Lynn equated the failure to achieve this with psychological disturbance.

There are types of parent-child relationships that encourage an appropriate sex identification. P. Sears (1953) noted that sons of fathers who were warm, permissive, and easygoing tended to behave in a manner appropriate to their sex. In the doll-play situation, boys who chose the maternal role came from homes in which the mother, but not the father, was high in warmth. In an earlier study, P. Sears (1951) observed that boys from homes lacking a father showed less fantasied aggression than boys whose fathers were living with them. Although her finding implied that the father served as the son's model for aggression, it might also indicate that a boy whose father was absent experienced fewer frustrations.

Social class influences sex identification. Rabban (1950) reported that lower-class children identified themselves with interests appropriate to their sex sooner than middle-class children. Perhaps there are stronger pressures brought at an earlier age in lower-class homes for behavior proper to the sex. Or it may be that a clearer distinction is made between the male and female roles in the lower class. Possibly there may be less tolerance of any deviation from a stereotyped norm among lower-class parents. Whatever the case, there is likely to be more difficulty of a psychological nature for the lower-class child who, for one reason or another, cannot make a suitable sex-role identification.

As to other behaviors springing from a child's identification with his parent, the Pattern Study examined the subject as it bore upon the development of inner control or conscience. Some support was found for the notion that warmth between mother and child and maternal acceptance of the youngster influence the development of conscience. The extent to which children adopt adult behavior in terms of enforcing rules broken by peers appears to be related to the strictness with which their parents enforced rules in early childhood (Maccoby, 1961). This enforcement-of-rules behavior in middle childhood is enhanced by an earlier dependency upon parents.

Girls, as we know, experience a stronger and longer-lasting identification with the mother, although both boys and girls spend more time with her than with the father. Consequently, incorporation of the mother's demands and values plays the largest part in the child's early development of conscience. It would follow from these considerations that conscience develops more strongly in girls than in boys. The Pattern Study found this to be so. Identification led to the development of conscience.

However, Hoffman (1971) has argued that several points require consideration before we can conclude that identification leads to conscience development. First, the identification must be strong enough to overcome the natural tendency to maximize pleasure and minimize pain; inhibition of natural impulses will not occur without strong internalization of parental standards. Second, the parent must communicate to the child his own value orientation with sufficient clarity so that it can serve as a model for the child. The child cannot adopt values he does not perceive or comprehend even though he may identify with the parent. This leads to the third point. The child's intellectual level helps to determine those parental behaviors which he observes and in turn interprets accurately. According to Hoffman, these conditions must be met before we can conclude that the child's identification with the parent will result in certain behavioral and personality characteristics.

In conclusion, several types of identification have been proposed, together with various antecedent conditions to account for its occurrence. Irrespective of theory, identification clearly serves an important function in the child's life. Gratification (increased security and sense of mastery) derives from behavior that emulates that of a significant adult; and, in practicing the behavior of an adult, as in doll play, a child learns something of his future adult role and acquires some understanding of it. Although initially children identify with their parents, other adults serve as models later. Moreover, there is never a one-to-one relation between the child's behavior and that of the adult with whom he identifies and whose behavior he imitates. The child is selective and innovative, modifying the imitated behavior in various ways to produce a novel and individualistic pattern. Although specific behaviors can be imitated, it seems unlikely that more general and pervasive (and therefore more important) personality characteristics of the adult can be discerned and imitated.

Discipline

Quite likely no topic holds more interest and concern for parents than discipline. Yet relatively little research has been undertaken in this lively area. Thus ideas and theories about discipline abound, but scientific knowledge to back them up is conspicuously scarce. Why research on the subject is scant is easy to understand. The obstacles to experimental investigation are virtually insurmountable. One could hardly ask a group of mothers to administer a certain type of discipline at fixed intervals while another group employed a different kind of discipline or none at all. And even if this could be done, measurement of the effects of discipline (the independent variable) on the child's behavior and attitudes (the dependent variables) would be full of booby traps. Moreover, it is clear that the effects of discipline depend upon the emotional context in which it is administered.

In current thinking, discipline is often equated with guidance. However, discipline might be more appropriately described as the methods used by parents to ensure their child's compliance with that guidance. The socialization process of getting the child to conform to what society expects of him creates conflicts between these social demands and the child's wishes and desires. Thus discipline becomes an inevitable aspect of the parent-child relationship. That discipline may take a vast number of forms and vary widely in the frequency of its use from parent to parent is also true.

What are the functions of discipline? Most obviously, parents use disciplinary methods to obtain conformity to their demands. Discipline also provides the child with cues to behavior. For maximum effectiveness these cues should apprise the child of what constitutes approved or acceptable behavior. However, when it takes the form of punishment, discipline supplies only the cues to unacceptable behavior. This leads to a distinction between the short-term and long-range goals of discipline. Whereas the former is conformity to parental demands, the latter is the development of self-control or inner discipline. Some types of discipline are more conducive to accomplishment of the short-term objectives; others are better suited to achieving the long-range goals.

Which disciplinary techniques receive the more frequent use? Table 10-2 contains a ranking of the 10 used most often at each of three age levels. The study from which the table is drawn (Clifford, 1959, p. 69) was based on records kept by

TABLE 10-2 The First 10 Methods of Control by Rank and Age of the Child

3-Year-Old Group		6-Year-Old Group		9-Year-Old Group	
Method	Rank	Method	Rank	Method	Rank
Reason	1	Reason	1	Reason	1
Scold	2	Scold	2	Scold	2
Coax	3	Coax	3	Take away privilege	4
Spank	4	Threaten	4	Coax	4
Divert	5	Ignore	5	Self-esteem	5.5
Threaten	6	Isolate	6	Threaten	5.5
Ignore	7	Spank	7	Ignore	7
Remove child forcibly	8	Divert	8	Remove difficulty	8
Isolate	9	Take away privilege	9	Humor	10
Remove difficulty	10	Humor	10.5	Isolate	10
		Order	10.5	Social disapproval	10

mothers over a three-week period. With the increasing age of the child, the table implies, the parent comes to rely more on verbal techniques and less on physical methods. The Pattern Study divided training techniques into positive sanctions—praise and tangible reward—and negative sanctions—physical punishment, deprivation of privileges, withdrawal of love, and isolation. Generally those mothers who were above average in the group in the use of positive sanctions were also above average in ratings on warmth and affection shown to children, on satisfaction with their roles of wife and mother, and on esteem felt for their husbands. This would suggest that the use of praise and rewards reflected a mother's satisfactory adjustment to her life situation. Perhaps, then, there may be some relation between a woman's adjustment to the mother role and the reasonableness of her behavior in it.

Why is discipline used and when is it most frequent throughout the day? Clearly the most important single reason for discipline is disobedience—the child's noncompliance with parental demands. The Clifford study identified the following 11 categories as areas requiring discipline: *sibling relationships*—that is, quarreling, aggression, interference; *eating*—refusal to eat, making a mess, leaving the table during the meal; *sleep*—refusal to go to bed, noise in bed; *dressing*—refusal to get dressed, soiling clothing, changing clothes; *activities*—conflict over television, Sunday School; *school*—preparing to go to school, refusal to go to school; *health*—medication, general health protection; *inappropriate behavior*—irritability, boisterousness, destructiveness, forbidden behavior; *adult interaction*—refusing an adult request, interference with adult activity, persistent demand of adult attention; *home*—neatness of home, refusal to put things away; *social*—inappropriate social behavior, insistence on own rights, interference with activities of others.

As to frequency of discipline, Figure 10-2 represents the periods throughout the day at which discipline is most often required for each of three age levels. As

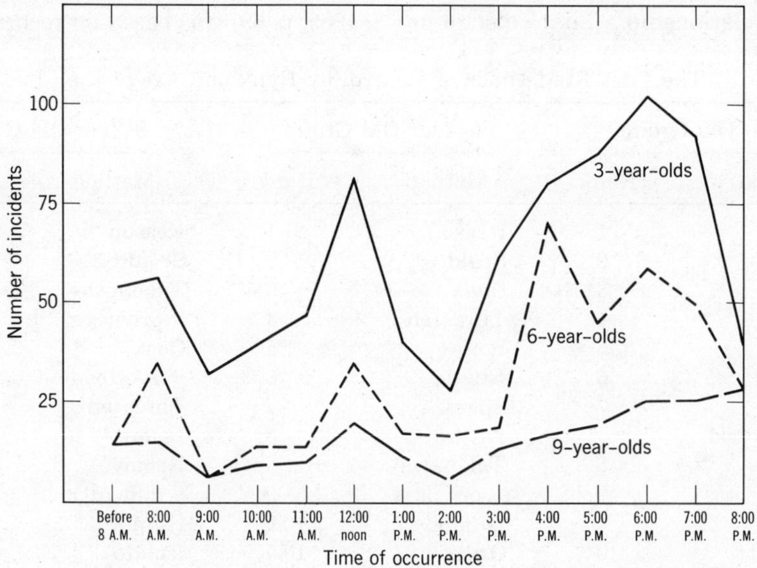

FIGURE 10-2 The frequency of discipline by the hour of occurrence and age (Clifford, 1959, p. 51).

the child grows older there is an apparent decrease in the frequency of situations requiring parental discipline. Perhaps this reflects a development of inner control with age; he is more aware of what is expected of him and is more able developmentally to conform to these expectations. Besides, as the child grows older, more of his time is spent interacting with others outside the home. The sheer quantity of his interaction with parents falls off. Now sanctions for inappropriate behavior spring increasingly from peers and from adults other than parents.

No discussion of discipline can ignore the effects of discipline on the child. Although discipline may achieve a behavioral goal, its accomplishment may be nullified by the emotional and attitudinal side effects it produces in the child. Several studies (Hollenberg & Sperry, 1951; R. R. Sears, 1950; Bandura & Walters, 1959; Becker, Peterson, Luria, Shoemaker, & Hellmer, 1962) have shown a positive correlation between aggressive behavior in children and severity of discipline in the home. There is little doubt that harsh, arbitrary, and inconsistent discipline arouses resentment, hostility, and anxiety in the child. Anger and crying were reported by mothers as responses to discipline (Clifford, 1959); and 63 percent of the preschool children interviewed in the Radke (1946) study said they were sad, unhappy, and pained by punishment, whereas only 14 percent reported feelings of penitence or resolutions for better behavior.

From strong discipline a child builds up a store of hostility that he directs toward others. This is borne out by a study conducted by Hoffman (1960). Mothers were rated according to how they coerced the child to change his entire current pattern of behavior immediately. A significant positive relation was found between a mother's use of what Hoffman called "unqualified power assertion" and the child's hostility toward others, his power assertiveness, and his resistance to the attempts of others to influence him. Thus the conforming, docile child at home may be a tiger on the outside.

Strict discipline by parents often leads to prejudiced, antidemocratic attitudes in the child (Harris, Gough, & Martin, 1950; Lyle & Levitt, 1955). This is another example of the displacement of aggression. Severe and punitive parental treatment awakens hostile and aggressive impulses in the child. Since these impulses cannot be directed toward the parent, they are leveled against others who are made into scapegoats and innocent victims. Other factors, such as the extent of prejudice in the parent and the degree to which the child identifies with the parent, are also important in the explanation of prejudicial attitudes; still, it is true that frequent use of parental discipline sensitizes the child to power relations along a strong-weak or superior-inferior dimension. In a study of social attitudes among an upper-class group of children (Epstein & Komorita, 1965), those who perceived parental punitiveness as moderate in degree showed the greatest amount of social distance toward a working-class group, as compared with those perceiving parental punitiveness as mild or severe. This finding can be explained in terms of Bronfenbrenner's notion (1961) of "optimal level of control." Parents using either lax or severe methods of control have less influence on their children than those using moderate control, in this case, in instilling class values.

Let us round out this review with some general comments about discipline and child management. These are not oracular preachments to govern one's handling of children, but broad considerations that might profit a parent or a teacher to ponder.

Behavior is motivated. There is a reason, a cause for every behavior. Usually these causes are not apparent at the conscious level: the child does not know why he does the things he does. To pinch his arm and ask, "Why did you do it?" is preposterous. If he knew why, he probably would not have had to act as he did in the first place. Yet the adult must try to ascertain and understand the cause. What is the child trying to achieve? Is he trying to gain acceptance? Attention? Recognition? Affection? Meanness is not a cause but an interpretation.

Discipline is concerned too frequently with actions. Feelings are disregarded. The action or behavior may be stopped, but what happens to the feelings? These must be dealt with, too. The child needs the opportunity to express them. He will feel better if he can air his feelings and adults may learn something in the process. Since restrictions are frustrating, the child needs to give vent to his feelings. The young child usually does so; the older child learns not to, but this does him no good.

Because restrictions are frustrating, they should be kept to a minimum. The fewer there are the better. The simpler they are the better. And they should always be geared to the child's level of understanding.

Then, too, the adult might examine his own thoughts. What are his motives? Are his demands reasonable? Was the child's behavior truly not permissible, or was the adult's level of tolerance unusually low? Too great a price may be charged for conformity.

Finally, the parent-child relationship is unique; all authority, all the power, all the weight is invested in only one individual, the parent. The child must obey. For a parent to take advantage of such a relationship reflects little basic human understanding. Physical punishment is violence. It breeds a response detrimental to the individual and the society of which he is a part. Kindness, respect, and sensitivity, on the other hand, are qualities worth cultivating in a growing human being, and these may well develop out of the intimate relationship between parent and child. They flourish in a climate of mutual trust, and for mutual trust to be truly mutual, it takes the full cooperation of both parties.

Education for Parenthood

Since one's role as a parent is undoubtedly the most important he will ever assume in terms of its impact on another individual, it is, indeed, amazing that so little provision is made for educating people for parenthood. As Kruger (1973) has so cogently pointed out, "more emphasis is placed upon the satisfactory completion of a driver education course than on parenthood education" (p. 5). Although a few courses dealing with child development and family relations are presently offered in a small number of high schools, they enroll a very small proportion of the teen-age population. According to Kruger, "In the entire country in 1970–1971, only 37,987 young men were enrolled in classes in family relations and only 5,503 in child development courses. Fewer than 3000 were enrolled in classes covering the care and guidance of children" (p. 6).

As noted at the beginning of this chapter, parents often model their behavior after their own parents. This helps account for certain similarities between parents and offspring in the manner in which they function in the parent role. While such generational continuity is not necessarily bad, exposure to different ways of viewing children and their relationship and interaction with adults should lead to new perspectives and new insights regarding child-rearing, enabling an individual to discard negative approaches and incorrect conceptions of child development and replacing these with more positive methods and more accurate views.

The Office of Child Development and the Office of Education have established a joint Education for Parenthood program. A major thrust will be to develop an appropriate curriculum for high school courses which will combine classroom instruction with actual work with children. Large-scale testing of the program will be conducted during the 1973–1974 school year, with the goal of reaching 500 public school districts by September, 1973 (Marland, 1973).

On the basis of a survey of existing exemplary parent education programs focusing on the question, "What do young people need to know to enable them to become effective parents?," the following topics were identified as important:

> Biological factors of human reproduction and the influences of heredity and environment.
>
> Pregnancy and childbirth and prenatal and postnatal care for mothers, including the influences of maternal nutrition.
>
> Prenatal development of the child.
>
> Infant care, emphasizing nutrition, health, protection and safety of children.
>
> Child growth and development (physical; perceptual and cognitive; and personal and social development).
>
> Individual differences in children.
>
> The handicapped child, including such topics as prevention of handicaps and working with handicapped children.
>
> Creative activities for children, including study of play, developmental toys, art, music, and dance.
>
> Family structure and functions, including the influence of family environment on child behavior.
>
> Parental roles and responsibilities.
>
> Family planning and population growth.
>
> Community resources to aid in parenting.
>
> Child care arrangements.
>
> Skills required for effective work with children, including learning by observation and counseling and tutoring the young child.
>
> (Kruger, 1973, pp. 6–7)

Whenever an adult works with or interacts with children, he must deal also with the child within himself—with his own childhood. Thus it would seem that education for parenthood would lead to greater self-understanding. The "facts" of child development are important but of nearly equal importance are an adult's attitudes toward these facts and toward himself.

High school courses dealing with parenthood should be only one aspect of a community "education for parenthood" program. "In-service" courses for parents of all ages should be available as well. One of the present authors has conducted surveys of various groups of mothers, eliciting from them some of their worries, problems, and concerns regarding child-rearing and child behavior. He has been greatly impressed with the tremendous number of daily concerns voiced by these mothers. Furthermore, an undercurrent of helplessness and, at times, despair seems evident in their attitudes because of the lack of available resources to which they can turn for information and support. Our country has neglected too long its role in providing adequate education for parenthood programs and ongoing programs for parents. The child abuse statistics alone attest to some of the stresses and strains which accompany child-rearing. A nation can ill afford to ignore the pressing needs of parents as they attempt to function in the parent role. Since it seems unlikely that our society would choose to replace parents and family life with large-scale parent-surrogate institutions such as orphanages, then appropriate training and supportive services must be provided for parents to ensure environments which will foster the optimal physical and psychological development of our children.

SUMMARY

Parenthood involves a host of functions and duties, and imposes a variety of demands on those individuals who fill its role. Some parents are abler than others to meet these demands. Quite naturally these experience greater satisfaction in the parent role.

Many factors influence a parent's behavior, among them his own childhood experiences and the behavior and attitudes of his parents. Personality structure and current child-rearing fads also influence an individual's demeanor as a parent.

Three principal variables were explored, with the research relevant to the relation of each of these—parent personality, parent attitudes, and parent behavior—to the child's personality and adjustment presented.

Two main dimensions emerged from factor analytic studies of parent attitude scores and parent behavior ratings. One of them, acceptance versus rejection, assessed the parent's attitude toward the child. The other, autonomy versus control, related to parental attitudes toward child rearing.

In view of the present state of knowledge, it would seem that assessment of the broad psychological atmospheres in the home is more revealing of effects on the child than is information on specific child-rearing practices. However, the ultimate goal of parent-child research is the identification of specific aspects of the parents, the family, and the home that exert a significant psychological impact on the child.

The chapter also surveyed three factors of importance to understanding parent-child relationships: children's perceptions of their parents, identification, and discipline. The relationship between parent and child holds much in common with any relationship between two people. Mutual trust, mutual understanding, and mutual acceptance are imperative if the relationship is to be satisfying and rewarding to both.

REFERENCES

Adorno, T. W., Frenkel-Brunswik, E., Levinson, D. J., & Sanford, R. N. *The authoritarian personality.* New York: Harper, 1950.

Arasteh, J. Parenthood: Some antecedents and consequences: A preliminary survey of the mental health literature. *Journal of Genetic Psychology,* 1971, **118**, 179–202.

Ausubel, D. *Theory and problems of child development.* New York: Grune & Stratton, 1958.

Ausubel, D., Balthazar, E. E., Rosenthal, I., Blackmore, L. S., Schpoont, S. H., & Welkowitz, J. Perceived parent attitudes as determinants of children's ego structure. *Child Development,* 1954, **25**, 173–183.

Baldwin, A. L., Kalhorn, J., & Breese, F. Patterns of parent behavior. *Psychological Monographs,* 1945, **58**, No. 3.

Baldwin, A. L., Kalhorn, J., & Breese, F. The appraisal of parent behavior. *Psychological Monographs,* 1949, **63**, No. 4.

Bandura, A., & Huston, A. Identification as a process of incidental learning. *Journal of Abnormal and Social Psychology,* 1961, **63**, 311–318.

Bandura, A., Ross, D., & Ross, S. A comparative test of the status envy, social power, and the secondary-reinforcement theories of identificatory learning. *Journal of Abnormal and Social Psychology,* 1963, **67**, 527-534.

Bandura, A., & Walters, R. *Adolescent aggression.* New York: Ronald, 1959.

Bandura, A., & Walters, R. *Social learning and personality development.* New York: Holt, 1963.

Baumrind, D. Effects of authoritative parental control on child behavior. *Child Development,* 1966, **37**, 887-907.

Baumrind, D. Child care practices anteceding three patterns of preschool behavior. *Genetic Psychology Monographs,* 1967, **75**, 43–88.

Baumrind, D. Harmonious parents and their preschool children. *Developmental Psychology,* 1971, **4**, 99–102. (a)

Baumrind, D. Current patterns of parental authority. *Developmental Psychology Monograph,* 1971, **4**, No. 1, Part 2. (b)

Baumrind, D., & Black, A. Socialization practices associated with dimensions of competence in preschool boys and girls. *Child Development,* 1967, **38**, 291–327.

Becker, W. C., Peterson, D. R., Hellmer, L. A., Shoemaker, D. J., & Quay, H. C. Factors in parental behavior and personality as related to problem behavior in children. *Journal of Consulting Psychology,* 1959, **23**, 107–118.

Becker, W. C., Peterson, D. R., Luria, Z., Shoemaker, D. J., & Hellmer, L. A. Relations of factors derived from parent-interview ratings to behavior problems of five-year-olds. *Child Development,* 1962, **33**, 509–535.

Behrens, M. L. Child rearing and the character structure of the mother. *Child Development,* 1954, **25**, 225–238.

Bell, R. Retrospective attitude studies of parent-child relations. *Child Development,* 1958, **29**, 323–338.

Bell, R. Structuring parent-child interaction situations for direct observation. *Child Development,* 1964, **35**, 1009–1020.

Biller, H. The mother-child relationship and the father-absent boy's personality development. *Merrill–Palmer Quarterly,* 1971, **17**, 227–241.

Biller, H., & Bahm, R. Father absence, perceived maternal behavior, and masculinity of self-concept among junior high school boys. *Developmental Psychology,* 1971, **4**, 178–181.

Bing, E. Effect of childrearing practices on development of differential cognitive abilities. *Child Development,* 1963, **34**, 631–648.

Bogue, D. J. (Ed.), Mass communication and motivation for birth control. *Proceedings of the summer workshops at the University of Chicago.* Chicago: Community and Family Study Center, University of Chicago, 1967.

Brody, G. Relationship between maternal attitudes and behavior. *Journal of Personality and Social Psychology,* 1965, **2**, 317–323.

Bronfenbrenner, U. Toward a theoretical model for the analysis of parent-child relationships in a social context. In J. C. Glidewell (Ed.), *Parental attitudes and child behavior.* Springfield, Ill.: Thomas, 1961.

Bronson, W. C., Kalten, E. S., & Livson, N. Patterns of authority and affection in two generations. *Journal of Abnormal and Social Psychology,* 1959, **58**, 143–152.

Burchinal, L. G. Mothers' and fathers' differences in parental acceptance of children for controlled comparisons based on parental and family characteristics. *Journal of Genetic Psychology,* 1958, **92**, 103–110.

Burger, G., & Armentrout, J. A factor analysis of fifth and sixth graders reports of parental child-rearing behaviors. *Developmental Psychology,* 1971, **4**, 483.

Butman, J. W. Summary, conclusions, and implications. Final report to DHEW, Grant #028, and to the McGregor Foundation, Detroit, Michigan, 1965.

Clifford, E. Discipline in the home: A controlled observational study of parental practices. *Journal of Genetic Psychology,* 1959, **95**, 45–82.

Cohler, B., Weiss, J., & Grunebaum, H. Child-care attitudes and emotional disturbance among mothers of young children. *Genetic Psychology Monographs,* 1970, **82**, 3–47.

Coleman, R. W., Kris, E., & Provence, S. The study of variations of early parental attitudes. *Psychoanalytic Study of the Child,* 1953, **8**, 20–47.

Cox, S. Intrafamily comparison of loving-rejecting child-rearing practices. *Child Development,* 1970, **41**, 437–448.

Delhees, K., Cattell, R., & Sweney, A. The structure of parents' intrafamilial attitudes and sentiments measured by objective tests and a vector model. *Journal of Social Psychology,* 1970, **82**, 231–252.

Droppelman, L., & Schaefer, E. Boys' and girls' reports of maternal and paternal behavior. *Journal of Abnormal and Social Psychology,* 1963, **67**, 648–654.

Eisenberg, J., Henderson, R., Kuhlmann, W., & Hill, J. Six- and ten-year-olds' attribution of punitiveness and nurturance to parents and other adults. *Journal of Genetic Psychology,* 1967, **111**, 233–240.

Emmerich, W. Young children's discrimination of parent and child roles. *Child Development,* 1959, **30**, 403–419.

Emmerich, W. Family role concepts of children ages six to ten. *Child Development,* 1961, **32**, 609–624.

Epstein, R., & Komorita, S. Parental discipline, stimulus characteristics of outgroups, and social distance in children. *Journal of Personality and Social Psychology,* 1965, **2**, 416–420.

Erikson, E. H. *Childhood and society.* New York: Norton, 1950.

Fawcett, J. T. *Psychology and population.* New York: Population Council, 1970.

Freeberg, N., & Payne, D. Dimensions of parental practice concerned with cognitive development in the preschool child. *Journal of Genetic Psychology,* 1967, **111**, 245–261.

Friedman, A. S. The family and the female delinquent: An overview. In O. Pollak & A. S. Friedman (Eds.), *Family Dynamics and female sexual delinquency.* Palo Alto, Calif.: Science and Behavior Books, 1969.

Gardner, L. P. An analysis of children's attitudes toward fathers. *Journal of Genetic Psychology,* 1947, **70**, 3–28.

Giel, R., & Kidd, C. Some psychiatric observations on pregnancy in the unmarried student. *American Journal of Psychiatry,* 1965, **111**, 591–594.

Gray, S. Perceived similarity to parents and adjustment. *Child Development,* 1959, **30**, 91–107.

Hanvik, L. J., & Byrum, M. MMPI profiles of parents of child psychiatric patients. *Journal of Clinical Psychology,* 1959, **15**, 427–431.

Harris, D. B., Gough, H. G., & Martin, W. E. Children's ethnic attitudes. II. Relationship to parental beliefs concerning child training. *Child Development,* 1950, **21**, 169–181.

Harris, D. B., & Tseng, S. C. Children's attitudes toward peers and parents as revealed by sentence completion. *Child Development,* 1957, **28**, 401–411.

Harris, I. D. *Normal children and mothers.* Glencoe, Ill.: Free Press, 1959.

Hatfield, J., Ferguson, L., & Alpert, R. Mother-child interaction and the socialization process. *Child Development,* 1967, **38**, 365–414.

Hawkes, G. R., Burchinal, L. G., & Gardner, B. Pre-adolescents' views of some of their relations with their parents. *Child Development,* 1957, **28**, 393–399.

Heaps, R. Some relationships among children's perceptions of parental characteristics. *Journal of Genetic Psychology,* 1970, **117**, 7–11.

Herzog, E., & Sudia, C. Fatherless homes: A review of research. *Children,* 1968, **15**, 177–187.

Hess, R., & Shipman, V. Early experience and the socialization of cognitive modes in children. *Child Development,* 1965, **36**, 869–886.

Hetherington, E. M. Effects of paternal absence on sex-typed behaviors in Negro and white pre-adolescent males. *Journal of Personality and Social Psychology,* 1966, **4**, 87–91.

Hetherington, E. M., & Deur, J. The effects of father absence on child development. *Young Children,* 1971, **26**, 233–248.

Hoffman, L., Rosen, S., & Lippitt, R. Parental coerciveness, child autonomy, and child's role at school. *Sociometry,* 1960, **23**, 15–22.

Hoffman, L. W. The value of children, women's roles, and motivations for fertility. Unpublished paper, Workshop on developing and educating psychologists for work in the population area. Chapel Hill, N.C., 1971.

Hoffman, M. Power assertion by the parent and its impact on the child. *Child Development,* 1960, **31**, 129–143.

Hoffman, M. Identification and conscience development. *Child Development,* 1971, **42**, 1071–1082.

Hollenberg, E., & Sperry, M. Some antecedents of aggression and effects of frustration in doll play. *Personality,* 1951, **1**, 32–43.

Hurley, J., & Hohn, R. Shifts in child-rearing attitudes linked with parenthood and occupation. *Developmental Psychology,* 1971, **4**, 324–328.

Ingersoll, H. L. A study of the transmission of authority patterns in the family. *Genetic Psychology Monographs,* 1948, **38**, 225–302.

Jungreis, J. E. The sexually delinquent female: Observations in therapy. In O. Pollak & A. S. Friedman (Eds.), *Family dynamics and female sexual delinquency.* Palo Alto: Science and Behavior Books, 1969.

Kagan, J. Children's perceptions of parents. *Journal of Abnormal and Social Psychology,* 1956, **53**, 257–259.

Kagan, J., Hosken, B., & Watson, S. Child's symbolic conceptualization of parents. *Child Development,* 1961, **32**, 625–636.

Kagan, J., & Lemkin, J. The child's differential perception of parental attributes. *Journal of Abnormal and Social Psychology,* 1960, **61**, 440–447.

Kagan, J., & Moss, H. *Birth to maturity.* New York: Wiley, 1962.

Khlentzos, M., & Pagliaro, M. Observations from psychotherapy with unwed mothers. *American Journal of Orthopsychiatry,* 1965, **35**, 779–786.

Kruger, W. S. Education for parenthood and the schools. *Children Today,* 1973, **2**, 4–7.

Lessing, E., Zagorin, S., & Nelson, D. WISC subtest and IQ score correlates of father absence. *Journal of Genetic Psychology,* 1970, **117**, 181–195.

Levine, J., Fishman, C., & Kagan, J. Sex of child and social class as determinants of maternal behavior. Paper presented at the American Orthopsychiatry Association meetings, Washington, D.C., March, 1967.

Lorr, M., & Jenkins, R. L. Three factors in parent behavior. *Journal of Consulting Psychology,* 1953, **17**, 306–308.

Lyle, W. H., & Levitt, E. E. Punitiveness, authoritarianism, and parental discipline of grade school children. *Journal of Abnormal and Social Psychology,* 1955, **51**, 42–46.

Lynn, D. B. Sex differences in identification development. *Sociometry,* 1961, **24**, 372–383.

Maccoby, E. The taking of adult roles in middle childhood. *Journal of Abnormal and Social Psychology,* 1961, **63**, 493–503.

Margolis, M. The mother-child relationship in bronchial asthma. *Journal of Abnormal and Social Psychology,* 1961, **63**, 360–367.

Marland, S. P., Jr. Education for parenthood. *Children Today,* 1973, **2**, 3.

McCord, W., McCord, J., & Verden, P. Family relationships and sexual deviance in lower-class adolescents. *International Journal of Social Psychiatry,* 1962, **8**, 165–179.

Medinnus, G. The relation between several parent measures and the child's early adjustment to school. *Journal of Educational Psychology,* 1961, **52**, 153–156.

Medinnus, G. Delinquents' perception of their parents. *Journal of Consulting Psychology,* 1965, **29**, 592–593.

Medinnus, G., & Curtis, F. J. The relation between maternal self-acceptance and child acceptance. *Journal of Consulting Psychology,* 1963, **27**, 542–544.

Meltzer, H. Sex differences in children's attitudes to parents. *Journal of Genetic Psychology,* 1943, **62**, 311–326.

Meyers, R. R. Intrafamily relationships and pupil adjustment. *Teachers College Contributions to Education,* 1935, No. 651.

Milton, G. A. A factor analytic study of child-rearing behavior. *Child Development,* 1958, **29**, 381–392.

Moll, K. L., & Darley, F. L. Attitudes of mothers of articulatory-impaired and speech-retarded children. *Journal of Speech and Hearing Disorders,* 1960, **25**, 377–384.

Morris, W. W., & Nicholas, A. L. Intra-family personality configurations among children with primary behavior disorders and their parents: A Rorschach investigation. *Journal of Clinical Psychology,* 1950, **6**, 309–319.

Nash, J. The father in contemporary culture and current psychological literature. *Child Development,* 1965, **36**, 261–297.

Paulsen, M. Legal protections against child abuse. *Children,* 1966, **13**, 42–48.

Payne, D., & Mussen, P. Parent-child relations and father identification among adolescent boys. *Journal of Abnormal and Social Psychology,* 1956, **52**, 358–362.

Peterson, D. R., Becker, W. C., Hellmer, L. A., Shoemaker, D. J., & Quay, H. C. Parental attitudes and child adjustment. *Child Development,* 1959, **30**, 119–130.

Phillips, E. L. Parent-child similarities in personality disturbances. *Journal of Clinical Psychology,* 1951, **7**, 188–190.

Pollak, O. Family structure: Its implications for mental health. In O. Pollak & A. S. Friedman (Eds.), *Family dynamics and female sexual delinquency.* Palo Alto: Science and Behavior Books, 1969.

Pollak, O., & Friedman, A. S. (Eds.), *Family dynamics and female sexual delinquency.* Palo Alto: Science and Behavior Books, 1969.

Rabban, M. Sex-role identification in young children in two diverse social groups. *Genetic Psychology Monographs,* 1950, **42**, 81–158.

Radke, M. J. *The relation of parental authority to children's behavior and attitudes.* Minneapolis: University of Minnesota Press, 1946.

Reppucci, N. Parental education, sex differences, and performance on cognitive tasks among two-year-old children. *Developmental Psychology,* 1971, **4**, 248–253.

Roe, A., & Siegelman, M. A Parent-Child Relations questionnaire. *Child Development,* 1963, **34**, 355–369.

Roff, M. A factorial study of the Fels Parent Behavior Scales. *Child Development,* 1949, **20**, 29–45.

Rothbart, M., & Maccoby, E. Parents' differential reactions to sons and daughters. *Journal of Personality and Social Psychology,* 1966, **4**, 237–243.

Sanford, N. The dynamics of identification. *Psychological Review,* 1955, **62**, 106–118.

Santrock, J. W. Paternal absence, sex typing, and identification. *Developmental Psychology,* 1970, **2**, 264–272.

Schaefer, E. A circumplex model for maternal behavior. *Journal of Abnormal and Social Psychology,* 1959, **59**, 226–235.

Schaefer, E. Children's reports of parental behavior: An inventory. *Child Development,* 1965, **36**, 413–424.

Schaefer, E., & Bayley, N. Maternal behavior, child behavior, and their intercorrelations from infancy through adolescence. *Monographs of the Society for Research in Child Development,* 1963, **28**, No. 3.

Schludermann, E., & Schludermann, S. Replicability of factors in children's report of parent behavior (CRPBI). *Journal of Psychology,* 1970, **76**, 239–249.

Sears, P. Doll-play aggression in normal young children: Influence of sex, age, sibling status, father's absence. *Psychological Monographs,* 1951, **65**, No. 6.

Sears, P. Child-rearing factors related to playing of sex-typed roles. *American Psychologist,* 1953, **8**, 431. (Abstract)

Sears, R. R. Relation of fantasy aggression to interpersonal aggression. *Child Development,* 1950, **21**, 5–6.

Sears, R. R., Maccoby, E., & Levin, H. *Patterns of child rearing.* Evanston, Ill.: Row, Peterson, 1957.

Siegelman, M. Evaluation of Bronfenbrenner's questionnaire for children concerning parental behavior. *Child Development,* 1965, **36**, 163–174. (a)

Siegelman, M. College student personality correlates of early parent-child relationship. *Journal of Consulting Psychology,* 1965, **29**, 558–564. (b)

Sutton-Smith, B., Rosenberg, B. G., & Landy, F. Father-absence effects in families of different sibling compositions. *Child Development,* 1968, **39**, 1213–1221.

Symonds, P. M. *The psychology of parent-child relationships.* New York: Appleton–Century–Crofts, 1939.

Symonds, P. M. *The dynamics of parent-child relationships.* New York: Appleton–Century–Crofts, 1949.

Whiting, J. W. M. Resource mediation and learning by identification. In I. Iscoe & H. Stevenson (Eds.), *Personality development in children.* Austin: University of Texas Press, 1960. Pp. 112–126.

Wolf, R. The identification and measurement of environmental process variables related to intelligence. Unpublished doctoral dissertation, University of Chicago, 1964.

Wolking, W., Dunteman, G., & Bailey, J. Multivariate analyses of parents' MMPI's based on the psychiatric diagnoses of their children. *Journal of Consulting Psychology,* 1967, **31**, 521–524.

Zunich, M. Relationship between maternal behavior and attitudes toward children. *Journal of Genetic Psychology,* 1962, **100**, 155–165.

section IV

societal influences on socialization

Although the family in Western culture imparts most of the society's values and beliefs and plays the largest role in molding personality and behavior, other social forces also make their impression on the child. The child's agemates, his school, and other outside influences including the community, religious experience, and exposure to the mass media all at times reinforce parental socialization. This is especially true of the school. At other times, the influence of these outside forces runs counter to that of the family. A child's peers, for example, often counter parental pressures, especially if the parents' behaviors and attitudes are deviant.

In this section, we shall consider these forces whose influence depends, to a large degree, on the adequacy of the parent-child relationship. Chapter 11 concerns the child and his agemates. Chapter 12 covers the school, and Chapter 13 is devoted to the community, the church, and the mass media. If parents are neglectful or so punitive that the child cannot have close relations with them, the influence of these social forces outside the home increases. How great an increase is determined by both the personality of the child and the behavior of the parents.

It seems reasonable to believe that the social influences forming the substance of this section are generally secondary in import to the family. Moreover, their effect is neither as deleterious as is sometimes maintained in the case of peers and the mass media nor as beneficial as is sometimes assumed in the case of school, school books, and religious instruction. More likely, these forces interacting with one another and with the family within the setting of the culture are each ambiguous in impact. Sometimes they conflict with each other, sometimes they reinforce each other. At times they dispose the child toward adaptive behavior, at other times toward maladaptive behavior.

chapter 11

the child among his peers

chapter 11

the child among his peers

chapter 11

the child among his peers

The society of children is clearly a primary group. As such, it features close, face-to-face contact, the ability to regulate or constrain the behavior of its members, and psychological support for them. In most cases, other than the family, it is the only primary group to which a child belongs. Obviously this society is of great significance in shaping a child's beliefs and behaviors. Yet psychologists have not flooded this important area with research. Indeed, far more is known about parent-child relationships, however vague this knowledge may be, than about the interaction of children with other children. Nevertheless, let us look into three facets of children's groups: their change in degree of involvement and type of activity, the question of acceptance by peers, and the functions such groups serve in the socialization process.

AGE CHANGES IN PEER INVOLVEMENT

The early developmental tasks of children are primarily phenomena of a maturational kind. Such things as the development of speech and locomotion result, in large part, from physical and motor maturation. As age advances, the types of developmental tasks change, becoming essentially social in character. The socialization process increases in importance; through it, the infant, terribly egocentric in its demands and unable to suffer delay or interference, ultimately acquires concern for others and becomes able to postpone or even reject gratification at someone else's expense. How is this socialization reflected in the changing interactions of the child with his agemates, and how do these interactions contribute to the molding of the end product, the human adult?

For many reasons, the young child does not interact too well with peers. Some of the more important ones are his rather greater distractability, his lower tolerance of frustration, his lesser ability to endure delay of gratification, and his inferior skill in communication. All these deficiencies may be related to the young child's inability to "take the role of the other." Because of a poorly developed capacity to discern the moods, motives, and feelings of others, the young child runs into the inevitable conflicts arising from social interaction. To put oneself in someone else's shoes or to empathize does much to reduce these difficulties.

Take this example. The mother is frantically attempting to cook dinner and at the same time cope with a two-year-old son with a cold who is lying on the kitchen floor, kicking his feet in the midst of a temper tantrum. The five-year-old daughter picks this moment to demand that her mother read a story, thus revealing her inability to "take the role of the other" and see the world at this juncture through the eyes of her mother. The two-year-old cannot be dealt with by arbitration; actually, as soon as he has been fed he will probably calm down anyway. But the five-year-old has come quite some way toward social maturity although this is not evident at the moment. If told, however, "I'm busy right now but I'll read you a story later; why don't you see if you can get your brother interested in something," she *may* respond maturely. The child is thus along the way to developing skills of empathy and in a few years may even be of some help to the mother in avoiding domestic crises of this sort.

From this, one can see that a pair of two-year-olds will engage in a fair amount of combat, since their personal needs generally cannot stand delay or compromise. By the time they are five, compromise and arbitration become possible, although usually these are not attempted until the efforts of either child to assert his rights have failed. While caring for a pair of five-year-olds, one of the writers kept track of the number of times they fought, made up, and reached a compromise solution to the problem engendering the conflict. In the course of the afternoon, this sequence occurred 14 times, even though both children were bright and pleasant, loved one another dearly, and both were having a "good day." Such activity is doubtless hard on the parent, but is probably of considerable value to the child since in the process he learns several things—to take the role of the other and show concern for the other's wishes, to delay gratification, to arbitrate difficulties, and to achieve compromises at his own expense in order to continue a desired activity and association.

As Barker and Wright (1955) and Anderson (1948) have emphasized, there is a tremendous amount of repetition of experience during childhood. Estimated quite conservatively, five-year-old children in free play enter into conflict with their agemates at least 20 times a day and manage to resolve most of these clashes successfully. Multiplied by 365 days, these figures yield a total of 7300 annual conflicts between children of the same age. No wonder most of us learn something of the art of diplomacy over the years!

Through growth of conceptual power and social skill, partly as a result of interaction with age equals, the child is able to increase still further his participation with his peers. This has been demonstrated by Parten's study (1929) of children's play. Because it involved one of the first uses of time sampling, the Parten project is of methodological interest besides having provided valuable information on child behavior. Over many brief intervals, Parten observed the play behaviors of children ranging in age from slightly under 2 to 4 years and 11 months and we saw that she could categorize this play according to amounts of social involvement. These were her categories (see also Figure 11-1):

Unoccupied Behavior—The child apparently is not playing at all, at least not in the usual sense, but occupies himself with watching anything which happens to be of momentary interest. When there is nothing exciting taking place, he plays with his own body, gets on and off chairs, just stands around, follows the teacher, or sits in one spot glancing around the room.

Solitary Play—The child plays alone and independently with toys that are different from those used by the children within speaking distance and makes no effort to get close to or speak to the other children. His interest is centered upon his own activity, and he pursues it without reference to what others are doing.

Onlooker Behavior—The child spends most of his time watching the others play. He often talks to the playing children, asks questions, or gives suggestions, but does not enter into the play himself. He stands or sits within speaking distance of the group so that he can see and hear all that is taking place. Thus he differs from the unoccupied child, who notices anything that happens to be exciting and is not especially interested in groups of children.

Parallel Play—The child plays independently, but the activity he chooses naturally brings him among other children. He plays with toys which are like those which the children around him are using, but he plays with the toys as he sees fit and does not try to influence the activity of the children near him. Thus he plays beside rather than with the other children (cf. solitary play above).

Associative Play—The child plays with other children. There are borrowing and lending of play material; following one another with trains and wagons; mild attempts to control which children may or may not play in the groups. All engage in similar if not identical activity; there is no division of labor and no organization of activity. Each child acts as he wishes,

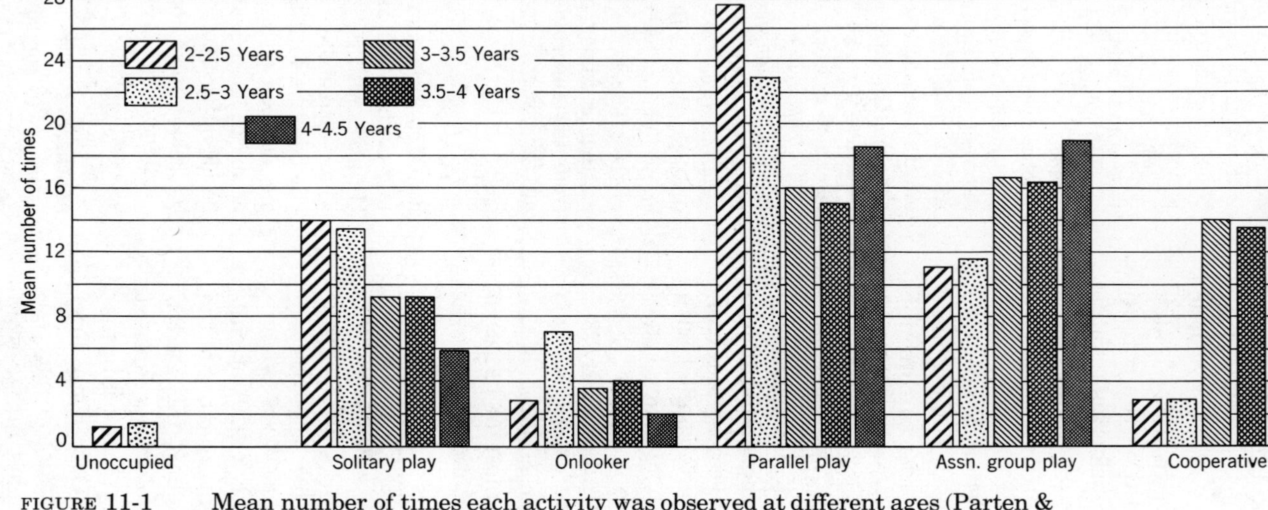

FIGURE 11-1 Mean number of times each activity was observed at different ages (Parten & Newhall, 1943, p. 517).

does not subordinate his interests to the group.

Cooperative or Organized Supplementary Play—The child plays in a group that is organized for the purpose of making some material product, of striving to attain some competitive goal, of dramatizing situations of adult or group life, or of playing formal games. There is a marked sense of belonging or not belonging to the group. The control of the group situation is in the hands of one or two members, who direct the activity of the others. The goal as well as the method of attaining it necessitates a division of labor, the taking of different roles by the various group members, and the organization of activity so that the efforts of one child are supplemented by those of another (Parten & Newhall, 1943).

Though increasingly interested in his peers, as seen in the development of parallel play, the young child does not have enough imaginative, role playing, arbitrational, or compromising skill to interact to any large degree at the more complex and intimate level of cooperative play. Interest in peers occurs early, but acquisition of the necessary skills requires time and practice. Developed largely through play, these skills open the door to future play and interaction of a more highly involved kind.

In the growing child, interest in peers awakens first and is followed by increasing interaction with them. From the greater interaction come improved social skills that in turn lead to even more interaction. Children who do not seek this interaction, who prefer adult company, are probably left behind more and more in their social learning, and are more often rejected by their peers (Marshall & McCandless, 1957).

From the one-year-old, uninterested in other one-year-olds and unable to maintain friendly contact with them because of a deficiency in social skill, the child becomes a two-year-old, who is now more interested in his peers but is still incapable of compromising his own needs sufficiently to sustain friendly or cooperative relations for any length of time. By five the child has become fully involved in the world of agemates and has made great gains in acquiring social adeptness. Later on in childhood and adolescence, through a codification of rules and a genuine feeling for one another, the neighborhood band emerges as a remarkably cohesive and influential primary group that performs many functions in the socialization process.

The process by which the peer "in-group" becomes such an important force in determining behavior is described in the classic "Robber's Cave" experiment of Sherif, Harvey, White, Hood, and Sherif (1961). This study was conducted at a boy's camp. The boys spent some time together in camp before beginning the experiment proper, which allowed them time to establish friendships. Then, after friendships had developed and groups coalesced, they were divided into two groups, cutting across friendship choices whenever possible, so that friends were on opposing teams. The two groups saw very little of each other except when meeting in competition. Prior cross-group friendships ended, and members of each team expressed real bitterness toward the other team. Social ties within each group became extremely strong. Finally, when the two groups were almost at the point of battle, Sherif and his associates provided situations of real importance to the boys in which cooperation between the two groups was necessary. After cooperative experiences had occurred, rivalry and animosity decreased markedly. Having an external enemy makes for strong ties within a group; cooperating with the enemy decreases hostility toward the outsider and decreases the strength of ties within the group as well.

That acceptance by one's peers is rewarding is demonstrated in the tremendous effort made by children to establish themselves when joining a new group of peers. Since the extent to which a child is involved with and accepted by his peers varies, the influence of the society of agemates also varies from child to child. It is to the personal qualities associated with such acceptance by peers that the discussion now moves.

ACCEPTANCE BY PEERS

The measure most often used to learn the degree to which an individual is accepted by others is the sociometric method devised by Moreno (1934). The device is simple. One merely asks a group of individuals a question, of which the following are typical:

> Whom would you like to have sit next to you in this classroom? (asked of sixth-grade children)
>
> Whom would you trust to fly at your wing position? (asked of a group of fighter pilots)
>
> Who is your best friend? (asked of kindergarten children)

How often a particular individual is chosen may be considered a measure of how much esteem he has in the group. Questions might be phrased negatively, but generally are not. The mere posing of a negative question such as "Whom would you least like to have sit next to you?" might serve to increase the overt rejection of the child, once his classmates compared notes. Therefore the actively rejected and the social isolate generally cannot be separated and studied as "types" in sociometric studies.

When choices are not limited to a specific group, the sociometric method can turn up information on the group's cohesiveness. For example, if Sunday school children were asked to name their best friends, few choices might be within the Sunday school group. Thus it would not be a very significant social group in the eyes of its members. On the other hand, if members of an informal, neighborhood group of peers were requested to name their best friends, most choices would fall within the society, for groups of peers have a great amount of cohesiveness and solidarity.

Sociometric studies also provide some indication of group morale and single out children within the group who need help to achieve a satisfactory adjustment. Figure 11-2 contains two sociograms of the same group of children. Note the change in the atmosphere of the group from October to March as the school year advanced. The number of isolates declined, the cliques disintegrated, and friendship choices increased.

A major reason for using measures of this sort is to ascertain the relative "healthiness" of a group. This healthiness is based on the satisfaction received by group members. What, then, happens to a group plagued by poor morale? If the group is a fighter squadron, it might be best to disband it and distribute its members among other groups, since their chances of physical survival would not be great if the original group remained intact. Dissolution of the group or removal of some members may also be a solution in children's groups. This applies especially to a younger child who suffers rejection or who is ignored.

Anderson (1956) said that one could not predict with any great amount of accuracy the adjustment or acceptance of a younger child, say one below the age of five. A child ignored within one group might be a highly accepted leader in another. However, this becomes less likely with increases in age. Accidental circumstances lose their importance; consistency in behavior gains; and the learning of social roles continues. The older rejected child is not likely to benefit greatly from transfer to another group, because he has developed certain roles and response tendencies that will probably persist in a new environment and lead to his rejection there. For this child, it might be preferable to teach him the skills valued by the original group, as was done by Jack (1934) and Page (1936), or to teach him mature responses, as was done by Keister and Updegraff (1937). In these areas social maturity is an important component of success.

Another rather widely employed measure of social acceptance is the "guess who" technique, first developed fully by Tryon (1939). To various classrooms of children aged 12 and 15, she put a number of questions such as, "Who always acts grown up?" By combining the "guess who" nominations with sociometric data on popularity, she discovered the traits and characteristics linked to popularity in boys and girls at the two age levels. In the eyes of the 12-year-olds, the ideal boy was aggressive, boisterous, unkempt, and, most important, skilled at games. The ideal girl, to the 12-year-olds, was friendly but demure and docile in social behavior, had quiet humor, and conformed to adult standards. At 15, the popular traits in boys did not change much from 12; the major emphasis was still on game skills. However, boisterousness and unkempt appearance were no longer positive virtues and some poise in dealing with girls became necessary. Meanwhile, the girl now had two highly acceptable new roles. First, she had to be a "girl's girl," a buoyant, rather aggressive pal of both boys and girls. The second was the role of the sophisticated and glamorous *femme fatale*. The demure conformist of 12 was now looked upon in a highly unfavorable light. Thus girls may have greater problems than boys in developing a consistent concept of the self. The role most rewarded at 12 and therefore most likely to be emulated leads to social defeat at 15.

More recent research (Tuddenham, 1951) has indicated the same clusters of traits related to boy and girl popularity, but with the shifts away from the "little lady" and the unkempt, boisterous boy occurring roughly by the age of 10. The pattern of socialization apparently had not changed but the sequence had accelerated.

Factors in Acceptance

Many personal characteristics of individuals affect their social acceptance or rejection. Discovery of these characteristics has various uses. First, it helps to solve the practical problem of enabling children to find some measure of acceptance. Second, it permits some inference about the values and orientation of a group from the personality traits it prizes.

Social Maturity. The prime requisite for social acceptance in childhood—and adulthood, for that matter—is social maturity as defined by the groups to which the individual belongs. Childhood is a time of sharp gradations of age, perhaps because age alone tells so much about the social behavior of a child. The following dialogue is not unfamiliar among children. Here *chronological age* affects social maturity:

George: Hi. My name is George.
Bill: Hi. My name is Bill.
George: How old are you?
Bill: Eight, going on nine (he had his eighth birthday last week). How old are you?
George: Nine, going on ten.

Both George and Bill enjoy playing with older kids, say 12-year-olds, and hold younger kids, say six-year-olds, in kindly contempt. There may be a sound reason

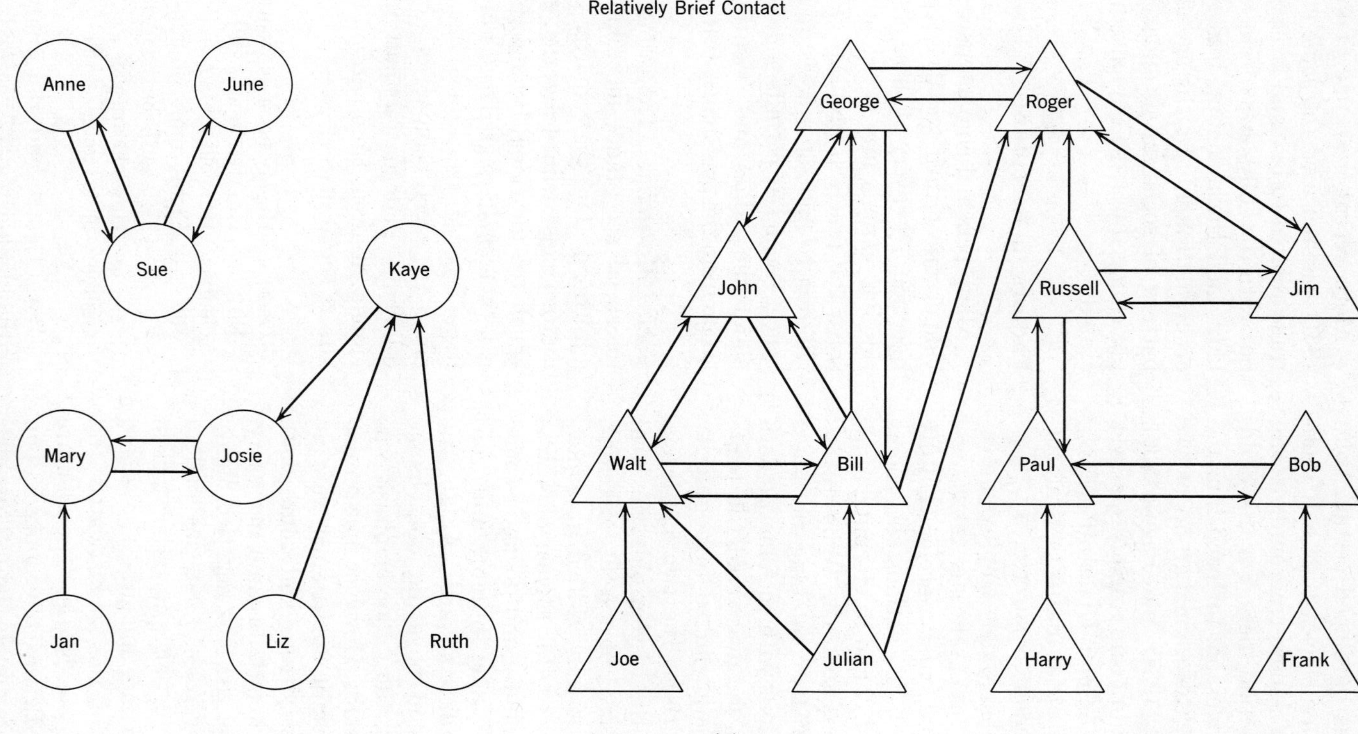

(a)

FIGURE 11-2 Changes in sociometric structure as length of time in contact increases.

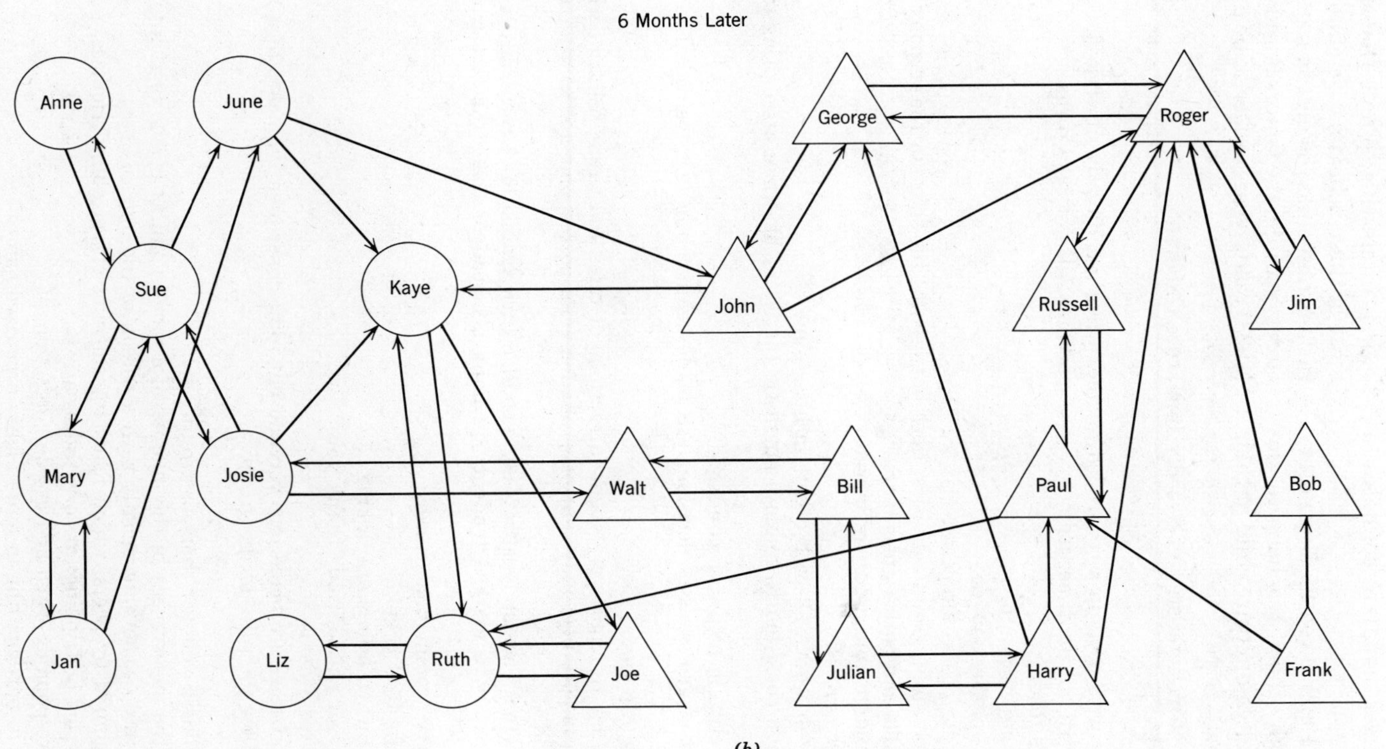

(b)

FIGURE 11-2 *(Continued)*

for this. Social maturity and game skills vary with age; thus, playing with older but not younger children connotes a learning situation.

Medinnus (1962) asked 25 elementary and junior-high-school teachers to describe the socially immature child in their respective grades. Table 11-1 lists those characteristics mentioned most often.

It is interesting to note that although most of these behaviors are child to child rather than child to adult in nature, they closely parallel the factors found by Koch (1933) many years earlier to be predictive

TABLE 11-1 Characteristics of Socially Immature Children*

Grades 1–3:

Does not play with peers in a controlled manner when not directly supervised.
Wants to be "It" all the time; jealousy when playing; will not take turns.
Will not share readily.
Withdraws from the group.
Inconsiderate–pushes shoves.
Lacks respect for others' property.
Does not cooperate in group activities; does not assume his share of the responsibility.
Interrupts; talks and bothers neighbors.
Plays with children younger than himself.

Grades 4–6:

Does not play or work well with others in his group:
(*a*) Picks fights; consistently employs pugilistic tactics rather than attempting to "talk it out."
(*b*) Uncooperative in planning games.
(*c*) Drops out of games when decisions are made against him (e.g., being called "out" in baseball).
(*d*) Wants his own way.
Tattles; tendency to report very slight infractions of rules and wrong behavior which is of little actual importance; judgment of wrong behavior corresponds to the evaluation of a younger child.
Rapid changes in friendship loyalties–i.e., a sudden turn against one's seemingly best friend.
Extreme shyness with marked tendency to hang his head or cover the face when asked questions.
Does not observe common courtesies:
(*a*) Walks in front of people.
(*b*) Interrupts when others are talking.
(*c*) Does not use "please" and "thank you."
Lacks respect for others.
Child feels that rules are made for everyone but him; consequently, makes own rules and does not follow the rules of the group.

Grades 7–9:

Plays with children younger than his group.
Interested in the opposite sex in the manner of a much younger person (e.g., would rather play tag than do something socially with a person of the opposite sex).
Child often ignored by peers, which leads to: showing off, giggling, grimaces, pushing or poking, slapping or tripping; or to withdrawal.
Hesitancy in responding when addressed or questioned.
Has difficulty in participating in more highly organized games.
Takes no responsibility for own conduct (must be reminded to be quiet, sit down, etc.).

*From Medinnus, 1962.

of unpopularity among preschool children. The following behavioral characteristics correlated negatively with popularity: the tendencies to play alone, to refuse or ignore the requests of other children, to attack other children or offer resistance to their attacks, to escape from undesirable situations, and to dawdle. Basically, social acceptance appears to be a reflection of social maturity.

Like chronological age, *mental age* is involved in social maturity. The diagnosis of mental deficiency stems from social competence. Thus a person of IQ 50 who behaved in a socially acceptable manner would not ordinarily be termed mentally defective, whereas another of IQ 100 who disclosed gross social incompetence might very well be considered so (Doll, 1935, 1941, Heber, 1959). Then, too, as the Terman study of genius (Terman et al., 1925) indicated, the association of popularity with high IQ (presumably indicative of social maturity in most cases), irrespective of chronological age, can be quite conclusively demonstrated. But this relation has an end point. In the opinion of Hollingworth (1942), as we have seen in Chapter 6, children above IQ 155 are neither social nor antisocial. Rather, they are asocial in their adjustment to their peers, apparently because they operate a different conceptual frame of reference.

Sex. Social maturity is not the only factor entering into acceptance by one's peers. One of the most potent determinants of how well one child is accepted by another during most of childhood is the sex of the children in question. In childhood sex cleavage in friendship is marked (Tuddenham, 1952). This cleavage is so readily observable that it becomes a defense, and may actually have been the basis of Freud's idea of latency —that once a child has rejected the parent of the opposite sex as a love object, it has also rejected all members of that sex until reaching an adult level of sexuality. Girls initially reject boys who, after several years of rejection, finally retaliate by rejecting girls. By early high-school years, girls again begin to accept boys, but boys, either because of social insensitivity or slower maturity, continue to reject girls for several more years (Harris & Tseng, 1957). Generally, these data show, girls are more rejecting than boys, turning away from other girls and parents as well as from boys. Because this also implies some rejection of themselves, girls are probably less satisfied by their roles and have lower morale, at least in Western culture at the present time.

Body build plays a surprisingly large role in social acceptance among boys; even at a relatively young age they assign favorable traits to mesomorphic (athletically built) boys, and unfavorable traits, either of a passive or aggressive character, to boys not of this body type (Staffieri, 1967). Perhaps this assignment is related to the fact that mesomorphs are reportedly more active (Walker, 1962, 1963), and young people place a high positive value on sheer activity level (Kuhlen & Lee, 1943).

Social Class. Class and caste also play a part in acceptance by peers. They begin to have considerable effect during childhood (Bonney, 1944) and increase their influence as children become more accurate judges of social class position (Hollingshead, 1949). Both class and color play large roles in acceptance partly because propinquity or closeness is an important element in determining choice of friendship. Since the chance of any two children being neighbors results in part from class and race, it is not surprising to find that the more stable choices of friendship in later childhood and adolescence depend somewhat on these two factors. This type of segregation on the basis of area of residence, does much to keep class and race differences in values (Ausubel, 1958, p. 433) and interests (Wilson, 1959) in existence. In communities in flux, as opposed to established communities, class barriers in contact play a lesser role (Udry, 1960).

Acceptance by peers is not all good, nor is rejection all bad. Achievement as an adult apparently depends to some extent on lack of involvement with peers (McCurdy, 1957). Yet a continuing rejection by one's peers seems to predict eventual maladjustment better than does an adult's diagnosis of "problem child" (Roff, 1961). The term *peer group* implies that one is being judged by his equals. These judges are harsh but generally accurate, perhaps because they judge less from the prejudices of society and more from individual merit than does the adult world.

CHILDREN'S GROUPS AND THE SOCIALIZATION PROCESS

Involvement with the Peer Group: Cultural and National Differences

Certain conditions must be met before a deep involvement with the peer group is likely to occur. These conditions include the amount of dependence on agemates, amount of contact with agemates, and autonomy from adult control. For example, among primitive (nonliterate) societies, greater contact with and dependence on agemates is seen in war-oriented cultures than in peaceful cultures; this is because in the former, one's agemates are likely to be fellow warriors during a lifetime military career (e.g., see the sections "Puberty" and "War and Peacemaking" in Mead & Calas, 1953). Perhaps for this reason, cultures with aggressive gods (warlike cultures) place greater value on independence from parents (autonomy), and presumably encourage greater peer influence than do cultures with more benevolent and pacifistic gods (Lambert, Triandis, & Wolf, 1959). Within contemporary societies, rich, industrial cultures have less use for child labor than older, agrarian cultures, and allow young persons more time for leisure, hence more time for peer contact.

Boehm (1957) offered evidence to show that autonomy from adult control was attained a good deal earlier in the United States than in Europe (in her study, Switzerland). She believed that American parents were less secure, less sure that their way was the right way; therefore they yielded more readily than European parents to pressure from their children. In the United States also the peer group was stronger than in Europe because most Europeans permitted far less interaction between agemates (see McKenney, 1953). Through greater contact, the American society of peers acquired more clearly articulated values and extra ability both to support and coerce members of the group. Under heavier peer pressure the American child encountered weaker parental resistance as he adapted to the demands of his friends. It is indeed possible that changes in the orientation of American culture over a period of time, as well as differences between American and European cultures, may result in part from the growing socializing role of peers in this country from generation to generation and from the greater function served by the peer society in the United States than in Europe.

In Western Europe, the United States, and Canada, a young person's peer-group involvement appears generally to be viewed as an index of his rebellion against adult values. Other cultures use the peer group as an ally in the inculcation of adult-held values. This appears to be the case in the age-graded child-rearing of the Israeli kibbutz (collective farm), where adult supervision guides a socialization process in which the peer group gains in significance at the expense of adult (especially parent) agents of socialization (Faigin, 1958; Spiro, 1958). In an analysis of child-rearing in the U.S.S.R., Bronfenbrenner (1962) notes that, especially in the school, the peer group is the chief source of values, of rewards, and of discipline. The adult in charge of a group of children establishes the nature of the behaviors to be rewarded, and does the rewarding, but does so through the group and on the basis of group effort. Children in a given row within the classroom are jointly responsible for one another's actions, so that if a child is falling behind in learning fractions, the row leader will provide tutoring either by himself or by the math expert of the row. It is advantageous to the row that all members of this "collective" learn fractions. If the laggard is inept, he is tutored; if lazy, he is disciplined by his fellow collective members. The rows that perform best are given recognition in the form of praise and rewards (special privileges) within the classroom. In the same way, classroom competes with classroom and school with school. Members of each collective (row, classroom, school) discipline and tutor one another, and are direct (teachers the indirect) source of reinforcement. The peer group in this case, as in that of the kibbutz, has as values such traits as responsibility and ability to delay gratification, which are more often part of the adult than the peer value system in most Western culture; thus the peer culture and adults need not be at odds in terms of values and role prescriptions. Bronfenbrenner's paper spells out procedures used to cause peer values to reflect more accurately the culture as a whole.

Involvement with the Peer Group: Individual Differences

Absence of the father from the home produces a situation in which the boy generally has no masculine figure to serve as a model for his behavior. It seems clear that father absence produces a somewhat "feminine" boy when it occurs early (Hetherington, 1966; Lynn & Sawrey, 1959). This "feminine" boy, aware that he is not competent in the masculine role, later develops strong ties with his male peer group, and, in adolescence and early adulthood shows a somewhat uneasy overcompensatory delinquent or "sociopathic" masculinity (Siegman, 1966). Father absence leads to a greater identification with the peer culture, and this overidentification seems likely to lead to delinquent behavior in America, although, as noted above it may not lead to the same problems in some of the other groups within the Western culture. The data suggesting that early "feminization" leads to later excessive involvement with and acceptance of the peer culture by boys allows one to make certain other predictions, as yet untested. Brim (1958) reanalyzed the data in a series of studies reported by Koch (e.g., see Koch, 1956) and demonstrated that boys with older sisters, in two-child families, are more feminine in early childhood than are boys in any other age-sex combination. If the idea of later overcompensatory masculinity holds, then boys with older sisters should develop the closest ties with the male peer group in later childhood and adolescence and should show the highest degree of delinquent behavior of any of the sex-by-age comparison groups (boy-boy, girl-girl, girl-boy; older versus younger in each sex pairing) at a later age.

During childhood, the peer group of equals is remarkably cohesive. This cohesion or solidarity is voluntary. Clearly the group must provide something of value to hold its members in line. What do peers offer?

Normalizing or Leveling Influence

The effect of other children on the development and adjustment of any one child is, first of all, to reduce the influence of parental idiosyncrasy in treatment. This normalizing or leveling influence, making children more similar to one another than might be expected, may prove detrimental to desirable goals. Children raised in homes free of racial prejudice, for example, learn quite quickly from their peers all the forms of bigotry to be found in the culture. Even if they also learn—perhaps more rapidly—to keep these ideas to themselves around home, certain damage has been done. They have been "normalized." A leveling process has occurred. To some moderate degree, they now hold the prejudices common to the culture.

Literature contains many illustrations of the shock of being removed from a tender and affectionate home into the rough-and-tumble society of peers. It seems equally clear that peers can moderate the influence of brutal, psychotic, neurotic, or otherwise deviant parents. Peer society provides a haven, at least for a time, from the unrealistic and arbitrary demands of the family. The child escapes temporarily into a world of agemates, where he undergoes basically the same experiences as all other children of his age. He becomes a member of the "gang" for better or worse—depending on what his home life was like before initiation.

In a similar vein, Harlow (1963) found that infant monkeys deprived of mothering nevertheless developed normally as long as they were allowed considerable contact with agemates during their "childhood" and "adolescence." Apparently, the influence of peers has as normalizing an effect on monkeys as on humans.

Only children appear to be deviant more often in both positive and negative directions than children with siblings. This may be because their parents' attentions, whether wholesome or harmful, are not diverted in any way. Similarly, children reared outside the world of agemates are more variable than other children, probably because they are more exclusively the products of parental pressures. Thus, although peers may teach prejudice to the unprejudiced and may divert genius, the "normalizing" effect of this society on child adjustment and behavior is generally good and ameliorative. Through it, the unjustly treated learns something of justice and the rejected finds acceptance.

Identification

To Freud (1935), the infant in his first groping thoughts believed that he was all powerful and that the world was merely an extension of himself. Piaget demonstrated (1954) that Freud's speculations had observable and testable validity. The child learned at about six months that he and the external world were not one. This was the point at which, in Freudian psychology, the ego or concept of self developed. Once having separated himself from the rest of the world, the child became aware of not being omnipotent, but rather of being impotent—a powerless creature in a threatening world.

Ausubel (1958) speculated that in response to this awareness of impotence, to escape the fear associated with helplessness, the child identified with his parents, the all-powerful beings of his universe, and thus vicariously regained a feeling of power and control. Some parents did not allow the child to identify himself with them; then the child remained anxious and fearful. Although Ausubel did not suggest it, the child denied this vicarious control might, as he got older, show greater concern for compulsively ordering and thus controlling his small world than might the undenied child. Gaining some measure of power and control in this way seems possible, but the cost is likely to be steep in terms of psychic well-being. If parents deny a child vicarious power, Ausubel suggested, it may be obtained through identification with one's peers. Research conducted by Lesser and Abelson (1959) provided experimental support for the notion that a child who has not identified closely with parents will be more likely to identify strongly with peers. It is probably for this reason that close parent-child ties serve to "insulate" the child from delinquency, high-crime areas (Scarpitti, Murray, Simon, & Reckless, 1960).

Children identifying with peers should differ from others whose main identification is with parents. Such children should be lacking in inner controls, or conscience, which to a considerable degree depend for their development on the child's love relationship with his parents (Hoffman, 1962). These controls are unlikely to evolve if the parents reject the child's efforts to identify. To use Riesman's (1950) distinction, such children should be more "other-directed" than "inner-directed." In Freudian terminology, this type of individual should have an *externalized superego;* that is, his standards would vary with the standards of the group to which he belonged at any particular time. One might predict that children denied early identification with parents would associate more with their peers as well as adhere more rigidly to the codes of the peer culture.

Ausubel's theory fits the facts. Quite probably rejected children identify more closely with agemates, and those who make this identification very close are likely to lack inner controls and become more conforming. In everyday life one sees the gangs of juvenile delinquents composed of youths from broken homes or with no parent ties at all. Yet other, simpler explanations may account for these facts. Correct or not, Ausubel's ideas seem at present to be an interesting, if unproved, attempt to bridge the gap between psychoanalytic theory and observed differences in the degree to which children identify with parents and peers. If Ausubel's views are correct, a child would pay a price of lack of autonomy and of inner controls for identification with peers, yet would find the identification worthwhile, for without it the world would be too threatening to face with equanimity. It is an interesting sidelight that six orphaned Jewish children (Freud & Dann, 1951) who were denied any opportunity to identify with adults while forced to live in the most threatening of all environments, a Nazi concentration camp in which 30,000 Jews perished, developed peer ties that were remarkable in their strength.

Thus far, the emphasis in this discussion of identification with peers has been on the pathological, on the indications of disturbances in function. However, some degree of identification with one's agemates is a normal and useful part of child development. A major aim of child-rearing in Western culture is to produce an autonomous or independent child. The child attempts to emancipate himself from parental control, while his parents gradually relinquish control in a rear-guard action to retain it. To borrow the language of Potter's *Gamesmanship* (1948), the child attempts to become one-up (dominant) with regard to parents, even when secretly desiring at times to remain one-down (submissive). The parents face the difficult task of teaching the child to be one-up by keeping him one-down until he has learned such "ploys" (maneuvers) that he bests them in the power struggle. At this point he is mature enough to be allowed to try out his ploys in the world at large: he is independent.

Identification with peers appears to be a prime force aiding in the emancipation from parents. It provides enough security for the child to risk the moderate parental rejection occasioned by each small victory in his development of independence. In the quest for emancipation, such identification forces the child to stick to the timetable used by agemates of the same sex. For example, a nine-year-old who is not allowed to go to Saturday movie matinees when other nine-year-olds are is made aware by his friends that his timetable lags. Pressing hard for this concession, he wins it after a few weeks and a number of encounters with his parents. He has thus taken one more step toward autonomy as a result of the combined coercion and support received from the peers with whom he identifies.

Learning

A vast amount of learning occurs among peers. Although this group has neither the traditional authority of the family nor the legal authority of the schools for teaching information and values, it manages to convey a substantial body of material to its members. Robert Paul Smith (1958) in his evocative, poignant book, *"Where Did You Go?" "Out." "What Did You Do?" "Nothing."*, described the learning process in this way:

> I don't remember being taught how to play mumbly-peg. (I know, I know. In the books they write it "mumblety-peg," but we said, and it *was*, "mumbly-peg.") When you were a little kid, you stood around while a covey of ancients of nine or ten played mumbly-peg, shifting from foot to foot and wiping your nose on your sleeve and hitching up your knickerbockers, saying, "Lemme do it, aw come on, lemme have a turn," until one of them struck you in a soft spot and you went home to sit under the porch by yourself, or found a smaller kid to torture, or loused up your sister's rope-skipping, or made a collection of small round stones. The small round stones were not *for* anything, it was just to have a collection of small round stones.
>
> One day you said, "Lemme have a turn, lemme have a turn," and some soft-hearted older brother, never your own, said, "Gowan, let the kid have a turn," and there, by all that was holy, you were playing mumbly-peg . . . (Smith, 1958, pp. 4–5).

What Smith learned in a "house" he and his friends built he tells of as follows:

> It was a pitiful wreck of a tarpaper hut, and in it I learned the difference between boys and girls, I learned that all fathers did that, I learned to swear, to play with myself, to sleep in the afternoon, I learned that some people were Catholics and some people were Protestants and some people were Jews, that people came from different places. I learned that other kids wondered, too, who they would have been if their fathers had not married their mothers, wondered if you could dig a hole right to the center of the earth, wondered if you could kill yourself by holding your breath. (None of us could.)
>
> I learned that with three people assembled, it was only for the briefest interludes that all three liked each other. Mitch and I were leagued against Simon. And then Simon and I against Mitch. And then —but you remember. I didn't know then just how to handle that situation. I still don't. It is my coldly comforting feeling that nobody still does, including nations, and that's what the trouble with the world is. That's what the trouble with the world

was then—when Mitch and Simon were the two and I was the one.

What else did I learn in the hut? That if two nails will not hold a board in place, three will probably not either, but the third nail will split the board. I think kids still do that. I think objects made of wood by children, left to their own devices, if such there be, will assay ten per cent wood, ninety per cent nails.

In the hut we looked and we learned. And drooled. I remember a picture of Clara Bow with one shoulder strap—and then there was Toby Wing—and look at Lily Damita—she's bending *way* over . . . (pp. 78–80).

Cultural and Individual Differences in Game Performance

The study of play, and of the functions of play, has led to a substantial recent literature on play. The recent books by Avedon and Sutton-Smith (1971), Herron and Sutton-Smith (1971) and Millar (1968) contain descriptions of this recent work, as well as much historic material.

One study (Roberts & Sutton-Smith, 1962) has to do with dimensions of culture as they relate to the presence of various types of games (games of physical skill, of physical skill and strategy, of strategy, and of chance) in the cultures studied. Numerous relations are established; for example, games of strategy are most frequently found in complex cultures that emphasize obedience training and use relatively severe, love-oriented discipline; games of physical skill are most emphasized in cultures with a high emphasis on achievement and high anxiety regarding failure to achieve.

Differences within as well as between cultures have been investigated. Sutton-Smith (1971; also see, Roberts, Sutton-Smith, & Kozelka, 1967) and his associates developed a multiple choice test by which it was possible to determine whether a child would use a strategy that would result in a win or a draw in the game of Tic-Tac-Toe. Some of the data that were obtained are shown in Table 11-2.

Sex differences in the correlations are marked. Sutton-Smith, in summarizing these data, notes that "the present study makes it clear that the most trivial game of pure strategy, the game of ticktacktoe is deviously implicated in the lives of its players. In the case of the winning boys, and the drawing boys and girls, the style of play at the game does seem to provide a parallel to other behaviors of these players. In these cases it seems not an unreasonable usage to say that the game models their general style of strategic competence. In the case of the winning girl, however, success at the game is merely a further illustration of her promethean-like tendency to dominate in many social matters. Here the game illustrates her power, but does not particularly model it (Sutton-Smith, 1971, p. 496).

Games and Social Learning

The chief voluntary occupation of children's groups is play. Yet children's games are among the most traditional and conservative of human institutions. It is difficult to establish the earliest historical mention of a game, but these are some of the macabre facts that have been found. *Hopscotch* seems to have originated in Greece or Crete, modeled after that most elaborate labyrinth of all, King Minos' (Spence, 1947). This mild game seems at one time to have been a method for selecting a sacrificial victim. Other games of the same original purpose abound. *London Bridge* seems very likely to be a remnant of those older times when a person chosen by this method each year was flung from the Bridge to

TABLE 11-2 Variables Associated with Playing for a Win at Ticktacktoe

Variable	Boys ($N = 25$)	Girls ($N = 25$)
A. *Status variables*		
Age	.10	.38
Intelligence	.08	−.19
Socioeconomic	.15	−.51†
B. *Motivational variable*		
Need achievement	.11	−.17
C. *Behavior variables*		
Achievement		
Concern with fine motor mastery	.20	−.37
Amount of time spent alone on tasks	.18	−.48*
Task persistence	.43*	−.46*
Independent achievement efforts	.34	−.33
Aggression		
Instigation of physical aggression	−.08	.54†
Instigation of verbal aggression	−.22	.47*
Activity passivity		
Associative play	−.08	.55†
Dominance of same sex peers	−.01	.53†
Uncontrolled motoriety	−.05	.53*
Concern with mastery of gross motor skills	−.03	−.41*
Withdrawal from social environment	−.01	−.64†
Withdrawal from aggressive attacks	−.16	−.60†

*Significant at .05 level (two-tailed tests).
†Significant at .01 level (two-tailed tests).

propitiate the gods. An identical "game" with the same purpose has been described in an Icelandic source, *The Vatnsdaela Saga,* dating from the eleventh century. *Blindman's bluff,* originally "hoodman's blind," or "executioner is blind," or "Blind Harry," began as a northern European "game" in which a sacrificial "lamb" was selected at random. The game of *jacks* also seems innocuous enough, yet in its original form of knucklebones it was a fifth century B.C. device for foretelling the future (David, 1955). One throw, the "throw of Zeus," meant one could kill one's enemy and escape detection. From this bizarre form of soothsaying sprang both dice and jacks.

In her book of jump-rope rhymes, Patricia Evans (1955) wrote that rope jumping began as a form of sympathetic magic. Farmers would jump rope in the spring, believing that their small grains would grow as high as they jumped. Jump-rope rhymes are interesting in their continuity and in their geographical dispersion. Evans mentioned that the earliest rhyme she could find dated from medieval England and started with the words, "Andy pandy, sugardy candy." Coincidentally, in San Francisco in 1955, a popular rhyme began with "Amos and Andy, sugar and candy." She recorded another rhyme used in San Francisco that was almost identical to one recorded by Opie and Opie (1959) in England at approximately the same time.

Charlie Chaplin went to France
To teach the ladies how to dance
First he did the rhumba,
Then he did the kicks,
Then he did the samba,
Then he did the splits
(Opie & Opie, 1959, p. 110)

Charlie Chaplin
Went to France
To teach the ladies
How to dance.
First the heel
And then the toe
Left foot forward
Out you go.
(Evans, 1955, p. 8)

Spence (1947) reported that *tag* at the time of its first reference in Germany involved touching iron, a medieval safeguard from witches and other supernatural beings, in order to be safe from from the *it* who was called the devil.

Since adults do not pay much attention to the games of children, it is hard to find literary reference to them. However, Virgil in Volume VII of *Aeneid* described spinning tops. Shakespeare mentioned a number of games including *hide* and *seek* (*Hamlet, IV, ii, 32*), *leap frog* (*Henry V, ii, 141–144*), *blindman's bluff* (*All's Well That Ends Well, IV, iii, 137–138*), *and prisoner's base* (*Cymbeline, V, iii, 19–20*).

Several books on children's games show their amazing continuity. A curious volume called *A Little Pretty Pocket Book* was published by Isaiah Thomas in 1787. (The book actually dates back to 1744 when it was written and published by John Newberry in London. Thomas pirated the book and published it in the United States.) This book describes the games and sports popular with children of that era. Of the 24 activities listed, 21 are still popular today. Two studies of games appeared at the turn of the century. One by Newell (1899) described the games of American children, and the other by Gomme, 1894, 1898) dealt with the games of English youngsters. There is a remarkable correspondence between the games contained in the two books. Moreover, most of them are still played today.

Change. Change does occur in children's games and game preferences (e.g., see Sutton–Smith & Rosenberg, 1961) but for the most part, only slowly. For example, both Newell and Gomme write of *Starlight, Moonlight,* a more complex version of hide and seek, which with the advent of traffic lights became known as *Red Light, Green Light.* Although Gomme stated her belief that traditional children's games would be forgotten with the increasing communication and urbanization of the English, these traditional games have shown an astonishing vitality. Despite modifications and changes, continuity is the rule. The Opies (1959) present an illustration of the continuity found in children's rhymes:

1725
Now he acts the *Grenadier,*
Calling for *a Pot of Beer:*
Where's his Money? He's forgot:
Get him gone, a Drunken Sot.

1907
Eenty, Teenty, tuppenny bun,
Pitching tatties doon the lum;
Who's there? John Blair.
What does he want? A bottle of beer.
Where's your money? I forgot.
Go downstairs, you drunken sot.

1939
A frog walked into a public
house
And asked for a pint of beer.
Where's your money?
In my pocket.
Where's your pocket,
I forgot it.
Well, please walk out.

1950
Mickey Mouse
In a public house
Drinking pints of beer.
Where's your money?
In my pocket.
Where's your pocket?
I forgot it.
Please walk out.
(Opie & Opie, 1959, p. 11)

On the other hand, if something is provided to children from the adult world, children may seize on it, change it in various ways, and make it part of their oral tradition. Witness the various verses devised by English youngsters to the tune of *Davy Crockett:*

Born on a roof top in Battersea,
Joined the Teds when he was only three,
Coshed a cop when he was only four
And now he's in Dartmoor for evermore.
Davy, Davy Crockett,
King of the Teddy boys.

Standing on the corner, swinging his chain,[1]
Along came a policeman and took his name;
He pulled out the razor and he slit the copper's throat,
Now he's wiping up the blood with his Teddy boy's coat.
Davy, Davy Crockett,
King of the Teddy boys.

Once part of the oral tradition of children, a game or rhyme is transmitted across generations of children with little variation, perhaps because the older child of 11 or 12 insists that the younger child of 6 or 7 learn it exactly. Frequently these games or rhymes are discarded aspects of the adult world. As Piaget (1932) showed, the young child is so impressed with the need for exactness that he often believes game rules are framed by God. Small wonder that child culture is conservative and allows little room for change. The question is, why are games so tradition-bound and conservative?

Perhaps games and rhymes transmit certain values of importance to the peer society. Only one person has explicitly stated this to be the case. Froebel (1898), founder of the kindergarten movement, believed that the child acquired a set of values from those inherent in the games played. For this reason he invented a series of games that he felt would teach a *better* set of values, a set involving knowledge of temporal and spatial relationships, of causality, and of human social interaction.

Information Learned. Piaget (1932) noted that game functions appeared to have vital significance for the socialization process. For him, as mentioned in Chapter 4, children were morally realistic, judging acts in terms of consequences, not motives. They also showed other signs of immature moral judgment. Such immaturity, Piaget believed, resulted from adult constraints as well as from the concreteness of children's own thought processes. This was countered, however, by the child's peers who, in part, helped him to achieve maturity in moral judgment. Among peers one was judged by and judged others, exposing the basic unfairness of moral realism. As Piaget saw it, one eventually learned

[1]Chain, i.e., bicycle chain, used as a weapon is street-gang warfare (Opie & Opie, 1958, p. 1190).

from contact with peers that game rules were not immutable. Rather they could be changed by mutual consent, or reciprocity. Through this knowledge an awareness of democratic processes and of fairness developed. From games, one learned arbitration.

Time spent at games is about equally divided between playing and arguing. Arguing over whether a pitched ball was a strike, over whose turn it is, over whether one has been tagged out, over whether one has been scalped by the Indians and must remain wounded for an indeterminate interval—all these are among the most common experiences of childhood. During these verbal battles, children acquire an understanding of the spirit of rules and the law, in contrast to the understanding of the letter of the law manifested by the young child. The child learns fairness and reciprocity, tact and diplomacy.

Children's games are not highly organized and are usually based on individual competition far more than on cooperative effort. If a choice is involved, most children will choose a game where the *it* role is made quite difficult and challenging (Sutton-Smith, 1955). Games youngsters like best, in contrast to those liked best by teachers and recreation leaders, are those in which a hierarchy of status on the basis of ability is manifest. Children, and in particular those children who find little chance for success at meeting adult demands, can find a position of status among their peers through skill and daring.

Most games share another characteristic, which might be referred to as "manageable fear." Although adults undertake such sport, children far more than their elders seem to relish frightening themselves as long as the fear is contained within bounds. Children's games are frequently of this sort. They create a vicarious danger that may provide the child with some of the information and strength needed to deal with real perils.

After a long lapse of interest children's games again are being investigated. One can measure age and sex differences in masculinity–femininity of game interests (Rosenberg & Sutton-Smith, 1959), and in toy preference (De Lucia, 1963), though important regional (Midwest versus East) differences exist in the masculinity-femininity of game choices between boys and girls of a given age group, and across age groups (Walker, 1964). Since a high proportion of children's time is spent in play, this increase in research interest should lead to a fuller understanding of the learning situations and values inherent in games.

Role Playing. The play activities of peers also open opportunities for role playing, and in so doing seem to fill a valuable function. The ability to play a role is apparently related to intellectual ability (Feffer & Gourevitch, 1960) and to adjustment. People differ in ability to play social roles; excessively poor role players are less adequately adjusted than individuals with some role-playing ability (Mann & Mann, 1960). Certainly the dramatic play of childhood is concerned chiefly with role playing. It provides the child with a rich variety of roles to tackle. To be a cowboy is easy. To be a railroad engineer or a parent is not much more difficult. But to be a sandbox, or something equally inanimate, may pose quite a challenge.

Most roles played offer some preparation for later roles in real life. Conceivably the play of girls with dolls, for example, provides a base for later care of real children both in attitudes toward infants and in knowledge of how to care for them. Even if a girl of four may leave her favorite "baby" out in the rain for a few days, the eight- or nine-year-old appears to have learned her maternal role quite adequately. For the boy, however, whose adult functions are not easily anticipated in play, unless he happens to become a cowboy as an adult, there is less to be gained from peer activities in this specific area, just as he probably benefits more than girls in learning arbitration, since his games are more complex and his rules more rigidly codified.

Peers as a Reality Check

A final form of learning to be discerned in the society of peers is that of growing more closely attuned to the reality about oneself. Parents may become so emotionally involved with the child that they cannot evaluate him in anything but the most favorable light. Or they may be so caught up in their own problems that they cannot evaluate him at all, or can evaluate him only negatively. Teachers seem to be moving away from comparing children with other children. But the one group that can be relied on to evaluate and to compare is the society of peers.

Seldom is it enjoyable to have reality brought home to oneself—"to see ourselves as others see us." Yet only upon becoming aware of others' opinions does one consider change. Peers are harsh but relatively unbiased judges. Any undesirable trait is quickly spotted by them and they are quite frank to deride it, thus heightening the possibility for change. The accuracy of their assessment has been indicated by a study by Roff (1961) showing that among adults who were considered behavior problems in their own childhood, one of the best auguries of adult adjustment was acceptance by peers. If a child is judged to be a problem child by adults but is accepted by his peers, his chances of making a normal adjustment are good. But if the peer society also considers him a problem his chances fall precipitously. Harsh as peer judgment and severe as its penalties may be, both seem relatively fair and accurate.

Psychologists have a vast, unexplored world to map, and the territory of peers is still largely unpenetrated. Yet it seems reasonable to believe from a brief sight of peer country that events occur to a child as a result of his interactions with other children of the same age that bear heavily on the process of growing up.

SUMMARY

Children are interested in other children early in life, yet their interactions are minimal because of their inadequate impulse control and their inability to have much feeling for the other person. With age, interaction increases, producing more quarrels and aggression as well as greater cooperation and sympathy. The degree of any child's involvement with agemates differs from age to age and also within any age group.

Children vary greatly in the degree to which they are accepted by children of the same age and to which they become involved in peer activity. Measuring devices enable the social scientist to assess the acceptance of children by their mates and to determine the personality traits associated with acceptance or rejection by peers.

By elementary school age, sex division begins to occur among children of the same age. From this time onward during childhood the influence of the peer society is principally that of agemates of the same sex.

The peer society plays a vital role in socialization. Peers have a normalizing or leveling effect. They allow the child an opportunity for identification. Peer society conveys to its members a large body of information and values. It provides a wide opportunity for the learning and playing of social roles. It makes available to the child a reality check from which he can judge his own behavior more accurately. The world of peers is largely unexplored by psychologists, but seems to be a harsh though fair one that has great significance for the socialization process.

REFERENCES

Anderson, J. E. Personality organization in children. *American Psychologist,* 1948, **3**, 409–416.

Anderson, J. E. Personal communication, 1956. Univ. of Minnesota.

Ausubel, D. P. *Ego development and the personality disorders.* New York: Grune & Stratton, 1952.

Ausubel, D. P. *Theory and problems of child development.* New York: Grune & Stratton, 1958.

Avedon, E. M. & Sutton-Smith, B. *The study of games.* New York: Wiley, 1971.

Barker, R. C., & Wright, H. F. *Midwest and its children: The psychological ecology of an American town.* New York: Row, Peterson, 1955.

Boehm, L. The development of independence: a comparative study. *Child Development,* 1957, **28**, 85–92.

Bonney, M. E. Relationships between social success, family size, socioeconomic background, and intelligence among school children in grades III to V. *Sociometry,* 1944, **7**, 26–39.

Brim, O. G., Jr. Family structure and sex role learning by children: A further analysis of Helen Koch's data. *Sociometry,* 1958, **21**, 1–16.

Bronfenbrenner, U. Soviet methods of character education: Some implications for research. *American Psychologist,* 1962, **17**, 550–564.

David, F. N. Studies in the history of probability and statistics. *Biometrika,* 1955, **42**, 1–32.

De Lucia, L. A. The toy preference test: A measure of sex role identification in children. *Child Development,* 1963, **34**, 107–117.

Doll, E. A. *The Vineland social maturity scale. Manual of directions.* Vineland, N.J.: The Training School, 1935.

Doll, E. A. The essentials of an inclusive concept of mental deficiency. *American Journal of Mental Deficiency,* 1941, **46**, 214–219.

Evans, P. *Jump rope rhymes.* San Francisco: Porpoise Book Shop, 1955.

Faigin, H. Social behavior of young children in the kibbutz. *Journal of Abnormal and Social Psychology,* 1958, **56**, 117–129.

Feffer, M. H., & Gourevitch, V. Cognitive aspects of role playing in children. *Journal of Personality,* 1960, **28**, 383–396.

Freud, A., & Dann, S. An experiment in group upbringing. *The psychoanalytic study of the child.* Vol. 6. New York: International Universities Press, 1951.

Freud, S. *The ego and the id.* London: Hogarth, 1935.

Froebel, F. *Mother play* (translated by H. R. Eliot & S. E. Blow). New York: Appleton, 1898.

Gomme, A. B. *Traditional games of England, Scotland, and Ireland* (Vols. 1 and 2). London: Methuen, 1894, 1898.

Gomme, A. B. *Old English singing games.* New York: Dodd Merrill, 1900.

Harlow, H. F. Effects of early experiences on personal-social, sexual, and maternal behavior. Paper read to the Society for Research in Child Development, Berkeley, Calif., April 11, 1963.

Harris, D. B., & Tseng, S. C. Children's attitudes toward peers and parents as revealed by sentence completions. *Child Development,* 1957, **28**, 401–411.

Heber, R. A manual on terminology and classification in mental retardation. *Monograph Supplement to the American Journal of Mental Deficiency,* 1959, **64**, No. 2.

Herron, R. E. & Sutton-Smith, B. *Child's play.* New York: Wiley, 1971.

Hetherington, E. M. Effects of paternal absence on sex-typed behaviors in Negro and white pre-adolescent boys. *Journal of Personality and Social Psychology,* 1966, **4**, 87–91.

Hoffman, M. L. The role of the parent in the child's moral growth. *Religious Education,* 1962, **57** (Research Supplement), S18–S33.

Hollingshead, A. deB. *Elmtown's youth: The impact of social classes on youth.* New York: Wiley, 1949.

Hollingworth, L. S. *Children above IQ 180.* New York: World Book, 1942.

Jack, L. M. An experimental study of ascendant behavior in preschool children. *University of Iowa Study in Child Welfare,* 1934, **9**, No. 3.

Keister, M. E., & Updegraff, R. A study of children's reactions to failure and an experimental attempt to modify them. *Child Development,* 1937, **8**, 241–248.

Koch, H. L. Popularity in children: Some related factors and a technique for its measurement. *Child Development,* 1933, **5**, 164–175.

Koch, H. L. Sissiness and tomboyishness in relation to sibling characteristics. *Journal of Genetic Psychology,* 1956, **88**, 231–244.

Kuhlen, R. G., & Lee, B. J. Personality characteristics and social acceptability in adolescence. *Journal of Educational Psychology,* 1943, **34**, 321–340.

Lambert, W. W., Triandis, L. M., & Wolf, M. Some correlates of beliefs in the malevolence or benevolence of supernatural beings: A cross social study. *Journal of Abnormal and Social Psychology,* 1959, **58**, 162–169.

Lesser, G. S., & Abelson, R. P. Personality correlates of persuasibility in children. In I. C. Janis & C. I. Hovland et al. (Eds.), *Personality and persuasibility.* New Haven: Yale University Press, 1959.

Lynn, D., & Sawrey, W. L. The effects of father-absence on Norwegian boys and girls. *Journal of Abnormal and Social Psychology,* 1959, **59**, 258–262.

McCurdy, H. G. The childhood pattern of genius. *Journal of the Elisha Mitchell Scientific Society,* 1957, **73**, 448–462. [Also in R. A. King (Ed.), *Readings for an introduction to psychology.* New York: McGraw-Hill, 1961.]

McKenney, R. Paris! City of children. *Holiday,* April 1953, 63–68. (Also in W. S. Martin & C. B. Stendler (Eds.), *Readings in child development.* New York: Harcourt, Brace, 1954.) Pp. 199–203.

Mann, J. H., & Mann, C. H. The relative effectiveness of role playing and task oriented group experience in producing personality and behavior change. *Journal of Social Psychology,* 1960, **51**, 313–317.

Marshall, H. R., & McCandless, B. R. Relationships between dependence on adults and social acceptance by peers. *Child Development,* 1957, **28,** 413–419.

Mead, M., & Calas, N. *Primitive heritage.* New York, Random House, 1953.

Medinnus, G. R. Behavioral indices of social immaturity. Unpublished manuscript, San Jose State College, San Jose, Calif., 1962.

Millar, S. *The psychology of play.* London: Pelican, 1968.

Moreno, J. L. *Who shall survive?* Washington, D.C.: Nervous and Mental Diseases Publishing, 1934.

Newell, W. *Games and songs of American children.* New York: Harper, 1899.

Opie, I., and Opie, P. *The lore and language of school children.* London: Oxford at the Clarenden Press, 1959.

Page, M. L. The modification of ascendant behavior in preschool children. *University of Iowa Study in Child Welfare,* 1936, **11,** No. 3.

Parten, M. An analysis of social participation, leadership, and other factors in pre-school play groups. Doctoral dissertation, University of Minnesota, 1929.

Parten, M. Social participation among pre-school children. *Journal of Abnormal and Social Psychology,* 1932, **27,** 243–269.

Parten, M., & Newhall, S. M. Social behavior of preschool children. In R. G. Barker, J. S. Kounin, & H. F. Wright (Eds.), *Child behavior and development.* New York: McGraw-Hill, 1943.

Piaget, J. *The moral judgment of the child.* New York: Harcourt, Brace, 1932.

Piaget, J. *The construction of reality in the child.* New York: Basic Books, 1954.

Potter, S. *The theory and art of gamesmanship.* New York: Holt, 1948.

Riesman, D. (with N. Glazer & R. Denny). *The lonely crowd.* New Haven: Yale University Press, 1950.

Roberts, J. M. & Sutton-Smith, B. Child training and game involvement. *Ethnology,* 1962, **2,** 166–185.

Roberts, J. M., Sutton-Smith, B., & Kozelka, R. M. Studies in an elementary game of strategy. *Genetic Psychology Monographs,* 1967, **75,** 3–42.

Roff, M. Childhood social interactions and young adult bad conduct. *Journal of Abnormal and Social Psychology,* 1961, **63,** 333–337.

Rosenberg, B. G., & Sutton-Smith, B. The measurement of masculinity and femininity in children. *Child Development,* 1959, **30,** 373–380.

Scarpitti, R. R., Murray, E., Simon, D., & Reckless, W. C. The "good" boy in a high delinquency area: Four years later. *American Sociological Review,* 1960, **25,** 555–558.

Sherif, M., Harvey, O. J., White, B. J., Hood, D. R., & Sherif, C. W. *Intergroup conflict and cooperation: The Robbers' Cave experiment,* Norman, Okla.: University of Oklahoma Press, 1961.

Siegman, A. W. Father absence during early childhood and anti-social behavior. *Journal of Abnormal Psychology,* 1966, **71,** 71–74.

Smith, R. P. *"Where did you go?" "Out." "What did you do?" "Nothing."* New York: Pocket Books, 1958 (first published by Norton, New York, 1957).

Spence, L. J. *Myth and ritual in dance, game, and rhyme.* London: Watts, 1947.

Spiro, M. E. *Children of the kibbutz.* Cambridge, Mass.: Harvard University Press, 1958.

Staffieri, J. R. A study of social stereotype of body image in children. *Journal of Personality and Social Psychology,* 1967, **7**, 101–104.

Sutton-Smith, B. The "it" role in children's games. *The Group,* 1955, **17**, 123–128.

Sutton-Smith, B. Achievement and strategic competence. In E. M. Avedon and B. Sutton-Smith (Eds.) *The study of games.* New York: Wiley, 1971.

Sutton-Smith, B., & Rosenberg, B. G. Sixty years of historical change in the game preferences of American children. *Journal of American Folklore,* 1961, **74**, 17–46.

Terman, L. M., et al. *Genetic studies of genius.* Vol. 1. *Mental and physical traits of a thousand gifted children.* Stanford, Calif.: Stanford University Press, 1925.

Thomas, I. *A little pretty pocketbook.* Worecester, Mass., 1787.

Tryon, C. M. Evaluation of adolescent personality by adolescents. *Monographs of the Society for Research in Child Development,* 1939, **4**, No. 4.

Tuddenham, R. D. Studies in reputation: III. Correlates of popularity among elementary school children. *Journal of Educational Psychology,* 1951, **42**, 257–276.

Tuddenham, R. D. Studies in reputation: I. Sex and grade differences in school children's evaluation of their peers. II. The diagnosis of social adjustment. *Psychological Monographs,* 1952, **66**, No. 333.

Udry, R. J. The importance of social class in a suburban school. *Journal of Educational Sociology,* 1960, **33**, 307–310.

Walker, R. N. Body build and behavior in young children: I. Body building and nursery school teachers' ratings. *Monographs of the Society for Research in Child Development,* 1962, **27**, No. 84.

Walker, R. N. Body build and behavior in young children: II. Body build and parents' ratings. *Child Development,* 1963, **34**, 1–23.

Walker, R. N. Measuring masculinity and femininity by children's games choices. *Child Development,* 1964, **35**, 961–969.

Wilson, A. B. Residential segregation of social classes and aspirations of high school boys. *American Sociological Review,* 1959, **24**, 836–845.

chapter 12

the child in the school

chapter 12

the child in the school

chapter 12

the child in the school

The school transmits the values of the society to each succeeding generation of children, thus perpetuating the basic facets of a culture. Its significance in the child's life becomes clear from the realization that it is the setting for much of his relationship with his peers. Because of the social interaction occurring within it, the school, through its personnel, attempts to guide and facilitate the personality development of its pupils. No longer the center of community life as it was in rural America, the school continues to play an important role in the lives of young people from five to 18.

The concern of the present chapter is essentially the various aspects of school experience that influence the child's development of personality. Nursery school, the beginning of formal schooling and what it means to the child, the teacher's role in the classroom, especially her part in establishing a psychological atmosphere, the factors involved in achievement, social-class membership, and competition—all these are considered in turn. Educational methodologies and materials are better left to texts on educational practice. Besides, the teacher's fund of knowledge, her enthusiasm, and the kind of psychological and emotional relationship existing between her and her pupils are the really crucial matters that most significantly affect the child in the classroom.

NURSERY-SCHOOL EXPERIENCE

In the 1930's child psychologists spent inordinate amounts of effort endeavoring to discover the relative contributions of heredity and environment to a child's intellectual development. One aspect of this issue—or indeed, controversy—was the effect of nursery-school experience. According to one camp (see Wellman, 1932; Skeels, Updegraff, Wellman, & Williams, 1938), nursery school produced a gain in IQ; according to another (see Olson & Hughes, 1940; Goodenough & Maurer, 1940) this was not necessarily so. More likely, attendance at nursery school may increase IQ scores although it probably does not exert any long-range influence on the functioning of the intellect. Actually, any increase in IQ scores flowing from such exposure may result from a variety of nonintellective factors, such as increased familiarity with the materials and tasks contained in intelligence tests and greater adult-child rapport.

The enriched nursery-school environment may have a salutary effect on children from deprived or impoverished backgrounds, but it is doubtful whether nursery-school experience will improve the IQs of children from homes offering an adequate amount of intellectual stimulation. Yet even if one were to concede that nursery school stimulates intellectual development, it would be difficult to identify the specific factors in the nursery-school environment that account for this.

By the 1940's, interest had shifted to the effect of nursery-school experience on the child's social and emotional adjustment. Even before that time M. E. Walsh (1931) had found a number of personality traits to be more pronounced in a group of children who had had six months of nursery-school training than in a similar group lacking such experience. The former group seemed more spontaneous in behavior and showed more independence, initiative, self-reliance, and curiosity than the control group. Other early studies noted similar differences (Hattwick, 1936; Van Alstyne & Hattwick, 1939). Later, Bonney and Nicholson (1958) saw some indications that elementary-school children who had had previous exposure to nursery school were more popular with their peers. However, this was not found to be the case in several earlier studies reviewed by them; these showed negative findings regarding the relation between preschool experience and pupil adjustment.

Notwithstanding the inconclusive nature of the research available, some comments seem to be in order. The very nature of the nursery-school situation, in which relatively large numbers of children interact under the supervision of one or two adults, would tend to encourage the development of independent behavior. In such a setting the child must learn to fend for himself. In addition, a certain amount of social learning inevitably occurs from participation in the group over a period of time. Some behaviors are discovered to be unacceptable to peers, whereas other behaviors result in pleasant, favorable responses and are thus reinforced. However, a follow-up study of a number of elementary-school children who had previously attended nursery school found consistency in behavior from nursery school through the elementary years, thus implying that peer responses alone may not suffice to remedy behavior difficulties (Van Alstyne & Hattwick, 1939). Since the source of such problems often lies in the parent-child relationship, which is a continuing one, influences outside the home cannot always counter those within it.

Nursery schools vary widely in goals and procedures. So do the behavioral results they hope to achieve in children. Certainly the quality of the school and the characteristics of the teacher determine the effects of this experience on the child. The importance of the teacher is reflected in an experimental study (Thompson, 1944) which analyzed the impact on nursery-school children of two different types of teacher-child relations. In one group the teacher was instructed to develop a warm relationship with each child and to stimulate the children's activities by providing information and assistance. In the other group contact between teacher and children remained at a minimum and the teacher participated in the children's activities only upon request. At the end of the school year the children in the first group, in contrast to those in the second, were seen to be more ascendant as well as more constructive in the face of possible failure. Moreover, they showed greater social participation and leadership. No noteworthy difference was detected between the two groups in nervous habits or IQ.

Attendance at a nursery school for at least part of the day may have some bearing on the relationship between mother and child. The time spent away from home may benefit both. The mother may enjoy temporary relief from her child-care responsibilities; the child enters a situation in which he learns to accommodate to the demands of an adult other than his parent. Like the effect of maternal employment on the child, the quality, not the quantity, of the mother-child interaction is the important thing. Quite possibly a reduction in quantity raises the level of the quality, or so it would seem from the typical report of mothers whose youngsters attend nursery school.

The nursery-school setting, through its equipment and type of supervision, is designed to reduce the amount of restrictions placed on a child and to encourage physical activity and self-expression. Few homes are arranged like it either with respect to schedule or physical facilities. In consequence, frictions present in the home, such as sibling rivalries or mother-child antagonisms centering about certain areas of behavior, can be minimized or avoided in the nursery-school setting.

However, this does not mean that compulsory school attendance should be lowered to the preschool years. Early child-rearing is a parental responsibility and should perhaps remain so. The value of the nursery-school experience is that it may enable the parent to gain some insight and understanding about the child-rearing process from a new perspective.

Preschool Programs for the Disadvantaged

A great surge of interest in the educational training of the preschool child is evident currently in public and professional circles. This interest has been stimulated by the fortunate confluence of two developments. First, there is a group of psychologists who have revised their thinking regarding intellectual development. Recognition has long been given to the effects of the child's early social and emotional experiences on his subsequent personality development and general adjustment. Only recently, however, have interest and research focused on the crucial importance of the early years in terms of the child's cognitive development. Second, the involvement of the federal government in the War on Poverty program has included Project Head Start, in which disadvantaged children are given preschool training during an eight-week summer period. Each of these two factors will be discussed in more detail.

Hunt (1961, 1964) has argued convincingly that certain traditional beliefs in psychology have prevented serious consideration of the value of preschool enrichment in stimulating intellectual development. These include the notion that intelligence is relatively fixed at birth and not subject to alteration by the environment. Further, the many early studies on the maturation versus environment issue concluded that development is predetermined; however, a majority of these studies dealt with simple motor skills and not with such complex abilities as intelligence. Hebb's (1949) emphasis on "primary learning" based on early perceptual experience and Harlow's (1950) principle of "learning to learn" both affirm the idea that early learning facilitates later learning and forms the foundation upon which subsequent learning is based.

Intellectual development does not proceed at a constant, linear rate. Rather, it is extremely rapid in the very early years and slows down markedly thereafter. Based on a careful review of research evidence, Bloom (1964) has estimated that half of adult intelligence is achieved by the age of four years. Moreover, Bloom has argued that environmental factors exert their greatest effect on a characteristic when it is developing most rapidly. Thus vitamin deficiency at ages 13–15 would have little effect on adult height, whereas such deficiency could affect terminal height if it occurred at ages 1–3. Similarly, environmental differences (enrichment or deprivation) in intellectual stimulation affect intellectual growth most markedly in the early years.

Since it now appears certain that the early years are extremely important in terms of intellectual stimulation, it is most appropriate that a number of large-scale studies are being conducted to determine the effects of various curricula for the disadvantaged preschool child. Among these investigators are Deutsch in New York, Gray and co-workers in Nashville, Bereiter and Engelmann in Illinois, and Nimnicht in Colorado.[1]

Two aspects of the federally sponsored Head Start program for disadvantaged four-year-olds merit comment. First, the importance of a low adult-child ratio

[1]For a discussion of some of these programs, see: Hess & Bear, 1968.

has been recognized. Thus the classes are limited to 15 children under the guidance of two adults, the teacher and a teacher's aide. The more individualized the instruction, the more profitable it is for the child. Second, parent involvement has been made an integral part of the Head Start program. The home and the school must cooperate in preparing the child for learning. The school's efforts probably are doomed to failure unless the parent is convinced of the value of learning and is aware of ways to facilitate learning in the child.

Philosophy of Preschool Enrichment Programs

Several issues concerning the educational philosophy of these preschool programs are tremendously important in determining their effectiveness. The first and most important concern deals with the extent to which cognitive stimulation is emphasized. The second focuses on the amount of structure in a program (Medinnus, 1970).

It is clear that intellectual development is most rapid in the first four years of life. It is also well documented that the disadvantaged child does not receive the kinds of stimulation and experiences that are necessary for school readiness. It must be concluded, therefore, that any program designed for the disadvantaged child must involve an intensive amount of intellectual stimulation. The skills required for school readiness are well known. They include language (vocabulary, knowledge of sentence structure), number concepts, form discrimination, listening skills, ability to attend to and follow simple directions, and general information. These general areas might well be used as the basis for designing a curriculum for the disadvantaged preschool child.

While the amount of structure is less important than the amount of cognitive stimulation, it is unlikely that the latter can occur in a completely unstructured setting. Regularity, predictability, and consistency frequently are lacking in the lower-class home. Yet these are important characteristics of the school situation as evidenced by time schedules, classroom routine, and expected patterns of behavior. Lawfulness and predictability of behavior and of events free the child to develop his unique qualities and abilities. Further, the relation between the self and the external world can best be understood in an atmosphere characterized by dependability of the environment.

Although a structured program has been misinterpreted to mean regimentation and sternness, this is certainly not the case. Rather, certain expectations are made clear to the child, such as paying attention at reading time. As Baumrind (1966) has pointed out, there is no evidence that a structured, authoritative approach robs the child of such desirable qualities as independence, creativity, self-assertiveness and individuality. In fact, it is possible that a predictable framework facilitates the development of these behaviors and attitudes because of the security and trust it provides the child.

Weikart (1967) has noted that most preschool programs can be divided into two types. The traditional type, emphasizing social, emotional, and motor development, involves such activities as free play, arts and crafts, block play, finger painting, cutting and pasting, and singing. These are typical nursery-school activities. The second, more structured approach, as illustrated in Figure 12-1, includes activities designed to accomplish specific goals focusing on the cognitive and language areas. After a careful examination of research studies, Weikart concluded that "the debate between the so-called traditional and structured curriculum methods seem to be over" (1967, p. 180). He feels that the evidence

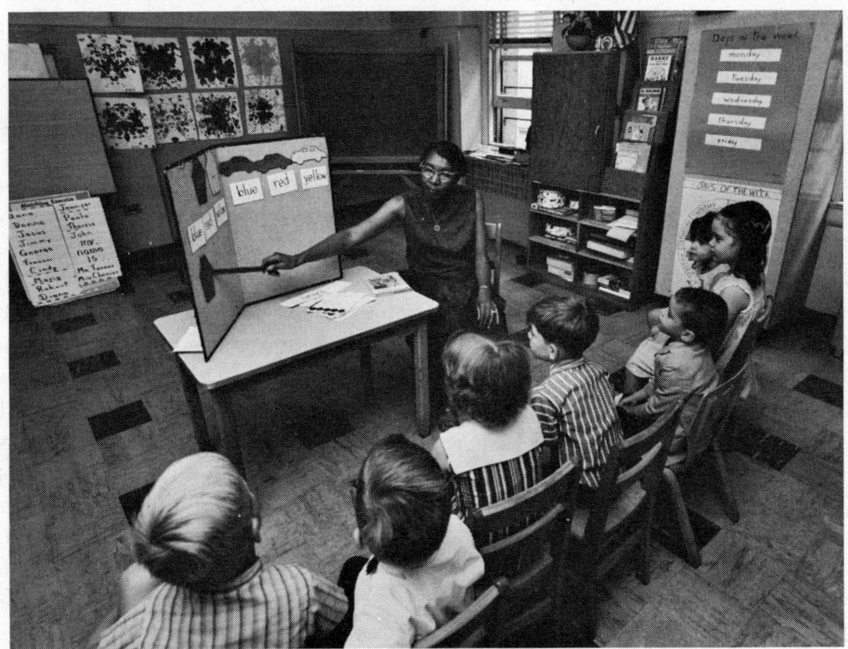

FIGURE 12-1 Preschool program of the structured type, with emphasis on the cognitive and language areas (photo by Ken Hyman).

is sufficiently strong to indicate that the traditional nursery school is effective in establishing initial rapport with the child but ineffective in accomplishing the goal of stimulating continued cognitive growth through a carefully programmed sequence of learning activities. In support of this conclusion, a study (Edwards & Stern, 1970) comparing the results of a structured curriculum with a traditional unstructured program with Head Start children found significantly greater gains on a number of measures in the group receiving the structured language curriculum. While initially nursery-school activities were not designed to facilitate cognitive development, the selling point of many private nursery schools today is that they prepare the child for school learning. Bereiter and Engelmann (1966) have pointed out that it is unwise, in programs for disadvantaged children, to focus on traditional nursery-school activities because they were intended for middle-class children who receive sufficient intellectual stimulation in the home. Deutsch has succinctly termed this the "built-in curriculum of the middle-class home." Indeed, the child's self concept and social and emotional development cannot be ignored; however, these can best be dealt with in a context of learning. The child who experiences school failure because of a lack of early stimulation will almost certainly suffer a lowered self-esteem. The only way to ensure permanent positive self-attitudes with regard to competency is to build in cognitive skills that enable the child to cope with the academic demands of school.

FORMAL SCHOOLING

The beginning of school marks the end of an era for the child chronologically and psychologically. Before the age of five the child interacts more with parents and siblings than anyone else. They are the greatest influence on him. To be sure, he has playmates in the neighborhood but his parents are the only adults he knows intimately. They set much of the pattern of his daily life. It is their approval that is most important to him. With the beginning of school the child's world expands and becomes more complex. He spends more of his time away from home in the company of people other than his immediate family. The opinions, approval, and demands of these people now become of increasing importance. Yet he may now need his parents more than ever before—at least they wish this.

> Entrance into the conventional first grade marks a sharp break in the actual structure of the child's experience. For the first time in the case of many children, they are expected to conform to a group pattern imposed by an adult who is in charge of too many children to be constantly aware of each child as an individual. Flash cards are flashed at the group all at once. Stories are told and everybody must listen whether he will or not. Drawing paper and crayons are meted out whether you happen to feel like drawing at that moment or not. One child who found this shift quite beyond endurance remarked after his first day in school, "It's awful; all you do is mind all day long." And another day he added, "It really is awful. All you do is sit and sit and sit" (Murphy, Murphy, & Newcomb, 1937, p. 652).

School Readiness

Some children adapt to the new conditions imposed by the start of formal education, whereas others encounter difficulties. How can these differences be explained? Are they predictable before school entrance so that some ameliorative measures may be applied? What sort of preschool experiences facilitate successful adjustment in the first grade? Although, of course, there are no final answers to these questions, data are available that permit some fairly certain conclusions.

One investigation that made use of anthropometric assessments of physique (Simon, 1959) found that students who were failing in first grade were less mature physically than a group of successful students. Thus physical maturity would seem to pertain to school readiness.

To check school readiness and adjustment to the first grade, Medinnus (1961a) subjected a small group of five-year-olds to a series of tests in the year before they started school. He also interviewed their mothers, made ratings of the psychological atmosphere of their homes, and had both parents complete a standard parent-attitude questionnaire. Upon the children's completion of the first grade, he correlated their scores on several criteria of achievement with their scores on academic skill type of tests. In addition, he related teacher ratings of general adjustment in the first grade to the scores obtained through assessment of the home psychological atmosphere. What he found was a moderate correlation of about +0.50 between the children's IQ scores on a Stanford–Binet test administered before school entrance and their achievement scores at the end of the first grade. Thus, although intelligence is important in academic success in the first grade, other factors such as motivation, interest, and application also seem to have relevance. Further, Medinnus noted that the amount of information possessed by a child before entering school predicted reading achievement by the end of the first grade.

To discover how much children knew before their entrance into first grade, Medinnus confronted them with a questionnaire that modified one used by

Templin (1958). These were some of its questions:

> How many pennies in a nickel?
> Friday, Saturday, Sunday—what day comes after Sunday?
> What are the colors in the flag?
> What is a helicopter?
> What are clouds made of?
> Whom was Red Riding Hood going to see?
> What was the name of the boy who climbed the beanstalk?
> What do we call a butterfly before it becomes a butterfly?
> What is butter made from?
> What is the brake on a car for?
> In what game do you have a home run?

Among 40 five-year-olds quizzed, Medinnus found a wide range of total scores. Because of a substantial correlation between the children's mental ages and their scores, it was impossible to attribute higher performance on the information test to a richer home environment. Of course, innately more intelligent children turn up more often in the better socioeconomic homes, where parents provide a fuller, more stimulating environment than is supplied by lower-class parents. However, irrespective of socioeconomic status, the amount of time a parent spends reading to a child and the variety of experiences to which the youngster is exposed—trips, museums, zoos—serve to expand the quantity of his information.

Although IQ predicts academic success in the first grade better than any other measure, the importance of an intellectually stimulating home environment must not be underestimated. First-grade children who scored high on a standard measure of mental maturity, Milner (1951) learned, came from homes with more books available; these children were read to more often by their parents and in general experienced a more positive emotional relationship with their parents than children who scored low. Time spent reading to a child accomplishes many things. It establishes a warm, friendly relationship between parent and child, which increases the child's sense of security. The child's questions and comments inspired by the reading aid the parent's understanding of the child. And the influence of parent reading to child is certainly evident in the child's record of achievement.

From what the mothers told him in their interview, Medinnus rated their homes on a number of the Fels Parent Rating Scales. The differences in the ratings of homes of well-adjusted and poorly adjusted first-graders showed a higher rating on a "dependence-encouraging factor" for those of the well-adjusted children (Medinnus, 1961b). This is borne out by Chance's (1961) study of academic achievement in the first grade. Mothers of the children who achieved above average in relation to intelligence favored later independence for them than mothers of children whose achievement on the basis of intelligence was low. Both findings seem to contradict the common notion that parents should stress early independence in their children to prepare them for school life. To Medinnus, great parental concern with the encouragement of independence perhaps reflected a basic rejection of the child. Parental clichés that children must learn to "stand on their own two feet," and "fight their own battles" may be attempts to justify an unwillingness to provide the child with emotional support, nurture, and acceptance. The teacher can teach the child to count but can never fully compensate for a lack of parental love and acceptance. Parents best prepare their children for school with affectional, accepting relationships.

Readiness Tests. A number of academic-readiness tests predict a child's capacity to master intellectual tasks and aid a teacher in identifying areas of strength and weakness in a particular child. Most of those tests at first-grade level assess reading readiness since reading is the primary preoccupation in the early elementary years. The principal element in most tests of reading readiness is the ability to discriminate word and letter forms. Comprehension and range of information are also included. Figure 12-2 illustrates the kind of item contained in a reading-readiness test.

Since the term *readiness* implies both level of maturity and prior experience, probably the best clues to academic achievement in first grade are scores of IQ tests and information tests. The former assesses mental maturity and the latter provides a measure of the range of the child's experiences. Correlations between certain tests administered to five-year-olds and the youngsters' achievement in reading at the end of first grade are presented in Table 12-1 (Medinnus, 1961a).

School Entrance and the Child

It is only natural to expect some changes in the child as a result of exposure to the formal school situation. Conformity to the demands of a new adult, intimate contact with a number of other

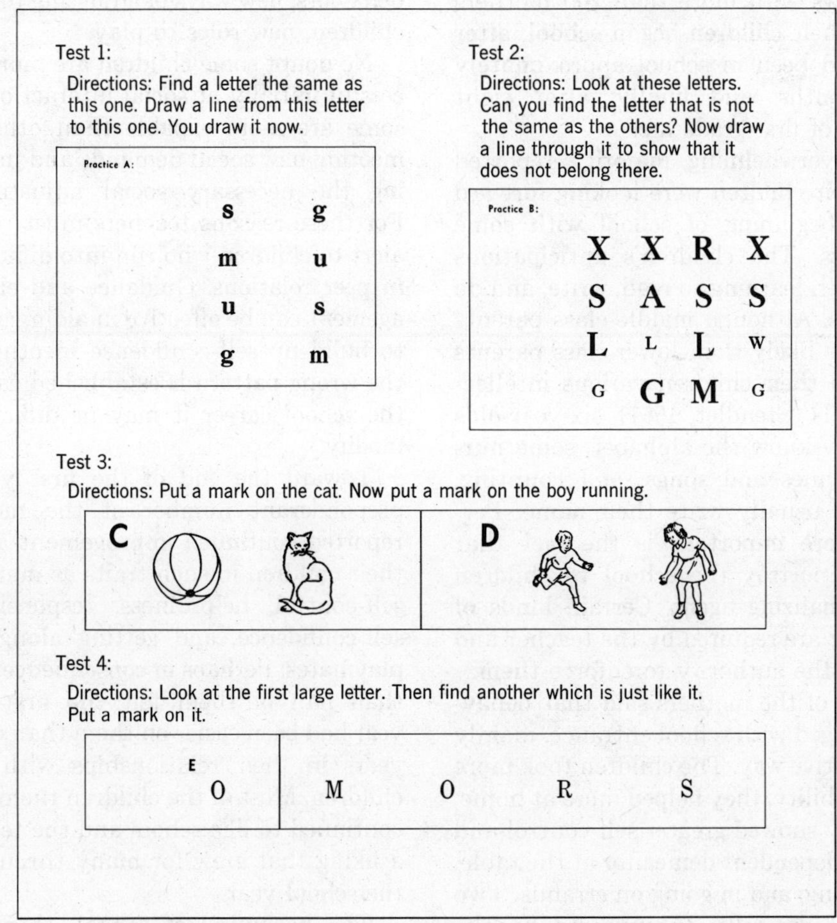

FIGURE 12-2 Sample items from the Lee–Clark Reading Readiness Test (Lee & Clark, 1951).

TABLE 12-1 Correlates of First-Grade Reading Achievement

Test Administered at Age 5	SRA Achievement Test			
	Language Perception	Verbal-Pictorial	Vocabulary	Comprehension
Stanford–Binet IQ	.51	.57	.41	.57
Gates Reading Readiness	.61	.57	.54	.64
Information test	.48	.51	.46	.42
Draw-A-Man IQ	.25	.36	.31	.22

children, separation from the mother for a substantial part of the day—all these must impinge on the child's behavior and his concept of the self. Information pertinent to this point was obtained by Stendler and Young (1950, 1959) in interviews with more than 200 mothers before their children began school, after they had been in school approximately two months, and finally, after eight months of first-grade life.

An overwhelming majority reported that their children were looking forward to the beginning of school with some eagerness. The children's anticipations dealt with learning to read, write, and do numbers. Although middle-class parents are more likely than lower-class parents to teach their children various intellectual skills (Stendler, 1951), six-year-olds generally know the alphabet, some nursery rhymes and songs, and counting, and can usually write their name. Perhaps more important is the fact that parents portray the school to children as a socializing agent. Certain kinds of behavior are required by the teacher and she has the authority to enforce them.

Most of the mothers said that behavior changed with school entrance, mainly in a positive way. The children took more responsibility, they helped more at home, and they showed greater self-control and more independent demeanor at the table, in dressing, and in going on errands. Two kinds of difficulty encountered by the child, both arising from social relations, were mentioned by the mothers. In more than half the interviews, they spoke of aggressiveness on the part of other children or of exclusion from a group. Thus school attendance clearly involves much social learning. The child learns new behaviors, new ways of adjusting to other children, new roles to play.

No doubt some children are more successful initially at social interaction and some are more capable than others in meeting new social demands and in making the necessary social adjustments. For these reasons teachers must remain alert to children who run into difficulties in peer relations. Guidance and encouragement can be effective in aiding a child to build up self-confidence in others. If the wrong pattern is established early in the school career it may be difficult to modify.

Toward the end of the first year, a preponderant number of the mothers reported continued improvement among their children in such traits as maturity, self-control, helpfulness, responsibility, self-confidence, and getting along with playmates. Perhaps in consequence, more than half of them felt the first-grade year had been easier on them than earlier years in their relationships with their children. Most of the children themselves continued to like school and the teacher, a liking that grew for many throughout the school year.

The beginning of school, then, is a significant moment for a child. Persons other than his immediate family begin to play an important role in the socialization process. His success in this new venture and his adjustment to its demands depend intimately on the skills and attitudes he brings to the new situation. However, the child's relationship with his parents continues to exert its influence on his behavior—and so it shall continue to be.

THE TEACHER

Throughout the child's days in school, especially during his early years there, the teacher without doubt exercises the most significant psychological influence on him. The physical plant of the school, the teaching materials, the classroom schedule and routine all wane in comparison with the potential impact of the teacher on the child—on his adjustment to school, on his personality development, and on his academic achievement. Interest and encouragement shown by a teacher may determine the choice of a career or a decision about values. Second only to the role of parent in its effect on the child, the teacher role becomes costly if filled by any but the very best people. It is the teacher more than the doctor, lawyer, journalist, or entertainer who can inspire the leaders of tomorrow, the new generation, and through these children influence the world of the future.

Teacher Functions

Both teachers and parents are concerned in Western culture with the psychological and emotional welfare of the child. Both constrain behavior. Both are in a position to enforce standards of conduct. Yet the functions assigned to each differ. The teacher does not have the responsibility for the child's physical welfare outside the school setting—that is a parent function—but is charged with stimulating and guiding the child's intellectual development. Moreover, because of the nature of the school situation, the teacher is influential in determining the child's attitudes and values.

How does this influence work? Obviously the teacher's values are communicated to the pupils directly through rules, comments, commands, and discussions. But perhaps what a teacher *says* is less important than what she *does*. The teacher serves as a model for the children; they identify with her and try to emulate her. Teacher approval is sought. Teacher disapproval is avoided. Indeed, the parent may feel somewhat rejected when his first-grade child declares, "I love my teacher more than anyone else in the world," or when a second-grader insists, "No, mother. My teacher wants me to do it this way and she's right." Nor is it any accident when a third-grader calls the teacher "mother." She is, in fact, a mother surrogate—a mother substitute—for the young, school-aged child. The child's attitudes toward his parents may extend to the teacher or the teacher may actually take the place of an absent or neglectful parent in a child's emotional life. As late as preadolescence, *hero worship* of a teacher may still appear in a child.

However, the functions of a teacher are limited by the primary function of teaching. The teacher is not a therapist. She cannot practice individual therapy with certain children. She can, of course, create an atmosphere in the classroom that is conducive to the mental health of the pupils. In general, the teacher can alleviate or aggravate children's problems. But she can never substitute fully for a parent who is either physically absent or psychologically inadequate. Teachers function most efficiently and effectively when parents discharge their responsibility to the child. Frequently they are heard to remark that although they are aware of a particular child's emotional needs, their responsibility to the remaining 30 or 35 members of the class prevents their taking as much action toward this child as they might like. Their job is to teach certain academic skills; though responsible to an extent for the emotional and psychological well-being of their pupils, teachers can be neither psychotherapists nor parent substitutes.

Teacher-Pupil Interactions

The praise, reward, disapproval, and punishment administered by the teacher inevitably affect the emotional adjustment and self concept of some, if not all, pupils. Are these forms of encouragement or discipline dispensed in equal measure to all pupils? Or are certain ones more likely to be praised or punished? Clearly, the teacher receives the most satisfaction from children who learn rapidly and who without difficulty grasp the material presented. After all, the teacher's sense of adequacy as a teacher depends in large part on how well she accomplishes her primary mission of teaching the academic skills.

A study of the pattern of teacher approval and disapproval supports this notion (DeGroat & Thompson, 1949). To a sixth-grade class a "guess who" technique of a dozen statements of teacher approval and an equal number of statements of teacher disapproval was applied. Some of these statements were: "Here is someone whose work is often pointed out as being very neat"; "Here is someone on whom the teacher calls when she wants the right answer"; "Here is someone whem the teacher often asks to do errands for her or to be monitor while she is out of the room"; "Here is someone whom the teacher often scolds for disturbing the class in some way (shooting paper wads, chewing gum, etc.)"; "Here is someone who is often suspected by the teacher when something happens while she is out of the room"; "Here is someone who is often pointed out as not doing [his] best work." By and large, relatively few children were nominated for either teacher approval or disapproval. This suggested that certain pupils enjoyed a much higher level of interaction with the teacher than others.

Several characteristics differentiated the high approval-low disapproval group from the low approval-low disapproval and high disapproval-low approval groups. Children of high approval were more intelligent; they rated higher in academic achievement and their scores on a personality-adjustment test were more favorable. Allowing for the tenuousness of cause-and-effect statements, this last point demonstrates a connection between teacher approval and pupil self-acceptance. This relationship may be viewed in various ways: those pupils who are more self-accepting elicit a favorable response in the teacher, or the teacher's good reaction to the child's behavior is conducive to an attitude of self-acceptance in the child. In any case, it seems unfortunate that teacher approval is limited to relatively few pupils—at least as perceived by the children themselves. Perhaps those who most need overt signs of teacher approval are least likely to receive them.

One investigation (Hoehn, 1954) found that teachers had more favorable contacts with children of high economic status than with those from lower economic backgrounds. Conversely, more conflict was seen between the teacher and the children of low economic status, especially among boys, than with youngsters of upper economic station. Hoehn concluded, however, that the basic factor in the contact between teacher and child was the latter's academic achievement.

Quantitatively there was more contact between the teacher and low achievers but qualitatively the tie between teacher and high achievers was more favorable.

In a study by Meyer and Thompson (1956) involving both the "guess who" technique and classroom observations of teacher-pupil interaction, boys were seen to receive more teacher disapproval than girls. It is not surprising, therefore, that girls express more positive attitudes toward school than boys (Antes, Anderson, & DeVault, 1965). The demands of school routine for orderliness and quiet are alien to the active, aggressive nature of boys. And when the resulting rebellious behavior brings forth blame and disapproval from the teacher, further hostility is generated. This is hardly likely to produce an atmosphere conducive to learning.

It has been shown that interaction between teacher and pupil relates to the pupil's acceptance by others as well as to his self-acceptance. Three studies, one at the first-grade level (Medinnus, 1962), another at sixth-grade level (Gronlund, 1950), and a third at tenth-grade level (Flanders and Havumaki, 1960), have all found that pupils receiving praise from teachers and preferred by teachers were more likely to be chosen by peers in a sociometric exercise, thus indicating greater acceptance by peers. To Medinnus this suggested that at the first-grade level children so identified with the teacher that her values became theirs. Behaviors praised by the teacher acquired positive, favorable value whereas those viewed negatively by her were similarly devalued by the pupils. In like manner, the teacher is able to influence the attitudes of the pupils in a great number of areas—attitudes toward minority-group children, personal likes and dislikes in others, attitudes toward handicapped or less favorably endowed children, and the like.

CLASSROOM ATMOSPHERE

Drawn from another science, the terms *atmosphere* and *climate* denote the sociopsychological relationships existing among the group in the classroom setting. Though perhaps applied somewhat awkwardly to the classroom, the two terms accurately suggest the pervasiveness of the psychological tone present in any single schoolroom. To a large extent it is the teacher who establishes the relationships that determine the prevailing psychological atmosphere.

Types of Atmosphere

What are the principal types of relationship that create a particular atmosphere in the classroom? Many categories have been used to measure the relationship between teacher and pupils. These categories have then become indices of the over-all classroom atmosphere. They include dominating, integrating, learner-centered, teacher-centered, democratic, *laissez faire,* authoritarian, and more. In one study of the social and emotional climate of classrooms (Withall, 1949), teacher behavior fell into seven main classes, of which six fitted into the categories of learner-centered and teacher-centered. The learner-centered behaviors were of three kinds: statements supporting the learner, which reassured or commended him; statements accepting and clarifying the pupil, which helped him refine his ideas and feelings and gave him the sense of being understood; and statements or questions about the structure of problems, which provided information or raised questions about a problem in a manner that facilitated its solution. The teacher-centered behaviors were also of three kinds: directive statements, which outlined a recommended course of action for the pupil to follow; reproving or deprecatory statements, intended to deter pupils from unacceptable behavior; and self-supporting statements, designed to justify the teacher's position or actions.

Teachers who establish positive social climates in the classroom are concerned about mental-health concepts and personality dynamics. They feel responsible for the personality growth and development of their pupils as well as their academic learning. Such teachers are alert and sensitive to their pupils' anxieties, self concepts, peer-group relations, and attitudes toward school.

A further study by Withall (1952), dealing with four seventh-grade classes, showed marked differences in the atmosphere under the four teachers. Yet from day to day there was a moderate amount of consistency for any one of them. Although knowledge is rather fragmentary on the effects of different classroom atmospheres on the emotional adjustment and academic accomplishments of pupils, certain kinds of psychological relations between teacher and children are far more conducive than others to the emotional and intellectual well-being of the youngsters in a school setting.

Anderson has distinguished between dominating and socially integrating behavior. Integrating behavior was described as "flexible, dynamic, yielding, spontaneous." The individual who showed this behavior sought and found "common purposes with another; he expended energy with another, not against another." Dominating behavior, on the other hand, was "rigid, fixed, static." The dominating individual neither respected nor attempted to understand another's individuality. Energy was expended against another individual; the conflict of differences grew. Each kind of behavior tended to elicit the same kind of behavior in someone else (Anderson, 1939b). Some tie was found between integrative scores of children and chronological age, suggesting that perhaps, in a developmental sense at least, an integrating behavior was a sign of maturity (Anderson, 1937a). Although developed originally to assess the social interaction of preschool children (Anderson, 1937a,b; 1939b), the two categories of dominating and socially integrating behavior have been applied pertinently to the classroom interaction of teacher and pupils.

A group of kindergarten children were making May baskets. Terry had folded his basket on the lines which had been drawn on the material the night before by the teacher. He had pasted the flaps as he had been instructed and had the handle fastened in place. The teacher had cut out of other paper a handful of diamond-shaped pieces which she had distributed four to a child. These were to serve as decorations to be pasted horizontally on the basket. As she walked about the room she noticed Terry pasting his diamond decoration vertically.

"Oh, oh, Terry," she said. "The decorations are to be pasted on lying down and not standing up."

"But I want to paste mine this way," said Terry.

"Well, that isn't the way they are supposed to go. Here now, just paste it this way." And she turned the diamond horizontally and pasted it before Terry seemed to know what had happened. She remained while Terry at her instructions pasted two more shapes horizontally. Then she turned away, leaving Terry to paste the fourth.

At the end of the period Terry had only three decorations on his basket. When the teacher inquired about his basket, Terry, pointing to the undecorated side of his basket, said that he did not want one there.

"Oh, but every basket should have four. Here is one your color. We'll just paste it on quickly." And with Terry speechless and transfixed she pasted it on quickly.

Mary Lou had observed that at her table several handles did not stick. "I guess I don't want a handle," she remarked to the boy seated next to her. She cut up the handle of her basket and pasted the pieces as decorations all over the basket. The teacher's remark to this *fait accompli* was, "Oh, you've spoiled yours, Mary Lou; yours is all messy and doesn't have a handle" (Anderson, 1943, p. 459).

Certainly the kind of teacher behavior described in the foregoing excerpt fits Withall's teacher-centered category. Noncompliance with goals defined by the teacher is castigated. No respect is shown for either the child's wishes or his individuality.

Through observation and recording of the interaction between teacher and pupils, Anderson (1939a,b) found teachers varying in dominating and integrating classroom behavior. In contacts with individual students, two teachers had twice as many dominating as integrating relationships, whereas a third teacher had five times as many dominating associations as integrating ones. In behavior toward their whole class, the dominating characteristic in all three teachers outdid the integrating by a ratio of five to one. Among pupils there were wide differences in the extent and nature of their contact with the teacher, as shown in Figure 12-3.

Children's Evaluation of Teachers

When asked to name reasons for disliking school, children mention the teacher more frequently than any other factor (Tenenbaum, 1940). Unfortunately, there appears to be increasing

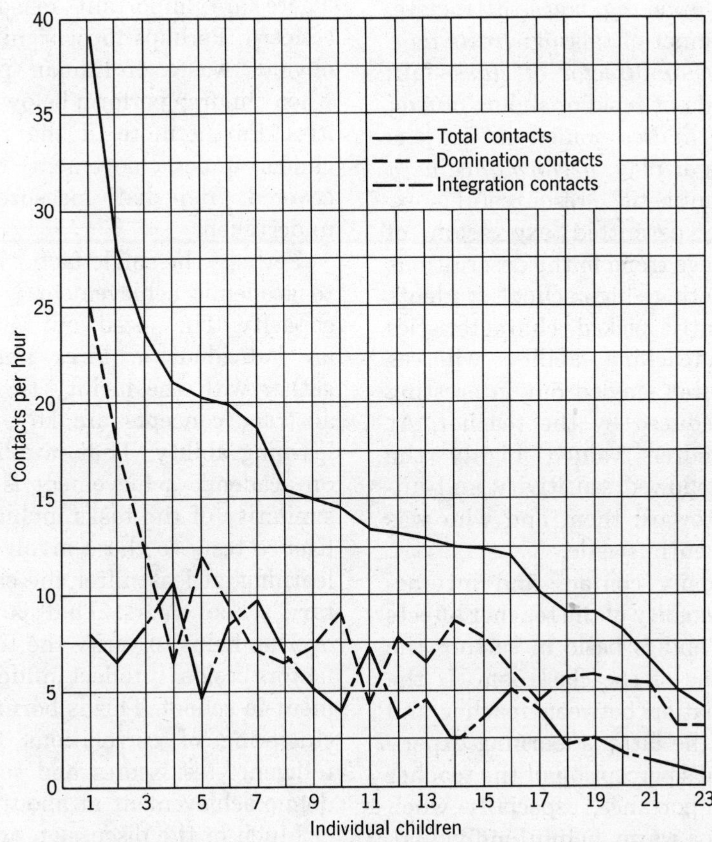

FIGURE 12-3 Mean number of contacts per hour which teacher A had with individual children enrolled in the morning session (Anderson, 1939b, p. 337).

dissatisfaction with the teacher from fourth through sixth grade, with older children rating their teacher less favorably than younger ones (Neale & Proshek, 1967). Children hold strong opinions about their teachers and the qualities they prefer in them. The qualities they single out refer as often to characteristics of the teacher as an individual as to the characteristics of her teaching ability. One study, in fact, noted that a majority of the traits used by elementary-school children to describe well-liked teachers covered personality and disposition (Leeds & Cook, 1947).

Jersild (1940) found elementary-school children mentioning these qualities as typical of the teachers they liked best: *human qualities as a person*—sympathetic, cheerful, good tempered; *physical appearance, grooming, voice*—attractive, neat, nice manner of talking; *traits as a disciplinarian or director of class*—fair, consistent, did not scold or shout; *participation in activities*—joined in or permitted games or play; *performance as a teacher*—enthusiastic, resourceful, explained well, permitted expression of opinion. The age trend in the descriptions was worth noting; high-school students more frequently picked characteristics bearing on teaching ability whereas younger children singled out interesting projects introduced by the teacher. At all ages children valued highly the teacher who showed sensitivity and understanding toward them and who was effective and enthusiastic.

Through daily contact and interaction, the personality of the teacher affects the children and is basic in setting the emotional tone of the classroom. If the emotional relation between teacher and pupil affects the latter's learning experience, the child's perception of the teacher is of vital importance, especially when the teacher is a warm, helpful individual. This is perhaps truer in elementary school, where the teacher indeed serves as a mother surrogate. An unsympathetic, ill-tempered, unfair, uninteresting teacher certainly cannot kindle children's interest in school and in the entire learning process.

SCHOOL ACHIEVEMENT

Since the primary goal of the school is the acquisition of academic skills by pupils, the extent to which this goal is attained reflects the success of the school's endeavor. It is not surprising, therefore, that great attention has been paid to academic achievement. Most research on the subject has sought to identify the factors responsible for differences in individual accomplishment. There are important reasons for this concern. Perhaps most significant is the obvious waste of human potentialities when children perform below their capacities. Furthermore, if the reason for a child's underachievement can be discovered, remedial measures may be undertaken.

Perhaps the single factor most related to academic achievement is intellectual capacity. The speed and level at which an individual acquires knowledge together with the facility to comprehend abstract concepts are key elements in learning ability. That intelligence bears on academic achievement is seen in the similarity of the tasks included in intelligence tests to those involved in school learning, at least after the early elementary school years. That is to say, the overlap helps to verify the tie. Yet other factors besides intellect influence achievement in school. This is borne out by the clustering of correlations between intelligence-test scores and scores of academic achievement at about +0.55.

Much of the discussion among educators about underachievement in the first grade and in the early elementary years has centered about the question of immaturity. The term needs definition. Few attempts have been made to define or evaluate emotional immaturity. Physiological and chronological immaturity are another matter. In a study comparing the scholastic achievement of 50 overage and 50 underage pupils in grades two–six, Carter (1956) found that 87 percent of the underaged did not measure up to the classroom performance of children of normal age. Carter further noted that chronological age had a greater effect on boys than on girls. Simon (1959) observed failing students to be less mature than successful ones on several measures of physiological configuration even when the two were matched on IQ and chronological age. Among third-grade children, Klausmeier and Check (1959) detected a connection between physical development and reading and arithmetic achievement in boys, yet not in girls. Medinnus (1961c) proposed that although chronological age might shape a child's initial adjustment to first grade, it might be less important than other factors by the end of the year. This is seen in the low correlation, +0.21, between chronological age and scores of adjustment after a year of schooling. Academic achievement, however, was only one of several factors entering into the assessment of general adjustment.

Parental Factors

A variety of parental factors influence a child's achievement in every school grade. These include the emotional relationship between parent and child, the attitudes of the parent toward school and school achievement, and parental concern for and interest in the child's performance.

Morrow and Wilson (1961) have provided support for this view in a study of the perceptions high-achieving and underachieving high-school boys have of their families. The former were more likely to see their family relationships in a positive light. They described their parents as approving, trusting, affectionate, relatively nonrestrictive, and encouraging–but not pressuring with respect to achievement. They said they accepted their parents' standards; in other words, they identified with them. In a similar study (Davids & Hainsworth, 1967), underachieving teenage boys perceived their mothers as high in control. Further, there was a much greater discrepancy for the underachievers than for the high achievers between the mother's report of several child-rearing attitudes and the son's perception of her attitudes. This suggests a lack of agreement and a lack of communication between the low-achieving boy and his mother.

Clinical studies of learning difficulties have commented that underachievement may signify a rebellion against parents. Despite only slight research support for this position, it seems reasonable to believe that excessive pressure for achievement unaccompanied by a satisfactory and rewarding relationship with parents may engender anxiety and resentment in the child. The anxiety may inhibit the child from working to full capacity, whereas the resentment may cause him to disappoint the parents by not meeting their expectations. Everyday observation of child behavior shows that rebellion may take a number of forms.

Personality and Emotional Factors

Notwithstanding the emotional and adjustment problems found in children who have difficulties in learning or achieving, the drawing of cause-and-effect conclusions is dangerous. In fact, in a study of 34 children admitted for inpatient care to a psychiatric hospital, it was observed that none of them was retarded in educational achievement (Tamkin, 1960). Conceivably, emotional problems and educational disabilities may be symptoms of the same underlying disturbance. Moreover, educational difficulties may be as frequent a cause of emotional problems as the other way around.

Within the limits of these precautions, several studies exemplify attempts to uncover emotional and personality factors as causes of scholastic underachievement. Among 20 high-school boys designated as underachievers, Kimball (1953) found the following significant things in their backgrounds. There was a poor relationship between father and son, marked by an absence of strong identification with the father; there were passivity, strong needs for dependency, propensities toward aggression, and pronounced feelings of inferiority. These characteristics described a child with a low concept of self, low self-esteem, and a lack of the personal security necessary to permit a manipulation of the environment in order to achieve. Feelings of dependency and inferiority prevent an individual from realizing his potential.

Other studies (Conklin, 1940; Walsh, 1956) have implied that underachievers have a history of disturbed personal relations, especially with respect to their parents. In consequence, they feel rejection and an inability to express their hostile and negative reactions. In a longitudinal study by Haggard (1957), high achievers, in distinction to low achievers, tended to be more responsive to the socialization pressures of their parents; they accepted parental values and endeavored to live up to them and to the expectations of their elders. Yet this seemed to bring on anxiety. At the level of the third grade, and more so by the seventh, there was evidence of hostility and antagonism toward adults among high-achieving children. By the seventh grade the anxiety apparent in these youngsters impeded their originality and creativity. By and large, they were aggressive, competitive, and persistent.

It would seem that the child who is relatively free from anxiety and other emotional upsets best concentrates on academic matters. Illustrating this point is a large-scale, longitudinal study (Feldhusen, Thurston, & Benning, 1970) which examined the relation between aggressiveness and school achievement as well as the relation between achievement and socially approved behavior. All third-, sixth-, and ninth-grade teachers in a single county were asked to nominate the two boys and two girls in their classes who most consistently displayed aggressive behavior and the two boys and two girls who most consistently displayed socially approved behavior. Aggressive behavior was defined as follows: "Disrupts class, bullies others, has temper tantrums, is overly dominant, is tardy or absent without excuse, talks back, lies, and is cruel." The child demonstrating socially approved behavior was described in these terms: "Industrious, productive, good-natured, ambitious, cooperative, truthful, and performs required tasks on time." Home background differences were noted between the two groups of children; the aggressive children ". . . had parents who displayed less affection toward them, offered inadequate supervision and discipline, were less able to develop a cohesive family relationship, were on lower educational and occupational levels, and were less effective participants in the life and services of the community" (Feldhusen *et al.*, 1970, p. 432). Five years later, comparisons were made between the aggressive and the socially approved children on school achievement as measured by school grades and scores on a standard achievement test. First, with respect to school grades, the aggressive children received lower grades than their socially approved peers in the four areas examined: English, science, mathematics, and social studies. This finding was corroborated by the results on the achievement test where the aggressive children scored lower on all five subtests: reading, writing, social studies, science, and mathematics. While several interpretations are plausible, it is likely that aggressive classroom behavior is of complex origin and that home problems combine with aggressive school behavior to affect adversely the child's school achievement. This whole process is circular in nature in that it leads to still poorer achievement.

Undoubtedly past experiences of success or failure in meeting the demands of a task, together with the attitudes toward these experiences, influence both an individual's performance and the level of achievement to which he aspires. Sears (1940) has demonstrated the effect of past experiences on one's setting of goals. She experimented with two groups of fourth-, fifth- and sixth-graders, requiring them to select a series of goals for performance following respective successful and failing experiences. One group had successful records of achievement in reading and arithmetic, the other had been much less successful. In the experimental situation, the successful group attempted as a unit to improve performance but set realistic goals. The failing group was less consistent; some members chose goals of a very low level in the hope of attaining them, whereas others selected goals of unrealistic challenge. Both goals were dictated by a desire to avoid failure.

A word is necessary about the effect of a series of repeated failures on the child's self-esteem. Demoralization sets in. One truly cannot condone any school curriculum in which certain children cannot avoid such failure. Perhaps teachers, because of the educational attainments demanded by their positions, are unable to understand the meaning of failure to a child and the impact it has on him. Naturally, every child does not have to be protected from failure, but success, in reality, is a relative term; it is relative to the goals set by the teacher, by the parent, and by the child himself. Although a sense of success certainly comes from achievement, it may derive also from having done a job to the best of one's ability. And ability varies in a classroom as much as height, weight, and color of one's eyes.

Miscellaneous Factors

Teachers affect the achievement of their pupils by the kind of contacts they have with them. Several investigations of high-school classrooms indicate that high achievers receive more motivation than low achievers from teacher approval (Battle, 1957), and that there is a closer kinship between the values held by the teacher and by high achievers than between those of the teacher and low achievers (McDavid, 1959). That is, the teacher tends to reward with approval those students most similar to himself in certain areas and this approval inspires them to strain for higher levels of performance.

Finally, there is the matter of interest. Generally, children—and adults too—do best those things in which they are most interested, and vice versa. School achievement is no exception. Girls prefer and do best in language and literature, boys in science and history. More important than sex differences is the interest value inhering in the academic materials. Children are not all interested in the same things, happily. It behooves the teacher, the builders of curriculum, and the authors of materials for academic use to ferret out the interests of pupils and also their *potential interests* in order to meet and stimulate these effectively in the classroom. There is little excuse for history, or for literature, or for science failing to hold the interest of pupils.

SOCIAL CLASS AND THE SCHOOL

To what extent does social-class membership affect the child's school achievement and his behavior in the school setting? Is the school meeting equally well the needs of children from different social classes?

The interest in educational circles on social-class differences in attitudes and behavior grew out of a series of publications in the 1940's that focused attention on such differences (see Davis & Havighurst, 1946; Davis & Dollard, 1940; Havighurst & Taba, 1949; Hollingshead, 1949; Warner, Havighurst, & Loeb, 1944). The data cited in these studies emphasized that the school was largely a middle-class institution with a middle-class bias in personnel, curriculum materials, and advocated values for child behavior. The result was that the middle-class child was rewarded with approval and support from the school, whereas the lower-class child, because of the discrepancy between his behavior and attitudes and those approved by the school, was neglected, punished, and misunderstood.

Stimulated in part by government concern for our economically disadvantaged, which resulted in the War on Poverty program, much recent research and discussion are available on this topic. Numerous action programs are in progress. While insufficient monies are available for such programs, public concern has been aroused to some extent and the problems involved are being attacked in a variety of ways. A number of broad issues related to social class and the school are receiving attention. Each of these will be discussed briefly.

Social Class Differences in Attitudes toward the School. On the basis of a careful review of social-class differences in child-rearing practices as they historically have affected the socialization process, Bronfenbrenner (1958) concluded that the gap may be narrowing. Some differences in values remain among the classes, but there is an overlap as well as wide variations within any single social class. Kohn (1959) discovered a broadly common set of values among working-class and middle-class mothers in parental ratings of child behavior. Both groups of mothers rated happiness, honesty, consideration, obedience, dependability, manners, and self-control as traits to be desired in children in the middle elementary-school years. Although the middle-class mothers emphasized self-control and the lower-class mothers were more likely to value obedience, *the similarities between the two groups were greater than the differences.*

The poor are becoming increasingly aware of and convinced of the importance of education. It is true that lower-class people are less likely to mention higher education when asked what is necessary to "get along well in the world." But, as Cloward and Jones (1963) point out, this is probably because lower-class individuals are oriented toward a lower occupational level. The middle-class person is oriented toward the "ideal" of a professional or semiprofessional occupation, which, indeed, requires more education. However, adequate recognition is not given to the fact that in surveys more than half of the lower-class respondents mention education as important for their children, especially for boys (Cloward & Jones, 1963). The lower-class individual has thus come to understand the need for education in getting a decent job, and to realize that education enables him to cope more adequately with a complex society (Riessman, 1962)—to understand the small print in the contract for a used-car purchase; to be informed about available welfare benefits; and to be informed about such issues as the draft, income tax, and legal rights.

A sample of mothers of children enrolled in a Head Start program in Santa Clara County, California, were surveyed with regard to their expectations for the program (Medinnus, 1967). They were asked, "What would you like to have your child get out of the Head Start program?" Their responses, emphasizing academic preparation (language, number concepts) and social skills (getting along with peers, increased independence), suggest that these mothers, primarily Mexican-American, were aware of the demands of the school situation. While not so well-informed or knowledgeable as better-educated middle-class mothers, these lower-class women were not ignorant of factors making for subsequent school success. The crucial difference between the two groups is that lower-class mothers, especially those of minority background, feel unqualified and unable to give their children the kinds of experience that will prepare them academically for school. These mothers are interested and motivated, but they lack the skills. The school must make a far greater effort to involve the lower-class parent in its activities. The Head Start program has attempted to do this, and with some success.

Middle-Class Values that Prevail in the School Prevent the Lower-Class Child from Functioning Adequately in This Situation. It is true that the middle-class child enjoys a continuity between his home experiences and values and those in the school. Frequent contradictions are experienced by the lower-class child, especially with regard to such values as long-term goals, emphasis on thinking rather than doing, seriousness attached to learning, individual competition, and language as a tool. The solution is not, however, to adopt lower-class values as the norm for our school systems. Awareness of these contradictions should enable the teacher and the school in general to gain a fuller understanding of the problems faced by these children, and to develop new techniques to cope with these problems. Positive aspects of lower-class culture should be recognized and fostered.

The Poor School Achievement of the Lower-Class Child is an Inevitable Consequence of His Background. It is extremely important for the school to be aware that the lower-class child's poor achievement is frequently caused by larger social forces such as poverty, family disintegration, urban blight, and poor housing. Only when these conditions are eliminated can we expect significant improvement in school performance. As Riessman (1962) points out, a number of subtle and not-so-subtle factors operating in the school situation work to the disadvantage of the lower-class child. Teacher turnover is far greater in schools in disadvantaged neighborhoods. New and inexperienced teachers predominate in these schools. For a variety of reasons intelligence tests are inappropriate for assessing the learning potential of these children. Much of the content of schoolbooks is alien to the experiences of the lower-class child. The teacher tends to favor those children who succeed in schoolwork.

The lower-class child has not had a reinforcement history conducive to school success. He has not been reinforced or rewarded by praise and approval for the kinds of behavior (counting, reading, studying, curiosity) that make for school success. Thus he is not prepared intellectually or motivationally to cope with school-type tasks.

With adequate recognition of the deficiencies of the disadvantaged child and the reasons for them, the school, with earnestness and imagination, can develop the kinds of program that will compensate for and overcome these deficiencies. And this will require the support of society as a whole.

It is important for the school to be aware of and to understand some of the value differences between social classes. The teacher must be aware of the conditions of lower-class life and the way in which these conditions affect the child. But the child must also be respected as an individual and not dealt with as a member of one social class or another. The low relationship between a child's social-class background and various personality indices (Sewell, 1961) suggests that knowledge of social class is of little use in understanding the individual child. Insofar as social class can tell anything about a child, the information should be obtained. But more important, what is the emotional relation between the child and his parents, and between the child and his siblings? How does he get along with his peers? What is the nature of the child's concept of himself?

The School: An Eye in the Storm

The past decade has witnessed a tremendous amount of ferment and controversy revolving around numerous aspects of our educational system, including the structure of the school, the classroom, and the school day; the curriculum; the goals of education; and the means for reaching these goals.

Even casual observation of our school system suggests that the present lockstep approach cannot, by its very nature, meet the varying needs of each child. For the most part, children enter school at the age of five; they move along from one grade to the next as a group; they are exposed to a standard curriculum and are expected to acquire certain academic skills; a teacher who has met certain educational requirements is in charge of a class of 30–35 children. And so on.

There is no question but what this approach does an adequate job of educating a majority of our children. It is equally true, however, that the school is failing a significant and important proportion of children. For whatever reason, these children are not learning the academic skills which the school is attempting to teach them. Moreover, as a result of frustrating and deeply unsatisfying experiences in the school situation, they lose interest in the learning process and, worse, they come to distrust the adults who perpetuate such a system. Descriptions of such children and their tragic school experiences can be found in the following accounts: *Thirty-six Children* by Herbert Kohl (1967); *Death At An Early Age* by Jonathan Kozol (1967); and *The Way It Spozed To Be* by James Herndon (1968).

School reform is being advocated by a great cross-section of individuals both within and outside of the school system. The positions taken range along a continuum from moderate restructuring of the present educational system to a complete dismantling of the system. The moderate position views as faulty our current conceptions of the learning process and the teacher's role in that process. A more child-centered curriculum in which children "become involved in their own education" is advocated. "Open classrooms," "organic teaching," and "self-directed learning" are terms used to denote some of the changes or innovations discussed. The more radical reformers, on the other hand, view the schools only as reflections of the larger sick society in which little concern is shown for the dignity and the value of the individual. Schools are seen as exerting a dehumanizing influence on children; the atmosphere is repressive; and the curriculum dull and irrelevant. Finally, a position which will be discussed at the end of this section contends that schools have very little impact, one way or another, on children.

Perhaps the following books by John Holt most clearly articulate the case for a more flexible child-oriented approach to learning: *How Children Learn* (1967), *The Underachieving School* (1969), *How Children Fail* (1970a), and *What Do I Do on Monday* (1970b). He argues that learning can be and should be a growth experience which fosters children's natural curiosity, promotes a positive self concept, and which actively involves children in the learning process. The following quote captures the essence of Holt's argument:

> To a very great degree, school is a place where children learn to be stupid. A dismal thought, but hard to escape. Infants are not stupid. Children of one, two, or even three throw the whole of themselves into everything they do. They embrace life, and devour it; it is why they learn so fast, and are such good company. Listlessness, boredom, apathy—these all come later. Children come to school *curious*; within a few years most of that curiosity is dead, or at least silent. Open a first or third grade to questions, and you will be deluged; fifth graders say nothing. They either have no questions or will not ask them. They think, "What's this leading up to? What's the catch?" Last year, thinking that self-consciousness and embarrassment might be silencing the children, I put a question box in the classroom, and said that I would answer any questions they put into it. In four months I got one question—"How long does a bear live?" While I was talking about the life span of bears and other creatures, one child said impatiently, "Come on, get to the point." The expressions on the children's faces seemed to say, "You've got us here in school; now make us do whatever it is that you want us to do." Curiosity, questions, speculation—these are for outside school, not inside.
>
> Boredom and resistance may cause as much stupidity in school as fear. Give a child the kind of task he gets in school, and whether he is afraid of it, or resists it, or is willing to do it but bored by it, he will do the task with only a small part of his attention, energy, and intelligence. In a word, he will do it stupidly—even if correctly. This soon becomes a habit. He gets used to working at low power, he develops strategies to enable him to get by this way. In time he even starts to think of himself as being stupid, which is what most fifth graders think of themselves, and to think that his low-power way of coping with school is the only possible way.
>
> It does no good to tell such students to pay attention and think about what they are doing. I can see myself now, in one of my ninth-grade algebra classes in Colorado, looking at one of my flunking students, a boy who had become frozen in his school stupidity, and saying to him in a loud voice, "Think! Think! Think!" Wasted breath; he had forgotten how. The stupid way—timid, unimaginative, defensive, evasive—in which he met and dealt with the problems of algebra were, by that time, the only way he knew of dealing with them. His strategies and expectations were fixed; he couldn't even imagine any others. He really was doing his dreadful best.
>
> We ask children to do for most of a day what few adults are able to do even for an hour. How many of us, attending, say, a lecture that doesn't interest us, can keep our minds from wandering? Hardly any. Not I, certainly. Yet children have far less awareness of and control of their

attention than we do. No use to shout at them to pay attention. If we want to get tough enough about it, as many schools do, we can terrorize a class of children into sitting still with their hands folded and their eyes glued on us, or somebody; but their minds will be far away. The attention of children must be lured, caught, and held, like a shy wild animal that must be coaxed with bait to come close. If the situations, the materials, the problems before a child do not interest him, his attention will slip off to what does interest him, and no amount of exhortation or threats will bring it back.

A child is most intelligent when the reality before him arouses in him a high degree of attention, interest, concentration, involvement—in short, when he cares most about what he is doing. This is why we should make schoolrooms and schoolwork as interesting and exciting as possible, not just so that school will be a pleasant place, but so that children in school will act intelligently and get into the *habit* of acting intelligently. The case against boredom in school is the same as the case against fear; it makes children behave stupidly, some on purpose, most because they cannot help it. If this goes on long enough, as it does in school, they forget what it is like to grasp at something, as they once grasped at everything, with all their minds and senses; they forget how to deal positively and aggressively with life and experience, to think and say, "I see it! I get it! I can do it!" (Holt in Gross & Gross, 1969, pp. 75–77)

British Infant Schools. The informal approach to education which characterizes the British Infant School for children from 5 to 7 years has a long history dating back to the early part of the nineteenth Century. Weber (1971), based on her careful observations of these schools, summarizes concisely the philosophy underlying informal education:

Informal, as I understand it, refers to the setting, the arrangements, the teacher-child and child-child relationships that maintain, restimulate if necessary, and extend what is considered to be the most intense form of learning, the already existing child's way of learning through play and through the experiences he seeks out for himself.

The active force of such learning is considered to be curiosity, interest, and the needs of a child's own research for definition and relevance. The school setting or environment must be rich enough to foster and maintain this curiosity; it must be free enough to allow and even to help each individual follow the path indicated by his curiosity. Entwined with the experience gained through a child's own use of the school environment is the learning of skills, because skills are needed in the process. *How* a child would learn in the school setting was also individual—he would learn in his *own* way, at his *own* pace, exploring his *own* interests, for his *own* purposes. (Weber, 1971, p. 11)

While it is difficult to summarize the many aspects which, taken together, reflect the actual ongoing format of the Infant Schools and which, in turn, reflect their basic philosophy, a number of points can be enumerated: (1) The classroom is arranged in an informal manner, and, in fact, the children do not even have assigned desks. (2) The buildings are designed for easy access to the out-of-doors; consequently a number of "learning" activities are conducted outside; (3) Admission is on a gradual basis depending upon the needs of the individual child and of the school. Parents are encouraged to accompany and remain with their child initially. (4) Family or mixed-age grouping is advocated. (5) Reading is encouraged but largely on an informal basis, with a great variety of books—not standard texts— provided. (6) Many intellectually stimulating activities are available to the child and he is permitted to choose from among them. (7) A close and informal relationship exists between parents and teacher. (8) No clear differentiation is made among various school subjects—reading, mathematics, social studies, and science are integrated. (9) Emphasis is placed on a smooth transition, first from the home to the Infant School, and later, from the Infant School to the Junior Schools (ages 7-11). (10) Concern is shown for the "whole child"—his health and physical status, his natural curiosity, his love of learning about and exploring his environment, his feelings about himself, his uniqueness and individuality.

The Infant School philosophy has influenced American nursery schools, and to some extent our primary education. Clearly, our more formal approach which characterizes the later elementary grades bears little relation to the Infant School. As Weber notes, American education still emphasizes "teaching" while British education emphasizes "learning." With the current pressure for change in our educational practice, it seems likely that the informal education of the British Infant Schools will be adopted or adapted in some measure in this country.

Community Control and Free Schools. Stemming in part from the dissatisfaction of many minority group parents, pressures are being exerted for "community control" of schools. Though it certainly makes a great deal of sense to involve parents in the decision-making process with regard to many aspects of the school system, it is too early to judge the long-range effects of this policy. The establishment of "alternate schools" or "free schools" might be viewed as a logical extension of the community control movement. In addition to the free schools developed in urban ghettoes, similar schools have been organized in rural and urban settings by white middle-class parents who, for a variety of reasons, prefer an alternate approach to education for their children. Perhaps for somewhat different reasons, young "counter-culture" parents have established schools, mostly in rural settings. Needless to say, free schools vary greatly in their philosophies of education, in their educational goals, and in their approach to the learning process. In his book entitled, *Free Schools*, Kozol (1972) describes his experiences in establishing a free school for urban black children in Boston.

Educational Vouchers.[2] The "voucher system" might be viewed as lying somewhere between the community control position and free schools. Essentially the voucher scheme permits parents to choose which school they would like their children to attend.

> Under the proposed voucher system, a publicly accountable agency would issue a voucher for a year's schooling for each eligible child. This voucher could be turned over to any school which had agreed to abide by the rules of the voucher system. Each school would turn in its vouchers for cash. Thus, parents would no longer be forced to send their children to the school around the corner simply because it was around the corner. If the school was attractive and desirable, it would not be seriously affected by the institution of a voucher plan. If not, attendance might fall, perhaps forcing the school to improve.
>
> Even if no new schools were established under the voucher system, the responsiveness of existing schools would probably increase. But new schools will be established. Some parents will get together to create schools reflecting their special perspectives or their children's special needs. Educators with new ideas—or old ideas that are now out of fashion in the public schools—will also be able to set up their own schools. Entrepreneurs who think they can teach children better and cheaper than the public schools do will also have an opportunity to do so. (Educational Vouchers, 1970, p. 2)

[2]For an extended discussion of this topic, see LaNoue, 1972.

A great many issues are involved in considering the merits and the feasibility of the voucher approach to education. Some of these issues strike at the very roots of several of the major criticisms of our present educational system. For example, who should decide the educational philosophy governing the school—parents, politicians, or professional educators? Are parents well enough informed and therefore in a position to know what the specific educational needs of their children are? Would the school and the individual teacher be at the mercy of the whims and demands of each and every parent? Would such community control become bogged down in endless discussions and controversy? What should be the rights and responsibilities of the various groups—students, parents, teachers, taxpayers—involved in public education? Should racial, ethnic, religious, social class, and other such group differences be encouraged or discouraged? Should the "melting pot" concept, which, overtly or covertly, seemed to underly our thinking in immigrant America, be abandoned in favor of cultural pluralism and diversity? To what extent are there common values which should be stressed in all our schools? Would the voucher system place our educational system in the competitive marketplace in the same way that private enterprise competes for the public's favor and hence their dollars?

There are as yet no answers to the above questions. Preliminary observations suggest that the voucher system may (1) make the schools more accountable to the people it serves, and (2) stimulate a high degree of parent involvement in the education of their children.

The first experiment with educational vouchers, funded by the United States Office of Economic Opportunity, is being conducted in the Alum Rock School District, San Jose, California. Various "mini-schools" offering different curriculum emphases are available options for parents. Despite such attractive innovations as schools which stress the fine arts, science, and bilingual education, approximately half of the parents have chosen schools which offer a "traditional" education. As with any new approach, the voucher system will undoubtedly undergo a great many modifications and revisions before a workable and satisfactory model is developed.

Is Formal Education The Answer?

Historically, education has been viewed in this country as the one sure avenue to upward mobility. Succeeding immigrant groups placed their faith, to lesser or greater degrees, in education as the great hope for their children. Statistics are frequently presented which purportedly show that the lifetime earnings of college graduates markedly exceed those of high school graduates which in turn are significantly greater than high school dropouts.

A number of recent trends and events have called into question the role of formal education as the equalizer, the leveler, and the answer in our quest for the key to individual success and to our nation's problems. One of the goals of the "counter-culture" appears to be a return to a simpler form of life in which people engage in occupations and enterprises which are personally satisfying and enriching. Many of these artisan type of activities do not require a lengthy period of formal education. Second, our recently fluctuating job market has witnessed a marked decline in job openings for individuals with graduate degrees in a number of fields. Although this is a generalization subject to change, the job future in such fields as social work, public school teaching, engineering, and related highly specialized technical areas, appears uncertain. The rate of unemployment among highly qualified (in terms of education) people does not encourage young people toward long-term educational goals. Finally, a recent book by Jencks and associates (1972) entitled, *Inequality: A Reassessment of the Effect of Family and Schooling in America,* argues that the effects of schooling are really quite minimal. A brief review of this position seems in order.

First, Jencks presents ample evidence for the inequality existing among our schools at all levels from preschool through college. Resources are not distributed equally, so that school expenditures vary markedly from one state to the next and from one school district to another. Thus, while the average American school spent $783 per pupil in 1969–1970, the average expenditure per pupil in New York state was $1,237 and in Alabama, $438. Even greater differences exist among school districts in any given state. Further, some children have far greater access to certain kinds of schools and certain kinds of curriculums than others. In sum, educational opportunities are unequal.

Second, schooling appears to have little effect on intellectual development. The IQ gains resulting from preschool experience are temporary; elementary school produces some gain in intellectual performance; and secondary schooling and college produce negligible gains. Further, an analysis was made of the relation between various school resources and policies and gains in student achievement scores. Few consistent relations were found, and the gains associated with any given resource were small. Thus, contrary to popular opinion, the following variables appear to be unrelated to academic achievement: physical facilities, libraries and library books, how much homework a school assigned, whether it had heterogeneous or homogeneous grouping, numbers and kinds of personnel, salaries, criteria for selecting teachers. Moreover, two other variables which have received a tremendous amount of public attention, tracking and desegregation, appear to have little effect on students' test scores. Jencks concludes that differences among adults in ability test scores and in achievement test scores are due to factors that schools do not control.

Third, and related to the above two points, the major determinant of the amount of education an individual attains is family background. Next in importance is the cognitive skills he possesses. The school itself seems not to be an important factor in differences among individuals in the amount of education they attain.

Fourth, while the occupational status an individual achieves is strongly related to the amount of education he attains, there are great differences among people of similar educational levels in (1) their occupational status, and (2) in their success on the job. Moreover, differences among male adults in earned income appear unrelated to family background, cognitive skills, or educational attainment. Luck (chance) and various personality factors are of major importance in this regard.

Jencks concludes that since schooling has only negligible impact on an individual's intellectual skills, job performance, and adult income, school reform cannot be expected to result in marked social changes with respect to greater overall equality among people in our society:

> There seem to be three reasons why school reform cannot make adults more equal. First, children seem to be far more influenced by what happens at home than by what happens in school. They may also be more influenced by what happens on the streets and by what they see on television. Second, reformers have very little

> control over those aspects of school life that affect children. Reallocating resources, reassigning pupils, and rewriting the curriculum seldom change the way teachers and students actually treat each other minute by minute. Third, even when a school exerts an unusual influence on children, the resulting changes are not likely to persist into adulthood. It takes a huge change in elementary school test scores, for example, to alter adult income by a significant amount. (Jencks, 1972, p. 255)

While it is difficult to evaluate the many ramifications of the Jencks thesis, the evidence and arguments presented must cause one to pause and reconsider the role, the function, and the results of our present educational system. Perhaps the effects of schooling are less marked than we had thought, or perhaps they are even greater in such subtle and less tangible areas as attitudes toward society, one's self concept, and in one's view regarding his eventual place in society. These are difficult to measure, but they may be more important over the long haul than gains in test performance.

MENTAL HEALTH PROGRAMS

In recent years a number of programs have been developed for use in the school setting to assist children in developing (1) an understanding of themselves and their relationships with others; (2) an understanding of their own feelings; and (3) a knowledge of ways to cope with problems and problem situations by seeking acceptable alternative solutions. Three such programs will be described.

Self Enhancing Education

Based on well-accepted principles of mental hygiene and counseling, the Self Enhancing Education (SEE) program (Randolph & Howe, 1966, 1968) was developed to help teachers and children understand themselves, their own feelings as well as the feelings of others, and their relationship with others. Stress is placed on the ability to express and experience two basic human emotions, love and hate, and on learning how to direct these toward positive growth and socialization rather than toward alienation. To aid her students in achieving these goals, the teacher is encouraged to employ the technique of "reflective listening" which is described as a way of hearing the underlying feelings a child is expressing (the message he is sending) and helping him understand and deal with these feelings. Traditional ways of responding to a child's messages are contrasted with the more effective technique of reflective listening. The following are examples of traditional responses:

> Child Talk: I'm real dumb.
>
> 1. Ordering or commanding: I don't want you to feel that way; or, stop pitying yourself.
> 2. Admonishing: You ought to be thankful you have the opportunity to learn at school.
> 3. Warning: You better stop talking like that.
> 4. Advising: If I were you I would talk with the counselor.
> 5. Instructing: You should think about it this way.
> 6. Criticizing and disagreeing: You are a bad boy for feeling that way.
> 7. Praising and agreeing: Boys often feel that way even when they are bright like you.
> 8. Name calling: You are acting like a baby.
> 9. Interpreting: You are just tired.
> 10. Reassuring, sympathizing: You'll feel better about school after vacation.
> 11. Probing or questioning: Why do you feel that way?
> 12. Diverting (Often by humor): You don't look like Dumbo to me. Go out and play.
>
> (Randolph & Howe, 1968, pp. 59–60)

In reflective listening, the feelings a child expresses are reflected back to him:

a. When we play ball I never get to bat.
Reflective listening: Pretty frustrating to be left out and passed over, huh?

b. Why do we have to do everything parents say?
Reflective listening: You feel parents are always telling you what to do? Bossing too much?

c. I have too many pages to write for that old English assignment.
Reflective listening: You are feeling overpowered by the work load?

d. I hate you!
Reflective listening: I've hurt your feelings and now you are very angry with me?

e. The other kids are always running me down.
Reflective listening: Pretty hurtful to be put down all the time?

(pp. 62–63)

The following are further examples contrasting traditional behavior with a reflective approach.

Child: I hate you!
Teacher: You can't talk to me that way. I'm your teacher. Go to the office and I'll deal with you later.
Note: In this interaction, the message, "I hate you," was interpreted by the adult as defiance of authority. Consequently, admonition and command followed the interpretation. Now let's stop interpreting the message as defiance of authority and hear the feeling:
Child: I hate you!
Teacher: I've hurt your feelings and now you are very angry with me?
Child: I sure am. You've been on my back all afternoon.
Teacher: You feel I've been a nagger? Hmmmmm. I wasn't really aware that I had been bossing so much.
Note: Let's consider what has been happening. The adult did not read the message as defiance. He heard the feeling and reflected it. As a result of the child's next input, the adult becomes more aware of his own behavior. The conflict can now be resolved by discussion and possibly a plan for a more comfortable afternoon.
Note: Now let's consider our traditional behavior when the message is a non-verbal one. Bobby, a first grader, is late for class. He is walking very slowly, dragging his feet. The yard teacher observes him.
Teacher: Bobby, hurry up! You are late for class!
Note: Bobby looked up but moved on in the same manner. Now let's make a different intervention:
Teacher: Good morning, Bobby.
Bobby: I'm not going to work today.
Teacher: A bad feeling this morning, Bobby?
Bobby: Yeh, my brother and I had a fight and my dad took his part. That's not fair. He started it!
Teacher: You feel your dad was unfair because he didn't understand the quarrel?
Bobby: Yeh. He shouldn't do that.
Note: Bobby waved and ran off to class. Often all that is needed, as in the above incident, is to stop interpreting the message as defiance of authority, hear the feeling and reflect it.

(pp. 82–83)

As a way of developing a sense of personal responsibility for one's feelings, actions, and behavior, children are encouraged to acknowledge their feelings, "to own them," to recognize them as legitimate, and to express these feelings. Forthright expression of feelings assists the child to understand and accept himself. When the teacher listens to the child and what he is trying to say, she is communicating to him the fact that she accepts him as a unique and worthwhile individual.

The SEE program describes a series of steps comprising an effective problem-solving process:

Step 1. Own the concern and state it
Step 2. Determine the social behavior for group discussion
Step 3. Invite discussion of what has been happening
Step 4. Reflect the feelings and perceptions
Step 5. Observe the trend of the data
Step 6. Clarify the hidden problem
Step 7. Let the participants vent
Step 8. Invite solutions
Step 9. Reflect the solutions without judgment
Step 10. Invite use of any appropriate solutions
Step 11. Set time to evaluate

(p. 87)

Specific examples of several of these steps include the following:

Step I
Owning the concern and stating it.

Example: I am troubled because yesterday when I had to be absent, your day with a substitute was not a very happy one for her or you either.

Example: Boys and girls, Ruth has a problem and she has asked me to pose it to you for your consideration. She feels that she has never been accepted by any group since she was in kindergarten and she is feeling that she is not being accepted by this fifth grade group either.

Step III
Inviting discussion.

Example: Ruth is asking for your help. Let's talk about what has been happening to cause Ruth to feel so lonesome.

Steps V and VI
Observe the trend of data and clarify.

Teacher talk: Boys and girls, from what you have been saying, I think I am perceiving the hidden problem with which you have been trying to cope. Let me tell you what I perceive and you must let me know if you agree.

Steps X and XI
Invite use of any solutions children feel are appropriate and set time for evaluation of how the solutions are working.

Teacher talk: Boys and girls, you have offered a number of solutions. How would it be if each one of you work with any one or several of the solutions that you feel might work for you. Then a week from now we will have a time to assess how we feel the solutions are working.

(pp. 110–115)

In summary, Self Enhancing Education is concerned with the development in each child of a sense of self worth and respect for the worth of others. The potential for personal growth is fostered by permitting the child to express his feelings and come to terms with them. Learning about oneself is seen as an important goal of education. Moreover, academic learning is facilitated in a psychological atmosphere which follows sound mental health principles.

Methods in Human Development

Similar to the Self Enhancing Education program described above in terms of basic concepts and goals is the approach developed by Bessell and Palomares (1967) called the Human Development Program. Essentially it consists of a series of lesson plan guides to be used by the classroom teacher in daily 20-minute sessions. Concerned primarily with motivational aspects of the child's school behavior, the program focuses on three main areas: awareness, self-confidence, and social interaction. The program is based on writings of a number of personality theorists which emphasize our basic strivings for mastery and approval.

> The curriculum with center around the fostering of a healthy self-concept in each child. It will dwell upon cultivating an awareness of self and others, upon an acceptance of self and others, and upon an appreciation of the similarities and differences between self and others. The concentration upon self and others as creatures of feelings, thoughts, and actions provides the child with the language of experience and expression. (Bessell & Palomares, 1967, p. 5)

A number of principles are listed for each of the three areas with which the program is concerned: (1) principles of effective communication: promoting awareness; (2) principles in the development of mastery: fostering self-confidence; and (3) principles of effective socialization: developing skills for interpersonal security. The principles for effective socialization are as follows:

PRINCIPLES OF EFFECTIVE SOCIALIZATION

Group I *Comprehension of Cause and Effect*

The effective child understands that the behavior of one person can produce feelings in another person.

Principles 1 through 4

The effective child understands that:

1 Some behaviors of another person can produce pleasant feelings in him.
2 Some behaviors of another person can produce unpleasant feelings in him.
3 Some of his behaviors can produce pleasant feelings in another person.
4 Some of his behaviors can produce unpleasant feelings in another person.

Group II *Ability to Discriminately Predict*

The effective child can predict on a discriminative basis whether a given action will produce a pleasant or unpleasant feeling in another person.

Principles 5 through 8

5 When another person behaves positively toward him.
6 When another person behaves negatively toward him.
7 When he behaves positively toward another person.
8 When he behaves negatively toward another person.

Group III *Comprehension of Connection Between Feelings and Approval and Disapproval*

The effective child understands that the kind of attitude (thought) that a person develops is directly related to the kinds of feelings that are produced in him.

Principles 9 and 10

9 The effective child understands that when a person has good feelings his attitude will almost certainly be one of approval.
10 The effective child understands that when a person has bad feelings his attitude will almost certainly be one of disapproval.

Group IV *Individual Differences in Approval and Disapproval*

The effective child appreciates and respects individual variations in terms of the way different people might react in feeling and attitude toward the same behavior.

Principles 11 through 13

11 The effective child knows that the same behavior may make one person feel good and think approvingly, while it may make another person feel badly and think disapprovingly.

12 The effective child knows that he could (for many possible reasons) respond differently in terms of feelings and attitude to the same behavior of two different people.

13 The effective child knows that a given behavior at one time may make another person feel a certain way at one time and have the opposite effect (for many possible reasons) at a different time.

Group V *Responsible Attitude About Control*

The effective child recognizes and believes in the importance of accepting responsibility for the effects that behaviors cause.

Principles 14 through 16

14 The effective child is able and willing to be held responsible for the bad feelings that his behavior produces in another person. He is not so insecure that he needs to deny, lie, rationalize or project about the responsibility for his actions.

15 The effective child recognizes that only insecurity (under-development) can cause another person to attempt to avoid his responsibility for behavior that he knows is making another person feel badly.

16 The effective child understands that society can function in a truly harmonious and productive fashion only if each and every individual member is able to recognize and accept the responsibility for his behavior.

(Bessell & Palomares, 1967, pp. 118–120)

Lesson plan guides have been developed for the elementary-school grades beginning with kindergarten. A "special session," is conducted, preferably at the same time each day. A group, composed of approximately 10 children, is seated in a circle. The sessions are 20 minutes in length. The following procedure is included in one of the first lessons at the kindergarten level. The lesson is designed to permit expression of positive feelings and to develop an awareness of these feelings.

UNIT 1
COMMUNICATION

First Week

Fourth Week: *Pleasant Feelings*

E: Procedure: Ten children are brought into a circle with the teacher. They may sit on chairs or on the floor. There should be no interruptions and no distractions. Leaving the circle during the session is not permissible except to go and get some object that gives him a good feeling, unless a child must go to the toilet or if there is some emergency. Interruptions or distractions will either weaken or ruin the session.

There should ideally be five boys and five girls. While this is not essential, the group should be as evenly balanced as possible. The emotionally mature person is one who has a broad range of exposure and appreciates the many personality variations within each sex.

The teacher will bring some object which is meaningful to her in a simple way such as her purse. She will say, *"Today we are going to each have a chance to tell how the thing we have gives us a good feeling. Here is my purse. It makes me feel good because it helps me to carry a lot of things that I need and it's nice to know that they are all in here."*

Have one child at a time leave the circle to go and bring back and show to the group some object that gives him a good feeling because he likes to touch it or play with it. Encourage him to tell in what way or why it gives him a good feeling.

It is essential to hold the interest of each child. Simple explanations of how or why an object makes a child feel good are most acceptable. If one or more children are not giving their attention the teacher should repeat what a child expressing himself is saying or she should amplify on it in some way to draw everyone's attention. Wandering attention and reluctance to participate will steadily become less and less of a problem as the children have more of these sessions and become accustomed to the procedure and what is expected. (p. 3)

While no statistical data are available at the present time showing the effectiveness of the Human Development program in accomplishing its goals, an examination of the theoretical foundations and the lesson guides suggest the value of this approach. The authors are correct in noting that healthy psychological development is too important to leave to chance. Because of the nature of a large class situation, undoubtedly many days and weeks may pass without a child receiving the kind of praise and attention from the teacher which facilitate the development of feelings of competence and self-worth.

Discovery Through Guidance

A third program entitled, *Discovery Through Guidance* (Bruck, 1968) includes four student activity booklets designed in the format of a workbook, with the student completing the various exercises. These workbooks are not handed in to the teacher; rather, the various topics serve as a basis for group discussion. Each workbook is appropriate for a different grade level. The first booklet consists of the following four units, with six exercises in each unit: "Unit I, Building Happiness and Success in School; Unit II, Building a "Me" I Can Always Respect; Unit III, Building My Life With Others; Unit IV, Building Into the Future." The following is an example of the kind of exercises in Unit I:

1 The Happiness Riddle

"Some kids are so unhappy in school," muttered Tom to Jack as they watched their classmates heading home. "There's Joe all alone as usual. He uses his brains to get into trouble instead of making good grades. The teachers are always after him."

"Why do you like school, Tom?" asked Jack. "You have to work like a dog to make passing grades, and you never have a gang around you. But no one has it in for you, and you always get along with the teachers."

"I try to get along with everyone, and I feel I have accomplished something when I finish my schoolwork."

Is Tom's happiness due to his own effort to learn and to get along with his classmates? Can you see why the teachers are pleased with Tom?

Where Do I Stand?

1. Am I reasonably happy in school? ______
2. If not, is it my own fault? ______
3. Is it possibly because I do not get along with my classmates? ______
4. Is it because I do not know how to study? ______
5. Could I be happier in school than I am at present? ______
6. Do I think happiness is worth working for? ______

Ideas to Discuss *(Jot down ideas to use for the discussion.)*

1. Happiness in school can be earned. How?
2. We earn the respect of others by our actions.
3. Friendless people are not happy people.
4. The first "success' is the hardest. Why?
5. Does happiness make success easier to accomplish? If so, why?
6. Happiness is "catching."

What Can I Do?

1. I would be happier in my relationship with my classmates if I ______ ______.
2. My teacher could be of more help to me if I ______ ______ ______.
3. If you do not wish to use either of the two preceding plans, think of a plan yourself to increase your happiness and success in school. ______ ______ ______.
4. Circle the number of the plan you have chosen: No. 1, No. 2, or No. 3.

How Well Did I Do? (*One week later.*)

1. Did I make an honest effort to carry out my chosen plan? ______
2. Was the plan worthwhile? ______
3. Did it make me feel happier? ______
4. Would it be a good idea to continue my plan? ______

(Bruck & Vogelsong, 1969, pp. 4–5)

The following six exercises are included under Unit II, Searchlight on Self, in the second booklet:

1. Jumping the Hurdles–
   Problem-solving and decision-making as parts of growing up
2. Facing Disappointments Gracefully–
   Developing tolerance to disappointment
3. Learning from My Mistakes–
   Considering mistakes as potential learning situations
4. Courage for What?–
   Understanding meaning and importance of courage in one's life
5. Discovering the Real Me–
   Facing reality by learning to know and accept oneself
6. Nature's Gifts–
   Appreciation of the gifts of nature

(Bruck, 1969, p. vii)

The Table of Contents of the fourth booklet entitled, *Focus*, are shown below.

At the end of each of the four booklets and several pages with a "problem-solving" outline designed to encourage the student to employ a systematic approach to solving various problems which he might face. The outline is given below:

1. Investigate: Identify and define the problem. State the problem in one clear sentence.
2. Analyze: Jot down all the facts you know about the problem. What? How? Where? When? Why?
3. Consider: What are the possible solutions?
   1.
   2.
   3.
   4.

   Evaluate each of the above solutions. What would happen if I chose: No. 1? No. 2? No. 3? No. 4?
4. Decide: After considering results of all possible solutions, choose the solutions that you think is best. Write it.
5. Evaluate Later: Am I glad I made this choice? If not, what would have been a better solution?
   Why?

Contents

UNIT I—EDUCATIONAL FOCUS

UNIT II—SOCIAL FOCUS

UNIT III—PERSONAL FOCUS

UNIT IV—VOCATIONAL FOCUS

Summary. It is clear that all three approaches deal with extremely important aspects of mental health. Learning can never be considered apart from the psychological atmosphere in which it takes place. If a child does not like himself, he will be ill-prepared for the long years of adulthood which lie ahead. Consequently, the school must play a vital role in ensuring the optimal psychological development of each child. No other social institution (family, church, etc.) is in a position to do this.

SUMMARY

The teacher's role in the classroom has been the main emphasis in this chapter. The teacher stimulates and guides the intellectual development of pupils, affects their attitudes and values, and exerts a marked influence on their emotional adjustment through the kind of psychological atmosphere established in the classroom and through differential rewards and punishments.

Many factors relate to academic achievement: intellectual ability, level of maturity, relationship with parents, emotional and personality factors, past success and failure, attitude toward school, the teacher, socioeconomic status, and patterns of interest. Because the primary function of the school is the teaching of academic skills, the extent to which a child learns these skills reflects the effectiveness of the school's endeavor and also bears heavily on the child's concept of himself.

The years spent in school are important ones. Teachers and parents must work together to make certain that for each child these years are fruitful and well used.

REFERENCES

Anderson, H. H. An experimental study of dominative and integrative behavior in children of preschool age. *Journal of Social Psychology*, 1937, **8**, 335–345. (a)

Anderson, H. H. Domination and integration in the social behavior of young children in an experimental play situation. *Genetic Psychology Monographs*, 1937, **19**, 341–408. (b)

Anderson, H. H. The measurement of domination and of socially integrative behavior in teachers' contacts with children. *Child Development*, 1939, **10**, 73–89. (a)

Anderson, H. H. Domination and social integration in the behavior of kindergarten children and teachers. *Genetic Psychology Monographs*, 1939, **21**, 287–385. (b)

Anderson, H. H. Domination and socially integrative behavior. In R. Barker, J. Kounin, & H. Wright (Eds.), *Child behavior and development.* New York: McGraw-Hill, 1943. Pp. 459–483.

Antes, J., Anderson, D., & DeVault, M. Elementary pupils' perceptions of the social-emotional environment of the classroom. *Psychology in the Schools*, 1965, **2**, 41–46.

Battle, H. Relation between personal values and scholastic achievements. *Journal of Experimental Education*, 1957, **26**, 27–41.

Baumrind, D. Effects of authoritative parental control on child behavior. *Child Development*, 1966, **37**, 887–907.

Bereiter, C., & Engelmann, S. *Teaching disadvantaged children in the preschool.* Englewood Cliffs, N.J.: Prentice-Hall, 1966.

Bessell, H., & Palomares, U. *Methods in human development.* San Diego: Human Development Training Institute, 1967.

Bloom, B. *Stability and change in human characteristics.* New York: Wiley, 1964.

Bonney, M. E., & Nicholson, E. L. Comparative social adjustments of elementary school pupils with and without preschool training. *Child Development*, 1958, **29**, 125–133.

Bronfenbrenner, U. Socialization and social class through time and space. In E. E. Maccoby, T. M. Newcomb, & E. L. Hartley (Eds.), *Readings in social psychology.* New York: Holt, 1958. Pp. 400–425.

Bruck, C. *Focus: Student activity book.* New York: Bruce, 1968.

Bruck, C., & Vogelsong, M. *Build: Student activity book.* New York: Bruce, 1968.

Carter, L. B. The effect of early school entrance on the scholastic achievement of elementary school children in the Austin public schools. *Journal of Educational Research*, 1956, **50**, 91–103.

Chance, J. E. Independence training and first graders' achievement. *Journal of Consulting Psychology*, 1961, **25**, 149–154.

Cloward, R., & Jones, J. Social class: Educational attitudes and participation. In A. H. Passow (Ed.), *Education in depressed areas.* New York: Teachers College Press, 1963. Pp. 190–216.

Conklin, A. M. Failures of highly intelligent pupils. *Teachers College Contributions to Education*, 1940, No. 792.

Davids, A., & Hainsworth, P. Maternal attitudes about family life and child rearing as avowed by mothers and perceived by their underachieving and high-achieving sons. *Journal of Consulting Psychology*, 1967, **31**, 29–37.

Davis, A., & Dollard, J. *Children of bondage.* Washington, D.C.: American Council on Education, 1940.

Davis, A., & Havighurst, R. Social class and color differences in child-rearing. *American Sociological Review*, 1946, **II**, 698–710.

DeGroat, A. F., & Thompson, G. G. A study of the distribution of teacher approval and disapproval among sixth-grade children. *Journal of Experimental Education*, 1949, **18**, 57–75.

Education Vouchers: A Preliminary Report on Financing Education by Payments to Parents. Cambridge, Mass.: Center for the Study of Public Policy, 1970.

Edwards, J., & Stern, C. A comparison of three intervention programs with disadvantaged preschool children. *Journal of Special Education*, 1970, **4**, 205–214.

Feldhusen, J., Thurston, J., & Benning, J. Aggressive classroom behavior and school achievement. *Journal of Special Education*, 1970, **4**, 431–439.

Flanders, N. A., & Havumaki, S. The effect of teacher-pupil contacts involving praise on the sociometric choices of students. *Journal of Educational Psychology*, 1960, **51**, 65–68.

Goodenough, F. L., & Maurer, K. M. The mental development of nursery-school children compared with that of non-nursery school children. *National Society for the Study of Education, 39th Yearbook*, 1940, Part II, 161–178.

Gronlund, N. E. The accuracy of teachers' judgments concerning the sociometric status of sixth-grade pupils. *Sociometry,* 1950, **13**, 197–225, 329–357.

Gross, B., & Gross, R. (Eds.) *Radical school reform.* New York: Simon & Schuster, 1969.

Haggard, E. A. Socialization, personality and achievement in gifted children. *School Review,* 1957, **65**, 318–414.

Harlow, H. Learning and satiation of response in intrinsically motivated complex puzzle performance by monkeys. *Journal of Comparative and Physiological Psychology,* 1950, **43**, 289–294.

Hattwick, L. A. The influence of nursery school attendance upon the behavior and personality of the preschool child. *Journal of Experimental Education,* 1936, **5**, 180–190.

Havighurst, R., & Taba, H. *Adolescent character and personality.* New York: Wiley, 1949.

Hebb, D. *The organization of behavior.* New York: Wiley, 1949.

Herndon, J. *The way it spozed to be.* New York: Simon & Schuster, 1968.

Hess, R. & Bear, R. (Eds.) *Early education.* Chicago: Aldine, 1968.

Hoehn, A. H. A study of social class differentiation in the classroom behavior of nineteen third-grade teachers. *Journal of Social Psychology,* 1954, **39**, 269–292.

Hollingshead, A. *Elmtown's youth: The impact of social classes on youth.* New York: Wiley, 1949.

Holt, J. *How children learn.* New York: Pitman, 1967.

Holt, J. *The underachieving school,* New York: Pitman, 1969.

Holt, J. *How children fail.* New York: Pitman, 1970. (a)

Holt, J. *What do I do Monday?* New York: Dutton, 1970. (b)

Hunt, J. McV. *Intelligence and experience.* New York: Ronald, 1961.

Hunt, J. McV. The psychological basis for using pre-school enrichment as an antidote for cultural deprivation. *Merrill–Palmer Quarterly,* 1964, **10**, 207–248.

Jencks, C. *Inequality: A reassessment of the effect of family and schooling in America.* New York: Basic Books, 1972.

Jersild, A. T. Characteristics of teachers who are "liked best" and "disliked most." *Journal of Experimental Education,* 1949, **9**, 139–151.

Kimball, B. Case studies in educational failure during adolescence. *American Journal of Orthopsychiatry,* 1953, **23**, 403–415.

Klausmeier, H. J., & Check, J. Relationships among physical, mental, achievement, and personality measures in children of low, average, and high intelligence. *American Journal of Mental Deficiency,* 1959, **63**, 647–656.

Kohl, H. *Thirty-six children.* New American Library, 1967.

Kohn, M. L. Social class and parental values. *American Journal of Sociology,* 1959, **64**, 337–351.

Kozol, J. *Death at an early age.* Boston: Houghton Mifflin, 1967.

Kozol, J. *Free schools.* Boston: Houghton Mifflin, 1972.

LaNoue, G. R. (Ed.) *Education vouchers: Concepts and controversies.* Columbia Univ.: Teachers College Press, 1972.

Lee, M. J., & Clark, W. W. *Lee–Clark Reading Readiness Test, Kindergarten and Grade I.* (1951 Rev.) Los Angeles: California Test Bureau, 1951.

Leeds, C. H., & Cook, W. W. The construction and differential value of a scale for determining teacher-pupil attitudes. *Journal of Experimental Education,* 1947, **16**, 149–159.

McDavid, J., Jr. Some relationships between social reinforcement and scholastic achievement. *Journal of Consulting Psychology,* 1959, **23**, 151–154.

Medinnus, G. R. An investigation of school readiness and first-grade adjustment. Unpublished manuscript, 1961. (a)

Medinnus, G. R. The relation between several parent measures and the child's early adjustment to school. *Journal of Educational Psychology,* 1961, **52**, 153–156. (b)

Medinnus, G. R. The development of a First-Grade Adjustment Scale. *Journal of Experimental Education,* 1961, **30**, 243–248. (c)

Medinnus, G. R. An examination of several correlates of sociometric status in a first grade group. *Journal of Genetic Psychology,* 1962, **101**, 3–13.

Medinnus, G. R. Evaluation of Santa Clara County Head Start. San Jose State College. Unpublished study, 1967.

Medinnus, G. R. Head Start: An examination of issues. In G. R. Medinnus & R. C. Johnson (Eds.), *Child and Adolescent Psychology: A Book of Readings.* New York: Wiley, 1970. Pp. 411–421.

Merrill, B. A measurement of mother-child interaction. *Journal of Abnormal and Social Psychology,* 1946, **41**, 37–49.

Meyer, W. J., & Thompson, G. G. Sex differences in the distribution of teacher approval and disapproval among sixth-grade children. *Journal of Educational Psychology,* 1956, **47**, 385–396.

Milner, E. A study of the relationship between reading readiness in grade one school children and patterns of parent-child interaction. *Child Development,* 1951, **22**, 95–112.

Murphy, G., Murphy, L. B., & Newcomb, T. *Experimental social psychology.* New York: Harper, 1937.

Neale, D., & Proshek, J. School-related attitudes of culturally disadvantaged elementary school children. *Journal of Educational Psychology,* 1967, **58**, 238–244.

Olson, W. C., & Hughes, B. O. Subsequent growth of children with and without nursery-school experience. *National Society for the Study of Education, 39th Yearbook,* 1940, Part II, 237–244.

Randolph, N., & Howe, W. *Self enhancing education.* Palo Alto: Stanford Press, 1966.

Randolph, N., & Howe, W. *Self enhancing education: A training manual.* Palo Alto: Stanford Press, 1968.

Riessman, F. *The culturally deprived child.* New York: Harper & Row, 1962.

Sears, P. S. Levels of aspiration in academically successful and unsuccessful children. *Journal of Abnormal and Social Psychology,* 1940, **35**, 498–536.

Sechrest, L. Studies of classroom atmosphere. *Psychology in the Schools,* 1964, **1**, 103–118.

Sewell, W. Social class and childhood personality. *Sociometry,* 1961, **24**, 340–356.

Simon, M. D. Body configuration and school readiness. *Child Development,* 1959, **30**, 493–512.

Skells, H. M., Updegraff, R., Wellman, B. L., & Williams, H. M. A study of environmental stimulation: An orphanage preschool project. *University of Iowa Study in Child Welfare,* 1938, **15**, No. 4.

Stendler, C. B. Social class differences in parental attitudes toward school at Grade I level. *Child Development,* 1951, **22**, 36–46.

Stendler, C. B., Damrin, D., & Haines, A. C. Studies in cooperation and competition: I. The effects of working for groups and individual rewards on the social climates of children's groups. *Journal of Genetic Psychology,* 1951, **79**, 173–197.

Stendler, C. B., & Young, N. Impact of first grade entrance upon the socialization of the child: Changes after eight months of school. *Child Development,* 1950, **22**, 113–122.

Stendler, C. B., & Young, N. The impact of beginning first grade upon socialization as reported by mothers. *Child Development,* 1959, **21**, 241–260.

Tamkin, A. S. A survey of educational disability in emotionally disturbed children. *Journal of Educational Research,* 1960, **53**, 313–315.

Templin, M. C. General information of kindergarten children: a comparison with the Probst study after 26 years. *Child Development,* 1958, **29**, 87–96.

Tenenbaum, S. Uncontrolled expressions of children's attitudes toward school. *Elementary School Journal,* 1940, **40**, 670–678.

Thompson, G. G. The social and emotional development of preschool children under two types of educational program. *Psychological Monographs: General and Applied,* 1944, **56**, No. 5.

Van Alstyne, D., & Hattwick, L. A. A follow-up study of the behavior of nursery school children. *Child Development,* 1939, **10**, 43–72.

Walsh, A. M. *Self-concepts of bright boys with learning difficulties.* New York: Bureau of Publication, Teachers College, Columbia University, 1956.

Walsh, M. E. The relation of nursery school training to the development of certain personality traits. *Child Development,* 1931, **2**, 72–73.

Warner, W., Havighurst, R., & Loeb, M. *Who shall be educated?* New York: Harper, 1944.

Weber, L. *The English infant school and informal education.* Englewood Cliffs, N.J.: Prentice-Hall, 1971.

Weikart, D. Preschool programs: preliminary findings. *Journal of special Education,* 1967, **1**, 163–181.

Wellman, B. L. The effect of preschool attendance upon the I.Q. *Journal of Experimental Education,* 1932, **I**, 48–69.

Withall, J. The development of a technique for the measurement of social-emotional climates in classrooms. *Journal of Experimental Education,* 1949, **17**, 347–361.

Withall, J. Assessment of the social-emotional climates experienced by a group of seventh graders as they moved from class to class. *Educational and Psychological Measurement,* 1952, **12**, 440–451.

chapter 13

other socializing influences

chapter 13

other socializing influences

chapter 13

other socializing influences

A growing child's family, his peers, and the school are not the only influences he encounters. A child grows up in a community. He is exposed to varying degrees of religious instruction. He takes cognizance of such organized groups as the Boy Scouts. He is confronted by the mass media of communication—books, comic books, movies, television. How much and in what way do these agencies of socialization affect his development?

THE COMMUNITY

The role of the community in the life of a young person depends largely on the child's parents. If they do not abdicate their responsibilities in the socialization process, the community serves more often to reinforce parental values than as a source of values themselves (Peck & Havighurst, 1960). Even if a community is a deteriorated slum fraught with delinquency and crime, the child appears to be largely shielded against its criminal influences as long as his parents provide him with a positive concept of the self through close, effective family interaction and high expectations (Reckless, Dinitz, & Murray, 1956; Scarpitti, Murray, Simon, & Reckless, 1960). It is when parents abandon their function in socializing the child that the community assumes a more central role. If the parents fail to provide values, or if they are lacking in the techniques for implanting them, the community, among other social forces, may take over by default. For children of this type of background the community has great importance.

As noted in Chapter 7, the pervasiveness and intensity of parental impact on the child at any single time has decreased, even though the period of parental control and influence has grown longer. If parental influence has fallen off, what social forces have taken its place? It is doubtful that the community has increased its influence. It does not seem likely that the other agencies to be considered in this chapter have gained much influence, either. Perhaps the major legatee has been the child's peers. The older primary-group community is vanishing because of the greater physical and social mobility and the increased urbanization of the American people. The urban *secondary-group* community does not teach values or reinforce existing values as adequately, even when these are not pathological, since the value system is not backed up by the consensus of a close-knit group. Only when filling a vacuum, only when providing values in the absence of any other source, does the community achieve any real significance in shaping behavior.

THE INFLUENCE OF RELIGIOUS EXPERIENCE

Since the days of G. Stanley Hall and his disciples (Daniels, 1893; Starbuck, 1899), all of whom believed religious conversion to be an almost necessary part of adolescent experience, psychologists have shown intermittent interest in the impact of religion on development. Actually, relatively little is known of the direct influence of religion on behavior because the problem of setting up a criterion is a difficult one. How does one separate the religious from the nonreligious to determine whether the two differ in behavior and values? One criterion of a religious orientation is the individual's own statement: does he or does he not claim religious affiliation?

In interviews and tests involving hundreds of delinquents, every one of them claimed some religious tie. This surely cannot validate the hypothesis that delinquents would not be delinquent if only they had some religious experience. But a bit of probing discloses that most of these delinquents do not enter a church once a year. Their affiliation is verbal, not behavioral. Some criterion other than affiliation is necessary.

Nor will church attendance, as cited in many studies, do. Some persons attend church for nonreligious reasons—as a result of habit, of pressure, of social aspirations, or in order to acquire feelings of superiority. There are studies using test scores of religious knowledge (McDowell, 1952), but even this approach cannot uncover true religious commitment. Although Godin (1962) offered other suggestions for a criterion, the problem has not been adequately dealt with in any study of which the authors are aware. Most of the data presented here must be viewed as containing information on the relation between certain formal aspects of religion and behavior—for example, churchgoing—rather than as presenting insights into the link between degree of religious involvement and behavior.

Religious experience might be expected to change both broad social attitudes, such as belief in the brotherhood of man, and specific behaviors, such as cheating on tests. Taking the social attitudes first, the case seems to be clear that church attendance does not increase acceptance of the Bill of Rights (Stouffer, 1955).

Wilson (1960) found a positive correlation between religion and anti-Semitism. In another study (Kelly, Ferson, & Holtzman, 1958), subjects favorable toward religion were seen to view Negroes more negatively than did persons less religiously committed. Finally, Jones (1958) observed that adults high in authoritarianism showed higher religious training and values, and lower interest in the theoretical and esthetic areas of personal experience, than did individuals of lesser authoritarian tendencies.

If respondents are divided as to those who go to church and those who do not, or as to those high versus low in religiosity, the results discussed above generally are obtained. However, if a more finely graded measure of religiosity is obtained, a curvilinear relationship between religious involvement and prejudice appears (see Allport & Ross, 1967); those persons who are deeply involved in religion (as indicated by regular participation) and those totally uninvolved are the least prejudiced, whereas church members who attend occasionally are the most prejudiced. Allport and Ross distinguished between the extrinsically religious (who find religion useful to provide security, sociability, or status) and the intrinsically religious (who are committed to religion because it provides an internalized guide to behavior). They found that the indiscriminately proreligious (who favor religion for both intrinsic and extrinsic reasons) are more prejudiced than the extrinsically religious, who in turn are more prejudiced than intrinsically religious persons. Salisbury (1962) distinguished among three major dimensions of religion: doctrine and belief, behavior and practice, and feelings and emotions.

Since those who never attend church and those who very frequently attend seem more "moral"—in the sense of being less afraid of and discriminating toward others than are the large mass of people who fall between the two extremes—it would appear unjust to say that religious involvement *causes* prejudice. Rather, it would seem that most of those persons who are occasional church attenders differ from persons at both extremes in that they are either indiscriminately ("muddle-headedly," to use Allport's and Ross's term) or extrinsically oriented toward religion and more concerned with doctrine and belief than in behavior and practices. Religiosity per se is not associated with prejudice; however, certain of the motivational forces that cause people to be avowedly religious seem to be the same as those forces that cause people to be prejudiced.

Turning to the specific behaviors, the studies by Hartshorne and May in the late 1920's (1928, 1929) must be cited. In their first study (1928) they ascertained through a number of ingeniously designed test situations the amount of cheating done by children who attended Sunday school and by those who did not. One sampling disclosed cheating among 31 percent and 40 percent of the two groups, respectively. A second sampling turned up respective findings of 38 percent and 43 percent. Although following the direction expected, the differences were negligible. In the subsequent experiment (1929) they observed that children who attended Sunday school regularly were more helpful than others whose attendance was irregular. Once again the difference was small. And even the minor positive results of these two studies might have been produced by inadequate matching.

Middleton and Putney (1962) suggest that research concentrating on delinquency, humanitarianism, and so on, has failed to reveal differences between religious and nonreligious persons because these issues are "moral" ones, and responses are determined by the "common religion"—the general social morality—rather than by specific denominational involvement.

To all those who believe in the positive value of religious instruction this may prove disappointing. That exposure to the teachings of religion is not efficacious in combatting intolerance or dishonesty is, however, not surprising. The young person, even if regularly attending church and Sunday school, is in contact with these religious institutions for less than one-fiftieth of his waking hours. Besides, there is an abundance of evidence dating back to Hall's original study (1882) that young children have an extremely low-level and primitive conception of God and of other religious symbols such as heaven, hell, and angels. This makes it quite difficult for the young child to grasp the moral issues involved in religion and to be influenced in his behavior by the religious resolution of these questions. All these studies suffer, as we have remarked, because of the difficulty in establishing a criterion for religious involvement. But even though attending church or Sunday school does not appear to influence moral behavior, it may be that the deeper criteria of religious commitment (such as amount of intrinsic orientation) will have considerable positive influence on behavior.

MASS MEDIA OF COMMUNICATION

Just as many consider religious experience a potent positive force in shaping behavior, so they look at most of the mass media of communication as a negative influence. As we shall see, the evidence against the mass media seems about as telling as the evidence supporting religious education.

Books

The oldest of the mass media is the printed word—books, newspapers, magazines. Despite the aura of wisdom surrounding books, the children's books that are acceptable to adults are not necessarily beneficial to children, if examined at close range. In an informative study, Child, Potter, and Levine (1946) checked the values portrayed in children's textbooks. They examined the stories presented in all third-grade readers published since 1930. Stories were broken down according to *thema*. Each theme formed a unit involving an individual confronted with a situation, behaving as a result of it, and feeling the consequences of the behavior. In the 914 stories reviewed there was a total of 3409 themes. In these themes, girls and women were depicted as being kind, sociable, inactive, unambitious, and uncreative. Boys, on the other hand, were oftener shown as being active, aggressive, and interested in achievement.

It is often proclaimed that the preeminence of men in all of the arts and sciences stems from the cliché belief that "it's a man's world." This is difficult to understand when one views the arts in America. Girls are rewarded at every turn for developing talent in the graphic arts and in music. Conversely, boys who display such interests are compelled to battle relentlessly against being considered effeminate. Nevertheless, there are virtually no women composers, painters, or sculptors of first rank. Even in the playing of musical instruments, perhaps a lesser accomplishment than composing, there are very few highly able woman performers. Sex distinctions in creativity may very well result from the roles that the culture attributes to girls and women in such media as children's readers.

If the analysis of the children's readers is any indication, society continually presents young women with a set of roles of being kindly, dependent, and passive, and should not be too surprised if women take these seriously. Amidst an outcry of need for scientists, the culture inadvertently may be losing a major portion of them through an influence that can, to a degree, be checked—and that, in fact, is apparently shifting rather sharply. It may not be possible to change the way that girls and women are portrayed in television, in novels, or in the other mass media, but it is possible to modify the values depicted in the books used in the public schools.

The themes of children's textbooks are unrealistic in other ways. They are inordinately Pollyanna-ish. The hero never suffers defeat. Moreover, children are rarely portrayed as aggressive and acquisitive. Adults are oftener cast in antisocial roles. The general conclusion inspired by the Child et al. study is that children's textbooks are—or were—laden with pap, sugar-coated fare of which the readers must tire.

A recent study by deCharms and Moeller (1962) resembles the Child et al. undertaking in that it, too, was based on an analysis of values expressed in children's textbooks. This study covered sample pages of readers used in the years 1800–1950. Striking changes in content occurred. The use of religious or moral sanctions diminished substantially during the century and a half, while material stressing the social ethic increasingly replaced them. Emphasis on achievement —the Protestant ethic—reached its apex about 1900 (as, incidentally, did the number of patents issued per million of persons) and has been on the decline since. Although the rise of the social ethic continued over a longer period of time than might have been expected, the conclusions reached about it in Chapter 7 seem confirmed, for the most part, by this analysis of children's reading materials (see Figure 13-1).

Comics and Comic Books

In every generation, young people have insisted on reading trash—penny dreadfuls, dime novels, big little-books, or comic books, each in their own day—at the expense of the literature approved by the school and their parents. Frederic Wertham, a New York psychiatrist, argued that comic books were a major cause of delinquency in his book *Seduction of the Innocent* (1953). In an earlier era, Healy (1915) and Healy and Bronner (1936) placed the onus of guilt on cheap novels and magazines. If this were the case, the challenges to the imagination would be great—think of how delinquency could be eliminated by censorship, blinding the multitude, or forbidding everyone

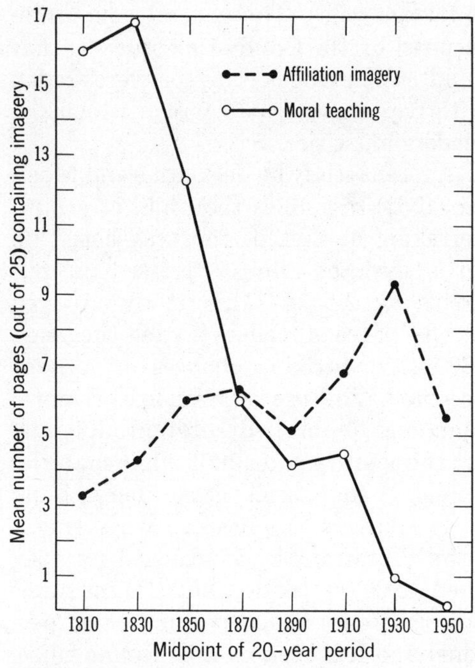

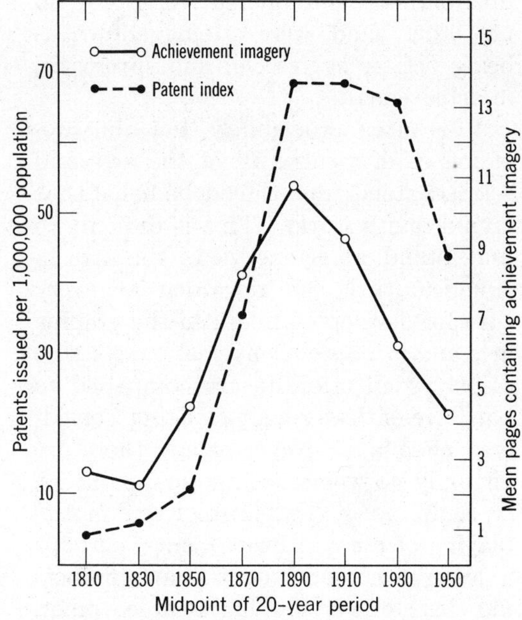

FIGURE 13-1

to learn to read! Obviously it oversimplifies the issue to blame comic books or other mass media for the existence of juvenile delinquency. Comics are a single, minor influence in the long sweep through which a child acquires a set of beliefs, values, and behaviors. What, then, is the real role that comics play?

To begin with, comic strips and comic books, as a rule, are neither funny nor amusing. They are exciting and contain a good deal of aggression. According to Bender and Lourie (1941) they fit the needs of children striving to understand the aggression of others and their own aggressive impulses. The comics and comic books share the characteristic of having justice prevail—the hero wins, the villain is punished. The vocabulary level of the typical comic book is high, about 10,000 words (Thorndike, 1941), and may be higher than the child is exposed to in conventional school texts.

Since the pictures provide cues to the words, and since the reader is highly motivated, many children unable to learn reading skills in a conventional classroom situation may gain from exposure to comic books. Although some of them and perhaps a few comic strips may center on sadism, masochism, or other pathological tendencies, and may at times provide an explicit blueprint for a specific crime, most comics for most children seem relatively harmless and, in some ways, beneficial. The question that arises is how much, if any, cenorship of comic books or any other of the mass media society should impose on the majority in order to safeguard the suggestible minority. But this, more properly, is a point of interest for sociologists, philosophers, and political scientists than for psychologists.

Movies

The moral character of movies first came under attack as a result of the peepshow "Dolorita in the Passion Dance" shown in Atlantic City in 1894 (Ramsaye, 1949). The attack intensified through the years until the late 1930's, when other problems of an economic nature plus a gradual public adaptation to movies caused a slackening of interest. Like the other mass media, movies are not closely bound to reality; in fact, movie theaters were once known as "dream palaces," which certainly indicated an awareness of the movies unreality. They portray a wide assortment of socially disapproved behaviors and at times present a master plan for criminal conduct. On the other hand, movies provide opportunities for other forms of social learning that are socially neutral or socially desirable.

As Blumer and Hauser (1934) said many years ago, movies can make a contribution to crime and delinquency.

> Through the display of crime techniques and criminal patterns of behavior; by arousing desires for easy money and luxury, and by suggesting questionable methods for their achievement; by inducing a spirit of bravado, thoroughness, and adventurousness; by arousing intense sexual desires; and by invoking daydreaming of criminal roles, motion pictures may create attitudes and furnish techniques conducive, quite, unwittingly, to delinquent or criminal behavior (Blumer & Hauser, 1934, p. 198).

Whether an individual is swayed depends on other, more basic aspects of individual personality and of the environment.

Television

After years during which the public has worried about the effects of television, information needed for evaluation purposes has become available. Three extensive studies, one in England (Himmelweit, Oppenheim, & Vince, 1958), one in the United States (Schramm, Lyle, & Parker, 1961), and one in Japan (Furu, 1962), contain reliable information on the impact of television on children's personality and behavior. As with the other mass media, the chief fear expressed by the individuals concerned is that young persons become passive, anxious, or delinquent as a result of television viewing. The actual influence of television in these areas of adjustment, together with its effect on aspects of cognitive functioning that are of less public concern, may be seen from the following data.

It has been maintained that spectator activities promote passivity (e.g., Whyte, 1956). There is not much evidence for this contention as it relates to television. However, Glynn (1956), a psychotherapist, had this to say:

> Warmth, sound, constancy, availability, a steady giving without ever a demand for return, the encouragement to complete passive surrender and development—all this and active fantasy besides. Watching these [viewers], one is deeply impressed by their acting out with the television set of their unconscious longings to be infants in their mothers' lap.
>
> These, then, are traits television can so easily satisfy in adults, or foster in children: traits of passivity, receptiveness, being fed, taking in and absorbing what is offered. Activity, self-reliance, and aggression are notably absent (Glynn, 1956, p. 178).

On the other hand, the Himmelweit group (1958) observed that television viewers were more curious about the world and showed a slightly wider variety of interests than a group of nonviewers or than they themselves had shown before becoming viewers. These are the only bits of information available on the matter of passivity and television viewing and they contradict each other. However, the

Himmelweit group reported data; Glynn reported an unsubstantiated personal opinion.

Much more information is at hand on the capacity of television to produce anxiety. There is no doubt that a great amount of violence is portrayed on television. The National Association of Educational Broadcasters (Purdue Opinion Panel, 1954) had a team of viewers watch all the television broadcasts visible in New York City for one week a year for four years. In the final year alone, 1954, during this one week 6868 incidents of a violent nature occurred on New York television screens. What is the general effect of this violence with respect to the production of anxiety among child viewers? The Himmelweit et al. study found one-fourth of the boys and one-third of the girls in a sample of more than 1000 young viewers aged 10–14 to have been frightened by the events seen on television.

Violence that follows a conventional pattern with a foreseeable outcome is not frightening. Although dripping with gore, Westerns frightened only seven of the whole sample, and of these, five were below average in ability (Himmelweit et al., 1958, p. 194). It is the more complex pattern of aggression such as that shown in adult dramas which is mentioned most often as productive of fear. Particularly upsetting for children is the serious verbal expression of hostility on the part of adults (Himmelweit et al., 1958, p. 204; pp. 461–462). Children appear to be far more impressed by verbal than physical hostility, perhaps because *they* have observed their parents in verbal but not physical conflicts, and the television experience recalls the real-life conflict to them. It was also discovered that real violence, as shown in news programs, was far more capable of producing anxiety than fictional violence of the same sort.

Clearly some children are made anxious and fearful by at least some television programs. So, too, were some children of an earlier era and are some children of today by such traditional fairy tales as "Bluebeard" and by such fairy-tale figures as "Little One Eye," a girl created by the brothers Grimm with one eye, as big as a saucer, in the middle of her forehead. But, as noted in Chapter 11, children seem to like and search for situations in which they can produce "manageable" fear. Consequently, there is no reason to believe that fear itself is necessarily bad or destructive.

Violence on television is also said to cause violence and delinquency in real life. "If the proverb is true that prison is a college of crime," said one psychiatrist, "then I believe that for young disturbed adolescents, T.V. is a preparatory school for delinquency" (Banay, 1955). As we have noted, comics and movies—and if we go farther back in time, for that matter, newspapers and stage productions—have also been blamed for delinquency. One large-scale study dealing with this issue failed to discover any more aggressive, maladjusted, or delinquent behavior among television viewers than among nonviewers (Himmelweit et al., 1958, p. 215). On the other hand, a long series of studies conducted by Bandura, Walters, and their associates (e.g., see Bandura, Ross, & Ross, 1963; Bandura & Walters, 1963) suggests that exposure to aggressive models causes the person so exposed to imitate the model and to become more aggressive. These data are contradictory. Perhaps the reason that Himmelweit et al. found no increase in aggression among television viewers (despite the presence of aggressive models) while the modeling studies cited did find an increase in aggression, is that in the modeling studies testing for aggression typically took place very shortly after exposure to the aggressive model in a laboratory situation in which few constraints were placed on aggression. In comparison, aggression following television viewing might more frequently require postponement, allowing the aggressive tendency some time to dissipate. Further, aggression in the real world, as compared with the experimental laboratory, probably would encounter more often the rather strong social sanctions placed on aggression. Finally, it may be that for some children, viewing of aggression on television provides catharsis—that is, reduces real-life aggression by providing a vicarious outlet—while other children imitate what they have seen and become more aggressive. If so, one would have to establish what other child characteristics determined whether catharisis or imitation resulted, before being able to predict the effects of televised aggression on the behavior of any given child. More recent researchers (e.g. Eron, Lefkowitz, Huesmann, & Walder, 1972) also have claimed to find that television violence promotes or increases individual aggression. As they put it, "the weight of evidence . . . supports the theory that during a critical period in a boy's development, regular viewing and liking of violent television leads to a formation of a more aggressive life style" (Eron et al., 1972, p. 262). This may be so; if so, imitation must occur more frequently than catharsis.

Now to the positive aspects of commercial television. So far as social learning is concerned, Shayon (1951) noted that television "is the shortest cut yet devised, the most accessible back door to the grown-up world. Television is never too busy to talk to our children. It never shuts them off because it has to prepare dinner. Television plays with them, shares its work with them. Television wants their attention, needs it, goes to any length to get it." As the child's back door to the adult world, television would seem likely to produce a distorted view. Surprisingly, it does not. Himmelweit and her colleagues presented the following findings: Viewers emphasized intelligence and bravery as important attributes for success in adulthood more often than did nonviewers (1958, p. 468); there were no differences between the two groups in attitudes toward school, school work, or teachers (p. 246); television viewing raised youngsters' levels of aspiration regarding employment (p. 258), and in older children of 13–14 it produced quite realistic worries and fears about the problems of being grown-up (p. 250).

Television has a leveling effect on class differences in general information and vocabulary, as was seen in Chapter 5. It also promotes a general elevation in vocabulary, with younger children gaining more than older ones, dull children more than bright ones, and heavy viewers more than light viewers (Schramm et al., 1961, pp. 75–97). Viewing, for American children, does not decrease the reading of books and of most magazines but does reduce the reading of comic books and pulp magazines (Schramm et al., p. 15). Viewing does seem to decrease study time and the reading of serious books (though only slightly) in Japan (Furu, 1962), possibly because Japanese children start at a somewhat higher base; that is, they study longer hours and read serious books a greater proportion of the time than do American or English children. As Maccoby (1964) notes, television tends to decrease those activities (e.g., comic books, movies) that are functionally equivalent to television in terms of their content and in their use by children.

All told, the influence of television does not seem to be as great or as deleterious as commonly believed. There are differences between viewers and nonviewers, but they are not marked, and the existing ones do not always favor the nonviewer.

Individual Susceptibility to the Media

The adverse effects of the mass media have been exaggerated, partly because most of the studies condemning them (Blumer & Hauser, 1934; Healy, 1915; Healy & Bronner, 1936; Wertham, 1953) have not used control groups and have dealt with small and deviant samples of the entire population. Wertham could hardly be expected not to have found all delinquency to be caused by comic books when he asked delinquent youngsters such leading questions that they could reply mainly in one way. If delinquents are asked whether reading comic books caused their delinquency, most of them will respond affirmatively. For that matter, if asked whether a phase of the moon caused their delinquency, most of them would also say yea, partly to be obliging, partly to shift the blame from themselves, and partly to avoid looking deeper into their own motivations.

Adequately designed studies do not show any considerable effect of the mass media on the behavior of most children, yet *some* youngsters are greatly influenced by them. Who are these children? These are the children who are addicted to the mass media. Those addicted to comic books showed marked tendencies toward neurosis as compared with nonaddicts; they were rather small and weak and identified with omnipotent heroism such as Superman (Wolf & Fiske, 1949). In television, Himmelweit et al. found addicts to have stronger feelings of rejection and insecurity than occasional viewers (1958, pp. 390–391). In a parallel study, they noted these characteristics in ardent movie goers, implying that children who must withdraw from real situations find solace in all the media. The "findings suggest that these differences were there before television came to the home and explain why the addict views so much more than others of his age, intelligence and social background. The parallel analysis of cinema addicts showed them to be very similar kinds of children. Television meets a need which the child without television satisfies through the cinema or the radio" (Himmelweit et al., 1958, p. 390).

In a study of the same type, Bailyn (1959) confirmed the Himmelweit observations. Children subjected to considerable frustration in the home viewed television more often than children not so greatly frustrated, at least in middle- and upper-class groups (Schramm et al., 1961, pp. 130–131; Maccoby, 1954, p. 303). Not only do frustrated children have more contact with the mass media, but there is also some conflicting evidence that suggests that they may concentrate on and be better able to recall the acts of violence they have seen (Maccoby, Levin, & Selya, 1955, 1956). Even if they do more adequately recall acts of violence, frustration need not lead to imitation of an aggressive model (Kuhn, Madsen, & Becker, 1967). The viewing of aggressive behavior may teach the child something concerning the aggressive role, but children learn many roles that they do not play (Maccoby, 1959; Whiting, 1960). Whether the child, frustrated or not, imitates an aggressive model probably depends on the way parents—particularly same-sex parents, respond to frustration.

One could argue that addicts are less social, more frustrated, and more beset by problems and neurotic tendencies than the nonaddicted *because* of their addiction, were it not for the fact that the Himmelweit study covered the same children before and after the introduction of television in their locale and showed the same problems to have existed *before* the advent of television. This type of pre-

and postexposure investigation allows a very different interpretation from the typical one conducted after exposure to the mass medium, which serves as a basis for attacking the mass media. In short, addiction to the mass media is a symptom rather than a cause of social disorder.

In sum, the negative effects of the mass media are fewer than is commonly believed. The mass media have some positive effects, but these are obscured by the media's major task of convincing readers and viewers that humans are overfed, undernourished, suffering from vitamin deficiencies, or, worst of all, prone to body odor.

SUMMARY

The influence of the community, voluntary associations, the church, and the mass media as agencies of socialization is secondary. If this conclusion seems to contradict the observations in Chapter 7 on the waning influence of parents on child behavior, the evidence seems to suggest that it is not the social forces discussed in this chapter that have gained ascendancy. Although the community, the voluntary associations, and the media may have acquired additional importance, the child's peers and his school have been the real beneficiaries of the parents' decline as a socializing influence.

Negative as the data may be on the influence of the social forces explored in this chapter, they are still worth knowing. Notwithstanding the array of pressures to which the child is exposed, the role of the family, though decreasing, remains primary in the socialization process. The community generally serves to reinforce parental values rather than as a source of values as long as parents meet their responsibility in child-rearing. Only when parents abandon their role does community influence become more significant. As the community loses its influence through urbanization, voluntary associations fill the void, to a degree.

Religious experience does not seem to make much of an inroad on values or behavior, possibly because of the small portion of time spent by the average child in religious setting or perhaps because researchers have not employed the proper criteria for religious commitment. Neither are the mass media, despite public outcry against them, of prime importance. However, continual influence in a fixed direction—that women should be passive and noncreative, that scientists are odd, or that violence is permissible—may ultimately bear fruit. Some young people, because of existing personal problems, show much greater interest in the mass media and appear to be more susceptible to their influence.

REFERENCES

Allport, G. W., & Ross, T. M. Personal religious orientation and prejudice. *Journal of Personality and Social Psychology*, 1967, **5**, 432–443.

Bailyn, L. Mass media and children: A study of exposure habits and cognitive effects. *Psychological Monographs*, 1959, **71**, 1–48.

Bandura, A., Ross, D., & Ross, S. Imitation of film mediated aggressive models.

Journal of Abnormal and Social Psychology, 1963, **66**, 3–11.

Bandura, A., & Walters, R. H. *Social learning and personality development.* New York: Holt, Rinehart & Winston, 1963.

Banay, R. S. Testimony before the Subcommittee to Investigate Juvenile Delinquency, of the Committee on the Judiciary, U. S. Senate, Eighty-fourth Congress. S. Res. 62. April 1955. Washington, D.C.: U.S. Government Printing Office, 1955.

Bender, L., & Lourie, R. S. The effect of comic books on the ideology of children. *American Journal of Orthopsychiatry*, 1941, **11**, 540–550.

Blumer, H., & Hauser, P. M. *Movies, delinquency, and crime.* New York: Macmillan, 1934.

Child, I., Potter, E. H., & Levine, E. M. Children's textbooks and personality development. *Psychological Monographs,* 1946, **60**, No. 3.

Daniels, A. D. The new life: A study of regeneration. *American Journal of Psychology*, 1893, **6**, 61–106.

deCharms, R., & Moeller, G. H. Values expressed in American children's readers: 1800–1950. *Journal of Abnormal and Social Psychology*, 1962, **64**, 136–142.

Eron, L. D., Lefkowitz, M. M., Huesmann, L. R., & Walder, L. O. Does television violence cause aggression? *American Psychologist*, 1972, **27**, 253–263.

Furu, T. *Television and children's life*. Tokyo: Radio and Television Central Research Institute, Japan Broadcasting Corp., 1962.

Glynn, E. E. Television and the American character–a psychiatrist looks at television. In W. T. Elliot (Ed.), *Television's impact on American culture*. East Lansing, Mich.: Michigan State University Press, 1956.

Godin, A. (S.J.). Importance and difficulty of scientific research in religious education: The problem of the "criterion." *Religious Education Supplement*, 1962, **57**, 166–174.

Hartshorne, H., & May, M. A. *Studies in service and self control.* Vol. 1, New York: Macmillan, 1928.

Hartshorne, H., & May, M. A. *Studies in service and self control.* Vol. 2, New York: Macmillan, 1929.

Healy, W. *The individual delinquent: A textbook of diagnosis for all concerned in understanding offenders.* Boston: Little, Brown, 1915.

Healy, W., & Bronner, A. F. *New light on delinquency and its treatment.* New Haven, Conn.: Yale University Press, 1936.

Himmelweit, H. T., Oppenheim, A. N., & Vince, P. *Television and the child.* London and New York: Oxford University Press, 1958.

Jones, M. B. Religious values and authoritarian tendency. *Journal of Social Psychology*, 1958, **48**, 83–89.

Kelly, J. G., Ferson, J. E., & Holtzman, W. H. The measurement of attitudes toward the Negro in the South. *Journal of Social Psychology*, 1958, **48**, 305–517.

Kuhn, D. Z., Madsen, C. H., Jr., & Becker, W. Effects of exposure to an aggressive model and "frustration" on children's aggressive behavior. *Child Development*, 1967, **38**, 739–745.

Maccoby, E. E. Why do children watch television? *Public Opinion Quarterly*, 1954, **18**, 239–244.

Maccoby, E. E. Role taking in childhood and its consequences for social learning. *Child Development*, 1959, **30**, 239–252.

Maccoby, E. E. Effects of mass media. In M. L. Hoffman & L. W. Hoffman (Eds.), *Review of child development research, Vol. 1.* New York: Russell Sage, 1964.

Maccoby, E. E., Levin, H., & Selya, B. V. The effect of emotional arousal on the retention of aggressive and nonaggressive movie content. (Abstract) *American Psychologist,* 1955, **10**, 359.

Maccoby, E. E., Levin, H., & Selya, B. V. The effects of emotional arousal on the retention of film content: A failure to replicate. *Journal of Abnormal and Social Psychology,* 1956, **53**, 373–374.

McDowell, J. B. *The development of the idea of God in the Catholic child.* Washington, D.C.: Catholic University of America Press, 1952.

Middleton, R., & Putney, A. Religion, normative values, and behavior. *Sociometry,* 1962, **25**, 141–152.

Morgan, W. Personality correlates of involvement in religious activities. Unpublished study, San Jose State College, San Jose, Calif., 1958.

Peck, R. F., & Havighurst, R. J. *The psychology of character development.* New York: Wiley, 1960.

Purdue Opinion Panel. *Four years of New York television.* Urbana, Ill.: National Association of Educational Broadcasters, 1954.

Ramsaye, T. The rise and place of the motion picture. In W. Schramm (Ed.), *Mass communications.* Urbana, Ill.: University of Illinois Press, 1949.

Reckless, W. C., Dinitz, S., & Murray, E. Self concept as an insulation against delinquency. *American Sociological Review,* 1956, **21**, 744–746.

Salisbury, W. S. Religiosity, regional sub-culture, and social behavior. *Journal for the Scientific Study of Religion,* 1962, **2**, 94–101.

Scarpitti, R. R., Murray, E., Simon, D., & Reckless, W. C. The "good" boy in a high delinquency area: Four years later. *American Sociological Review,* 1960, **25**, 555–558.

Schramm, W., Lyle, J., & Parker, E. G. *Television in the lives of our children.* Stanford, Calif.: Stanford University Press, 1961.

Shayon, R. L. *Television and our children.* New York: Longmans, Green, 1951.

Stanley-Hall, G. The moral and religious training of children. *Princeton Review,* 1882, **10**, 26–48.

Starbuck, E. D. *Psychology of religion.* New York: Scribner's, 1899.

Stouffer, S. *Communism, conformity, and civil liberties.* New York: 1955.

Thorndike, E. L. Words and the comics. *Journal of Experimental Education,* 1941, **17**, 110–113.

Thrasher, F. L. *The gang.* Chicago: University of Chicago Press, 1927.

Wertham, F. *Seduction of the innocent.* New York: Rinehart, 1953.

Whiting, J. W. M. Resource mediation and learning by identification. In I. Iscoe & H. W. Stevenson (Eds.), *Personality development in children.* Austin: Univeristy of Texas Press, 1960.

Whyte, W. F. *Street corner society.* Chicago: University of Chicago Press, 1943.

Whyte, W. H. *The organization man.* New York: Simon and Schuster, 1956.

Wilson, W. C. Extrinsic religious values and prejudice. *Journal of Abnormal and Social Psychology,* 1960, **60**, 286–288.

Wolf, K., & Fiske, M. The children talk about comics. In P. F. Lazarsfeld & F. N. Stanton (Eds.), *Communications research, 1948–1940.* New York: Harper, 1949.

section V*

the emerging self

The previous sections of this book have investigated the forces affecting the human being—his inheritance, his growth and maturation, his learning and motivation, his language, his intelligence—and his unique pattern of response to the world around him: his personality. In this section we shall take a deeper look into the child's emerging personality. The first of the section's three chapters is devoted to a study of how the individual is appraised as an infant, as a young child, and in the school years. The second chapter, concerning personality development, covers two main facets of personality change occurring with age. These are an increasingly rich and diversified but consistent response to the world and the development of a self concept based on consistent attitudes toward the self and the world. The third chapter of the section deals with the psychological problems met in the course of the developmental process. It explores their causes, diagnosis, and probability of solution, either through therapy or the individual's own inner resources.

chapter 14

individual appraisal

chapter 14

individual appraisal

chapter 14

individual appraisal

Child psychologists and others concerned with the diagnosis of children's problems are often asked, "Is this child developing or progressing normally?" The question requires as accurate an answer as possible. To get at it psychologists have developed techniques for assessing the various aspects of child development. For early infancy, they have placed the accent on physical and motor development. For the period of early childhood, they have concerned themselves with intellectual functioning. And for the elementary-school years, they have shifted the attention to evaluation of the child's social, emotional, and personality adjustment. In this chapter we consider each of these areas of individual appraisal in turn, beginning with assessment of infant procedures.

INFANT ASSESSMENT

In this country, Arnold Gesell played a major role in the devising of techniques to evaluate the growth and physical development of infants. Because of his training and dedication as a man of medicine, his methods stressed the diagnosis of deviation from normality rather than an evaluation of levels of normality. In addition, Gesell's emphasis tended toward the medical rather than the psychological aspects of development. Nevertheless, from his accent on the "lawfulness of growth" evolved the notion that growth and development were predictable.

The Gesell Development Schedules (Gesell, 1940; Gesell and Amatruda, 1947) are concerned with four major areas of behavior: motor characteristics, adaptive behavior, language, and personal-social behavior. In examining motor behavior the primary concern is the infant's increasing control of posture in the areas of locomotion and prehension. Head control comes first, followed by sitting posture and, later, upright posture. In prehension, the infant reaches out before it is able to grasp an object accurately. Through underlying neurological development he acquires coordination that permits increasing accuracy of arm and hand movements. How these motor behaviors are executed and the ages at which they appear supply clues to the maturity level of the infant. Deviation may signify an abnormality in development.

Adaptive behaviors involve some adjustment to the environment. Their presence is detected in the child's ability to manipulate blocks by arranging them in simple structures. Tests of simple number concepts and requiring a child to copy a circle and a cross are used at a later time.

In assessing language maturity, a number of aspects are taken into consideration. One observes the child's articulation, vocabulary, use of language in communication, and comprehension. Language development is reflected by an increase in the size of vocabulary, in the length and complexity of sentence structure, and by an increase in comprehension as revealed by the ability to respond to verbal directions and commands.

Personal-social behavior embraces such matters as feeding, dressing, toilet procedure, and play. In all of these maturity is judged by increased self-reliance and independence. Since environment plays a more influential part than maturation in these areas of behavior, deviations in development frequently furnish clues to the kind of psychological atmosphere in which the child is being reared.

Gesell devised the notion of a Developmental Quotient (DQ) which expresses the ratio between the child's *maturity age* and his actual age. Maturity age is based on a child's performance on a series of developmental tests, which is then compared with the norms obtained from the administration of these tests to a number of children at various age levels. The DQ reflects the proportion of normal development attained at any given age level. By Gesell's own admission the DQ may be useful in predicting the course of future development only if no complicating factors arise. Since fluctuations in development are more common than not, maturity assessed at any one point in time may be more or less typical of any infant's developmental rate. All told, the DQ adequately assesses the infant's current rate of development, taking into account its variability, complexity, and unevenness.

To Gesell, the developmental examination served not only to establish rate of development, as in the spotting of precocity and retardation, but also to diagnose neurological difficulties and other disturbances of development. Although not much information is available on the long-term predictive ability of the Gesell Developmental Schedules, they have achieved widespread use for the evaluation of the developmental status of infants. They have been used, for example, also as a measure for validation in a Developmental Questionnaire for infants of 40 weeks devised by Knobloch and Pasamanick (1955).

While some infant tests yield developmental age or mental age scores, others have been designed to permit the identification of delayed development. One such test is the Denver Developmental Screening Test (DDST) which is a short, easily administered measure of physical, motor, perceptual, and cognitive development in preschool aged children (Frankenburg & Dodds, 1967). It provides scores in four areas: gross motor, fine motor-adaptive, language, and personal-social (see Figure 14-1). The DDST is used as a screening device in which development is scored as normal, questionable, or abnormal. Research has shown the DDST to possess high inter-tester agreement and high stability over time (Frankenburg, Camp, Van Natta, Demersseman, & Voorhees, 1971). Further, scores on the DDST show high agreement with such standardized tests as the Stanford–Binet, Bayley Scale of Infant Tests, and the Cattell Infant Intelligence Scale (Frankenburg, Camp, & Van Natta, 1971). To administer the test, a vertical line is drawn on the examination sheet representing the child's chronological age. The items to be administered are those through which the child's chronological age line passes. Each item is marked either pass or fail on the examination blank which provides a visual picture of the child's development in each of the four areas.

INTELLIGENCE AND SCHOOL-RELATED TESTS

Mental testing had many beginnings. However, the work of Alfred Binet in France represents the clearest and most direct forerunner of contemporary intelligence tests. In the closing decade of the nineteenth century, Binet and Simon investigated a variety of measures to differentiate bright from dull schoolchildren. These early efforts came to a head soon after the turn of the century when, in 1904, the Minister of Public Instruction in Paris appointed a commission to study the advisability of establishing special schools for children incapable of profiting from instruction in the public-school classroom. Some means of identifying such children was clearly needed. Binet and Simon were consulted, with the result that a formal scale for testing the intelligence of children was constructed. The aim of this scale was to obtain an estimate of the child's level of mental development. Although a wide variety of tasks tapping different areas of ability was included in

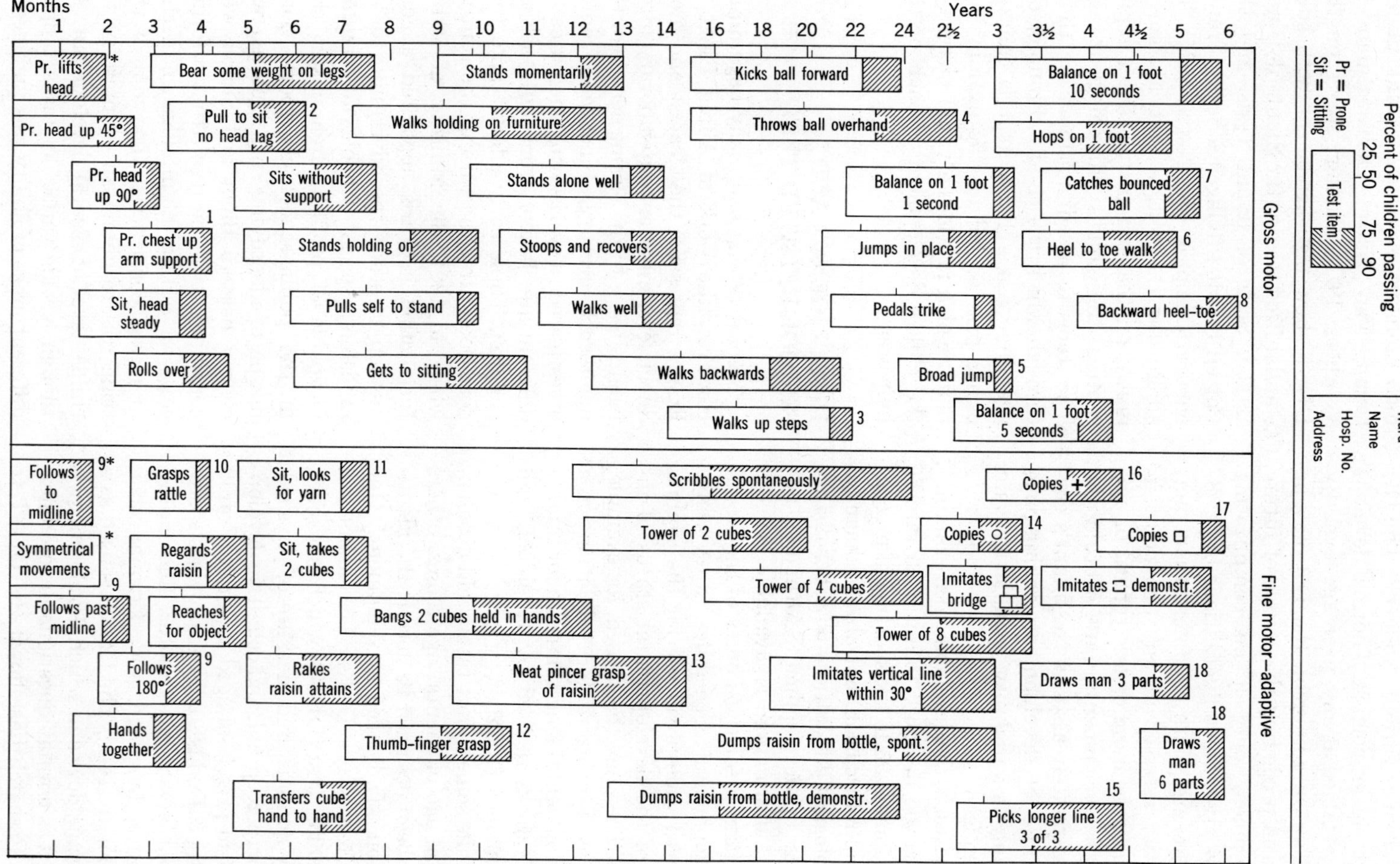

FIGURE 14-1 Denver Developmental Screening Test.

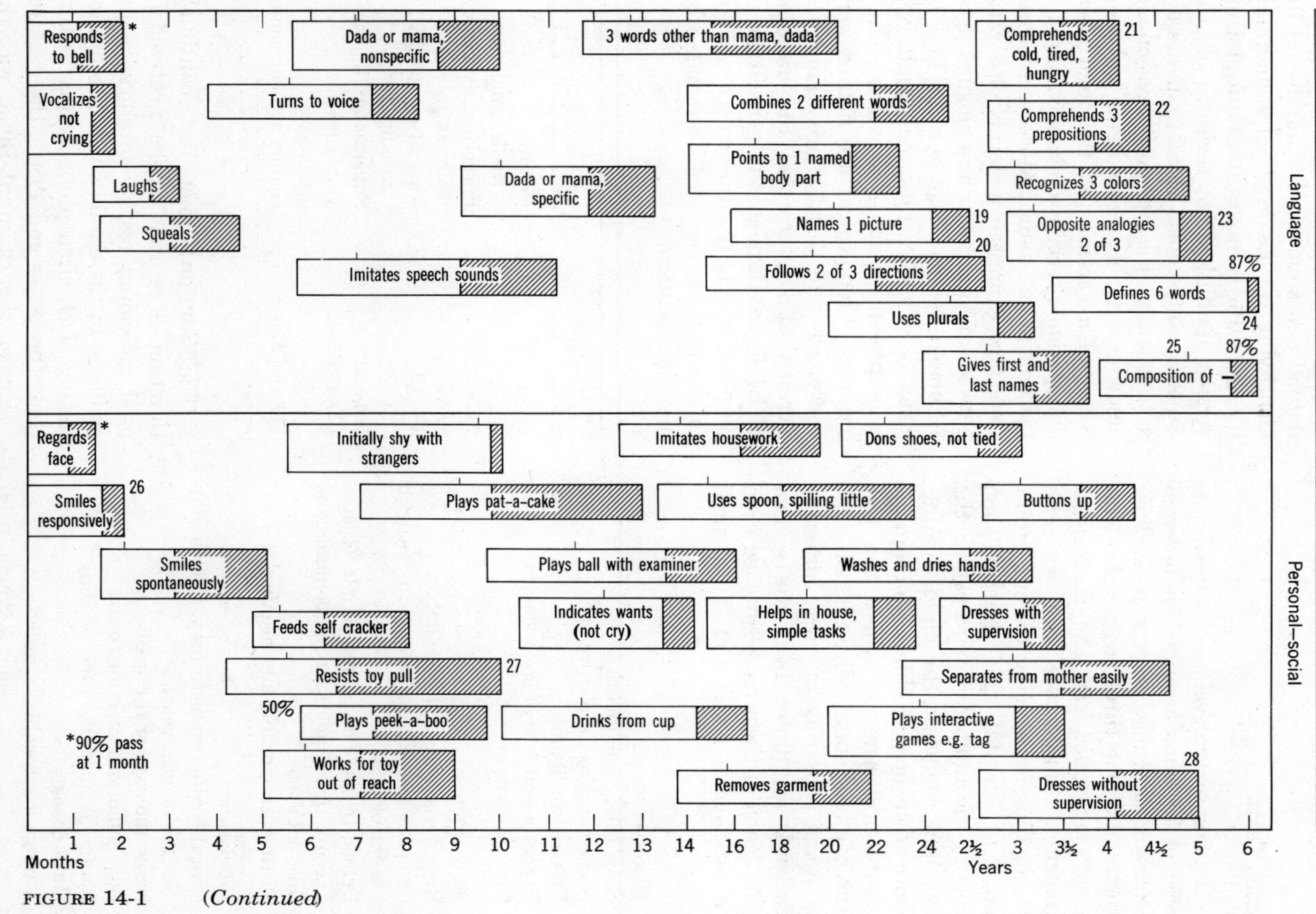

FIGURE 14-1 (*Continued*)

the scale, Binet and Simon formulated a rather clear definition of intelligence: "To judge well, to comprehend well, to reason well, these are the essential activities of intelligence."

Binet Tests

The first scale, developed in 1905, consisted of 30 items arranged in order of increasing difficulty. It was revised by Binet and Simon three years later. New items were added and the method of arranging them by age level was employed, thus introducing the important notion of "mental age." Rather than denoting the number of items passed, the score now compared the child's performance with those of children of various chronological ages on whom the test items had been standardized. The following items appearing at three different age levels are drawn from the revised scale. Many of them have survived even the most recent revision of the original scale.

Three years:
Show eyes, nose, mouth
Name objects in a picture
Repeat two figures
Repeat a sentence of six syllables
Give last name

Six years:
Repeat a sentence of 16 syllables
Compare two figures from an esthetic point of view
Define, by use only, some simple objects
Execute three simultaneous commissions
Give one's age
Distinguish morning and evening

Nine years:
Give the date complete (day, month, day of the month, year)
Name the days of the week
Give definitions superior to use
Retain six memories after reading
Make change
Arrange five weights in order

(Binet & Simon, 1948)

The Binet-Simon scale made its debut in English at the Vineland Training School in New Jersey, where Goddard put it to use as a diagnostic instrument for distinguishing between intellectually normal and subnormal children and for identifying various levels of subnormality. In 1916 Terman, at Stanford University, published a revision of the Binet-Simon scales. More than merely a translation, the Stanford revision included a number of new items and, as a result of a careful and thorough standardization procedure, changed the age placement of items. Moreover, scores were now expressed in terms of a ratio between mental and chronological ages. Although Terman was not the first to conceive of such a ratio, he popularized it by presenting tables in which mental age and chronological age figures were converted into Intelligence Quotients. Terman also interpreted the meaning of IQ levels through the percentage of people receiving the various scores. The following table contains Terman's original classification.

IQ range	*Classification*
Below 70	Definite feeble-mindedness
70–80	Borderline deficiency
80–90	Dullness
90–110	Normal or average intelligence
110–120	Superior intelligence
120–140	Very superior intelligence
140 and above	Genius or near genius

The Stanford–Binet test continues to retain its position as the most widely used individual test of intelligence for children. In the era in which intelligence testing of children probably reached its peak, the 1940's and 1950's, the 1937 revision of the Stanford–Binet was the test used (Terman & Merrill, 1937). Although this was superseded by a 1960 revision, much of what follows applies to both.

Perhaps one of the most notable features of the Stanford–Binet is its precision of administration and of scoring. Clear instructions are provided for the examiner on the exact wording of his questions and the extent to which urging and further questioning are permissible. The scoring manual is detailed, with numerous examples supplied to assist in scoring the child's responses. Both features tend to reduce as much as possible the effects on IQ scores of such factors as differences among examiners in the administration and scoring of tests. The kind of rapport established by the examiner with the child is important, however; for this and other reasons only a trained and experienced individual is qualified to administer an intelligence test.

The nature of the Stanford–Binet test items, especially at the younger age levels, is such that they are intrinsically interesting to children. Because of this it is usually possible to hold children's attention throughout the administration of the test which lasts approximately one hour. The 1960 revision consists of six test items at each half-year age level from 2 to 5 and six tests at each year level from 5 to 14.

Several points of importance in evaluating any intelligence test are worth noting. First, as to test reliability, Terman and Merrill (1937) reported reliability coefficients ranging from +0.90 to +0.98 for the children used to set up the standardization procedure. A median coefficient of +0.91 resulted from correlating the two forms of the 1937 revision, Forms L and M, for each of the 21 groups involved in the standardization effort. It is apparent that the Stanford–Binet is a highly reliable measuring instrument. Nevertheless, individual performances on the test may show fluctuations over a period of time. IQ scores do change upon retesting. In Terman's 1916 standardization group half of the children deviated by five IQ points or more on retesting; 16 percent deviated by 10 points or more, 6.2 percent by 15 points or more, and 1.85 percent by 20 points or more. Thus caution must be exercised in interpreting the meaning of a single assessment of a child's intelligence and in making predictions on the basis of a single score. Furthermore, as noted in Chapter 6, the later the age at which a test is administered, the more closely it correlates with an IQ score obtained at the age of 18. Scores of IQ tests show a sharp increase in long-term predictive power around five or six. Before then, they should be viewed with reserve.

The next important aspect of any test is its validity. Evaluating the validity of the Stanford–Binet is far more difficult than assessing its reliability. There is no definition of intelligence on which there is general agreement. In fact, there are as many views of intelligence as there are tests to measure it. This has led to the quip that intelligence is what intelligence tests measure. Such a belief is unduly pessimistic. IQ test scores have the ability to predict such things as school achievement and later intellectual functioning. Correlations between Stanford–Binet scores and achievement in first grade imply the moderate success of IQ scores in predicting school achievement. In this sense, the Stanford–Binet possesses *predictive validity*. The Stanford–Binet also possesses what is called *construct validity*; that is, it contains items capable of measuring the kinds of abilities that Binet, and later Terman, termed as intelligence.

Finally, a number of cautions and criticisms should be noted. Although Binet attempted originally to assess a child's inborn or native capacity, an IQ is apparently only a measure of the child's *present level of functioning*, despite being moderately predictive of later functioning as well. A related point is that the Stanford–Binet assumes background experience similar to that of the children on whom the test was standardized. Many of its test materials presuppose a general familiarity with the American culture. Hence scores of children whose backgrounds depart in any degree from the American norm should be viewed with suspicion. Although IQ scores of children of recently arrived Mexican laborers in California, for example, may fall below those of typical white, middle-class, urban youngsters, such results are not really valid indications of a difference between the two groups.

The Stanford–Binet has been charged with predicting neither social nor personality adjustment, nor success in life. Such criticisms lack validity. Binet, as we have seen, designed his test originally to identify levels of academic performance. In this respect, the test continues to do an adequate job. The intelligence test was never designed to assess personality factors, musical ability, or a host of other individual qualities. There are separate tests for these things.

Another criticism of the Stanford–Binet is its preponderance of items involving verbal ability. This is thought to penalize those children whose strengths lie in other areas of functioning. Although some children, such as those from bilingual homes or afflicted with hearing deficiencies, may be handicapped by the test's verbal biases, language facility remains a major factor in academic pursuits. To predict a child's success in such endeavors, an intelligence test must measure a child's potentialities in coping with their language demands. Besides, as noted in Chapter 5, the ability to deal with and to manipulate such abstract symbols as words is distinctly human and may be man's greatest glory. Thus it is hardly inappropriate for intelligence tests to be weighted heavily in linguistic content. However, performance tests, as we shall see presently, have been developed to give a fair indication of the intellectual ability of children whose verbal facility may be limited.

One last caution. Although IQ tests and other tests differ in a number of ways, they also have many similarities. A child's performance on an IQ test, like his performance on any other test, depends, in part, on how he feels at the moment, on his mood, on his motivation, and on many similar incidental factors. An IQ result has maximal significance only if all conditions surrounding the test are optimal. It reveals no sacred, immutable truth about a child. It is only an index to one area of a child's functioning, an important area, to be sure, but one best interpreted when seen as the basis for a broad understanding of the child's behavior and personality.

Performance Tests

Although the term *performance* is something of a misnomer since performance tests require abstract abilities plus knowledge and understanding, manipulation of objects has considerable importance in these tests. Verbal facility is a very important part of general intelligence, as has been observed, yet the evaluation of other skills uncovers valuable information regarding other areas of the child's capabilities. Studying the child's performance in the types of task usually contained in performance tests provides clinical insights into the techniques employed by the child in approaching a problem of this kind.

Appropriate for children between the ages of 5 and 15 is the Wechsler Intelligence Scale for Children (WISC) (Wechsler, 1949). The WISC includes both verbal and performance scales, of which the latter is probably the most widely used test of its kind at the present time.

The performance scale is comprised of five subtests—picture arrangement, picture completion, block design, digit symbol, and object assembly. Figure 14-2 illustrates the administration of the WISC.

Because of the nature of the abilities measured by the WISC performance scale, it correlates less highly with the Stanford–Binet test than does the verbal scale. Similarly the IQs of the performance scale do not relate as well as the IQs of the verbal scale or the Stanford–Binet to school achievement. In view of the importance of verbal abilities in scholastic achievement this situation is quite understandable; even so, the lesser bearing of the performance IQs downgrades their predictive usefulness.

More recently the Wechsler Preschool and Primary Scale of Intelligence (WPPSI) (Wechsler, 1967) has been developed for the four- to six-and-a-half-year level. Although in part a downward extension of the WISC, the WPPSI is a separate scale consisting of six verbal and five performance subtests.

Another performance test, the Goodenough Draw-A-Man test (Goodenough, 1926), was one of the first such developed. The test requires the child to draw "the best man he can." In the main the scoring is based on the number of details included in the drawing. The test is relatively simple to administer and score. Although Goodenough originally obtained rather high correlations between the Draw-A-Man IQs and scores on the Stanford–Binet, Medinnus (1961a) found correlations ranging between +0.26 and +0.57 for a group of five-year-olds. Low correlations were also seen between Draw-A-Man IQs and subsequent first-grade achievement. Thus, though IQ scores obtained from children's drawings may be useful for gross estimates of ability and for general screening purposes, they do not serve the end for which intelligence tests were originally developed because they do not correlate highly with academic achievement. Samples of a child's Draw-A-Man products over a 10-month period appear in Figure 14-3.

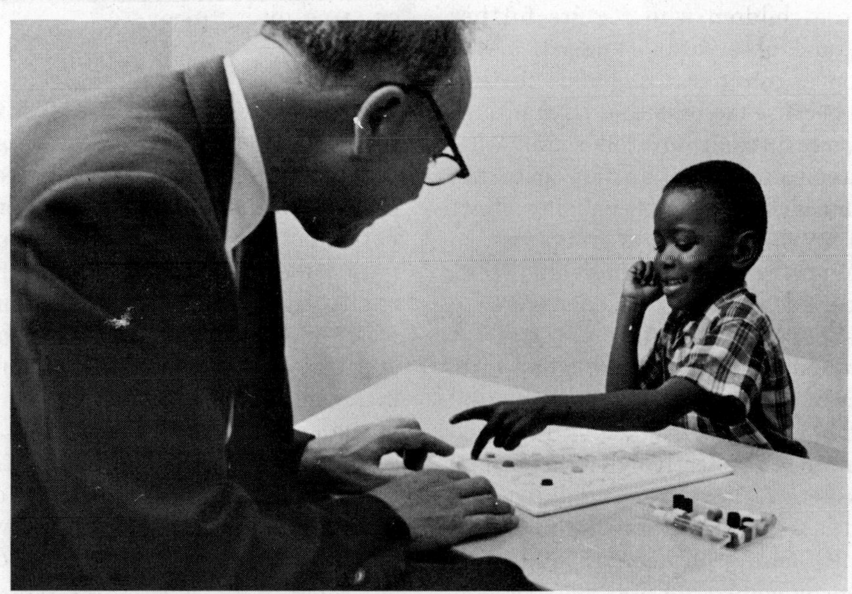

FIGURE 14-2 Administration of the WISC (by permission of The Psychological Corporation).

FIGURE 14-3 Three Draw-A-Man samples, by the same child over a period of 10 months.

Group Tests

Time is often a precious commodity. There is rarely enough of it to do what one wishes. To use time economically, tests have been developed to measure the ability of a large number of children simultaneously. Even if some of the advantages of individually administered tests are lost, group tests function as productive screening devices to single out those children who require further testing and observation. Indeed, a low score on a group test demands further testing because factors other than intelligence may intrude on the score. Misunderstood directions, anxiety over the test, and lack of motivation may effect a child's performance on a group test. In the administration of an individual test, an experienced examiner endeavors to eliminate such intrusions.

Commonly one hears that group tests are never as satisfactory as individual tests. Nevertheless, IQ scores obtained from group tests effectively predict school achievement. The closer similarity between the testing situation and nature of group IQ and achievement tests than between individual IQ and achievement tests may contribute to this predictability. Besides, in the day-to-day school situation the child does not enjoy the individual attention and encouragement that are present in the individual test situation. In school, the child's achievement rests in part on his capacity to follow directions, function independently, and apply himself to the task before him.

Figure 14-4 contains items extracted from a group test, the California Short-From Test of Mental Maturity (Sullivan, Clark, & Tiegs, 1963).

School Readiness Tests. Most kindergarten and first-grade readiness tests deal specifically with reading readiness because reading is the primary preoccupation in the early elementary years. The principal element in most tests of reading readiness is the ability to discriminate word and letter forms. Comprehension and range of information frequently are included also. While readiness to read is of major importance in assessing school readiness, other kinds of information are useful in determining whether a child is ready for school entrance or whether an additional year of maturity would be advisable. Two general tests of school readiness are described here.

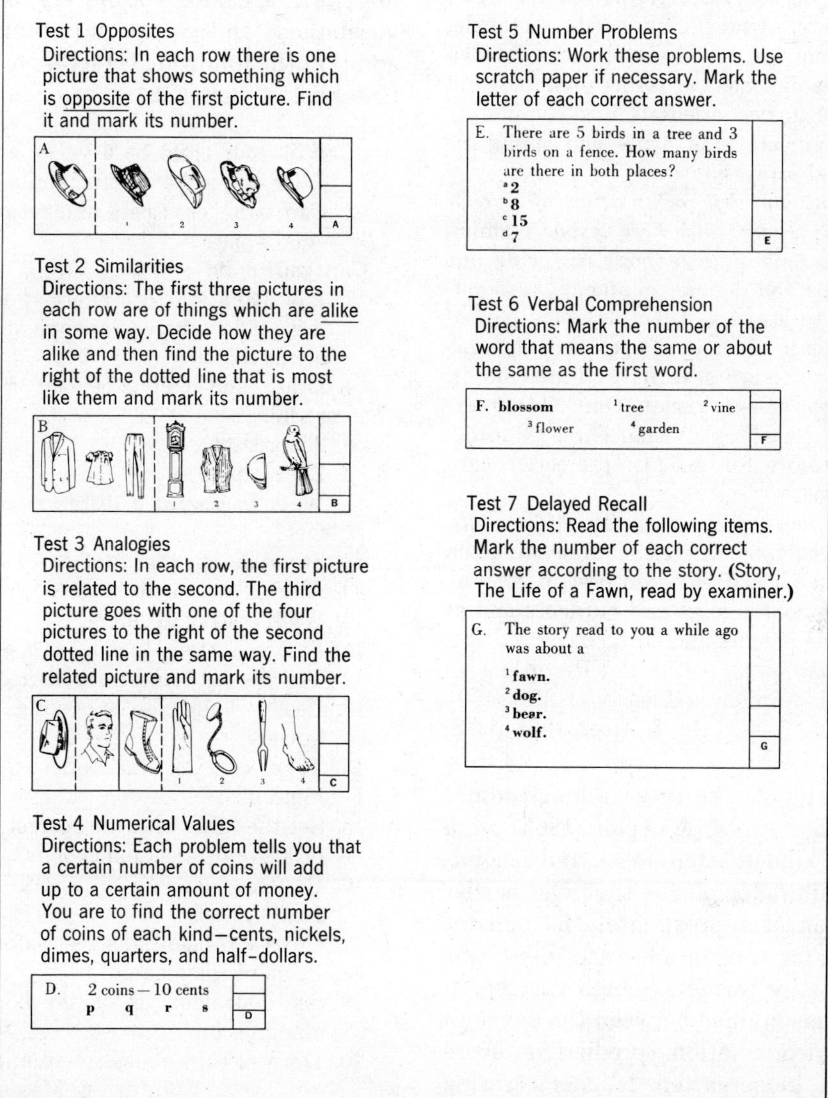

Test 1 Opposites
Directions: In each row there is one picture that shows something which is opposite of the first picture. Find it and mark its number.

A 1 2 3 4 A

Test 2 Similarities
Directions: The first three pictures in each row are of things which are alike in some way. Decide how they are alike and then find the picture to the right of the dotted line that is most like them and mark its number.

B 1 2 3 4 B

Test 3 Analogies
Directions: In each row, the first picture is related to the second. The third picture goes with one of the four pictures to the right of the second dotted line in the same way. Find the related picture and mark its number.

C 1 2 3 4 C

Test 4 Numerical Values
Directions: Each problem tells you that a certain number of coins will add up to a certain amount of money. You are to find the correct number of coins of each kind—cents, nickels, dimes, quarters, and half-dollars.

D. 2 coins—10 cents
p q r s D

Test 5 Number Problems
Directions: Work these problems. Use scratch paper if necessary. Mark the letter of each correct answer.

E. There are 5 birds in a tree and 3 birds on a fence. How many birds are there in both places?
a 2
b 8
c 15
d 7
E

Test 6 Verbal Comprehension
Directions: Mark the number of the word that means the same or about the same as the first word.

F. **blossom** 1 tree 2 vine 3 flower 4 garden F

Test 7 Delayed Recall
Directions: Read the following items. Mark the number of each correct answer according to the story. (Story, The Life of a Fawn, read by examiner.)

G. The story read to you a while ago was about a
1 **fawn.**
2 **dog.**
3 **bear.**
4 **wolf.**
G

FIGURE 14-4 Sample items from the California Short-Form Test of Mental Maturity.

As a result of their clinical work since 1950, the staff at the Gesell Institute have observed that at least 50 percent of those children referred as school behavior problems are overplaced as to grade. This overplacement resulted from determination of school entrance by chronological age alone. The Gesell Institute Developmental Examination was devised in order to provide a more adequate basis for determining readiness for school. The examination is divided into the following seven parts:

1. *The initial interview.* Questions about abe, birth date, birthday party, including favorite activity and present received; siblings—names and ages; father's occupation.
2. *Pencil and paper tests.* Writing name or letters and address; numbers 1 to 20;

copying six basic forms (circle, cross, square, triangle, divided rectangle, diamond in two orientations), and two three-dimensional forms (cylinder and cube in two orientations); completing Incomplete Man figure and giving his facial expression.

3. *Right and left (adaptation of Jacobson's Right and Left tests).* Naming parts and sides of body, carrying out single and double commands, responding to a series of pictures of a pair of hands in which two fingers are touching. Response is first verbal and then motor.
4. *Form tests.* Visual One (Monroe)–matching forms; Visual Three (Monroe) –memory for designs; projection into forms.
5. *Naming of animals for 60 seconds.*
6. *Concluding interview.* Reporting on what child likes to do best in general, at school indoors and outdoors and at home indoors and outdoors.
7. *Examination of teeth.* Recording of both eruption and decay or fillings.

(Ilg & Ames, 1964, p. 35)

The results of a three-year longitudinal study (Ilg, Ames, & Apell, 1965) of a group of kindergarten, first-, and second-grade children indicate that the earlier impression of approximately 50 percent unready for their grade placement was substantially correct. A high correspondence was obtained between the developmental examination prediction score and the kindergarten teacher's rating of the children's progress throughout the year. As would be expected from previous literature dealing with sex differences in development, girls were considerably accelerated over boys in terms of school readiness.

A novel approach to answering the parents' question, "Should I keep Johnny out of school for another year?" is a readiness test designed for parents to administer to preschool children (Jordan & Massey, 1967). Readiness is assessed in seven areas: Number concepts, discrimination of form, color naming, symbol matching, speaking vocabulary, listening vocabulary, and general information. In addition the following General Readiness Checklist is included:

1. Will your child be 5 years 3 months older when he begins kindergarten?
2. Can strangers easily understand your child's speech?

Can your child:

3. Pay attention to a short story when it is read, and answer simple questions about it?
4. Draw and color, beyond a simple scribble?
5. Tie a knot?
6. Zip a zipper?
7. Walk backward a distance of 5 or 6 feet?
8. Stand on one foot for 5 to 10 seconds?
9. Alternate feet walking down stairs?
10. Walk a straight line?
11. Fasten buttons that he can see?
12. Tell his left hand from his right?
13. Use a knife for spreading jam or butter?
14. Take care of his toilet needs by himself?
15. Set the table with the correct number of knives, forks, and spoons?
16. Be away from you 2 or 3 hours without being upset?
17. Cross a residential street safely?
18. Print his first name?
19. See a straight pin on the floor while standing up?
20. Draw or copy a plus, a box, and a ball?

(Jordan & Massey, 1967)

Games and activities for facilitating development in each of the areas are provided. Thus the parent is given specific suggestions for ways in which he may improve his child's school readiness.

Tests for Specific Learning Disabilities

While the intelligence tests described above provide a global assessment of the child's level of intellectual functioning, tests have been developed more recently to identify areas of specific disability. Most of these have arisen out of a school learning context, in which certain language and perceptual deficiencies retard the child's ability to master learning skills. For both of the tests we describe here, exercises have been developed to remediate specific deficiencies that the tests identify.

The Frostig Developmental Test of Visual Perception. This test (Frostig, Maslow, Lefever, & Whittlesey, 1964) resulted from the observation that many children with learning difficulties manifested visual or auditory perceptual disturbances. The test measures five perceptual skill areas: eye-motor coordination, figure-ground, constancy of shape, position in space, and spatial relationships. Test items illustrating each of these subtests are shown in Figure 14-5. The Frostig Test is designed for group administration, although it should be administered individually to disturbed or handicapped children. It is appropriate for children from 3 through 10 years of age. Normative data provide the basis for converting raw scores into Perceptual Age scores, which yield a Perceptual Quotient when divided by the child's chronological age.

The test-retest reliability correlations for the Frostig Test appear to be satisfactory. With regard to validity, the scores are significantly related to teacher's ratings of the child's coordination and intellectual functioning. However, the test is not a good predictor of later reading ability (Olson & Johnson, 1970) which restricts its usefulness. This poor predictive usefulness may be due in part to the fact that, though it is composed of five subtests, the Frostig measures primarily visual perceptual ability (Olson, 1969) which is somewhat less important to reading achievement than abilities involving verbal comprehension. Children with severe learning difficulties and neurologically handicapped children have been found to score low on the test.

Graded materials are available (Frostig & Horne, 1964) to facilitate development in the various areas identified through testing. A pilot study using these perceptual training materials with a group of kindergarten children showed that the experimental group gained significantly more than the control group.

The Illinois Test of Psycholinguistic Ability. The ITPA was designed to identify "psycholinguistic abilities and disabilities in children between the ages of two and one-half and nine" (McCarthy & Kirk, 1963, p. 1). The test yields scores for nine different language skills plus a total language age score.

Tests at the Representational Level. These tests assess the individual's ability to deal with linguistic symbols.

Test 1. Auditory Decoding—the ability to understand the spoken word. The words are presented in simple sentences to which the subject responds yes or no.

Examples: "Do airplanes fly?" "Do bicycles drink?"

Test 2. Visual Decoding—the ability to comprehend pictures and written words. A stimulus picture is presented, followed by four comparison pictures. The task is to select the comparison picture that is most meaningfully related to the stimulus picture.

Example: a silver knife and a jackknife

The Association Tests. These tests tap the ability to relate visual or auditory symbols in a meaningful way.

Test 3. Auditory-Vocal Association—the ability to relate spoken words is assessed through an analogies test graded for level of difficulty.

Example: Soup is hot;
ice cream is ______.

Test 4. Visual-Motor Association—the ability to relate visual symbols in a

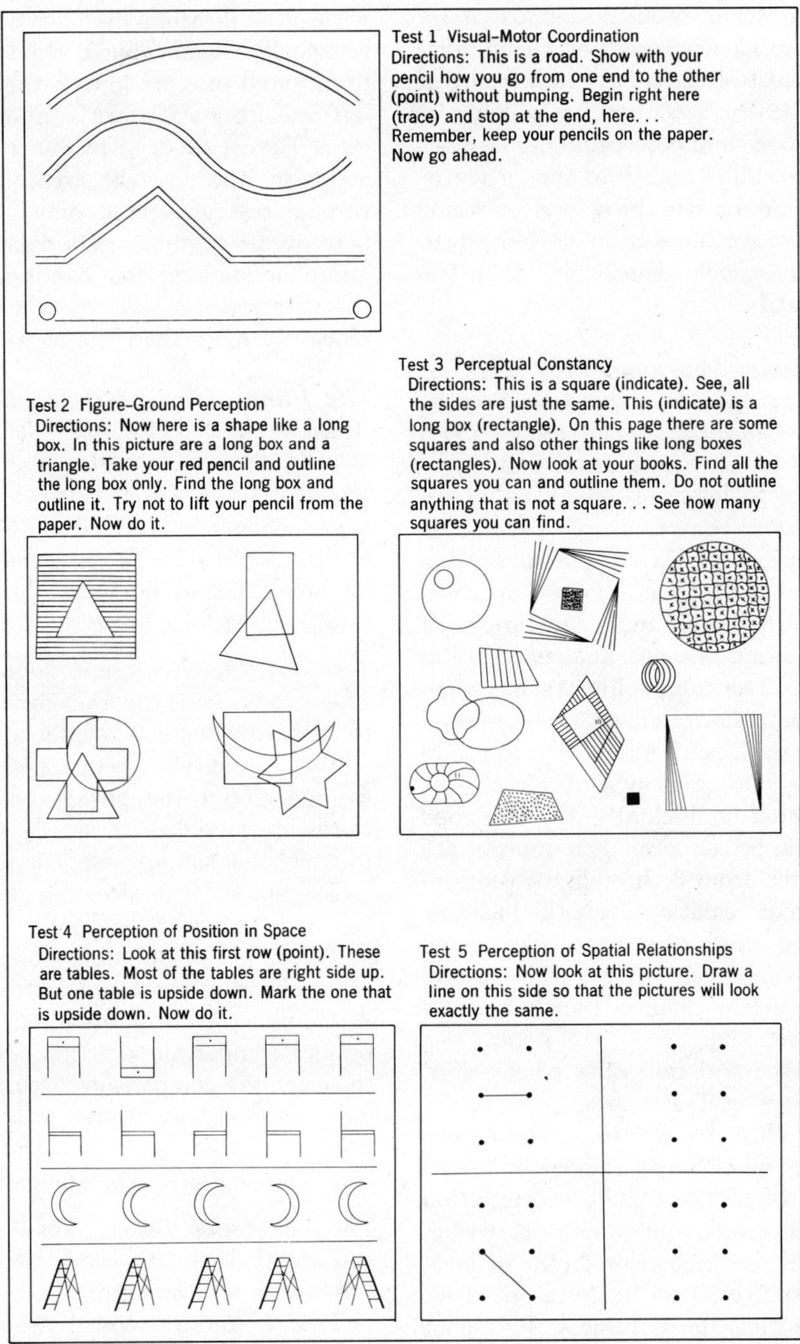

Test 1 Visual–Motor Coordination
Directions: This is a road. Show with your pencil how you go from one end to the other (point) without bumping. Begin right here (trace) and stop at the end, here. . . Remember, keep your pencils on the paper. Now go ahead.
Test 2 Figure-Ground Perception
Directions: Now here is a shape like a long box. In this picture are a long box and a triangle. Take your red pencil and outline the long box only. Find the long box and outline it. Try not to lift your pencil from the paper. Now do it.
Test 3 Perceptual Constancy
Directions: This is a square (indicate). See, all the sides are just the same. This (indicate) is a long box (rectangle). On this page there are some squares and also other things like long boxes (rectangles). Now look at your books. Find all the squares you can and outline them. Do not outline anything that is not a square. . . See how many squares you can find.
Test 4 Perception of Position in Space
Directions: Look at this first row (point). These are tables. Most of the tables are right side up. But one table is upside down. Mark the one that is upside down. Now do it.
Test 5 Perception of Spatial Relationships
Directions: Now look at this picture. Draw a line on this side so that the pictures will look exactly the same.

FIGURE 14-5 Sample items from the Frostig Developmental Test of Visual Perception.

meaningful way. A picture association test requires the subject to select from among four pictures the one which is most meaningfully related to the stimulus picture.

Examples: sock and shoe; hammer and nail

The Encoding Tests. These involve the ability to put ideas into words or gestures.

Test 5. Vocal Encoding—the ability to express ideas in spoken words is measured by asking the subject to describe simple objects.

Examples: ball, chalk, block

Test 6. Motor Encoding—the ability to express ideas in gestures. The subject is shown a picture of an object and asked to, "Show me what you should do with this."

Examples: drinking from a cup; strumming a guitar

Tests at the Automatic Sequential Level.

Test 7. Auditory-Vocal Automatic—a grammar test involving the ability to supply the correct linguistic form of a word.

Examples: Here is an apple. Here are two _______.
Father is opening the can. Now the can has been _______.

Test 8. Auditory-Vocal Sequencing—the ability to repeat a sequence of symbols is measured by a digit memory test.

Test 9. Visual-Motor Sequencing—the ability to reproduce a series of symbols is measured by requiring the subject to duplicate a sequence of pictures or geometrical designs presented by the examiner and then removed.

Although the ITPA is composed of the above nine subtests, factor analyses of children's scores on the total test have revealed only two–five factors, or separate abilities, depending on age level (Ryckman & Wiegerink, 1969). Only two factors, a general language ability and a visual-motor ability, were noted at the three-year level. Other factors emerged at later age levels, indicating increasing differentiation with age.

A number of remedial exercises have been suggested to facilitate development in the specific areas measured by the ITPA. These procedures should be useful for developing a remedial curriculum for children manifesting specific language deficiencies as well as those from culturally disadvantaged backgrounds who show general language retardation.

While some questions have been raised regarding the reliability and validity of the ITPA (Weener, Barritt, & Semmel, 1967), the test is a fruitful attempt to assess level of functioning in the language area—an area that is receiving increased attention among educators and psychologists.

Achievement Tests

The rapid increase in the testing of achievement during the 1950's stemmed partly from the self-critical, self-evaluative attitude of the nation's public schools. How effective are teaching techniques? How much have children learned from a particular course? Which areas of course content have pupils failed to assimilate? Such questions have spurred the drive to wider testing of achievement. In addition, knowledge of pupil achievement proves useful in counseling children and helps to make pertinent decisions about a child's academic strengths and weaknesses.

An indication of the importance attached to the assessment of achievement was a law passed by the California legislature in 1961 setting up a mandatory testing program throughout the state's public-school system. California school districts are now required to administer standardized achievement tests in English and mathematics as well as intelligence tests at the fifth-, eighth-, and eleventh-grade levels. The State Board of Education has certified an approved list of tests from which school districts must select those to be used. Scores must be recorded in the pupils' cumulative records.

In the early elementary years achievement tests concentrate on the child's reading ability. One test commonly used at the primary level (Metropolitan

Achievement Tests, 1959) isolates and measures four aspects of reading: word knowledge, word discrimination, sentence reading, and story reading. Later, achievement tests assess a number of fairly specific skills. A test considered appropriate for junior-high-school students (Tiegs & Clark, 1957) covers three main areas: reading, arithmetic, and language, each of which is divided into the following subtests.

Reading
- Reading Vocabulary: Mathematics; Science; Social Science; General.
- Reading Comprehension: Following Directions; Reference Skills; Interpretations.

Arithmetic
- Arithmetic Reasoning: Meanings; Symbols, Rules, and Equations; Problems.
- Arithmetic Fundamentals: Addition, Subtraction; Multiplication; Division.

Language
- Mechanics of English: Capitalization; Punctuation; Word Usage.
- Spelling.

Sample items drawn from two achievement tests are shown in Figure 14-6.

It may seem unnecessary to speak of the validity of achievement tests. Obviously they must be valid if they measure the amount of subject matter a child has learned from a course. Yet achievement tests have been criticized because too often they measure only a child's retention of isolated facts without concern for other possible goals of the course. How much, for example, has the course stimulated the child's interest and curiosity? To what extent has the child gained a broad understanding of the principles involved? To what extent is the child able to apply the information he has learned to the solving of problems in a specific area? Since all these are reasonable educational goals, an educational achievement test, to be valid, might well assess a child's proficiency in these regions. In all fairness, it must be pointed out that authors of achievement tests have grown increasingly concerned with some of these matters. Another discernible trend is the measuring of a child's knowledge in such broad areas as natural science and social science rather than in fields of specific subject fare.

Achievement-test scores are typically interpreted on the basis of *grade norms.* The child's raw score is converted into one showing the grade level at which such a score is oftenest obtained. Despite the valid criticisms to which this method may be subjected, it has the advantage in the educational setting of denoting, at least approximately, a child's acceleration or retardation in a particular area of academic activity.

PERSONALITY APPRAISAL

The techniques devised to access personality do not compare in effectiveness with those that appraise intellect. To begin with, personality is less clearly defined than intelligence; psychological theorists cannot agree on what constitutes personality. Furthermore, personality seems to be a subtler and more complex notion than intelligence, requiring more indirect methods of assessment (Goodenough, 1949b). Of the many appraisal techniques developed, each often assesses but one aspect of personality. Thus such measures fall short of the mark because personality is the sum of several different traits in the individual.

The methods of personality appraisal also fail to measure up to the ideal for a historical reason. Many of them grew out of a clinical need for appraising or diagnosing children referred to child guidance or child clinical centers. However, a tool

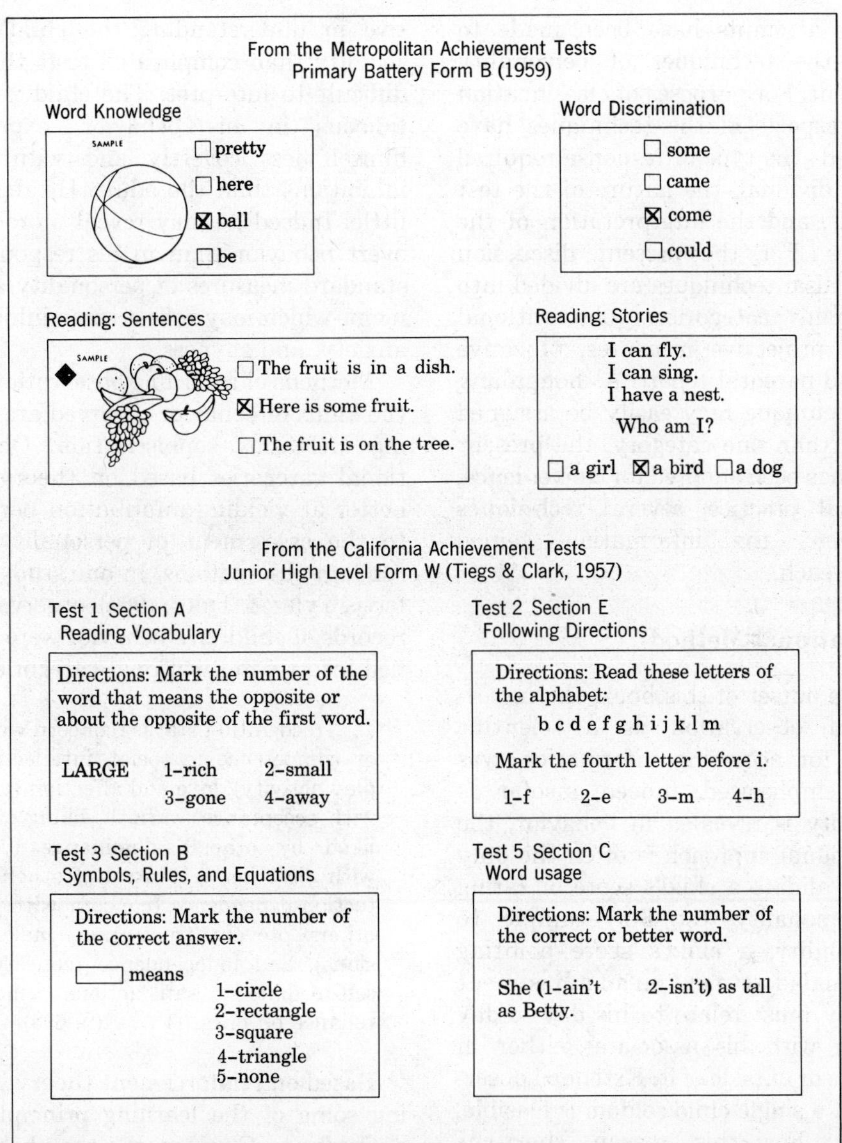
From the Metropolitan Achievement Tests
Primary Battery Form B (1959)

Word Knowledge

SAMPLE
☐ pretty
☐ here
☒ ball
☐ be

Word Discrimination

☐ some
☐ came
☒ come
☐ could

Reading: Sentences

SAMPLE
☐ The fruit is in a dish.
☒ Here is some fruit.
☐ The fruit is on the tree.

Reading: Stories

I can fly.
I can sing.
I have a nest.
Who am I?

☐ a girl ☒ a bird ☐ a dog

From the California Achievement Tests
Junior High Level Form W (Tiegs & Clark, 1957)

Test 1 Section A
Reading Vocabulary

Directions: Mark the number of the word that means the opposite or about the opposite of the first word.

LARGE 1–rich 2–small
3–gone 4–away

Test 2 Section E
Following Directions

Directions: Read these letters of the alphabet:

b c d e f g h i j k l m

Mark the fourth letter before i.

1–f 2–e 3–m 4–h

Test 3 Section B
Symbols, Rules, and Equations

Directions: Mark the number of the correct answer.

▭ means
1–circle
2–rectangle
3–square
4–triangle
5–none

Test 5 Section C
Word usage

Directions: Mark the number of the correct or better word.

She (1–ain't 2–isn't) as tall as Betty.

FIGURE 14-6 Items illustrating two school achievement tests.

useful for clinical diagnosis of the nature of a child's psychological problems may not be equally productive for appraising the personality of nonproblem children. More recent research has gone beyond the applied nature of clinical diagnosis, looking to the development of more refined and precise instruments.

Finally, personality appraisal in children presents problems not found in the appraisal of adult personality. Yet many measures developed for the adult level have been adapted for use with children. Paper-and-pencil tests, for example, are inappropriate at the younger age levels. They limit the use of self-reporting techniques. And the problems of interpretation and validation are more numerous and more difficult at the child than at the adult level.

Many attempts have been made to classify the techniques of personality assessment. For purposes of classification various aspects of the techniques have been used—the type of response required of the individual, the nature of the test materials, and the interpretation of the responses. For the present discussion the appraisal techniques are divided into four main categories: observational method, projective measures, objective tests, and parental report. Although any single technique may easily be assigned to more than one category, the present scheme has been adopted for convenience. In actual practice, several techniques supplement the information gained through each.

Observational Method

At the outset of this book, the importance of observation as a scientific method for acquiring information was heavily emphasized. Indeed, insofar as personality is revealed in behavior, the observational approach is often the only way to validate a child's score or rating on a personality test. For example, to have validity, a child's score pointing toward maladjustment on an adjustment inventory must relate to his day-to-day behavior with his associates either in the home or outside of it. Extended observation of a single child seldom is feasible, however. For this reason short-cut methods are developed. But one should never forget that an instrument is no more useful than its ability to yield information similar to that obtained by the more cumbersome approach of long-term observation of the individual.

Life Situations. Observation of the child's behavior in his day-to-day environment remains one of the most commonly used methods of personality appraisal. In fact, observation may be more productive in understanding the child's personality than complicated tests that are difficult to interpret. The child is spontaneous in his behavior, expressing himself less covertly and with fewer inhibitions than the adult. He represses little. Indeed he may reveal more in his overt behavior than in his responses to standard measures of personality assessment, which may reflect some inhibition, anxiety, and shyness.

Methods of recording observations and the kinds of behavior observed are showing increasing sophistication. Observational categories based on theory seem better at yielding information pertinent to the assessment of personality than random observations. In one study (Rafferty, Tyler, & Tyler, 1960), observational records of children's behavior were classified into six motivational categories.

> . . . recognition-status (concern with skill or competence in social, intellectual, or play activity), love and affection (concern with acceptance, warmth, liking or being liked by others), dominance (concern with direction or control of others), protection-dependence (concern with having others prevent frustration, make decisions), and independence (concern with self-mediated satisfactions including reliance on oneself) . . . (p. 693).

Based on reinforcement theory involving some of the learning principles described in Chapter 4, the behavior-modification approach frequently uses observational recording to identify reinforcement contingencies, that is, the extent to which the frequency of a response or an action is dependent or contingent upon the consequences of that response. Rewarding a certain behavior increases the likelihood that such behavior will occur again, while negative reinforcement (e.g., punishment) weakens a given response. Recent research has shown that a great variety of behaviors, including tantrums, crying, social withdrawal, and aggressive behavior, may be controlled by using reinforcement principles. One example of the way in which observation is conducted in such studies will serve to illustrate this approach. Theorizing that assertive behavior is the product of a reinforcement history in which a child has been rewarded for such behavior by parents, siblings, and peers, Patterson, Littman, and Bricker (1967) hypothesized that when a nursery-school child's aggressive-assertive behavior toward another child (e.g., hitting, pushing, grabbing toys) is followed by positive reinforcement (victim cries, relinquishes toy), the aggressor is likely to select that child again as a target for his aggression. If such aggressive behavior is followed by negative reinforcement (victim retaliates), the aggressor is likely to select another child as the target. Their procedure involved observation of the children's free play in a nursery school. Using a face-mask microphone in conjunction with a portable tape recorder, the observer dictated a detailed description of each aggressive episode. The aggressor was identified, as was the nature of the aggressive behavior. The consequences provided by the victim were described. Following each observational session the taped record was transcribed onto 3 × 5 cards, with a separate card for each episode of action and consequence. Judges independently coded all of the episodes according to the form of the aggressive attack and the victim's reaction. The categories used are shown in Table 14-1.

Frequently impressions gained through observation are quantified through the use of check lists or rating scales designed to describe the child's behavior on the basis of a limited number of traits. The following is an illustration

TABLE 14-1*

Category	Example
I. Aggressor's behavior (instigation):	
A. Bodily attack	Ag hits V. Ag pushes V. Also includes spitting, kicking, biting, punching, jumping on, grabbing, and choking.
B. Attack with an object	Ag hits V with a book.
C. Verbal or symbolic	Ag verbally threatens V. Also includes derogations, assertive demands, or threatening gestures.
D. Infringement of property or invasion of territory	Ag takes toy from V.
II. Target's response-consequences:	
A. Passive	Ag hits V. V does not respond to Ag or V withdraws or V gives up toy.
B. Cries	Ag hits V. V cries.
C. Defensive postures	Ag hits V. V covers his head. Also includes verbal protest.
D. Telling the teacher	
E. Recover property	Ag takes truck away from V. V grabs truck back from Ag.
R. Retaliation	Ag hits V. V hits Ag back.

*From Patterson et al., 1967, p. 14.

of a check list developed to find a child's position with respect to ascendant or submissive behavior.

1. Submits to any child who takes the initiative.
2. Even submits to younger children.
3. Dominates children more mature than himself.
4. Submits to a leader only after a struggle to dominate.
5. Usually leads a small group.
6. Decides who shall participate in the group activities.
7. Is a leader in any group.
8. Directs all activity about him.
9. Neither leads nor follows; plays alone.
10. Other children make many appeals to him for information.
11. Dominates other children through his ability to talk effectively.
12. Other children appeal to him to make decisions for the group.
13. Dominates other children through their love or admiration for him.
14. Dominates other children through his wealth of ideas.
15. Definitely schemes to get others to carry out his plans.
16. Gives commands with an air of finality.
17. Helpless unless someone organizes activity for him.
18. Hesitates to initiate activity.
19. Hesitates to make suggestions to other children.
20. Usually follows the ideas of others for activity.
21. Can take the initiative if it is absolutely necessary.
22. Usually takes the initiative.
23. Seeks the approval of the leader before he acts.
24. Does not push the issue in case of opposition.
25. Stands aside to let others participate.
26. Fights for his place as leader.
27. Opposition spurs him on to greater activity.
28. Insists that other children do as he wishes.
29. Does not defend his own rights with other children.
30. Gets willing cooperation easily.

(Stott & Ball, 1957, p. 261)

Ascendance-submission check-list data were available on 60 children over a 10-year interval from the age of 2 or 3 to over 13. Ascendant behavior increased throughout the three-year period of nursery-school attendance, with a very low frequency of interactive behavior at the age of three and under, increasing sharply up to the age of five. With the change from nursery school to kindergarten, ascendant behavior became less frequent. There were no consistent changes in the frequency of ascendant-submissive behavior after the age of five (Stott & Ball, 1957).

Observational rating scales are widely used in personality appraisal. Since the information obtained through them is purely descriptive in nature, the value of such scales is limited. Ratings of behavior do not interpret behavior in terms of its causes and the type of personality underlying it. Even so, note the following items drawn from a scale (Haggerty–Olson–Wickman Behavior Rating Schedules) designed to identify problem behavior in school children and to assess 35 physical, mental, social, and emotional characteristics (Haggerty, Olson, & Wickman, 1930).

How does he accept authority?

Defiant	Critical of authority	Ordinarily obedient	Respectful, complies by habit	Entirely resigned, accepts all authority

How does he react to frustrations or to unpleasant situations?

Very submissive, long-suffering	Tolerant, rarely blows up	Generally self-controlled	Impatient	Easily irritated, hot-headed, explosive

Is he suspicious or trustful?

Very suspicious, distrustful	Has to be assured	Generally unsuspicious and trustful	Somewhat gullible	Accepts everything without question

Does he act impulsively or cautiously?

Impulsive, bolts, acts on the spur of the moment	Frequently unreflective and imprudent	Acts with reasonable care	Deliberate	Very cautious and calculating

Miniature Life Situations. Although any interference with behavior in its natural setting introduces possible error in the accuracy of interpretation, control of a situation frequently increases the precision and significance of the data obtained. For this reason, real-life situations have been simulated in order to make appraisals of personality. The use of a miniature life situation assumes a relation between the individual's behavior in this experimental environment and his behavior outside of it. It is also argued that the child will reveal various personality characteristics by his manipulation of the materials at hand or by his solution of the problems presented.

In the Hartshorne and May (1928) study of deceit in children between the ages of 8 and 11, a variety of methods were employed. One of the measures of deception involved four athletic tests: the dynamometer test, the spirometer test, pull-ups, and standing broad jump. The children were led to believe the tests were part of a real athletic contest in which badges were to be awarded to the winners of the four events. The directions for each test were given to the children individually and they were asked to try each procedure, the examiner taking mental note of their performance. Subsequently, the child was told to proceed alone, recording the best of several trials. The difference between the examiner's rating and the child's own was the measure of deception.

Selected general findings of the study indicated older children to be slightly more deceptive than younger ones. The sex differences were few. The more intelligent children cheated less. Children who showed symptoms of emotional instability were more likely to be deceitful than others, and children from low socioeconomic backgrounds demonstrated less honesty than those from higher levels.

Observation of Play. This technique presents the child with a wide range of play materials including toys, paints, dough, and cold cream. Freedom is permitted in their use. If he so chooses, the child may arrange, build, destroy, or smear. The rationale for this freedom is that the natural language of children is behavior and that the child will disclose his needs, attitudes, feelings, and problems through the manner in which he approaches and deals with play materials. If a completely permissive and accepting atmosphere is established, the child will have no need to conceal his feelings; the restrictions in the world of reality will not be present.

What are some of the aspects of personality revealed in a child's play? An alert observer can identify differences among children in a great many personality areas. If a child is observed playing with toys representing real-life objects, such as a doll house with dolls suggesting the family unit, one can follow the enactment of situations and events, the treatment of the various dolls, the child's emotional expressions, and his verbal behavior. When manipulating such tactile materials as clay and finger paint, the child's attitude toward middle-class strictures against dirtiness and messiness may be disclosed through the spontaneity with which he approaches these materials. Is he inhibited, anxious, relaxed, aggressive? Is he secure enough to explore the possible artistic uses of such amorphous substances or is his behavior rigid and stereotyped?

The following excerpt describes a young child's reaction to playing with dough.

> Another little girl whispered "I can't" at first, and approached the dough almost tentatively. She ran her hand in a gingerly way through the mess, and did not squeeze the dough until the experimenter had done so. However, when she did, she squeezed *very* hard, with a kind of aggressive violence which no other child showed. After more play she volunteered, however, "I don't think it's nice." Yet when the experimenter started to put away the pan, she resisted: "I'm not all finished yet." She took her hands through the mess saying, "Gooey, gooey, gooey!" She squeezed, made balls of the dough. But at the end, after she had washed her hands, she said, "I never want to do that again . . . why did you do this to me?" Her expressive face appeared "mildy horrified and puzzled," wanting rapport at the beginning; after being released by the experimenter's example she was definitely aggressive with the paste, in contrast to the other children, and then seemed to develop a sense of guilt as she went on, apparently feeling this was naughty. Among other comments made in the context of cleaning up after the dough, she said, "My mother spanks me if I'm naughty . . . I cry so the neighbors hear . . . sometimes I scratch her and she spanks me" (Murphy, 1956, p. 124).

Sometimes situations are provided that specifically encourage the release of aggressive, destructive feelings. The intensity in the child of these tendencies, his fear or anxiety over exhibiting such behavior, and the sequence of his behavior through which some control is achieved can be observed.

There is no question that the child reveals his personality through play. Problems arise, however, in the interpretation of such behavior. For example, a child who shows little aggression in his play either may have little need for aggressive outlets or he may be restrained from expressing aggression by anxiety or fear of punishment. Therefore, data obtained from observing a child's play must be used in conjunction with information from other sources, essentially from techniques that are more objective as to scoring and interpretation. We now turn to some of these.

Projective Assessment Techniques

The idea that individuals will bring structure to ambiguous, diffuse stimuli on the basis of individual needs, feelings, and personality patterns is popular in psychology. The individual imposes on the environment his own psychological outlook, organization, and meanings. In a formless cloud the child sees the friendly face of a man and in the shadow on the wall a vicious animal about to pounce on its prey. This idea of projection is accepted widely as an approach to the assessment of personality because the individual is least willing or least able to reveal through interview or questionnaire those of his aspects that most adequately describe the uniqueness of his personality (Frank, 1939). This idea, that projective tests allow one to assess aspects of the respondent that he either is unwilling or unable to reveal through direct measures, has relatively weak support (see Kidder, & Campbell, 1970; Mischel, 1968, 1972; Scott and Johnson, 1972). It may well be that the easiest and most accurate assessment of personality involves questioning the respondent directly about those domains of personality under investigation.

Whether the position taken above is correct or not, a tremendous growth has taken place in the development and use of projective techniques.[1] As a result, a great number and variety of projective instruments are now available. Taking the cue from Allport's (1961) classification, let us describe several examples of these techniques under three main headings: perceptive, apperceptive, and productive.

Perceptive Techniques. The child is confronted with ambiguous material and is asked to tell what it means to him. Either auditory or visual stimuli may be used; the latter is commoner. The most widely used instrument of this description is the Rorschach Ink Blot Test developed in 1921. The test consists of a series of 10 cards, 5 colored and 5 achromatic. These are presented in sequence, and the individual is instructed to describe what he sees in the ink blots. Later, the child identifies on the card the location of what he saw and the clues used in his response. In scoring the child's responses, a variety of categories are employed, including the location and determinants of the response, its originality, and the time required for the individual to respond. From an interpretation of the record of the responses a full description of the individual's personality is construced. The following account is a description of a nine-year-old boy referred to a child guidance clinic by his teacher because of his difficulties in the classroom.

> Jim's thinking is fairly well organized and there is no evidence of bizarreness or morbidity in his fantasies. He is able to see things as most people do and there are indications of a very early inculcation of adult standards concerning propriety, right and wrong, and how one should behave.
>
> Despite Jim's attempts to maintain a facade of happiness, willingness and compliance, he is rather vulnerable to emotional stimuli and is apt to react largely in terms of his feelings of the moment with immature expression of his emotions. However, when possible, Jim attempts to handle emotional impact in a superficial, behavioral way that is not essentially related to his own feelings. That is, he responds in terms of what he feels is demanded by the situation without a genuine integration of his own feelings with the realistic demands of the situation.
>
> Jim is very concerned about handling sexual and aggressive impulses and a good deal of tension and anxiety is associated with such impulses. His great concern about aggression is reflected in Rorschach

[1] A fuller treatment of projective techniques appropriate at the child level may be found in Rabin & Haworth, 1960.

responses such as "Volcanoes," "Fire burning up the ground," and "Like they were in Africa and killed a bear." Jim is fearful of his own aggressive impulses and defends strongly against their direct expression. It appears that his fear of aggression has led to a generalized inhibition of most forms of assertiveness so that even socially acceptable strivings for attainment are inhibited. Hence, Jim's aggression is expressed primarily in indirect ways through passive resistance or passive negativism.

In part, Jim's fearfulness of aggression appears to stem from unresolved Oedipal conflicts in which castration anxiety plays a major role. While Jim would like to be able to compete aggressively against father figures, he is quite apprehensive about such wishes, fearing that his castration or destruction will be the outcome of such competition. He views father figures as quite dangerous. But despite his fearfulness of father figures, Jim seems to want father's permission (and probably father's encouragement and support) in expressing himself in a more masculine way.

Apperceptive Techniques. These techniques require the individual to respond to less amorphous material by contributing some interpretation of his own. Figure 14-7 shows a picture from a series intended to assess parent-child relations (Alexander, 1952). The subject is asked to develop a story about a picture, explaining what led up to the scene, what is occurring, and what will happen.

FIGURE 14-7 Sample picture from the Alexander Adult-Child Interaction test.

The story is to include the thoughts and feelings of the characters. Stories are then evaluated for the approach used to solve their problems, the nature of the emotional expressions conveyed, whether positive or negative, and the way in which the characters in them are viewed—as friendly or hostile. The following is an Alexander summary about an 11-year-old boy.

> Ronald found thinking about the stimuli in the cards a threatening experience. He used only the main stimuli (mainly the fingers) in the cards and added few stimuli in an effort to account for the ones presented. Emotional expressions were few in number and most of them were negative. Adults and parents are viewed as hostile and he has aggressive and hostile feelings in return. He tries to solve his problems by avoidance and escape (Alexander, 1952, p. 18).

Incomplete sentences have been used to elicit children's attitudes and feelings toward people and toward other aspects of their environment Stems of sentences are provided, which the child is required to complete. The following list of stems represents a test intended to assess parent-child relations (Hoeflin & Kell, 1959, p. 12). The responses are scored on the bases of how the child conceives of the parent and child relationship, whether it promotes growth or is autocratic, and of the positiveness or negativeness of feeling.

1. Our family
2. As a child I enjoyed
3. My mother
4. Being a child
5. Obedience
6. Children should not
7. If my father
8. When I was in high school
9. I wish my parents had
10. Being a (boy) (girl)
11. Discipline
12. Teen-agers
13. My father
14. Making high grades in school
15. Punishment
16. As a child I disliked
17. A democratic family
18. If my mother
19. Being at home
20. Making decisions in the home

Productive Techniques. As the wording implies, the child produces something in these tests which the examiner then interprets. Long before the formal beginnigs of psychology, interest was shown in analyzing people's handwriting. Yet not much progress has been made through the years toward developing an objective analysis and valid interpretation of handwriting. Similarly, numerous difficulties are met in attempting to construct a valid measure of personality from children's drawings although several drawing tests are in current use. The rationale for relying on these tests is that children divulge important aspects of their personalities through the way they express themselves artistically.

Most widely used among children is the Draw-A-Person Test (DAP), a descendant of Goodenough's original Draw-A-Man Test (1926) which, as we saw, was designed to assess intelligence in young children. This method for evaluating children's drawings on the basis of hints of several personality traits was devised by Machover (1949). To her, the child's drawing of the human figure represented his image of himself in relation to his environment. Things noted about the drawing include the kinds of line employed, the part of the page covered, and the dimensions, proportions, and perspective of the figure. After the drawing has been completed, the examiner elicits from the child various associations he may have in connection with his picture. He is requested to describe the feelings and mood of the figure drawn and other such characteristics. There are no objective scoring norms for the DAP

Test; its use is primarily as a clinical aid in understanding the individual child.

Several interesting findings emerged from a study that endeavored to develop a scale of sexual differentiation from the DAP Test (Haworth & Normington, 1961). Pairs of drawings, male and female figures, were obtained from 312 children ranging in age from 7 through 12. Four levels of sexual differentiation were detected, from the lowest level of "figures nearly the same, no apparent sex," to the highest level of "each figure well differentiated as to sex," with such items as mustache or pants fly for the male and breasts and jewelry for the female. With age an increase in sex differentiation was noted, girls consistently showing greater differentiation than boys and also placing greater emphasis on figures of their own sex.

Objective Tests

Objective paper-and-pencil tests are perhaps the oldest approach to the assessment of personality. Their development related to the early success in constructing tests to appraise intelligence. Because these tests presumably provided valid assessments of intelligence, it was only natural that psychologists should make the effort to apply their technique to personality measurement. However, the relative value of objective and projective tests has generated lively controversy. Adherents of the projective approach contend that measurement of separate traits does injustice to the complexity of personality and to the interaction among personality factors. The opposite position notes the difficulty of scoring and interpreting the projective material obtained; without objectivity, it holds, a scientific assessment of personality can never be attained. Both views contain strengths as well as limitations. For the present, at least, adequate evaluation of a child's personality involves the use of a wide variety of instruments.

Personality Inventories. A personality inventory is expected to uncover a specific number of elements considered to be important by the builder of the test. Two of the tests used most commonly with children, the California Test of Personality and the Rogers Test of Personality Adjustment, have some validity. There is evidence (Smith, 1958) that both are significantly, and at the least, moderately, related to teacher and peer nomination of well- and poorly adjusted children (see Chapter 12). Because of the nature of objective tests, they obviously cannot be used below the seven- or eight-year level, although in the California Test the questions can be read to children by the examiner.

California Test. The California Test of Personality has various forms appropriate for use from kindergarten through the adult level. Its organization has been described in the following way by its authors (Thorpe, Clark, & Tiegs, 1953):

1. Self Adjustment: Based on feelings of personal security	A. Self-reliance B. Sense of personal worth C. Sense of personal freedom D. Feeling of belonging E. Freedom from withdrawing tendencies F. Freedom from nervous symptoms
Life Adjustment: A balance between self and social adjustment	A. Social standards B. Social skills

2. Social Adjustment: Based on feelings of social security	C. Freedom from anti-social tendencies
	D. Family relations
	E. School relations
	F. Community relations

The test is comprised of a series of questions that are answered by checking blanks marked "yes" or "no." The test's primary purpose, said its authors, is to indicate the extent to which a child is adjusting to the problems confronting him and to which he is developing a well-adjusted, socially effective personality. Fifteen raw scores, for which keys are provided, are converted into percentiles based on norms in order to be plotted on so-called *profile* sheets. Examination of a child's profile aids the teacher in ascertaining specifically where guidance or remedial effort is needed. The following items are typical of those contained in the primary series, kindergarten to grade three.

Is it hard for you to look out for yourself?	YES	NO
Do the children forget to ask you to play with them?	YES	NO
Do you feel bad because you can't do things well enough?	YES	NO
Does your stomach ache often?	YES	NO
Do you feel that some of the teachers have it in for you?	YES	NO

Rogers Test. The Rogers Test of Personality Adjustment (Rogers, 1931), designed for children from 9 through 13, is one of the oldest personality tests available for youngsters. From it, four scores and a total score can be derived. A personal inferiority score indicates the degree to which the child perceives himself as physically or mentally less capable than his peers. The score of social maladjustment is an index to the child's feelings about his social relations with other children. The family-relations score represents the child's reports of conflict and dissatisfaction in his relations with his parents and siblings. The daydreaming score reflects the child's indulgence in fantasies and unrealistic thinking. The total score indexes the seriousness of the child's maladjustment. As the intent of the items, as a rule, is rather concealed, the responses are probably more meaningful and valid than if the test simply required yes or no answers.

The Rogers Test of Personality Adjustment was administered to 256 fifth-graders from small towns and rural areas in the Midwest. In general, children from higher social-class backgrounds showed fewer signs of personality maladjustment than children from lower-class homes. However, those children whose fathers had the highest educational achievement showed greater maladjustment than many of the children whose fathers were less well educated. Pressures for achievement exerted by high-achieving parents on their children may be detrimental to healthy personality development (Burchinal, Gardner, & Hawkes, 1958).

Self-Ratings. Self-ratings or check lists, while less objective than personality inventories, reveal the way the individual sees himself. Information thus obtained about the concept of the self helps a youngster to a better understanding of himself. The Mooney Problem Check List (Mooney & Gordon, 1950) represents an instrument designed for this purpose. Its form for junior high school consists of 30 items in each of seven problem areas: health and physical development; school; home and family; money, work, and the future; boy and girl relations; relations to people in general; and self-centered concerns. The youngster underlines items that he feels cause him some personal concern and circles the number of items that he considers as serious problems for himself.

Parental Report

Many of the more formal personality tests used with some success among adults are unsuitable for children, especially at the younger age levels, because of the young child's inability to read and write and respond in a manner relevant to the questions posed to him. However, information acquired from persons intimate with the behavior of children is frequently of great value in appraising a child's approach to people and to his environment in general. Clearly, parents are in a position to furnish such information. Although data of this type are obtained indirectly and parental impressions of a child may not be entirely unbiased or objective, a parent's perception of the young child exposes a great deal about the youngster's personality and about the kind of psychological environment in which the child's personality is formed. Parental report may vary from freeflowing discussions to the use of objective instruments.

Interview. As a technique for appraisal, the interview can provide information about a child that is obtainable in no other way. The child's reaction to intimate interactions and situations within the family, the events that have been important in the shaping of his current level of adjustment, his characteristic mode of response to frustration and stress—all these and more may be discerned most directly from parental interviews. The alert interviewer will endeavor to separate facts from attitudes toward them. Both are valuable, perhaps equally so, but as the main interest is an appraisal of the child's personality, knowledge of a parent's attitude toward the child may help to explain rather than to assess his personality.

An interview may be totally unplanned, in which the interviewee is free to pursue any topic he wishes or it may be confined to a predetermined list of questions. Each type has its advantages and disadvantages and, in actual practice, the interview is seldom completely one or the other. Frequently in the initial stages of an interview, rapport is established by letting the parent discuss those areas he selects; later the interviewer may wish to dig further into certain points or to obtain information where gaps exist.

Since the information gathered through interviews is not easily quantified, except through the tedious procedure of rating the transcript of the taped interview, examiners frequently employ more objective methods of assessing the child's personality as revealed through parental report. Two of these are the *semantic differential* and the *Q-sort* techniques. The semantic differential technique was designed originally as a device for measuring the meaning of various concepts (see Osgood, Suci, & Tannenbaum, 1957). As its name implies, the technique helps to discern the differences in meaning that an individual holds toward two concepts. The individual discloses his attitude toward a concept or the meaning the concept has for him by rating it on a number of polarized scales. The discrepancy between an individual's ratings of two separate concepts is taken as representative of the extent to which their meanings differ to him.

In a study of the relation between maternal self-acceptance and maternal acceptance of her child, Medinnus and Curtis (1963) asked 56 mothers of preschool children to describe "My child (as he is)" by rating him on 20 bipolar scales. Then the mothers were asked to repeat the procedure, now describing "My child (as I would like him to be)." The item-by-item discrepancy in their ratings of the two concepts was taken as a measure of maternal acceptance of the child. Moderate and statistically significant correlations were obtained between two measures of maternal self-acceptance and adjustment, and the "semantic differential" measure of child acceptance. As we have already seen, the mothers who were most accepting of their children were those who scored highest in self-acceptance. These were some of the bipolar scales used:

friendly	____ :	____ :	____ :	____ :	____ :	____ :	____	hostile
trustful	____ :	____ :	____ :	____ :	____ :	____ :	____	suspicious
deliberate	____ :	____ :	____ :	____ :	____ :	____ :	____	impulsive
submissive	____ :	____ :	____ :	____ :	____ :	____ :	____	assertive
sociable	____ :	____ :	____ :	____ :	____ :	____ :	____	shy
mature emotionally	____ :	____ :	____ :	____ :	____ :	____ :	____	infantile

The Q-sort technique elicits an individual's view of himself or of others through a rating-type approach. Originally developed by Stephenson (1935), the technique requires the person to sort a large variety of descriptive phrases along a continuum from, say, "most like myself" to "least like myself." Rogers (1951) used this technique to obtain a picture of an individual's self-perceptions before and after therapy, as well as of his view of the "ideal self." The technique is particularly productive in collecting parental descriptions of their child and conceptions of the "ideal child." The latter sorting uncovers interesting information on the kinds of behavior and characteristics to which the parent attaches greatest significance. Moreover, discrepancy between two parents in their descriptions of their child and of the ideal child sheds some light on certain aspects of the psychological atmosphere in which the child is reared.

Thirty-eight sets of parents of five-year-olds sorted two pools of 42 items each to describe their own child and the ideal five-year-old (Medinnus, 1961b). Parental agreement was higher for the "real sort" describing their own child than for the "ideal sort," indicating that parents agree more in their perceptions of their children than in their expectations and goals for them. There was generally greater agreement between parents of boys than of girls. The item ranked as most important for the ideal five-year-old was: "is in good physical condition; is usually healthy."

OTHER APPRAISAL METHODS

Several further methods of gaining information about the child's behavioral development warrant brief mention, either because of general usefulness or because they attempt to appriase areas of behavior often overlooked in discussions of personality development.

Vineland Social Maturity Scale

Working with mentally retarded children, Doll observed great differences in the social competence of children of the same intellectual capacity. And since social competence is of particular importance to children of inferior intellectual ability, as we have seen, Doll recognized the need for a practical instrument to assess this area. First published in 1935, the Vineland Social Maturity Scale (Doll,

1935) consists of a series of items of growing difficulty representing progressive social independence in the following areas of behavior: self-help (eating, dressing), self-direction, locomotion, occupation, communication, and social relations.

Through interviews with parents, information about a child's behavior and development is obtained. The child is given a plus or minus for each item based on his ability to perform the task in question. The total score, representing the sum of the items passed, is translated into a Social Quotient (SQ) by converting the total score into a "social age" figure and dividing this by the chronological age of the child. The SQ, similar in computation to the IQ, compares the child's social competence with others of his chronological age. Thus a child of average social maturity for his age level would receive an SQ of 100. These are items contained in the three- to five-year levels:

III–IV

Walks downstairs one step per tread
Plays cooperatively at kindergarten level
Buttons coat or dress
Helps at little household tasks
"Performs" for others
Washes hands unaided

IV–V

Cares for self at toilet
Washes face unassisted
Goes about neighborhood unattended
Dresses self except for tying
Uses pencil or crayon for drawing
Plays competitive exercise games

(Doll, 1953)

Sociometric Tests

A child's acceptance by and popularity among his agemates is an important part of his behavior and adjustment. Although adjustment to peers is only one facet of a child's personality, his relationship with others serves well as a measure of his general adjustment. Children who rank low in popularity frequently exhibit, as we have observed, a variety of maladaptive and maladjusted behaviors.

It would be rare, especially in elementary schools, for teachers to have no notion of how well a child is accepted by his peers. However, as an additional aid, data furnished by a sociometric measure specify quite clearly how any child is accepted by his peers. The Guess Who method also discloses information about how a child is perceived. Is a particular child seen as possessing primarily positive, acceptable qualities or characteristics? Or are the characteristics attributed to him by his peers largely negative?

Peer ratings spot areas of strength and weakness in any child's behavior as perceived by his agemates. This information assists a teacher in her efforts to manipulate a child's social environment to produce positive changes in his behavior. It also helps her to establish in the classroom an atmosphere that is conducive to the development of healthy psychological adjustment in all the children. Among older children, the teacher or counselor may use the information gained from sociometric tests and Guess Who devices to aid the child in gaining insight into his behavior, especially with regard to those characteristics that impede his acceptance by his peers.

The Children's Manifest Anxiety Scale, the Children's Self-Concept Scale and a sociometric ranking were administered to 111 fourth-, fifth-, and sixth-graders. The less popular children tended to be more anxious and they tended to hold poorer self concepts. These findings were true for both sexes and for the three grade levels. However, the low magnitude of the correlations suggested that the interrelations are complex and that other variables are of considerable importance in affecting a child's sociometric standing (Horowitz, 1962).

School Anecdotal Records

As a trained person, the teacher is in a particularly advantageous position to observe a child's behavior in a variety of day-to-day situations. Both in the formal classroom setting and on the informal playground, the child displays his general response to his environment. Specifically, he demonstrates his response to frustration, his resourcefulness in meeting new situations, his level of persistence, his attitudes of independence, his sense of responsibility, and his social and emotional adjustment.

Anecdotal records keep track of these behaviors. They are diary-like accounts of crucial observations and impressions of a child's performance. Frequently the incidents entered into the record are highly significant in understanding the personality and adjustment of a particular child. The usefulness of these records depends, however, on the objectivity of the recorder and his observations, and on the relevance of the incidents recorded. When anecdotal records are accumulated over a period of time, they present a rich, factual, detailed picture of the child. Recurring patterns of behavior can be noted and a broad understanding can be gained of a child's characteristic manner and level of functioning. The following entries in an anecdotal record of a youngster kept by her third-grade teacher illustrate the types of information generally included in such accounts.

March 1: Reading group three was in the front of the room having its phonics lesson while the other two reading groups were working at their desks. Debbie had volunteered to divide a word into syllables on the chalkboard. Julie, seated in the reading circle behind Debbie, repeatedly swung her crossed leg, hitting Debbie's posterior. Julie's behavior ceased when I remonstrated with her. (Julie's behavior was caused apparently by her jealousy of Debbie who this time won their ceaseless struggle to sit next to me in the reading circle.)

March 17: Julie and her best friend, Paulia, quarreled over a problem related to a difficulty between the two families while entering the school grounds in the morning. Characteristically, Julie impulsively and in anger slapped Paulia forcefully in the face. This provoked a battle between the two girls requiring intervention by the yard teacher.

April 4: Jimmy, on courtesy patrol in the hall outside of Julie's third-grade room, reported to me an incident which had occurred between him and Julie. When Jimmy attempted to prevent Julie from running in the hall, she refused to comply and when Jimmy attempted to enforce his command, Julie added insult to injury by defiantly calling him "stupid."

April 23: By actual count, Julie left her seat to socialize with other children ten times in the space of one hour this morning —this despite the fact I ordered her to return to and to remain in her seat each time. (Little wonder that she seldom completes her seatwork satisfactorily!)

June 3: This morning it was Julie's turn to be in charge of one of the balls during recess. She agreed to play "four square" with a small group of children. When Julie was "out" she became angry and upset and took the ball and ran to an isolated section of the playground. (One of the playground rules of our school forbids the breaking up of a school game.)

Ann came to me in tears during afternoon recess because Julie pushed her out of the line of children waiting to jump rope. (Though Julie desperately needs friends, the two incidents today illustrate her negative approach to others which antagonizes her classmates and makes an adequate social adjustment for Julie seem even more remote.)

SUMMARY

Three main areas of appraisal have been explored: infant assessment, assessment of intellectual ability, and assessment of personality. Despite the fruitless efforts of psychologists to predict future ability from tests administered to infants, Gesell's methods for measuring rate of general development in infancy have value in assessing developmental progress.

The mental testing movement originally developed IQ tests to discern levels of academic ability. Although intelligence tests have been charged with failing to assess a wide range of characteristics, such tests continue to predict adequately a child's level of performance in the school setting, the purpose for which they were originally intended.

Four broad techniques for appraising personality were examined: observational methods, projective measures, objective tests, and parental report. For a number of reasons the techniques devised to evaluate personality have not proved as satisfactory as those used for appraising the intellect. Even though each technique falls short of adequate assessment of the dynamic interrelation and interaction among an individual's personality traits, in the actual practice of diagnosing personality a number of the techniques described supplement one another. The result is that a fairly distinct picture of the child's personality structure unfolds.

REFERENCES

Alexander, T. The Adult-Child Interaction Test. *Monographs of the Society for Research in Child Development*, 1952, **17**, No. 2 (Serial No. 55).

Allport, G. W. *Pattern and growth in personality*. New York: Holt, 1961.

Anderson, J. E. The limitations of infant and preschool tests in the measurement of intelligence. *Journal of Psychology*, 1939, **8**, 351–379.

Bayley, N. *California First-Year Mental Scale*. Berkeley: University of California Press, 1933. (a)

Bayley, N. Mental growth during the first three years. A developmental study of sixty-one children by repeated tests. *Genetic Psychology Monographs*, 1933, **14**, No. 1. (b)

Binet, A., & Simon, T. The development of the Binet–Simon scale. In W. Dennis (Ed.), *Readings in the history of psychology*. New York: Appleton–Century–Crofts, 1948. Pp. 412–424.

Burchinal, L., Gardner, B., & Hawkes, G. Children's personality adjustment and the socio-economic status of their families. *Journal of Genetic Psychology*, 1958, **92**, 149–159.

Cattell, P. *Cattell Infant Intelligence Scale*. New York: Psychological Corporation, 1947.

Doll, E. A. A genetic scale of social maturity. *American Journal of Orthopsychiatry*, 1935, **5**, 180–188.

Doll, E. A. *The measurement of social competence*. Minneapolis: Educational Test Bureau, 1953.

Escalona, S. The use of infant tests for predictive purposes. *Bulletin of the Menninger Clinic,* 1950, **14**, 117–128.

Frank, L. K. Projective methods for the study of personality. *Journal of Psychology,* 1939, **8**, 389–413.

Frankenburg, W. K., Camp, B., & Van Natta, P. Validity of the Denver developmental screening test. *Child Development,* 1971, **42**, 475–485.

Frankenburg, W. K., Camp, B., Van Natta, P., Demersseman, J., & Voorhees, S. Reliability and stability of the Denver developmental screening test. *Child Development,* 1971, **42**, 1315–1325.

Frankenburg, W. K., & Dodds, J. B. The Denver developmental screening test. *Journal of Pediatrics,* 1967, **71**, 181–191.

Frostig, M., & Horne, D. *The Frostig program for the development of visual perception.* Chicago: Follett, 1964.

Frostig, M., Maslow, P., Lefever, D., & Whittlesey, J. *The Marianne Frostig Developmental Test of Visual Perception.* Palo Alto: Consulting Psychologists Press, 1964.

Gesell, A. *The first five years of life.* New York: Harper, 1940.

Gesell, A., & Amatruda, C. S. *Developmental diagnosis.* New York: Hoeber, 1947.

Gilliland, A. R. The measurement of the mentality of infants. *Child Development,* 1948, **19**, 155–158.

Goodenough, F. L. *Measurement of intelligence by drawings.* Tarrytown-on-Hudson, N.Y.: World Book, 1926.

Goodenough, F. L. *Mental testing.* New York: Rinehart, 1949. (a)

Goodenough, F. L. The appraisal of child personality. *Psychological Review,* 1949, **56**, 123–131. (b)

Griffiths, R. *Griffiths Mental Development Scale.* London: University of London Press, 1954.

Haggerty, M. E., Olson, W. C., & Wickman, E. K. Haggerty–Olson–Wickman Behavior Rating Schedules. Yonkers, N.Y.: World Book, 1930.

Hartshorne, H., & May, M. A. *Studies in the nature of character.* I. *Studies in deceit.* New York: Macmillan, 1928.

Haworth, M. R., & Normington, C. J. A sexual differentiation scale for the D-A-P Test. *Journal of Projective Techniques,* 1961, **25**, 441–450.

Hoeflin, R., & Kell, L. The Kell–Hoeflin Incomplete Sentences Blank: Youth-Parent Relations. *Monographs of the Society for Research in Child Development,* 1959, **24**, No. 3.

Hofstaetter, P. R. The changing composition of "intelligence": A study in T technique. *Journal of Genetic Psychology,* 1954, **85**, 159–164.

Horowitz, F. D. The relationship of anxiety, self-concept, and sociometric status among fourth, fifth, and sixth grade children. *Journal of Abnormal and Social Psychology,* 1962, **65**, 212–214.

Ilg, F., & Ames, L. B. *School readiness.* New York: Harper & Row, 1964.

Ilg, F., Ames, L. B., & Apell, R. School readiness as evaluated by Gesell developmental, visual, and projective tests. *Genetic Psychology Monographs,* 1965, **71**, 61–92.

Illingworth, R. S. *The development of the infant and young child.* London: Livingston, 1960.

Jordan, F., & Massey, J. *School readiness survey.* Palo Alto: Consulting Psychologists Press, 1967.

Kidder, L. H., & Campbell, D. T. The indirect testing of social attitudes. In G. F. Summers (Ed.), *Attitude measurement.* New York: Rand, McNally, 1970.

Knobloch, H., & Pasamanick, B. A developmental questionnaire for infants forty weeks of age: An evaluation. *Monographs of the Society for Research in Child Development,* 1955, **20**, No. 2.

McCarthy, J., & Kirk, S. *The construction, standardization and statistical characteristics of the Illinois Test of Psycholinguistic Abilities,* 1963.

Machover, K. *Personality projection in the drawing of the human figure.* Springfield, Ill.: Thomas, 1949.

MacRae, J. M. Retests of children given mental tests as infants. *Journal of Genetic Psychology,* 1955, **87**, 111–119.

Medinnus, G. R. An investigation of school readiness and first grade adjustment. Unpublished manuscript, 1961. (a)

Medinnus, G. R. Q-sort descriptions of five-year-old children by their parents. *Child Development,* 1961, **32**, 473–489. (b)

Medinnus, G. R., & Curtis, F. The relation between maternal self-acceptance and child acceptance. *Journal of Consulting Psychology,* 1963, **27**, 542–544.

Metropolitan Achievement Tests. Yonkers, N.Y.: World Book, 1959.

Mischel, W. *Personality and assessment.* New York: Wiley, 1968.

Mischel, W. Direct versus indirect personality assessment: Evidence and implications. *Journal of Clinical and Consulting Psychology,* 1972, **38**, 319–324.

Mooney, R. L., & Gordon, L. V. Mooney Problem Check List: 1950 Revision. New York: Psychological Corporation, 1950.

Murphy, L. B. *Personality in young children.* Vol. 1. *Methods for the study of personality in young children.* New York: Basic Books, 1956.

Olson, A. Factor analytic studies of the Frostig Test of Visual Perception. *Journal of Special Education,* 1969, **2**, 429–433.

Olson, A., & Johnson, C. Structure and predictive validity of the Frostig Developmental Test of Visual Perception in Grades One and Three. *Journal of Special Education,* 1970, **4**, 49–52.

Osgood, C., Suci, G., & Tannenbaum, P. *The measurement of meaning.* Urbana: University of Illinois Press, 1957.

Patterson, G., Littman, R., & Bricker, W. Assertive behavior in children: A step toward a theory of aggression. *Monographs of the Society for Research in Child Development,* 1967, **32**, No. 5.

Rabin, A. I. & Haworth, M. R. (Eds.) *Projective techniques with children.* New York: Grune & Stratton, 1960.

Rafferty, J. E., Tyler, B. B., & Tyler, F. B. Personality assessment from free play observations. *Child Development,* 1960, **31**, 691–702.

Rogers, C. R. Measuring personality adjustment in children nine to thirteen years of age. *Teachers College Contribution to Education,* 1931.

Rogers, C. R. *Client-centered therapy.* Boston: Houghton Mifflin, 1951.

Ryckman, D., & Wiegerink, R. The factors of the Illinois Test of Psycholinguistic Abilities: A comparison of 18 factor analyses. *Exceptional Children,* 1969, **36**, 107–113.

Scott, W. A., & Johnson, R. C. Comparative validities of direct and indirect personality tests. *Journal of Consulting and Clinical Psychology,* 1972, **38**, 301–318.

Smith, L. M. The concurrent validity of six personality and adjustment tests for children. *Psychological Monographs: General and Applied,* 1958, **72**, (4), 1–30.

Stephenson, W. *The study of behavior.* Chicago: University of Chicago Press, 1935.

Stott, L. H., & Ball, R. S. Consistency and change in ascendance-submission in the social interaction of children. *Child Development,* 1957, **28**, 259–272.

Sullivan, E. T., Clark, W. W., & Tiegs, E. W. California Short-Form Test of Mental Maturity. Level 2. Monterey, Calif.: California Test Bureau, 1963.

Terman, L. M., & Merrill, M. A. *Measuring intelligence.* Boston: Houghton Mifflin, 1937.

Thorpe, L., Clark, W., & Tiegs, E. California Test of Personality. Primary, Form B. Los Angeles: California Test Bureau, 1953.

Tiegs, E. W., & Clark, W. W. California Achievement Tests. Complete Battery. Junior High Level, Form W. Los Angeles: California Test Bureau, 1957.

Wechsler, D. *Wechsler Intelligence Scale for Children.* New York: Psychological Corporation, 1949.

Wechsler, D. *Manual for the Wechsler Preschool and Primary Scale of Intelligence.* New York: Psychological Corporation, 1967.

Weener, P., Barritt, L., & Semmel, M. A critical evaluation of the Illinois Test of Psycholinguistic Abilities. *Exceptional Children,* 1967, **33**, 373–384.

chapter 15

personality development

chapter 15

personality development

chapter 15

personality development

Perhaps no concept in psychology is as important or as elusive as personality. Like intelligence, personality might be thought of as a "hypothetical construct." Psychologists observe an individual's behavior and on the basis of their observations draw inferences about his personality. However, too often personality is more than a descriptive concept; it becomes explanatory.

"Susie stays apart from the other third-graders because she has an introverted personality." Thus, the child's behavior has been explained by assuming that it reflects her "basic nature" and by attaching a label to it. Further, she can be linked with other children who are introverts. She has been typed, pigeonholed. Her behavior has been elucidated. This, of course, is one of the perils of employing the concept of personality. Inferences are drawn from selected observations of behavior in which attention is focused on only one aspect or characteristic. The notion of personality, however, is really thought to include all aspects of the individual.

To understand this child more fully necessitates rating her on many different bases. It is not enough to consider just her tendency to remain apart from others in a group situation. This neither explains her behavior nor describes her personality. Nor will a summation of her characteristics constitute a portrait of the individual. The interaction among these characteristics, their organization, and the unique manner in which each modifies and alters the others is what truly matters.

For the purposes of this chapter, personality may be defined as the distinct and unique organization of traits in an individual as reflected in how he reacts to himself and others and in how they react to him, and also in how he meets frustrations and conflicts—that is, in how he adjusts to his environment. The chapter is divided into three general areas: first, a reprise of the antecedents of personality; second, an analysis of the self concept and of self-consistency; and third, a treatment of those phases of personality that appear to be of particular significance in development.

Many attempts have been made to describe stages in personality development. It is not certain whether there are specific, inevitable, well-defined stages, but one assumption concerning their existence is worth attention. This assumes that an individual can move on to the next, more mature stage only after having successfully completed the demands of the previous stage or having satisfactorily met its requirements. For understanding the personality development of children, this is invaluable. It also has far-reaching implications for understanding adult behavior and adjustment.

Erikson (1950) described the following eight stages in personality development, each with its own distinctive goal normally to be attained in that period.

Infancy:	a basic sense of trust
Early childhood:	a sense of autonomy
Play age:	a sense of initiative
School age:	industry and competence
Adolescence:	personal identity
Young adult:	intimacy
Adulthood:	generativity
Mature age:	integrity and acceptance

The advanced stages of psychological maturity cannot be approached unless the goals of the preceding period have been met successfully. For example, a sense of trust is necessary before a child feels sufficiently secure to strive for autonomy. This is a trust in both the reliability of people and the satisfaction of basic physiological and psychological needs. Security gives freedom. The child who is led to mistrust others and his universe may be wedded forever to a need to seek the security he lacks.

In the normal progression to personality adjustment as a mature adult, an individual may be more vulnerable to certain influences during some periods of his life than during others. For example, some say, as noted earlier, that the effects of maternal deprivation are more severe in the second half of the child's first year. Perhaps in general a child cannot move on to a new and higher phase of personality development until he has achieved a certain amount of personality integration at his current level. Perhaps also the appearance of a more mature phase may be blocked or retarded by the interference of some event with the child's present degree of adjustment. The same principles apply as the child grows. Not just the first year or two of his life but the entire period from infancy through adolescence lays the groundwork for adult personality.

PERSONALITY ANTECEDENTS

In a sense, the entire book to this point could be considered as composed of antecedents of personality: maturation, learning, cultural factors, the home and family setting, including parental and sibling influences, the peer society, and finally, aspects of community. It may be argued, however, that the influences that occur earliest in a child's life tend to have the broadest impact on the individual's personality because they are the first incorporated into it and thus play a part in determining the effects of subsequent experiences.

Because personality is conceived of as the product of interaction between hereditary and environmental factors, let us examine both areas of influence. Since from birth onward, heredity and environment interact, it is impossible even at the age of two to say how much of a child's personality is attributable to one or the other. A child may inherit an irritable temperament from his father, but it is his mother who reacts to it, with resulting consequences for the child's personality.

Innate Predispositional Factors

An infant, as we have noted in Chapter 9, is an active energy system that affects its environment and in turn is affected by it. Flexible and resilient, the infant selects those aspects of the environment to which he responds. Innate characteristics determine both this selectivity and the infant's initial responses to the environment.

Endocrine and Nervous System. Malfunctioning of the endocrine glands produces deviant behavior in only a limited number of individuals. Nevertheless, there is a link between behavior and glandular secretion. An underactive thyroid, for example, causes a low rate of metabolism, resulting in sluggish behavior and lack of endurance. Contrarily, too high a rate of thyroid secretion engenders restlessness and "nervousness."

Hormonal secretion from the gonads, though it can be changed by environmental factors, stems primarily from innate sources. The sex hormones influence a number of behaviors and characteristics. Secondary sex manifestations, such as lower voice pitch, facial hair growth, and growth in musculature appearing in boys at puberty, exert broad influences on personality and adjustment. Further, the rate of sexual maturation, which is largely determined by hereditary forces, bears an important relation to certain personality tendencies at adolescence.

Findings from the California Adolescent Growth Study indicate that the girl who matures early and the boy who matures late both encounter problems of adjustment (Bayley & Tuddenham, 1944). Marked behavioral differences were noted by Jones and Bayley (1950) between boys who matured early and those who matured late. Late maturers persisted in childlike patterns of activity, eager and animated. Their peers considered them restless, talkative, and attention-seeking while viewing early maturers as popular and as having older friends, a sense of humor about themselves, and good appearance. Quite clearly the rate of maturity relates to several aspects of adolescent personality because of the premium on "maturity" at this age level. Thus we have an excellent example of the interplay between innate factors—maturity level—and environmental factors—social responses based on values and social expectations—which then affects personality adjustment. Moreover, while age of reaching puberty is unimportant in itself in adulthood, its effect on adjustment at adolescence may leave long-lasting consequences. A longitudinal follow-up of the subjects in the California Adolescent Studies found differences in favor of the early as compared with the late maturer. On a standard personality test administered at age 30, early maturers described themselves as able to make a good impression, as poised, responsible, achieving in conformity to society's expectations, and as relatively free from neurotic symptoms (M. C. Jones, 1957). By their late thirties, the late maturers showed ability to cope with various situations, although their adaptability was accompanied by some fearfulness and vulnerability to threat (M. C. Jones, 1965). Though the late maturer was in a less favorable position at adolescence, his striving for social acceptance (which the early maturer was readily accorded) resulted in a certain adaptability and flexibility later. Thus the effects of age of maturation may diminish with age but are apparent even in adulthood; however, the advantages are not wholly on the side of the early maturer over the long run.

Among infants the differences in the reactive tendencies of their nervous systems influence both their responses to their enviornments and the manner in which the significant individuals in their environments respond to them. Newborns differ widely in level of activity, irritability, and general emotional excitability—all of which reflect differences in nervous systems. Whether or not these particular characteristics have long-term consistency in the individual, their influence on the child's psychological surroundings and, in turn, on his personality at one point in his development suggests they have some importance. For example, Stewart (1953) concluded from her observations of crying behavior in infants that too much crying tended to generate insecurity in the mother which, in turn, is transmitted back to the offspring.

There is no doubt that emotionality, the physiological portions of emotional experience, has a base in the autonomic nervous system. This is borne out by a study by Gottesman (1960) in which identical twins resembled one another more than fraternal twins, especially with respect to sociability versus withdrawal. It does not mean, however, that differences among adults in emotional behavior are due exclusively to constitutional factors. Environmental factors play a tremendous part. Nevertheless, infants and children differ in the functioning of their autonomic nervous system, thus occasioning differences in emotionality and in the responses of adults (see Wenger, 1947; H. E. Jones, 1960).

Finally, any trait or characteristic based on the structure and operation of the nervous system is hereditary in origin. Admittedly, research has hardly scratched the surface in detecting relations between behavior and organic structure. But there seems to be enough evidence to conclude, for example, that intelligence has a physiological source in the central nervous system whereas such a trait as selfishness almost certainly has not.

Body Structure and Physical Abilities. The child's basic physique is primarily a product of hereditary. Despite a history of efforts to link type of body to personality and temperament, present evidence indicates only a slight relationship between physical and psychological make-up. Sheldon, the leading protagonist of the body-type theory of personality (Sheldon, Stevens, & Tucker, 1940), devised a scheme for ascertaining the portion of each of three body types in an individual's physique: *endomorphic*—a roundish build weak in bony and muscular development; *mesomorphic*—large bones and muscles with an athletic physique; and *ectomorphic*—long, slender extremities, lacking in muscular development. In addition, three basic types of temperament were described, each associated with one of the body types: with the endomorphic, *viscerotonic*—sociable, relaxed, love of comfort, slow reaction; with the mesomorphic, *somatotonic*—need for activity and action, assertive, courageous, energetic; and with the ectomorphic, *cerebrotonic*—restrained, inhibited, tense, preferring solitude.

The Gluecks found at least twice as many mesomorphic physiques among delinquent boys as among nondelinquents (Glueck & Glueck, 1956). Another investigation observed some differences in IQ test performances of seven-year-old boys grouped into the three categories of body types (Davidson, McInnes, & Parnell, 1957). In addition, more signs of emotional disturbance in the boys were reported by mothers of the ectomorphic group. Support for Sheldon's original contention was obtained in a study of high-school senior boys and a sample of college girls (Cortes & Gatti, 1965). Endomorphs rated themselves significantly more often as kind, relaxed, warm, soft-hearted; mesomorphs as confident, energetic, adventurous, enterprising; and ectomorphs as detached, tense, shy, and reserved. Mesomorphs were found also to demonstrate a higher need for achievement than the other two body types (Cortes & Gatti, 1966).

In an extensive study linking body build and behavior (Walker, 1962), 125 preschool children were rated by their teachers on 64 behavior items. The somatotyping used Sheldon's classification system. With regard to the relations between the behavioral and physique data, many more of the predictions were confirmed for boys than for girls, suggesting that physical factors are more important in affecting the behavior of boys. Certainly our cultural stereotypes and expectations concerning physique and behavior are more firmly established for males (despite the popular concern for female measurements). The mesomorphic body build showed the strongest relationship to the behavioral ratings, especially for boys.

> Characteristic of both boys and girls high in mesomorphy is a dominating assertiveness (leader in play, competitive, self-assertive, easily angered, attacks others, etc.), high energy output, openness of expression, and fearlessness. The girls combine this assertiveness with socialness, cheerfulness, and warmth. The boys' items give more suggestion of hostility (quarrelsome, revengeful, inconsiderate) and of an impulsive, headlong quality to their activity (daring, noisy, quick, accident prone, self-confident, etc.) (Walker, 1962, p. 78).

Some relationships were evident for the ectomorphic physique:

> In common for both sexes are items suggesting a certain aloofness. . . . For boys, the items in general define a cautious, quiet child, not self-assertive, hesitant to give offense, looking to adults rather than to children for approval, sensitive, slow to recover from upsets. He appears lacking in energy reserves. . . . For girls, the composite picture is similar but tends more to indicate a somberness of outlook–unfriendly, tense, not gay or cheerful, irritable (p. 78).

Some additional support for the relation between personality and body type was obtained from mothers' ratings of these same children (Walker, 1963).

Digman (1963) demonstrated that excitability and "outgoingness" were related only minimally to parent attitudes, whereas other traits, such as empathy, and clusters of traits, such as meeting cultural demands, were closely related to them. Possibly excitability and outgoingness result more from genetic factors–perhaps body type–than from strictly social forces.

Some physiques more than others permit an individual to perform certain motor and physical behaviors successfully. Competence in the motor area is an important attribute in childhood, especially among boys (see Hardy, 1937; Sanford, Adkins, Miller, Cobb, et al., 1943). The competence of the mesomorph wins favorable reaction from the group. This leads him to solicit further approval in the particular area of activity; thus, an assertiveness induced by social considerations may emanate from the self-confidence he develops. Similarly, a child who is unsuccessful in the motor area will seek rewarding experience elsewhere. Success in the classroom may compensate for failure on the playground.

A second and related factor is social expectation. The stereotypes of the jolly, plump individual, the thin bookworm, and the aggressive mesomorph may not be scientifically derived, but they establish certain expectations of behavior for children of these body types. For example, a father is less likely to spur an ectomorphic son than a mesomorphic son to athletic prowess. These cultural stereotypes are adopted early by children. When asked to identify the photograph, from three representing chubby, average, and thin body builds, which they would not want to look like, kindergarteners show a marked aversion to the chubby physique (Lerner & Gellert, 1969; Lerner & Schroeder, 1971). Moreover, children as young as 6–11 years of age agree closely in assigning personality traits to body types (Staffieri, 1967, 1972). In general the behavior adjectives assigned to the mesomorph (which was the preferred body build) were positive, while those assigned to the ectomorph and endomorph were unfavorable. The following characteristics were among those assigned to mesomorphs: best friend, lots of friends, happy, helps others, polite, brave, good looking, smart, and neat. Ectomorphs were seen as quiet and weak, while endomorphs were perceived in these terms: fights, cheats, worries, argues, gets teased, lonely, lazy, lies, sloppy, mean, ugly, dirty, and stupid. Clearly, social stereotypes dictate social expectations so that individuals are responded to on the basis of a "cultural transmission" of body-build–behavior relations rather than on the basis of one's actual experiences with persons having different body builds.

Attractive appearance has been seen to have some relation to popularity among children (Tryon, 1939; Hardy, 1937). Although popularity may be a result rather than a cause of an individual's personality, the extent to which a child is accepted by his peers, as noted in Chapter 11, exerts some influence on his self-acceptance. This, in turn, affects his subsequent personality development.

Intelligence. To consider intelligence as an innate predispositional factor is not to imply that intellectual functioning is entirely inherited. Indeed, it is an excellent example of the continual interaction of hereditary and environmental factors. Yet it is probable that heredity, by determining an individual's central nervous structure, imposes limits within which environmental influences work.

It is not easy to determine the precise role of intelligence in the development of personality. Despite the conclusion from a survey of 200 studies that no uniform relation exists between intelligence and emotional and personality traits (Lorge, 1940), there is evidence that shows a tie between intelligence and adjustment. J. E. Anderson (1960), in studying prediction of adjustment over a seven-year span, found IQ to be a significant prognosticator of adjustment and concluded: "Our results can be interpreted either as showing how difficult it is to separate out an intelligence factor from the complex of personality characteristics with which we are dealing when we talk about adjustment, or as indicating how important intelligence is in the adjustive process" (p. 64). Through factor analysis of various personality ratings and measures of analysis, Cattell (1945) has shown intelligence to correlate highly with self-control, reliability, industriousness, emotional independence, conscientiousness, and perseverance—all of which are traits of character. Intelligence was less closely associated, however, with basic emotional integration and adjustment.

Several explanations account for the relation of intelligence to adjustment in American society. First, brighter children have brighter parents who handle the emotional problems of childhood more wisely, thus establishing a sounder psychological foundation in childhood. Second, brighter children perceive social expectation more accurately and conform accordingly. Their behavior is rewarded, which leads to good adjustment to the demands made of them. Third, brighter children are more resourceful in meeting social expectations and demands; therefore, they are more likely to be successful. Fourth, a moderate relation exists between intelligence and ingenuity, curiosity, and creativity, traits that abet popularity and adjustment in peer society. Fifth, a closer relation between intelligence and adjustment may be postulated for middle-class than for lower-class children because of middle-class emphasis on academic achievement and educational progress.

Just as intelligence exerts a broad and complex influence on personality development, aspects of personality affect intellectual functioning. In a longitudinal study of mental growth and personality development, children who gained or lost in IQ during elementary-school years were seen to differ significantly in the following personality traits: independence, aggressiveness, self-initiative, problem solving, anticipation, and competitiveness (Sontag, Baker, & Nelson, 1958). And in Terman and Oden's 20-year follow-up (1947) of a group of highly gifted children, comparisons were made between successful and unsuccessful male adults, the measure for success being the extent to which an individual has made use of his superior intellectual ability. The successful received higher ratings on perseverance, self-confidence, integration toward goals, and absence of inferiority feelings, leading to the conclusion that the two groups differed markedly in achievement drive and all-around social adjustment.

To be sure, the interaction between intellect and personality is complex, and a great variance in personality adjustment exists at all levels of intelligence. Certain problems of emotional adjustment are more frequent at the lower intellectual levels, yet highly endowed individuals are not entirely immune from personality difficulties. Thus it is apparent that even if there is no clear-cut tie between aspects of intellect and personality, intelligence does influence an individual's interactions with other people; it also affects adjustment to the demands of the environment.

Environmental Factors

What a child brings to a situation helps to shape the responses of others to him in the situation. This, in turn, determines how he will approach future situations. Let us deal here, then, with the social influences that bear on personality development. These include social expectations for child behavior as well as some cultural differences in expectations for behavior and personality. First, we should mention several nonpsychological factors that have some potential psychological bearing.

Organic Factors. Anything that affects the individual's willingness or ability to respond to his environment is certain to influence his view of himself and his interaction with others. For example, vitamin deficiences may be reflected in such psychological symptoms as depression and irritability. More important perhaps is the lowered vitality of a child suffering from general nutritional deficiency. Illness, injury, and physical handicap undoubtedly impede the child's personality development. Yet research that has sought to find the precise impact of these factors on personality development is largely inconclusive.

To begin with, information concerning the child's personality development prior to illness or injury is seldom available. This limits the extent to which certain aspects of a child's personality may be attributed to them. The use of a control group, of course, would be advantageous, but it is difficult to obtain an adequate one suitably matched with the experimental group. Furthermore, present instruments for assessing personality are largely inadequate in this area of research. The children on whom personality measures were standardized are not comparable with, say, children with physical handicaps. Comparisons are therefore inappropriate. Similar responses by a healthy and a handicapped child on a personality inventory may have entirely different meanings for the two.

Prolonged illness reduces the child's contact with the environment and his interaction, which results in decreased stimulation. Coupled with increased bodily concern, this induces the child to withdraw his interest from the world about him and focus it upon himself. Egocentricity, selfishness, and undue concern with himself follow. Because illness handicaps, feelings of helplessness and dependency are born. These, together with parental resentment, rejection, overconcern, or overprotection, may have long-range effects on the child. Beverly (1936) found, for example, that an overwhelming majority of hospitalized children whom she interviewed answered the question, "Why do children get sick?" with the assertion, "Because they are bad." Indeed such an attitude can pervade the child's concept of himself and his sense of self-worth.

In discussions of the effect of physical injury or handicap on personality the notion of *body image* has often been invoked. An infant gradually becomes aware of his physical self through a variety of physical sensations. At first the distinction between *me* and *not me* is not a sharp one. Then experience furnishes countless clues that assist in the process of self-differentiation. Later, psychological attitudes toward the physical self develop out of the child's social interaction with others so that ultimately the most significant aspects of one's body image are those psychological attitudes that involve evaluation and consequent acceptance or rejection.

Because of the circular nature of an individual's attitude toward himself and the attitude of others toward him, there is not necessarily a close correspondence between the objective aspects of one's physical composition and the psychological attitudes associated with it. In any case, the image of one's physical self becomes increasingly consistent throughout childhood. For this reason any alteration in one's body requires some adjustments in body image. Perhaps one of the most difficult and yet most imperative adjustments is acceptance of the changed physical condition. This requires acknowledgment of dependency on others when physically handicapped and recognition of the fact that participation and achievement in some areas of life are impossible (Mussen & Newman, 1958). Realization of this avoids needless frustration.

Acceptance. Too frequently physical handicap engenders resentment and frustration in the child. Deviation from normality, especially if it restricts and curtails the child's active participation with his peers, can affect personality development. So can parental nonacceptance of the child and his handicap, which is particularly damaging to the child's sense of self-worth. The underlying psychological mechanism of this nonacceptance is complicated. Parents blame themselves for abnormality in their offspring. This was the case, for example, with mothers of children with cleft palate (Tisza, Selverstone, Rosenblum, & Hanlon, 1958). Actually, any condition in the child that adds to child-care responsibilities often irks the parent. This irksomeness is bound to affect the parent's attitude toward the child. The point is that parental acceptance or rejection, as we have seen in Chapter 10, influences the child's attitude toward himself, which is a significant factor in personality development.

Similarly, peer acceptance is an important element in self-acceptance, though it is not always clear which causes which. Perhaps the child's lower self-acceptance may generate hostility and resentment that reduce his acceptance by his peers. Sociometric studies have shown that children with speech defects are chosen less often than children without them when play and friendship are the bases for selection (Woods & Carrow, 1959), and that children with defective hearing are not as acceptable among peers as those whose hearing is normal (Elser, 1959).

Case studies spotlight strong differences in the degree to which physical handicaps become psychological burdens among children. What causes these differences? The major factor is doubtless the parent's attitude toward the child—the extent to which they accept him prior to and then with a handicap. Though bodily injury or physical handicap may exacerbate and complicate a previously hostile, nonaccepting parent-child relationship, it is doubtful whether a real acceptance of the child for his own sake would be substantially altered by such an occurrence. One five-year-old, severely afflicted with cerebral palsy, was lighthearted, gay, and full of mischief. With much effort and exertion he would manage to propel himself up the ladder of a slide and then slide down, screaming with delight, to land at the bottom, arms and legs twisted appallingly. Every day at 5:30 his father came to fetch him at the day-care nursery center, engulf the child in his arms, and wipe away the boy's uncontrolled saliva as the youngster jabbered on about the day's events. He would never watch his son hit a home run or score a touchdown, but, because of his acceptance of the boy, he would be able to see him grow and develop into a fine, worthwhile young man.

Sociocultural Factors

The differences among cultures are so strong and pervasive that *modal* personality types are often noted by anthropologists. They use the adjective *modal* to signify "common" or "fashionable" as in a la mode. This modal type may be essentially paranoid and suspicious, as among the Dobuans studied by Fortune (1932), or open and guileless, as were some of the Dobuans' neighbors studied by Malinowski (1922). It has been suggested that there is a modal American personality, which is changing largely as a result of technological, educational, and economic development within the culture. The specific behavioral pattern of an individual, based on his unique biological composition and social experience, takes form within the range of behaviors deemed acceptable by the culture.

Behavior and personality vary among individuals within a culture. Some of this variance results from social class, occupation, racial background, and place of residence. These broad sociological variables, as previously noted, have considerable bearing in the creation of individual differences in personality and behavior. Also contributing to the shaping of an individual's web of responses are various aspects in the family setting.

The biological forces on one side and the social forces on the other fix the limits within which parents and others in intimate association with the child may mold character and personality. Parental personality, attitudes, and behavior all influence the developing child. The development of dependence or independence, of activity level, and of ability to resist stress result, in part, from the child's interaction with his parents.

THE SELF CONCEPT

The term *self concept* has many definitions, sometimes conflicting. For the purpose of this discussion, we shall call the self concept an individual's attitude toward his physical self and his own behavior. In recent perusals of literature concerning the self concept (e.g., Hall & Lindzey, 1957; Wylie, 1961; Shlien, 1962), investigators have hit upon two bases for it: the social roles and attempts to synthesize them; and the body image, "the body as a psychological experience . . . the individual's feelings and attitudes toward his own body" (Fisher & Cleveland, 1958, p. x). In the pages that follow we shall dwell on these two aspects of the self and then turn to the relation of the self concept to behavior.

Role Theory

"All the world's a stage, and every man's a player." Centuries after Shakespeare, the scientific study of roles and the use of role theory as an explanatory device had its beginnings in the work of such sociologists as Durkheim and Tonnies. Their thoughts were first elucidated clearly by Cooley (1902), to be further developed in the social psychology of George H. Mead. Mead did not publish his ideas himself; after his death, his lecture notes were edited by his students (see Strauss, 1956).

Cooley originated the notion of the social or "looking glass" self. To him, man's ideas about himself were reflections of how others saw him. Mead divided personality structure into the *I* and the *me.* The *I* was the part of the self that was partly—perhaps largely—genetic in origin, the continuing part of personality present in every special situation. The *me* was basically social, a reflection of society's demands. Each individual was made up of many *me's*, as many as he had distinct social roles. The expectations and demands of all social groups of significance to the individual influenced his behavior at all times, but their relative influences shifted with the behavioral situation and the roles it required.

The *me* that is in the forefront at any time depends on the composition of the group toward which an individual's behavior is directed. For example, a boy in a Little League game has his teammates as his main *reference group.* They provide him with the most accurate information about how he is playing his particular role as baseball player. The Little League loses its power as a reference group as the boy's role changes to son, brother, or pupil, while other groups such as family, teachers, or classmates gain in influence.

Whiting (1960) suggests that we most adequately learn and portray the roles of people whom we envy or admire—often those people, usually our parents, who control the resources in the environment when we are children. It appears that Whiting's position may explain some types of role learning, such as "like father, like son," but does not adequately explain the learning of other, maladaptive roles, such as "stutterer" or "delinquent." Role assignment has much to do with personality. This has been clearly shown at many points throughout this book; individuals have a strong disposition to perform the roles assigned to them, even when the roles are damaging to self-esteem, as in the case of the stutterer, or to adjustment. As noted in Chapter 8, one major problem of members of minority groups is that, having been assigned roles as inferiors, they often accept such roles and attempt to live up to them.

A wide range of social and biological factors, as well as chance, enters into the roles assigned to an individual. Once he has had his roles assigned, however, the individual tends to respond in terms of these roles. This makes for regular, consistent behavior, as long as the roles are clearly defined and do not clash too sharply. Across those situations the *I* aspect of personality persists. And a good thing, too! One can see that the individual whose behavior is determined only by the demands of the social group would be the ultimate of the other-directed person, with no core of personal integrity. To use Freudian terms, this type of person would have an "externalized superego": a conscience dependent only on the values of the group to which he belongs at the time.

The roles assigned to an individual determine a fair portion of his behavior; when roles are central and significant and yet conflict directly with one another, there is behavioral disturbance. *Romeo and Juliet* is a classic example of role conflict in which romantic love and family honor collide; it is of little significance today, since family honor means less now than it did to individuals in Shakespeare's day—and perhaps the same is true of romantic love. *Crime and Punishment* is more pertinent to us because Raskolnikov's conflict between conventional upper-middle-class values and those of the poverty-stricken, amoral student world is more immediate in contemporary life. The classic primary-group tragedy involving a clash of central roles still exists, and along with it in contemporary industrial society goes the problem of nonexistent roles and a loss of personal identity. The breakdown occurring as a result of ambiguous role definitions has been well described by Dunham (1959) and forms the basis of most contemporary literature. Kafka's heroes, on trial for some unnamed crime, or changing overnight into a gigantic cockroach, are the ancestors of Beckett's and Sartre's existential men–individuals without a governing set of roles and values. Whereas having clear and conflicting roles is one basis for tragedy, the tragic nature and emptiness of a life in which one has no roles to play is doubtless greater.

The Body Image

Awareness of the physical self and its separation from the nonself comes about, in part, from body movements, internal changes such as hunger, and such things as laryngeal activity in which the infant feels movement simultaneously with hearing sound (Schilder, 1935). It also comes from observing the effects of one's behavior on the external world (Piaget, 1954).

Degree of awareness of one's own body appears to be related to sex, with males being more aware of certain aspects of the physical self, and making greater use of such things as body orientation to structure the environment (Witkin, Dyke, Faterson, Goodenough, & Karp, 1962).

Generally the body image is assumed to be closely tied to physical reality; distortions in it relate to psychological disturbance. In the following case a distorted body image seemed to be the source of some otherwise inexplicable behavior.

Rudy was a man in his early twenties. He was 5′ 4″ tall and weighed about 135 pounds, and had an athletic body build. He did not seek trouble to any noticeable extent, but certainly did nothing to avoid it. He had had his nose broken twice and his upper front teeth knocked out in fist fights with fellows who outweighed him by about 100 pounds. These fights could have been avoided without "losing face." The writer wondered why Rudy did not do so, and why he continued to get into difficulties of this sort, until one day the writer noticed something. Rudy always stooped when he went through a doorway. Watching Rudy maneuver about made one fact obvious. Rudy thought he was 7′ tall, and no number of losses made him the least concerned over someone a mere 6′ 2″. Occasionally distortion of body image can be discerned in an individual and explain behavior that appears highly unreasonable and illogical. Hence, body image exists–though not tied as closely to the physical self as is widely assumed.

Attempts to assess body image in a scientific manner and to predict behavior from it have not always been successful. Frequently, individuals are requested to draw a human figure; it is assumed that they will project into the drawing their own ideas about their physical selves. These drawings are then interpreted. If, for example, the individual draws his figure with hands concealed behind the back, he is believed to disclose a feeling of impotence, of inability to deal with problems. Perhaps the individual feels impotent only in the fine art of drawing hands! Very few individuals represent their own bodies when instructed to draw a person, suggested Swenson (1957). Even when they do, the interpretations of their drawings seem largely based on conjecture (Levy, 1950).

Other approaches to the measurement of the body image have been used less frequently, but have proved more useful. Fisher and Cleveland (1958) were concerned with measuring the boundaries of the body exterior (does the individual view his body self as merging into the environment surrounding the body self, or as rigidly separated from the nonself?)

through the analysis of Rorschach (see p. 532) responses. They hypothesized that persons whose psychosomatic symptoms involved the body interior (ulcers, etc.) would perceive their bodies merging with the environment and as being easily penetrated, while those whose symptoms involved a body exterior (skin disorders, etc.) would conceive of their bodies as surrounded by a rigid protective barrier that would "protect them from the world." Their data strongly supported their beliefs. In another approach to the measurement of the body image, Secord and Jourard (1953) developed a test aimed at measuring satisfaction with the physical self. Secord (1953) also developed a measure of concern for the physical self. He used homonyms—words such as *mole, trunk,* and *graft,* which have two or more meanings, one of which associates the word with a body part or function. The number of times that the body meaning is used in defining homonyms is an index of concern for one's own body. From the Secord and Jourard measures we can obtain some knowledge of the individual's interest in and attitude toward the physical self that does allow us to make predictions about such things as reactions to mutilation of the body, as in operations (Shaub, 1967). Further, these measures have been used to demonstrate that individual's valuation of the body and of the self tend to be commensurate (Secord, 1953). The Secord and Jourard measures seem to be the best presently available measures of the body image that can be scored objectively. Results obtained from studies in which these scales have been used generally support the belief that the body image is an important determinant of behavior.

One further point on body image. If body image determines behavior, and especially the self concept, which promotes consistency in behavior, then the behavior of individuals should become more variable as the physical self changes more rapidly. This is what happens in adolescence; rapid shifts in children's behavior often baffle parents. And, of course data cited earlier on the relation of physical maturity to social adjustment are themselves suggestive of the impact on adjustment of the physical self and one's attitudes toward it.

The Self Concept and Adjustment

To many who are interested in psychotherapy (see, e.g., Rogers, 1951; Shlien, 1961), the self concept plays a vital role in adjustment. They say that the fundamental problem of the neurotic is that he is self-rejecting. The objective of their therapy is to cause him to come to terms with himself and adjust his behavior and perception of himself to the point at which he is able to accept himself. Raimy (1948) demonstrated that successful cases in psychotherapy enabled patients to acquire a more favorable view of themselves, whereas unsuccessful cases did not.

The overwhelming evidence from Wylie's (1961) review of the literature on the self suggested that self-acceptance was related to adjustment. A high regard of the self generally meant a high level of adjustment, except in a few cases where high self-esteem worked as adversely as self-rejection. In general, moreover, those individuals who were self-accepting were seen to be accepting of others (e.g., Wylie, 1957). What this means, of course, is that the individual who can accept himself can withstand aggression and disparagement from others; his personal psychological security grants him an objective view of the behavior of others and an understanding of the bases for their behavior. Such an individual can also sustain adversity better than a self-rejecting person. He can return aggression directly toward others, if necessary. He therefore need not develop neurotic defenses or take out his hostility on innocent victims.

Quite obviously it would be to the benefit of the culture to raise children who are self-accepting. From McCurdy's work (1957) on extremely creative individuals as well as from the researches of those directly concerned with the self concept (Maris, 1958; Coopersmith, 1967; Sears, 1970), it would appear that children who experience a warm and affectionate relationship with their parents, who are accepted by their parents and who are aware of their parents' attitudes toward them are most accepting of themselves. Early and continued parental acceptance contributes to a child's self-acceptance which in turn enables him to be accepting of others. A positive self concept in terms of self-esteem and self-acceptance is the foundation for healthy personality development.

PRINCIPAL COMPONENTS OF PERSONALITY IN CHILDREN

Personality seems to gain complexity and consistency as the years pass. It grows more complex because the number and range of its antecedents increase, producing more intricate interactions. It increases in consistency because, as physical growth terminates, the body image becomes stable and roles played become clearer, more consonant with one another, and more tightly incorporated into the self concept.

Considerable research has been amassed on particular components of personality that seem to be central in the personality fabric of childhood, yet relatively independent of one another. These are dependence-independence, aggression, anxiety, conscience development, dominance-submission, and social acceptability. We propose to explore each in some detail, with emphasis on their antecedents.

Dependence-Independence

Dependency is the condition of the human infant. The infant is *instrumentally* dependent on his mother. Because he associates her with the satisfaction of his basic biological needs, the infant also develops a rewarding *emotional* dependence on her (Heathers, 1955b). How then does independent behavior develop? It comes about through maturation and learning. The young child grows increasingly capable of functioning independently. Speaking of the mammalian infant in general, Rheingold and Eckerman (1970) point out that the infant's leaving the mother is universal. At some point in his early life the infant leaves the mother to explore the world about him. As we pointed out in our earlier discussion of infant-mother attachment (see pp. 263–269), such exploration served, in man's long evolutionary history, a survival function. At first the excursion from the mother is brief; it increases in frequency and duration with age. Since the separation is voluntary on the part of the infant, it does not produce "separation anxiety." Differences exist among cultures in the extent to which the mother separates herself from the infant in the early years. In some, the infant spends no time away from the mother since she carries him about with her, while such separation is common in our society. In all cases, however, the infant attempts to separate himself from his mother when he is physically able to do so (crawling behavior in the human infant appears some time after the first half year of life).

Much remains to be learned about factors promoting early independence. Some of these rest in the infant's early relation with his mother; the attractiveness of the environment, in both a physical and a psychological sense, is important also.

> If we look beyond the period of infancy, the full significance of the child's separating himself from his mother comes into view. Leaving her side is but the first step in the continuous process of achieving psychological independence. (Rheingold & Eckerman, 1970, p. 83)

Independent behavior is in itself rewarding to the child because of the satisfaction gained from exploring and manipulating the environment and from interacting with peers. Normally, therefore, there is an increase in independent behavior with age (Steth & Conner, 1962). In nursery school, children exhibit less behavior reflecting infantile reliance on adults and a shift toward a more active, assertive dependence on peers (Heathers, 1955a). However, emotional or psychological independence does not invariably accompany physical or instrumental independence. Further, some children manifest greater independence of behavior than others.

A Cultural Phenomenon. The concern of American psychologists over dependence versus independence reflects the importance attached by society to the development of independent behavior. The individual who is able to operate as an independent agent is regarded as a mature adult. However, anthropologists have shown that American emphasis on early independent training is not shared by all other cultures. Take this illustration, for example, of the attitude and behavior of parents in a New Guinea tribe.

> When the child begins to walk the quiet continuous rhythm of its life changes somewhat. It is now becoming a little heavy for the mother to carry about with her on long trips to the garden, and furthermore it can be expected to live without suckling for an hour or so. The mother leaves the child in the village with the father, or with some other relative, while she goes to the garden or for firewood. . . . As the child grows older, it is no longer confined so closely to the care of its own parents. Children are lent about. An aunt comes to visit and takes home the four-year-old for a week's stay, handing him on to some other relative for eventual return to his parents. This means that a child learns to think of the world as filled with parents, not merely a place in which all of his safety and happiness depend upon the continuance of his relationship to his own particular parents. . . . There is no insistence at all upon children's growing up rapidly, or acquiring special skills or proficiencies, and there is a corresponding lack of techniques for training them physically. . . . The result is that the child grows up with a sense of emotional security in the care of others, not in its own control over the environment (quoted in Whiting & Child, 1953, from Mead, 1935).

Similarly, a study of child-rearing practices in Puerto Rico (Landy, 1959) found little parental encouragement of independent behavior in the young child. Children are not given regular tasks to perform and little is expected of them. This stems partly from the culture's view of the child: *sin capacidad*-without capacity.

The following are examples of the kinds of items included in a recently developed scale for assessing dependency in children (Golightly, Nelson, & Johnson, 1970): "I like to be just a little sick so I can have meals in bed. My mother brings me to school. If I get up first I get my own breakfast. My parents let me go to the movies by myself. My mother doesn't let the other kids pick on me. I would like to be five years old again. Drawing is more fun when the teacher tells us what to draw. I like to go exploring by myself." Preliminary results with the scale support other findings concerning dependency: girls score higher than boys and there is a decrease with age in dependency scores.

Symptoms and Causes. What are the earmarks of dependent behavior? Of independent behavior? To Beller (1955) the following behaviors were signs of dependency: seeking help, seeking physical contact, seeking proximity, seeking attention, and seeking recognition. These were the behaviors denoting independence: taking initiative, trying to overcome obstacles in the environment, trying to carry activities to completion, getting satisfaction from work, and trying to do routine tasks by oneself. By and large, dependent behavior is characterized by reliance on someone else for assistance and assurance. A child is said to be dependent when he manifests behavior that, at his age level, should have been superseded by independent behavior. The six-year-old who does not dress himself alone, the four-year-old who does not feed himself, the five-year-old who does not play with his peers unattended by his mother all exhibit dependency.

Why does dependent behavior persist? No single explanation accounts either for dependence in children in general or its occurrence in any one child. All explanations, interestingly enough, have focused on various aspects of the parent-child relationship. An early study (Heathers, 1953) concluded that dependent behavior resulted from maternal overconcern; the mother was not only permissive about dependency behavior but also encouraged it. This view was reached by identifying independent and dependent behavior in children and then applying Fels ratings to the psychological atmosphere of their homes. The homes of the dependent youngsters rated higher on child-centered and babying counts. Others (Gavalas & Briggs, 1966) have argued that the extent to which dependency persists in a child is a function of the degree to which parents reward dependent behavior and fail to reward competent (achievement-oriented) behavior.

Widely held at the present time is the view that dependency increases and is intensified when the parent does not adequately meet the dependency needs of the child. Frustrated through lack of parental warmth, nurture, and affection, the child cannot proceed to greater emotional independence. This notion has supporting evidence, even though the results of various studies are not in full agreement. In an experimental study with preschool children, an increase in imitative behavior was noted in children who exhibited greater dependency behavior after an adult withdrew of nurturance and attention (Stein & Wright, 1964). This suggests that one reason for children's imitation of adults is to relieve dependency anxiety; incorporation of the adult behavior provides some measure of security. This interpretation is supported in a study showing strong similarity in values between mothers and sons when the mother trains the child early in independence (Rosen, 1964). Presumably, the early independence training arouses anxiety in the boy that is reduced by internalizing the mother's expectations and values.

In an extensive study of the antecedents of dependency and aggression (Sears, Whiting, Nowlis, & Sears, 1953), the amount of dependent behavior in nursery-school children correlated positively with the severity of their weaning in infancy. However, no such relation was found with respect to toilet training. And even the weaning finding was not supported by data obtained in the Pattern Study (Sears, Maccoby, & Levin, 1957). Conceivably the extent of the frustration of a child's early dependency needs is not adequately assessed through the mother's feeding and toilet-training practices.

Some Conclusions about Dependency Antecedents. To begin with, there is probably a curvilinear relationship within the normal range of dependency behavior between how parents meet or frustrate a child's early dependency needs and the persistence of such needs in the child. If the parent strongly rewards dependent behavior and takes a permissive attitude toward it, preventing or discouraging independence, dependency persists. Similarly, frustration of the infant's needs for dependence might intensify the yearning for dependency. The Pattern Study, for example, found dependency increased in children whose mothers punished them for such behavior; the same thing applied to children of homes where rejection was evident and withdrawal of love was used as a disciplinary technique. Parental conflict and rejection of the child were prominent in the family backgrounds of extremely dependent boys (McCord, McCord, & Verden, 1962). Low parental esteem for one another and for the child pervaded their homes. From this point of view dependent behavior was a manifestation of feelings of insecurity in the parent-child relationship. Gewirtz (1956) noted a high frequency of attention seeking in children when the adult was relatively unavailable. Thus dependence on adults appeared to increase when the children perceived them as psychologically distant.

Although the socialization process is characterized ordinarily by increasing independence in the child, certain parental attitudes impede this development. Stendler (1952) maintained that there are critical periods during the early years when overdependency may result. The first of these occurs toward the end of the first year of life when the child becomes aware of his dependence on his mother. Recognizing her importance, the child tests her to see if he can really depend on her. Separation at this time might produce a child low in ego strength and toleration of frustration. The second critical period appears between the ages of two and three. At this time the pressure of the culture for independent behavior increases on the child. Disturbances in his relation of dependency with his mother during this period might touch off attempts to cope with the resulting anxiety by developing an extremely strong conscience. To support this notion of a critical period, Stendler (1954) showed that a larger number of discontinuities in personality adjustment turned up in dependent children than in others. Moreover, her data corroborated those of Bandura and Walters in noting the importance of paternal influence in the learning of dependency.

Two further considerations merit brief attention. First, because independence grows out of dependence, the two must not be considered distinct from each other. Several studies (Beller, 1955; Heathers, 1955a) have observed that despite a negative correlation between the amount of independent and dependent behavior shown by nursery-school youngsters, the two are not entirely inversely related. That is, even though some children display generally less dependent behavior than others, some of both kinds of behavior can be seen in all children.

Second, long-term consistency in dependent behavior is of great concern to child psychologists interested in predicting behavior. In their study of the display of passive and dependent behavior in 54 adults, Kagan and Moss (1960) collected information on how much dependency these individuals had shown as children between the ages of 3 and 10. Comparisons of the two sets of data indicated that passive and dependent behaviors remained stable over the years among women but not necessarily among men. Kagan and Moss inferred that passive and dependent behavior was punishable in males while perhaps actually being encouraged in females. More males proportionately than females shifted from high dependency in childhood to independence in adulthood, implying a sex difference in the extent to which pressures for independence are applied in America. Even in adolescence, girls enjoy less independence than boys.

Dependency and Other Behaviors. Is independent or dependent behavior related to other aspects of behavior? Among preschool children a negative connection has been shown between dependence on adults and popularity among peers (Marshall & McCandless, 1957; McCandless, Bilous, & Bennett, 1961). Actually, those children depending most on adults participate least with peers. Thus dependence on adults presumably hinders a child's interaction with his peers, whereas independence seems to be a valued trait even at the preschool level. In adolescence, independence and popularity go together; however, the inverse relation between dependence on adults and popularity is by no means a simple one. Dependent boys were seen in the McCord study (McCord et al., 1962) to display heightened anxiety and internal stress, which perhaps interfered with peer relations.

Independence relates to achievement and motivation for achieving. High-achieving nursery-school children depended less on adults for help and emotional support than did children lower in achievement in a study conducted by Crandall, Preston, and Rabson (1960). Experimental research (Todd & Nakamura, 1970) has shown dependent children to be more responsive than independent children to reinforcement from adults, particularly if it involves social approval. Furthermore, children who rated high in emotional independence from parents showed increases in IQ during preschool years (Sontag et al., 1958). One might infer that independence as a sign of security enables the child to function autonomously and apply effort toward personal accomplishment and attainment of goals. This interpretation is supported by an experimental study (DiBartolo & Vinacke, 1969) which found that, as compared with preschoolers rated as independent, the performance of dependent preschoolers on a complex task (solving jigsaw puzzles) was markedly affected by the change from a nurturant adult condition (gave child attention, verbal praise, smiled at child) to a condition where the adult ignored the child's attempt to solve the puzzle. Apparently dependent children are alert to and highly sensitive to changes in the extent to which an adult provides warmth and nurturance, and their task performance is affected by such change.

Aggressive Behavior

Our culture seems uncertain as to how aggressive behavior should be regarded. During childhood aggression is discouraged; attitudes toward it are highly restrictive. Yet aggressiveness carries a premium in adult society. The ambitious, hard-driving, aggressive male represents the epitome of success in the competitive, free-enterprise system. His quiet, contemplative, introverted opposite is outdistanced in the race to the top. Aggressiveness appears to be approved in covert, sophisticated forms, but frowned upon in the overt, primitive, physical sorts that characterize children's behavior, except in such formalized events as athletic contests and war.

Aggression may be defined as any act or behavior that is intended to harm or injure. Thus defined, it is inimical to friendly, social intercourse. The rights and wishes of others are ignored or abridged. In this sense, aggressive behavior is maladaptive. There is also evidence that the behavior of highly aggressive children is inflexible and stereotyped (Dittmann & Goodrich, 1961). The implication is that children evincing a great amount of aggression have failed to develop inner controls and have not learned more appropriate, adaptable, and acceptable types of behavior.

The social interaction of young children is marked by aggressive, conflict-ridden behavior. Anger, hostility, quarrelling, and combativeness are observable frequently in children's relations with each other. It is impossible to determine how early these aggressive feelings appear in the child. However, the infant lashes out very early at the source of events that frustrate, restrict, or irritate him. The child uses any means at his command to eliminate unpleasant and undesirable stimuli. In the young child this usually means crying, screaming, and direct physical attack.

As children grow older overt aggression decreases. Inner controls are learned. More effective and more socially acceptable ways of solving conflicts are developed, and rules governing the rights of property become incorporated. However, at every age there are wide disparities among individuals in the amount of aggressive behavior, and in some children a marked persistence of aggression pervades a great number of behaviors. Children differ, too, in the extent to which they will manifest aggressive behavior in situations where retaliation may or may not occur. Boys low in aggression have been found to inhibit aggression when retaliation is likely, while high aggressive boys aggress more when retaliation is expected than when it is not (Peterson, 1971). Clearly, a given situation calls forth different behaviors in children depending upon their typical mode of behavior which, in turn, is related to their past histories.

Among the notions advanced to explain aggression in children, three stress various aspects of the parent-child relationship. In the first, *frustration-aggression*, any situation, condition, relationship, or experience that produces frustration in an individual is seen to generate aggression. The second notion emphasizes the *parent as a model* for the child; identifying with the parent, the child models his own behavior after the parent's. Third, parental *permissiveness of aggression* is said to increase the child's tendency to behave aggressively. Clearly all three notions are centered in the environment since these stress the child's learning experiences, particularly as they occur in the family setting. Furthermore, there is evidence that the three are interrelated. An adult who creates frustrations for the child is likely also to demonstrate aggressive behavior and to permit, and even reward, aggressive behavior in the child. This evidence was provided by a study (Cohen, 1972) in which fourth- and sixth-grade boys were interviewed regarding three aspects (frustration, modeling, permissiveness or reinforcement of aggression) of aggression-related experiences. Representative questions included (a) "Does your (social agent) hit or slap you when angry." (b) "When mad, does your (social agent) yell or scream at other children?" (c) "Does your social agent expect you to fight for your rights?" Questions dealing with four primary socialization agents were used: mother, father, teacher, and peers. The principal finding was that "socialization agents perceived as frustrating were also seen as salient models of aggression toward others and advocates of interpersonal aggression." The interviews also indicated that there are plentiful examples of aggressive behavior in the child's environment.

There is also an argument for a biological basis for aggression. Diamond (1957), who examined studies among animals, found strain and sex differences in aggressiveness and concluded that genetic factors were influential in determining aggressive behavior, even though learning experiences were important. However, reviewing some of the same research, Berkowitz (1962) saw no evidence of an instinctive drive to hostility or aggression in animals. He accounted for the relatively rare occurrence of spontaneous aggression by frustration or through prior learning that rewarded aggressive behavior.

Although environmental factors contribute heavily to the appearance of aggressive behavior, it would be a mistake to overlook inherent differences in individuals that might indirectly increase their tendency to react aggressively to environmental events. Certain innate characteristics, then, may determine the kinds of learning experience to which the child is exposed and these, in turn, influence behavior and personality. Among nursery-school children, Walker (1962) obtained significant correlations between mesomorphic type and clusters of behavioral triats labeled "energetic-active" and "aggressive-assertive." He concluded that "variations in physical energy, in bodily effectiveness for assertive or dominating behavior, and in bodily sensitivity appear as important mediating links between physique structure and general behavior" (p. 79). Whereas no cause-and-effect statements can be drawn from studies showing a relationship between physical factors and personality, it is not possible to ignore entirely the role such factors play in molding responses to the environment.

Frustration-Aggression. Most people experience frustration in the course of a day's events. Goals are blocked. Rewards are not received. Desires remain unfulfilled. Developed by the Yale group (Dollard, Doob, Miller, Mowrer, & Sears, 1939), the frustration-aggression hypothesis holds that aggressive behavior is the typical response to frustration. Support for the hypothesis appears in experimental studies as well as in observation. To mention one briefly (Otis & McCandless, 1955), 63 preschool children were exposed to eight consecutive repetitions of a mildly frustrating situation. Observed and recorded for manifestations of aggressiveness, the children displayed an increase in aggressive conduct from the first four to the last four trials. Quite likely this finding is particularly significant in supporting the Yale group's hypothesis because the frustration was mild and the children were not greatly involved in the situation. Certainly plausible, then, are findings that point out the severe consequences of parental frustrations of the child's emotional needs.

The findings of several parent-child research studies concur in noting a bond between aggressive behavior in children and punishment for aggression. The Pattern Study explained this relationship along the following lines: the child receives some reward in resorting to aggression through the satisfaction realized from hurting others or expressing anger. But when this aggressive behavior incurs punishment, great frustration is felt, which incites the child to further aggression. Moreover, the Pattern Study noted a tendency for severe punishment of aggression toward parents to be one aspect of general strictness in child-rearing.

One study relating parental behaviors to aggressiveness in school children (Eron, Banta, Walder, & Laulicht, 1961) found agressive boys likely to have fathers who severely punished aggressive deportment in the home. That there was no significant correlation between aggression at school and maternal punishment of aggressive behavior at home suggested that fathers, more than mothers, were an important source of frustration in the home, especially for boys. In addition to the effects of harsh punishment on aggression, there is evidence that inconsistent punishment tends to reduce its inhibiting effects (Deur & Parke, 1970). That is, punishment does not reduce aggression in children who have a past history of inconsistent parental behavior in which aggressive is alternately punished, rewarded, and ignored.

So much for restrictive and autocratic techniques producing frustration. As we have seen, the young child is totally dependent on his parents. When one or both parents fail him, frustration results. Hostile, aggressive behavior appears. In their book on adolescent aggression, Bandura and Walters (1959) attributed the development of aggressive behavior to disruption of the child's dependency relation with his parents. Their thesis is corroborated by the findings of another study of family correlates of aggression in nondelinquent boys (McCord, McCord, & Howard, 1961). Here, 95 percent of the aggressive boys come from homes in which at least one parent was emotionally rejecting.

Thus there seems to be evidence for the frustration-aggression hypothesis. It is clear, however, that frustration does not lead inevitably to aggression. Depending upon the nature of the frustration, it may lead to an inhibition of aggressive behavior, especially if the frustration is seen by the child as punishment for aggression (Kuhn, Madsen, & Becker, 1967). While frustration may well lead to an intensification of hostile feeling, this may not be translated immediately into action. However, whether the frustration stems from a rejection of the child's need for dependency and affection or from a restrictive home atmosphere, the effects on the child's personality development are harmful.

The Parent as a Model. The parent serves as a model for the child, who adopts his parent's values and imitates his behavior, irrespective of whether such behavior is rewarded or expected. In general, adults set examples for children. Logically, then, it would seem that the more aggressive the adult's behavior, the more aggressive the child's. This view is supported by several studies (Bandura & Huston, 1961; Bandura, Ross, & Ross, 1961) in which preschool children imitated or reproduced the behavior of the conductor of the experiment, who was their model. An aggressive model elicited a greater amount of aggressive behavior than a nonaggressive model (see Figure 15-1). Failure in a competitive situation has been found to increase the likelihood that children will imitate the aggressive behavior of a model (Nelson, Gelfand, & Hartman, 1969). This supports the notion discussed above that conditions promoting aggressive behavior (e.g., frustration and modeling) often are found in combination in the child's environment.

Interestingly enough, boys show more aggression than girls after exposure to an aggressive *male* model. In the development of aggressive behavior the father plays a particularly pivotal role, just as he is a more important source of frustration than the mother. Indeed, a correlation of +0.33 was obtained by Eron et al. (1961) between ratings of paternal aggression and child aggressiveness at home. And Winder and Rau (1962), in a study of the parental attitudes of deviant preadolescent boys, found parents of the aggressive boys to score higher in aggressiveness than parents of nonaggressive counterparts.

In one study pertinent to the notion that parents serve as models for a child's aggression, it was observed that children most closely identified with their parents displayed the most aggression in the doll-play sessions (Levin & Sears, 1956).

FIGURE 15-1 (By permission of the American Psychological Association and Albert Bandura.)

This was particularly true for boys whose fathers did the punishing. Since boys from homes in which the father was absent showed less aggression in doll play than boys from intact homes (Sears, 1951; Bach, 1946), boys might be thought less likely to act aggressively in the absence of an aggressive male model. In similar manner, more aggression is evident in lower-class children than in those from the middle class (McKee & Leader, 1955) because the lower-class male serves as the model is seen as typically aggressive, at least in the overt physical mannerisms that might prove most significant.

While the discussion here has focused upon parents as models, everyday observation indicates that the child may imitate others in his environment as well. Siblings, peers, and other adults may serve as models. In fact, several studies with preschoolers have shown that exposure to aggressive behavior in another child is highly effective in eliciting imitative aggressive behavior (Hicks, 1965; Dubanoski & Parton, 1971). It seems that, in general, the more the child is exposed to aggressive behavior in others, the more likely he is to manifest such behavior himself.

Permissiveness of Aggression. This notion rests on the fact that aggression is more likely to occur when it is permitted. An increase in doll-play aggression in a permissive situation has been observed from session to session. This has been taken to signify that in a permissive atmosphere the child's fear of punishment for aggressive behavior diminishes and his inhibitions concerning the show of aggression lessen. The accepting, nonreproachful attitude of the adult is perceived by the child as granting him permission to exhibit aggression.

However, another interpretation is plausible. The amount of session-to-session aggression manifested by pairs of 7- to 10-year-old boys in a permissive, free-play situation was observed under two conditions (Siegel & Kohn, 1959): the presence of a permissive adult and the absence of any adult. Under the former condition, the typical increase of aggression in playing with dolls was noted from one session to the next. Under the latter condition, however, there was a drop in aggressive behavior from the first session to the second. Thus when an adult is present the child presumably tends to transfer certain ego functions, such as control of disapproved or punishable behavior, to him. In the absence of the adult the child must exercise his own self-control.

The Fels studies (Baldwin, 1948) indicated that one effect of democracy in the home was to raise the child's activity level. Since there is a connection between sheer level of activity and aggressiveness, this helps to explain the greater aggression noted in children from democratic or permissive homes. Democratic parents incline toward tolerating all child behaviors, including quarreling, activeness, and aggression. In the Pattern Study a slight relationship was seen between aggressive conduct in the child and the mother's permissiveness of aggression. Sears argued that maternal permissiveness signaled the child that aggressive behavior was acceptable; it was not punishable and was expected by the mother to occur. Yet Lynn (1961), in testing the Pattern Study's finding, could not discover such a link between aggression in children and maternal permissiveness of aggressive behavior. However, Lynn did observe a relationship between scores of a mother's extroversion and both her tendency to be permissive and her child's aggression in school. Lynn suggested the existence of a genetic factor since other studies also found a connection between extroversion and aggression.

The case for the notion that aggressiveness in children is abetted by a permissive atmosphere in the home is not clear-cut. The idea does not explain the original onset of aggression. Possibly, however, parental reluctance to punish various sorts of child behavior tacitly encourages such behaviors when their exercise is rewarding to the child. Regarding aggression, a child's frustrations are relieved by striking someone interfering with or interrupting his activity. If this behavior is allowed by parents, the tendency for aggressive behavior to recur in similar situations is reinforced.

Sex Differences. That boys are more aggressive than girls appears early in life and can be observed in a variety of settings and situations. Besides, children themselves perceive boys as the more aggressive of the sexes. Studies of the middle childhood years (Winder & Rau, 1962) and also of adolescence (Eron et al., 1961) show peers nominating boys oftener than girls as deporting themselves aggressively. It is likely that the sources of this greater male aggressiveness are both environmental and biological.

The boy's identification with his father signifies association of himself with a relatively aggressive model for his eventual role. Moreover, at least in America, it is the cultural expectation that boys will display more aggressiveness than girls. Indeed, aggression is tolerated and often urged on boys; their show of aggression is reinforced. And in the Pattern Study mothers appeared to be less permissive of aggression in girls than in boys. Following up the 5-year-olds of the Pattern Study when they were 12, Sears (1961) rated boys higher in antisocial aggression and girls higher in anxiety over aggression. Apparently the unwillingness to permit aggressive behavior in girls gave them greater anxiety over its exhibition.

Kagan and Moss (1962) in their longitudinal study from childhood to adulthood reported greater long-term stability of aggressive conduct in males than females. Conceivably aggression is allowed in boys during their developmental years, but not in girls; it does not fit the cultural cliché of feminine, ladylike deportment. In fact, one experimental study (Martin, Gelfand, & Hartmann, 1971) showed that girls are less likely than boys to display aggressive behavior in the presence of an adult. The frustration-aggression hypothesis may help account for sex differences in aggression. The higher activity level of boys may engulf them in more frustrating situations. This might explain Fite's (1940) assertion of a relationship between aggression and level of activity. Then, too, the fact that parents in general and fathers in particular have greater expectations for their sons than for their daughters may produce frustration in boys.

The point was made that biological determinants of aggression cannot be ignored. Activity level rests in part on the nervous system. Greater nervous irritability may be typical of the male. Sex differences in longevity and in incidence of certain illnesses suggest that males may be more susceptible biologically to environmental pressures. Thus a complex interaction of biological and environmental forces may cause sex differences as well as individual differences in behavior—including aggressive behavior.

Aggression and Popularity. The hostile feelings underlying aggression do not promote positive social exchange. Aggression is likely to incur counteraggression. Not surprisingly, the relation between popularity and aggression through childhood and adolescence is negative (Winder & Rau, 1962; Eron et al., 1961). Among lower-class fifth- and sixth-graders, Lesser (1959) gathered Guess Who nominations for five categories of aggressive activity; *provoked physical aggression*—to attack or injure physically upon provocation; *outburst aggression*—to explode in an uncontrolled temper tantrum; *unprovoked physical aggression*—to attack or harm physically without provocation; *verbal aggression*—to attack or damage verbally; and *indirect aggression*—to attack or injure through some other person or object. Between popularity and provoked physical aggression the correlation was positive; the relation of popularity to the other four categories was negative. Most disapproved was indirect aggression, with verbal, unprovoked physical, and outburst aggression following in that order.

Too much aggressive behavior implies some basic maladjustment. Either the child has not learned better ways of responding to environmental forces or his need for aggression is so strong that he cannot behave otherwise. However this may be, it is not looked upon with favor by the child's peers.

Anxiety

This has been called the "age of anxiety." Commemorated in Auden's verse, intoned in Bernstein's music, encapsulated in Robbin's choreography, it has also received a great amount of attention in popular literature as well as in the writings of psychologists, sociologists, and philosophers. Modern man is beset by intense feelings of anxiety that arise from a plethora of causes ranging from the threat of nuclear annihilation to the insecurities resulting from the breakdown of the family as a social unit. The main concern here are the signs, symptoms, and antecedents of anxiety in children.

Psychological Theories. Freud made a distinction between fear and anxiety (see May, 1950). In fear, the individual's concern is drawn to the threat arising from a specific object. Anxiety, on the other hand, may be considered a generalized fear, which is a condition within the individual. Freud further distinguished objective anxiety from neurotic anxiety. The former is a reaction to external dangers, a protective, self-preservation mechanism, whereas neurotic anxiety appears in the absence of any apparent danger and is anticipatory in nature. Freud held that although the capacity for anxiety is innate, its appearance is the result of learning—learning stemming primarily from the child's early emotional relations with the parents. Describing a number of causes of anxiety, Freud stressed the importance in neurotic anxiety of the child's fear of loss of or separation from the mother.

To Rank, best known for his notion of *birth trauma,* anxiety arises from the individual's fear of the endless number of separations that occur from early childhood onward in the process of acquiring autonomy, independence, and individuality. The beginning of school may be one such threatening experience, involving as it does a partial disruption of the child's previous closeness with the mother.

Adler, in a sense, equated anxiety with neurotic feelings of inferiority that arise from the child's evaluation of himself as weaker and less competent than others. Basic anxiety, according to Horney, is a product of the child's conflict between dependence on parents and hostile feelings toward them. In general, anxiety arises from any threat to the individual's security. Sullivan thought that such threats originate in the infant even before the development of conscious awareness and result from his fear of disapproval from the important persons in his interpersonal environment. Because approval, especially from the mother, is of such crucial importance to the child, he tends to mold his behavior to conform to her demands and expectations. Anxiety arises whenever there are tendencies that may bring disapproval from others. These tendencies are therefore repressed, and such repression imposes a restriction on the child's awareness and on his developing sense of the self. As Sullivan saw it, anxiety is antithetical to emotional health, which denotes personal awareness and personal growth.

Finally, in his early work with the notion of anxiety, Mowrer saw anxiety as a conditioned form of reaction to pain. It is a strong motivating force for behavior since the organism seeks to reduce the level of anxiety and reinforces any behavior serving that purpose. Later Mowrer cited the origin of anxiety as repressed fears and the guilt associated with them.

Thus anxiety that arises initially in infancy or early childhood is an outgrowth of the child's relations with his parent. Whereas fear is a response to specific environmental danger, anxiety is a reaction to a pervasive threat to the individual's security. Certain fears are normal and desirable in the growing child. Anxiety, however, is restrictive rather than constructive.

Signs of Anxiety. Two broad types of behavior indicating anxiety can be discerned in children. In the first, the child avoids a large number of situations and experiences as though each possessed some potential danger. His world becomes restricted as a result; he retreats from life and his conduct becomes rigid and stereotyped. In the second type, the child's demeanor resembles "flight reaction"; he is restless, hyperactive, nervous, and uneasy. In both types, attention to the task at hand, persistence of a constructive nature, and interpersonal relations are all disrupted and impaired. Such children, of course, remain in a state of emotional conflict.

Characteristics of Anxiety. Evolving from the Taylor Manifest Anxiety Scale (Taylor, 1953) for identifying the strength of the anxiety drive in adults, several scales have been devised to assess the characteristics of anxious children. One of these, consisting of 53 items, requires the child to respond either "yes" or "no" to such statements as the following:

> It is hard for me to keep my mind on anything.
> I worry most of the time.
> My feelings get hurt easily.
> Often I feel sick in my stomach.
> I have bad dreams.
> (Castenada, McCandless, & Palermo, 1956, pp. 318–319)

Another test was designed expressly to detect the amount of anxiety experienced by children in a school test situation (Sarason, Davidson, Lighthall, & Waite, 1958a). Subsequent studies have examined various characteristics differentiating children who score high and low on an anxiety scale.

The effects of anxiety on intelligence and learning have received considerable attention. Despite some contradictory results, there has been a consistent negative correlation between anxiety and both intelligence and school achievement at the elementary-school level (McCandless & Castenada, 1956; Feldhusen & Klausmeier, 1962) and also at the senior-high level (Sarason, 1963). It is likely that anxiety impairs a child's intellectual functioning—as though so much of his attention and effort is diverted to coping with his problems that he cannot apply himself sufficiently to other tasks. In this sense the child is certainly emotionally handicapped. However, there is some evidence that a moderate degree of anxiety concerning achievement may be useful for certain children. In a study of third-grade boys (Messer, 1970), anxiety concerning performance was induced by exposing them to a failure experience. On a subsequent task, highly impulsive boys made fewer errors and they tended to behave in a more reflective manner than they had earlier. This suggests that for these impulsive children, anxiety served a positive function by increasing their attentiveness to the task, and they approached the task more cautiously and more deliberately. Several reports of a longitudinal study examining the relation between test anxiety and IQ and school achievement are now available (Sarason, Hill, & Zimbardo, 1964; Hill & Sarason, 1966). Though the findings are complex, several patterns emerge clearly: (1) The negative correlation typically obtained between test anxiety and both IQ and school achievement increases in magnitude throughout the elementary-school years, indicating that the effects of anxiety become increasingly detrimental to adequate school performance throughout this period; (2) extreme shifts in anxiety are related to reciprocal changes in IQ and achievement, so that, for example, a child who decreased markedly in anxiety level over time showed a corresponding increase in IQ and school achievement; (3) anxiety depresses reading achievement more noticeably than it affects scores on arithmetic subtests, suggesting that more emphasis and pressure are placed on the child by parent and teacher in the area of reading than in other academic skills. Another possibility is that reading is a more complex task than arithmetic and therefore it is affected to a greater extent by anxiety. An experimental study (Cotler, 1969) involving oral reading by high- and low-anxious fourth- through sixth-grade boys found that the high-anxious boys read more slowly and more inaccurately than the low-anxious boys. These findings suggest also that lessons requiring oral performance (recitation, oral reading) are emotionally upsetting to anxious children because of the stress produced; consequently, written lessons might be preferable.

Experimental studies on the relation of anxiety to learning have concluded that school children high in anxiety—that is, in motivation—surpass those low in anxiety on simple tasks but prove inferior on complex ones (Castenada, Palermo, & McCandless, 1956). This does not appear to be the case, however, in studies of college students (Buskirk, 1961; Sarason, 1961). From these investigations, the conclusion was reached that anxious subjects did not necessarily perform less well on complex tasks but that their performance was inferior on tasks entailing threats to their feelings of adequacy. This fits with the position that anxiety results from any threat to individual security. Clearly, therefore, in a school situation children, particularly anxious ones, function best in a secure, nonthreatening atmosphere.

Research relating anxiety to other personality characteristics falls into a consistent pattern. Highly anxious children are less popular with peers than children of low anxiety (McCandless, Castenada, & Palermo, 1956). They have less positive self concepts (Lipsitt, 1958; Horowitz, 1962); they express more dissatification with themselves and others (Phillips, Hindsman, & Jennings, 1960); and in general they express more negative feelings than less anxious children (Barnard, Zimbardo, & Sarason, 1961). At the middle elementary-school level significant correlations have been obtained between scores on the Children's Manifest Anxiety Test and teacher ratings of adjustment as well as scores of the California Test of Personality (Iscoe & Cochran, 1960; Cowen, Zax, Klein, Izzo,

& Trost, 1965). The more anxious children were rated as more maladjusted by their teachers who, in part, defined maladjustment on the basis of restlessness, lack of attention, and inability or unwillingness to "settle down."

In classroom observations, highly anxious boys show less orientation toward tasks than boys of low anxiety; they also display greater insecurity in their relation with their teacher. Among girls, however, the highly anxious are less distractible and evince a stronger need for achievement than those low in anxiety (Sarason, Davidson, Lighthall, & Waite, 1958b). Apparently anxiety operates in different ways with respect to sex. Psychoanalytic writers have argued that boys and girls handle anxiety differently. Girls are said to employ *autoplastic* defenses–defenses involving the individual herself, as in daydreaming–whereas boys handle anxiety through *alloplastic* defenses–defenses in which the individual turns outward toward other persons or objects, as in rebelliousness. Covert versus overt behavior may distinguish between boys and girls in this respect. Consistently, girls score higher on anxiety scales (Castenada et al., 1956), implying that in American society it is easier for females than males to admit they are anxious (Davidson, Sarason, Lighthall, Waite, & Sarnoff, 1958; L'Abate, 1960). Nervousness is a woman's prerogative, whereas it is the man who develops an ulcer.

The idea that anxiety exerts a constricting influence on behavior is buttressed by studies indicating that the more anxious children score higher on scales measuring "rigidity of thinking" (Kitano, 1960). These children also show greater rigidity in their drawings (Fox, Davidson, Lighthall, Waite, & Sarason, 1958) and in their behavior (Smock, 1958); and they prefer familiar rather than novel stimuli (Mendel, 1965). Related to this is the finding that dependency characterizes the behavior of anxious children (Sarason et al., 1958b). Since dependency is often a sign of insecurity, anxiety, dependency, and insecurity are interrelated causally. They constrict and restrict the child's behavior and his world.

Parental Antecedents. Not much has been turned up so far in research regarding parental antecedents of anxiety, perhaps partly because mothers of highly anxious children have taken a highly defensive stance in interviews (Davidson, 1959). They are less frank in their responses and are less willing to divulge information about themselves. Possibly they are themselves anxious and insecure or they may be defensive for reasons of guilt over nonacceptance of their children. Mothers of children low in anxiety indicated that their children were free to express feelings of anger and aggression (Davidson, 1959). That family influences on the development of anxiety in children merit intensive examination was emphasized in a study (Adams & Sarason, 1963) that found significant correlations between anxiety test scores of high-school students, especially girls, and their mothers. Apparently anxious mothers extablish the kind of home atmosphere that produces anxiety in the children. Anxiety may well be contagious.

Conscience Development

Conscience is sometimes defined with tongue in cheek as "that which keeps us from doing what we shouldn't do even when no one is looking." Indeed, this definition lights upon a major element in the idea of conscience: inner controls based on an individual's acceptance of values concerning right and wrong behavior. Yet there are other kinds of control of behavior. Control may be external in origin, resting in the prohibitions and demands of others. In Chapter 7 the distinction was noted between *guilt* and *shame* cultures, the latter controlling behavior by shame—fear of punishment, ridicule, ostracism, retribution—and the former by internalizing society's standards. One other point about conscience: inner controls are learned, as are the values to which they relate.

Between the Hartshorne and May (1928) study and the late 1950's, little concern was shown over conscience development in children. Matters of values and conscience were apparently not thought to be appropriate topics for scientific research. Then Sears (1960) noted that the identification of the child-rearing antecedents of inner controls and sanctions signified "one of the most important problems facing students of personality development today" (p. 97). Miller and Swanson (1960) saw moral standards in terms of inner conflict. Three reasons were advanced for this approach: moral needs, that is, internalized standards, are frequently the cause of conflict within the individual; the manner in which these conflicts are resolved depends on the particular moral values held by the individual; and each individual employs characteristic ways of resolving conflicts, and these are thought of as his "character structure."

Among adults, some are faced more frequently than others with conflicts over moral issues. Such conflicts are likelier, however, to involve a position taken on some moral issue than overt behavior, as in childhood. For example, is racial discrimination in public housing acceptable? Is nuclear war justified? Can unfair business competition be condoned? Most likely the mature adult resolves such issues in a rather consistent manner, and when he does employ defenses such as rationalization to avoid facing a conflict, they are a stable part of his personality. No wonder an understanding of conscience is essential to an understanding of human behavior.

Antecedents. There are three principal elements that affect the development of conscience. First, a culture's values or standards form an important part of the legacy transmitted to a child by his parents; one culture may discourage aggressiveness, another emphasize self-effacement, a third espouse personal recognition. The second factor is the child's intellectual development. An older, more intellectually mature child is better able to perceive what is expected of him; he can understand the reasons for certain restrictions and standards; he is able to generalize a principle and apply it to a variety of situations. More than a younger child, the older one can comprehend some of the abstract concepts behind social issues—unselfishness, equality, justice, truth. Third is the child's relations with his parents. Several research techniques have been used to study parental influences on development of conscience. In the Pattern Study, mothers were asked to indicate signs of conscience in their childhood. Two criteria were used; the child's tendency to "act the parental role," that is, his attempt to teach parental standards to siblings and friends; and the child's behavior following a wrongdoing, that is, his attempts to confess, apologize, or make amends. Evidence of the development of a conscience was rated on the following scale (Sears et al., 1957, p. 381):

1. No evidence. Child hides, denies, does not seem unhappy when naughty.
2. Little evidence of conscience.
3. Moderate conscience development. May not confess directly but looks sheepish; seldom denies.
4. Considerable conscience.
5. Strong conscience. Child feels miserable when naughty; always confesses; never denies; strong need for forgiveness.

The concept employed most frequently to explain the child's internalization of adult standards is identification. Factors producing a strong identification with the parent tend to encourage development of conscience. Kindergarten boys who were highly masculine, presumably because of identification with their fathers, were also high in conscience development (Mussen & Distler, 1960). Moreover, boys from father-absent homes have been found to be somewhat retarded in conscience as compared with boys from father-present homes (Hoffman, 1971a). No such effect has been found for girls, suggesting that conscience development in the girl derives from her identification with her mother.

Research on the relation between identification and moral behavior has been somewhat inconclusive (Hoffman, 1971b). This may be due to several factors: (1) Identification is not an all-or-none process. For whatever reason, children may identify with some aspects of his parents' behavior and not with others; thus, he may adopt only some of their behaviors. (2) The behaviors or values under consideration must be obvious and clear-cut to the child before he will adopt them. Thus, the child is more likely to adopt his parents' value orientation if they communicate these values clearly to him. (3) Inconsistency between parents may lead to behavior in the child which is dissimilar to that of either parent.

There is some experimental evidence that in a temptation situation children will imitate a model who yields to temptation (Stein, 1967). This suggests that parents serve rather directly as models for their children with regard to moral behavior. Research has dealt with two factors in particular regarding this antecedent of conscience development: the type of parental discipline and the warmth of the parent-child relationship.

As to disciplinary activity in the home, the Pattern Study indicated that psychological or love-oriented techniques exemplified in praise, isolation, and withdrawal of love aided the development of conscience more than the materialistic or physical methods embodied in tangible rewards, deprivation, and physical punishment. MacKinnon's (1938) investigation of college students found that those who transgressed prohibitions in an experimental setting were likelier to be children of fathers whose disciplinary tactics had been physical rather than psychological. Yet a study of four-year-olds (Burton, Maccoby, & Allinsmith, 1961) on resistance to cheating did not support these findings. In this investigation, scolding and physical punishment were more closely related to resistance to temptation than were psychological punishments or use of reasoning. Direct, physical techniques seemed most effective in the young child, although psychological techniques encouraging identification with the parent took over as the child grew older and gained in cognitive development.

Most efforts to link conscience development to specific child-rearing practices, such as the age and severity of toilet training, have not borne fruit (Grinder, 1962; Burton et al., 1961). Perhaps, as noted in the chapters on parental influences on children, the general psychological atmosphere of the home may be more important. In the Pattern Study, the threat to withdraw love, a psychological device, had little effect if the mother was relatively cold and rejecting. Conversely, it proved most effective when the child's relationship with his mother was warm and accepting. Thus the non-accepted child has little to lose by displaying disapproved behavior. Only 18 percent of the rejected children covered in the Pattern Study were judged as having "high conscience," compared with 31 percent of the accepted group. And in support of the MacKinnon (1938) finding about the import of the kind of discipline practiced by the father, stronger consciences were observed in boys with accepting fathers than boys with fathers who tended to reject them. No such difference was detected, however, in girls.

Two major family qualities are tied to a strong superego in children, that is, to the "presence of an effectively behavior-guiding conscience"—a combination of mutal trust and approval, and consistency (Peck, 1958). An atmosphere of mutual trust inspires the child to absorb his parents' values and standards, which the child accepts for his own. Logically, a consistent pattern of parental control and expectations provides a clear-cut setting for the development of positive conduct.

> A useful distinction could be made, for example, between intraparental and interparental inconsistency. The former type would include such behaviors as punishing a given behavior on one occasion but not another; not following through on threats and warnings of punishment; and saying one thing and doing something else, perhaps even the direct opposite of what was said. Interparental inconsistency might involve one of the parents punishing and the other rewarding a given behavior; one of the parents verbally prohibiting a given behavior while the other parent engages in the forbidden act; and the issuance of discrepant verbal instructions to the child—for example, one parent permitting and the other parent prohibiting a given behavior. (Stouwie, 1971, p. 1518).

Predicted results were obtained in a study (Stouwie, 1971) of the effect of inconsistent verbal instructions on children's resistance to temptation behavior. These instructions were given by a male and a female experimenter to children in four different groups regarding playing with toys available in the experimental room:

Consistent Prohibitive:

F: While you're waiting here, you may not play with the toys.

M: Yes, don't play with the toys.

F: Remember now, don't play with them.

M: That's right, they probably belong to someone else.

Consistent Permissive:

F: While you're waiting here, you can play with the toys.

M: Yes, go ahead, play with the toys.

F: It's OK, you can play with them.

M: That's right, they probably don't belong to anybody else.

Inconsistent, Permissive First:

F: While you're waiting here, you can play with the toys.

M: No, you better not play with the toys. The probably belong to someone else.

F: Oh, it's OK, you may play with them. They probably don't belong to anybody else.

M: Remember now, don't play with them.

Inconsistent, Prohibitive First:

F: While you're waiting here, you may not play with the toys.

M: Oh, you can play with the toys. They probably don't belong to anybody else.

F: No, don't play with them. They probably belong to someone else.

M: Oh, it's OK, go ahead and play with them.

(Stouwie, 1971, p. 1522)

Following the instructions, the experimenters left the room and observed the children's behavior for 15 minutes through a one-way vision window.

The children who received the permissive instructions showed the longest duration of playing with the toys; those receiving the prohibitive instructions playing with the toys the least; and those given inconsistent instructions were intermediate between these two groups. In addition, the children in the inconsistent group showed signs of conflict and uncertainty; approach-avoidance behavior, in the form of reaching out toward the toys and quickly drawing back, was evident. Clearly, children face the difficult task of attempting to resolve the conflict produced by inconsistent parental demands, prohibitions, and expectations. Similar conflict results when there are inconsistencies between home and school in standards of behavior.

Relationship With Other Variables

Research has examined the relation between moral behavior and a great many other variables including sex differences, school grades, motivation for achievement, IQ, ability to delay reward, and internal-external locus of control (the extent to which the individual feels he is in control of his own destiny).

First, with regard to sex differences, the findings are inconclusive. The early pioneer work by Hartshorne and May (1928) on deceit in children found few sex differences. The findings of subsequent studies have been contradictory, and it appears likely that sex differences in tendency to cheat depend in part on the measures employed. For example, Medinnus (1966) found that girls were more likely to cheat on a measure asking them to check the number of books they had read, while boys cheated more on a target-shooting task. In other words, tendency to cheat was related to the extent to which the children felt ego involved in the task and wished to perform well on it. There is some evidence that girls more than boys are motivated to cheat in order to gain social approval (Keasey, 1971).

In a study of cheating among fifth-graders (Johnson & Gormely, 1972), a relation was found between cheating and school grades, with a greater frequency of cheating among students with low school marks. There is a contamination here with intelligence, and, in general, a relation has been found between IQ and honesty, with brighter children less likely to cheat. It is not clear whether brighter children are more honest; whether they are more clever in their cheating techniques and thus are less likely to be detected; or whether they feel less need for cheating because of their ability to perform well without doing so.

Research evidence has been obtained showing that children cheat to avoid unfavorable comparison with peers (Shelton & Hill, 1969). This suggests that cheating is more likely to occur in situations where a premium is placed on high achievement and where the rankings of students on performance is made available to the group.

Certainly such situational variables as the value the child attaches to the reward for good performance plays a part in determining whether he will cheat in order to receive the reward (Dmitruk, 1971). At all age levels, including adulthood, it is pursuit of the highly desired object that most tempts one to falsify and deceive.

Another important variable is the extent to which a child observes the results of dishonesty by others. If no dire consequences result from dishonest behavior on the part of one individual, others are more likely to follow his example than if the individual is punished for yielding to temptation. Research has shown that boys are particularly vulnerable to imitating the behavior of others, depending upon the consequences of the model's behavior (Slaby & Parke, 1971).

Summary. Development of conscience, then, needs to be understood in order to understand the development of personality, for the manner in which the individual resolves a moral conflict is a stable aspect of his personality. As significant as are the cultural lessons transmitted by parents, the child's own intellectual growth, and also his identification with parents, which leads to adoption of their values and to acquisition of inner controls, nothing counts as much as an atmosphere of warmth in the relationship between parents and child. Mutual trust, acceptance, and consistency combined with warmth are likely to assure strong conscience when childhood gives way to adolescence.

Dominant-Submissive Behavior

A hierarchy of behavior ranging from dominance to submissiveness has been seen many times in the social interaction of a wide assortment of organisms including rats, dogs, monkeys, domestic fowl, and humans. Implied in this pecking order is the jockeying for position, the maneuvering for power that is virtually an integral part of all social interaction, regardless of species. Here, too, we see the structure of groups, whose members can be ranked with respect to dominance and submission.

Factor analyses of personality tests and ratings almost invariably find a factor designated ascendance, or dominance, or assertiveness both at child (Cattell & Gruen, 1953; Cattell & Coan, 1957) and adult (Cattell, 1957) levels. In the paragraphs that follow we shall summarize some of the early studies that contributed methodologically to the investigation of ascendant behavior in children, and then turn to the antecedents of dominance and submissiveness and to the characteristics of leadership.

Experimental Studies. A noteworthy study is Jack's (1934), which sought experimentally to modify behavior. Jack observed four-year-olds in pairs in a room supplied with a sandbox and three types of toy. The following eight types of behavior were used in defining ascendance.

1. Verbal attempts to secure play material.
2. Forceful attempts to secure play materials.
3. Success in securing material from companion's possession.
4. Defense and snatching back of materials taken from one's possession.
5. Verbal attempts to direct behavior of companion.
6. Companion compliance with direction.
7. Forbidding, criticizing, reproving companion.
8. Providing pattern of behavior which companion imitates.

Concluding that the most significant difference between ascendant and nonascendant children was degree of self-confidence, Jack applied special training materials in her effort to modify the behavior of the five least ascendant youngsters. Later, when she paired them again in the experimental room, the ascendance scores of these particular youngsters showed significant gain.

Page (1936) achieved similar results among three- and four-year-olds. Yet Page noted that teacher ratings of ascendance away from the experimental setting did not change as a result of the modification of the children's behavior through training. Therefore she questioned whether the results of the training spread to the environment beyond the training room. Though lacking data on long-term effects of training, psychologists find it significant that by increasing a child's self-confidence through developing certain skills and proficiencies in him, they can alter his behavior in a social situation.

Similar modification of behavior was reported by Chittenden (1942). She provided special tutelage to 10 preschool children who were most dominating in their relations with other children. Conflicts involving dolls were analyzed, with the social and emotional consequences of certain kinds of behavior emphasized. Tests conducted after the training disclosed that these children had increased their cooperative behavior.

An interesting study (Blum & Kennedy, 1967) found that dominative behavior can be increased through reinforcement. Children were rewarded when the choice made by the nondominant member of a pair prevailed. Subsequently, the nondominant member made an increasing number of dominant responses. While the early studies emphasized training in dominative or assertive behavior, it appears that administering reinforcement (reward) for dominative behavior is effective in increasing its likelihood of occurrence, thus modifying a child's behavior on this dimension.

Dominant-Submissive Antecedents. Dominant behavior is observable in children at least as young as three years of age. It is also observable in lower organisms. Conceivably, therefore, constitutional factors predisposing an individual to dominance play a role in such behavior. Nevertheless, this does not eliminate the role of environmental antecedents.

Part of the problem of identifying the antecedents of ascendant behavior results from a confusion in nomenclature. Jack clearly did not differentiate between acceptable and unacceptable kinds of behavior in the types she selected to define ascendance. This distinction largely appeared later. Chittenden (1942) embraced both dominating and cooperative behavior in the term "assertiveness." H. H. Anderson (1937, 1939, 1946), it will be recalled, distinguished dominating from integrating behavior. In a similar vein, Parten (1932) described two types of leader: the bully, who used brute force and bossing, and the diplomat, who used artful and indirect suggestion. Finally, Mummery (1947) spoke of socially acceptable and socially unacceptable behavior.

Various distinctions between socially positive and socially negative types of domination aid in resolving some of the disagreement over parental antecedents of dominating behavior. From some of the Fels studies, Baldwin (1948, 1949) concluded that democracy in the home, expecially an actively democratic home, tended to produce an active, aggressive child, likely to be a leader. Children from restrictive, controlled homes tend to be unaggressive and fearful. Baldwin reasoned that freedom in the home encouraged active exploration of the environment and a high degree of social participation. In agreement with the Fels data, Miles (in H. H. Anderson, 1946) noted that parents of adolescent leaders were less restrictive in handling their children. The child enjoyed the freedom to make his own decisions and judgments and to experiment with new opportunities.

These findings, however, contradicted those of an investigation by Meyer (1947) who, in rating homes of 29 preschool children on the 30 Fels Parent Behavior Scales, found significant negative correlations between their dominating responses under experimental conditions and such home atmosphere as democracy of policy, readiness of explanation, understanding of child's problems, and rapport with child. The homes of the dominant children were characterized by disciplinary friction and general discord. Similarly, Radke (1946) reported that children from autocratic homes tended to dominate their companions more readily than children from democratic homes. They were also less considerate of their peers. To Mummery (1954) the chief effect of democracy in the home was perhaps to influence the child's self concept in terms of self-acceptance and self-confidence. Because democratic parents respect the individuality of the child, it is likely that he will show respect for his peers in social situations. If such a child displays assertive behavior it will generally be socially acceptable, integrating, and cooperative in nature.

Leadership Behavior. Although not synonymous with dominating behavior, leadership has much in common with it. Leadership implies the successful use of techniques to guide and direct the behavior of others toward an agreed goal. Dominating behavior, on the other hand, may or may not succeed and may or may not involve a shared goal. Whether children who are dominating in the preschool period assume leadership in elementary-school years is not certain from the scant evidence at hand. Equally sparse is evidence relating to the transferability of leadership from one group to another.

Yet leadership is a topic of interest to social psychologists who deal with adult behavior. In general, there are two approaches to the subject (Allen, 1952). *Structuralists* regard leadership as a trait or a set of traits. *Functionalists* view it as a function of the situation. The two positions may be synthesized if leadership is considered in terms of role theory and role expectancy. It is likely that children who later become leaders possess in childhood the earmarks of leadership. The inclusion of leadership capacities in the child's concept of the self results from the successful use of these characteristics in opportunities to lead. Effective leadership in one situation inspires the child to assert it in others. Through repeated successes the notion of leadership becomes an integral part of the self concept. Furthermore, as others expect an individual to continue to lead, this contributes to further exhibition of leadership demeanor. Reputation occasions the repeated display of specific behaviors in children even if the repute is undeserved.

Having reviewed the available data on the qualities inherent in leaders, Stogdill (1948) listed these characteristics in which leaders surpassed the average members of their groups: intelligence, scholarship, dependability in exercising responsibilities, activity and social participation, socioeconomic status, initiative, persistence, knowing how to get things done, self-confidence, alertness to and insight into situations, cooperativeness, popularity, adaptability, verbal facility, athletic ability, originality, desire to excel, judgment, humor, chronological age, height, weight, appearance, energy, dominance, integrity, and mood control. These factors, Stogdill (1948, p. 64) concluded, could probably be classified under the following headings.

1. Capacity (intelligence, alertness, verbal facility, originality, judgment).
2. Achievement (scholarship, knowledge, athletic accomplishments).
3. Responsibility (dependability, initiative, persistence, aggressiveness, self-confidence, desire to excel).
4. Participation (activity, sociability, cooperation, adaptability, humor).
5. Status (socio-economic position, popularity).
6. Situation (mental level, status, skills, needs and interests of followers, objectives to be achieved, etc).

As much as the traits seem to support the structuralist approach to leadership, Stogdill pointed out that the qualities and skills enabling an individual to function as a leader depended on the demands of the group and the situation. In preschool years, mere activity level is enough to determine leadership (Parten, 1932); in late elementary-school years and throughout adolescence, athletic ability and physical prowess are the important requisites for leadership among boys (Partridge, 1934); in college empathy is the key to leadership (Bell & Hall, 1954). Since the functionalists are also correct, leaders are made as well as born.

Social Acceptance

Social psychologists who contend that Americans place too much emphasis on sociability, adjustment to the group, and "other-directedness" support their complaint by pointing to the amount of research on social acceptance in the field of child psychology. Yet there are a number of reasons to believe that a child's degree of acceptance by his peers is of more than fleeting or superficial significance. Children not well accepted by their peers tend to express less positive feelings toward them (Lippitt & Gold, 1959), and it is reasonable to consider positive feelings toward others as one sign of mental health. Moreover, a significant relation has been found between self-acceptance and acceptance by others, with children holding a low self concept designated as "least popular" by peers (Guardo, 1969). In the classroom, poor pupil-to-pupil relationships is one indication of an unfavorable climate for learning and for positive group interaction (Spector, 1953).

The second reason for attaching importance to peer relationships is that early adjustment to peers is a good barometer for adjustment in adult life. Roff (1957, 1960, 1961) has been able to predict the adjustment of individuals to military service from comments made about them years before concerning their childhood relations with their peers. Early detection of difficulties in adult adjustment is possible, Roff held, from knowledge of the attitudes and opinions of an individual's associates regarding him. Undoubtedly, a vast number of persons who are not highly accepted by their peers in childhood make an adequate adjustment to adult life. There is a difference, though, between lack of acceptance and active rejection. The Roff data seem to indicate that it was active rejection to which he referred.

Finally, it is important to find the personality correlates of social acceptance because knowledge of them may make it possible to help children develop better relations with their peers. We have seen the negative correlations between social acceptance and aggressiveness, anxiety, and dependence. How can these aspects of personality be altered, modified, or altogether prevented?

Correlates of Social Acceptance. Efforts to isolate the factors bearing on social acceptance go back to the 1920's and the early 1930's. Furfey (1927) noted a tendency among preadolescent boys to elect chums of the same size, age, intelligence, and maturity as themselves. Challman (1932) found preschool children to be similar to their friends in chronological age, sociability, and physical activity. Similarities in mental age, height, extroversion, attractiveness of personality, IQ, and frequency of laughter mattered little in preschool choices of friendship. Lippitt (1941) noted cooperation in routines to be most clearly related to popularity in a group of preschool youngsters. Other correlates of social acceptance in children included socioeconomic status, school achievement, responsibility, cooperativeness, freedom from fears and anxieties, good health, attractiveness of appearance, and empathy. The following characteristics were closely related to popularity in a study of six-graders: athletic ability, answers questions in class, clean and neat, best school work, acts grown-up, best looking, and gregarious (Brozovich, 1970). Interestingly enough, the social desirability of a child's first name appears to be related to popularity (McDavid & Harari, 1966). Favorable or unfavorable connotations become attached to personal names, so that a child bearing an unpopular or unpleasant name may be handicapped in his social interactions with peers. Sex difference is also important, since there is an increasing separation by sex in friendship choices throughout the early elementary-school years. Further, girls receive higher social acceptance scores than boys. Table 15-1 lists the traits designated by a group of 13- to 15-year-old boys as characterizing their most acceptable peers.

In contrast to earlier studies, the more recent ones have tried to single out the antecedents causing different levels of social acceptance. In an interesting study of the extent of orientation toward self or parents versus peers (Hollander & Marcia, 1970), a group of fifth-graders were presented with six problematic situations which they had to resolve by choosing between peer values on the one hand and either their own or their parents' values on the other. The following are two examples of the situations used:

The Summer Camp

Suppose you have a chance to go to camp this summer. There are two possibilities. One camp has special things to do that you are interested in, but your friends are going to the other camp. Your friends want you to come with them. Put just one X mark below to show what you would really do.

GO TO THE CAMP
WITH MY FRIENDS

________ : ________ : ________

absolutely — fairly sure — maybe

GO TO THE CAMP
WITH THINGS I'M
INTERESTED IN

________ : ________ : ________

maybe — fairly sure — absolutely sure

The Halloween Prank

Suppose you are out with your friends on Halloween night. They want to soap some windows. Your parents have told you that it is wrong to hurt other people's property. Put just one X mark below to show what you would really do.

SOAP WINDOWS
WITH MY FRIENDS

________ : ________ : ________ :

absolutely sure — fairly sure — maybe

NOT SOAP WINDOWS
WITH MY FRIENDS

: ________ : ________ : ________

maybe — fairly sure — absolutely sure

(Hollander & Marcia, 1970, p. 294)

In addition, the extent to which the children's parents were peer-oriented was determined by three interview questions dealing with "a recent activity that the child had been forbidden to do, what the parents said, and did, and finally whether the argument that "the other kids can do it" was employed. Then the child was asked if this argument was successful in this instance or in similar ones" (p. 293). Sociometric ratings were made by having the children rate their classmates on each of the following descriptions: "(a) This is a classmate who does things independently. (b) This is a classmate who gets other children to do things. (c) This is a classmate who goes along with what the other children are doing. (d) This is a classmate who does what grown-ups think is right. (e) This is a classmate who gets along with other children." (p. 294). In general, a strong relation was found between the parents' peer-orientation and the children's peer-orientation. This suggests that the importance of "going along with the crowd" versus "be your own boss" is transmitted to the child from his parents. Children of parents low in

TABLE 15-1* Correlates of Social Acceptance in 13- to 15-Year-Old Boys

Identifying Number	Name	Illustrative Terms
1	Intelligent	Intelligent, keen, bright vs. Dumb, stupid
2	Sociable	Friendly, sociable vs. Unfriendly, too quiet, stiff
3	Minds own business	Minds own business vs. Annoying, pest
4	Plays fair	Good sport, plays fair vs. Poor sport, plays unfair
5	Quiet	Quiet vs. Loud, noisy, overtalkative
6	Witty	Humorous, witty, good joker vs. Not humorous, no sense of humor
7	Athletic	Athletic, ball player vs. Not athletic
8	Helpful	Helpful vs. Not helpful
9	Unconceited	Humble, doesn't show off vs. Conceited, stuck up
10	Good Company	Good company, fun to be with vs. No fun, poor company
11	Serious	Serious, not silly vs. Silly, foolish
12	Conscientious	Conscientious, good worker vs. Lazy, listless
13	Masculine	Real man, has guts vs. Sissy, helpless, girlish, fairy
14	Stays out of trouble	Stays out of trouble vs. Always in trouble
15	Talks well	Can talk, talks well vs. Can't talk
16	Honest	Honest, doesn't cheat vs. Dishonest, cheats, lies
17	Clean	Clean, neat vs. Sloppy, dirty
18	Doesn't fight	Doesn't fight vs. Always fighting
19	Kind	Kind, considerate vs. Unkind, not considerate, mean
20	Trustworthy	Trustworthy, keeps his word vs. Unreliable

*From Feinberg, Smith, & Schmidt, 1958.

peer-orientation were rated as independent by peers. Moreover, children who were parent- rather than peer-oriented were seen by the other children as "doing what grown-ups think is right." Interestingly, children high in peer-orientation

TABLE 15-1 *(Continued)*

Identifying Number	Name	Illustrative Terms
21	Gets along well with others	Gets along well with others vs. Can't get along
22	Leader	Leader vs. Not a leader
23	Cheerful	Cheerful vs. Grumpy, complains
24	Cooperative	Cooperative vs. Not cooperative
25	Good scholar	Good scholar, student vs. Poor scholar, student
26	Common interests	Same interests vs. Not same interests
27	Interesting	Interesting vs. Not interesting, dull
28	Good manners	Good manners vs. Poor manners
29	Pleasant, agreeable	Pleasant, agreeable vs. Argues, insults
30	Can take a joke	Can take a joke vs. Can't take a joke
31	Mature	Mature, grownup vs. Immature, babyish
32	Generous	Generous, unselfish vs. Tight, selfish
33	Good-looking	Good-looking, clean cut vs. Ugly
34	Good character	Good character vs. Poor character
35	Understanding	Understanding vs. Not understanding
36	Participates in activities	All around vs. No activities, doesn't take part
37	Calm	Calm, doesn't get excited, easy-going vs. Bad tempered, gets excited
38	Sincere	Sincere, means what he says vs. Insincere
39	Well dressed	Good dresser, sharp clothes vs. Poor dresser
40	Other specific terms used infrequently	
41	General nonspecific terms	Swell, good friend vs. No good, real drip

whose parents were also high in peer-orientation were least likely to be chosen as friends. Apparently too strong a need to be liked by others only leads to rejection. A secure independence is more desirable.

In another example, studying family influences on adjustment to peers, Hoffman (1961) noted that children from homes dominated by the mother experienced difficulties in their relations with the opposite sex. This was equally true for boys and girls. Influential as was an affectional relationship with the father on the adjustment of both boys and girls to peers, it was especially so for boys. An affectional relationship with the mother augured well for her daughter's adjustment to peers.

The rejected, unpopular child is often shy, recessive, socially disinterested, and self-centered. Even if he is noisy and energetic, his attempts at social acceptance by his agemates go unheeded. This may be because the behavior of such children is motivated by strong needs for attention and social approval. Usually they are unable to share, to take turns, and to comply with rules and regulations, thus disclosing an underlying insecurity. Whether lack of acceptance or unacceptable behavior comes first is hard to ascertain. It is likely that both are causes and both are effects: undesirable behavior leads to unpopularity, which leads to more undesirable behavior. The importance of therapeutic intervention by a trained adult is obvious.

The following two personality sketches are drawn from a study that investigated the personalities of five popular and five unpopular children. Their contents will add meaning to this discussion of the correlates of social acceptance.

> David is about average size for his age, and is quite good-looking. Always neat and clean, but not fussy or overly nice in appearance. Has a happy expression which radiates friendliness and good humor.
>
> David is outstanding in friendliness and social interest. He is "smooth" in interpersonal relationships; carries on a conversation with ease and poise. Shows more initiative than most children in meeting new-comers who enter the room. Goes out of his way to make them feel welcome, and to show them around the building. Never snubs anyone, but still he does not try to establish intimate relationships with those to whom he is not especially attracted. Would never consciously hurt anyone. Is always very courteous in his relations with both teachers and children. Shows more sympathetic concern for others than most children of his age. Sometimes he asks the teacher to allow him to help another child who has difficulty in his school work. Also, he has been observed to pull a larger boy off a smaller one on the playground when his sense of fairness has been violated. As a patrol leader in the halls, he has shown a marked interest in aiding the smallest children. In spite of these characteristics, it must also be stated that David is described as "egocentric" and "bull-headed" at times. One of his most frequent companions states that he has lots of quarrels with David because "David gets mad if you disagree with him." Also, David does not usually react very well to criticism. He shows some resentment and acts like he considers it unwarranted, but seldom says anything.
>
> David has a number of abilities which bring him group recognition. Is outstanding in dramatics. Often takes leading roles. Always knows his lines perfectly, and helps carry the entire performance. Also sings very well. Is a member of the school choir. Enjoys entertaining others. Likes to be before his public. Sometimes acts as an announcer. Has frequently been elected to class offices. He takes these obligations seriously and performs his duties well. As a patrolman in the sixth grade, he has been especially watchful and has shown marked ability in directing others and in getting them to do the right thing without antagonizing them. Is not bossy or dominating.
>
> In classroom academic work, David is not especially brilliant, but his work is nearly always better than average. He makes good contributions to class discussions. Is very dependable in having his written work in on time. Takes pride in

doing good school work and in making good grades. Also, he likes to please the teacher. Although David's application to his academic work is generally steady and conscientious, he seldom shows any initiative or originality. Prefers to be told what to do. Neither does he show much drive in trying to overcome problems that are very difficult. Is inclined to quit, and wait for the teacher to help him.

David conforms well to school regulations, but is not a perfectly behaved child. In the fourth grade he was paddled a number of times for impertinence to the teacher. This trait has not been much in evidence since. He is mischievous at times, both in the classroom and on the playground, but he never does anything of serious proportions and always does things above-board rather than pulling tricks behind the teacher's back. Never sneaking or under-handed. When caught in some kind of mischief, he readily confesses and does not try to shift blame to others (Bonney, 1947, pp. 14–16).

Eugene is a sturdy type of boy about average height. His appearance is somewhat marred by blackheads which he frequently picks at. Has a pleasant, but weak facial expression. His ambling gait, poor carriage, and lackadaisical manner cause others to think of him as a boy who has never taken life or its obligations very seriously. Does not appear unhappy, but he gives the impression of being insecure and uncertain of himself.

Eugene's personality structure is primarily that of an effeminate boy. He has never engaged in out-door boyish activities and refuses to play aggressive group games. He participates a little in simpler games like dodge ball or chase, but does not do well in these. Has a "don't care" attitude in respect to all playground activities. He is not uncoordinated or physically weak; he just doesn't identify himself with such things. When left alone at play period, he plays on the teeter-totter, swings, or teases the girls. When forced to participate in a group game such as baseball, he "puts on an act," tries to be cute, does a lot of irrelevant talking, and makes an "out" every time. The other boys laugh at him to his face, and deride him, but he shrugs it all off and pretends not to care. Never fights, never gets angry or argues about a point, and never attacks others. Has a minimum of courage and daring.

Eugene is characterized by emotional instability and immaturity. He is frequently restless in class, does quite a lot of "doodling," jabbers under his breath, and sometimes annoys other children by putting his arm on their desks. Is seriously lacking in persistency of effort. He will work very well at a task which he likes, but not for long. Once he was given an important part in a play, but he never learned his lines, even though he had much help and urging from the teacher. He got some of his lines right, but he improvised so much that the other players had a hard time catching their cues from him. This disgusted the other children. He did, however, show good dramatic sense and entered into the spirit of his part exceptionally well.

Eugene's emotional and social immaturity is emphasized by several other traits. One of these is his strong persistency in wanting his own way in group projects, club meetings, or indoor games. He does not take "no" for an answer from the teacher or the group, but will argue, cajole, or plead for hours to have what he wants. Another evidence of his emotional immaturity is his very naive identification with certain strong, capable boys. One day he told his special reading teacher with obvious elation how he had sat next to one of these admired boys in the picture show the day before. The fact that his sitting next to this boy was purely accidental made his mention of it all the more significant—and pathetic. Additional evidence of Eugene's inadequate social development is found in his excessive eating and in his playing with children much younger than himself. Several investigations have emphasized the relation between excessive eating and social inferiority. Eugene's eating certainly fits the diagnosis of a substitute pleasure for social failure. He frequently brings a mid-morning lunch in addition to eating a big lunch at noon. That there is some degree of unconscious compulsion in his eating is indicated by the fact that several times he said to his sixth grade teacher, "I feel better today; I didn't eat so much."

Eugene has a number of abilities which could be developed into real assets except for his inadequate personality structure. As previously stated, he has unusually good dramatic sense. Also he draws and paints quite well, but he will seldom work at anything long enough to achieve a praise-worthy product. At times he makes interesting and unusual contributions to class discussions. He may come forth with some rare bit of information which he has picked up from the radio or other sources, or he may see unusual, significant relationships in material being discussed in class; but these performances are very irregular (Bonney, 1947, pp. 46–48).

Constancy of Social Acceptance. Several factors indicate the likelihood of relative constancy in social acceptance from one group to another and one time to the next (Northway, 1946). First, Bonney (1943) found that a child's social position in grades two, three, and five was as constant as his intellectual and academic achievement throughout the elementary-school years. Years later, upon interviewing 25 first-grade children throughout the school year, Medinnus (1962) obtained correlations of about +0.85 between scores of social acceptance from one interview to the next. Thus there is certainly short-term constancy in social acceptance. Second, a number of studies concur on the personality characteristics associated with acceptance and nonacceptance. Further, researches into children's friendships report an increasing constancy in friendship choices throughout childhood and adolescence (Horrocks & Thompson, 1946; Thompson & Horrocks, 1947; Horrocks & Buker, 1951). Before school age, constancy probably results from the restricted range of choices imposed by limitations in mobility. Later it may be accounted for by the increasing consistency of personality. In adolescence, friends are chosen on a deeper basis—on aspects of personality that are fairly stable.

That social acceptance is fairly constant while growing up points to its influence on the child's personality and adjustment. As awareness of social position increases with age (Ausubel, Schiff, & Gasser, 1952), a long-term pattern of acceptance and nonacceptance exerts direct and indirect influence on behavior, until knowledge of one's social status becomes an important part of one's self concept.

Modifying Social Acceptance. If social rejection reflects basic maladjustment of personality, raising the level of an individual's social acceptance is not easily accomplished. Because of the role of antecedent parent-child relationships in social acceptance, changes may involve the entire family. But this may be true only of extreme social rejection. For children in the intermediate zone, it may be profitable to concentrate on the self concept. Increasing their self-confidence, self-assurance, and self-esteem is most desirable. Children who manifest unacceptable behaviors usually know that they elicit unfavorable reactions from others but are unable to change. Feelings of inadequacy interfere with behavior and lead to deeper feelings of inadequacy. Somehow the treadmill must be stopped. And it is likely that modifications in self-feelings and in behavior are best achieved in the early elementary years.

The results of recent studies attempting to enhance a child's social acceptance are guarded. For example, through sociometric measures, Bonney (1971) identified third through sixth-grade children who were low in acceptance by peers. Working with the classroom teacher, various techniques were attempted to increase these children's social acceptance. Interviews were held with the children and with their mothers; individual play therapy and counseling sessions were conducted; the children were given special assignments; they were involved in cooperative activities with other children; they were seated near those they had mentioned as liking in the sociometric measure; and they were given special praise by the teacher. At the end of approximately four months, readministration of the earlier sociometric test revealed no change in popularity status of these children identified as low in acceptance by peers. Bonney concluded that the way in which an individual's performance in the classroom is perceived by others is predetermined by the way in which that person is expected to perform, and this generalized expectancy or perception is not readily altered. The child high in social status is responded to favorably regardless of the quality of his behavior or performance at any one time. He functions in an atmosphere of positive social acceptance and expectations. In marked contrast, the child low in social prestige is often ignored by others; his contributions are rejected out of hand; and he operates under a pall of negative social expectations.

The findings of other studies using more specific approaches have been somewhat more promising. One study (Hansen, Niland, & Zana, 1969) compared the effectiveness of group discussions involving low-status sixth-graders only with similar discussion groups involving both high- and low-status children. Over a four-week period, the latter group was effective in enhancing the popularity of low-status children. No change in status was found for those in the homogeneous discussion group. Using low-status seventh-graders, another study (Alden, Pettigrew, & Skiba, 1970) found that praising these children for right answers in front of the class, with the entire class receiving a reward, increased the sociometric status of the less popular children. Apparently the effectiveness of this technique resulted from the favorable recognition given these children by the teacher, combined with the fact that their good performance accrued to the benefit of the other children. Finally, a study of preschoolers (Blau & Rafferty, 1970) paired the children on a cooperative task for which they were rewarded. This technique served to increase the friendship scores of the less popular children.

SUMMARY

The first part of this chapter recapitulated to a large degree material discussed in earlier parts of the book, which was brought together here in order to deal in one place with references to the relation of specific antecedents to that continuing and unique pattern of traits called personality. Differences in personality are evident at birth as a result of hereditary and congenital forces, and these early behavioral tendencies are responded to by the social forces impinging on the child.

The notion of personality implies consistency. Evidence points to the moderate consistency of human behavior, with consistency obtained earlier in some traits than in others, but with younger individuals generally showing less consistency than older ones. The existence of the self concept is often posited as a major basis for consistency. The self concept is composed, in part, of the body image—ideas about and acceptance of the physical self. With age and a decreased amount of bodily change, a relatively stable body image develops, which, in turn, increases stability of behavior.

The self concept also includes social roles. Through reward, people tend to play roles more frequently and with greater degrees of accuracy. If possible, contradictory roles are resolved and an emotional commitment to the roles played is developed. As roles are better defined and better played, consistency increases.

Finally, the chapter examined six areas of personality that appear to be major in childhood and for which considerable information is available. These are: dependence-independence, aggression, anxiety, conscience development, dominance-submission, and social acceptance. In each of these areas we have attempted to trace the emergence of these personality characteristics of psychological conditions in the home and to the child's relations with his parents.

REFERENCES

Adams, E. B., & Sarason, I. Relation between anxiety in children and their parents. *Child Development*, 1963, **34**, 237–246.

Alden, S., Pettigrew, L., & Skiba, E. The effect of individual-contingent group reinforcement on popularity. *Child Development*, 1970, **41**, 1191–1196.

Allen, P. J. The leadership pattern. *American Sociological Review*, 1952, **17**, 93–96.

Anderson, H. H. Domination and integration in the social behavior of young children in an experimental play situation. *Genetic Psychology Monographs*, 1937, **19**, 341–408.

Anderson, H. H. Domination and social integration in the behavior of kindergarten children and teachers. *Genetic Psychology Monographs*, 1939, **21**, 287–385.

Anderson, H. H. Socially integrative behavior. *Journal of Abnormal and Social Psychology*, 1946, **41**, 379–384.

Anderson, J. E. Parents' attitudes on child behavior: A report of three studies. *Child Development*, 1946, **17**, 91–97.

Anderson, J. E. The prediction of adjustment over time. In I. Iscoe & H. Stevenson (Eds.), *Personality development in children*. Austin: Unisity of Texas Press, 1960. Pp. 28–72.

Ausubel, D. P., Schiff, H. M., & Gasser, E. G. A preliminary study of developmental trends in sociopathy: Accuracy of perception of own and others' sociometric status. *Child Development*, 1952, **23**, 111–128.

Bach, G. R. Father-fantasies and father-typing in father-separated children. *Child Development*, 1946, **17**, 63–80.

Baldwin, A. L. Socialization and the parent-child relationship. *Child Development*, 1948, **19**, 127–136.

Baldwin, A. L. The effect of home environment on nursery school behavior. *Child Development*, 1949, **20**, 49–61.

Bandura, A., & Huston, A. C. Identification as a process of incidental learning. *Journal of Abnormal and Social Psychology*, 1961, **63**, 311–318.

Bandura, A., Ross, D., & Ross, S. A. Transmission of aggression through imitation of aggressive models. *Journal of Abnormal and Social Psychology*, 1961, **63**, 575–582.

Bandura, A., & Walters, R. H. *Adolescent aggression.* New York: Ronald, 1959.

Barnard, J., Zimbardo, P., & Sarason, S. Anxiety and verbal behavior in children. *Child Development*, 1961, **32**, 379–392.

Bayley, N., & Tuddenham, R. Adolescent changes in body build. In *National Society for the Study of Education, 43rd Yearbook, Part I, Adolescence.* Chicago: University of Chicago Press, 1944.

Bell, G. B., & Hall, H. E. The relationship between leadership and latency. *Journal of Abnormal and Social Psychology*, 1954, **49**, 156–157.

Beller, E. K. Dependence and independence in young children. *Journal of Genetic Psychology*, 1955, **87**, 25–35.

Berkowitz, L. *Aggression: A social psychological analysis.* New York: McGraw-Hill, 1952.

Beverly, B. I. The effect of illness on emotional development. *Journal of Pediatrics*, 1936, **8**, 533–544.

Blau, B., & Rafferty, J. Changes in friendship status as a function of reinforcement. *Child Development*, 1970, **41**, 113–121.

Blum, E., & Kennedy, W. Modification of dominant behavior in school children. *Journal of Personality and Social Psychology*, 1967, **7**, 275–281.

Bonney, M. E. The relative stability of social, intellectual, and academic status in grades II to IV, and the interrelationships between these various forms of growth. *Journal of Educational Psychology*, 1943, **34**, 88–102.

Bonney, M. E. Popular and unpopular children, a sociometric study. *Sociometric Monographs*, No. 9. New York: Beacon House, 1947.

Bonney, M. Assessment of efforts to aid socially isolated elementary school pupils. *Journal of Educational Research*, 1971, **64**, 359–364.

Brozovich, R. Characteristics associated with popularity among different social and socioeconomic groups of children. *Journal of Educational Research*, 1970, **63**, 441–444.

Burton, R., Maccoby, E. E., & Allinsmith, W. Antecedents of resistance to temptation in four-year-old children. *Child Development*, 1961, **32**, 689–710.

Buskirk, C. V. Performance on complex reasoning tasks as a function of anxiety. *Journal of Abnormal and Social Psychology*, 1961, **62**, 201–209.

Castenada, A., McCandless, B., & Palermo, D. The children's form of the Manifest Anxiety Scale. *Child Development*, 1956, **27**, 317–326.

Castenada, A., Palermo, D., & McCandless, B. Complex learning and performance as a function of anxiety in children and task difficulty. *Child Development*, 1956, **27**, 327–332.

Cattell, R. B. Personality traits associated with abilities. I. With intelligence and drawing abilities. *Educational and Psychological Measurement*, 1945, **5**, 131–146.

Cattell, R. B. *Personality and motivation structure and measurement.* Yonkers, N.Y.: World Book, 1957.

Cattell, R. B., & Coan, R. A. Child personality structure as revealed in teachers' rating. *Journal of Clinical Psychology*, 1957, **13**, 315–327.

Cattell, R. B., & Gruen, W. The personality structure of 11-year-old children in terms of behavior rating data. *Journal of Clinical Psychology*, 1953, **9**, 256–266.

Challman, R. C. Factors influencing friendships among preschool children. *Child Development*, 1932, **3**, 146–158.

Chittenden, G. E. An experimental study in measuring and modifying assertive behavior in young children. *Monographs of the Society for Research in Child Development*, 1942, **7**, No. 1.

Cohen, S. Children's observation and integration of aggressive experiences. *Developmental Psychology*, 1972, **6**, 362.

Cooley, C. H. *Human nature and the social order*. New York: Scribner's, 1902.

Coopersmith, S. *The antecedents of self-esteem*. San Francisco: Freeman, 1967.

Cortes, J., & Gatti, F. M. Physique and self-description of temperament. *Journal of Consulting Psychology*, 1965, **29**, 432–439.

Cortes, J., & Gatti, F. M. Physique and motivation. *Journal of Consulting Psychology*, 1966, **30**, 408–414.

Cotler, S. The effects of positive and negative reinforcement and test anxiety on the reading performance of male elementary school children. *Genetic Psychology Monographs*, 1969, **80**, 29–50.

Cowen, E., Zax, M., Klein, R., Izzo, L., & Trost, M. The relation of anxiety in school children to school record, achievement, and behavioral measures. *Child Development*, 1965, **36**, 685–695.

Crandall, V., Preston, A., & Rabson, A. Maternal reactions and the development of independence and achievement behavior in young children. *Child Development*, 1960, **31**, 243–251.

Davidson, K. Interviews of parents of high anxious and low anxious children. *Child Development*. 1959, **30**, 341–351.

Davidson, K., Sarason, S., Lighthall, F., Waite, R., & Sarnoff, I. Differences between mothers' and fathers' ratings of low anxious and high anxious children. *Child Development*, 1958, **29**, 155–160.

Davidson, M. A., McInnes, R. G., & Parnell, R. W. The distribution of personality traits in seven-year-old children: A combined psychological, psychiatric and somatotype study. *British Journal of Educational Psychology*, 1957, **27**, 48–61.

Deur, J., & Parke, R. Effects of inconsistent punishment on aggression in children. *Developmental Psychology*, 1970, **2**, 403–411.

Diamond, S. *Personality and temperament*. New York: Harper, 1957.

Dibartolo, R., & Vinacke, W. Relationship between adult nurturance and dependency and performance of the preschool child. *Developmental Psychology*, 1969, **1**, 247–252.

Digman, J. M. Principal dimensions of child personality as inferred from teachers' judgments. *Child Development*, 1963, **34**, 43–60.

Dittman, A., & Goodrich, D. A comparison of social behavior in normal and hyperaggressive preadolescent boys. *Child Devleopment*, 1961, **32**, 315–327.

Dmitruk, V. Incentive preference and resistance to temptation. *Child Development*, 1971, **42**, 625–628.

Dollard, J., Doob, L. W., Miller, N. E., Mowrer, O. H., & Sears, R. R. *Frustration and aggression*. New Haven, Conn.: Yale University Press, 1939.

Dubanoski, R., & Parton, D. Imitative aggression in children as a function of observing a human model. *Developmental Psychology*, 1971, **4**, 489.

Dunham H. W. *Sociological theory and mental disorder*. Detroit: Wayne University Press, 1959.

Elser, R. The social position of hearing-handicapped children in the regular grades. *Exceptional Children*, 1959, **25**, 305–309.

Erikson, E. H. *Childhood and society*. New York: Norton, 1950.

Eron, L. D., Banta, T. J., Walder, L. O., & Laulicht, J. H. Comparison of data obtained from mothers and fathers on childrearing practices and their relation to child aggression. *Child Development*, 1961, **32**, 457–472.

Feinberg, M., Smith, M., & Schmidt, R. An analysis of expressions used by adolescents at varying economic levels to describe accepted and rejected peers. *Journal of Genetic Psychology*, 1958, **93**, 133–148.

Feldhusen, J., & Klausmeier, H. Anxiety, intelligence, and achievement in children of low, average, and high intelligence. *Child Development*, 1962, **33**, 403–409.

Fisher, S., & Cleveland, S. E. *Body image and personality*. Princeton, N.J.: Van Nostrand, 1958.

Fite, M.D. Aggressive behavior in young children and children's attitudes toward aggression. *Genetic Psychology Monographs*, 1940, **22**, 151–319.

Fortune, R. F. *Sorcerers of Dobu*. New York: Dutton, 1932.

Fox, C., Davidson, K., Lighthall, F., Waite, R., & Sarason, S. Human figure drawings of high and low anxious children. *Children Development*, 1958, **29**, 297–301.

Furfey, P. H. Some factors influencing the selection of boys' chums. *Journal of Applied Psychology*, 1927, **11**, 47–51.

Gavalas, R., & Briggs, P. Concurrent schedules of reinforcement: a new concept of dependency. *Merrill-Palmer Quarterly*, 1966, **12**, 97–121.

Gewirtz, J. L. A factor analysis of some attention-seeking behaviors of young children. *Child Development*, 1956, **27**, 17–36.

Glueck, S., & Glueck, E. *Physique and delinquency*. New York: Harper, 1956.

Golightly, C., Nelson, D., & Johnson, J. The Children's Dependency Scale. *Developmental Psychology*, 1970, **3**, 114-118.

Gottesman, I. I. The psychogenics of personality. Unpublished doctoral dissertation, University of Minnesota, 1960.

Grinder, R. E. Parental childrearing practices, conscience, and resistance to temptation of sixth-grade children. *Child Development*, 1962, **33**, 803–820.

Guardo, C. Sociometric status and self-concept in sixth graders. *Journal of Educational Research*, 1969, **62**, 320–322.

Hall, C. S., & Lindzey, G. *Theories of personality*. New York: Wiley, 1957.

Hansen, J., Niland, T., & Zana, L. Model reinforcement in group counseling with elementary school children. *Personnel and Guidance Journal*, 1969, **47**, 741–744.

Hardy, M. C. Social recognition at the elementary school age. *Journal of Social Psychology*, 1937, **8**, 365–384.

Hartshorne, H., & May, M. A. *Studies in the nature of character: Vol. I. Studies in deciet*. New York: Macmillan, 1928.

Heathers, G. Emotional dependence and independence in a physical threat situation. *Child Development*, 1953, **24**, 169–179.

Heathers, G. Emotional dependence and independence in nursery school play. *Journal of Genetic Psychology*, 1955, **87**, 37–57. (a)

Heathers, G. Acquiring dependence and independence: A theoretical orientation. *Journal of Genetic Psychology*, 1955, **87**, 277–291. (b)

Hicks, D. Imitation and retention of film-mediated aggressive peer and adult models. *Journal of personality and Social Psychology*, 1965, **2**, 97–100.

Hill, K., & Sarason, S. The relation of test anxiety and defensiveness to test and school performance over the elementary-school years. *Monographs of the Society for Research in Child Development*, 1966, **31**, No. 2.

Hoffman, L. W. The father's role in the family and the child's peer-group adjustment. *Merrill-Palmer Quarterly*, 1961, **7**, 97–105.

Hoffman, M. Father absence and conscience development. *Developmental Psychology*, 1971, **4**, 400–401. (a)

Hoffman, M. Identification and conscience development. *Child Development*, 1971, **42**, 1071–1082. (b)

Hollander, E., & Marcia, J. Parental determinants of peer-orientation and self-orientation among preadolescents. *Developmental Psychology*, 1970, **2**, 292–302.

Horowitz, F. D. The relationship of anxiety, self-concept, and sociometric status among fourth, fifth, and sixth grade children. *Journal of Abnormal and Social Psychology*, 1962, **65**, 212–214.

Horrocks, J. E., & Buker, M. E. A study of the friendship fluctuations of preadolescents. *Journal of Genetic Psychology*, 1951, **78**, 131–144.

Horrocks, J. E., & Thompson, G. G. A study of the friendship fluctuations of rural boys and girls. *Journal of Genetic Psychology*, 1946, **69**, 189–198.

Iscoe, I., & Cochran, I. Some correlates of manifest anxiety in children. *Journal of Consulting Psychology*, 1960, **24**,97.

Jack, L. An experimental study of ascendant behavior in preschool children. In L. Jack, E. M. Manwell, I. G. Mengert, et al., Behavior of the preschool child. *University of Iowa Study in Child Welfare*, 1934, **9**, 7–65.

Johnson, C., & Gormely, J. Academic cheating. *Developmental Psychology*, 1972, **6**, 320–325.

Jones, H. E. The longitudinal method in the study of personality. In I. Iscoe & H. Stevenson (Eds.), *Personality development in children.* Austin: University of Texas Press, 1960. Pp. 3–27.

Jones, M. C. The later careers of boys who were early- or late-maturing. *Child Development*, 1957, **28**, 113–128.

Jones, M. C. Psychological correlates of somatic development. *Child Development*, 1965, **36**, 899–911.

Jones, M. C., & Bayley, N. Physical maturing among boys as related to behavior. *Journal of Educational Psychology*, 1950, **41**, 129–148.

Kagan, J., & Moss, H. A. The stability of passive and dependent behavior from childhood through adulthood. *Child Development*, 1960, **31**, 577–591.

Kagan, J., & Moss, H. A. *Birth to maturity.* New York: Wiley, 1962.

Keasey, C. Social participation as a factor in the moral development of preadolescents. *Developmental Psychology*, 1971, **5**, 216–220.

Kitano, H. Validity of the Children's Manifest Anxiety Scale and the Modified Revised California Inventory. *Child Development*, 1960, **31**, 67–72.

Koch, H. I. Popularity in preschool children: Some related factors and a technique for its measurement. *Child Development*, 1933, **4**, 164–175.

Kuhn, D., Madsen, C., & Becker, W. Effects of exposure to an aggressive model and "frustration" on children's aggressive behavior. *Child Development*, 1967, **38**, 739–745.

L'Abate, L. Personality correlates of manifest anxiety in children. *Journal of Consulting Psychology*, 1960, **24**, 342–348.

Landy, D. *Tropical childhood.* Chapel Hill: University of North Carolina Press, 1959.

Lerner, R., & Gellert, E. Body build identification, preference, and aversion in children. *Developmental Psychology*, 1969, **1**, 456–462.

Lerner, R., & Schroeder, C. Physique identification, preference, and aversion in kindergarten children. *Developmental Psychology*, 1971, **5**, 538.

Lesser, G. S. The relationships between various forms of aggression and popularity among lower-class children. *Journal of Educational Psychology*, 1959, **50**, 20–25.

Levin, H., & Sears, R. R. Identification with parents as a determinant of doll play aggression. *Child Development*, 1956, **27**, 135–153.

Levy, S. Figure drawing as a projective test. In L. E. Abt & L. Bellak (Eds.), *Projective psychology*. New York: Knopf, 1950.

Lippitt, R. Popularity among preschool children. *Child Development*, 1941, **12**, 305–332.

Lippitt, R., & Gold, M. Classroom social structure as a mental health problem. *Journal of Social Issues*, 1959, **15** (1), 40–49.

Lipsitt, L. A Self-Concept Scale for Children and its relationship to the children's form of the Manifest Anxiety Scale. *Child Development*, 1958, **29**, 463–472.

Lorge, I. Intelligence and personality as revealed in questionnaires and inventories. *National Society for the Study of Education, 39th Yearbook*, 1940, Part II, 275–281.

Lynn, R. Personality characteristics of the mothers of aggressive and nonaggressive children. *Journal of Genetic Psychology*, 1961, **99**, 159–164.

McCandless, B. R., Bilous, C. B., & Bennett, H. L. Peer popularity and dependence on adults in preschool-age socialization. *Child Development*, 1961, **32**, 511–518.

McCandless, B., & Castenada, A. Anxiety in children, school achievement, and intelligence. *Child Development*, 1956, **27**, 379–382.

McCandless, B., Castenada, A., & Palermo, D. Anxiety in children and social status. *Child Development*, **27**, 385–391.

McCord, W., McCord, J., & Howard, A. Familial correlates of aggression in non-delinquent male children. *Journal of Abnormal and Social Psychology*, 1961, **62**, 79–93.

McCord, W., McCord, J., & Verden, P. Familial and behavioral correlates of dependency in male children. *Child Development*, 1962, **33**, 313–326.

McCurdy, H. G. The childhood pattern of genius. *Journal of the Elisha Mitchell Scientific Society*, 1957, **73**, 448–462. Also in R. A. King (Ed.), *Readings for an introduction to psychology*. New York: McGraw-Hill, 1961. Pp. 269–278.

McDavid, J., & Harari, H. Stereotyping of names and popularity in grade-school children. *Child Development*, 1966, **37**, 453–459.

McKee, J. P., & Leader, F. B. The relationship of socioeconomic status and aggression to the competitive behavior of preschool children. *Child Development*, 1955, **26**, 135–142.

MacKinnon, D. Violations of prohibitions. In H. A. Murray et al., *Explorations in personality*. New York: Oxford University Press, 1938.

Malinowski, B. *Argonauts of the western Pacific*. New York: Dutton, 1922.

Maris, M. Personal adjustment, assumed similarity to parents, and inferred parental evaluations of the self. *Journal of Consulting Psychology*, 1958, **22**, 481–485.

Marshall, H. R., & McCandless, B. R. Relationships between dependence on adults and social acceptance by peers. *Child Development*, 1957, **28**, 413–419.

Martin, M., Gelfand, D., & Hartmann, D. Effects of adult and peer observers on boys' and girls' responses to an aggressive model. *Child Development*, 1971, **42**, 1271–1275.

Martin, W. S. Singularity and stability of profiles of social behavior. In

C. B. Stendler (Ed.), *Readings in child behavior and development.* (2nd ed.) New York: Harcourt, Brace, 1964. Pp. 444–465.

May, R. *The meaning of anxiety.* New York: Ronald, 1950.

Mead, M. *Sex and temperament in three primitive societies.* New York: Morrow, 1935.

Medinnus, G. R. An examination of several correlates of sociometric status in a first grade group. *Journal of Genetic Psychology,* 1962, **101**, 3–13.

Medinnus, G. R. Age and sex differences in conscience development. *Journal of Genetic Psychology,* 1966, **109**, 117–118.

Mendel, G. Children's preferences for differing degrees of novelty. *Child Development,* 1965, **36**, 453–465.

Messer, S. The effect of anxiety over intellectual performance on reflection-impulsivity in children. *Child Development,* 1970, **41**, 723–735.

Meyer, C. T. The assertive behavior of children as related to parent behavior. *Journal of Home Economics,* 1947, **7**, 77–80.

Miller, D. R., & Swanson, G. E. *Inner conflict and defense.* New York: Holt, 1960.

Mummery, D. V. An analytical study of ascendant behavior of preschool children. *Child Development,* 1947, **18**, 40–81.

Mummery, D. V. Family backgrounds of assertive and nonassertive children. *Child Development,* 1954, **25**, 63–80.

Mussen, P., & Distler, L. Child-rearing antecedents of masculine identification in kindergarten boys. *Child Development,* 1960, **31**, 89–100.

Mussen, P., & Newman, D. Handicap: Motivation, and adjustment in physically disabled children. *Exceptional Children,* 1958, **24**, 255–260, 277–279.

Nelson, J., Gelfand, D., & Hartmann, D. Children's aggression following competition and exposure to an aggressive model. *Child Development,* 1969, **40**, 1085–1097.

Northway, M. L. Sociometry and some challenging problems of social relationships. *Sociometry,* 1946, **9**, 187–198.

Otis, N. B., & McCandless, B. R. Responses to repeated frustrations of young children differentiated according to need area. *Journal of Abnormal and Social Psychology,* 1955, **50**, 349–353.

Page, M. The modification of ascendant behavior in preschool children. *University of Iowa Study in Child Welfare,* 1936, **12** (3), 69.

Parten, M. B. Leadership among preschool children. *Journal of Abnormal and Social Psychology,* 1932, **27**, 430–440.

Partridge, E. D. Leadership among adolescent boys. *Teachers College Contributions to Education,* 1934, No. 608.

Peck, R. F. Family patterns correlated with adolescent personality structure. *Journal of Abnormal and Social Psychology,* 1958, **57**, 347–350.

Peterson, R. Aggression as a function of expected retaliation and aggression level of target and aggression. *Developmental Psychology,* 1971, **5**, 161–166.

Phillips, B., Hindsman, E., & Jennings, E. Influence of intelligence on anxiety and perception of self and others. *Child Development,* 1960, **31**, 41–46.

Piaget, J. *The construction of reality in the child.* New York: Basic Books, 1954 (originally published in English in 1937).

Radke, M. J. The relation of parental authority to children's behavior and attitudes. *University of Minnesota Child Welfare Monographs,* 1946, No. 22.

Raimy, V. C. Self reference in counseling interviews. *Journal of Consulting Psychology*, 1948, **12**, 153–163.

Rheingold, H., & Eckerman, C. The infant separates himself from his mother. *Science*, 1970, **168**, 78–83.

Roff, M. Preservice personality and subsequent adjustments to military service: The prediction of psychoneurotic reactions. *USAF School of Aviation Medicine Report,* 1957, No. 57–136.

Roff, M. Relations between certain preservice factors and psychoneurosis during military duty. *Armed Forces Medical Journal,* 1960, **II**, 152–160.

Roff, M. Childhood social interactions and young adult bad conduct. *Journal of Abnormal and Social Psychology,* 1961, **63**, 333–337.

Rogers, C. R. *Client-centered therapy.* Boston: Houghton Mifflin, 1951.

Rosen, B. Family structure and value transmission. *Merrill-Palmer Quarterly,* 1964, **10**, 59–76.

Sanford, R. N., Adkins, M. M., Miller, R. B., Cobb, E. A., et al. Physique, personality and scholarship: A cooperative study of school children. *Monographs of the Society for Research in Child Development,* 1943, **8**, No. 1.

Sarason, I. The effects of anxiety and threat on the solution of a difficult task. *Journal of Abnormal and Social Psychology,* 1961, **62**, 165–168.

Sarason, I. Test anxiety and intellectual performance. *Journal of Abnormal and Social Psychology,* 1963, **66**, 73–75.

Sarason, S., Davidson, K., Lighthall, F., & Waite, R. A Test Anxiety Scale for Children. *Child Development,* 1958, **29**, 105–113. (a)

Sarason, S., Davidson, K., Lighthall, F., & Waite, R. Classroom observations of high and low anxious children. *Child Development,* 1958, **29**, 287–295. (b)

Sarason, S., Hill, K., & Zimbardo, P. A longitudinal study of the relation of test anxiety to performance on intelligence and achievement tests. *Monographs of the Society for Research in Child Development,* 1964, **29**, No. 7.

Schilder, P. *The image and appearance of the human body.* London: Kegan, Paul, 1935.

Sears, P. S. Doll play aggression in normal young children: Influence of sex, age, sibling status, father's absence. *Psychological Monographs: General and Applied,* 1951, **65**, No. 6.

Sears, R. R. The growth of conscience. In I. Iscoe & H. W. Stevenson (Eds.), *Personality development in children.* Austin: University of Texas Press, 1960. Pp. 92–111.

Sears, R. R. Relation of early socialization experiences to aggression in middle childhood. *Journal of Abnormal and Social Psychology,* 1961, **63**, 466–492.

Sears, R. R. Relation of early socialization experiences to self-concepts and gender role in middle childhood. *Child Development,* 1970, **41**, 267–289.

Sears, R. R., Maccoby, E. E., & Levin, H. *Patterns of child rearing.* Evanston, Ill.: Row, Peterson, 1957.

Sears, R. R., Whiting, J. W. M., Nowlis, V., & Sears, P. S. Some child-rearing antecedents of aggression and dependency in young children. *Genetic Psychology Monographs,* 1953, **47**, 135–234.

Secord, P. Objectification of word association procedures by the use of homonyms in a measure of body cathexis. *Journal of Personality,* 1953, **21**, 479–495.

Secord, P., & Jourard, S. The appraisal of body cathexis: Body cathexis and the self. *Journal of Consulting Psychology,* 1953, **17**, 343–347.

Shaub, R. R. Kidney donors: Body image and psychopathology. Unpublished master's thesis, University of Colorado, 1967.

Sheldon, W. H., Stevens, S. S., & Tucker, W. B. *The varieties of human physique.* New York: Harper, 1940.

Shelton, J., & Hill, J. Effects on cheating of achievement anxiety and knowledge of peer performance. *Developmental Psychology,* 1969, **1**, 449–455.

Shirley, M. M. *The first two years: A study of twenty-five babies.* Vol. 3. *Personality manifestations.* Minneapolis: University of Minnesota Press, 1933.

Shlien, J. A client-centered approach to schizophrenia: first approximation. In A. Burton (Ed.), *Psychotherapy of the psychoses.* New York: Basic Books, 1961.

Shlien, J. The self concept in relation to behavior: Theoretical and empirical research. *Religion Education, Research Supplement,* 1962, **17**, S111–S127.

Siegel, A. A., & Kohn, L. G. Permissiveness, permission, and aggression: The effect of adult presence or absence on aggression in children's play. *Child Development,* 1959, **30**, 131–141.

Slaby, R., & Parke, R. Effect on resistance to deviation of observing models' affective reaction to response consequences. *Developmental Psychology,* 1971, **5**, 40–47.

Smock, C. Perceptual rigidity and closure phenomenon as a function of manifest anxiety in children. *Child Development,* 1958, **29**, 237–247.

Sontag, L. W., Baker, C. T., & Nelson, V. L. Mental growth and personality development: A longitudinal study. *Monographs of the Society for Research in Child Development,* 1958, **23**, No. 68.

Spector, S. I. Climate and social acceptability. *Journal of Educational Sociology,* 1953, **27**, 108–114.

Staffieri, J. A study of social stereotype of body image in children. *Journal of Personality and Social Psychology,* 1967, **7**, 101–104.

Staffieri, J. R. Body build and behavioral expectancies in young females. *Developmental Psychology,* 1972, **6**, 125–127.

Stein, A. Imitation of resistance to temptation. *Child Development,* 1967, **38**, 157–169.

Stein, A., & Wright, J. Imitative learning under conditions of nurturance and nurturance withdrawal. *Child Development,* 1964, **35**, 927–938.

Stendler, C. B. Critical periods in socialization and over-dependency. *Child Development,* 1952, **23**, 3–12.

Stendler, C. B. Possible causes of over-dependency in young children. *Child Development,* 1954, **25**, 125–146.

Steth, M., & Connor, R. Dependency and helpfulness in young children. *Child Development,* 1962, **33**, 15–20.

Stewart, A. Excessive crying in infants—a family disease. In M. Senn (Ed.), *Sixth conference on problems of infancy and childhood.* New York: Josiah Macy, Jr., Foundation, 1953. Pp. 138–160.

Stogdill, R. M. Personal factors associated with leadership: A survey of the literature. *Journal of Psychology,* 1948, **25**, 35–71.

Stouwie, R. Inconsistent verbal instructions and children's resistance-to-temptation behavior. *Child Development,* 1971, **42**, 1517–1531.

Strauss, A. (Ed.). *The social psychology of George Herbert Mead.* Chicago: University of Chicago Press, 1956.

Swensen, C. H., Jr. Empirical evaluations of human figure drawings. *Psychological Bulletin,* 1957, **54**, 431–466.

Taylor, J. A. A personality scale of manifest anxiety. *Journal of Abnormal and Social Psychology,* 1953, **48**, 285–290.

Terman, L. M., & Oden, M. H. *The gifted child grows up.* Stanford, Calif.: Stanford University Press, 1947.

Thompson, G. G., & Horrocks, J. E. A study of the friendship fluctuations of urban boys and girls. *Journal of Genetic Psychology,* 1947, **70**, 53–63.

Tisza, V. B., Selverstone, B., Rosenblum, G., & Hanlon, N. Psychiatric observations of children with cleft palate. *American Journal of Orthopsychiatry,* 1958, **28**, 416–423.

Todd, J., & Nakamura, C. Interactive effects of informational and affective components of social and nonsocial reinforcers on independent and dependent children. *Child Development,* 1970, **41**, 365–376.

Tryon, C. M. Evaluation of adolescent personality by adolescents. *Monographs of the Society for Research in Child Development,* 1939, **4**, No. 4, p. 88.

Tuddenham, R. D. Studies in reputation. III. Correlates of popularity among elementary school children. *Journal of Educational Psychology,* 1951, **42**, 257–276.

Walker, R. N. Body build and behavior in young children: I. Body build and nursery school teachers' ratings. *Monographs of the Society for Research in Child Development,* 1962, **27**, No. 3.

Walker, R. N. Body build and behavior in young children: II. Body build and parents' ratings. *Child Development,* 1963, **34**, 1–23.

Wenger, M. A. Preliminary study of the significance of autonomic balance. *Psychosomatic Medicine,* 1947, **9**, 301–309.

Whiting, J. W. M. Resource mediation and learning by identification. In I. Iscoe & H. W. Stevenson (Eds.), *Personality development in children.* Austin: University of Texas Press, 1960.

Whiting, J. W. M., & Child, I. *Child training and personality.* New Haven, Conn.: Yale University Press, 1953.

Winder, C. L., & Rau, L. Parental attitudes associated with social deviance in preadolescent boys. *Journal of Abnormal and Social Psychology,* 1962, **64**, 418–424.

Witkin, H. A., Dyke, R. B., Faterson, H. F., Goodenough, D. R., & Karp, S. A. *Psychological differentiation.* New York: Wiley, 1962.

Woods, F. J., & Carrow, M. A. The choice-rejection status of speech-defective children. *Exceptional Children,* 1959, **25**, 279–283.

Wylie, R. C. Some relationships between defensiveness and self-concept discrepancies. *Journal of Personality,* 1957, **25**, 600–616.

Whylie, R. C. *The self concept: A critical survey of pertinent literature.* Lincoln: University of Nebraska Press, 1961.

chapter 16

disturbances in development

chapter 16

disturbances in development

chapter 16

disturbances in development

As development progresses psychological problems often emerge. Disturbances set in motion problem behavior. How such behavior is caused, how it is diagnosed, how it is treated, and the probability of its cure constitute the substance of this chapter. These subjects will be considered under four general headings: causes, diagnosis, treatment techniques, and prognosis.

CAUSES OF BEHAVIORAL PROBLEMS

Only rarely do we find a disturbed individual with one specific form of maladjustment and no other symptoms. Oftener a patient will have a dominant set of problems accompanied by other, less well-developed signs of disturbance. So, too, with causation. Seldom can we say about any one problem of any one patient that this and only this aspect of his background produced the disturbance. Far more frequently a variety of factors contribute to the production of a given kind of problem.

A fine illustration of the diversity of factors that may be seen in the background of an individual appears in the autobiography of Carryl Chessman (1955), a robber who was convicted and executed for kidnapping. Chessman attributed his long record of crime to having been reared in a Los Angeles slum and to overcompensation for being a small, picked-on child. Although he placed no emphasis on the fact, Chessman did have a severe attack of encephalitis as a child, a disease that frequently produces undesirable behavioral changes in its victims. Thus all those who believe in sociological forces, feelings of inferiority, or organic factors as the prime cause of problem behavior are satisfied by Chessman's explanation of his deviant behavior. In addition, certain aspects of his family relationship support a Freudian interpretation of his conduct.

Although numerous forces combine to produce many behavioral problems, the effect of any one force differs from behavior to behavior. Hence the statement that "Problem A has much more of an innate physiological component, and is less influenced by the social milieu of the patient than Problem B." The relative import of the several forces believed to cause specific problem disorders can be, but seldom has been, determined.

Genetic Factors

Many problem behaviors relate to affective, or emotional, maladjustment. The individual may "feel too much" and be devastated by events that bring no concern to others. Or he may "feel too little" and not have much attachment for others, in which case he is not greatly affected by social approval or disapproval and shows incompetence at learning social roles. The disturbed, fearful, neurotic youngster and the psychopathic delinquent have one thing in common: neither is influenced by the attitudes of others toward them or by inner standards in the same way that better-adjusted children are influenced. Individual differences in emotionality and emotional stability have a fairly substantial genetic base (Vandenberg, 1967). In this broad sense, genetic forces may underlie many varieties of problem behavior.

More specifically, the role of heredity is evident in many cases of schizophrenia. If one of a pair of siblings becomes schizophrenic, the chances are roughly one in seven that the other will become so. For fraternal twins the probability is the same. For stepbrothers and sisters growing up in the same home, the probability is approximately one in 50. Among identical twins, it is seven in eight. Although these findings by Kallman and by others (reviewed by Rosenthal, 1962) have been attacked for various reasons (Pastore, 1949; Jackson, 1964), their general conclusions appear to have been upheld, though more current studies (Gottesman & Shields, 1966; Kringlen, 1966) show a lesser influence of heredity than did Kallman's research. As noted above, not all twin pairs, even among identicals, are concordant (alike) in the sense that either both members of the pair are normal or else both members are schizophrenic. Rosenthal (1959) studied pairs of concordant (both schizophrenic) and discordant (only one schizophrenic) identical (MZ) twins. Differences in family structure and in the treatment of the twins were found between the two groups. Further, schizophrenics from discordant pairs (in which schizophrenia was presumably more a result of environmental pathology than it was among concordant schizophrenic twins) had a later onset and more favorable prognosis than did members of concordant pairs. Rosenthal's (1963) study of the "Genain" quadruplets, all of whom were schizophrenic, should be mentioned here. The intensive study of these four young women led to the conclusion that susceptibility to schizophrenic breakdown is genetically determined, but that the severity of the manifestations of the disturbance, for each of the quadruplets, was determined chiefly by the amount of environmental stress. As discussed in Chapter 2, the tendency to approach or withdraw from stimuli, as well as general emotionality and activity level, seem to be rather strongly determined by heredity. Since these aspects of personality are related to schizophrenic behavior, it is not surprising that at least some types of schizophrenic disturbance have a strong hereditary component.

It has been suggested that taking the position that a given problem behavior has a substantial genetic basis is a counsel of despair (e.g., see McCandless, 1964, pp. 175–176). The discussion of phenylketonuria on p. 8 of this volume demonstrates that this point of view has little support in fact: the metabolic basis of PKU has been established, the genetic mechanisms of PKU have been explored, the existence of different subtypes of PKU demonstrated, dietary therapeutic regimens tested and found effective, means of finding carriers validated. To be sure, PKU accounts for only about 1 percent of severe retardation (Johnson, 1969); even so, to have established the basis of and the prevention and the treatment of a significant form of retardation is hardly a counsel of despair.

Other genetic influences on problem behavior of various sorts may have substantially greater generality; their investigation may also result in effective treatment. For example, see Ahern and Johnson (1973), regarding the much more frequent—as compared to PKU—familial retardation. It was hypothesized that one of the causes of what usually is called familial retardation might be an inherited tendency, on the part of females in the family lines, to produce an inadequate uterine environment and hence produce a high proportion of retarded offspring. If so, one would expect sisters and aunts, as compared with brothers and uncles, of retarded individuals to produce a higher proportion of retarded (as well as spontaneously aborted, stillborn, or neonatal casualty) offspring. An analysis of data from Reed and Reed, *Mental Retardation: A Family Study* (1965), supports the hypothesis.

The results of the study point out a possible cause of defective development—a hereditary tendency to produce a defective offspring—and reveal an especially high-risk group—female relatives of retarded propositi. Typically, in preventive medicine, following the discovery of a high-risk group efforts are made to discover the basis of this high risk (many alternate research avenues are open, as shown in Barnes, 1968, *Intrauterine Development*) and provide the high-risk group with special care in order to attempt to reduce the risk (here, too, data are already available regarding the efficacy of remedial efforts—see Kaplan, 1972).

It may be that those individuals who are retarded as a result of maternal uterine inadequacy differ from the remainder of the retarded individuals who make up such gross and heterogeneous categories as "cultural familial retarded." If so, they might show different profiles of ability in tests of sensory processes or in factor-pure tests of cognition. Presumably, individuals of this sort would make up a larger portion of those retardates found in pedigrees with a highly disproportionate percent of defective offspring of male versus female members than of retardates for whom the ratio was equal (environmental factors as well as other genetic factors not associated with uterine environmental adequacy might be expected to be more involved here). If so, the particular attributes of the "uterine inadequacy" versus "other" types of retardation might be more clearly delineated by, say, a comparison of retardates from families where the percent of retarded offspring of relatives of a given propositus was at least twice as great for members of the propositus' female line as compared with the male line with retardates where the percent of retarded offspring was approximately equal for female as opposed to male relatives of the propositus. Such a procedure might refine the categorization of the "at risk" group and further facilitate treatment. Bessman's (1972) theories concerning failures of amino acid justification (see Chapter 3, p. 70) also could be brought to bear in establishing risk.

A genetic interpretation need not be a counsel of despair.

Congenital Factors

As discussed in Chapter 3, it is difficult to separate hereditary from congenital factors, since symptoms of both become apparent at birth or some time after it. As noted in Chapter 3, the most thorough study so far of the connection between congential factors and problem behavior was undertaken by a group headed by Pasamanick. Kawi and Pasamanick (1959) stated that there was within the uterus a continuum of maldevelopment "with a lethal component consisting of abortions, still births, and neonatal deaths, and a sublethal component consisting of cerebral palsy, epilepsy, mental deficiency, and behavior disorders in children." A frequent sequel to malnutrition and to complications in pregnancy is hyperactivity, confusion, and disorganization in the children (Pasamanick, Rogers, & Lilienfeld, 1956), symptoms that might often be confused with certain hereditary disorders or with postnatal brain injury.

Postnatal Physical Factors

Brain injury suffered in the uterus, at birth, or after birth appears to produce deviant behavior as well as mental deficiency, as Kawi and Pasamanick (1959) observed. Since brain injury results not only from tumors but also from diseases, such as encephalitis and meningitis, and from physical damage, it is a factor of relevance in the study of behavioral problems. On the other hand, it is the favored cause in diagnoses made by parents. *All* children have bad falls and high fevers; hence parents with a problem child can always assuage their guilt by blaming a fall or a fever rather than their own behavior. Although brain injury may be a valid cause and must be considered a possibility during diagnosis, unsubstantiated parental statements of injury or pressures to attribute the problem to it call for a wary attitude in the diagnostician.

The influence of biological factors in postnatal life is reinforced by Hebb's citation (1949, p. 262) of evidence that shows neurotic or psychotic behavior to have been associated, at least on occasion, with a large number of physical diseases. Whether inherited, congenital, or postnatal, physical conditions are obviously related to behavior disorders. For this reason it is not redundant to emphasize again the necessity of determining the physical state of the youngster who is referred to a social agency or clinic as a "problem child."

Family Factors

Ever since Freud's day, it has been believed that the basis of pathology lies in the family setting. Contemporary theory attributes pathology in the child to the behavior of the parents, especially that of the mother. It is rather surprising to find parental guilt and responsibility increasingly emphasized at the same time that the person with the problem, whether child or adult, is absolved of responsibility. Although, in many cases, parental deviations contribute to problem behavior in their children, these parental behaviors should be judged on the same basis as the child's problems—as being caused.

Further defense of the parents lies in the fact that the cause-and-effect relationship between parental behavior and child problems is often unclear. For example, "three-month colic," a term used by parents to describe a disorder in which the infant howls, in apparent agony, for roughly 20 out of every 24 hours in its first three months of life and then suddenly ceases without reason, illustrates the difficulties of attributing cause and effect to parental influences on child behavior problems. Lakin (1957) found that mothers of colicky infants, in contrast to mothers of noncolicky infants, were less accepting of the female role, felt less adequate, were less happy with their husbands and with their parents, and were less motherly in their attitudes. He concluded that these attributes of mothers produced the colic in their infants. However, could it not be that having an infant cry for 20 out of 24 hours for a few months might have produced the differences in attitude?

Similarly, several studies (e.g., Heilbrun, 1960; Kohn & Clausen, 1956) have shown mothers of schizophrenics to be both harsher and more overprotective than mothers of normal children. Aside from the obviously important fact that these judgments usually occur *after* the schizophrenic onset, there is still the matter of cause and effect. Fish (1959) produced evidence to corroborate Bender's (1947) contention that certain characteristic deviations of behavior were observable at or shortly after birth in a child who would later become schizophrenic. Other evidence indicates that a child who will later succumb to schizophrenia suffers no more traumatic experience than normal siblings, but will more probably react pathologically to any change in the environment and *invite a special response* from parents that further impairs an innately weak capacity to resist stress (Prout & White, 1956). Although it is unpopular to attribute pathological behavior to hereditary factors, genetic sources cannot be easily dismissed.

In other instances, a social interpretation of familial influences seems quite clear-cut. As Ackerman (1958) pointed out, the parent often produces a kind of pathology in the child that fills certain parental needs. A clear illustration of this "secondary" gain by the parent is seen in cases in which the parent has a dislike for authority figures, yet cannot bring this dislike out into the open. By providing subtle reinforcement, the parent produces a rebellious child. It does not take much talent or imagination on the part of the youngster to recognize a green light when a parent laughs and says, "Oh, you shouldn't have hit the high school principal in the nose." Verbal protest notwithstanding, the parent finds hitting an authority figure to be a rather pleasant prospect.

In other instances, parents produce deviation by providing the child with a deviant behavior model. Roebuck and Johnson (1964) show that individuals who as youths and adults have operated as "con men" have learned from parents a life-style centered on deceit. As one con man related:

> I learned from my mother that "front" and how you carry yourself is the main thing with the marks (suckers). She'd buy $10 worth of groceries and while I held them walk up to the man and give him a rubber check for $50. She talked fast, smooth, and bold. You know, like she had a million. Of course she always dressed the part. She had such a way about her that the clerks in stores where she stole dresses were afraid to question her though they had a good idea she had their "rags" under her coat. She always said, "son if you get in the life (life in the underworld) get a soft hustle. No rough stuff" (Roebuck & Johnson, 1964, p. 241).

This is clearly an example of imitation and direct social learning, not so much of one type of criminality but a way of life predicated on cheating. Another life-style learned in much the same manner is that of hypochondria. Observing a parent using a certain style of response to life, the child sees that the behavior pays and adopts it as his own.

In other instances of psychological disturbance caused by family circumstances, the fault is not so much in the individual family members as it is in the pattern of interaction within the family.

One aspect of interaction is the "double bind," in which the child is told, in essence, that if he behaves in way X, he will be punished, and that if he does not behave in this way, he'll also be punished. Here is a case in point:

> A young man who had fairly well recovered from an acute schizophrenic episode was visited in the hospital by his mother. He was glad to see her and impulsively put his arm around her shoulders, whereupon she stiffened. He withdrew his arm, and she asked, "Don't you love me any more?" He then blushed, and she said, "Dear, you must not be so easily embarrassed and afraid of your feelings" (Bateson, Jackson, Haley, & Weakland, 1956, p. 259).

Other patterns of communication that are said to produce psychological disturbance include "disconfirmation," in which the parent or parents respond to the child's behavior as though the behavior is irrelevant, and "disqualification" (Haley, 1959), as illustrated below:

> Typically in these families the mother tends to initiate what happens, while indicating either that she isn't, or that someone else should. The father will invite her to initiate what happens while condemning her when she does. Often they suggest the child take the lead, and then disqualify his attempts (Haley, 1963).

These are only several of the many theories of family interaction. It should be noted that, although the two examples above show the mothers to be the villains, these theories have to do with the entire family—the father, mother, and siblings.

Disorders in communication within the family may well be important sources of confusion for the child. Yet it seems entirely possible that all families have frequent disorders of this sort, and, for that matter, that all other groups do, too.

Schofield's and Balian's (1959) research, showing that highly normal males have as many supposedly pathological factors in their home environment as do institutionalized patients, suggests that many phenomena, such as the double bind, are relatively common experiences for all of us. If so, they do not in themselves produce psychological disturbance. Rather, they produce disturbance in *some* people, and our problem is to determine why these people are so severely and adversely affected.

One further important aspect of the family situation is the role of the parent as diagnostician. The only common element in all behavioral problems is that they are diagnosed by someone. Every clinician sees many children whose behavior is representative of children in general, yet who are viewed as severe problems by parents or, less often, by teachers. Other children seen as "holy terrors" by the world at large are angels to their parents. In this respect, an item on the "Lie" scale of a well-known personality test rests on the fact that nearly all adults confess to having indulged in petty theft at some time during childhood; thus, in a statistical sense, this behavior is normal. The same thing may be said for the findings of the Kinsey reports (1948, 1953) in which most children admitted to indulging in many varieties of sexual behavior at some time in development prior to reaching maturity. Yet if any of these behaviors are detected by parents and made to symbolize an evil nature, the child may well accept the parental diagnosis of being evil or delinquent and live up to the role thus assigned him.

A final illustration of a problem created primarily by diagnosis is found in feeding. Clinical psychologists are familiar with the maternal complaint: "He hasn't eaten anything for two days and he never does more than pick at his food. I'm afraid he'll become ill if he doesn't eat more." The starving child who accompanies her to the consultation nearly always turns out to be highly active, healthy, and obviously well nourished. The mother's diagnosis, though clearly having no foundation in reality, is certainly of great concern to her.

The high frequency of feeding problems (25 percent of all children are diagnosed as feeding problems by someone, usually parents, according to Kanner, 1957) is associated with aspects of the culture as well as of the mother-child relationship. Most of the world goes to bed hungry, whereas Americans, as a nation, have more than enough. Because of this affluence, food is urged on children and its consumption is heavily emphasized. Advertising and other social forces make a fetish of nutrition in what is perhaps the best-fed society of all. This becomes an area of parental concern when many children shift from having a remarkable appetite (in the parent's view) for the first few years of life to a much reduced food intake at three and after as growth rate shows down and a high peak of metabolic efficiency is attained. The parent is concerned; the child feels it. The parent assigns the role of feeding problem to the child and the child accepts it. Since feeding problems occur only in food-rich societies, it seems likely that they do not originate with the child but with parental responses to the child's eating habits.

The problem in all these examples is more in diagnosis than in child behavior. Yet once the diagnosis has been made the child is treated differently and may accept the "problem child" role and become a genuine problem. The child judged doomed to perdition begins to think that he might as well live up to the reputation. The child diagnosed a stutterer stutters; the child considered a dullard may become a nonachiever (see Lecky, 1945), and the one deemed a feeding problem very likely becomes one (see Kanner,

1957, pp. 470–477). Adults should, therefore, exercise extreme caution in diagnosis.

One final point regarding the role of family factors in producing behavior problems. Why is it that the mother is so frequently viewed as being the cause of the child's problem? The child, terror though he may be, is treated as the victim of a pathological mother. She, on the other hand, is seen as pathological not because of environmental forces acting on her, but because of her own free will and accord. Some of Roe's (1953) data suggest that social scientists generally have grown up in a mother-dominated home. (Physical and biological scientists, on the other hand, have grown up in father-dominated homes.) Further, social scientists generally have had a rather stormy relationship with their mothers. As Roe points out, it may be that social scientists' theories of pathology, generally emphasizing maternal causes of disturbance, do not reflect reality with regard to the world at large so much as they reflect the social scientist's own life situation, in which a major influence is a dominative and difficult mother. It may be, however, that theories implicating the mothers as the chief causal agent in the production of neurotic disturbance are correct, even though the theories have been developed, in part, for the wrong reasons. Data (Medinnus, 1965; Brigham, Ricketts, & Johnson, 1967) suggest that psychopathic acting-out problems among boys are associated with poor father-son relationships, but that more neurotic kinds of disturbance are associated with poor mother-son relationships.

Sociological Factors

Sociologists have argued that most delinquents are psychologically "normal" but that they come from slum areas in which certain operative forces dispose an individual to become involved in illegal behaviors. Among children from depressed and criminal slum environments, it hardly seems necessary to seek strictly psychological forces to account for delinquency, and the subcultural delinquent is perhaps the commonest sociological problem.

Social class and subcultural differences in values frequently may cause lower-class children, especially from minority groups, to behave in ways that cause them to be judged as deviant by members of the majority culture.

The causes for any type of behavior problem are multiple, often interacting with one another. Yet careful study of prior conditions leading to problem behavior will, for many types of problem, yield discrete categories, as we shall presently observe, each with its own major cause and each with its own treatment.

DIAGNOSIS

The term *diagnosis* comes from a Greek word which means to "know one from another." As the term itself indicates, the task of the diagnostician is to observe the symptomatic behavior closely and to establish the particular type of disorder most probably associated with the evident symptoms. Psychotherapists have not succeeded well in fulfilling this task. Sometimes they believe the challenge to be insurmountable. Yet medical doctors have faced and largely mastered the same problem.

Differential Diagnosis in Medicine

There are a number of varieties of fever, just as there are a number of varieties of mental deficiency and, probably, of schizophrenia. Fever, mental retardation, and schizophrenia have one thing in common: each has a single dominant symptom—high temperature, inability to learn adequately, and dissociation, respectively. Beneath the surface similarity of high temperature, closely observing physicians discerned secondary symptoms that allowed them to differentiate types of fever within the broad phenotype of fever. Malaria began with chills accompanied by blueness of the skin and cyclical vomiting, then showed high fever followed by normal or subnormal temperature until the next paroxysm. Typhoid showed some similarity to malaria in early symptoms, since chills are common to both. Unlike malaria, however, typhoid also produces early symptoms of tiredness and loss of appetite; as the disease advances, there are pains in the limbs and severe headaches. The cyclical quality of malaria is missing. Later, in typhoid, lethargy increases, pulse rate rises slightly, and temperature climbs higher. There is nervousness and delirium, and a rash on the chest and abdomen. Recovery is gradual.

A third fever, yellow fever, resembles typhoid in many respects, since early symptoms of both include severe headaches. However, victims of yellow fever feel pain in the back and neck rather than in the limbs, and the pulse rate drops rather than rises. In its early stages, yellow fever also resembles malaria; vomiting is a symptom of each. But jaundice accompanies yellow fever, as compared with the blueness of malaria.

By observing *all* the symptoms, one can detect a specific configuration that accompanies each disorder and allows for a clear differential diagnosis—a "telling one from the other." This diagnosis *could not* be arrived at by observing only the dominant symptom, fever, nor by observing most of the individual secondary symptoms. One can differentiate these fevers from one another and note the effectiveness of specific treatment techniques on each. Since no treatment suffices for all of them, any treatment is necessarily a failure in most cases until the subspecies of fever are distinguished so that one of them susceptible to a particular type of treatment can be singled out from the rest. Causes can then be discovered and steps taken for prevention as well as cure. The same point applies to psychological problems.

Differential Diagnosis and the Medical Model of Psychological Disturbance

Disorders that show considerable similarity in their manifest symptomatology may differ markedly in causation, in how they are most effectively treated, and in prognosis. Therefore it would seem highly advantageous to differentiate superficially similar sets of symptoms in order to find effective treatment techniques for each.

Arguments can be raised against differential diagnosis: Many attempts at developing systems of differential diagnosis have proved fruitless; different psychological problems are not caused by different physical agents (as is the case with physical disorders and "germs"), and may seem to be caused by the same kind of psychosocial problems (e.g., feelings of estrangement from others); all kinds of psychological disturbance may basically be one, though the symptoms vary somewhat, and therefore may be expected to yield to the same treatment procedures. For these reasons many psychologists believe that differential diagnosis is futile and without value. Each of these arguments is dealt with, in turn, below.

Attempts at developing systems of differential diagnosis *have* proved fruitless, but usually because the systems are based almost entirely on the symptoms present when the diagnosis is made. These symptoms frequently change from day to day and from examiner to examiner. Other, more recent systems for the differentiation of problem behaviors have proved to be of value. A system of differential diagnosis presently in use, in which schizophrenic disturbances are divided into two major categories (process and reaction), has shown that problems in the process category show a greater genetic component and a longer period of onset than in the reaction category. Individuals in the former category have a tendency to blame others for their problems, a longer period of institutionalization, a lower likelihood of release, and a poorer prognosis. In the same fashion, an awareness of subtle phenotypical differences between groups has allowed for a distinction to be made between childhood schizophrenia and autism (see Rimland, 1964), two disorders with differing probable causes (etiology), differing treatment possibilities, and differing prognosis. Other examples of the utility of differential diagnosis are given below.

It is true that psychological disturbances are not all caused by their own highly specific agents, as is the case with physical diseases. However, sometimes they are (e.g., phenylketonuria, caused by a pair of recessive genes), and sometimes it is possible to see the relative weighting of influence of different agents (as in hereditary and environmental factors in process and reactive schizophrenia). The fact that disorders sometimes can be separated from one another in terms of their causes, most effective therapies, and prognosis suggests that it is valuable to attempt to do so more often, to make use of the most effective treatment technique for a given kind of problem, to evaluate adequately the effectiveness of the technique, and to give the parents the most accurate statement of prognosis possible.

The whole concept of differential diagnosis is sometimes rejected because a therapist believes that his form of therapy is equally effective for all problems and therefore that diagnosis is pointless. In contrast, Eysenck (1961, 1965) has demonstrated in excellent reviews of the literature that about as many people who receive *no* therapy recover from their problems as people who do receive therapy. Eysenck's conclusion was that "talking therapy" has no positive value, and may even be harmful. An alternative conclusion that can be drawn from the data that Eysenck presents is that some people get worse, some are unchanged, and some gain from each variant of psychotherapy. If this latter conclusion is correct, our task is to discover what kind of person, with what kind of problem, benefits from each type of therapy—again a problem of differential diagnosis.

Other Instances of the Differential Diagnosis of Psychological Problems. Two groups of theories exist about the major causes of juvenile delinquency. Sociological theories stress the notion that a delinquent is usually a normal, well-integrated member of a subculture that accepts values judged to be delinquent by the majority culture. Psychological theories consider personal maladjustment as the basis for the delinquency. There has been little effort to fragmentize the broad category, delinquent, into various subtypes in order to determine the relative seriousness of each—how many remain delinquent and later become criminals, to what degree deviant behaviors are dangerous to others—or to learn whether specific varieties of delinquency respond better to one kind of treatment than another.

Johnson (1950) noted a phenotypical difference of some apparent significance among delinquents: solitary delinquents seemed to differ considerably from those who acted in concert with others. Further research (Randolph, Richardson, & Johnson, 1961) found that the simple division of delinquents into those who committed their delinquencies alone and those who did not was sufficient to uncover two distinct groups on the basis of backgrounds, however gross and simple this phenotypical classification might be. Solitary performers usually come from an ostensibly normal, middle-class environment. They report disturbed relations with both mother and father (Brigham et al., 1967). They are of average ability and disclose a very high degree of pathology in their responses to personality tests; they are *psychological* delinquents. Social delinquents generally come from lower-class homes in high-delinquency areas. They report disturbed relations with their fathers but generally normal psychological relations with their mothers (Medinnus, 1965; Brigham et al., 1967). They are usually dull to normal in ability and show few pathological signs on a standardized personality inventory; these are *sociological* delinquents.

The division is certainly a crude categorization, but far better than none at all. Solitary delinquents evince a much higher degree of *recidivism*—that is, a stronger tendency to be delinquent or criminal again in the future—indicating that solitary delinquency is a more serious problem. The psychological nature of the solitary delinquent's problems points to the advisability of some form of psychotherapy as a technique for treatment. Since the social delinquent's problems appear to be largely the product of a deviant crimogenic environment, direct manipulation of the setting, such as some form of placement outside the home, might serve more effectively as an ameliorating approach.

Another area in need of more adequate differential diagnosis is the separation of schizophrenia from mental deficiency in children and also, within the schizophrenic type of disturbances in childhood, the separation of various subtypes. Each of these types would be expected to have a distinctly different basis, a differing rate of spontaneous recovery without specific treatment, a differing accessibility to treatment, and would perhaps require a unique form of treatment. Without subdividing schizophrenia but separating it from mental deficiency, Schachter, Meyer, and Loomis (1962) characterized the schizophrenic child as follows:

1. Prolonged withdrawal reaction (physical, social and/or emotional).
2. Consistently and characteristically bizarre motility patterns.
3. Prolonged, seriously disturbed sleep patterns.
4. Extraordinary resistance to change.
5. Speech (where present) characterized by pronominal reversal, immediate or delayed cholalia, failure to be used for conventional communication, and bizarre associations.
6. Cataclysmic panic reactions.
7. Low spontaneity, affective flatness and/or inappropriateness.
8. Persistent marked negativism.
9. Absence of demonstrable organic brain damage.

They characterized the mentally defective child, on the other hand, in this manner:

1. Reasonably symmetrical general retardation in emotional and intellectual development to patterns more typical of younger children.
2. Speech development slow and appropriate to younger age period.
3. Absence of marked social withdrawal, negativism, bizarreness, or other evidence of psychosis.
4. Absence of demonstrable organic brain damage.

In a free-play situation, the mentally retarded children resembled a control group of normal children in their responses to people and resembled schizophrenics in their responses to objects. In contrast, the schizophrenics show a grave impairment in responses both to things and people. As might be expected, the schizophrenic children displayed more variability in performance on intelligence tests.

Differential diagnosis of mentally defective and of schizophrenic children is clearly possible. Although the two groups generally resemble one another in inability to benefit much from training and in being somewhat unresponsive, they differ in many ways. First, unlike most severely retarded children, schizophrenics have no apparent abnormalities of physical development. Second, they display a great deal of variability in level of ability; a 10-year-old may function like a 10-year-old in some test situations and like a two-year-old in others. Third, they exhibit movements typical of schizophrenics—whirling, walking in circles, and other perseverative motor habits. They are less interested in people than are more genuinely defective children. Yet there is a fair amount of misdiagnosis; children who are schizophrenic, or perhaps schizophrenic *and* retarded, are placed in mentally retarded programs even though a number of easily observable symptoms might be used to differentiate the two groups.

Thus, despite the possibilities for relatively accurate differential diagnosis, it is not always made. Schizophrenic or schizoid children do not benefit as a rule from placement in mentally retarded educational programs and those programs suffer from their presence. Only through precise differentiation of two superficially similar problem groups can the genotype of each be ascertained and the most suitable treatment method be applied.

TREATMENT

While the medical model for differential diagnosis may not be entirely analogous to diagnosis of psychological problems, the data cited above strongly suggest that a separation of problem groups into subphenotypes, based on different causes, may improve the effectiveness of treatment. Perhaps we should act "as if" the medical model holds true.

Differential treatment, to be of maximal benefit, must be preceded by differential diagnosis. Diagnoses, of course, are made by many people, and those of parents and teachers are markedly different from those of clinicians with respect to the seriousness of behavioral problems. Even when parents or teachers recognize a bona fide problem, the evidence suggests that neither knows where to obtain help (e.g., Stendler, 1949). This section, therefore, describes various types of therapists and then considers various forms of therapy.

Quacks: How to Avoid Them

Charlatans, frauds, quacks, and crackpots abound in the field of diagnosing psychological disturbances and providing treatment for them (David, 1954; David & Springfield, 1958).

One reason for the prevalence of quacks is that many forms of therapy are in use and the relative efficacy of any one kind is hard to evaluate. With any luck at all, a quack who sets himself up as a therapist will find that at least half of his patients will improve, since there is evidence that, on the average, at least 50 percent of neurotic individuals whose problems have no organic antecedent get well even without treatment (see Eysenck, 1961, pp. 697–725, especially 704–705). That people often get well by themselves, have a *spontaneous remission*, works to the advantage of all therapists, including quacks.

Quacks fall into two main categories: commercial types in the business of therapy for money alone and single-minded crackpots who believe they have *the* answer to all of the world's ills but are being persecuted by better educated but jealous contemporaries. Both generally have college degrees of a sort, often from unaccredited institutions. Brophy and Durfee (1960) listed the various mail-order degrees purporting to qualify one for the practice of psychotherapy. In one of these diploma mills, they noted, four doctoral degrees—PsD, MsD, DD, and PhD—could be acquired in 20 months for $250. At this price, any quack could afford a doctor's degree. Some were not even graduates of elementary school.

One generally can avoid quacks by obtaining information regarding available legitimate professional help. The National Association for Mental Health in New York City publishes a directory of out-patient psychiatric clinics. The American Board of Psychological Services in St. Louis publishes a similar directory of psychological services. City or county medical associations can provide information regarding competent therapists. Many school systems now have their own staff psychologists and counselors. Numerous cities and counties have mental-health clinics, child-guidance centers, or family services where free or inexpensive treatment is obtainable.

Legitimate Therapists

Individuals engaged in legitimate mental-healing endeavors fall into four major categories; psychiatry, psychoanalysis, social work, and psychology. Their relative effectiveness, in terms of professional affiliation, generally is unclear (see Eysenck, 1961), as is that of more peripheral groups of trained psychotherapists such as pastoral counselors and pediatricians. The first three of the four major groups most frequently are involved in analytically oriented "directive" therapy; the last group, psychologists, in nondirective therapy and in behavior therapy.

Forms of Psychotherapy

However psychotherapists may differ from each other in professional affiliation, they all are confronted by the same problem: how to change the patient's behavior, or the behavior of the people interacting most closely with the patient, or both. The therapist's approach to this task depends on his conception of the role he can play and of the nature of problem behavior.

Directive Therapy. Directive or analytic therapists are most frequently psychiatrists and psychoanalysts. Since Freud, practitioners of this type of therapy have believed that if a problem is treated without finding its cause, the specific problem behavior that makes up the symptom may be "cured," but another symptom will take its place—as a nervous person who has been able to stop smoking may develop ulcers instead. Directive therapists generally believe that they know, within their own orientation or philosophy, the cause of a given problem. Whether their core of belief is around the Rankian birth trauma, the Freudian Oedipal complex, or some other concept that seems to them central as a cause of the behavior, their assignment is to direct the patient's flow of thoughts and associations in such a way that he also becomes aware of the cause. Once he has a conscious awareness, the patient need not expend psychic energy in repressing his feelings and can function normally.

Nondirective Therapy. The nondirective or client-centered therapist is usually a psychologist. He does not claim to know the cause of a disorder, but believes that in a supportive relationship with the patient he can reflect back to the patient the latter's own comments and behavior in a way that will help him to develop insight into his own problems. By understanding his problems, the patient will thus solve them.

Nondirective Play Therapy. Play is the child's commonest activity, and much treatment of children centers on play therapy. Although some play therapists are directive (see Kanner, 1957, p. 231), more commonly play therapy is nondirective. Axline's (1947) description of the theoretical basis and techniques of nondirective play therapy is classic. Like that of many contemporary therapists, her position was that the basis for problem behavior was in the environment, usually the home, and that the child's play often revealed the cause of the problem. Furthermore, in a nondirective atmosphere the child could resolve his problems. The therapist reflected back to the child the child's own statements so that the child could understand himself better. Play provided catharsis, an outpouring of feeling; this in itself was important. Finally, though the therapist was not essentially concerned with the learning of adequate social roles, this learning undoubtedly occurred, especially in a group play-therapy situation. The nondirective credo to the contrary, certain kinds of verbal and physical behavior are rewarded while others are extinguished through nonreinforcement during the therapy sessions, as shown by Truax (1966).

Behavior Therapy. The behavior therapist believes that his chief concern is with the patient's present behavior and not with the causes of the deviant behavior. To him, the symptoms *are* the disorder—these symptoms have been learned in the same way that all other behavior is learned, and the same rules operate in causing patients to stop manifesting their symptoms as operate in the extinction of any other behavior. This is a markedly different point of view from that of either the analytic or the nondirective therapist; if the behavior therapist changes the deviant behavior, he is satisfied.

It should be noted that some analytic and nondirective therapists do treat symptoms, but this is usually in conjunction with other efforts aimed at getting at the cause of a disturbance. We discuss behavior therapy at length here because it is currently receiving much attention from social scientists.

Behavior therapy developed gradually rather than all at once, but if it could be said to have one originator, he probably would be Wolpe. Wolpe was a Freudian when he first became a member of the South African contingent fighting Nazi Germany in the Libyan desert. With Pavlov as his chief source of reading material during the campaign, he emerged a behavior therapist within the Pavlovian tradition of conditioned reflex therapy (see Chapter 4). Wolpe's (1958) approach is concerned chiefly with reciprocal inhibition—basically, teaching the disturbed person to relax in tense situations, often through the use of Jacobson's (1938) *progressive relaxation* techniques, or else through the use of *desensitization*, which meant gradually exposing the disturbed individual to stimuli that progressively become more anxiety or fear producing as the means of causing anxiety reduction. Other kinds of behavior therapy involve causing the patient to model his behavior, in some adaptive fashion, after individuals in the environment (see Bandura, 1965; see also Slavson, 1952; Moreno, 1946; and Garland, Koloday, & Waldfogel, 1962), and shaping behavior by reward, by punishment, or by a combination of reward and punishment or reward and nonreinforcement. The purpose of all types of behavior therapy is to change the frequency with which certain behaviors occur.

Examples of each kind of procedure are given below. Further case studies (many of them dealing with children) and discussions of the principles of behavior therapy can be found in Wolpe (1958), Eysenck (1960), Eysenck and Rachman (1965), Krasner and Ullman (1965), and Ullman and Krasner (1965). An example of the use of reciprocal inhibition as a therapeutic technique is found in Jones' (1924) work with her subject, Peter, in which social reassurance served as a tension reducer or counter-conditioning force and ultimately caused the disappearance of certain fears. Some form of supportive and affectional behavior often serves as the anxiety-reducing agent (and/or as a reward for performing the feared behavior) in younger children, sometimes in combination with desensitization procedures. Desensitization alone is used more frequently with older children.

Reciprocal inhibition through affection plus desensitization occurred in a study by Bentler (1962). An 11-and-a-half-month-old girl, Margaret, developed a strong fear of water, for reasons possibly associated with separation from the mother as well as from slipping and falling in the bathtub. The response strengthened and generalized (she feared handbasins, faucets, water, and a wading pool as well as the bathtub). She was treated through reciprocal inhibition of the fear response by associating the feared object with pleasure (favorite toys) and through desensitization (she was exposed first to the empty tub and then to the filled kitchen sink, then she was placed in the sink, then washed in the sink, and finally returned to being bathed in a tub). A number of experiences were required at each level of contact with the feared situation, but she recovered within approximately one month and again enjoyed bathing in the tub and playing in her wading pool. All symptoms of her phobic response to water disappeared and did not recur.

A more clear-cut use of desensitization therapy is reported by Greer (1964). A girl had a fear of becoming infested by lice. This fear reached the point that she could not bear physical proximity to others, and was unable to do such things as attend school. A hierarchy of anxiety-producing stimuli was developed (e.g., a stimulus situation low in the hierarchy would be "Imagine yourself looking through a microscope at a dead louse mounted on a slide"; one high in the hierarchy might be "Imagine that your arms, shoulders, and neck are covered with lice, all crawling up to get in your hair"). Once a hierarchy has been developed, the patient begins by visualizing least anxiety-producing situation and continues to do this until the visualization of the imagined situation no longer produces anxiety, then visualizes the next most anxiety-producing situation, until finally even the most anxiety-producing situation can be imagined without fear. Often following, but sometimes simultaneously with the imagining, the patient also works through a hierarchy of behaviors (e.g., in the case mentioned above, an analogous behavioral hierarchy might range from dissecting a louse to allowing lice to crawl on her). Desensitization techniques seem more appropriate for fears and phobias than for other problems, but seem highly effective in this limited area and of fair value elsewhere.

The reciprocal inhibition and desensitization techniques described above are based, for the most part, on classical conditioning. Other kinds of behavior therapy have a close connection with the operant type of learning investigated by B. F. Skinner (see Chapter 4 for a discussion of operant and respondent learning). Behavior therapists of this latter persuasion are chiefiy concerned with manipulating behavior through combinations of positive reinforcement, negative reinforcement, and nonreinforcement. An example of an emphasis on positive reinforcement for correct responses is found in a study by Neale (1963), in which a nine-year-old boy regained bowel control after being encopretic (soiling himself) for 18 months. First, the boy was encouraged to go to the toilet at four specified times each day. Success in defecation resulted in a variety of rewards. Later, he again learned to be aware of and to respond to a sense of rectal fullness, so the specified times were discontinued. Success in defecation in the toilet continued to be rewarded. Soiling of the clothes *never* was punished, once the training procedure had been initiated. Complete success was achieved within three months after treatment was begun.

An example of a technique emphasizing the use of negative reinforcement in order to produce a desired behavior is found in the work of Lovaas, Schaeffer, and Simmons (1965). Lovaas and his associates treat autistic children—children who do not respond socially or affectionally to other individuals. Briefly, Lovaa's original technique was to shock the autistic child through an electrified floor until he moved toward other people and until, somewhat later in training, he interacted in specified ways with other people. More recent work by Lovaas and his associates has placed less emphasis on negative reinforcement and more on reward.

Nonreinforcement of an undesirable response, leading to the extinction of the response, is illustrated by Williams (1959). A 21-month-old boy would cry and have tantrums if his parents left him in his bed before he went to sleep. One of the parents or an aunt who shared care of the child had to spend anywhere from one-half to two hours waiting in the bedroom each time he went to sleep. Treatment consisted of ignoring the crying and tantrums. When the child needed to be put to bed he was put to bed in a pleasant fashion and then the door was closed. The duration of crying on each successive occasion is shown in Figure 16-1. Two extinction series are shown, since the aunt rewarded his tantrum behavior on one occasion by remaining with him until he went to sleep. This re-evoked the behavior, but it was extinguished again through nonreinforcement. Most behavior therapists in the Skinnerian tradition use some combination of these three procedures—positive reinforcement of the desired behavior, negative reinforcement of the undesirable behavior, and nonreinforcement of the undesirable behavior.

The aim of behavior therapy is to eliminate socially undesirable behaviors ("symptoms") and to build in socially

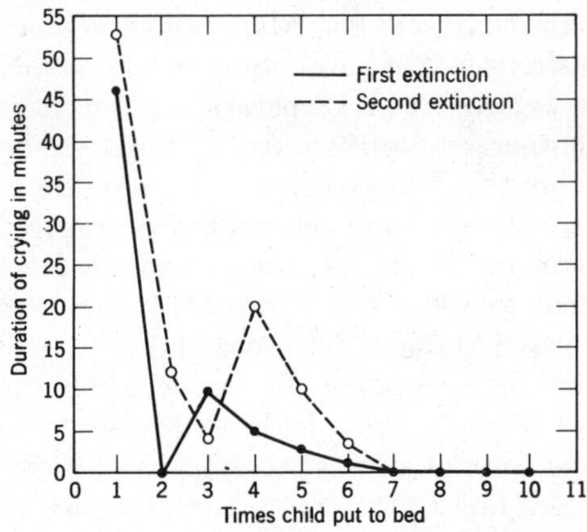

FIGURE 16-1 Length of crying in two extinction series as a function of successive occasions of being put to bed (Williams, 1959, p. 269).

desirable behaviors. As noted above, other types of therapist generally believe that the undesirable behavior is a sign of some deeper psychic disturbance, and that if the symptom is eliminated without getting at the cause of the symptom, another problem will spring up in place of the one that was eliminated. However, Eysenck (1960, p. 9), a behavior therapist, says, *"Get rid of the symptom and you have eliminated the neurosis."* Further, according to Ullman and Krasner (1965, pp. 13–14), symptom substitution does not seem to occur, Freudian theory to the contrary.

As a result of a concern for symptoms, of a high level of success in treating symptoms, and of finding no basis for the notion of symptom substitution, behavior therapists generally are opposed to the idea of differential diagnosis, as espoused in this chapter. However, behavior therapy is not universally effective in the treatment of any kind of disorder; it is less effective for some kinds of problem than for others; and, when effective inside the laboratory situation, it may or may not generalize to behavior in the larger social milieu. All these matters depend on the personality of the patient, the kind of psychological disturbance, and the relative weighting of the possible different types of behavior therapy used. Therefore, even though behavior therapy has proved to be far more effective than other approaches acorss a wide range of problem behaviors, the problem of determining what kind of disturbance benefits most from what kind of treatment remains a valid one.

Finally, with regard to behavior therapy, it should be noted that it is avowedly based on learning theory. It probably is true, as Breger and McGaugh say (see Breger & McGaugh, 1965, 1966; Rachman & Eysenck, 1966) that behavior therapy is based on overly simplified and, in part, inaccurate notions about the way that humans learn. Even so, behavior therapy seems effective. As in the case of many other human accomplishments, such as the prehistoric development of metallurgy, effective practice can precede complete theretical understanding. Based on a set of testable ideas, behavior therapy appears to have the potential to develop into a still more effective procedure than it is at present.

The Behavior Therapy Approach to Problem Behavior

Here is the way that a behavior therapist might approach a problem.

Let's say that the problem, as first described, is that, according to the classroom teacher and the school principal, nine-year-old John is a "troublemaker in the classroom." The first step is to specify what in the world they mean by "troublemaker in the classroom." This label could mean anything from telling the teacher that she was factually incorrect when she was factually incorrect in making a statement to threatening to cut the teacher's ears off with a switch blade. The behavior must be specified. In this case, let us say that the term *troublemaker* in the classroom has three major components: 1. talking when he should be quiet, 2. clowning around–making noise and making faces that get the class to laughing, 3. not remaining seated–continually being up and about when the rest of the class is seated.

One might tackle all three of these behaviors at once. Ackerman (1972, pp. 40–41), among others, suggests that it is best to start on one, rather than to deal with them all at once. He suggests that one should choose the one behavior that is first to be changed on the basis of

1. Annoyance value. Why not try to eliminate, first, the most annoying

behavior? This will positively reinforce the behavior changer.

2. Available reinforcers. The person desiring to change the behavior must have some control over reinforcement contingencies (rewards, punishment, nonreinforcement) associated with the behavior; if not, it is unlikely that the behavior can be modified.
3. Behavior rate. Choose a behavior that occurs at a relatively high frequency. After all, the behavior must occur before it can be modified.
4. Alterability. Choose a behavior that appears relatively easy to alter.

Let's say that, on the basis of unsystematic observation and subjective feelings of annoyance, the teacher chooses "out-of-seat" behavior as the first behavior to modify. It is annoying, disruptive, occurs with substantial frequency, and since most children will stay in their seats when they're supposed to do so, there must be available reinforcers available in the classroom that make the behavior alterable.

The first step is to obtain a baseline rate of frequency for the behavior to be changed. One can only establish the effects, if any, of an intervention effort, if one has solid data in how frequently the behavior occurred prior to intervention. Since out-of-the-seat behavior was a frequent behavior for John, the teacher might well use time sampling (see Chapter 1, pp. 18) to establish a base rate. Out-of-the seat behavior occurs during study and recitation time. The teacher should divide that portion of the school day devoted in behavior requiring that the student stay seated, for the most part, into segments of, say, three minutes each. Each day before going to school, the teacher then in some random fashion, chooses, 10 three-minute segments during which the frequency of out-of-the-seat behavior is recorded. The teacher also should choose at random, some extra time periods. The needs of other children will cause the teacher to forget some of the time periods, so that some of the original 10 intervals will remain unrecorded; the addition intervals will serve as replacements. Once the intervals have been chosen for a given day, the teacher can mark a 3 × 5 card every time the behavior occurs, using a different row for each segment of time (see Table 16-1). Observation should be as inobtrusive as possible.

Five days of this kind of time sampling should be enough to establish a base rate against which to evaluate one's intervention techniques. If one finds consistency across days (e.g., more getting out of the seat and wandering about the room in the morning then in the afternoon, more in reading than in math, more in solitary preparation than in discussion) one also may ascertain the conditions most likely to trigger the behavior.

While observing the frequency with which out-of-the-seat behavior occurs, the teacher also should observe, as systematically as possible, the specific events that trigger the behavior, and the consequences of the behavior. This also can be done when the behavior occurs during those times in which the teacher is obtaining baseline data. The first may be difficult; the second generally can be done. Let's say, that over a period of one week, the teacher finds that about one-third of the time, he or she admonishes John and says "John, sit down!" The admonition, when it occurs, always brings John to the attention of his classmates. About one admonition out of every three evokes a titter from the class. About one time in six, following the teacher's response to John, a neighbor begins talking to him as soon as he is seated. John is receiving plenty of enjoyable positive reinforcement. The reinforcement from classmates is intermittent (see Chapter 4, pp. 123); this will keep the behavior going at a high rate and make it resistant to extinction. Further, all of the different

TABLE 16-1

Time Sampling Sheet	Behavior Out of Seat	
Student name *John*	Day *Monday*	Date 10/18
Time	*Activity*	*Frequency*
1. 9:09–9:12	Reading period	1111
2. 9:27–9:30	Discussion of story read	1
3. 10:18–10:21	Practice at writing letter	~~1111~~ 1
4. 11:24–11:27	Reading history lesson	111
5. 11:45–11:48	Discussion of history unit	1
6. 12:48–12:51	Spelling practice	111
7. 12:57–1:00	Spelling test	———
8. 1:15–1:54	Free reading period	1
9. 1:51–1:54	Doing arithmetic problems at desk	11
10. 2:09–2:12	Division problems at blackboard	111
	Total for the day	24
	Rate per minute	.8

observable reinforcements may well be positive. Being admonished, scolded, or nagged does not, on the face of it, appear to be rewarding. But attention per se, may be rewarding. Buys (1970), in a behavior modification study, dealt with the very worst behavior problems in an elementary school. In establishing baselines he discovered that some of these children received no reinforcements at all from the teacher except when they misbehaved. No positive exchanges occurred between a problem child and the teacher throughout a fairly long (long enough, in some cases, for the child to receive up to a thousand negative responses) baseline observation period. Any interaction may be far more rewarding than none.

So now we have some clues as to what keeps the behavior going. The problem, now, is to alter the reinforcement contingencies so that out-of-the-seat behavior becomes less rewarding: sitting in the seat and doing one's work becomes more rewarding. It might be more scientific to systematically vary one thing at a time in order to determine the effects of each environment change on the behavior in question. But generally one is dealing with a real-life problem that requires moderately rapid remediation. Therefore, typically, many things are varied at once. For example, in this particular instance, a variety of things can be done.

There are some things that the teacher can do. Yelling at John for the behavior hasn't decreased the behavior. Not responding to the behavior may do so. This means no yelling, no attention, complete ignoring. Nonreinforcement, if given enough time, presumably will cause the behavior to cease. Also, building in a desired behavior incompatible with out-of-the-seat behavior should hasten the cessation of the undesired behavior. Praising John for periods in which he remains in his seat and works at his lesson certainly will increase these behaviors. As noted above, Buys found that some school children receive *no* positive reinforcement. The teacher may wish to "make a contract"; to agree, to oneself, not to perform some desired behavior, such as taking a coffee break, until John has been praised at least twice for the day. Ultimately, the praising of desired behavior will become habitual. The recipient won't be startled. The teacher will no longer have to make a contract in order to make sure it is done.

There are some things that John's classmates can do. The teacher can be honest and say, "John has trouble learning as well as he might because he's always in and out of his seat when he's supposed to be sitting and working. We can help John. One of the reasons that John does this is that we watch him, I yell at him, and you laugh and talk about it. I'm not going to yell at John. What I want you to do is to not pay any attention when he gets up, even when he seems to want your attention. On days when you all help John (and me) by not paying attention when he does something he's not supposed to do, I'm going to reward you with an extra 5 minutes of recess." This usually is enough of an incentive to get class cooperation, once the rewards have been forthcoming.

John can do something about his behavior, too. Most classroom terrors would prefer another role—they won't fight change, once change seems possible. There must be a number of things that John would like to do inside the classroom far more than he likes disrupting the classroom. These usually can be ascertained. Does he like to draw? If so, one could establish a contract with John —One minute at the easel for every five minutes spent without getting out of his seat (since his base rate is up out of the seat every 0.8 minutes, this would be quite an improvement); a half minute loss of earned time for every time up.

As the nature of the reinforcements change, it is very likely that John's behavior will change—that he will cease this constantly being in and out of his seat. Then, on to the next behavior to be changed. Ackerman (1972) and Watson and Tharp (1972) provide many more examples than those given above regarding means by which behavior can be modified through changing reinforcement contingencies. Further, they describe means of "thinning"—of reducing what at times are essentially somewhat artificial rewards (e.g., extra recess for the class) for prosocial behavior. They describe the means of checking the effectiveness of the intervention, by graphing changes in behavior frequency from the baseline rate, and many other aspects of behavior modification not covered in this section. But this section gives some of the flavor of behavior therapy—of the concentration on the behavior to be modified and the manipulation of the rewards and punishments found in the environment in order that this modification occur.

PROGNOSIS

As noted in Chapter 15, humans show a good deal of consistency in their behavior. This consistency is undoubtedly related to the fact that, for any given individual certain behaviors lead to reward or positive reinforcement. This reinforcement may come from the self or from others who reward the individual's consistency because it makes behavior more orderly and predictable. Reinforcement may also take the form of "secondary gain" as, for instance, when an individual thinks to himself, "I feel less tense now that I've stolen a car."

So long as behaviors judged by society as deviant and maladaptive reward a specific individual, it is unlikely that change will occur. The therapeutic process, by rewarding a new class of behaviors, by extinguishing an old set through nonreinforcement, or by both, endeavors to reduce deviant behavior. Quite likely changes in age alone, without therapeutic assistance, produce new demands on the individual that reduce the rewards of certain deviant behaviors and increase the rewards of others. In considering prognosis—the probability of recovery—one attempts to distinguish the problems that persist over time, despite therapeutic aid and the shifts that accompany age, from those problem behaviors that are easily extinguishable through therapy or that disappear of their own accord as the patient grows older.

Looming large on the list of clinical referrals are problem behaviors that result largely from adult misunderstanding of child behavior—from judging normal acts to be atypical and deviant. These problems do not become problems until diagnosed. Next come the genuine problems that will decrease in severity or even disappear in most cases without any treatment whatsoever. Then there are the problems that are severe but transient and those that are mild but long-term. Finally, there are the severe, persisting problems that do not yield easily to treatment.

Physicians have long distinguished between chronic and transient disorders. Perhaps psychologists need to follow the example of medical practice. As long as therapists are in short supply, it would be of great value to have normative data on the duration and degree of debilitation of various problem disorders. Lacking this information, one cannot make a judicious use of therapy time. Without knowledge of how frequently various problems disappear by themselves, it is not possible even to evaluate the effects of therapy.

Acting Out and Withdrawn Behaviors

So broad a division of behavioral problems into acting out and withdrawal behaviors may not serve much purpose in permitting the prediction of severity or outcome of specific disorders. Yet the relative seriousness of each of these two broad categories warrants consideration, especially since the subject has aroused considerable controversy.

In one of the first studies aimed at finding the views of various individuals toward the seriousness of problems, Wickman (1928) found teachers and clinicians differing widely in their judgments of problem severity (see Chapter 12). From the rather large collection of problem behaviors rated, those judged as among the most serious by one group were often considered as among the least serious by the other. Although later studies (e.g., Beilin, 1959) have shown teachers and clinicians to be more in agreement nowadays than in Wickman's time, some of the differences he noted remain (Ritholz, 1959). The Ritholz study further demonstrated that parents and even children themselves agreed with the teachers. Whereas clinicians consider psychological conditions resulting in withdrawn behavior as the most serious, teachers, parents, and children are more concerned with actual conduct, generally aggressive in character.

In general the clinicians' assessment of problem seriousness appears correct, though incorrect in some particulars. The entire cluster of traits composing "withdrawal" seems to be a poor sign in prognosis. From among 73 children referred to a clinic, Brown (1960) took 20 who were doing well and an equal number who were doing poorly and compared them in symptoms exhibited at the time of original referral to the clinic. The worst cases manifested greater withdrawal in every respect. The best, on the other hand, oftener showed inhibition and caution—behaviors that have come to be associated with withdrawal. Whereas it might be argued that inhibited, cautious behavior will predict withdrawal, this is not true. These symptoms more accurately reflect a lesser frequency of the discharge of tension through total and diffuse motor behavior. Withdrawn behavior does appear to be quite serious, as clinicians maintain, but the clinicians seem wrong, in part, in their analyses of its constituent traits.

In the Wickman study, clinicians rated shyness as a rather serious problem. Some of them may have believed shyness itself to be pathological. Many more probably rated it as a serious problem because they believed that the shy, introverted individual was prone to schizophrenic disorders. This is questionable. The idea that the shy introvert is more susceptible to schizophrenia than the more extroverted individual is doubtful; both older (Ackerson, 1931) and more recent (Michael, Morris, & Soroker, 1957) studies indicate that shyness has a strong tendency to vanish of its own accord as an individual ages, and that it in no way predicts later schizophrenia. The withdrawn child who *can* relate to others, but does not do so, is withdrawn in a very different sense from the child who does not relate to others because of a general confusion and inability to respond. The latter kind of withdrawn behavior is more serious than acting out behaviors.

Despite the belief frequently held by therapists that acting out behaviors are more amenable to therapy than are neurotic or withdrawn behaviors, one of the most extensive follow-up studies of deviant children (Robbins, 1966) shows that basically psychopathic or sociopathic acting out kinds of problems have by far the poorest prognosis of problem types. This, of course, is what we would expect from Mowrer's position (see Chapter 7).

In any broad category of behavior, certain subtypes have good prognosis and others are less promising of successful recovery. Table 16-2 lists behaviors ranging from simple problems of habit formation to relatively severe disorders. Accompanying them is evidence concerning their probability of remission—that is, recovery—in most cases, without treatment.

Only when it is known that individuals can recover by themselves from a number of problems can the effectiveness of therapy be determined. Some studies suggest that therapy is of little value (e.g., Levitt, Bieser, & Robertson, 1959; Robins & O'Neal, 1958). Other studies claim high rates of remission (e.g., Rexford, Schleifer, & Van Amerongen, 1956; Cunningham, Westerman, & Fischhoff, 1956). Either is hard to evaluate without knowing the frequency with which various problems arose among the children studied, the rate of spontaneous remission of these problems, and the type of therapy used.

SUMMARY

Hereditary, physiological, familial, and sociological factors all operate in the production of problem behavior. Their respective contributions vary from one disorder to the next. Moreover, as skill is developed in differentiating between superficially similar disorders, specific or relatively specific single causes may be found in the background of each of the subtypes of disorder composing a broad phenotypical category.

Clinicians differ from other individuals in their judgments of the seriousness of various disorders. Although perhaps incorrect about specifics, the clinicians seem generally correct in their assessment of problem severity. Unlike others who deal with children, the clinician uses systematic observation and is committed to scientific rules of evidence. Thus he is potentially capable of developing adequate diagnostic and therapeutic techniques.

In diagnosis, so far, emphasis on broad phenotypical categories has impeded the development of effective treatment meth-

TABLE 16-2 Behavior Problems and Their Probability of Remission

Investigator	High Probability of Remission	Low Probability of Remission
MacFarlane, Allen & Honzik, 1955 (an extensive longitudinal study)	Timidity Specific fears Tantrums Speech problems Enuresis Bad dreams Restlessness in sleep Poor appetite, "finicky" eating Thumb sucking Destructiveness Excessive demanding of attention Excessive activity Lying Masturbation	Excessive modesty Excessive dependence Oversensitiveness Nail biting Jealousy Somberness
Ackerson, 1931 (an extensive cross-sectional study)	Restlessness Shyness Distractibility Fearfulness Tantrums Finicky eating habits Negativism Cruelty to younger children	Depression Seclusiveness Unresponsiveness Oversensitiveness Daydreaming Sullenness Egocentricity Emotional lability Boastfulness Irritability Selfishness
Johnson, 1950	Social delinquent	Solitary delinquent
Michael, Morris, & Soroker, 1957	Shyness	
Bender, 1947		Childhood schizophrenia
Kanner & Eisenberg, 1955	Autism, if child verbal by age 5	Autism, if child still mute at age 5
Berkowitz, 1955	"Predelinquent" behavior (76% had no record as delinquents)	
Griffiths, 1952	Upper- and lower-class "delinquency-related" behaviors	Middle-class "delinquency-related" behaviors

ods. Differential diagnosis, based on observation within the phenotype, leads to discovery of various genotypes and permits development of specific treatment aimed at one genotypical variety of problem.

As far as most problem behaviors are concerned, there are two general approaches to treatment of children—some form of play therapy or some form of behavior therapy. The value of play therapy is not entirely certain, while that of behavior therapy, in most of its aspects, seems well demonstrated. Fortunately, many problem behaviors disappear without treatment. Despite the present lack of knowledge of problem behavior and its treatment, there is reason to hope that present skills in treatment can be greatly improved.

REFERENCES

Ackerman, J. M. *Operant conditioning techniques for the classroom teacher.* Glenview, Ill.: Scott, Foresman, 1972.

Ackerman, N. W. *The psychodynamics of family life.* New York: Basic Books, 1958.

Ackerson, L. *Children's behavior problems. I. Incidence, genetic, and intellectual factors.* Chicago: University of Chicago Press, 1931.

Ahern, F. M. & Johnson, R. C. Inherited uterine inadequacy: An alternate explanation for a portion of cases of defect. *Behavior Genetics,* 1973, **3**, 1-12.

Axline, V. M. *Play therapy.* Boston: Houghton Mifflin, 1947.

Bandura, A. Behavior modification through modeling procedures. In L. Krasner & L. P. Ullman (Eds.), *Research in behavior modification.* New York: Holt, Rinehart and Winston, 1965.

Barnes, A. C. *Intra-uterine development.* Philadelphia: Lea & Febiger, 1968.

Bateson, G., Jackson, D. D., Haley, J., & Weakland, J. Toward a theory of schizophrenia. *Behavioral Science,* **1**, 251-264.

Beilin, H. Teacher's and clinician's attitudes toward behavior problems of children: a reappraisal. *Child Development,* 1959, **30**, 9–25.

Bender, L. R. Childhood schizophrenia; clinical study of one hundred schizophrenic children. *American Journal of Orthopsychiatry,* 1947, **17**, 40–56.

Bentler, P. M. An infant's phobia treated with reciprocal inhibition therapy. *Journal of Child Psychology and Psychiatry,* 1962, **3**, 185–189.

Berkowitz, B. The Juvenile Aid Bureau of the New York City Police. *Nervous Child,* 1955, **11**, 42–48.

Bessman, S. J., Genetic failure of fetal amino acid "justification": a common basis for many forms of metabolic, nutritional, and "nonspecific" mental retardation. *Journal of Pediatrics,* 1972, **81**, 834–842.

Breger, L., & McGaugh, J. L. Critique and reformulation of "learning theory" approaches to psychotherapy and neurosis. *Psychological Bulletin,* 1965, **63**, 338–358.

Breger, L., & McGaugh, J. L. Learning theory and behavior therapy: A reply to Rachman and Eysenck. *Psychological Bulletin,* 1966, **65**, 170–173.

Brigham, J. C., Ricketts, J. L., & Johnson, R. C. Reported maternal and paternal behaviors of solitary and social delinquents. *Journal of Consulting Psychology,* 1967, **31**, 420–422.

Brophy, A. L., & Durfee, R. A. Mail order training in psychotherapy. *American Psychologist,* 1960, **15**, 356–360.

Brown, J. L. Prognosis from presenting symptoms of preschool children with atypical development. *American Journal of Orthopsychiatry,* 1960, **30**, 382–390.

Buys, C. J. Effects of teacher reinforcement on classroom behaviors and attitudes. Unpublished doctoral dissertation, University of Colorado, Boulder, Colorado, 1970.

Chessman, C., *Cell 2455, death row*. New York: Pocket Books, 1955.

Cunningham, J. M., Westerman, Hester H., & Fischhoff, J. A follow up study of patients seen in a psychiatric clinic for children. *American Journal of Orthopsychiatry*, 1956, **26**, 602–611.

David, H. P. Phones, phonies, and psychologists. *American Psychologist*, 1954, **9**, 237–240.

David, H. P., & Springfield, F. B. Phones, phonies and psychologists: H. Four years later. *American Psychologist*, 1958, **13**, 61–64.

Eysenck, H. J. *Behavior therapy and the neuroses*. Oxford, England: Pergamon, 1960.

Eysenck, H. J. *Handbook of abnormal psychology*. New York: Basic Books, 1961.

Eysenck, H. J. The effects of psychotherapy. *International Journal of Psychiatry*, 1965, **1**, 97–144.

Eysenck, H. J., & Rachman, S. *The causes and cures of neuroses*. San Diego, California: Knapp, 1965.

Fish, B. Longitudinal observations of biological deviations in a schizophrenic infant. *American Journal of Psychiatry*, 1959, **116**, 25–31.

Garland, J. A., Kolodny, R. L., & Waldfogel, S. Social group work as adjunctive treatment for the emotionally disturbed adolescent: The experience of a specialized group work department. *American Journal of Orthopsychiatry*, 1962, **32**, 691–706.

Gottesman, I. I. Heritability of personality: A demonstration. *Psychological Monographs*, 1963, **77**, Whole No. 572.

Gottesman, I., & Shields, J. In pursuit of the schizophrenic genotype. Paper presented at the second Louisville conference on human behavior genetics, 1966.

Greer, J. H. Phobia treated by reciprocal inhibition. *Journal of Abnormal and Social Psychology*, 1964, **69**, 642–645.

Griffiths, W. *Behavior difficulties of children as perceived and judged by parents, teachers, and children themselves*. Minneapolis: University of Minnesota Press, 1952.

Haley, J. The family of the schizophrenic: A model system. *Journal of Nervous and Mental Disease*, 1959, **129**, 357–374.

Haley, J. *Strategies of psychotherapy*. New York: Grune & Stratton, 1963.

Hebb, D. O. *The organization of behavior*. New York: Wiley, 1949.

Heilbrun, A. G., Jr. Perceptual distortion and schizophrenia. *American Journal of Orthopsychiatry*, 1960, **30**, 412–418.

Hobbs, N. Helping disturbed children: Psychological and ecological strategies. *American Psychologist*, 1966, **21**, 1105–1115.

Jackson, D. D. *Myths of madness: New facts for old fallacies*. New York: Macmillan, 1964.

Jacobson, E. *Progressive relaxation*. Chicago: University of Chicago Press, 1938.

Johnson, R. C. Causal factors in the delinquency of fifty Denver boys. Unpublished master's thesis, Denver University, 1950.

Johnson, R. C. Behavioral characteristics of phenylketonurics and matched controls. *American Journal of Mental Deficiency*, 1969, **74**, 17–19.

Jones, M. C. A laboratory study of fear: The case of Peter. *Pedagogical Seminary and Journal of Genetic Psychology*, 1924, **31**, 308–315.

Kanner, L. *Child psychiatry*. Springfield, Ill.: Thomas, 1957.

Kanner, L., & Eisenberg, L. Notes on the follow-up studies of autistic children. In P. H. Hoch & J. Zubin (Eds.), *Psychopathology of childhood.* New York: Grune & Stratton, 1955.

Kaplan, B. J. Malnutrition and mental retardation. *Psychological Bulletin,* 1972, **78**, 321–334.

Kawi, A. A., & Pasamanick, B. Prenatal and paranatal factors in the development of childhood reading disorders. *Monographs of the Society for Research in Child Development,* 1959, **24**, No. 4.

Kinsey, A. C., Pomeroy, W. B., & Martin, C. E. *Sexual behavior in the human male.* Philadelphia: Saunders, 1948.

Kinsey, A. C., Pomeroy, W. B., Martin, C. E., & Gebhard, P. H. *Sexual behavior in the human female.* Philadelphia: Saunders, 1953.

Kohn, M. L., & Clausen, J. A. Parental authority behavior and schizophrenia. *American Journal of Orthopsychiatry,* 1956, **26**, 297–313.

Krasner, L., & Ullman, L. P. *Research in Behavior Modification.* New York: Holt, Rinehart & Winston, 1965.

Kringlen, E. Schizophrenia in twins: An epidemiological clinical study. *Psychiatry,* 1966, **29**, 172–184.

Lakin, M. Personality factors in mothers of excessively crying (colicky) infants. *Monographs of the Society for Research in Child Development,* 1957, **22**, No. 1.

Lecky, P. *Self consistency, a theory of personality.* New York: Island Press, 1945.

Levitt, E. E., Bieser, H., & Robertson, R. A follow-up evaluation of cases treated at a community child guidance clinic. *American Journal of Orthopsychiatry,* 1959, **29**, 337–346.

Lovaas, O. I., Schaeffer, B., & Simmons, J. Q. Building social behavior in autistic children by use of electric shock. *Journal of Experimental Research in Personality,* 1965, **1**, 99–109.

MacFarlane, J. W. Allen, L., & Honzik, M. *A developmental study of behavior problems of normal children between 21 months and 14 years.* Berkeley: University of California Press, 1955.

McCandless, B. R. Relation of environmental factors to intellectual functioning. In H. A. Stevens and R. Heber (Eds.) *Mental retardation: A review of research,* Chicago, University of Chicago Press, 1964. Pp. 175–213.

Medinnus, G. R. Delinquents' perceptions of their parents. *Journal of Consulting Psychology,* 1965, **29**, 592–593.

Michael, C. M., Morris, D. P., & Soroker, E. Follow-up studies of shy, withdrawn children. II. Relative incidence of schizophrenia. *American Journal of Orthopsychiatry,* 1957, **27**, 331–337.

Moreno, J. L. *Psychodrama.* New York: Beacon House, 1946.

Mowrer, O. H. "Sin," the lesser of two evils. *American Psychologist,* 1960, **15**, 301–304.

Neale, D. H. Behavior therapy and encopresis in children. *Behavior Research Therapy,* 1963, **1**, 139–150.

Pasamanick, B., Rogers, M., & Lilienfeld, A. Pregnancy experience and the development of behavior disorder in children. *American Journal of Psychiatry,* 1956, **112**, 613–617.

Pastore, N. Genetics of schizophrenia. *Psychological Bulletin,* 1949, **46**, 285–302.

Pavlov, I. P. *Conditioned reflexes and psychiatry* (translated by W. H. Gant). New York: International Publishers, 1941.

Prout, C. T., & White, M. A. The schizophrenic's siblings. *Journal of Nervous and Mental Diseases*, 1956, **123**, 162–170.

Rachman, S., & Eysenck, H. J. Reply to a "critique and reformulation" of behavior therapy. *Psychological Bulletin*, 1966, **65**, 165–169.

Randolph, M. H., Richardson, H., & Johnson, R. C. A comparison of social and solitary male delinquents. *Journal of Consulting Psychology*, 1961, **25**, 293–295.

Reed, E. W. & Reed, S. C. *Mental retardation: A family study.* Philadelphia: Saunders, 1965.

Rexford, E. N., Schleifer, M., & Van Amerongen, S. T. A follow-up of a psychiatric study of 57 antisocial young children. *Mental Hygiene*, 1956, **40**, 196–214.

Rimland, B. *Infantile autism.* New York: Appleton-Century-Crofts, 1964.

Ritholz, S. *Children's behavior.* New York: Bookman, 1959.

Robins, L. N. *Deviant children grown up.* Baltimore: Williams & Wilkins, 1966.

Robins, L. N., & O'Neal, P. The marital history of former problem children. *Social Problem*, 1958, **5**, 347–358.

Roe, A. A psychological study of eminent psychologists and anthropologists, and a comparison with biologists and physical scientists. *Psychological Monographs*, 1953, **57**, No. 2.

Roebuck, J. B., & Johnson, R. C. The short con man. *Crime and Delinquency*, 1964, **10**, 235–248.

Rogers, C. R. *Client centered therapy.* Boston: Houghton Mifflin, 1951.

Rosenthal, D. Some factors associated with concordance and discordance with respect to schizophrenia in monozygotic twins. *Journal of Nervous and Mental Diseases*, 1959, **129**, 1–10.

Rosenthal, D. Problems of sampling and diagnosis in the major twin studies of schizophrenia. *Journal of Psychiatric Research*, 1962, **1**, 115–134.

Rosenthal, D. (Ed.). *The Genain quadruplets.* New York: Basic Books, 1963.

Schachter, F. F., Meyer, L. R., & Loomis, E. A., Jr. Childhood schizophrenia and mental retardation: Differential diagnosis before and after one year of psychotherapy. *American Journal of Orthopsychiatry*, 1962, **32**, 584–594.

Schofield, W., & Balian, L. A comparative study of the personal histories of schizophrenic and nonpsychiatric patients. *Journal of Abnormal and Social Psychology*, 1959, **59**, 216–225.

Slavson, S. R. *Child psychotherapy.* New York: Columbia University Press, 1952.

Stendler, C. B. How well do elementary school teachers understand child behavior? *Journal of Educational Psychology*, 1949, **40**, 489–498.

Truax, C. B. Reinforcement and nonreinforcement in Rogerian psychotherapy. *Journal of Abnormal Psychology*, 1966, **71**, 1–9.

Ullman, L. P., & Krasner, L. *Case studies in behavior modification.* New York: Holt, Rinehart & Winston, 1965.

Vandenberg, S. G. Hereditary factors in normal personality traits (as measured by inventories). In *Recent advances in biological psychology*, Vol. 9. New York: Plenum, 1967. Pp. 65–104.

Watson, D. & Tharp, R. *Sefl-directed behavior.* Monterey, Calif.: Brooks/Cole, 1972.

Wickman, E. K. *Children's behavior and teacher's attitudes.* New York: Commonwealth Fund, 1928.

Williams, C. D. The elimination of tantrum behavior by extinction procedures. *Journal of Abnormal and Social Psychology*, 1959, **59**, 269.

Wolpe, J. *Psychotherapy by reciprocal inhibition*. Stanford, Calif.: Stanford University Press, 1958.

chapter 17

summing up

chapter 17

summing up

chapter 17

summing up

The aim of science is to understand natural phenomena. The scientist assumes that the universe is orderly and that natural phenomena, ultimately, are predictable and lawful. Understanding and prediction come from the use of the scientific method. The scientific method is merely a set of rules by which scientists attempt to eliminate bias from there observations and thus view nature as it is, not as they wish it to be.

Systematic observation of unbiased samples of the phenomenon under investigation is the key to an accurate understanding of the universe. Experiments are the form of observation most commonly used in science, since in experiments uncontrolled or unknown sources of variance are reduced to a minimum. Further, experiments, far more than naturalistic observation, may be directed to highly specific problems whose solution may provide the information needed to decide which of two or more conflicting theories is the most accurate portrayal of the relations between natural phenomena.

On the negative side, an emphasis on experimentation may cause the neglect, for the most part, of those natural phenomena that do not readily fit within conventional experimental design. This is illustrated in the psychology of learning; there is a plethora of experiments dealing with forms of learning common to all species but few dealing with those complex forms of cognition that set mankind apart from other species.

We observe, systematically and without bias. From this observation we attempt to understand, predict, and, at times, control the phenomena with which we deal. In psychology, especially in child psychology, there are grave ethical problems involved in scientifically controlling behavior. It seems reasonable to believe that the level of development of a science should be judged by the degree to which that science allows understanding and predictions.

This book has attempted to provide information about the known and the predictable in child psychology. In general, although at a lesser stage of development than the physical or biological sciences, child psychology has much to be proud of. It has steadily increased the rigor of its methods of investigation and the accuracy of its predictions. From the scattered anecdotes and unsupported folk beliefs of a century ago, and from the scanty array of methods and information available at the turn of the century, it has developed adequate research methods, a vast store of facts, and a few theories useful for knitting together at least some of the facts in an orderly fashion. Child psychology appears to be at the stage where theories, more accurate and inclusive than those now available, can be evolved and proved valuable rather than merely blinding people to those natural events for which they cannot account.

The child psychologist has to deal with two major questions. First, in what ways are humans all alike, and why? Second, within this framework of similarity, how do individual differences arise? These are the two problems that this book has attempted to deal with as best possible in the light of imperfect knowledge.

Two sets of forces work upon mankind, those that are biological-genetic, and those that are social. The biological-genetic forces are chiefly influential in producing a basic similarity between all humans; they also serve to produce a biological core of individual difference, which is further increased by each individual's unique set of social experiences. Social forces also produce similarity between humans. We share the characteristic of growing up within some primary group, of being cared for by one or more parents or parent-surrogates; we all must face the challenge of moving from a position of dependence to one of comparative independence. Further similarity results from being brought up within one specific culture, with its own pattern of relieving social stresses. However alike humans may be, as a result of the similarity in the way they are socialized, it is their unique social environment that greatly enlarges the individual differences that are hereditary in nature.

Humans are alike. We are bipedal, with stereoscopic vision and with sensitive hands, free to manipulate objects in the environment. We follow the same general course of growth and maturation. We share with all other animals certain ways of learning, such as operant and respondent learning, but are different from all nonprimates in other areas, such as in the ease of formation of learning sets. We are like one another, but unlike all other organisms, in the ease with which we deal with abstract concepts, delayed reactions, and complex and creative problem solving. This human uniqueness appears to be the result of the fact that only humans are capable of symbolic behavior. Language is again an inherited ability, causing humans to share a broad social heritage, built up across generations, and to show similarity in social and intellectual responses to the world. We are manipulative, curious, and arousal seeking. Within this framework of similarity, individual differences occur.

We are different. Genetic inheritance makes individuals differ from one another in obvious ways, as in eye color, skin color, size, and physical attractiveness, and in less obvious but more significant ways, as in intelligence and in activity level. Certain innate differences are present, and these differences are enhanced by the environment.

The contemporary American child grows up in a rich, urban, industrial society in which there is little need for early economic productivity. This society is becoming milder in its approach to child rearing, although it may still be considered relatively harsh in some areas if judged by cross-cultural standards. The child is less subject to parental pressures and more subject to the influences of such agents of socialization as his peers and the school. Although parental influences are probably somewhat less pervasive than previously at any given time in the child's early life, the period of dependency on parents has lengthened considerably.

Within the areas of similarity within the culture, forces producing diversity operate. The sex of the child, his ordinal position, the characteristics of his siblings, and the economic well-being and marital adjustment of the parents are all important factors producing differences in the way the child is treated within the family—and thus, in causing variation in personality, adjustment, and behavior, both in childhood and in later years. These sociological factors within the family setting, interacting with the child's innate characteristics and with parental personalities, attitudes toward child-rearing, and behaviors, help make each child unique. The family, and especially the parents, plays the major role of shaping the child and producing that complex set of traits called personality.

Other agents of socialization also operate on the child. Certainly, for most individuals, agemates play an important role in socialization. Although the peer group is often viewed as a "bad" influence, it has a number of useful functions. It conveys information and value, provides the child with a source of identification and, perhaps the most important of all, serves as a buffer and a normalizer of deviant parent attitudes.

The school is a second extrafamilial grouping that has considerable influence on the development of the child. Both information and values are transmitted. By exposing all children to a relatively uniform set of experiences, the school helps to produce a more homogeneous culture—one that is in some ways increasingly oriented toward a middle-class value system based on a belief in hard work, delayed gratification, and social mobility. The educational system engenders a drive for mobility and provides the formal education necessary for its achievement.

The community, religious institutions, and mass media of communication also have some influence on the socialization process. However, the effect of these last social forces appears to be less than is commonly believed. Further, the effects of the so-called "good" forces such as schoolbooks and religious instruction are not all good, nor are the effects of movies, television, and comics as uniformly pernicious as is often assumed. The effects are ambiguous and generally rather minor. Some few children, however, are deeply influenced by such things as community setting or television. These children appear to be young people whose parents have largely abdicated the responsibility of providing values and security, or are individuals with a fair degree of psychological disturbance, or both.

Although genetic inheritance sets the limits within which individuals vary from one another, it also produces a substantial portion of the resulting variation. Upon this genetic variation multifarious environmental forces act to make each of us unique. The complex and interactive play of environmental and hereditary forces, plus the interaction between the many environmental factors themselves, combine to produce the individual. Family and friends, community and school, and books and comic books are only a small sampling of the social influences encountered by a child. Influences may be short-term or long-range, gradual or sudden, mild or traumatic. Further, the child is not merely a weak and passive recipient of stimulation but is a vigorous and active organism that determines, to a considerable extent, the kind of stimulation it is to receive and the degree of impact that stimuli will have in changing behavior.

From these crosscurrents of stimulation the child broadens his sphere of activity. The child develops a personality—a unique set of traits. He develops a self concept—a set of ideas concerning the physical self and a set of self-expectations concerning behavior; this makes him relatively consistent and predictable in behavior. He tends to respond in ways consistent with this self concept and thus develops a more rigid and clearly delineated set of social roles with age.

The humans born weak, small, and totally dependent, masters his developmental tasks and emerges as a tough and strong organism, resistant to stress and capable of self-repair and of manipulating the environment to shape it closer to his heart's desire—social, yet independent; unique, yet part of the stream of life.

We have attempted to map the course of child development. The problems faced in understanding and predicting child behavior are complex and although some questions, such as the influence of maturation on physical development, have been largely answered, others, such as the bases of personality deviation in childhood, are far from solution. We believe that all scientific problems are potentially solvable, and hope that at least some of the *terra incognito* of child psychology will by mapped by students who have read this book.

author index

author index

author index

subject index

subject index

subject index